Critical Issues in Human Resource Management

Edited by
Ian Roper, Rea Prouska and Uracha Chatrakul Na Ayudhya

Ian Roper is Principal Lecturer in the Department of HRM at Middlesex University Business School.

Rea Prouska is Senior Lecturer in the Department of HRM at Middlesex University Business School.

Uracha Chatrakul Na Ayudhya is Lecturer in the Department of HRM at Middlesex University Business School.

The Chartered Institute of Personnel and Development is the leading publisher of books and reports for personnel and training professionals, students, and all those concerned with the effective management and development of people at work. For details of all our titles, please contact the publishing department:

tel: 020 8612 6204
email: publish@cipd.co.uk
The catalogue of all CIPD titles can be viewed on the CIPD website:
www.cipd.co.uk/bookstore

Critical Issues in Human Resource Management

Edited by
Ian Roper, Rea Prouska and Uracha Chatrakul Na Ayudhya

Chartered Institute of Personnel and Development

Published by the Chartered Institute of Personnel and Development,
151, The Broadway, London, SW19 1JQ

This edition first published 2010

Typeset by Fakenham Photosetting Ltd, Norfolk

Printed in Malta by Gutenberg Press Ltd.

British Library Cataloguing in Publication Data
A catalogue of this publication is available from the British Library

ISBN 978 1 84398 242 5

The views expressed in this publication are the authors' own and may not necessarily reflect those of the CIPD.

Chartered Institute of Personnel and Development, CIPD House,
151 The Broadway, London, SW19 1JQ

Tel: 020 8612 6200
Email: cipd@cipd.co.uk
Website: www.cipd.co.uk
Incorporated by Royal Charter
Registered Charity No. 1079797

Contents

List of boxes, tables and figures

Acknowledgements

The editors would like to thank the following groups of people.

Firstly, we would like to thank past students on taught module 'Contemporary Issues in Human Resource Management' for their feedback and interactions with us, which led to the idea for creating this book. Secondly, we would like to thank all the contributory authors, without which this book would not be possible.

In addition, we would like to thank the anonymous reviewers, particularly 'Reviewer 3', for their extensive comments on draft chapters. Of course, the usual disclaimer applies: any errors that remain are those of the authors and/or editors. Finally, we would like to thank the CIPD editorial team, particularly Kirsty Smy, whose encouragement and prompts ensured the book was published on time.

Ian, Rea and Uracha

Notes on contributors

Uracha Chatrakul Na Ayudhya, PhD, is Lecturer in the Department of HRM at Middlesex University Business School. Her main research interests focus on understanding the experiences of work–life balance and transitions in and out of employment among women and men across the life course.

Elizabeth Cotton is Senior Lecturer in the Department of HRM at Middlesex University Business School. She has worked in International Development for many years and was the Head of Education and Programmes for the International Federation of Chemical, Energy, Mine and General Workers' Unions (ICEM).

Richard Croucher, PhD, is Professor of Comparative Employment Relations and Associate Dean of Research at Middlesex University Business School.

Ian Cunningham, PhD, is Senior Lecturer in the Department of HRM at the University of Strathclyde. His research interests include managing employee relations in the voluntary sector.

Anne Daguerre, PhD, is Senior Lecturer in the Department of HRM at Middlesex University Business School. Her research interests are in labour market policies.

Matt Flynn, PhD, is Senior Lecturer in the Department of HRM at Middlesex University Business School. His main research interests are in age management and the transition to retirement.

Sebastian Fuchs is Lecturer in the Department of HRM at Middlesex University Business School and is currently reading for a PhD at King's College London. His research interests include organisational citizenship behaviour, employee withdrawal behaviour, organisational change management and cross-cultural management.

John Grahl is Professor of European Integration at Middlesex University Business School. His research interests include the Eurozone and its financial integration, financial markets and globalisation, financial change and European employment relations, and labour market policies in the EU.

Mary Hartog, PhD, is Head of the Department of HRM at Middlesex University Business School. Her research interests include reflective practice, building learning communities and business ethics.

Qian (Lydia) He is a doctoral candidate at the Centre for Industrial Relations and Human Resources, University of Toronto, Canada.

Phil James is Professor of Employment Relations at Oxford Brookes University. He has a range of research interests but particularly includes the area of HRM and occupational health and safety.

Susie Leigh is Senior Lecturer in the Department of HRM at Middlesex University Business School. She is co-editor of *Human Resource Management: A Case Study Approach* (CIPD). She has a particular research interest in HR practices in the NHS.

Suzan Lewis, PhD, is Professor of Organisational Psychology at Middlesex University Business School. Her research focuses on work–personal life issues and workplace practice, culture and change in different workplace and national social policy contexts. She is currently a member of a European Union Expert Group on Women in Science, Engineering and Technology.

Miguel MARTÍNEZ-LUCIO, PhD, is Professor of International HRM at Manchester University Business School. He has researched and written widely on public sector employment relations in the UK and Europe.

Lola-Peach MARTINS, PhD, is Lecturer in the Department of HRM at Middlesex University Business School. She has over 10 years' teaching and research experience and consultancy/practitioner experience in large service and manufacturing companies. She is Chartered Member of the CIPD.

Michael MULLER-CAMEN, PhD, is Professor of International HRM at Middlesex University Business School. His main research interests are comparative HRM, age management and Green HRM.

Sepideh PARSA, PhD, is Principal Lecturer in the Department of Accounting and Finance at Middlesex University Business School. Her research interests are in corporate governance and social and environmental reporting.

Rea PROUSKA, PhD, is Senior Lecturer in the Department of HRM at Middlesex University Business School. Her main research interests are in HR outsourcing, offshoring, HRM practices and gender, and graduate employability.

Ian ROPER, PhD, is Principal Lecturer in the Department of HRM at Middlesex University Business School. He is co-editor of *Modernising Work in Public Services* and *Contesting Public Sector Reforms* (Palgrave Macmillan). His research interests include public service employment relations and working-time flexibility rights.

Asiya SIDDIQUEE, PhD, is Lecturer in Psychology at Manchester Metropolitan University. Her main research interests are social justice, marginalisation, digital technologies and community psychology.

Martin UPCHURCH, PhD, is Professor of International Employment Relations at Middlesex University Business School. He is co-author of *New Unions, New Workplaces* (Routledge), *The Realities of Partnership at Work* (Palgrave Macmillan), and *The Crisis of Social Democratic Trade Unionism in Western Europe* (Ashgate).

Anil VERMA, PhD, is Professor at the Rotman School of Management and Centre for Industrial Relations and Human Resources, University of Toronto. He is also Visiting Professor, Middlesex University Business School.

Geoff WHITE, PhD, is Professor of Reward Management at the University of Greenwich. His main research interest is in reward management, especially in the public sector, and he has published widely in the fields of pay and employee relations.

Doirean WILSON is Senior Lecturer in the HRM Department at Middlesex University Business School. She is a Chartered Fellow of the CIPD. Her research interests include cultural diversity, gender disparity, leadership and management.

Geoff WOOD, PhD, is Professor and Associate Dean at the School of Management, University of Sheffield, and Visiting Professor at Nelson Mandela University, South Africa. His current interests centre on the relationship between institutional setting, corporate governance and firm level practice.

Walkthrough of textbook features and online resources

OVERVIEW

This chapter begins with a comparison of different definitions of corporate governance, arguing that governance structures are the end results of social and political processes. The chapter then moves on to discuss different corporate governance mechanisms and how employees in each mechanism are considered. Three governance mechanisms, namely the Anglo-Saxon mechanism in the UK, the stakeholder approach in Germany and the Japanese corporate governance mechanism, are discussed. This is followed by a review of the development of those aspects of the regulatory codes that could have impacts on employees. The chapter ends with a section on three theoretical perspectives that are commonly used in corporate governance literature and how employees are positioned in governance structure within each theoretical perspective.

OVERVIEW

Each chapter opens with an overview outlining the purpose and content of the chapter.

LEARNING OBJECTIVES

Reading this chapter will enable the reader to:

- critically evaluate theoretical definitions of corporate governance and apply their relevance to HR decision-making
- appreciate major corporate governance mechanisms and their potential impacts on employees
- compare and contrast several theoretical arguments that are commonly used in corporate governance and are pertinent to employees and their relationships with company.

LEARNING OBJECTIVES

A bulleted set of learning objectives summarises what you can expect to learn from the proceeding chapter, helping you to track your progress.

HRM IN THE MEDIA

'OIL GIANT REWARDS EXECUTIVES BUT RISKS EMPLOYEES' SAFETY'

In April 2010, the oil giant BP was responsible for one the worst oil spills ever in their Gulf of Mexico oil platform 'Deepwater Horizon'. While much negative publicity surrounded the company on the pollution involved in this disaster, the original event leading to this spill involved the death of 11 workers and further injury to others.

The disaster focused attention on the company's general approach to risk and reward: while the company had made

workers died, and in 2006 in the Alaska pipeline spill.

Following the capping of the 2010 spill, the chief executive of BP was reported to be leaving the company on agreed terms. The terms were said to include being appointed chief executive of a Russian subsidiary of BP (*Financial Times* 26 July 2010). BP was facing considerable costs from the spill and damage to its share price.

HRM IN THE MEDIA

At the beginning of each chapter, a contemporary HR news story with related questions is introduced. These stories open up current debate in HR and problematise the core HRM topics, getting you thinking about them in a more critical and sophisticated way.

HRM IN THE MEDIA

CRITICAL REFLECTIONS

BP, as a British company operating in the US, can be assumed to operate on shareholder-value assumptions of corporate governance, and accountability is therefore based on ensuring that shareholder interests are the only legitimate interests that need to be protected by corporate governance structures. Agency theory suggests that the separation of ownership and control meant that managers had access to corporate information that allowed them to make strategic decisions related to the relative risks posed by operational costs, safety costs and the likelihood and cost of an accident. With falling oil prices, these relative risks made health and safety costs relatively more expensive and the risk was tilted more towards cost-cutting in this area. As prescribed by the regulatory codes, the non-executive directors who were expected to play the monitoring role and mitigate the utility-maximising behaviour of managers failed to have an effective role. Despite the regulatory codes of conduct, the weaknesses in corporate governance still allowed substantial pension packages.

HRM IN THE MEDIA: CRITICAL REFLECTIONS

As you read the main body of each chapter, you will gain the in-depth knowledge and critical thinking skills needed to join in the debate presented at the beginning of each chapter. Critical reflections boxes will help you to relate your learning back to the opening questions.

EXPLORE FURTHER

SPARROW, P., BREWSTER, C. and HARRIS, H. (eds) (2004) *Globalising human resource management*. London: Routledge.

This book provides a broad, coherent overview of the field of international HRM and a detailed, practical analysis of what is needed to be successful in this crucial area of modern management.

JACKSON, S.E., LUO, Y. and SCHULER, R.S. (eds) (2003) *Managing human resources in cross-border alliances*. London: Routledge.

This book provides a comprehensive treatment of HR issues in international alliances.

BREWSTER, C., MAYRHOFER, W. and MORLEY, M. (eds) (2004), *HRM in Europe: evidence of convergence?* Oxford: Butterworth-Heinemann.

This book presents HR issues in a wide variety of European countries.

EXPLORE FURTHER

Explore further boxes contain suggestions for further reading and useful websites, so that you can develop your understanding of the issues and debates raised in each chapter.

ONLINE RESOURCES FOR STUDENTS

● Annotated web links – access a wealth of journal articles and other useful sources of information in order to develop your understanding of the debates and issues raised.

Visit **www.cipd.co.uk/sss**.

ONLINE RESOURCES FOR TUTORS

LECTURER'S GUIDE

● Guidance on the HRM in the Media features in the book, as well as theoretical outlines, additional seminar activities and discussion topics.

● Case studies – use these additional cases with accompanying questions to enliven your lectures and really engage students with critical issues in HRM.

● PowerPoint slides – design your programme around these ready-made lectures.

Visit **www.cipd.co.uk/tss**.

CHAPTER 1

Introduction

Ian Roper, Rea Prouska and Uracha Chatrakul Na Ayudhya

OVERVIEW

This chapter provides an introduction and overview of the contents of the book. It introduces the reader to some underlying themes that define what the authors mean by 'critical issues' and explains how a critical approach applies to the study of human resource management (HRM). It suggests how the reader can use prior knowledge and understandings gained from previous studies in the functions of HRM and consider what additional considerations need to be taken into consideration when confronted with more acute circumstances – a situation that human resource (HR) managers could reasonably be expected to face in real-world situations. The chapter finishes by mapping the structure of the book and providing a rationale to the topics that will be encountered throughout the remainder of the book.

PURPOSE OF THE BOOK

Welcome to *Critical Issues in Human Resource Management*. This edited textbook has been written specifically to cover the subject area of HRM from a critical point of view. The reader in mind for this book is a final-year undergraduate studying HRM as a specialist subject, or perhaps a postgraduate HRM student who is looking for supplementary text to support his or her core reading. In either case the reader will be assumed to have already studied some HRM and will know some of the topics. The aim, within the book, is to problematise otherwise familiar topics and to confront higher-level problems that could face HR professionals. By engaging with this text, it should be possible for the reader to integrate his or her prior understanding of some key operational aspects of HRM with the wider institutional and social contexts in which they occur (at the level of the firm, industry sector, nation and international) by reference to wider social science and business theories. The book concentrates predominantly on HR practice in the UK, but consciously views the UK experiences within (a) the convergence pressures of globalisation and (b) the counter tendencies of cross-national divergence.

SCOPE OF THE BOOK

The book covers topics considered emerging and important within the particular subjects addressed in each chapter. It is not within the scope of this book to repeat core theories in managing HR, although some background to the concepts explored is provided in each chapter to refresh the reader's memory of such theories surrounding the particular topic. Rather, the book aims to present significant new developments in the field, which are and will remain at the forefront of managing HR in the coming years.

For example, Part 1 of the book deals with the influences on and shapers of HR practice and strategy. A core HRM textbook targeted at levels 1 and 2 undergraduate students would perhaps focus on a more general discussion, introducing theories of organisational, business and corporate strategies and how these link to HR strategies. What the current book is exploring, though, is the range of issues considered emerging and important for organisations. Topics such as corporate governance, corporate social responsibility and financialisation, for example, could be seen as being more influential on mainstream HR policy in the future as the dominant management paradigms leading up to the 2008 financial crisis are successively reflected upon (for example, see Currie et al 2010). Similarly, while globalisation, technology, politics and demography are frequently cited in mainstream HR textbooks as important background factors influencing the way that HR policy-makers need to plan, it is less often described and explained what these trends are.

The 'critical approach' is slightly different in Part 2 of the book. Here, it moves away from exploring basic concepts in the core HRM activities that present a definitive guide to managing HR processes, to a critical approach of emerging issues in these areas.

Here, the particular approach taken on each topic is personal to each author and reflects the contributors' diverse adopted positionings of HRM, which are multidisciplinary in nature. However, in all cases, there is reason to believe that the issue under discussion will remain relevant and not a passing fad: it is difficult to see the demise of *offshoring* as a most contentious aspect of resourcing policy, or that the issue of defining *performance* within *performance management* will suddenly reach consensus and be unworthy of further discussion.

Part 3 of the book completes this critical approach to exploring current HR issues by providing a sector-by-sector analysis. The intent of this section is to demonstrate to the reader that there is no 'one best way' to manage HR. Rather, the particularities of sectors need to be taken into consideration before implementing HR strategies. This part, therefore, explores the four main sectors present in the UK economy (manufacturing, private services, public services and not-for-profit sector) and discusses in particular how HR is managed in each of these sectors.

WHAT IS MEANT BY 'CRITICAL'?

The term 'critical' requires some explanation. Critical could be taken to mean a number of things in the broad social science disciplines that are embedded within the discourse of contemporary HRM. In contrast, 'criticality' takes on a looser, broadly analytical meaning when used in a learning context. Criticality also implies an approach to the selection of evidence used to demonstrate (or refute) assumptions in general practice. These will now be considered in turn.

CRITICAL THEORY, CRITICAL REALISM, CRITIQUE

One definition of critical would be that associated with the philosophical notion of *critique* more generally – applied as a challenge to assuming orthodox views on a subject. This definition stretches from the use applied by Kant, through to Marx and later applied to a more specific definition of 'critical theory' associated with the Frankfurt School (Habermas 1984). More recently approaches associated with the term 'critical' have varied from postmodernism to the now apparent turn away from postmodernism towards critical realism (Bhaskar 1986). Within the broad academic areas that are relevant to the study of HRM, a number of these critical approaches have been prominent over the years: from the early 1980s, a whole new area opened up under the broad umbrella of 'the labour process debate'. Initially influenced by Braverman's (1974) contention that modern work in capitalist society is subject to a continuous process of degradation through the essential nature of the managerial imperative, this debate widened with a significant alternative narrative influenced by Foucault, turning to examine the fundamental importance of employee subjectivity and managerial *discourses* – in precedence over *processes* – as being of primary importance (Knights and Willmott 1989). Most recently there has been a further turn towards *critical realism* as both a rejection of Foucaultian relativism and an attempt to link the analysis of workplace relationships back to the political economy of the forces determining managerial behaviour (Fleetwood and Ackroyd 2004; Thompson and Vincent 2010).

There are, therefore, a number of definitions and approaches associated with the notion of 'critical' when considering how we think about studying HRM – and just from the overview above, it can be seen that adopting one particular approach would be putting itself in contestation of another approach. The editors have their own views and preferences on these issues, but this was not a consideration when inviting contributors for the large range of topics contained in this book. In all cases, chapters are presented, to a greater or lesser degree, in such a way that is intended to challenge an assumption about orthodox views of HR practice, but not by adherence to any one specific philosophical view.

CRITICALITY AS A PEDAGOGIC PROCESS

At a more pragmatic level, criticality is used to define the level of engagement that the *reader* is expected to make. It is intended that the reader will aspire to be 'thinking critically' and therefore it is anticipated that the reader will read in a critical way (Wallace and Wray 2006).

It is expected that the reader has some prior exposure to the study of HRM: that they may have studied the basic functions and what processes are involved in HRM and that they know the kinds of activities that an HR manager may be responsible for and may do on a day-to-day basis.

The 'critical' aspect of the content of the chapters in this book is that of taking the reader beyond the operational aspects of HR. This is not the same as 'being strategic' – though there is a link. Being strategic requires a consideration of 'the big picture'. Thinking critically sometimes requires thinking about the bigger picture – what larger forces are at work when considering an operational decision about outsourcing, absenteeism, pay awards, and so on – but also may involve a consideration of the micro effects of strategic decisions – the reason that workers may react differently to a *change management* initiative because of differing workforce composition, workplace dynamics, demographic factors or other characteristics.

CRITICAL CASE SCENARIOS

A special feature of this edited textbook is 'HRM in the media', a section in each chapter that presents a relatively contemporary HR news story that has been communicated in the news media. The chapter structure aspires, in a broad sense, to a problem-based learning approach (Boud and Feletti 1991). Each news story relates directly to the topic of the chapter. News stories were selected based on the scope for discussion they present. Questions for discussion follow these news stories, which are then revisited at the end of the chapter in the 'HRM in the media: critical reflections' section. Readers need to remember that it is not the purpose of this textbook to prescribe definitive answers regarding the particular critical HR issues raised. Instead, the purpose is to present current debates in HR and illustrate the complexities of these contemporary HR policies and practices and to encourage the reader to look deeper into the issue to uncover further evidence in order to attempt to understand the reasons for the apparent differences.

The use of this 'HRM in the media' device has two components and two important caveats. The first component is, by the reasoning that a story relating to the chapter subject has appeared in the news media, that there must be something within the chosen topic to make it contentious in some way: stories tend not to appear 'on the news' if they are routine and unproblematic. There is, then, the potential for the topic under discussion, for outcomes of HR policy, to sometimes not go according to prescribed best practice. Thinking critically should allow the reader to consider the reasons for this. The second component is the realisation that, by virtue of the fact that such linked stories are available, further stories are also almost certainly available. A carefully written case study by a tutor to draw readers' attention to a topic is a good pedagogic device, but potentially better still is the existence of real-life events that readers can research themselves. Modern electronic searching facilities make this task relatively easy, in contrast to the painstaking archive research required for such a task in the past. Indeed, being able to make such a search should be considered an important research and study skill in its own right, provided appropriate caution is taken by understanding the limitations of the technology involved (Devine and Egger-Sider 2009).

It is taken as given (notwithstanding the induction/deduction dilemma) that being familiar with *theory* is essential to a full understanding of an event; but that also in being able to apply an abstract theory to explain (or at least to gain more considered insight into) a real-life situation is equally important to being fully able to grasp what a theory means *in practice*. Given the ease with which electronic searches are possible, students of HRM using this book should be able to embed their understanding of theory by reflecting upon the reported examples and searching more for themselves.

The first caveat to the above is to acknowledge the limitations of trusting the news media as an indication of 'facts'. For the first part – and as an important corrective to the point made above – an event being reported in the media, while indicating that what may be assumed to be unproblematic could be demonstrated not always to be so, it also needs to be remembered that the other reason why such an event is being reported is that it is not necessarily 'normal'. A second important caveat is that news media sources should not be assumed to be objective conduits of 'the truth'. It has long been established that news outlets distort events around their own ideological (and commercial) interests (Eldridge 1993). Even those sources bound by the principle of 'due impartiality' – public service broadcasting organisations such as the BBC – are still subject to 'agenda-setting' by the more overtly biased source – particularly the tabloid press. This tendency was linked explicitly to the reporting of industrial relations, for example, in the first of the well-known Glasgow University Media Group's 'Bad News' series (1976). Some HR-related stories make for obviously 'juicy' news stories: strikes, moral panic over 'compensation culture', or the offshoring of British call-centre jobs. But does the story reflect the background reality? Strikes are the product of discontent about a previous – and unreported – situation; headline stories about large payoffs of unfairly treated employees do not convey the reality from the statistics showing that the vast majority of unfair dismissal claims put through the employment tribunal service in the UK are unsuccessful and those that are successful tend to pay modest levels of compensation (see www.employmenttribunals.gov.uk); and in addition to offshored call-centre work, it is less well known that during the 2000s, more UK jobs were created in this industry than were exported from it.

So using media sources requires critical thinking and a degree of 'filtering' in order to properly judge how it may link to the topic in question. The overall approach offered would be:

- Be aware of the subject material taken by formal study.
- Be vigilant and observe media stories that appear relevant to study topics.
- Are there differences between formal theory and apparent practice observed via the media?
- Be critical of the theory: does the apparent difference indicate that theory is inadequate in its present form?
- Examine the back story: what lies behind the reported story? To what extent is the story informed by 'moral panic'?
- Dig deeper. What other sources can be found on this story? What similar stories on this topic are there?
- Integrate the accumulated findings of the news stories and academic theory. What do you now understand about this subject?

CHAPTER FORMAT

Each chapter is structured in a way that is intended to stimulate interest in the topic, provoke further enquiry and embed previous knowledge. Each chapter starts with an overview, follows with three to four key learning objectives – which are expected to be achieved through the reader not just reading the chapter, but engaging with the subject more generally. There then follows a short case study extracted from a media source: 'HRM in the media'. The main body of the chapter then follows – with an introduction following the case study. Each chapter then follows a series of subheadings specific to the topic in question and, after the conclusion section, the HRM case study is returned to with some reflections. Some suggested further reading is then provided. As explained, above, the use of the 'HRM in the media' device has two purposes. Firstly, it is intended to demonstrate that a seemingly straightforward technical aspect of HR practice – perhaps already known to the reader – does not always go according to plan and that a critical approach to a particular topic enables a deeper understanding of the topic if such problems are to be resolved or avoided. Secondly, it is intended to challenge the reader to seek out other such dilemmas, notwithstanding the important caveats made about over-reliance on media-based stories as being representative.

STRUCTURE OF THE BOOK

The book follows the following structure: Part 1 focuses on the influences on, and shapers of, HR strategy and sets the scene for the book. This is intended to mirror what students studying at this level, or an HR practitioner, would need as prerequisite knowledge: an understanding of some critical determining factors that shape the choice of HR policy and practice within a specific organisational context. Chapter 2 by Sepideh Parsa discusses corporate governance and how the differing approaches to the accountability structures of large corporations go on to shape the relationship that such companies choose to have with their stakeholders – including employees. The underlying assumptions that shape these accountability structures go on to shape HR policies and practices. Chapter 3 by Elizabeth Cotton analyses corporate social responsibility (CSR) and its link to HRM. CSR has become a significant feature of management in large – especially multinational – enterprises, and one of the fundamental issues within CSR is the treatment of labour – whether that be direct employees or contract labour; yet this topic is rarely considered and discussed in conventional HR literature. Chapter 4 by Geoff Wood addresses issues in managing HR in different national contexts and considers, in particular, the importance of the influence that differing national business systems can have on HR practices at firm level. Chapter 5 by Martin Upchurch explores the impact that information technology has had in work organisations and its implications for the nature of contemporary work and organisations. Chapters 6, 7 and 8 focus on the more specific themes influenced by the preceding chapters. Chapter 6 by John Grahl considers the significance of the dominance of shareholder value for the way that HRM is conducted in the UK. Chapter 7 by Phil James and Ian Roper considers the ways in which national-level politics have – and will continue to have – an influence on HR policy in firms in the UK. Chapter 8 by Matt Flynn and Michael Muller-Camen considers one of the emerging socio-demographic features of modern advanced economies: the ageing workforce and age diversity as an emerging issue for management. Finally, Chapter 9 by Anne Daguerre concludes the first part of the book with a discussion on HR strategy and the business environment and makes a case for why external forces need to be considered in planning and implementing any HR processes.

Part 2 of the book focuses on critical aspects of HR practices and policies. This section covers topics that students studying HRM would be likely to have covered in previous studies: the core operational functions of the HR practitioner, defined here under the recognisable terms used over a long period and codified by the Chartered Institute of Personnel and Development (CIPD). However, where previous studies should have equipped the student with an understanding of the important foundations in the issues of *people resourcing*, *employee relations*, *employee reward* and *learning and development*, the chapters in this section of the book attempt to take students into particular areas of these subjects. It is not claimed that these chapters represent the final word on the subjects. What they attempt to do, however, is take an aspect of the subject and consider, from each author's own perspective, an issue that could be seen as problematic or critical in the subject. Chapters 10 and 11 explore critical issues in people resourcing. They look particularly at how performance can be identified in performance management (Chapter 10 by Sebastian Fuchs) and at the dilemmas associated with the most acute aspect of hiring and firing: that of outsourcing and offshoring (Chapter 11 by Rea Prouska). Chapters 12 and 13 investigate critical issues in employee relations. Chapter 12 by Susie Leigh and Ian Roper explores the dilemmas associated with an individualised workforce and the attempts to rectify such problems with the notion of employee engagement. Chapter 13 by Richard Croucher looks at the often neglected issue within the notion of global HRM, that of global labour institutions. Chapter 14 by Mary Hartog examines critical issues in learning and development and centres its discussion on the learning organisation. Chapter 15 by Geoff White introduces the debate surrounding reward management and explores the background to the phenomenon of 'new pay' and considers whether future pressures may force a return to some older concerns of equity and voice. The remaining chapters in Part 2 critically deal with equality and diversity and consider: the issue of gender equity and its inter-relationship with the problematic work–life-balance narrative (Chapter 16 by Uracha Chatrakul Na Ayudhya and Suzan Lewis); the far from straightforward issue of institutional racism (Chapter 17 by Doirean Wilson); and the often taken-for-granted issue of disability discrimination in the modern workplace (Chapter 18 by Asiya Siddiquee and Uracha Chatrakul Na Ayudhya). Having three chapters on these aspects of equality and diversity may seem to some as excessive. Yet, as the motive bases of discrimination, of good and bad practice, are different in each case (economic, cultural, social, respectively), covering all categories of equality and diversity as one unified issue would not, ultimately, lead to particularly helpful insights as to how to promote inclusiveness in any one of these areas at the level of study intended in this book. Of course, this does lead to the editors needing to acknowledge the omission of equally pertinent areas of equality and diversity: the issues of sexuality and religious belief being the most prominent. Ideally, it would have been possible to include all aspects of diversity, but space restrictions constrain how much of a book on critical HRM could be dedicated to the equality and diversity agenda without jeopardising the quality of the critical treatment of other aspects of HRM.

Finally, Part 3 is structured around a sectoral analysis of HRM. Past experience has led the editors to believe that students attempting to apply aspects of HRM theory into a specific workplace context often fail to grasp the contextual differences in explaining the manner in which specific HR practices may be applied. This error is either by way of an over-reliance on prescriptive HR models and/or an assumption that ideal-type best practice will necessarily be embraced (or even possible) in a particular organisational setting. For example, an assumption could be made, on prescribed best practice, that a 'social partnership' approach to employee relations would be welcomed by management in a small non-union retail organisation; or that an off-the-shelf 'change management' programme will be welcomed by staff in a unionised public service organisation with a recent history of staff redundancies. Of course, the application of context is not unique to this subject – or indeed this book. And the editors of this book would also not suggest that any serious student should not take their own initiative in investigating important organisational contexts when applying theory to practice. However, the manner in which much HR practice is presented in many textbooks suggests universal applicability. In some cases, this may be as the author intends and that there are universally applicable 'rules' that can apply. In most cases, however, it is due to the author undoubtedly assuming that the reader would need to do the extra sector-specific reading to complete the full picture. This final section therefore provides an overview of the external contexts and resulting HRM practices associated with these particular sectors. Chapters 19, 20, 21 and 22 introduce the particularities of HRM in the manufacturing sector (Lola Peach Martins and Geoff Wood), private services (Sebastian Fuchs), public services (Miguel Martinez-Lucio and Ian Roper), and the not-for-profit sector (Ian Cunningham) respectively.

Part 4 concludes the book with a one-chapter afterword devoted to what, in the view of Anil Verma and Qian He, constitute the 'big issues' facing HR in the coming decades. This chapter is not presented as others: it has no learning objectives or case study. The big issues covered in this chapter – migration, precarious work, lifelong learning and work–life balance – are considered from a global perspective. All of these themes are covered elsewhere in the book individually, but this chapter integrates them. If some readers of this book find themselves selectively reading certain chapters, they would be encouraged to read this chapter in conjunction with the specialist chapter of choice.

PART ONE

THE INFLUENCES ON AND SHAPERS OF HR STRATEGY

CHAPTER 2

Ethics (1): Corporate Governance and HRM

Sepideh Parsa

OVERVIEW

This chapter begins with a comparison of different definitions of corporate governance, arguing that governance structures are the end results of social and political processes. The chapter then moves on to discuss different corporate governance mechanisms and how employees in each mechanism are considered. Three governance mechanisms, namely the Anglo-Saxon mechanism in the UK, the stakeholder approach in Germany and the Japanese corporate governance mechanism, are discussed. This is followed by a review of the development of those aspects of the regulatory codes that could have impacts on employees. The chapter ends with a section on three theoretical perspectives that are commonly used in corporate governance literature and how employees are positioned in governance structure within each theoretical perspective.

LEARNING OBJECTIVES

Reading this chapter will enable the reader to:

- critically evaluate theoretical definitions of corporate governance and apply their relevance to HR decision-making
- appreciate major corporate governance mechanisms and their potential impacts on employees
- compare and contrast several theoretical arguments that are commonly used in corporate governance and are pertinent to employees and their relationships with company.

HRM IN THE MEDIA

'OIL GIANT REWARDS EXECUTIVES BUT RISKS EMPLOYEES' SAFETY'

In April 2010, the oil giant BP was responsible for one the worst oil spills ever in their Gulf of Mexico oil platform 'Deepwater Horizon'. While much negative publicity surrounded the company on the pollution involved in this disaster, the original event leading to this spill involved the death of 11 workers and further injury to others.

The disaster focused attention on the company's general approach to risk and reward: while the company had made strenuous efforts to ensure good returns for investors, it had done this with higher-risk projects. Arguably, it had done this by not making a reasonable balance of interests in its risk assessment. In 2006, for example, after a series of highly publicised accidents, BP publicly admitted that it needed to improve its safety measures. This highlighted its previously poor safety record following accidents in 2005 in Texas, where

15 workers died, and in 2006 in the Alaska pipeline spill.

Following the capping of the 2010 spill, the chief executive of BP was reported to be leaving the company on agreed terms. The terms were said to include being appointed chief executive of a Russian subsidiary of BP (*Financial Times* 26 July 2010). BP was facing considerable costs from the spill and damage to its share price.

Questions

1 As a British company operating in the US, what assumptions could be made about how BP weighed the interests of shareholders and employees in assessing risks?

2 How may alternative governance mechanisms have led to different outcomes?

INTRODUCTION

What we understand by the term 'corporate governance' underlines our perception of how companies operating in any society can have an impact on the manner in which people are managed within organisations. In the UK the corporate governance codes of conduct have been devised primarily to protect shareholders' interests over the interests of other parties, including employees. In countries such as Germany and Japan, the governance mechanisms are designed in a way that employees' rights and interests are protected. This is achieved by the inclusion of employees in the governance mechanisms so that they can take part in the decision-making processes and voice their views and concerns so that their long-term interests can be protected. A better understanding of different types of governance mechanism and how they operate and treat their employees can be attained by looking at the justification and reasoning that are argued under different theoretical perspectives. Hence, this chapter reviews agency theory, stakeholder theory and resource dependence theory.

DEFINITIONS AND CONCEPTS

The HRM policies of a company are pertinent to the overall strategic management approach adopted by the company. If strategic management is defined as the process through which a company develops its critical goals and resources (Boxall and Purcell 2006, p55), the HRM policies are determined by these corporate goals and the resources that the company has chosen to access. The decision on the choice of corporate goals and which resources to access is made at the top managerial level, or what is commonly regarded as corporate governance. The approach taken to corporate governance will determine the content and approach taken on HRM-related issues, such as the hiring, firing and outsourcing of elements of the workforce, the training of the workforce, employee voice issues and pay and reward packages. The next section presents discussions on what is meant by the term corporate governance.

CORPORATE GOVERNANCE

Corporate governance originated in the nineteenth century when the need for legislation and regulation arose with the advent of limited liability companies. The term 'corporate governance' came out of a seminal analysis by Berle and Means (1932), who drew attention to a managerial revolution whereby control was transferred from owners to managers. A common ownership model is that of 'disbursed shareholding' whereby ownership is held by a wide range of remote shareholders rather than an owner on the premises. In such companies, professional managers assume the responsibility of running the company. Traditionally, most definitions of corporate governance allude to the interest of shareholders and how managers are entrusted with the responsibilities and duties to manage the company in a way that serves the shareholders' interests. The regulatory codes of conduct, for example, define corporate governance as '…the system by which companies are directed and controlled' (Committee on the Financial Aspects of Corporate Governance [Cadbury Report] 1992). According to the Higgs Report (Committee on Corporate Governance 2003, p11), 'corporate governance provides an architecture of accountability – the structures and processes to ensure companies are managed in the interest of their owners'. Sheik and Rees (1995, p5) take a similar view and state that corporate governance is a '…system whereby directors are entrusted with responsibilities and duties in relation to the direction of the company's affairs. It is founded on a system of accountability primarily directed towards shareholders in addition to maximising shareholders' welfare.'

Considering the pivotal role of corporate governance in distribution of wealth and creation of opportunities, everyone has an interest in how governance mechanisms are structured (Sheik and Rees 2005). A broad definition is given by Burchell et al (1991, pviii), who state that '…governance is an activity and an art which concerns all and touches each. And it is an art which presupposes thought.' Governance, in the view of Starkey (1995, p843), '…is more than the legitimation of authority or taming of power. It lies at the heart of the organizations we work in and live our lives through. What we expect and demand of governance will determine what kind of society we and our children shall live in.' In other words, corporate governance can entail the interests of a range of groups rather than merely shareholders. A similar view is adopted by Tricker (1984), who makes the distinction between management and governance and argues that the management role is pertinent to decision-making to run the business operations efficiently within the company borders. By contrast, he argues, governance is about monitoring the actions of corporate managers and satisfying the legitimate expectations of accountability beyond the company borders. According to Tricker (1984), corporate governance comprises four principal activities: (1) direction, which deals with formulating the long-term strategic direction of a company; (2) executive action, which relates to the crucial executive decisions; (3) supervision, which involves monitoring and oversight of management performance; and (4) accountability, which is concerned with recognising responsibilities to those making a legitimate demand for accountability.

For Keasey et al (1997, p2), corporate governance is the formal mechanism through which senior managers are held accountable to shareholders first and foremost and embraces the entire network of formal and informal relations, which involves the corporate sector and their consequences for society in general. By this definition, a wider range of stakeholders are taken into consideration. Keasey et al's (1997) definition goes a step further than the traditional definition of corporate governance, which mainly addresses the separation of ownership and control in the concept of principle–agent within agency theory framework. Another broad definition is by Sheridan and Kendall (1998, p27), who describe corporate governance as a system of structuring, operating and controlling a company in order to '(1) fulfil the long term strategic goal of the owners, (2) consider and care for the interests of employees, (3) take account of the needs of the environment and the local community, (4) work to maintain excellent relations with both customers and suppliers, and (5) maintain proper compliance with all the applicable legal and regulatory requirements'. A similar view is adopted by the OECD (2004), where corporate governance is defined as a structure involving a set of relationships between corporate managers, its shareholders as well as other stakeholders through which company objectives are set and eventually attained. According to the OECD (2004, p11), 'governance mechanisms should be designed in a manner that improves economic efficiency and growth as well as enhancing investor confidence...[whereby]...synergy between macroeconomic and structural policies in achieving fundamental policy gaols [can be achieved]'.

When ownership takes the form of disbursed shareholding and professional managers assume the responsibility of running the company, it becomes necessary to have a system of control over those managers to ensure that the company is managed in the best interest of the shareholders. The concept of corporate governance appears to have gone further than its traditional perspective where shareholders are regarded as the only parties to whom companies pay attention and are held accountable.

CORPORATE GOVERNANCE STRUCTURES

Most traditional definitions of corporate governance adhere to Anglo-Saxon governance structures whereby mechanisms are designed to mitigate the problems arising from separation of ownership from control, which could ultimately lead to poor communication and hence information asymmetry between owners and managers with lack of trust between the two groups. In countries with Anglo-Saxon corporate governance mechanisms, for example the UK and US, shareholders rely on boards of directors as the primary source of management oversight and accountability. In Anglo-Saxon structures, managers, given the opportunity, are assumed to maximise their own utility rather than acting in the best interest of the owners. In order to ensure that managers act in the best interest of shareholders, it is imperative that governance structures are designed in such a way that they would ensure that managers act in the best interest of shareholders.

In the UK, all the regulations regarding managerial conduct within corporations take the form of voluntary codes that do not have the status of law or regulations. From a statutory point of view, the interests of employees are considered, but '...only their "relationship" with the company's needs is to be considered, and then only as an adjunct to the aim of shareholder profit maximization' (Wedderburn 2004, p43). Also known as the 'comply or explain' approach, the use of voluntary codes ensures the greater likelihood of companies obeying the spirit, rather than just the letter of the law (Kirkbride and Letza 2003). The governance regulations in the UK developed after a series of corporate scandals in the 1990s. The number of corporate governance committees established, and the resulting codes of best practice, attest to the importance attached to the subject of corporate governance over the years, yet critics argue that the various committees set up to reform corporate governance have been shaped by histories, conflicts and politics (Sikka 2008) and that employees, or their representatives, have been continuously kept out of governance mechanisms, leading to inequalities in the distribution of wealth and income within and beyond the corporations. At European level, a number of attempts have been made to facilitate an element of employee representation on UK boards, going back as far as 1975, but have been resisted.

In contrast to the Anglo-Saxon structure, the German model adopts an approach where companies are required to act in the interest of all 'stakeholders'. The central characteristic of the German corporate governance model is that all interested stakeholders – managers, employees, creditors, suppliers and customers – are able to monitor corporate performance (Clarke 2007, p181). The German model was formed after the Second World War and formally recognises workers' participation in managerial decision-making. The German corporate governance mechanism '...is not only bank based, but also has weak rights for minority shareholders, a lower rate of return for shareholders and weakly developed market for corporate control' (Beyer and Hassel 2002, p310). It has a system of '...centralised wage bargaining which gives labour a prominent role in the firm's decisions on restructuring and pursuing product market strategies' (Beyer and Hassel 2002, p310).

Under this model, employee representatives fill half of the seats on companies' supervisory boards. A separate management board is responsible for running the business day to day. German employees can influence managerial decision-making through mechanisms that are legally recognised. The law specifies the particular roles of workers and managers and how workers can influence managerial decision-making. Employees' participation is not always mandatory but employees are given the legal right to have works councils if they choose so (Blair and Roe 1999). There is a dual system in which unions and employers negotiate wages while works councils oversee working conditions.

The Japanese corporate governance mechanism, also adopting a stakeholder approach, was developed in its current format after the Second World War, when economic policies were devised through strong but informal links between the Liberal Democratic Party, government ministries and industry (Aoki 2001). This promoted a 'cohesive and solidaristic model of national political economy' (Jackson and Miyajima 2007, p5).

In the Japanese governance mechanism employees play a central role (Dore 2000) while shareholders have a limited role in monitoring and controlling corporate managers. By contrast to the German system, the Japanese system embodies an informal approach to the inclusion of employees whereby employees' participation is assured through a set of conventions that are not legally recognised but where the level of employees' participation is high due to the emphasis on long-term relationships with employees. The concept of 'lifetime employment' implies that employees stay with their company until retirement, reflecting strict legal constraints on dismissals, and 'seniority wage' applies as long as employees stay with the same company; in return the company organises training sessions for them to ensure that their skills are developed so that they can move on to other jobs within the company if they wish to or if there is a need for them to do so (Jackson and Miyajima 2007). The successful co-operation of employees can be attributed to the way employees are perceived to belong to the 'company community' (Shishido 2000), which embraces a coalition of trading partners (*keiretsu* members), management, board members, core employees, banks and other creditors (Blair and Roe 1999).

UK REGULATORY PERSPECTIVES

The UK's approach to addressing corporate governance issues has been described as committee-creation strategy, involving consultations among potentially important stakeholders from a business ethics point of view (Solomon 2007). The evolution of the footprint of UK corporate governance codes and guidelines is discussed below.

THE CADBURY REPORT (1992)

Although the majority of attention to regulatory reform had originated in the US, the commissioning of the Cadbury Report established the UK as a world leader. Loss of investor confidence in the financial reporting system following corporate collapses and scandals ensured the set-up of the Financial Aspects of Corporate Governance Committee by the Financial Reporting Council, London Stock Exchange and the accounting profession, which, after the Maxwell and BCCI cases, expanded its horizon to include all remits of corporate governance (Mallin 2007).

Though not legally binding, the resultant code of corporate governance was incorporated in the listing rules of the Stock Exchange and required all publicly listed companies to communicate their level of adoption of the code, or otherwise (Solomon 2007). This is commonly regarded as the 'comply or explain' approach. The report covered issues related to the structure and responsibilities of the boards and aimed to increase the transparency of the boards' decision-making and boost shareholders' confidence in the governance process (Laing and Weir 1999). The report aimed to achieve this by focusing on four core elements: (i) CEO duality, that is, separation of ownership of the chairman and chief executive post; (ii) representation of non-executive directors (NEDs) on the board; (iii) introduction of the audit; and (iv) nomination and remuneration committees as well as the role of institutional shareholders.

Later collapses were to reveal further weaknesses in the UK corporate governance framework, despite the reforms prescribed by the Cadbury Report and high levels of subsequent compliance, confirming the committee's concluding opinion that no governance mechanism is fraud, but structures/processes can be instituted to discourage aberrations via quick identification and to minimise the risks and resultant effects (see the Cadbury Report 1992, para. 7.2).

THE GREENBURY REPORT (1995)

The Greenbury Report was published after concerns were raised over the substantial payments British Gas directors received in 1995. The report was not aimed at reducing directors' salaries, as it was that particular pay levels were required to attract quality of talent, but rather the establishment of a balance between directors' salaries and their performance to curb 'fat cattery' (Solomon 2007). The core theme of the report was the improvement of accountability in the process of determining remuneration in two ways: (i) the establishment of remuneration committees composed solely of independent NEDs (with shareholder disclosure requirements); and (ii) the linkage of remuneration to performance-related measures to align interests of the shareholders and directors (Mallin 2007; Greenbury 1995).

Though UK companies responded speedily to the recommendation of remuneration committee structure, 'fat cattery' remains prevalent in the UK, and various transparency initiatives that were put in place have not been effective (Thompson 2005).

HAMPEL REPORT (1998) AND COMBINED CODE (1998, 2003, 2006)

The Hampel Report reviewed the implementation of the earlier reports and endorsed a majority of their findings, as well as presented its own recommendations. The report sought to 'correct the balance' of accountability and business prosperity perspectives more in favour of the latter (Spira 2001). In response to the failure of Barings Bank in 1995, issues related to risk management and internal control systems were also addressed, but with little emphasis on the mechanisms.

The first version of the Combined Code gave recommendations on internal control, director evaluation and risk management. The code was revised in 2003 and the structure and profile of the board and its subcommittees, appointment and remuneration processes for the board as well as the role of the chairman and senior independent director were the main thrusts of the revised code (Mallin 2007), with particular focus on greater empowerment of independent NEDs as a means of strengthening transparency, disclosure, accountability and attention to shareholders' interests (Pass 2006). The Combined Code was further revised in early 2006, and the final revised code comprised three changes: (i) allowing the chairman to sit on the remuneration committee; (ii) including the vote-withheld option in proxy forms; and (iii) the publishing of resolution made by a vote of showing of hands.

THEORETICAL PERSPECTIVES

The study of corporate governance is complicated by the fact that the structure, role and impact of boards have been studied from various theoretical angles, resulting in a number of sometimes competing corporate governance theories (Kiel and Nicholson 2003). This multi-theoretic approach is considered by Kiel and Nicholson (2003) as vital for identifying the many mechanisms and structures that may serve to improve the proper functioning of organisations. Agency theory, stewardship theory, stakeholder theory and resource dependence theory are the ubiquitous theoretical perspectives in corporate governance literature.

AGENCY THEORY

Agency theory is the dominant theoretical perspective in corporate governance. Its popularity is due to its simplicity based on the assumption that human behaviour is motivated by rational self-interest (Daily et al 2003). It was born out of the existence of the shareholder-owned corporation defined by Berle and Means (1932). The agency relationship is described as one in which '…one or more persons (the principal(s)) engage another person (the agent) to perform some service on their behalf which involves delegating some decision making authority' (Jensen and Meckling 1976, p308). The shareholders' lack of active involvement in the company's affairs results in information asymmetry, whereby management is better informed about the opportunities, prospects and performance of the company than the shareholders. Healy and Palepu (2001) maintain that the demand for financial reporting and disclosure arises from information asymmetry and conflicts between managers and outside investors.

The crux of agency theory is that managers as agents of shareholders can exhibit behaviour and take decisions that may not maximise shareholder wealth.

Opportunities for managers to abscond with shareholders' funds or squander them on non-wealth-maximising activities are plentiful and well documented (Shleifer and Vishny 1997). The implication of the agency theory for corporate governance is that adequate monitoring or control mechanisms need to be established to protect shareholders from management's conflict of interest (Kiel and Nicholson 2003). In other words, there is the need for a large group of corporate outsiders (shareholders) to be able to control the incentives of a large group of insiders (management) (Weinberg 2003). Hence, Denis and McConnell (2003, p2) define corporate governance as 'the set of mechanisms...that induce the self-interested controllers of a company (those that make decisions regarding how the company will be operated) to make decisions that maximise the value of the company to its owners...'.

These control mechanisms could be either internal or external. Internal mechanisms include an effectively structured board, equity-based and performance-related compensation contracts, and concentrated ownership holdings that encourage active monitoring of managerial decisions (Hendry and Kiel 2004; Kiel and Nicholson 2003; Shleifer and Vishny 1997). The market for corporate control, which commonly takes the form of corporate takeovers, proxy contests and a legal system that guarantees investor rights (Shleifer and Vishny 1997), are external mechanisms that come into play when internal mechanisms fail (Daily et al 2003).

To say that a corporate governance mechanism is effective is to say that the benefits of such mechanisms outweigh the costs. The ultimate corporate governance mechanism therefore does not necessarily eliminate the agency problem but rather is a rational best response to the problem that attempts to balance the costs and benefits of managerial discretion (Weinberg 2003).

STEWARDSHIP THEORY

Stewardship theory, which gains its insights from the field of sociology and psychology (Sundaramurthy and Lewis 2003), has attracted researchers' attention both as a complement and a contrast to the agency theory (Daily et al 2003). The theory recognises that there exist non-financial motives for managerial behaviour. These include the need for achievement, recognition, the intrinsic satisfaction of successful performance, respect for authority and the work ethic (Muth and Donaldson 1998), and reputation (Daily et al 2003). The steward managers intend to maximise corporate performance, believing that they will ultimately benefit when their companies thrive. For example, in order to protect their reputation as expert decision-makers, executives and directors are more likely to run the company in a manner that maximises the company's financial performance. Essentially, to the degree that an executive feels that their future fortunes are bound to their current corporate employers, the executive may consider their interest as aligned with that of the corporation and shareholders even in the absence of any shareholding (Donaldson and Davis 1991).

Based on the assumption that managers may have other motives beyond self-interest, stewardship theorists suggest that goal conflict may not be inherent in the separation of ownership from control (Muth and Donaldson 1998). Thus, while the agency theory advocates corporate governance structures that control and monitor the actions of management, stewardship theory advocates the empowerment of management. The steward manager is empowered with the information, the tools and the authority to make good decisions for the organisation. The principal (that is, corporate owner) will fully enable the steward (that is, managers) to act in the best interest of the company, trusting that the steward will make choices that maximise the long-term return of the company. It is argued that devising control mechanisms on stewards will significantly demotivate the steward and be counterproductive for both the steward and for the company (Argyris 1964). Stewardship theorists strongly believe that having control empowers management to maximise corporate profits. Consequently, they favour CEO duality (Donaldson and Davis 1991) and insider-dominated boards, arguing that compared with outside directors, inside directors contribute a greater depth of knowledge, expertise and commitment to the company (Hendry and Kiel 2004).

Stewardship theory, according to Smallman (2004), is primarily an argument for a balanced governance where stewards balance tension between different beneficiaries and interest groups to produce firm performance that 'satisfies' the interests of all parties. Trust, open communication, empowerment, long-term orientation and performance enhancement are regarded as factors that characterise management philosophy of stewardship (Davis et al 1997). All these factors appear to be imperative if loyalty and commitment are to be attained in the workplace. For example, open communication and empowerment imply a high level of commitment by employees in organisations (Walton 1985).

STAKEHOLDER THEORY

Stakeholder theory has its roots in politics, law and management organisation studies. Its prominence in organisation studies is attributed to Freeman's (1984) study in which a stakeholder is defined as any group or individual who can affect or is affected by the organisation's objectives. Under stakeholder theory, companies owe some degree of accountability to a range of groups connected with their business other than shareholders. Proponents of the stakeholder theory argue that shareholders are the stakeholders with the least commitment to the company and the greatest mobility. According to stakeholder theory, companies can be viewed as having multilateral agreements with their multiple stakeholders. The relationship between a company and its internal stakeholders is regarded as being either formal or informal depending on the history of the relationship. It is the nature of these relationships that is argued to create strategic possibilities for companies (Clarke 2007). For instance, while managers rely on their shareholders for financial resources, they should rely on their employees and their expertise to achieve their strategic goals. As Blair (1995) advocates, companies are institutional arrangements that exist for governing the relationships between all the groups that contribute to companies' operations. Among these groups, employees with specialised skills can be regarded as an important group which makes the attainment of strategic goals plausible. If managers aim to fulfil their fiduciary duty, which is to maximise their companies' wealth rather than shareholders' wealth, they are expected to consider the impacts managerial decisions may have on all stakeholder groups. One criticism that could be laid against this line of argument is that management is left with too much freedom to manoeuvre. Sternberg (1997), a critic of stakeholder theory, claims that because it denies that companies should be primarily accountable to their owners, the key concept of corporate governance is lost as accountability to everyone is accountability to no one. Further criticism is levied against stakeholder theory that even if stakeholders could be categorised according to their degree of importance to the company, directors (as agents) would be attempting to serve too many principals, and in doing so they may fail to satisfy those with a genuine claim on the organisation (Smallman 2004).

RESOURCE DEPENDENCE THEORY

Resource dependence theory gains its prominence from economics and sociology (Zahra and Pearce 1989). This theory draws attention to interdependencies of companies by focusing on the relationship between an organisation and its constituencies. According to resource dependence theory, resource exchanges are central to these relationships (Pfeffer and Cohen 1984). Under this theory, groups or organisations gain power over each other by controlling valued resources. For large public limited companies, access to scarce external resources is secured through the presence of outsiders, that is, non-executive directors. Corporate boards act as co-optative mechanisms that allow companies to interact with their external environments in order to secure vital resources for their operations and hence gain competitive advantage (Stiles and Taylor 2001).

Most of the literature is on top management and how, for instance, non-executive directors are expected to bring in external resources that aid the company in gaining competitive advantage and achieving goals (Hillman et al 2000). Little attention has been paid to how employees within a company can get hold of vital resources, such as knowledge and expertise that are imperative for the smooth running of operations, and how they continuously need to keep themselves up to date with the latest advances in their field of expertise. Any stakeholder group that holds resources vital to the operations of a company is believed to hold power over the company and powerful stakeholders are to be taken seriously by companies (Boxall and Purcell 2008; Schuler and Jackson 2007). Employees, through their skills and motivation, have the power to affect corporate performance in significant ways. Hence, a company that intends to be successful should choose HR strategies, such as how to recruit, organise and motivate employees over time, that are appropriate and serve the best interest of the company and makes the attainment of corporate goals plausible.

IMPLICATIONS FOR HRM

The approach that an organisation takes to corporate governance strongly influences the kinds of HR policies it will adopt. As is explained in Chapter 1, it is generally accepted that the core functional activities of HR can be subdivided into: (1) employee relations, (2) people resourcing, (3) employee reward and (4) learning and development (Marchington and Wilkinson 2008), and these are the subcategories used by the CIPD in its Professional Standards.

Under agency theory, which dominates Anglo-Saxon governance mechanisms in the UK and US, the separation of ownership and control implies that managers are the only ones taking decisions about HR. Thus, in terms of reward, an apparent polarisation between the fortunes of senior managers and ordinary employees has grown (see Chapter 15). The assertion that senior managers need to be highly rewarded in order to align their interests with shareholders is based upon the assumption of their rational utility-maximising behaviour. In contrast, while we have witnessed many cases in Anglo-Saxon countries where senior management have received substantial pay packages, ordinary employees have faced the threat of redundancy (hence a resourcing issue) with modest, if any, compensation. This can be particularly the case when companies face financial difficulties. The images of staff clearing their desks and leaving their jobs with no notice at the London branch of the failed Lehman Brothers in 2008 contrasts starkly with the public outrage at other finance houses – some whose risks were borne by the taxpayer, not shareholders or executives – paying six-figure bonuses to senior staff in 2009. The contrast is directly attributable to the model of corporate governance taken.

For employee relations, corporate governance is directly relevant. Companies governed under the principle of shareholder value will generally wish to resist employee relations approaches that have strong mechanisms for employee voice. Stakeholder versions will see strong employee voice as important and, while rare examples of companies such as John Lewis have established a reputation for strong employee voice through non-union staff representation, for the most part trade union recognition remains the most significant form of employee voice in the UK (Kersley et al 2005). In the absence of any legal backing and considering that they are not represented in the governance mechanisms, employees have little say on issues related to them under the Anglo-Saxon model. In the UK, as elsewhere, trade unions have long been the dominant representative voice of employees. However, as is explained in Chapter 12, union influence has declined significantly in recent decades.

Regarding issues related to learning and development, companies decide to have training and development programmes with the view that doing so will enhance the productivity and performance of their employees, which will ultimately result in higher share prices. In comparison to agency theory, the stewardship theory views the whole situation from the opposite end of the spectrum, whereby managers are argued to act as stewards who endeavour to strike the balance between different interests. Hence, managers are expected to deploy the culture of openness and trust whereby dialogue and communication with employees are held on a regular basis and employees are expected to participate in training programmes to enhance their efficiencies and progress their careers and are eventually rewarded for improved performance. Employees are viewed as valuable resources whose motivation and loyalty can get a company through difficult times and put it ahead of its competitors in times of difficulty. Although the governance mechanisms of the Anglo-Saxon countries are predominantly analysed using agency theory, there are exceptional companies (for example John Lewis, Cadbury's) that make the effort to treat their employees well and their behaviour can be analysed using stewardship theories. In the case of Cadbury's, it will be interesting to see how these values will be affected by its high-profile takeover by the American company Kraft – adhering to the shareholder-value approach to corporate governance. Nonetheless, it is important to note that in Anglo-Saxon systems, the absence of any employees from the governance mechanisms implies that employees are always at the mercy of their top managers.

In countries such as Germany and Japan, the stakeholder approach, commonly discussed under stakeholder theory, implies that, unlike Anglo-Saxon structures, employees are actively involved in the decision-making process with the supporting legislation, mitigating managers' positions as the only ones in charge of decision-making. For instance in Germany, the presence of trade unions on the supervisory board ensures employees' involvement in the decision-making process. This would ultimately mean a flow of information between managers and employees (Davies 2000). Similarly in Japan, the concept of lifetime employment is conflated with employees' loyalty where managers continuously seek the views of their employees. In such structures, managers cannot easily fire employees at their discretion. For example, German work councils resist short-term layoffs and mandate redeployment through retraining and transfers, and any redundancy would be illegal unless the approval of the work councils is obtained (Jackson et al 2004). Japanese employees are regularly retrained and redeployed to other parts of the organisation when necessary and there are strict laws against redundancies. The retraining of employees is ubiquitous in a stakeholder approach and is regarded as a means of maintaining employees' loyalty. For example, in Germany, training takes place within a multi-employer and quasi-public system of occupational training and the skills are portable and related to broad occupations rather than being firm-specific (Jackson et al 2004, p8).

Another common characteristic of stakeholder approach systems is the concept of fair pay and reward to employees. In Germany, for example, substantial pay and reward differences between senior and ordinary employees are not observable (Jackson 2003). Minimum rates with high thresholds, as well as outlining basic provisions and premium pay (for example overtime, shift work rates, and holidays) for each grade of employees, are set through collective agreements (Jackson et al 2004). Criteria for firms to categorise jobs into standardised grades by job evaluation methods, including detailed weightings for skill, knowledge, responsibility and factors in the work environment (dust, gases, noise, vibration, and so on), are specified through collective agreements and works councils play an active role of monitoring the implementation of industry-wide agreements at the company level (Jackson et al 2004). This considerably reduces the scope for firm-level variation of wages and working conditions. At the same time, individual variability of pay is also reduced. As there tends to be a high level of union commitment to principles of equal pay for equal work, company seniority, unlike in Anglo-Saxon structures, plays little or no formal role in the determination of individual pay. Overall, income inequality is low given the flat wage structure and relatively high wages.

CONCLUSION

This chapter presented an overview of the main governance mechanisms, where employees are located and hence treated in each mechanism. Discussions were presented on different definitions of corporate governance and distinctions were made between the traditional views, where shareholders are regarded as the main focus, and the more modern definitions, where a range of stakeholders are considered. The chapter draws attention to two main governance mechanisms: the Anglo-Saxon mechanism and the stakeholder approaches in Germany and Japan. It was illustrated that in the Anglo-Saxon structure, which is predominant in the UK and US, most of the attention is on shareholders and the interests of other stakeholders may be taken into account as long as doing so is in the interest of shareholders. In comparison with the Anglo-Saxon mechanism, employees lie at the heart of corporate governance in Germany and Japan. In Germany, employees at different levels have the legal right to be represented at top managerial level and can actively take part in decision-making processes, and in Japan, corporate governance is convoluted with the concept of lifetime employment with strict laws against redundancies. The chapter also presented a brief review of the development of those aspects of corporate governance codes that could be related to employees or could reflect managerial decision-making that could have implications for employees. The review revealed that shareholders are the main stakeholders to whom corporate managers are held accountable, and all the monitoring and incentive mechanisms are devised to curb the utility-maximising behaviour of managers and ensure that their interests are in alignment with those of the corporate owners, that is, shareholders. It was later contended that the idea for UK corporate governance has transcended from the traditional agency theory, and this is despite the arguments by the stakeholder theory and resource dependence theory stating that increasing attention is paid to the importance of stakeholders and the impacts they can have on the long-term success of a company.

CRITICAL REFLECTIONS

BP, as a British company operating in the US, can be assumed to operate on shareholder-value assumptions of corporate governance, and accountability is therefore based on ensuring that shareholder interests are the only legitimate interests that need to be protected by corporate governance structures. Agency theory suggests that the separation of ownership and control meant that managers had access to corporate information that allowed them to make strategic decisions related to the relative risks posed by operational costs, safety costs and the likelihood and cost of an accident. With falling oil prices, these relative risks made health and safety costs relatively more expensive and the risk was tilted more towards cost-cutting in this area. As prescribed by the regulatory codes, the non-executive directors who were expected to play the monitoring role and mitigate the utility-maximising behaviour of managers failed to have an effective role. Despite the regulatory codes of conduct, the weaknesses in corporate governance still allowed substantial pension packages.

The absence of employees on the corporate board, and their exclusion from governance mechanisms in general, coupled with the absence of strict statute to protect redundancies can be regarded as factors contributing to the way that risk was weighed against the interests of employees.

Comparisons with German and Japanese corporate governance mechanisms could be made in relation to 'alternative outcomes'. In these systems employees do have a voice and their views are counted, if not directly taken into consideration. They are expected to make proposals as to how employees' views can be considered in decision-making in an Anglo-Saxon structure – it may be that employees can have representatives in governance mechanisms, or codes of best practice can be modified so that their views can be considered.

Regarding alternative approaches to corporate governance we could note that stewardship theory would suggest that managers did not act as stewards of the shareholders as they put the company in disrepute over the long run. Stakeholder theory suggests that little evidence can be found to indicate that employees' views were formally taken into consideration in strategic decision-making. Resource dependence theory suggests that employees can be regarded as one of the most precious resources that companies have because they offer their wealth of knowledge and expertise. Had BP weighted more in favour of its employees' technical views with regard to safety and less in favour of the costs associated with better safety, they would have been less likely to have experienced so many accidents over the period.

EXPLORE FURTHER

TRICKER, R.I. (1984) *Corporate governance*. Aldershot: Gower.

This is one of the core texts covering the models of corporate governance.

AGLIETTA, M. and REBÉRIOUX, A. (2005) *Corporate governance adrift: a critique of shareholder value*. Northampton, MA.: Edward Elgar Publishing.

As the title suggests, this is a critique of the shareholder-value view of the firm and society from a well-known writer in the institutionalist school of thought.

SIKKA, P. (2008) Corporate governance: what about the workers? *Accounting, Auditing and Accountability Journal*. Vol 21, No 7. pp955–977.

Makes a strong case for the inadequacy of the Anglo-Saxon governance mechanisms from the point of view of workers.

FRIEDMAN, M. (2007) The social responsibility of business is to increase its profits. In: ZIMMERLI, W., HOLZINGER, M. and RICHTER, K. (eds). *Corporate ethics and corporate governance*. Berlin: Springer.

A reprinted version of Friedman's classic defence of the principle behind the shareholder-value view of governance.

CHAPTER 3

Ethics (2): Corporate Social Responsibility and HRM

Elizabeth Cotton

OVERVIEW

The aim of this chapter is to examine some contemporary issues around corporate social responsibility (CSR) and its impact on employment practices. The chapter takes an international perspective on the growth and development of CSR, principally in relation to the working practices of multinational companies (MNCs).It looks at the human rights basis of many existing CSR mechanisms and provide some ways of approaching a critical analysis of their effectiveness and credibility. It does this principally through exploring the changing nature of the employment relationship and its 'externalisation' and the weak protection that CSR offers to this category of workers. A case study and detailed information about the UN's Global Compact is included.

LEARNING OBJECTIVES

Reading this chapter will enable the reader to:

- critically examine the shift in paradigms of CSR during this century
- critically analyse the main CSR mechanisms currently in place
- critically evaluate the impact of the 'externalisation' of the employment relationship on the scope of CSR
- form a critical perspective about the effectiveness of CSR in influencing the employment relations climate.

'NATIONAL TRADE UNION TIGLU SIGNS AGREEMENT TO REPRESENT WORKERS IN THAI PLANTS'

According to ICEM online news (2008), in early 2008 Thai Industrial Gases (TIG/Linde), Thailand's biggest provider of industrial gases and a subsidiary of a German multinational company, signed a milestone agreement with the national trade union TIGLU to represent workers in their Thai plants. The agreement, which only came after a struggle, secured their rights to organise TIG workers across Thailand.

In one situation, jobs had been contracted out first to Adecco, one of the world's largest temporary employment agencies. Adecco was then replaced by an unknown agency, whose address turned out to be a building under construction. This made the agency seem a sham, making it appear that this was an attempt by TIG/Linde to circumvent the union. Most workers signed the new work agreements, but nine refused and were fired. Reportedly, some who did sign were threatened with dismissal if they got involved in union activities. In the end, TIG/Linde agreed to reinstate the nine dismissed workers, to not victimise workers by transferring them, and to give the 19 agency workers the same conditions as TIG's regular employees.

TIGLU has also used the Thai labour inspection service to counter bad employment practices at a TIG branch in which agency workers had received lower overtime pay, no sick leave payments and were issued with inadequate safety equipment. After the inspection, the employment agency paid the workers in full, but then retaliated by giving them contracts that had to be renewed every three months.

Questions

1 Is the TIC and the agency violating the human rights of the contract workers? If yes, how?

2 What responsibility does the German parent company have for the situation presented in the case study?

3 What does this case study indicate to us regarding CSR policies?

INTRODUCTION

The central argument of this chapter is that changes in the nature of employment relationship mean that the scope of CSR, in relation to employees, is limited and therefore is not a significant driver to promote better working practices and labour relations. Specifically, the global trend towards an 'externalisation' (Theron 2005) of the labour relationship, primarily through outsourcing and contracting out of labour, allows companies to limit their social responsibilities to direct employees only, an increasingly small percentage of the people who carry out work for them. As a result a company that applies CSR practices and policies only to its direct employees will be able to avoid penalties for poor employment relations practices carried out by contractors, suppliers and in some cases subsidiaries.

PARADIGM SHIFTS

During the 1990s CSR was promoted as a key process of risk management, particularly for international business vulnerable to shareholder action or consumer boycotts. That is, it had become an increased and increasingly costly risk for companies to be using unacceptable working practices in any part of the world. This was straightforwardly quantifiable in companies producing consumer goods or retailers where exposure to using child labour, say, was seen to have a direct impact on share value and consumer patterns. This increase in risk was directly linked to an explosion of ethical consumer initiatives developed at that time, ranging from anti-sweat shop campaigns in the clothing industry to environmental action against mining companies. The 1990s were the time, particularly in the UK, of the non-governmental organisation (NGO), where thousands of small campaigns and organisations, including networks and virtual groups, were set up in response to the practices of business. In addition, the large charitable agencies, such as Oxfam, Save the Children and Amnesty International, all started to turn their attention to the work of companies, in addition to their more traditional charitable and aid work.

One of the key objectives of these campaigns was to raise awareness of corporate employment practices outside of their home countries. This was facilitated by an upsurge in information exchange through the Internet and cyber campaigning where ordinary, primarily young, people could easily get access to information about how companies were acting towards workers abroad. It was becoming relatively easy for people to distribute and also to read information from a local level.

One of the dominant campaign themes at this time was the use of child labour in the garment and textiles industries. International non-governmental organisations (INGOs) and trade unions took up the issue extensively, often targeting MNCs who relied on their good reputation with consumers to generate sales (Werther and Chandler 2005). Two of the earliest campaigns exposing the use of child labour related to North American companies Nike and Levi's.

By the early 2000s CSR was in full flow, with increasingly robust ideas and policies being put in place. By 2008, CSR was being heralded as a key component to development and pulling millions of people out of poverty. This idea was supported by the work of Jeffrey Sachs (2005) and the campaigning around the increasingly important G8 and G20 meetings at this time, all pushing not only for taxpayer and governmental responses to poverty but also promoting heavily the role of the private company in providing good jobs and incomes for poor people.

This philosophy is encapsulated in the press statements coming out of the World Economic Forum (WEF) in Davos in 2008, where great claims were made about the impact of the practices of MNCs carrying out their work in a socially responsible way.

This was spearheaded by what became known as the 'philanthrocapitalists', corporate and philanthropic leaders who paid for and also promoted the work of private companies in aid and development. The most famous at that time was

Bill Gates from Microsoft who, through the Bill and Melinda Gates Foundation, channelled millions of private dollars into work around inequalities and HIV/AIDS, malaria and tuberculosis. This represented a major paradigm shift in the idea of CSR as a mechanism for protecting MNCs from risk, particularly shareholder action, towards a more inflated idea of CSR as the way in which large corporations contribute to poverty alleviation and the development of poor countries. The CSR and aid worlds share a common language of human rights and sustainable development. CSR and aid ideologies reinforce each other, founded on a core belief that poverty is fundamentally a problem of geography or difference rather than a structural problem with the free market. It is only possible to believe that poverty can be solved by individuals and individual programmes if you also believe that it is not structurally caused. That is, that the source of these philanthropic funds is not, at least in part, responsible for the poverty that they are trying to alleviate.

There were many organisations and people who argued critically against this picture of CSR, including trade unions, which provided evidence for apparently socially responsible corporations not adhering to the basic human rights of their own workers. Although it is not true that this grand version of CSR was purely a public relations exercise, it is true to say that the experience of many workers in developing countries stood in stark contrast to these developmental ambitions. That is, there was already clear evidence that the labour practices of many foreign companies operating in developing countries did not respect even basic human rights.

By 2009 the context within which CSR was operating had changed as a consequence of the recession triggered by the financial crisis from 2007. Moving away from grand claims about the impact on development of socially responsible business, the model of CSR became reduced to a more modest idea of 'social business'. The same WEF event in 2009 presented quietly a reduced idea of CSR as 'social business'.

This conceptualisation of 'social business' is at best vague. It appears to be the idea that businesses need to be able to sell their goods to increasingly impoverished markets. In essence this seems to amount to the idea that companies expanding their production and markets to poorer regions of the world is in itself a social good. That is, by doing business in the developing world developing countries will inherently benefit. Whether we agree with this or not, what is important here is the contrast between this modest and business-like approach to global business, with the grand claims made in 2008 about the role of business in global development objectives.

CSR AND EMPLOYEES

In the main CSR has been driven by and applied to multinational companies (MNCs). This is partly due to the increased risk that large companies face in terms of their reputation if their practices are seen to be irresponsible. That is, large companies have a larger market presence and therefore carry a greater cost from losing 'moral capital' (Godfrey et al 2009; Backhaus and Tikoo 2004).

It is also because MNCs are most likely to have operations in developing countries, where there may be a deficit of labour and other standards. This lack of regulation exposes MNCs to working practices that would not be acceptable either legally or culturally in the developed world, where the majority are headquartered. In developing countries most large-scale CSR activities are being carried out by foreign multinational companies as part of their global policy. Small and medium-size enterprises are much less active, although this does not necessarily point to a lack of social responsibility, but more to a limitation on dedicated resources. Since the early 1990s CSR has developed into a sector in its own right. In developed countries most large firms will have dedicated staff and even departments responsible for CSR, often using titles such as community relations, governance and external relations. Even for relatively small firms you will find that someone at senior level is responsible for managing the company's relationship with various stakeholders, including shareholders, consumers and employees.

The CSR structures of companies are rarely explicitly linked to HR departments or functions, focusing almost exclusively on external rather than internal relations. It is common that in the CSR reports or policies you will not find many references to employees and certainly not to trade unions, which have a presence in most parts of the world. The culture of CSR does not pay great attention to the issue of employment relations and labour standards, raising the question as to whether CSR does anything to improve the position of working people.

CSR AND HUMAN RIGHTS

Social responsibility is understood through a human rights framework. That is, the responsibilities of companies are spelled out with reference to human rights and the responsibilities that they entail. The most up-to-date summary of how human rights relate to the responsibilities of companies is John Ruggie's report from April 2008. This report, written by the then Special Advisor to Kofi Annan (previously the Secretary General of the United Nations), outlines the current thinking around which human rights relate to business practices and their relative success in influencing company behaviour, both internally and externally.

The main human rights as they relate to employees are framed using the International Labour Organization's (ILO) Core Labour Conventions. The ILO, part of the United Nations responsible for human rights and practice within the workplace, is a tripartite body made up of employers, governments and trade unions. The key function of the ILO is to negotiate and develop international standards for work, primarily in the form of conventions, which are then ratified by national governments and enshrined in national law. The body, although regarded as a weak enforcement mechanism, is accepted internationally as the setter of standards. It should be noted, however, that these standards are minimum ones, below which a company's practices are internationally recognised as unacceptable.

Box 3.1 ILO Core Labour Conventions

The eight Core Labour Conventions are regarded as being fundamental to the rights of all working people regardless of national context and traditions. Even if a country does not ratify them, these conventions are regarded as binding to all governments. The conventions are:

- Convention 29 Forced Labour 1930
- Convention 87 Freedom of Association and Protection of the Right to Organize 1948
- Convention 98 Right to Organize and Collective Bargaining 1949
- Convention 100 Equal Remuneration 1951
- Convention 105 Abolition of Forced Labour 1957
- Convention 111 Discrimination (Employment and Occupation) 1958
- Convention 138 Minimum Age Convention 1973
- Convention 182 Elimination of the Worst Forms of Child Labour 1999

Source: International Labour Organization (2010)

For trade unions the two conventions relating to the right to join a trade union and for that union to bargain collectively on their behalf are crucial minimum standards allowing union organising in many parts of the world. Particularly in those countries where trade union rights are weak or not enshrined, these international standards are important in creating a possibility for people to form and join trade unions.

When these conventions are not adhered to, unions and groups can submit a complaint to the ILO's Committee of Experts or the Committee for Freedom of Association. Complaints are then investigated by these committees and a formal report submitted to the ILO's Governing Body for their attention. This system, although well established and respected, is seen as a weak one because of its lack of penalties beyond the embarrassment felt by individual governments if found to have contravened basic human rights.

CSR MECHANISMS

By 2000 there existed hundreds of thousands of CSR policies, programmes and initiatives used by companies to implement their principles. The majority of these were unilateral company codes of conduct, which were drawn up by companies as a statement of their core principles and commitments. Although most companies continue to have these codes, they have a relatively weak level of support precisely because of their unilateral nature, that they are entirely managed by the company itself.

Partly in response to this, a wide range of voluntary initiatives were set up in the late 1990s and early part of 2000 on a multilateral basis – that is, involving more than one organisation and based on common principles held by them (Ruggie 1993). These ranged from sector-specific initiatives such as Fairtrade labelling in the food sector to the Extractive Industries Transparency Initiative (EITI), where the focus was on promoting better company practices in specific sectors addressing sector-specific issues. In the case of the extractive industries, for example, a key issue faced by companies was that of corruption and transparency in dealing with national governments and indigenous groups. The EITI was an attempt, initiated by the British Government, to help the industry regulate itself by setting its own standards.

Another response to the weakness of unilateral codes has been the push towards more binding agreements, ones that are signed and agreed between parties. There are relatively few binding agreements currently in place, with the most extensively used being International Framework Agreements (IFAs). IFAs are based on a negotiated agreement between MNC senior management and national and international trade unions. Over 70 agreements currently exist with major MNCs, mainly from western Europe. IFAs are significant international agreements because they are signed and have monitoring mechanisms but also because they include in their content core labour standards and employment-related clauses such as equal opportunities, living wages and exchange of information between unions and employers (Croucher and Cotton 2009).

In addition to these agreements and policies, many companies carry out direct programmes in areas affected by company operations. Well promoted in annual reports, companies such as Unilever and Shell have carried out local community programmes ranging from access to water and primary education for many years. But the programmes are not just limited to what can be seen as charitable acts for local people. In one of the most advanced CSR programmes of an MNC, there is the example of Anglo American, which provides extensive treatment and support services on HIV/AIDS for its employees and, increasingly, mining communities. Although there is an economic argument in the case of Anglo American to do this, it still stands as one of the most progressive and extensive CSR programmes in the industry (Croucher and Cotton 2009)

ISSUES FOR CSR MECHANISMS

For workers, there are three key issues that determine whether a particular CSR mechanism is credible or not.

The first is whether the mechanism includes within it some commitment to follow the eight Core Labour Standards as they are set out by the ILO. ILO research shows that of 300 company codes and policies, approximately only 10% included the eight core conventions. That means that an estimated 90% of company codes make no reference to labour standards (ILO 2003). In other voluntary codes, such as the Global Compact (which we look at below) and the IFAs, the eight Core Labour Conventions form an important part.

The second issue is about the usability of the mechanisms. In most workplaces in the world there is limited specialist knowledge about human rights and the United Nations. It is crucially important, therefore, that the CSR policies or agreements that companies adopt are understandable and useable by the people that are working in their operations at worker, trade union and management levels. This places a requirement on companies for a high degree of clarity and information provision about its CSR commitments in order for the company to successfully follow its own policies.

The third key issue is who monitors or audits the company's practices against their commitments. Particularly in large-scale companies where senior management and CSR staff are not present on a daily basis, it is important that company practices are monitored and an assessment made about whether they reach the standards set. The most obvious question that we might have about monitoring is, who does it? For example, can the company itself be relied upon to monitor its own practices? There has been much international debate about this, with the trade union position being predominantly that the trade unions need to be part of the monitoring process because of their unique position in the workplace. Trade unions are present in the workplace on a daily basis and are also independent of company management, giving them an important role in monitoring company practices. In addition, many independent companies and NGOs offer auditing and monitoring services to companies with fairly specific processes and degrees of effectiveness.

Linked to this is an issue that has been debated over the last ten years about what indicators are used to measure social responsibility. In recent years the Global Reporting Initiative (GRI) index has been used extensively by companies, particularly those signed up to the Global Compact, in order to provide an internationally accepted measurement of social responsibility. In our case study, for example, Linde uses the Global Compact principles and the GRI indicators to measure its social responsibility.

The Global Compact

One of the most widely used CSR mechanisms is the Global Compact, with over 5,200 companies from 130 countries signed up to this voluntary initiative. This is partly due to its credible origins in the office of the previous Secretary General of the United Nations (UN), Kofi Annan, a much respected international figure in both the human rights and business arenas. The initiative was set up to try to include companies in the United Nations' human rights work. Remember that the membership of the UN is made up of national governments and there was previously no direct way of linking private companies to the UN's human rights programmes. The Global Compact is also felt to be highly pragmatic and useable, based on a system of national, regional and international networks aimed at promoting best practice. Although varied between countries, NGOs and trade unions are not excluded from these platforms and provide an important point of dialogue between the different CSR stakeholders.

The Global Compact is regarded by trade unions as one of the stronger CSR mechanisms because of its inclusion of the eight Core Labour Conventions, the inclusion of trade unions in the Global Compact's own advisory board and its usability in the workplace.

EXTERNALISATION: CONTRACT AND AGENCY WORK

Externalisation encapsulates the processes by which a company obtains and uses labour from outside the organisation (see Chapter 11). The particular processes that we are going to look at in this section, which have a major impact on employment relations, relate to the use of contract and agency labour.

There are hundreds of ways that a company can use the labour of workers that are not directly employed by them, depending on national contexts, law and sectors. The common forms of externalised labour that are seen in most parts of the world include arrangements such as contracting out functions to other companies (off-site and on-site), disguised employment training contracts, on-call/daily hire, home-working and temporary labour contracts.

Although there is not comprehensive research on the use of externalised labour (ILO 2007), there are pockets of data, often researched by unions and global union federations. For example, it is estimated that 70% of labour used by Nestlé to manufacture, package and distribute products are not directly employed by them (Greenfield 2006). The International Metalworkers Federation (IMF) estimates that 44% of workers in the metal sectors work under 'precarious' or externalised contracts (IMF 2008). We also know that the use of contract and agency labour is increasing globally, with regions such as Asia and Eastern Europe facing externalised work for the first time in their history.

Two key categories of precarious or externalised labour are contract and agency labour. Here it is important to understand what we mean by these terms, although it should be noted that because of the huge diversity and complexity of the various forms there are no internationally accepted definitions in place. The ILO itself has struggled to find a definition of contract work that applies globally and in most cases the use of the terms 'contract labour' and 'agency labour' need to be clarified. For the purposes of this chapter, contracting out is where a company gives work to another employer. The work may or may not be done at the same location. Sometimes the new employer may take on the existing permanent workers to carry out this work. This is often linked to outsourcing, which is where a company decides to have work done in another location. This may or may not be owned by the present employer and may or may not be in the same country. Agency labour is where a company needs workers and, rather than employ them directly, it asks an agency to send the required number of workers. These workers are employed by the agency.

Contract and agency labour is often precarious in character, but is not necessarily so. In some cases, such as specialist technical staff working in the extractive industries, contract workers are highly paid and valued. However, in the majority of cases contract and agency workers are used because of the cost savings to the company. Not only are workers likely to be paid a low rate, contracting companies are not liable to pay certain social security or employers' costs, and most importantly only have to use contract and agency workers at those times when they require it.

One significant consequence of this is the high level of job insecurity that contract and agency workers face, with the ever-present pressure to accept lower pay and conditions in order to secure paid work. This job insecurity exists even where contract and agency workers have been working in the same workplace for long periods, with short-term contracts extended for many years. Even in this case of 'permatemps', the reality is that once a short-term contract ends there is no legal obligation on the company to renew it. There are even examples where employers will change the contractor regularly in order to avoid any legal complication with long-term renewal of temporary contracts. One ILO complaint in Korea was submitted where a worker had been nominally employed by seven subcontractors while he continued to carry out the same job in Kiryung Electronics for many years (ICEM 2008).

This also has a major impact on union membership and the scope of collective bargaining. The majority of contract and agency workers are not union members, often concerned about losing work because of their affiliation with a union. In some cases unions have also been reluctant to represent contract and agency workers, given that they are often replacing permanent and organised workers. This is a dilemma for both the workers and the trade unions. One example of this is the textile and clothing sector in Turkey, which has seen a shrinking of the number of workers covered by a collective bargaining agreement (CBA) from 150,000 in 1986 to fewer than 50,000 in 2006, in part due to the extensive use of subcontracting in the sector (Koçer and Fransen 2009). What it does mean is that by far the majority of contract and agency workers are not covered by any collective agreement and are therefore unlikely to see an improvement of their pay and conditions.

Externalised workers are often not protected by national labour legislation in the way that 'standard' workers are. This is because most employment and commercial law is based on a standard definition of the employment relationship. Where this relationship is externalised to another employer or to self-employed workers, the consequence is a shift in the employment relationship that places it outside of the existing legislation. This does not mean that the use of externalised labour becomes illegal, rather that it places certain forms of employment contracts outside of the law such that companies are able to circumnavigate their responsibilities as employers.

Table 3.1 Key multinationals supplying labour

Multinational	2004	2006/07
Adecco	5,800 offices	7,000 offices (2007)
Manpower	4,300 offices	4,400 offices (2007)
Vedior *	2,200 offices	2,433 offices (2006)
Randstad		1,827 offices (2006) 2,670 offices (2007)

* Vedior was purchased by Randstad in December 2007.

Source: Company annual reports and websites; Croucher and Cotton (2009)

We can also see this expansion of contract and agency labour through the massive growth in employment agencies, a number of which are themselves large MNCs. Table 3.1 lists some of the largest agencies operating globally.

In the main, however, labour agencies are small-scale national companies, with many operating outside of the law. Some extreme examples of this are contractors operating in the mining sector in Colombia and 'gangmasters' operating in most regions of the world, including western Europe. These agencies often target vulnerable groups, including migrants and women, exploiting the particular difficulties that they face in securing paid work.

Often, when legal frameworks are weak, it can be difficult for contract and agency workers to even establish who the real employer is. Even in relatively simple operations, the commercial agreements with subcontractors can be vaguely formulated and employment contracts non-existent, making it difficult to prove where legally the responsibilities lie. In our case study the agency that employs the TIG contract workers is registered to a construction site and as such is likely to be simply a mechanism to externalise the responsibilities of the employer.

This externalisation of the employment relationship is reflected in the increase in disputes and industrial action taken by workers in response to companies contracting out jobs. Information about current campaigns against contracting out and cases of abuses of contract and agency workers can be accessed easily by looking at the online news facilities of the Global Union Federations and the Trade Union Advisory Committee (TUAC) (www.global-unions.org).

What this means in terms of CSR is that companies that extensively use contract and agency labour are able to limit their responsibilities for ensuring acceptable standards and conditions of work to only those workers that are directly employed by them. By signing an agreement with an employment agency or by subcontracting work to local suppliers, the contracting company is able to distance itself from the conditions under which contract and agency workers are forced to work, claiming that the responsibility lies with the contractor or agency.

CONCLUSION

The central argument of this chapter has been that despite the important cultural shift that has taken place in relation to the social responsibilities of companies over the last 30 years in creating a more aware and rights-based corporate practice, the positive gains for workers have been minimal. This is, in part, because the existing CSR policies and mechanisms as they relate to employees cover only a small minority of often privileged workers, those that work directly for an MNC. A much greater percentage of people work indirectly for MNCs, through contractors and agencies, therefore falling outside the scope of current CSR mechanisms. As the externalisation of labour grows globally, we see a conversant shrinking of the percentage of workers covered by CSR mechanisms and international labour standards.

Given the cost savings to companies that comes with externalisation, we should anticipate that in the current recession these trends will intensify. Since 2008 we have been living within a global recession with an estimated 50 million people becoming unemployed during 2009, 200 million working people living in extreme poverty and over 1.4 billion people earning below 2 US dollars a day (ILO 2010). People who are precariously employed have been the first victims of the crisis, regarded as 'disposable' workers because of the lack of protections they have (Global Unions 2009). A recession of this scale brings with it profound challenges to any conceptualisation of social responsibility as it affects labour standards.

The argument has been in this chapter that given the increased 'externalisation' of employment relations, the current conceptualisation of corporate social responsibility is not a sufficiently substantial one to govern the complexities of today's employment relationships. CSR is primarily driven by MNCs, rather than the great majority of small and domestic companies. Given that most domestic firms are not vulnerable to the impact of codes, a change in their employment practices for the better is realistically dependent on their relationship with foreign and multinational companies. That is, it is only when MNCs require of their suppliers the same standards they set for their own employees that working standards will be raised for more working people.

HRM IN THE MEDIA

CRITICAL REFLECTIONS

Relating to the first question of the opening case study, the nature of the employment relationships is unclear. The agency that legally employed the contract workers involved in this case was unknown and likely to be a purely paper exercise to externalise the employment relationship away from TIG. It had the impact that the contract workers did not know who their employer was.

We also have a situation where the contracting company, Thai Industrial Gases (TIG), is contravening basic labour standards by discriminating against contract workers. Not only were nine workers sacked for refusing to sign new temporary contracts, but the agency workers then received lower overtime pay, no sick leave payments and were issued with inadequate safety equipment. At the end of this dispute, following an inspection and ruling by the Thai labour inspectorate, TIG and the employment agency were forced to provide the same conditions to agency workers as TIG's regular employees.

Both TIG and the agency are breaking the human rights of the contract workers by not facilitating their rights to join a trade union and to have them bargain on their behalf. These rights are summarised in the two core labour standards relating to trade union activity, ILO Conventions 87 and 98. Workers were reportedly advised by TIG management not to join TIGLU if they wanted to have their contracts renewed, a clear contravention of Convention 87. Management also refused for more than one year to negotiate with TIGLU, IGBCE and ICEM on behalf of the sacked workers, contravening Convention 98.

Regarding the second question of the opening case study, TIG is a subsidiary of Linde AG, a German multinational company operating in the chemicals sector. Its reputation is as a responsible company, particularly in relation to health and safety, which is typical of companies producing chemicals potentially dangerous to the environment. In its 2008 annual CSR report, Linde AG is proud of its achievements in both its European and developing country operations. Linde AG is a member of the Global Compact and every year reports on its CSR practices using the GRI indicators (Linde 2008). Linde states in this report its commitment to respecting employee rights globally.

Despite this, Linde management in Germany has only reluctantly accepted that, as the parent company, it might have to extend these employee rights to people working for subsidiaries in Thailand and also those working in their operations via employment agencies. This is surprising if you consider the strength of employment relations in a German context, where there are strong relationships between management and worker representatives by law and also corporate culture. It was only after sustained international trade union activity, involving the IGBCE, the powerful German trade union representing Linde's German workers, and the Global Union Federation, the ICEM, which TIGLU is affiliated to, that management was able to make a commitment to respect the human rights of TIG workers.

As far as the third question is concerned, what this case study indicates to us is that CSR policies and reporting do not in themselves lead to good employment practices. This is due in part to a number of national factors. In Thailand, people work in a highly externalised workforce, where workers are predominantly employed within industry on the basis of temporary contracts or through employment agencies. In addition, trade union activity is severely restricted, both by law and the widespread victimisation of trade unionists. The Thai unions are small and struggle to recruit contract and agency workers, who fear the loss of work because of their involvement with a union. This is reflected in the management practices within MNCs operating in Thailand, who are predominantly hostile to bargaining with unions and recognising their right to represent working people.

In an employment relations context such as this, the impact of CSR in and of itself is minimal.

For many trade unions, such as TIGLU, the CSR pronouncements of employers based in western Europe ring hollow when contrasted with the state of local employment relations in the developing world.

EXPLORE FURTHER

CRANE, A., MATTEN, D. and SPENCE, L.J. (2008) *Corporate social responsibility: readings and cases in a global context.* London and New York: Routledge.

This book provides a good basic introduction to CSR.

INTERNATIONAL LABOUR ORGANIZATION. (2010) *Global employment trends.* January 2010. Geneva: International Labour Organization.

This document provides up-to-date statistics and predictions relating to employment within the current recession.

Ethical Trading Initiative, available online at **www.ethicaltrade.org/**

This website provides information on how the UK stakeholders have set up a CSR organisation.

ICEM, available online at **http://cal.icem.org/**

This is the global union website of the ICEM and it provides up-to-date information on how contract and agency work affects jobs and working conditions.

London School of Economics Podcasts, available online at **www.lse.ac.uk/ resources/podcasts/publicLecturesAndEvents.htm**

This website provides podcasts covering contemporary issues on CSR.

CHAPTER 4

Managing HR in Different National Contexts

Geoff Wood

OVERVIEW

This chapter provides a review of contemporary issues and debates in comparative HRM. It focuses particular attention on the types of HRM likely to be encountered in neo-liberal economics, and those found in alternative types of economic organisation. It explores the different categorisations of national economy that have been devised to explain differences in HRM. Central to this chapter is a critique of cultural-based explanations for understanding differences in HR practices, and institutionally orientated alternatives. The chapter concludes with a review of recent advances in institutional theory, which seek to explain the co-existence of alternative HRM paradigms within specific national settings.

LEARNING OBJECTIVES

Reading this chapter will enable the reader to:

- critically analyse cultural explanations of diversity in HR practice
- critically examine accounts that predict convergence in HR practice
- critically evaluate rational choice-based explanations of the effects of institutions on HRM
- critically discuss regulationist accounts of the effects of institutions on HRM
- critically discuss varieties of capitalism approaches to understanding the effects of institutions on HRM.

'THE ABORTIVE SALE OF OPEL'

According to BBC News (2009), during the 2008 financial crisis General Motors was forced to consider the sale of its European wing, Opel (including the British brand, Vauxhall). This led to a great deal of controversy as to possible job losses in the latter. While the British Government favoured a private-equity-led takeover, the German government (and unions) favoured one involving a Canadian car parts maker (Magna) and a Russian motor industry player. Given that the German Government was prepared to provide more financial backing in the event of the latter, the Magna-led offer was ultimately accepted by GM. The worry, particularly of Vauxhall workers and their unions, was that the new deal would be more likely to lead to job losses in the UK. Later, however, GM withdrew from the deal, on account of a modest upturn in its own performance. The case of Opel highlighted the relative extent to which different governments were prepared to get involved in safeguarding jobs – and established ways of managing people – in different national contexts.

Questions

1 Why did the German and British governments differ in their handling of the potential sale of Opel?

2 What aspects of the German and British employment systems led British unions to fear that they would be more likely to bear the brunt of jobs cuts?

INTRODUCTION

Comparative HRM seeks to understand why and how companies manage their people in different national contexts. At the end of the Cold War, writers from a neo-liberal starting point were quick to claim that all countries would ultimately merge towards a neo-liberal ideal (see Fukuyama 2000). The latter would be characterised by deregulated labour markets and generally hands-off governmental policies, giving firms a free hand to utilise or dispose of their labour in the manner they wished (Friedman 1997). Even if this meant workers would be worse off in the short term, it was held that, as firms would operate more efficiently, profits would be higher and more secure, with the benefits trickling down across the economy. While firmly rejecting neo-liberals, pessimistic radical accounts made similar assumptions regarding convergence; general deregulation would give employers more room to manage their people as they wished. However, it was argued that the end state of convergence would result in increasingly uniform labour repression, with resources across society being increasingly concentrated in the hands of a small elite (Moody 1997).

At the time of writing, almost two decades since the end of the Cold War, global convergence in terms of management strategies, and more specifically, people management policies and practices, appears remote. In much of the world, reduced state involvement has meant that employees are indeed very much worse off in terms of both job tenure and terms and conditions of service, with little sign of beneficial trickle down. But, alternative higher-value-added production paradigms persist. And, there are important differences in terms of the way firms are run, both on national and regional lines. This has refocused attention on what makes for persistent diversity in HRM. In practice, the existing literature on comparative HRM can be divided into two broad camps: cultural and institutional approaches. After revisiting these two core concepts – culture and institutions – this chapter provides a review of recent theoretical and empirical research in these areas, and a critique thereof.

COMPREHENDING CULTURE AND INSTITUTIONS

Given the centrality of the concepts of culture and institutions to comparative HRM, it is worth exploring what these terms actually mean and the theoretical challenges associated with using either concept.

Culture may be understood from three basic starting points. Within the broad functionalist tradition, Parsons held that the cultural system was one of four primary systems that fit together, the others being the social system, the personality system and the behavioural organism itself (Wallace and Wolf 1995, p28; Parsons 1951). Central to culture is the basic concept of meaning, for example, language, religion or national values; through a process of socialisation culture is internalised by a society's members (Wallace and Wolf 1995, p28). What does this mean in practice? Basically, for society to 'work' (in other words, produce and distribute the resources required for survival and social life), members have to share basic values. This means that in any exchange relationship – such as the employment contract – each side can know what to expect in a range of areas from the other party. And, culture is a mediating influence; in other words, culture ensures people will rein in short-term opportunism, preventing society from collapsing into destructively competitive rivalries for resources (Wallace and Wolf 1995, p28).

As can be seen from Parsons' analysis, there are likely to be important distinctions in culture on national and regional lines. But Parsons (1951) saw society as composed of many different component parts, work organisations being one of them. Work systems will have specific subcultures of their own, which, again, are essential in maintaining solidarity and effectiveness. For societies to continue 'working', cultures need to persist. This involves a process of socialisation, basically training new members to fit in. What can this tell us about HRM? A classic functionalist account would suggest that as long as societies are at least functional for a significant component thereof, predominant cultures and hence, specific patterns of decisions and practices are likely to persist (Parsons 1951). This means that similar types of HRM are likely to be encountered in a particular setting, with innovation being reined in, in the interests of order and predictability. In practice, functionalist approaches towards culture have tended to veer towards conservatism, concerned with understanding how deviant behaviours are reined in (Ritzer 1992; Ashley and Orenstein 1995).

Interactionist approaches have seen cultures as always being contested and remade through the decisions of individual social actors. This means that culture will be fluid and adaptable (Wallace and Wolf 1995, pp204–205). While this would make comparisons in terms of culture and HR practice across settings more difficult, such approaches do highlight the extent to which culture may be remade to suit changing needs and purposes of individuals and their associations. Even if an organisation's culture appears to have stayed the same over a period of time, it may in fact have been subject to subtle alterations with, over time, interpretations of rules changing dramatically, even if the rules themselves stay the same.

In his classic writings, Marx saw culture as one of the mechanisms that serve to preserve social order (Turner 1998; Ritzer 1992). However, unlike Parsons, who saw this process as essential for economic life, Marx primarily saw culture as a means of perpetuating social injustice; even if they are in objective terms, poorly off, an organisation's employees will be reluctant to challenge this – or indeed, wider social injustice – if they have been subtly inculcated with the attitudes, norms and values that support the present order (Turner 1998; Ashley and Orenstein 1995). In other words, while culture may make for persistent practice, culture often serves to perpetuate repression, making it ultimately open to challenge. Later, critical theory built on these assumptions, but focused on the psychological basis both for perpetuating and challenging cultural norms (Ritzer 1992; Turner 1998).

In practice, if we want to deploy concepts of culture to understand differences in HRM practice on national and organisational lines, a crucial distinction is whether culture is conceived of in functionalist terms, as a necessary prerequisite for social order and, hence, mutual benefit, within and beyond the workplace, or as a mechanism for securing domination and control of one grouping at the expense of another.

Institutions represent systems of interactions 'that endure over time, and that distribute people over space' (Turner 1998, p495). In other words, institutions are formalised clusters of behaviour that are embedded and persist; for example, a country's education and training system may be seen as an institution. From a functionalist perspective, different institutions may be seen as each playing a specific role within a particular context. For example, the dominant cultural system within a particular context would be an institution (Turner 1998; Wallace and Wolf 1995). Following from Parsons, culture would be seen as a necessary prerequisite for ensuring social order. Other institutions would supplement this role; in a functional society institutions support each other, rather than dynamically interact or challenge each other. Within his later work, Parsons argued that the cultural system regulated and controlled other systems of action (Turner 1998, p32; Parsons 1951). Hence, from a functionalist perspective, it could be argued that in trying to understand differences in behaviour in different contexts, culture is particularly important (Ashley and Orenstein 1995). Indeed, in comparing differences in HRM practice in different contexts, one could focus primarily on culture, rather than on a range of other institutional features.

While the radical tradition would be similarly concerned with the role of institutions as the basis for social order, it is held that their operation will rarely be 'fair' or in any way mutually beneficial. This means that the basis of social order will be regularly challenged. In other words, institutional mediation is likely to be temporary and contested.

Other approaches to institutions, building on the works of Georg Simmel, have suggested that while institutions may provide an essential mechanism for mediating the interests of competing individuals and collectives, their continuation and role is subject to regular remaking, reflecting the differing agendas and concerns of subordinates (Turner 1998, p276). In other words, what takes place at the firm represents the product of objective circumstances and subjective choices, and reinterpretations (Simmel 1980).

CULTURAL ACCOUNTS AND HRM IN PRACTICE

While much earlier work was sceptical as to the possibilities of neatly describing and summarising core cultural features, Hofstede claimed to have uncovered four distinct dimensions that make up national cultures; the number of dimensions later increased to five (McSweeney 2002). These five dimensions are power distance, uncertainty avoidance, individualism/collectivism, masculinity/femininity and long-/short-term orientation (Hofstede 1991). Central to Hofstede's work is that culture determines social actions (McSweeney 2002). In other words, stemming from certain embedded cultural values, firms will manage their people in a specific way in a particular socio-cultural setting. For example, cultures that have a more short-term orientation would set less store on the relative seniority and experience of their employees or on long-term HR planning. National cultures are assumed to be stable and internally uniform (Tung 2008); in other words, within a particular society, people management is likely to have common characteristics, in line with prevailing cultural norms and values. This could include a reluctance, say, to engage in confrontations and/or a greater emphasis on formal hierarchies. New entrants into a particular market will be gradually impelled to fit in; in other words, firms entering a particular cultural context will have to adapt their HR and other policies and practices in line with accepted ways of doing things, or simply exit (Wöcke et al 2007).

It has further been argued that business failures by firms entering new markets represent a lack of cross-cultural competence, in other words, a lack of understanding of different norms and accepted ways of doing things in different parts of the world (Johnson et al 2006). Culture plays a central role in mediating conflict and in balancing the pressures of work and social life (Jackson 2002). Key cultural factors would include the relative individualism or collectivism in society, control orientation, achievement orientation (in other words, how much and how individual achievement is prized) and commitment to egalitarianism (Jackson 2002). Arguably, a strength of cultural approaches is that they highlight the extent to which Western ways of doing things are simply not appropriate in different parts of the world, and the value – and underlying functionality of – alternative cultures.

By focusing on resilient cultural differences, the Hofstede approach discounts the effects of transfers of knowledge, ideas and ways of doing things across national borders (Fang 2007). In response, some writers in the culturalist tradition have begun to explore the extent to which aspects of culture may be transferred across contexts, and the extent to which hybridisation of cultures may take place (Jackson 2002; Woldu et al 2006). The global transformation and restructuring of the world is eroding the confidence of cultural accounts that focus on the national level and on predetermined cultural rigidities. Again, Budhwar and Sparrow (2002, p604) note that culture does not simply impose norms on people; how HR managers (and others) subjectively interpret these norms actually determines practice. And, although there is increasing scholarly unease with many of the foundations of cross-cultural HRM, many of these critics have been reluctant to depart from the camp totally; rather there has been a move towards a more psychologically orientated approach to culture, drawing on social psychology (see Budhwar and Sparrow 2002). But, to date, only limited attention has been devoted to understanding variations at the local and supernational level. A notable exception is the study of Woldu et al (2006), which highlighted variations in the relative embeddedness of culture at social and organisational level. In some sectors, a high transnational division of labour and specific technologies have done much to promote cross-fertilisation (Woldu et al 2006).

LIMITS OF CULTURAL ACCOUNTS

In view of the above, it is evident that there are a number of limitations to cultural approaches to comparative HRM. It is clear that the bulk of the literature from a culturalist starting point is unashamedly and unreconstructedly functionalist. What does this mean? Firstly, cultures provide the basis for social order; as long as an economy is functional at least for a core of powerful interests, structures will persist. This means that the specific cultures identified in different parts of the world identified by writers such as Hofstede (1991) are likely to persist; this will preclude firms from innovating beyond the confines of a particular cultural framework. Quite simply, firms have to work with what they are given, and employees are likely to comply with the status quo at the workplace. Indeed, given that societies tend to function for mutual benefit, challenging or contesting the status quo would simply be 'irrational', prompted by incomplete understandings or misinterpretations (Turner 1998).

Such a starting point has led to the overpromotion of the beneficial effects of communication – or, alternatively, greater cultural awareness – within the HRM literature. It is assumed that conflict in the workplace is largely due to poor communication or misunderstandings that can be readily solved through better mechanisms for information dissemination, rather than having to deal with the material conditions faced by employees (Reder 1980).

Secondly, while functionalists do assume that systems have to 'work' in order to persist, what 'works' may be open to debate. Cross-cultural accounts assume that what a lot of what firms do depends on culture; given that there is considerable variation in the performance of national economies, it could be argued that some cultures are better suited to the activities of modern organisations than others. This would suggest that in some way, some cultures are defective, representing blind alleys, which will ultimately be extinguished, or only partly developed. Such assumptions are ethnocentric and fail to take account of the manner in which systems may reinvent themselves. For example, in the 1920s and 1930s, the Austrian national economy performed very poorly; this could lead to all sorts of negative conclusions regarding the quality and efficacy of Austrian culture. Today, Austria is a prosperous country; even though there are many cultural continuities, it is evident that much has been redefined in the face of external shocks and choices by internal actors. In short, culture may be a dynamic thing, redefined and reconstituted through social action, made and remade through external pressure and internal innovations (Sorge 2005). Cultural approaches to comparative HRM tend to ignore or downplay the effects of systemic evolution and change, focusing instead on existing potentially beneficial features of the status quo. In short, much of this literature has both an impoverished notion of change within and beyond the firm, and embodies inherently conservative assumptions as to the desirability of the status quo. Finally, the methodologies underlying the empirical evidence marshalled to support cross-cultural accounts can be dismissed as flawed or pseudoscientific: very ambitious claims are made as to the state of the world of the basis of very partial and selective evidence (McSweeney 2002).

INSTITUTIONAL ACCOUNTS

Institutional approaches to understanding national difference in HRM have tended to see culture as only one of many institutions within particular contexts that have overlapping roles, and interact with each other and social actors, the outcome framing the choices owners, managers and other stakeholders in the firm make. Within this broad school of thinking, a core distinction is between those approaches rooted in orthodox rational choice economics and heterodox socio-economic alternatives.

RATIONAL CHOICE ACCOUNTS

The persistence of difference both in terms of firm-level practices and macro-economic outcomes led to the rise in the 1990s of rational choice approaches that recognise the effects of social institutions. Already in 1990, North (1990) argued that the institutional foundation of property rights was a central factor in defining the fortunes of nations. North held that in contexts where property rights were strong, firms were likely to do better, and where they were weak, firms would perform poorly. To North, institutions provide incentives or disincentives to rational actors; strong property rights would provide incentives to individuals to accumulate wealth, a process which would ultimately be beneficial to all. Such approaches to institutions are hierarchical in that they assume a particular dimension – in this case property rights – will override all others.

If one believes that strong property rights are essential for strong firm performance and overall economic growth, then it follows that anything that diminishes it – such as rights for employees and other stakeholders in the firm – are counterproductive. Or, as Goergen et al (2009) note, owner and employee rights are seen as a zero-sum game; if owners are strong, employees must necessarily be weak and vice versa. How do managers fit into this picture? Agency theories suggest that left to their own devices, managers will seek to 'empire build', to make the organisation as large as possible; employees are likely to co-operate and collude with management in this process, as larger firms are likely to pay more and offer greater job security (Roe 2003; Goergen et al 2009). In turn, profits that should be returned to owners are ploughed into making far larger and ever less efficient organisations. Such approaches are, of course, inherently conservative in that they assume employee rights are counterproductive; in the long term, employees will be better off (as organisations are likely to prosper, and the resultant growth will trickle down across society) if they have less job protection and more-flexible wages.

But, how are property rights secured? Central to property rights is the law and associated institutions for making and securing it. In practice, there have been two ways in which this process has been understood, the first focusing on national legal traditions and the second on the nature of political processes and structures and how they impact on the type of legislation passed.

But, how might one distinguish legal traditions? To La Porta et al (1999), legal traditions can be broadly divided between common and civil law ones. Whatever one may feel about rational choice approaches, this distinction is an important one. Within common law, a central strand has been the strong emphasis on private property rights (Johnson et al 2006). Common law systems rely heavily not just on statutory law (that is, legislation) but also case law (in other words, on the earlier decisions of the courts). This makes litigation central in informing and securing rights. From an employee perspective, this means that not only are your rights not always clearly defined (as they represent not just the product of formal laws, but many court cases), but you may have to resort to litigation to enforce them. Of course, employers are likely to have very much more resources at their disposal and may retaliate in subtle ways should an individual employee decide to remain in their job afterwards (Harcourt and Wood 2004; Johnson et al 2006); litigation is likely to permanently damage the employment relationship. A founding principle of civil law was the importance of social order and solidarity. Given the central role of France in the foundation and dissemination of civil law, La Porta et al (1999) see French civil law as an archetype of systems that trade off owner rights against those of other interests in society. Other civil law systems include German and Scandinavian civil law; both are somewhat removed from the French ideal, the latter particularly so.

From this starting point, Botero et al (2004) compare and contrast the rights of individual employees and their collectives (for example, rights to free association and unionisation) according to legal system. Given that they see employee and employer rights as mutually antagonistic, they suggest that employee rights are strongest in French civil law ones, and weakest in common law ones.

This means that the type of HRM encountered in common law countries would centre on insecure and flexible contracting (that is, weak job security, with firms having an ability to readily upsize and downsize), with wages being readily adjustable upward and downward in line with market conditions, and individual pay being tied to performance or simply limited to the minimum the market will bear (in other words, the minimum that can be paid while still enticing individuals to stay in the job) (Goergen et al 2009). In contrast, the type of HRM encountered in civil law ones would be more likely to be associated with job security (and, hence, longer-term relations between the firm and the employee), and trade unions engaged in collective bargaining (and hence, making compromises and, in effect, sharing power) with owners and their representatives.

La Porta et al (1999) and Botero et al (2004) categorise the legal traditions of central and eastern Europe as 'post-communist'. This is perhaps not a very helpful categorisation, given that there is a major difference between countries such as Slovenia and Slovakia, where the law since 1990 has tended towards promoting co-operation and compromise between employer and employee, and others, such as the Czech Republic and the Baltic states, which have drifted closer to neo-liberalism and weak employee rights. A further limitation with this approach is the limited evidence base in which it founds its assertion that firms within all civil-law countries will generally perform better. This broad grouping includes the somewhat dysfunctional economies from francophone West Africa in the French civil-law camp. An analysis of European economies on their own would reveal that civil law countries have not performed much worse – and in some cases better – than common law ones over the past two decades (OECD 2007).

Roe (2003) argues that it is not so much legal tradition that matters, but legislation. Right-wing governments are more likely to pass laws that favour property owners, and left-wing ones that favour employees and unions. In practical terms, this means that firms are more likely to opt for hard-line HRM policies when right-wing governments are in power, and be deterred from them (and, hence, by default, lapsing into softer-line ones) under left-wing governments. A problem with such an approach is how one defines right and left wing; while there are numerous indices, inadequate attention is often accorded to national traditions and experiences. For example, a right-wing politician in continental Europe could be considered (economically) leftward in the United States. And there is little doubt that a conservative politician in the United States would be relegated to the unelectable fringe in Canada.

Alternatively, what drives legislation may be seen primarily as a product of the electoral system. Pagano and Volpin (2005) argue that in 'first past the post' electoral systems, the rights of property owners are stronger. In contrast, in proportional electoral systems, employees and other stakeholders in the firm are likely to have stronger rights. In 'first past the post' systems, elections are decided by fickle swing voters who are unlikely to have the interests of a particular social class in mind, but who may be brought over by those with more resources at their disposal. In contrast, in proportional systems, political parties have to reach compromises with each other. This means that invariably, the rights of property owners will be diluted, as a means of reaching compromises with others. This will mean that legislation and government interventions will similarly promote compromises, leading to more co-operative – as adverse to instrumental, owner-interest-driven – HRM within the workplace.

What are the limits with such approaches? Firstly, as noted above, while rational-hierarchical approaches assume that economies where owner rights are stronger will work better, the actual economic evidence is somewhat mixed. With their usual obliviousness to facts, neo-liberals in the 1990s and early 2000s claimed that owner/shareholder-dominant economies performed better than ones that allowed for more stakeholder rights; in reality the differences were either marginal (for example the US and UK vs Germany) or in fact the opposite of what might be expected (for example Sweden vs the UK and US). It is often argued by neo-liberals that where employers are freer to fire employees, they are also more likely to take the risk of hiring them; in other words, weak job security and deregulated labour markets is more conducive to job creation. However, the apparently impressive job creation record by the US during this time period was not nearly as good as might at first seem; a prison population of 2 million, an equally bloated and inefficient army, and a large number of part-time jobs and discouraged unemployed meant that what appeared to be a good job-creation record was in fact among the worst in the developed world (Wood 2003).

Finally, approaches that prioritise a single institutional dimension – the law, and, hence, the legal tradition or government policy and legislation – assume that laws work and are enforced. In practice, within large areas of southern Europe – let alone the developed world – many employers ignore the law with impunity. In other words, there are instances where, while owner rights are heavily circumscribed by the law, employers may act with impunity. In contrast, employees may be unable to enforce their rights even when they are clearly delineated in legislation. Even within more developed economies, such as the UK, there is considerable evidence to suggest that large numbers of SMEs flout employment law on a regular basis (Toynbee 2003).

HETERODOX ALTERNATIVES

Regulation theory

It can be seen that there are many limitations to approaches that seek to explain differences in corporate governance and employee rights, and, hence, the practice of HRM, in terms of a rational-hierarchical conceptualisation of institutions. We saw earlier that the radical political economy tradition saw social order as founded on inequality and, hence, open to contestation and radical change. In other words, any institutional mediation is open to challenge and reconfiguration. Building on and developing these strands of thinking, and other approaches that emphasise the importance not only of economic profit but also social relations on what individuals and firms do, and theories of economic long waves, regulation theory argues that phases of economic growth will inevitably be followed by extended periods of adjustment, mediocre growth and recession (Jessop 2001). Periods of growth are supported by an assembly (rather than just one) of institutions, that mediate and reconcile the interests of differing groupings, but always on a spatially and temporarily confined basis (Boyer 2006). After a period of time, such institutional frameworks are likely to stop working owing to changes in technology, external pressures and/or the breakdown of internal compromises (Jessop 2001).

Regulation theory would suggest that there are likely to be profound differences in the manner in which societies and firms are governed and what they do, according to time and place. While, as with much of the rational hierarchical literature, they accord a great deal of importance to what happens at national level, developments and extensions of regulationist thinking have drawn attention to the 'nested' nature of institutions; in other words, institutions operate on a subnational (for example regional government), national and supra-national (for example international financial institutions, and transnational bodies such as the European Union) (Hollingsworth and Boyer 1997). These different levels interact with each other. Hence, there are pressures both towards a common European model of work and employment relations (which may either be co-operative or less regulated) and towards regional difference (regional development policies may encourage specific firm activities in specific regions within a particular country) (Hollingsworth and Boyer 1997).

Finally, given that institutional arrangements regularly break down, societies are not only likely to be subject to incremental evolution, but also rupture; unlike cultural approaches, it is held that societies do not evolve on a linear and confined basis (Hollingsworth 2006). In practice, regulationist thinking has been used to explain changes in work and employment organisation in a range of different national contexts.

For example, in South Africa, it has been argued that apartheid was associated with a system called racial Fordism: that is, Fordist mass production combined with a racial division of labour (with blacks being confined to low-level jobs) and the political exclusion of blacks within wider society (facilitating repression in the workplace) (Gelb 1989). This proved highly functional to large areas of agriculture, manufacturing and mining (Gelb 1989). By the mid-1970s, in response to both changes in the global economy and internal pressures, the system began to break down, ultimately leading to economic decline and the collapse of apartheid.

In the UK, Hudson (2006) argues that specific political pressures and regional industrial traditions in the north-east (a reliance on mining and heavy industry) led to fundamental differences in national government policies to the region when compared with others; in practice, this has led to more active developmental approaches aimed at promoting employment and skills.

Shareholder and stakeholder capitalism

According similar importance to the effects of institutions, writers such as Lincoln and Kalleberg (1990) and Dore (2000) have focused more on the practical outcomes of institutional mediation. To a large part, these writings were prompted by a desire to promote alternatives to neo-liberalism and by the success of more co-operative economies such as Germany and Japan in high-value-added manufacturing. These writers argued that there were fundamental differences between shareholder and stakeholder capitalism. Within the former, Anglo-American style capitalism, shareholder rights are stronger; this means that a stronger emphasis is placed on returning value to owners, to pursuing profits rather than organisational growth, a prediction not far removed from rational-hierarchical accounts. However, a fundamental departure from the latter is that it is assumed that this is not always necessarily functional to firms or, indeed, society at large (Lincoln and Kalleberg 1990). Indeed, in such contexts, a reluctance to reinvest may make high-quality production more difficult. Poor well-being for other stakeholders is likely to have knock-on effects in terms of lower commitment to the organisation and reduced incentives for human capital development. If jobs are insecure, firms are reluctant to invest in their people, while the latter will be more concerned with developing externally marketable skills than skills genuinely needed by the firm.

The varieties of capitalism literature

Similarly – but more implicitly – inspired by the need to promote alternatives to neo-liberalism, an influential 2001 edited volume by Hall and Soskice (2001) presented the 'varieties of capitalism' approach. This book made a similar distinction between lightly regulated, owner-dominant liberal market economies (LMEs), and more co-operative, co-ordinated market economies (CMEs). Examples of the former would include the US and the UK, and the latter the developed economies of north-western Europe (for example Germany, the Netherlands) and Scandinavia, and the Far East (for example Japan, South Korea, Taiwan). Central to Hall and Soskice's (2001) account is the assumption of the possibility of complementarity that different institutions and practices may, in working together, yield greater results than a sum of their constituent parts. This means that even some features that appear marginal on their own may in fact have great importance at an overall systematic level. Given that the sum may be very much greater than the constituent parts, this would suggest that a number of alternative systems may be equally viable, for example, CMEs may be just as viable as LMEs.

What distinguishes Hall and Soskice (2001) from Lincoln and Kalleberg (1990) and Dore (2000) is that the former account is less vested with a moral purpose: it is more concerned with presenting viable alternatives than promoting a specific alternative.

How is HRM likely to vary between LMEs and CMEs? Firstly, as predicted by rational-hierarchical accounts, job security is weaker in the former. This means that an individual is likely to have many more jobs over a working career. The benefits for firms are that upsizing and downsizing of workforces in response to changes in demand are easier, and that skills and knowledge get gradually disseminated across an economy (Thelen 2004). However, a cost for firms is that they are constantly being drained of organisation-specific skills and knowledge; in LMEs, the value of the latter is constantly discounted, when in reality skills and knowledge are not readily substitutable via the external labour market (Harcourt and Wood 2007). Secondly, because labour is treated as a readily disposable commodity, firms are reluctant to invest in their people. At the same time, high staff turnover rates mean that firms have to devote a large amount of resources to basic induction training: it is a myth to say that firms in LMEs are likely to have lower training bills (Goergen et al 2009). Thirdly, weaker unions and union rights mean that there will be a lower incidence of collective bargaining; this means that either a greater emphasis will be focused on involving employees as individuals through meetings, briefings and other non-representative voice mechanisms, or, possibly more plausibly, denying them a voice at all (see Chapter 12 and Brewster et al 2007).

In the case of CMEs, stronger job security means that both individual employees and their employers have an interest in organisation-specific human capital development. In other words, rather than honing externally marketable skills, employees will have a strong interest in developing skills that make them useful to the organisation and that are likely to facilitate a career therein. This means that the costs of building needed organisation-specific skills can be spread over many years (Goergen et al 2009). Strong vocational training systems provide a solid base of industry-specific skills that firms can build upon. Again, stronger unions mean that meaningful collective bargaining is more likely to occur; indeed, collective bargaining may be supplemented by other forms of representative voice that provide a forum for negotiation of issues of work organisation (Brewster et al 2007). Quite simply, this allows employee representatives to bargain over a greater range of topics than issues to do with the employment contract – in other words, terms and conditions of service.

A limitation of dichotomous or two-archetype accounts is that these categorisations are extremely broad. There is quite a lot of difference between Scandinavia and Germany, for example, let alone between north-western Europe and the Far East. This has led to the development of alternative, multi-variety models. Drawing to a greater extent on the developments of the functionalist tradition that accord greater attention to the effects of social action and the dynamic nature of systemic evolution, Whitley's (1999) business systems theory argues that, *inter alia*, Far Eastern economies can be divided into at least two distinct categories in their own right, reflecting differing degrees of state interventionism and firm size (for example the differences in the evolution of the Japanese and Hong Kong economies have made for very different types of firm-level HR practice today). Again, the highly prosperous northern Italian economy is quite different from the economies of north-western Europe.

However, Whitley continues to combine Scandinavia and north-western continental Europe into one category. An alternative multi-variety approach, by Amable (2003), argues that Scandinavia and continental north-western Europe represent distinct varieties of capitalism. Key differences in terms of HR practice include variations in access to skills and training; in continental north-western Europe, strong pre-employment vocational training systems means that firms can count on a pool of job-seekers with a broad industry-relevant foundation of skills and aptitudes (Amable 2003). In Scandinavia, while vocational training systems are generally weaker, governments devote more attention to ensuring that individuals have access to opportunities for updating their skills, to ensure their continued relevance both within their firm and within the external labour market.

There have been recent attempts to apply business systems theory to the developing world, and more specifically, tropical Africa, which can be referred to as a segmented business system (Wood and Frynas 2006). As Wood and Frynas (2006, p255) note:

> Employment relations in segmented business systems are dualistic in nature, reflecting the divide between relatively large organisations in the TNC and state sectors, and indigenous private firms, most of which are small and/or family owned. ... In the latter, employee relations are particularly likely to be firmly unitarist in orientation; that is, authority in the workplace is firmly vested in the hands of management. ... In segmented business systems, trade unions have a very narrow social footprint, with their activities being largely confined to the state sector and the manufacturing sector.

CONCLUSION

There is a growing consensus that HRM practices are neither converging across the world into a single ideal type, nor a worst type, for that matter. However, while there is a lot of variety in the practice of HRM within and between contexts, there is similarly little evidence of diffuse diversity (Lane and Wood 2009). In other words, while there is variety in HR practice, this is bounded or constrained. In specific times and places, the bulk of firms will broadly follow one of a limited range of broad alternative models for managing their people. What determines HRM has been described as the result of embedded cultures: ultimately a product of private property rights, or as the outcome of a complex web of social relations. The author is sceptical of the first two points of view. Rather, it is believed that the rehashing of 1950s functionalist interpretations of culture, which sees it as both rigid and deterministic, resulted in crude stereotypes of the outlooks of individuals and groups in specific parts of the world. Rather, culture is seen as something contested and fluid, with it being remade to suit changes in technology, in global markets and changes in governance and ownership. Again, a prioritisation of property rights may make for cut-throat competition that may make it difficult for firms to progress from labour-repressive people management to higher-value-added approaches that provide a firm's people with dignity and the means to consume (in turn propping up demand across an economy), and the firm with a reliable, committed and quality-conscious workforce. Central in this is the question of social action. Managers and workers make real choices within particular settings. While the range of choices may be somewhat confined by formal and informal rules, there is still room to innovate. On the side of management, there are fundamental choices around the relative degree of co-operation and control that is deemed necessary in a wide range of areas (Thompson and Smith 2010). On the side of employees, there is not just the question of co-operation, but also resistance. Even in highly repressive contexts, employees have a range of options for challenging what managers do, which, in turn, may reinforce or force a change in managerial strategies (Thompson and Smith 2010).

While socio-economic approaches are more convincing, at the same time the importance of recent work that points to bounded diversity within national contexts should be emphasised (HR practice is likely to differ considerably between industries and regions within particular national contexts), and the uneven, contested and episodic nature of systemic change (Lane and Wood 2009). Finally, in any analysis of this nature, one always faces the difficulty in accurately summarising the rules and norms governing what firms and other associations do, and the actual practice of HRM, yet retaining useful analytical categories. This is a broader problem of theory: the challenge of providing summaries and predictions that are coherent and usable, while not resorting to crude stereotypes of the richness of practice.

HRM IN THE MEDIA

CRITICAL REFLECTIONS

In relation to the first question, it could be observed that within co-ordinated market economies (CMEs) such as Germany, the state has exhibited a greater willingness to actively intervene in support of industry and industrial jobs. Such intervention includes those that preserve the core features of people management associated with the German paradigm – particularly the long-term investment in skills. In part, this reflects the greater power of unions, but it also reflects a broader commitment to actively promoting compromises and sustainability than is commonly encountered in liberal market economies (LMEs) such as the UK. The various theories outlined above all provide alternative accounts of the reasons underlying these differences.

In relation to the second question, British unions feared that British jobs would be more vulnerable than German jobs partly because of the obvious factor of government support in Germany but also about the relative costs associated with making workers redundant in each country: despite the lower wage costs of British workers, the German system makes it more expensive to lay workers off. This is a reflection of the two systems: the LME system encouraging high labour market mobility and the CME favouring lower labour market mobility, but higher functional flexibility.

EXPLORE FURTHER

SPARROW, P., BREWSTER, C. and HARRIS, H. (eds) (2004) *Globalising human resource management*. London: Routledge.

This book provides a broad, coherent overview of the field of international HRM and a detailed, practical analysis of what is needed to be successful in this crucial area of modern management.

JACKSON, S.E., LUO, Y. and SCHULER, R.S. (eds) (2003) *Managing human resources in cross-border alliances*. London: Routledge.

This book provides a comprehensive treatment of HR issues in international alliances.

BREWSTER, C., MAYRHOFER, W. and MORLEY, M. (eds) (2004), *HRM in Europe: evidence of convergence?* Oxford: Butterworth-Heinemann.

This book presents HR issues in a wide variety of European countries.

HALL, P.A. and SOSKICE, D. (eds) (2001) *Varieties of capitalism: the institutional foundations of comparative advantage*. Oxford: Oxford University Press.

This book highlights the role of business in national economies and explores the relationships between politics, economics and business.

SCHULER, R.S., BRISCOE, D.R. and CLAUS, L. (eds) (2008) *International human resource management*. 3rd ed. Oxford: Routledge.

This book focuses on international HRM within multinational enterprises (MNEs) from throughout the world.

CHAPTER 5

Technology and Work: Is the Future Certain?

Martin Upchurch

OVERVIEW

This chapter looks at developments in information and communication technology (ICT) in the workplace from an HR perspective. The recent history of ICT innovation is presented and some theoretical frameworks for the implications of the organisation of work are assessed. These frameworks include aspects of the 'information society' and approaches to understanding knowledge-based work and the 'knowledge worker'. The use and potential use of ICT by HR departments is then recorded and reflections are made on the positive and negative aspects of usage. Guidelines for effective and efficient use of ICT by HR departments are presented. The chapter concludes with an examination of the effects of Web 2.0 developments and social networking in the workplace.

LEARNING OBJECTIVES

Reading this chapter will enable the reader to:

- critically examine the development of new forms of ICT and their impact in the workplace
- critically examine the dilemmas posed to HR departments in managing the introduction of ICT
- critically analyse the use of ICT in the workplace through its 'dark side'
- critically synthesise an ICT strategy for the workplace in the light of Web 2.0 developments

'RETAIL WAREHOUSE STAFF MONITORED'

A report in 2005 by Professor Michael Blakemore at Durham University found many instances of retail warehouse staff being monitored by their employers using radio and satellite-based tracking technology. Ten thousand warehouse workers were found to be wearing electronic tags as they move around accessing stock. Professor Blakemore suggests that such a system can be used to estimate the amount of time it takes a worker to load products. In such fashion the electronic eye can police workers' movements. Paul Kenny, the general secretary of the trade union GMB, stated: 'The GMB is not a Luddite organisation, but we will not stand idly by to see our members reduced to robots with heartbeats.' A spokesperson for Ocado, one of the organisations using the system, denied that workers were being turned into robots and that the purpose of using the electronic device is to make sure that staff pick the right stock (*Guardian* 2005).

Questions

1 What are the HR implications of the case above?

2 Is the system used by the retailers ethical?

INTRODUCTION

Contemporary workplaces are increasingly subject to management processes that utilise information and communication technology (ICT). The spread of ICT has led many commentators to suggest that a new workplace paradigm has been created. This new workplace creates a socio-technical dynamic whereby ICT-based skills and knowledge are contained within a framework of value-adding 'knowledge-based work' in a 'post-industrial society' (Bell 1973). Knowledge-based work, dependent on IT skills, is purported by many social theorists to have then created a divide between advantaged workers, who have accommodated to the new regime, and disadvantaged workers, who have not. Professional workers are likely to be beneficiaries of this new regime as they are able to use ICT to enhance and specialise their knowledge within the internal labour market. As such, commentators such as Castells (2001) refer to the dawn of the IT age as the 'third industrial revolution', whereby knowledge work dependent on ICT is an essential ingredient of advanced capitalism and its importance follows the invention of the steam engine (first revolution) and then electricity (second revolution). Other commentators have cast doubt on the notion of paradigm shift linked to ICT and new technologies. ICT may simply be an additional way of applying technology to work organisation and there is nothing 'new' about such a process to justify paradigm shift (Nolan and Wood 2003). The definition of 'knowledge work' is obscure, as most workers apply varying degrees of knowledge to their work. There is also a 'dark side' to ICT in the workplace, summarised by surveillance, monitoring and control and associated with the displacement of workers' jobs.

Box 5.1 Timeline of ICT

1956 First fully automatic mobile phone system commercially released by Ericsson in Sweden.

1958 Silicon chip invented (integrated electronic circuit on a silicon wafer) in USA

1958 'Pocket' version of mobile phone developed in USSR

1969 Stanford Research Institute, USA, first computer-to-computer remote communication

1973 Britain connected through Arpanet from University College London to Stanford

1977 Apple computer launched

1977 PC modem for sale

1978 First spam email

1983 Launch of JANET, the UK university network

1985 First dot.com registration

1989 Hypertext enables development of World Wide Web, whereby you can 'click on a link'

1991 First webpage at info.cern.ch

1991 World's first SMS text message sent in the UK

1992 Demon Internet – Britain's first commercial Internet server

1993 Mosaic Internet browser launched

1994 First cyber cafe

1995 amazon.com launched

1998 Google search engine launched

1999 Social network sites such as Friends Reunited appear

2002 First person to be dismissed at work, or 'dooced', as a result of what was written on personal blog

2004 Facebook started by Harvard student Mark Zuckerberg

2005 Launch of YouTube

2007 BBC launches iPlayer

2009 East Africa gets first broadband connection

In this chapter we explore the implications of the introduction of ICT in the workplace. We deal first with the social organisation of work that has been enabled by ICT, and consider its implications for human resource management. We then examine what might be termed the 'dark side' of ICT in the workplace, namely surveillance, monitoring and control of the workforce. Then we examine the extracurricular aspects of workplace ICT, such as the use of social networking, and see how employers and employees might respond to these developments.

VIRTUAL COMMUNICATION IN THE WORKPLACE

The invention in 1958 and subsequent mass production of the silicon chip allowed a great leap forward in communication possibilities within the workplace. Progress actually took place over a 30- or 40-year period until

Internet-based communication became the workplace norm. The first email, for example, was sent in 1971 but it was not until the mid-to-late 1990s that the use of email became widespread in Western industrial societies. A report by Robert Taylor (2002), summarising the ESRC 'Future of Work' programme, recorded that (in 2000) 'two thirds of men and women in the workforce say the new technologies have become "essential" for the accomplishment of their jobs compared with only 35% of women and 28% of men who believed this was so in the 1997 ESRC sponsored skills survey carried out at Leicester University'. One of the first casualties of this new technology in the late 1970s onwards was the typing pool. The widespread introduction of word processing technology and the positioning of desktop computers linked to a central server spelled the death knell of the typist and the typewriter. In design and engineering, the skills of the draughtsmen and draughtswomen were rapidly replaced with computer-aided design, while machine operators began tuning the computers working the machines rather than the machines themselves. In the print industry, too, hot metal techniques of typesetting led to the demise of the craft of printing, as typesetting was now conducted entirely by journalists as they wrote the text. Major industrial disputes occurred when the 'hot metal' printers fought unsuccessfully to try and preserve their jobs. Digitalisation also allowed the rapid transfer of images by electronic means, obviating the need for physical transfer of paper. The paper-based memorandum and letter were replaced by fax machine, email and scanner. An example of how this may speed up work comes from the insurance industry, where new insurance claims are scanned on receipt and then directed electronically to the insurance clerk's computer. When the clerk has finished processing the claim, another immediately pops up on the monitor screen. Parallel developments in satellite and other forms of communication technology liberated people from land-based telephone lines, enabling widespread use of cellular technology and the mobile phone. Within a period of less than 30 years, communications were transformed. Time and distance became compressed with these technological developments.

ICT has enabled more effective control systems to be established, creating efficiencies through such techniques as business process re-engineering. Workloads and work speeds are now recorded more effectively by management. An example might be bar code information recorded at checkout tills in supermarkets, which not only record stock levels and sales, but also the speed of checkout assistants in processing sales and the volume of sales at different times of the day. The latter is essential information for HR in planning staffing requirements. As such, ICT has enabled Taylorist processes at work, whereby time taken for specific tasks can be monitored, and control checks placed against individual employees. An example is the ability to scan documents and then send them for processing to remote computers of individual staff. In this way insurance claims and applications, for example, are processed within the insurance industry.

In addition, ICT has enabled more possibilities for home-based and mobile working, whereby workers are linked to the central organisation virtually. According to the Government's *Labour Force Surveys* in 1981, around 1 in 25 people used their homes in this way; by 2002, this had risen to 1 in 10. There are now about 1 million workers who work solely at home in the UK, the vast majority of whom are women. The numbers have increased significantly since the 1980s, reflecting the use of the home-based computer. Many more spend part of the week working at home. Some home-based work is routine outsourced work, such as data processing. Other work could be labelled as 'creative', such as consultant home-based graphic design or web design. A parallel development is that of 'hot-desking', whereby workers visit the office only occasionally and share a desk and computer. In some offices this has been transformed to 'touch-down' desks or even 'stand-up' areas where employees have space to stand up and plug in their laptops whenever they are in the office. In this way the spread of ICT is used by organisations to save office space and restructure the working environment.

Furthermore, mobile working in particular is likely to create problems in dividing personal time between work time and non-work time. As the speed of communication gathered pace, it enabled the workforce to use their time more intensively and extensively, even on the move as email became accessible through the mobile phone. This has implications for work–life balance, whereby the mobile phone is never switched off and employees are expected to respond 24/7.

Moreover, the spread of ICT-based information systems is argued by some to have enabled new forms of post-bureaucratic management (Semler 2003; Zohar and Marshall 2005). ICT enables cross-functional and time/distance contact to be compressed in virtual organisation, leading to new forms of networking which eschew traditional bureaucratic structures and hierarchies and enable 'communities of practice' (Wenger 1998). In such organisations old hierarchies of communication and authority can break down as employees are able to communicate with each other both laterally and vertically across and between organisations, and without mediation through their superiors.

Also, employees (again, especially professional workers) are encouraged to utilise ICT to express their creativity and apply their knowledge.

Furthermore, distributed teamworking is included within this process, and is utilised as a vehicle to develop synergy of technical expertise, often across organisation and even national boundaries. Such networks are intended to add value by innovation and knowledge creation.

Finally, the development of Web 2.0 technology has enabled interactive use of the Internet through such functions as social networking, YouTube, LinkedIn, Second Life and wikis. This has posed fresh challenges for the management of ICT in the workplace.

These rapid developments were placed into theoretical frameworks by academics. Peter Drucker first coined the term 'knowledge worker' in 1968, which he applied to '...productive work, ideas, concepts, and information rather than manual skill or brawn'. The term later became associated with the use of information technology, such that knowledge work is alleged to 'favor strong non-routine cognitive skills, such as abstract reasoning, problem-solving, communication and collaboration' (Karoly and Panis 2004, pxiv). The implication of these definitions was that knowledge work belonged to the future, whereas manual work belonged to the past, and in an increasingly precarious world of work the 'knowledge worker' would be more likely to survive. However, there are confusing and overlapping boundaries between *knowledge* work, *creative* work and *access to information* enabled by ICT. Only a relatively small proportion of workers may use ICT for problem-solving or creative and abstract reasoning. Examples might be film animators or academic researchers. Many workers will use ICT in their work, but they may have routinised jobs, which do not necessitate the use of knowledge, as they may simply be processing information. Others may have certain skill sets for which access to the Internet is required to exercise those skills. An example might be a gas engineer who stores information on a computer about different gas boilers, or an insurance salesperson who can access a laptop to gain information on different products to sell to customers. 'Knowledge' is also difficult to define, crossing boundaries of understanding, skills and intelligence. Blackler (1995), for example, has attempted to define different types of knowledge:

- **embrained** – abstract and conceptual knowledge needed to solve problems

- **embodied** – practical skills obtained from experience

- **encultured** – shared understanding about how things are done within the organisation

- **embedded** – routine ability to complete a task, reflecting a combination of knowledge, learning and skill

- **encoded** – ability to decode information given in the form of codes and symbols.

While more and more workers use ICT in the workplace, the use may still vary considerably between occupation and grade (see Table 5.1). The report for the Economic and Social Research Council (ESRC), with data from the year 2000, found that while 69% of higher professional and managers used the Internet for work, only 29% of administrators and 14% of skilled manual workers did so. The use of email showed similar variation, with scores of 83%, 51% and 10% respectively for the same groups. However, 46% of skilled workers had a PC at home, compared with 80% of higher professionals. These latter figures would indicate that although computer-based skills are widespread in the UK, and their use at work has increased, the *reliance* of workers on ICT for their work remains concentrated in professional grades.

The importance of skill-based training and education in ICT has been recognised by the Government in its response to the Leitch Review of Skills in England in changes made to core learning objectives. ICT now sits alongside English and maths as a core subject at GCSE level in secondary schools and on diplomas and apprenticeships. This approach is parallel with wider initiatives as part of the Lisbon Process in the European Union to upgrade skills and 'human capital' in order to enhance individual 'employability' and national business competitiveness. As such it recognises the dangers of the development of a 'digital

Table 5.1 Users of new technology in the workplace in 2000, UK

Percentage of employees	Internet	Email	Pager/mobile	PC at home
Higher management/professional	69	83	53	80
Lower management/professional	52	55	49	70
Administrative	29	51	26	51
Routine non-manual	20	17	23	61
Technicians and supervisors	18	33	52	50
Skilled manual	14	10	33	46
Semi- and unskilled manual	15	8	27	41

Source: Taylor (2002, Table 7)

divide' between those with and without ICT skills in the new economy. Indeed this 'digital divide' has an international as well as national dimension. This divide at global level can be measured simply by the number of Internet users per head of population in each country. In 2009, internetworldstats.com reported that the country with the highest proportion of Internet users was Iceland, with 90% of the population using the Internet. The USA recorded a percentage use of 73.9% and the EU average was 63.2%. The UK recorded 71.8%. However, poorer countries have hardly entered the field. India recorded only 7.1%, Nigeria 6.8% and Mozambique 0.9%.

THE HRM FUNCTION AND ICT

There are three major aspects to consider when understanding the role of the HR function in relation to information and communication technology. First, HR managers need to be aware of tools or techniques that can act as an aid to the encouragement of knowledge work and the management of knowledge workers. Second, the function of HR itself can be subject to ICT and can be utilised effectively to improve HR practice within the organisation. Third, HR professionals must be aware of the social impacts of ICT within the workplace, and seek to manage the impact of electronic means of communication within the organisation.

In terms of the *management of knowledge work* and workers, the starting point for HR is that ICT can be used to enhance and retain knowledge within the organisation. In other words, we can use the power of ICT to enhance and develop human capital within an organisation, either by improving, capturing and sharing the general knowledge of employees, or by improving the organisational knowledge of systems, practices and best way methods of getting things done (see CIPD 2002). E-learning, training and development, together with web-based learning packages thus enable increased opportunity for self-directed learning and knowledge enhancement within organisations. ICT can improve an organisation's ability to capture and codify knowledge by enabling easy storage of such captured and coded information to be quickly accessed by employees through such vehicles as organisational intranets and HR service applications. The sharing of knowledge, however, goes beyond simple coding and electronic storage and is in fact a social process through which conversation, conflict and argument play an equally important role. Knowledge-sharing must therefore be encouraged in an organisation, and HR may have a role to play in the design of incentive and competency schemes that emphasise such knowledge-sharing and organisational learning. 'Communities of practice' (Wenger 1998) and task-based teams are a social formation for which encouragement is needed to participate, either in the form of organisational incentives or through constructed bonding engendered within the organisation 'culture'.

E-HR

The HR department of an organisation can effectively prepare itself for the potential of ICT by constructing its own *HR information system*. Primarily such a system may be a simple database that stores personnel information on individual job history, pay and reward records, sickness, absence, education and training, disciplinary incidence, expenses claims, medical history, pensions profile and performance assessment scores. A CIPD survey in 2005 found that 77% of organisations surveyed use ICT for HR-related functions, which, as well as use for personnel record-keeping, might include systems for e-recruitment and selection, learning and development (e-learning) and performance management. As important is the construction of such systems that might allow self-recording and self-access by individual members of staff through an organisation intranet. In designing such systems HR professionals must take full notice of the provisions of the 1998 Data Protection Act, which stipulates, *inter alia*, that data may only be used for the specific purpose for which it is collected; that data should not be disclosed to other parties without the consent of the individual; that individuals have the right of access to information held about them (excluding data related to prevention or detection of crime); and that adequate security measures (such as firewalls) must be put in place to protect data security. Once such a system is established it may allow HR to develop synergies in the workplace by the creation of an *enterprise resource planning system*. Such a system would allow an HR officer to be in a position to construct project teams from within an organisation based on the competency and skill profiles of individual staff members held on the system. Personnel-based IT systems may also allow more effective succession planning and recruitment strategies within an organisation. Projected retirement ages of key staff, computed against average figures for general staff turnover, when programmed through efficient software programs, can help predict likely shortfalls of skills and competencies within an organisation, and so better prepare the HR department for planning recruitment strategies for the future. Electronic-based performance management systems may be used specifically for lower-level jobs by storing information on outputs, times for production, and error and wastage rates. Appraisal forms may also be converted to electronic format, providing opportunities for 360-degree feedback, as well as to construct control measures such as absence, lateness, grievance and staff turnover.

Issues *of network security*, data protection and use of the Internet must all be approached with detailed policy and advice. Email activity, for example, may be subject to HR advice on private use, content and distribution and even 'style' of written work on email, as well as disclosure of email addresses and laws on defamation. In order to enforce policy, disciplinary procedures must be constructed together with a system of monitoring use and providing disclaimers. Finally, HR must develop strategies to cope with the 'softer' effects of ICT in the workplace characterised by the general diffusion of information, the 'extraneous' use of ICT by employees in work time, and the structured or unstructured use of Web 2.0 technology, which enables social networking through Facebook, Twitter, and so on. These aspects are dealt with in a later section.

THE DARK SIDE

Some commentators argue that there is a possible 'dark side' to the use of ICT in the workplace. Rifkin (1996), for example, sees the widespread introduction of ICT in the workplace as a precursor to widespread unemployment – as robotic, information and computer technology take the place of human labour. His views may be overstated, as more workers are needed to design and make new technology in that sector. The UK, for example, now has many new jobs in the computer games industry. Capitalism is also very dynamic, constantly reforming itself as new products are created in new and otherwise unpredictable industrial sectors. However, for the individual workplace it is true that new technology can replace workers. An example is the auto industry, where robots have replaced assembly line workers, or retail supermarkets, where self-service checkouts may replace cashiers. Control over the pace of work is also enhanced by IT and work is intensified as a result. Work outputs and targets can be instantly measured and monitored by management, so that workers have less time during the day to engage in 'non-work' activity. Professional workers are particularly subject to the resulting tension between this employer control and personal creativity. Teamworking, for example, rather than becoming a collective liberation for workers, transforms into reformed Taylorist routine (Danford et al 2003). This is because teams too have monitored targets for quantity of output, and meeting those targets may conflict with finding time to be creative. The use of email as an interactive form of communication may also allow for horizontal communication across traditional workplace hierarchies. As such, it could act to liberate employees from bureaucratic and hierarchical workplace regimes. However, Zuboff (1988), in a major study of ICT in the workplace, observed that email usage quickly took on the hierarchical characteristics of the workplace, with suggestions to subordinates from managers being interpreted as commands. Most importantly, ICT is used as a method of workforce surveillance, by measuring work output, by listening in to telephone conversations or recording email traffic, or even by electronically tagging (RFID) workers to trace their movements.

Figure 5.1 The panopticon

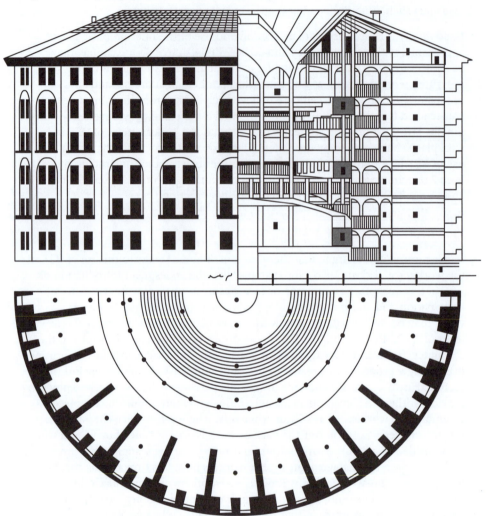

Source: Bentham, J. (1843; originally 1791): 'Plan of Panopticon' in *The Works of Jeremy Bentham*, vol. IV, pp172–3.

It is these latter effects that have been equated with Jeremy Bentham's panopticon. The constant surveillance from the internal watchtower, in this model, places the worker in a virtual prison, whereby they are driven to self-discipline and compliance (Foucault 1995). The hidden watchtower, it may be suggested, even acts on our unconscious and induces an 'assembly line in the head'.

Particular interest has been generated in such surveillance effects by the growth in the number of workers in the UK employed in call centres. Call centres integrate VDU and telephone technology to enable rapid and automated response to incoming and outgoing telephone calls, often utilising systems of automatic call distribution (ACD) and interactive voice recognition (IAVR) as part of the operation. Estimates suggest that about 2.3% of the UK workforce were employed in various types of call centres in 2002. The nature of routinised, automated work in call centres, combined with the ability of supervisors to listen in to conversations has led some commentators to define the working conditions as similar to Bentham's prison panopticon predicting a grim 'vision of the future' (Fernie and Metcalf 1997, p3). Such conclusions have been challenged by other studies of call centre workers. Taylor and Bain (1997, p115), for example, agree that call centre work is often routinised, pre-scripted and heavily monitored and also point to the 'emotional labour' that call centre workers are meant to apply when talking to customers. They find that the typical call centre worker is '... young and female...and working complex shift patterns which correspond to the peaks of consumer demand...She has to concentrate hard on what is being said, jump from page to page on a screen, making sure...that she has said the right things in a pleasant manner...'. But there is a contradictory process identified by the authors defined by the tension between quality and quantity of service, which allows for call centre workers to overcome the constant monitoring, either by individual acts of resistance, the use of humour or by joining trade unions to collectively fight for better working conditions and pay (Taylor and Bain 1997, 2003).

ICT and 'countersurveillance'

The use of humour or non-referential language by individuals against their organisation may be a conscious precursor to more serious collectivised resistance within the workplace, giving workers space to conduct activities as part of personal survival strategies or against the corporate cultural 'norms' (Thompson and Ackroyd 1995). Individuals taking such action have been typologised in different frames. Outside the traditional misbehaviour–resistance spectrum Lenhart and Fox (2006), for example, record much Internet-based behaviour as acts of creative self-expression. From cultural theory, whistleblowing behaviour has been characterised as acts performed by 'egalitarians' with high regard for workplace collectivity and low regard for workplace hierarchy (Thompson et al 1990; Evans 2008). Downward surveillance from above can thus be reversed and employees and workers become able to use the benefits of ICT to monitor and sometimes expose employer behaviour and organisation wrongdoing. Mathieson (1997) referred to such reversion as synoptic. Arguably, we should refer to such effects as a 'reverse panopticon' whereby employers themselves become constrained in their behaviours by the very processes celebrated in the workplace ICT 'revolution'. The workplace thus becomes a focus of 'distributed discourse' whereby information is disseminated widely across the organisation both formally and *informally* through ICT networks, thus opening up opportunities for new ways of collective resistance to management prerogative (Greene et al 2003). There are distinct mechanisms and processes connected with ICT that encourage or ease this activity. The Internet can be used at low money cost to both record and disseminate inappropriate or embarrassing employer behaviour at high speed and with wide and uncontrolled external access. Such exposure and countersurveillance is controversial within the workplace. It challenges authority and, as such, is subject to varieties of meaning, which is reflected in language and discourse. We might term such behaviour *inter alia* as sabotage, countersurveillance, individual misbehaviour or collective resistance.

A parallel and related phenomenon of workplace use of the Internet is the recent explosion of virtual social networking sites. The growth of such social networking has been phenomenal. For example, Facebook was founded in a Harvard University dormitory room by Mark Zuckerberg and friends in February 2004. By the end of the year, it had 1 million users. In 2010, Facebook claims to have 400 million active users, each with an average 130 friends. Seventy per cent of active users are outside the USA. In 2009 Twitter was the fastest growing social network site, recording 54 million visits per month. Many companies and organisations have also established social networking groups and encourage their staff to register. However, such social networking sites cause potential problems for employers if they are used to comment on employer behaviour, or on fellow employees or staff. Cases have emerged of employers taking disciplinary action against staff for using such sites 'inappropriately'. For example, high-profile dismissals of bloggers or Internet-based social networkers have already occurred in the UK of employees at Waterstone's bookstore, Argos retailers, the Prison Service, Argyll and Bute Education Authority, and Virgin Airways through the 'inappropriate' use of Facebook or blogs. Such 'inappropriate' use has usually involved alleged abusive remarks by employees directed at clients, customers, students or service users. However, the 2010 British Airways cabin crew dispute involved more than 55 disciplinary cases, including dismissals of cabin crew staff, for using Facebook and SMS to denigrate fellow workers who were allegedly strike-breaking. Further cases involving social networking sites so far include *Hays Specialist Recruitment (Holdings) Ltd v Ions*, where a former employee copied confidential business contacts to his LinkedIn account, and *PennWell Publishing (UK) Ltd v Ornstein*, which examined who had the right to contacts made during the course of employment (CIPD 2009).

For individuals, the opportunity, means and propensity to whistleblow on the employer may be correspondingly enhanced, adding to already existing employer uncertainty towards policy approach (Lewis 2002). Most existing legislation continues to be framed to address 'conventional' forms of whistleblowing. However, Internet-based activity complicates matters. Instead of whistleblowing through third parties (for example the traditional media, trade unions, government regulators or employer-supported 'hotlines'), ICT enhancement allows the immediate release of information to a worldwide audience. Such information is therefore unmediated and unrestricted. The implications of this are beginning to be recognised by many legal commentators. In Australia, for example, para 8.22 of the Dreyfus Report on Whistleblowing Protection (published February 2009) states *inter alia* that 'If the Commonwealth does not legislate on disclosures to the media, it may be overtaken by technological advances enabling the anonymous disclosure of official information on the Internet on such sites as Wikileaks. The Wikileaks website contains measures to protect the identities of its contributors and does not include any Australian filtering mechanism' (transcript of evidence of Dr Rimmer on 10 October 2008, page 10). A conflict ensues framed by contradictory pressures on employer and employee alike. In the process a number of dilemmas are posed. For example, within the discourse and practice of corporate social responsibility and public service accountability it may be difficult to determine the boundaries of acceptable or reasonable practice when employees reveal potentially unsavoury aspects of employer behaviour. Such boundaries are between employer and employee rights and responsibilities, and embrace a variety of legislation covering data protection, public interest disclosure, privacy, intellectual property and human rights. These dilemmas are reflected in potential confusion at policy level as the boundaries in the legal status of electronically available information and data between the public, corporate and private domain become difficult to define and delineate. For example, SMS texts and instant messages will likely fall within the scope of a 'document' for UK court disclosure. Courts may also order social networking sites to disclose the identity of account holders and details of profiles and blogs. Yet in much of western Europe, individual privacy appears more important. In France, the data protection regulator requires employees' express consent to monitoring while in Sweden, the Data Inspections Board considers an individual's Internet provider address to be personal data.

HR and Web 2.0

For the HR officer in UK organisations, such dilemmas need policy responses to cover the use of social network sites and Internet-based communication in the workplace. Many companies have embraced Web 2.0 advances by establishing their in-house social networking. An example is Cisco Systems in California's Silicon Valley, which operates its own network, IZone, by encouraging all employees to respond to new ideas for innovation and production within the company. However, many more organisations are extremely cautious about social networking, and a recent study by the Internet security company Clearswift found that two-thirds of British companies have banned employees from using social networking sites. Half of all the HR professionals in the survey had disciplined workers for wasting time on social networking while at work.

The CIPD has recently begun to research the uses of Web 2.0 applications in the workplace. The initial discussion paper (Martin et al n.d.) reports that some companies (for example Cadbury) have now begun to use blogs as an additional means of recruitment and internal communications. Podcasts are also used by some organisations as a learning tool as well as social bookmarks (webpages shared privately across a network). The Government has responded to the dilemmas posed by Web 2.0 facilities in the workplace by producing guidelines for social networking (Government Communication Network 2007):

- develop a strategic, evidence-based approach, integrating existing activities and communications strategies
- educate managers by raising awareness of what Web 2.0 technologies are available, the opportunities they offer and the risks they raise
- develop a code of conduct and toolkit for the use of Web 2.0, providing a clear

steer to employees and managers on the use of social media for work and personal use

- learn to listen by adopting focused and sustained efforts to understand, map and track the use of relevant Web 2.0 technologies

- set out a business case for using Web 2.0 technologies, including a phased implementation of access to social media tools

- avoid replication by engaging with existing technologies before developing in-house ones

- regularly evaluate the use and effectiveness of Web 2.0 technologies in the organisation.

Alternatively, or perhaps in parallel with the government guideline approach, is the approach of Enterprise 2.0, which encourages the use of bespoke development of social network software that can link organisations both internally with their employees and externally with their customers. Enterprise 2.0 is a term usually associated with Andrew McAfee of Harvard University, who recommends such an approach because it avoids the problems of information-sharing and distributed discourse associated with open social networks such as Facebook, while at the same time allows organisations to harness the potential advantages of Web 2.0 interaction for the organisation. An example of Enterprise 2.0 comes from Pfizer, the pharmaceutical company, which has developed an application called Pfizerpedia (similar to Wikipedia) as a shared knowledge repository among its research scientists.

CONCLUSION

We have seen that the use of ICT in the workplace has occurred very rapidly in the last three decades. Some have argued that this has created a third industrial revolution of a networked society with advantaged knowledge workers. However, others have disputed this perspective. There are alternative forms and interpretations of ICT-based knowledge, all of which have implications for the modern workplace and HR policy. We have also seen the 'dark side' of ICT, characterised by monitoring, surveillance and control and reflected on its implications. Finally, we have reviewed the potential impact of interactive Web 2.0 technology in the workplace, with all its potential to expand creative potential

CRITICAL REFLECTIONS

Relating to the first question of the opening case study, HR is clearly using ICT as a tool to monitor and control staff movements and activities. Clear justification needs to be given of the reasons why such a system of monitoring is necessary, and HR will need to brief managers and affected staff accordingly. HR will also have to consider which, if any, disciplinary routes they are likely to suggest should the monitoring expose any individual wrongdoing by staff.

Regarding the second question, HR is within its rights to monitor output of individual employees. However, the means chosen could be considered unethical if it is perceived by staff, their union or the wider population to be an infringement of personal liberty. The employer will need to justify use of the tags and explain why such use is preferable to more conventional ways of monitoring by supervisors.

CASTELLS, M. (2001) *The rise of the network society.* Oxford: Wiley-Blackwell.

This book provides a systemic analysis of the global informational capitalism that emerged in the last half of the twentieth century.

CIPD. (2002) *Training in the knowledge economy.* Research report. London: CIPD.

This research report highlights issues that employers face in training their workforce in the knowledge economy era.

CIPD. (2005) *Technology and people management: the opportunity and the challenge.* London: CIPD.

This report examines the opportunities and challenges that technology presents to the management of human resources.

KAROLY, L. and PANIS, C. (2004) *The 21st century at work: forces shaping the future workforce and workplace in the United States.* Santa Monica, CA: Rand.

This book examined the likely evolution of the US workforce and workplace over the next 10 to 15 years, focusing on demographics, technology and globalisation.

RIFKIN, J. (1996) *The end of work: the decline of the global labour force and the dawn of a post-market era.* New York: G.P. Putnam.

This report examines the implications that the new computer-based and communications technologies will have on worldwide unemployment.

ZUBOFF, S. (1988) *In the age of the smart machine: the future of work and power.* Oxford: Heinemann.

This book documents the pitfalls and promise of computerised technology in business life.

in the workplace, and to create dangers of unmediated organisational behaviour. The further reading below provides further exploration of the issues raised in this chapter, and the websites are useful sources of policy advice for the practitioner HR specialist.

PERMISSIONS

CHAPTER 6

Employment Relations, Finance and the Corporation

John Grahl

OVERVIEW

This chapter will consider classical studies of how ownership and control factors have influenced HR decisions. It will then move on to consider how these trends have led to a blurring of the lines between the structures dealing with organisational accountability and the discourses used for critically analysing organisations. The emerging dominance of the shareholder value view of the firm and the HR implications of this are considered, before finally reflecting upon how all of these trends have fed into the financial crisis of 2008 and beyond.

LEARNING OBJECTIVES

Reading this chapter will enable the reader to:

- critically evaluate the HR implications of ownership and control on HR decisions
- critically evaluate the influence and importance of the 'shareholder value' view of the firm
- critically evaluate how the financial crisis of 2008 might challenge existing assumptions about the dominance of 'shareholder value'.

HRM IN THE MEDIA

'PROTESTS AT CORPORATE TAKEOVER'

In late 2009/early 2010, the internationally known confectioner, Cadbury's, was subject to a widely reported hostile takeover bid by the even larger multinational food production firm Kraft (for example see BBC News 2009). The law for corporate takeover in the UK has long been one of a free and open market. The argument for such an open policy has been that the threat of corporate takeover makes domestic firms more competitive, that restricting such takeovers risks British takeovers elsewhere and that firms that are taken over are made more efficient as a result. Among a number of objections raised, however, has been that the new owners would need to make up the costs of the takeover in cutting costs at the new acquisition; that an overseas owner will be less likely to prioritise key value-adding activities such as research in the new acquisition (preferring to consolidate such activities in the home country) and that they will be more remote to potential pressure from key stakeholders – principally employees.

Questions

1 What may explain what is 'rational' for Kraft to do in terms of employment decisions at Cadbury's?

2 How inevitable is downsizing as a consequence of a corporate takeover such as this?

INTRODUCTION

At least since the twentieth century, it has been widely accepted that two questions are very closely linked: (1) what is the nature of the employment relationship, and (2) what is the essential nature of the business enterprise (Putterman and Kroszner 1996)? Ronald Coase (1937) initiated an important line of economic thinking when he pointed out that the standard neoclassical 'theory of the firm' was at variance with the notion of the employment contract as a means of organising work, as the employment contract specifies only the possibilities that workers offer for the transformation of inputs into outputs. That is, why do entrepreneurs find it more efficient, in practice, to hire people as employees in a company rather than to offer a series of contracts for services in the open market? Coase's contribution accounted for the existence of business enterprises as resulting from the costs of using the market – functions are internalised when transaction costs make it disadvantageous to outsource them. The argument clearly includes an explanation of the boundaries of the firm and one consequence is found in the dilemmas faced by firms: when would you outsource and when would you keep in-house (see Chapter 11)?

Aspects of the employment relationship are closely related to this view. Coase suggested both that the alternative to the use of markets was a hierarchical form of organisation and that enterprises would avoid a narrow specification of workers' tasks in order to avoid the costs of re-contracting when the circumstances of the enterprise changed. Thus the theory of the firm offered suggestions as to how one might account for aspects of the employment relationship as it is generally understood – in this case both the subordination of employees and the wide indeterminacy of employment contracts.

Alchian and Demsetz (1972) made the theory more specific by focusing on the need to reduce opportunistic behaviour within team production and to adjust the contracts of the team members in the light of changing circumstances. With this reformulation the enterprise becomes in essence not a hierarchical organisation, but a 'nexus of contracts'. This may seem a very abstract characterisation but time has worked in its favour. Most of the dominant firms of last century were undoubtedly served by immense bureaucratic hierarchies of an impressive solidity. But recent decades have seen a transformation of enterprise control systems. Although the bureaucratic hierarchies subsist in very many cases, they have often been reduced in scale and density, and in some other significant cases much lighter and more fluid forms of organisation have emerged. The 'nexus of contracts', on the other hand, remains central to the interpretation of the new forms, as of the old. It even becomes a surprisingly concrete description of certain 'hollow' corporations controlling complex production, marketing and sales networks in which, however, all the specific activities have been externalised.

Despite the apparently obvious unequal power relationship existing between employer and employee, Alchian and Demsetz (1972) strenuously denied that the employment relationship involved subordination (of the employee) in the sense of a loss of freedom; they insisted that the constraints accepted by the employee were basically contractual and voluntary. Surely a practical assessment of this issue depends on the alternatives available on the external labour market. When these are attenuated, the terse offer from the employer, 'take it or leave it', assumes all the sinister force it has in the pages of Marx.

The same correlation between employment and the business enterprise can be found in later contributions to the same current of thought. Grossman and Hart (1986) gave a more precise account of subordination in terms of the managerial prerogatives of the firm's proprietor as 'residual claimant': if other factors of production were rewarded according to contracts more or less closely tied to external markets then the firm's owner receiving the profits or losses that remained bore most of the risks of the enterprise. It was efficient to concentrate decision-making on this risk-bearer, who had the greatest incentive to get things right.

The contributions of Williamson (1985) to the same general research programme emphasise elements of conflict in the interpretation of the enterprise and of employment relations. 'Monitoring' of employee performance becomes a key enterprise function (by 'residual claimant' logic, attributed to the party with most to lose). It is true that Coase already invokes monitoring costs but, for him, these were in the first instance costs of using the market, to be avoided by bringing activities in-house. And there is an emphasis in Williamson on firm-specific investments by both proprietors and workers: sunk costs on the part of the owner are the basis of the residual claimant position, but employment relations must be managed to induce the co-operation of the workforce in a context where 'hold-ups' are possible on the basis of vertical integration and workforce capacities that cannot be easily replaced on external markets. There is an interesting convergence between Williamson's views and the more radical interpretation of the enterprise by Bowles and Gintis (1990), although of course the two latter have a very different perspective on the market economy and the corporation.

The correlation suggested here between theories of the enterprise and employment is, however, not absolute. A specific historical objection to it arises from the work of Deakin, who insists that the enterprise and the modern contract of employment do not have the same history. The latter gradually emerges from the early modern status relationship of master and servant. The former is deeply shaped by the nineteenth-century introduction of limited liability. Deakin (2004) sees their convergence as only taking place in the twentieth century as an economic, partly contractual, understanding of employment displaces earlier conceptions of a subordination determined by differences in status.

There is surely also a limit to any derivation of institutions from purely economic premises. Contracts and market exchange presuppose some effective socialisation of the agents involved; and even institutions with a primarily economic function will be more successful if they can reinforce existing social ties (Granovetter 1985). Thus, a purely economic account even of an essentially economic institution such as the enterprise may be unavoidably incomplete.

Nevertheless, the present chapter traces some recent developments in the status of corporations and sketches some of the possible consequences for employment relations. The focus is on US experience, which provides the most general case, and on changes in corporate finance, which are taken as a compressed representation of corporate change as a whole. It falls into five sections: the starting point is the separation of ownership and control in the large US corporation, which is in the background to subsequent developments; there followed an era where the direction of change was towards a strong assimilation of the large corporation into national growth systems, with a corresponding codification of their employment relations; the challenge to the structures that emerged at that time took the form of a reassertion of the role of capital markets, expressed firstly in a drive for bond-financed takeovers and secondly in the movement for shareholder value; the recent collapse of the global financial system calls this model into question in its turn, so that it is possible to conclude that the status and role of the large corporation today are still deeply problematic.

BERLE AND MEANS

In 1932 Berle and Means published *The Modern Corporation and Private Property* – one of the classic studies of the US corporation. When this was republished in 1992, it contained a new introduction by Mark Jensen, who suggested that although the central theme of the work – the separation of ownership and control in the large corporation with dispersed shareholders – remained topical, Berle and Means' treatment of this theme was now 'obsolete'. Jensen's judgement was based on the view that more recent analysis, centred on the principal–agent paradigm, was decisively superior to that of the 1930s. This 'reappraisal' seems questionable today.

The central problem is that of ownership and control. How do shareholders, as the owners of the corporation, ensure that those who control it, the board of directors, run the company in such a way that shareholders get a fair return? How can they be sure that they are not running the corporation in the personal interests of the directors themselves? Dispersed ownership of a corporation's shares (that is, through shares) depends on the prior establishment of 'limited liability', which endows the corporation with a legal personality. In itself limited liability disturbs the notion of the proprietor as 'residual claimant' since, in the event of insolvency, it is the creditors who absorb losses. The dangers of this institution, which even at the start of the twentieth century only covered a minority of business enterprises, have recently been emphasised by Blankenburg and Plesch (2007): risks and liabilities may become harder to read, especially when parent corporations only accept limited liability for their own subsidiaries; when a corporation's debt is held by a bank or other sophisticated investor, the risks may be accurately assessed but this is much less likely when credit is supplied by suppliers or employees.

Nevertheless, limited liability on its own, as Berle and Means put it, merely as a legal device 'through which the private business transactions may be carried on', would not suffice to alter significantly the employment practices of the enterprise. When, however, limited liability becomes the support of widely dispersed share ownership, two essential changes take place – in scale and in the allocation of responsibility. A huge concentration of economic power extends and completes the transformation of independent workers into wage labourers.

A most significant part of Berle and Means' analysis is their assertion that the ceding of control by shareholders is made acceptable to them by a compensating advantage – the liquidity of their holdings. A key interest of the shareholder is 'that his stock should remain freely marketable at a fair price'. The consequence is a kind of Faustian pact, where control and effective participation in decision-making is yielded in exchange for the ready marketability of the securities concerned. It will be suggested below that this transaction, of voice against exit, to use the terminology introduced later by Hirschman, has only been confirmed by the increasing role today of institutional investors.

This abdication of the proprietors gives rise to a key problem of accountability. When the management of giant corporations is no longer subordinated to the interests of the shareholders as nominal owners, in whose interests is their power exercised? The most alarming answer, that this is simply unaccountable economic power held by self-perpetuating elites, is rendered more plausible by the legal relations carefully explored by Berle and Means. The courts, particularly in the US, were and are deeply reluctant to challenge the decisions of incumbent managements provided these are in accordance with the law. To second-guess these decisions would imply the responsibility of the authorities for the conduct of business – only fraud or other breaches of the criminal law are therefore normally subject to judicial sanction.

Berle and Means therefore identify the following dilemma: in the view of the corporations themselves and the lawyers who spoke for them, new relations had emerged 'giving to the groups in control powers which are absolute and not limited by any implied obligation with respect to their use'. In a traditional view, on the other hand, these groups should act as the trustees for a class of absentee proprietors with less and less engagement in the actual working of the industrial system. They had no hesitation in preferring the second of these as 'the lesser of two evils'. But they also foresaw an evolution of the corporation to 'serve not alone the owners of the corporation but all society'. This would involve the controlling managements evolving 'into a purely neutral technocracy, balancing a variety of claims by various groups in the community and assigning to each a portion of the income stream on the basis of public policy rather than private cupidity'.

This is a remarkable anticipation of what is now called the 'stakeholder' view of the enterprise. Berle and Means saw this evolution of the corporation in this direction as driven by conflict: 'A constant warfare has existed between the individuals wielding power, in whatever form, and the subjects of that power.... This pressure, constant in ecclesiastical and political history, is already making its appearance in many guises in the economic field.' This conflict presumably includes that between corporate managements and their increasingly organised workforces and would contribute to the assertion of the 'larger interests of society' within the large corporation as the 'dominant form of social organisation'.

THE RISE OF TECHNOCRACY

The 50 years following the publication of *The Modern Corporation and Private Property* seemed in general to confirm its central hypotheses on the evolution of the corporation. The corporate system was stabilised, managerial procedures normalised and reduced to predictable routines. The interactions among corporations became more dense and seemed to unify them into a single, coherent system, governed by leaderships evolving into a technocracy of the kind foreseen. Across a range of disciplines, new analyses and investigations confirmed this general line of development. In economics, for example, the standard view of firms as maximising profits was called into question: Baumol's (1962) postulate of sales maximisation reflected a clear departure from the priorities of shareholders but at the same time a certain alignment with wider social interests since it supported continuous economic growth, which, with the associated stabilisation of employment, was the main economic priority of most of the population. Critical sociologists, such as C. Wright Mills (1951) and William Whyte (1956), found that the effects of the organisational changes involved on the well-being, the social interactions and the conduct of those subjected to corporate hierarchies were in many respects questionable – but these critiques themselves presupposed that an important transformation in economic life had taken place.

Much of the cross-disciplinary work of Herbert Simon can be related to the same pattern of development. Corporations as complex organisations which could no longer be seen as primarily directed towards a straightforward proprietorial interest provided a context in which such notions as bounded rationality and 'satisficing' found fruitful application. However, perhaps the most comprehensive account of the developing corporate structure is found in the writings of J.K. Galbraith; his *The New Industrial State*, in particular, with its view that the business elite was evolving into a 'technostructure', can be related to the perspective of Berle and Means in the closing pages of their book.

A certain politicisation of economic life is recognised by many of these writers – the issue is the power of the corporation that is not sufficiently constrained by output or factor markets. Galbraith (1967) postulated the emergence of countervailing power – requiring the aggregation interests by consumers, employees or other groups but not necessarily centralised action. The Zeitgeist is reflected in the strong fiscal incentives in most countries to restrict the distribution of dividends in favour of the reinvestment of retained earnings: such measures clearly subordinate shareholder interests to the general interest in economic growth.

There were sceptics both among free market conservatives and Marxists. Among the latter, Baran and Sweezy (1966) gave the ironic title 'the soulful corporation' to a chapter of *Monopoly Capital*, debunking the notion of publicly spirited corporations. However, it is significant that they saw the continuity of capitalist social relations not in the survival of a class of shareholders but in the accumulation of capital by the large corporation itself – in this they were followed by most other Marxists; it was the top managements of the large corporations who were seen as the bearers of the capital relation, the shareholding proprietors being regarded as of marginal significance. From the opposing standpoint, conservative critics, such as George Stigler (1962), identified the dysfunctions arising from a close association of corporate power with government agencies.

The emergence of this corporate system is associated with a strong codification of employment relations and under the control of corporate bureaucracies. Sanford Jacoby (2004) speaks of a 'transformation'. In his view, the key issue was job security. At least in the US, the first efforts of corporate leaderships were directed against the unions – in the hope that measures to standardise working conditions and enhance the security of employees could forestall unionisation. However, partly because the new corporate system facilitated union organisation in the largest firms, the entry of the unions was achieved on a widespread basis and they even became to some extent participants in personnel management tasks, relieving the actual managerial hierarchy of some detailed responsibilities affecting individual employees. Of course, these corporate developments did not call into question the subordination of wage earners within the employment relationship. In many ways they reinforced it, as is testified by both the sociological accounts referred to above, concerned especially with fate of junior corporate functionaries, and by the growing critique of Fordism with reference to factory operatives. But a relatively clear settlement between capital and organised labour could be discerned, essentially compensating for continuing subordination by higher wages and enhanced security, and it was possible to believe that the further evolution of the system would, by gradual reform or radical challenge, start to erode the absence of workers' autonomy within the productive sphere itself.

THE REIGN OF FINANCE

Discussion of financial pressures on the contemporary corporation, especially in Europe, tends to centre on the movement for shareholder value. For present purposes, however, this is a rather narrow focus and may even obscure some of the key issues involved. In the US, in particular, the reassertion of financial relations came in two waves. In the first of these the key financial instrument was the junk bond – issued precisely in order to buy out dispersed holdings of equity and thus institute top managements reuniting ownership and control. This was the era of the corporate raiders, as Carl Icahn and T. Boone Pickens stalked even the largest and most prestigious members of the corporate elite. None of the very biggest giants was brought down in this assault, but the raiders amassed huge fortunes as some of the besieged leaderships paid them handsomely to go away. At the same time the conduct and ethos of US business moved away from the patterns of the technocratic era.

The conjuncture helps to illuminate the main features of the shift. The huge productivity gap between the US and other industrial countries had been rapidly narrowed during the 1950s and 1960s. The previously unchallenged supremacy of US industry was now called into question by the super-efficient industrial systems of Germany and Japan, in the context of a general decline in profitability and of threats to the dollar. The patterns of investment of the post-war decades, financed for the most part out of retained profits, no longer yielded the routine gains in productivity that had been achieved in the past. The new priority was not expansion as such but restructuring – and this gave a new importance to the capital markets.

These circumstances help to clarify the critique of established corporate leaderships by Michael Jensen, the most influential academic advocate of the leverage buyout (LBO) as an instrument of structural change. A representative target for Jensen – and likewise for the raiders – was a large, profitable enterprise whose managerial procedures were dominated by routine. The profits arose from market power and the industrial assets accumulated in the past, but the yield on repeated investment in the same direction might be low. However, even a low positive return might be acceptable to a management more preoccupied with expansion than with efficiency, and insulated from investor pressures by the dispersion and disorganisation of the shareholders.

In these circumstances, a more effective use of corporate assets and investment resources could be promoted by two linked forces – the capital markets and the market for corporate control. To make the first effective, it was necessary to break down the partition between retained profits and the monetary resources of the capital markets. All profits should be regarded as potentially flowing on to the capital markets and company profits retained only if there were internal investment projects with returns better than those available from external placements. For Jensen (1986), 'free cash flow' – revenues available to corporate managements to use at their discretion – would often be put to unproductive use. He advocated extensive use of debt finance – this would place contractual restrictions on the use of company earnings and help to focus top management on the efficiency of resource use rather than the scale of operations, while bond-holders as a group would, in their own interests, subject the company's balance sheets to close scrutiny.

The market for corporate control would reinforce these disciplines. Corporate leaderships whose positions were contestable would concentrate on increasing the value of the firm's activities and, in the event of failure, would be displaced by more capable teams. The mechanism for this circulation of elites was again to be found in the bond market. LBOs would be financed by the large-scale issue of bonds. Thus the unimpeded functioning of security markets and the removal of barriers to hostile takeovers were necessary for a successful renewal of the US economic system.

In its historical context, this approach – one of the most influential and incisive aspects of the neo-liberal agenda – had some elements in common with Marxist views current at the same time, which also traced a connection between economic crisis and capital restructuring. In the neo-liberal case, however, the restructuring was seen as an essentially beneficial process in that capital market evaluations were perceived as a true measure of corporate performance and a reliable guide to the necessary reforms. In the works of Jensen and Eugene Fama, efficient capital markets provided the basis for a kind of social Darwinism – the capital markets would select those organisational and institutional forms that offered the best prospects of economic adaptation (Fama and Jensen 1983).

Note that, for a large part of the 1980s, the emphasis was not on the equity markets but on corporate bond markets. The problems arising from the separation of ownership and control were to be resolved by reuniting them in the hands of new corporate leaderships who would buy out dispersed shareholdings and once again concentrate ownership in the hands of the controlling groups. At one point, Jensen even prophesised the demise of the publicly quoted company. He even, on one occasion, expressed his respect for the Japanese forms of corporate organisation, where equity was closely held within financial groups. Even though the capital market was attenuated in such circumstances, the close relations between owners and management reduced the 'principal-agent' problems arising with dispersed shareholdings.

THE DRIVE FOR SHAREHOLDER VALUE

Thus the theme of shareholder value (Williams 2000), increasingly important in the corporate world of the 1990s, represented a significant change of direction in capital market-led restructuring. The participation of dispersed investors via the equity markets rather than the corporate bond markets was now accepted and the elimination of the public company deferred. Principal–agent problems were now to be addressed not by recombining the two roles but by subjecting the agents – CEOs and other corporate leaders – to effective scrutiny and offering them appropriate incentives. The romance of the corporate raiders gave way to the more prosaic theme of corporate governance.

A range of factors help to explain this shift. Hostile takeovers, often leading to plant closures and the transfer of jobs overseas, became increasingly unpopular in the US. After the Supreme Court modified its position on takeovers, most states legislated to permit incumbent managements to use various forms of defence. Scandals tarnished the reputation of some of the raiders, such as Ivan Boesky and Michael ('Greed is OK') Milken, who were imprisoned, and the collapse of investment bank Drexel Burnham Lambert in 1990 almost closed down the junk bond market. Private equity continued – partly in the sphere of venture capital start-ups, where a new bubble began to inflate – partly as a form of intervention in smaller companies. However, in the world of giant corporations, it was henceforth only a relatively minor adjunct to the normal prevalence of dispersed shareholdings.

It was now suggested, however, that the principal–agent problem could be contained by appropriate governance arrangements and managerial incentives. Codes of practice detailing the procedures required proliferated in the advanced economies. Investor relations departments were established in the big companies (although one sceptical commentator saw this simply as the standard corporate response to any new external challenge – 'comply and disconnect'). The increasing importance of institutional investors as holders of corporate securities may also have encouraged the shareholder value drive because the big institutions could, to a certain extent, aggregate the interests of the households who were the final suppliers of the financial resources involved.

Takeovers remained important in this new phase of financialisation, but now the emphasis was less on LBOs and more on restructuring among the big corporations themselves, the most daring case being perhaps the purchase of Mannesmann by the much smaller Vodafone. The continuing importance of the capital markets from the 1980s into the 1990s found one expression in the large equity buy-backs carried out by large corporations, and another in a sharper concern with the quarterly earnings reports made to investors.

How was corporate practice affected by these waves of financialisation? It should first of all be recognised that the very weight of corporations as economic structures makes for a certain continuity in their internal organisation and their strategies – thus many routine aspects of management were unaffected by either the threats of the corporate raiders or the new priority accorded to shareholder returns. It is also necessary not to take the declared devotion to shareholder interests too literally. Vast reallocations of capital are brought about by disposals, mergers and acquisitions, but it is difficult to show that these corresponded to any clear shareholder interest: on the contrary, the announcement of any major acquisition often depresses the share price of the purchaser. The era is certainly one of finance-led restructuring and reorganisation but there is abundant evidence, especially from the dot.com boom and bust and the associated scandals, that the protection of shareholders has hardly been the first priority of company leaderships.

Generally recognised impacts on corporate strategy include an increased readiness to accept risks, remuneration linked to financial performance, the outsourcing of non-core service inputs, and a move away from conglomerate structures towards a sharper focus on central activities (Grahl 2006, 2009). Consequently the previous direction of change in employment relations was called into question. This was true, above all, of its primary emphasis on job security. Wage differentials widened as core workers, able to influence corporate performance, made gains and those with peripheral functions, more easy to replace, were pinned back to the pay levels available on outside markets. The introduction of 'flat hierarchies', destabilising career structures, reflected this attenuation of internal labour markets.

The meaning of these changes in the longer term is more difficult to determine. The era, on the face of things, is one of disorganisation and chaotic restructuring. Its self-understanding made the individual corporate enterprise the key actor, almost the only significant actor, in the socio-economic system. In the view of leading interpreters, such as Michael Jensen, acute competition among enterprises – on the markets for output, labour and, above all, finance – was the essence of the process. They held to a kind of social Darwinism, where the financial markets worked to select successful organisational developments and eliminate the failures.

However, the financial system not only selects; it also connects. One feature of the previous, 'technocratic' era was that each giant corporation, however finely organised it might be internally, was a world apart. Some of the sociological criticism of the time reflects on the sense of isolation of corporate functionaries – closely integrated into the organisation, but often feeling divorced from the wider society. In financial terms, that had been the era of retained earnings; internal labour markets expanded at the expense of external ones and something similar happened to financial markets as Wall Street was almost marginalised within the national economy. The huge transfers of capital from enterprise to enterprise that have taken place since the 1980s were largely effected through the capital markets, giving these a key role in the allocation of capital even though they raised very little new industrial capital from the public.

Although the subjective aspects of restructuring – individual success or failure, the promotion or relegation of members of the business elite – understandably attract attention, there are objective features that correspond not to some dramatic struggle among enterprises but to a reshaping of economic systems as a whole as the sectoral and regional balances of the economy and its technological basis were reconfigured. The severe global financial crisis of 2008 made clear this integrative role: in spite of the highly dysfunctional practices of international banks and liberalised financial markets, virtually all actors were determined to avoid a fragmentation of the global system, which, in spite of massive losses and disturbances, was regarded as an indispensable support of international economic relations.

Thus, in spite of the sharp light that financial developments threw on the performance of individual enterprises, in the longer run it might be seen as making for a higher degree of integration in the corporate sector and for a fuller and more coherent response to pressures for restructuring. Employees, however, did not benefit from this embryonic emergence of a structurally unified corporate economy. Their past links to individual corporations had been weakened and, in many cases, broken. No general or collective institutions existed to validate their role in the economic system as a whole. Indeed, it was the imposition of many of the heavy adjustment costs associated with restructuring on to employees and local communities – in the most arbitrary way – that did most to discredit the ideologies of financial control.

THE DEBACLE AND AFTER

The claim that financial markets are the best guides to economic restructuring depends on these markets exhibiting, if not efficiency in the senses of economic theory, then at least some measure of consistency and some minimum level of rationality. Until the new century the crises of globalised finance were centred outside the West and could be attributed to the immaturity of developing or post-socialist economies. However, the high-tech boom in late 1990s America, leading to a dramatic bust in 2000–01, and the corporate scandals that followed already tended to subvert the more Panglossian interpretations of deregulated financial systems. The sub-prime fiasco of 2007–08 was on a much greater scale because it impaired the whole of real estate finance in North America, by far the largest sector of the world's financial system.

Michael Jensen himself, perhaps the most influential advocate of a central role for financial market evaluations in corporate life, had to acknowledge that many of his previous positions had been called into question. One key example can be given: the 'market for corporate control' or the exposure of inadequate corporate leaderships to displacement in the course of a hostile takeover – this was a central mechanism in both phases of financial market domination of the corporation. Consider, however, a stock market that systematically overvalues corporate equity. Jensen (2004) now dryly observes, 'It is difficult, to say the least, to buy up an overvalued company, eliminate its overvaluation and make a profit.' In efficient financial markets, overvaluation would soon be removed by short-selling. But in this context it is now impossible to refute the argument of Shleifer and the behavioural school of finance: it is risky to try to exploit financial market disequilibria because one cannot know how long they will last or whether they will widen before they narrow.

The shareholder interpretation of the enterprise is still asserted today but this may be to avoid recognising the absence of any clear account of corporate power or of how it should be exercised. A critique of this position by Aglietta and

Rebérioux (2005) centres on a reassertion of the argument of Berle and Means some 80 years before. The dispersed shareholders of giant corporations cannot be seen as in any way sovereigns for whom corporate managements would simply be the representatives. The fact that today much corporate equity is held by pension funds and other institutional investors in no way resolves this problem; on the contrary, these institutions trade intensively and are even more preoccupied with market liquidity than individuals. This concern sets a structural limit to their activism: the institutions will always demand that the markets are fully informed about corporate developments; they would avoid any role in the formulation of strategy that might give them privileged access to information and thus impair their ability to trade their shares.

This state of affairs leaves unanswered the question of corporate power; in whose interests is it exercised? In terms of employment relations, the closer interactions among corporations and the higher responsiveness of economic systems as a whole has accompanied a continuing attenuation of the links between individual employees and individual employers. Recent developments within the corporation push this process further but at the same time start to suggest some possible responses.

INTANGIBLE CAPITAL AND THE NETWORK ENTERPRISE

In a survey of current problems in the theory of the firm, Luigi Zingales (2000) uses what might seem a very extreme example. The celebrated advertising expert, Maurice Saatchi, in dispute with the institutional shareholders of the Saatchi & Saatchi corporation, simply resigned, along with his brother and other leading executives, and established a new advertising agency. The shareholders suffered substantial losses.

Of course, there are few individuals with as much power to reverse the traditional relationship between employees and corporations, but if one thinks not only of exceptional individuals but of teams and networks of key workers, then the example may point to a general trend. In the giant corporations of the past, the control of vast complexes of physical capital, most of it sunk irrevocably into the specific purposes of the enterprise, established the decision-making rights of the owners or, when these were dispersed 'absentee' shareholders, of the senior management.

There are, of course, still many such corporations today, but the expansion of the service sector and the deployment of new technologies have moved economic systems decisively away from this pattern. Corporate assets are increasingly intangible and impossible to separate from the value produced in the enterprise as a going concern: human capital, especially in firm-specific forms, and the organisational capital involved in the combination of individual workers into productive teams (Brynjolfsson et al 2002). Zingales (2000, p34) characterises the development of such enterprises as depending, in the first instance, on the entrepreneur's control over some critical asset, itself often intangible, which makes it possible to elicit firm-specific investments from key specialists. 'In this framework, power is maintained and increased by having more and more people specialising; thus at some point the critical resource becomes the web of specific investment itself.' The corporation that employs the workers is then simply their own collective productive potential. Zingales suggests that growth is an economic necessity for such firms: the prospect of growth underpins the promise to workers making firm-specific investments that these will not be devalued, but rewarded out of rising revenues.

Such organisational developments validate a certain type of stakeholder theory; when a firm's key stakeholders are all those, employees and others, who have made investments specific to its success, then it is these stakeholders who will share the rewards.

However, there is a sharp contrast between this view and standard stakeholder theories. In the latter, the stakeholders are all those who depend on the enterprise, rather than those on whom the enterprise depends. The difference threatens to have very adverse implications for the distribution of income. There are higher rewards for the key specialists, who in effect cease to be subordinated employees and participate in decision-making and control. For the rest, rewards are determined on external markets. Zingales (2000, p39) suggests that in the new corporation, 'the primary role of a governance system is to ensure an alignment between the ability to capture the opportunities and the reward stemming from them'. This seems dystopian – it suggests a world of situational rents, with only the most tenuous link to effort, merit or need. Massive negative externalities for corporations as a whole can result just from this externalisation of those workers without critical specialisations tying them to the firm.

As the Saatchi example suggests, the increasing importance of intangible capital seems to further weaken the position of dispersed shareholders and thus to render even more implausible any interpretation of corporate managements as the 'agents' of shareholder 'principals'. Zingales suggests that shareholders may find a new role in defending the integrity of the enterprise – but it seems that a certain concentration of share ownership might be necessary for this. Dispersed shareholders might be reduced to a purely financial role, defined by the specific risk characteristics of their investment, and even further alienated from corporate control.

The issue of enterprise integrity points to a key vulnerability of corporations today – fragmentation of the structured assembly of key specialists, which constitutes their organisational capital. The new salience of network forms of organisation (Castells) increases this danger from centrifugal forces at the same time as it contributes to the importance of intangible investments. A wide measure of autonomy has often to be conceded to networks of workers within the firm, and these may seek to advance their own interests at the firm's expense. Meanwhile, the firm as a whole may find it necessary to build network relationships with others, again with a possibly damaging loss of autonomy. But the most critical case may be the emergence of networks across enterprise boundaries, where productive systems involve dense linkages between workers inside and outside the firm. A very good example of the risks involved is the case where a corporation's customers have expert knowledge, indispensable to the design and delivery of the product or service they are purchasing; the relevant group of workers inside the corporation, together with the account manager or marketing specialist can then form a closely integrated group with the customer's representatives, threatening to downplay or marginalise the interests of the corporation as a whole. Other functions, such as research, procurement or the establishment of subsidiaries are exposed to analogous risks.

Thus corporations face two dangers: on the one hand, the increasing permeability of their own boundaries can destabilise the fragile assemblies of specialists at the core of their productive systems; on the other, the continuing externalisation of routine functions, under financial pressure, makes for a world of exclusion, where replaceable workers are exposed to the harshest competitive conditions.

It may be justified to see in the current movement for corporate social responsibility (CSR) an awareness of these threats, although not yet a coherent response to them. There are other interpretations of CSR – it is sometimes seen as responding to legitimacy problems, sometimes as attempting to forestall official regulation (for a critical survey, see Blowfield and Murray 2008). But the consciousness that the external environment is becoming more uncertain, often as a result of corporate strategies themselves, may be one source of the concern to stabilise and pacify that environment.

CONCLUSION

In the present era, the significance of corporations has grown beyond all measure. Regarded, a generation ago, simply as providing a functional institutional frame for economic activity, they have been promoted to become the key agents, almost the only agents, of economic development and social change. All other institutions – schools, political parties, football clubs, orchestras – have been pressed to conform to corporate models and to adopt essentially corporate strategies. Corporations, in practice, displaced the competitive markets that were supposed to lie at the heart of economic reform: instead of the rule of competition, we have had the dominion of business.

Actual economic events, however, call this primacy into question. The financial forces that were supposed to constrain the corporate world and shape its development are exposed as arbitrary and irrational. With the failure of the shareholder concept of the corporation, no compelling rationale can be found for the power of corporate elites. Trends in corporate organisation and strategy call into question their relevance to the key problems of employment.

Moreover, it may soon become necessary to adopt a more complex view of socio-economic agency. Deep economic changes leave the corporation as an indispensable legal and financial instrument, but make it difficult to interpret as a coherent productive system. In this situation, two contrasting lines of development need to be considered: either a further evolution of corporations that would restore their ability to provide solutions to the problems of employment – its quantity, its quality and its security – or the emergence of new institutions, working both outside corporations and across their boundaries, in a reassertion of 'the larger interests of society' within 'the dominant form of social organisation'.

HRM IN THE MEDIA

CRITICAL REFLECTIONS

The answer to the first question depends on what we mean by 'rational'. What may be 'rational' from the 'shareholder value' view of the firm, integrating all of Kraft's European operations could be 'rational'. This integration could involve large-scale redundancies of the Cadbury's workforce. On the other hand, since this was a very high-profile and controversial takeover, it could also be 'rational' to ensure that a sustainable future is possible for the Cadbury's workforce, at least in the medium term, because of the adverse effects that the event could have on the company's reputation.

In relation to the second question, there is a cost-based logic to downsizing in a corporate takeover such as the one presented in the opening case study. However, there is also the risk of compromising organisational capacity. Cadbury's was always seen as a very successful organisation and this was partly due to the people employed in it. Other factors to take into consideration include the social capital that works in Cadbury's and that has established company reputation. In addition, takeovers such as this one often see industrial action taken to resist downsizing measures.

EXPLORE FURTHER

AGLIETTA, M. and REBÉRIOUX, A. (2005) *Corporate governance adrift: a critique of shareholder value.* Cheltenham: Edward Elgar.

This book is basic reading for anyone interested in industrial organisation and strategy of the firm, finance and corporate governance.

HUTTON, W. and GIDDENS, A. (eds) (2001) *Global capitalism.* New York: New Press.

This book deals with the financial and cultural effects of globalisation.

Economy and Society Journal. UK: Routledge.

This journal addresses issues ranging from economic governance to developments in the life sciences and beyond, and publishes new work on current political issues throughout the world.

BLOWFIELD, M. and MURRAY, A. (2008) *Corporate responsibility: a critical introduction.* Oxford: Oxford University Press.

This book examines the dimensions of corporate responsibility, creating a framework that presents a historical and interdisciplinary overview of the field, a summary of different management approaches, and a review of the key actors and trends worldwide.

GRAHL, J. (ed.) (2009) *Global finance and social Europe*. Cheltenham: Edward Elgar.

This book provides a critical account of the relationship between global financial developments, the emergent European financial system and the implications of the operation of these for the European social model and its future.

CHAPTER 7

Politics, the Regulatory Environment and HRM

Phil James and Ian Roper

OVERVIEW

After presenting a media-based case study, this chapter considers the key mechanisms by which the state regulates the employment relationship – which includes the scale and scope of intervention and the role of ideology and party politics – before considering the major theoretical interventions on the issues – primarily being those approaches claiming that minimal intervention by the state will allow optimum outcomes versus those approaches claiming that intervention is needed to correct for the unequal market position held by employers leading to distorting and inefficient outcomes.

LEARNING OBJECTIVES

Reading this chapter will enable the reader to:

- have a critical understanding of the different motives that the state has for intervening in the area of employment rights
- critically compare and contrast the differing objectives that were intended by various governments since 1979
- based on the knowledge of long-term trends in employment regulation, make a critical assessment of what could be considered to be reasonable expectations of medium-term future trends in employment regulation.

HRM IN THE MEDIA

'BOSSES TOLD TO IMPROVE WORK–LIFE BALANCE'

In October 2009, bosses in British companies were told to make better use of part-time working opportunities for working parents as a means of enhancing employee work–life balance at the same time as providing more creative ways of dealing with the ongoing economic downturn (Hinsliff 2009). This announcement was made in conjunction with the extension of government regulations extending the rights of new parents to be able to request flexible working hours to better balance work commitments with childcare responsibilities. Previously, the Business Secretary had considered reviewing these new measures after employers' organisations had complained about the latest extension of these rights, stating that

the costs in doing this would be too heavy a burden on employers during a recession (BBC News 2008).

Questions

1 What reasons would the Government have in trying to influence employers' policies on work–life balance?

2 Does this intervention suggest that the Government always sides with the employee against the employer when it intervenes?

3 To what extent could HR plan in relation to likely and unlikely future changes to employment regulation?

INTRODUCTION

The news story above highlights a number of issues relating to state influence on HR policy. It draws attention to a range of important facts: that employment laws invariably serve to influence, and constrain, the HR policies and actions of employers; that the development of such laws is the product of political decisions; and that such decisions are themselves the outcome of political dynamics encompassing conflicting views and beliefs. It also demonstrates that how organisations approach the management of HR cannot be sensibly understood without reference to both the regulatory frameworks that govern employment relations and the political considerations that influence the nature of these frameworks and the way in which they change over time.

This chapter has four central objectives: (1) to locate government policy towards employment regulation within the broader set of political concerns of governments, the key interests of employers and workers, and the wider dynamics of party political allegiances; (2) to more narrowly explore how the action taken (and not taken) in the sphere of employment regulation links to differing perspectives relating to its economic and social desirability; (3) to examine the way in which such regulation has evolved over the post-1945 period and how this process of evolution has been shaped by these differing perspectives, concerns, interests and dynamics; and (4) by way of conclusion, to briefly explore how it may evolve in the immediate future.

MECHANISMS FOR REGULATING EMPLOYMENT

Before considering the array of factors that influence *how much* employment regulation there could or should be, and what kinds of employment regulation this should be, a brief overview of the mechanisms which governments have in order to regulate employment is needed.

The most obvious way in which governments aim to regulate in the area of employment is through primary legislation: an *Act of Parliament*. Such Acts that are aimed specifically at employment have generally been named under 'industrial relations' or 'employment' Acts, depending on whether their focus has tended to be on collective issues – primarily relating to trade unions – or individual rights. In addition, employment rights have also been affected by legislation promoting wider social issues – the Race Relations, Sex Discrimination and Disability Discrimination Acts have all been good examples of these. In recent decades – technically since 1973 – a further source of regulation has been through the European Union (EU). This has accelerated since the introduction of the Social Chapter of the Maastricht Treaty. Various directives have been adopted at EU level and these are then interpreted at national level. Regulations originating from the EU include the Working Time Regulations (1998/2008) and Transfer of Undertakings – Protection of Employment (TUPE) Regulations – which have been regularly amended.

Finally, there are actions and policies pursued by governments, sometimes without the need for primary legislation, which, while having no directly stated employment agenda, have nevertheless had profound – intended – consequences for employment. In this category, 'actions' may include the general management of the economy: arguably, one of the most profound influences on 'deregulating' the labour market in the 1980s, for example, was the effect of high levels of unemployment dampening workers' expectations. This category also includes government policy aimed at restructuring the state itself; privatisation, competitive tendering, public–private partnerships and the Private Finance Initiative. The schemes that such policy has introduced have had complex implications for large sections of employees who work within the public sector (see Chapter 21) and also for increasing numbers who work in private or voluntary sector organisations that operate closely with the public sector (see Chapter 22).

THE SCALE AND SCOPE OF STATE INTERVENTION ON EMPLOYMENT ISSUES

In considering the motives for state intervention, a basic recognition needs to be made of what is being considered here. What is 'the state' and what are its 'interests'? This may seem to be going beyond the normal knowledge base required of the HR practitioner and into the subject of politics. However, it is important to understand some fundamentals in order to understand the outcomes of political decisions made at government level in order to then understand the likely effect on the possible HR implications at organisational level.

The state could be considered, at a most basic level, the element within a society that can claim 'a monopoly of legitimate violence' (Weber 1964). This language may seem a little dramatic but consider what this means: the state is the only part of a society that the population overall would consider as having the means and the will to use force to achieve the common good. All states have this: their visible manifestations are the military and the police. Clearly, though, a state relying just on coercive forces to maintain its position would suggest a somewhat unstable situation. Thus 'modern' states incorporate a whole range of supporting functions to enhance their legitimacy: from the administration of legal systems, to welfare systems, to education and transport infrastructures. Within liberal democracies the state is also legitimised by democratic institutions of one sort or another via the election of representatives to form legislative assemblies and/ or governments: people vote in elections and governments are elected. While this again may seem obvious and not directly linked to HR practice, consider the implications of a change of government to one with radically different policies on employment policy than the government in office. Looked at this way, such events could be considered a major source of uncertainty for HR planning. Considering why different governments interfere in issues relating to employment, how they balance apparently competing interests within civil society, why the balance shifts over time and what mechanisms are used is very important.

In terms of the employment relationship, the most basic interest that the state is attempting to reconcile is that between capital and labour. While this crude economic dichotomy is rarely used in contemporary HR literature, it does provide the basis of describing the most basic problem in the employment relationship. First, there are interests associated with employers. These could be summarised as the right to be able to make a profit, the right to have discretion over who can be employed, the right to determine wages, the right to dismiss workers who are not wanted, the right to establish 'the rules' that they wish workers should be subject to within their business. Second, there are interests associated with workers. At basic levels – using the International Labour Organization's (ILO) Core Labour Standards (see Chapter 13) – these are the absence of forced labour, the absence of child labour, freedom from discrimination and 'freedom of association' accompanied with the right to the effective recognition of collective bargaining. How do these sets of employer/ worker rights compare and how may the state mediate between them? Forced labour is a feudal practice that would not be used directly by any established business in a liberal democracy, and child labour occupies a similar status – though further down the supply chain of respectable businesses lie more difficult problems (see Chapter 13). Discrimination is something that employers in democracies would not claim to do – but here the issue is more complex as it involves an interpretation of discrimination that may not be matched between employer and employee. Finally, the last of the ILO standards effectively means the right for an individual to be a member of a trade union and the right of that union to be allowed to effectively represent its members. As a matter of principle, this is the aspect of worker rights that tends to remain the most contentious. The employee's right to be represented by a union may well clash with the company's right to be able to determine, unilaterally, the 'rules' and remuneration of those that it employs (see Chapter 12). In addition, the right of the employee to be represented by a union is invariably accompanied – as a matter of principle – with the sanction most commonly associated with a union: the right to strike.

Beyond the more basic balance of rights issues, the state has a further set of interests to balance. The news story at the beginning of the chapter relates to the issue of part-time employment, and therefore a layer of additional issues also presents itself: what areas of employment do governments intervene into? Is there a settled view as to the balance struck between employer discretion and government prescription? To what degree should workers be protected against unscrupulous employers? Why do certain issues seem to be more fashionable at different times? This then extends the potential scope of government intervention. So what mechanisms are available to governments and what are the broad choices available? Broadly, the choices that are made relate to the priorities that governments make and this is defined by ideology. Below are a series of issues that government may wish to pursue:

- the preservation of order
- the protection or promotion of the rights of particular groups
- the promotion of economic efficiency
- the promotion of social cohesion.

This is not an exhaustive list but even using this, if the possible combinations of these are considered, it demonstrates the range of possibilities that could face anyone attempting to predict any straightforward balance of outcomes from these priorities. Governments representing different interests within society and promoting different values make prioritising these differing agendas contentious. They also form the basis of ideologies presented by different political parties when in government or opposition.

The state's interest in the *preservation of order* can be seen to have fed into policies regulating the activities of trade unions – whether in terms of unions' ability to mobilise their members into strike action or just in terms of the extent to which freedom of association is permitted. As an absolute right, both of these rights have not been universally available in all periods in advanced economies and are certainly still not universally available in all parts of the world.

In relation to the *protection or promotion of particular groups' rights*, this has fed into the arena of state intervention on employment through – at different times – the promotion or restriction of the rights of trade unions, the rights of businesses in relation to a union, the rights of individuals in relation their treatment by an employer and the rights of individual workers in relation to a union.

The *promotion of efficiency* feeds into a whole range of policies relevant to HR, though strong ideological influences defining what is economically efficient means that policies under this heading can vary hugely. For example, just considering the UK since 1945, promoting efficiency has meant, at different times, the active promotion of 'full employment', reducing employment protection to promote flexible labour markets, privatising state industries, nationalising 'strategic' private industries, promoting employer-led vocational training, providing state-led training, actively promoting partnership between unions and employers, and actively discouraging union involvement. Finally, if promoting *social cohesion* is the objective, this could be associated with equalising wage differentials through collective bargaining, or the enhancement of equality rights at work.

If this, by no means exhaustive, list of values were assumed to be combined by governments in a random manner, the level of uncertainty would be bewildering. In practice, however, these values are combined by political parties in a broadly predictable way through the combination of ideology and partisanship. In all liberal democracies parties are ideologically distinguished, broadly, in terms of left and right. Left parties tend to prioritise equality and social cohesion as the means towards economic efficiency, whereas right parties will tend to emphasise the primary importance of promoting 'business leaders' as the means to economic efficiency. As a general rule, left parties have tended to favour a significant role for the state in promoting its agenda, while right parties have tended to favour a reduced role of the state, though this distinction is sometimes overstated.

Political parties' association with particular economic interests adds the dimension of partisanship. The left has tended to have been associated with the interests of organised labour (unions) while the right has tended to have been associated with business interests. In the UK the Conservatives have long been associated with the wealthier elements of society and with 'big business' and they receive funding primarily from these sources. The Labour Party was established by a special conference of the Trades Union Council in 1900 to promote the interests of organised labour (unions) in Parliament. Labour remains predominantly funded by the unions. It is not therefore surprising to discover that the Conservatives' attitude towards unions is broadly hostile.

CHANGING INFLUENCES ON PARTY POLITICS

To understand what the broad current policy positions of the major parties are, it is important to recognise some longer-term changes that have taken place in UK party politics and how these have invariably reflected political influences of key actors over long periods of time. The first shift has been demography. Where the Labour Party was established to champion the interests of the working class, and the Conservatives established their appeal among the middle classes, the profile of what constitutes the differences between these categories of social class blurred progressively over the latter twentieth century. Thus, the working class that was predominantly associated with manual trades declined in numbers; with the economy shifting increasingly away from manufacturing to services, other categories increased. While it remains debatable whether this meant a change in the composition within the class structure or just a redefinition of what constitutes working class (Goldthorpe et al 1969), the net effect was a blurring of class allegiances to both Labour and Conservatives in what political scientists have termed 'partisan de-alignment' (Crewe et al 1977).

A second shift has been in international issues. In addition to the ubiquitous issue of 'globalisation', Britain's changing position in the world has had a big effect on the ways that the political parties have identified themselves. This has probably been most marked for the Conservatives, who have had the most difficulty in adjusting their traditional association with 'empire' and in finding its new world view in reconciling its view about Britain's relationship with the USA, with Europe and with the various constituent nations of the UK (Gamble 2003). This has, in turn, influenced its view on the role of the state in regulating employment and, in particular, in wishing to emulate a US-style deregulated approach and to opposing the influence of EU employment regulation.

For Labour, from 1980, there was also a rapid decline in the traditional base of its support – the unions – to compound its difficulties in its diminishing traditional class base. This was to a large degree a direct result of the changes introduced by the Conservatives. Following 10 years of opposition, Labour rebranded itself as 'New Labour', making a conscious shift away from its identification with 'class' politics – and especially its direct association with the trade unions – into something apparently more suitable to what its strategists were advising were the changing demographics of society. In particular, the whole project was informed by a view of changing forces within society know as 'the third way' and associated, in particular, with Anthony Giddens (1998). This rebranding was also to have a significant influence on Labour's policy on employment when it replaced the Conservatives in government in 1997 – shifting emphasis from collective rights to individual ones.

PERSPECTIVES ON EMPLOYMENT REGULATION

Views concerning the desirability, or otherwise, of legally regulating employment relationships, at both the individual and collective levels, can be seen to differ widely. The same is true with regard to opinions concerning the extent and nature of such regulation.

These differing views and opinions can be seen to be intimately connected to broader ones concerning the economic and social desirability of governments intervening to shape the nature of employer–worker relations. These broader views and opinions can usefully be highlighted by reference to two related areas of debate, namely whether employment regulation is, at the general level, harmful or supportive of organisational and national economic performance, and whether it is supportive or damaging to wider 'social welfare' (of the population as a whole).

REGULATION AND ECONOMIC PERFORMANCE

Any examination of the debates surrounding employment-related proposals reveals that an inevitable focus of attention within them is the issue of whether they will serve to enhance or harm the economic performance of employers, as well as the economy more generally. To a large extent the differing views expressed in this area, in turn, can be seen to link to the broader question of whether it is desirable, via the imposition of regulatory requirements, to interfere with the operation of 'free' market forces.

Those who argue that such interference is undesirable effectively accept the central tenets of neo-classical economic theory: these being that the laws of supply and demand operate, in the context of competitive labour and product markets, to create 'market clearing' terms and conditions for workers that serve, thereby, to maximise the use of available labour resources in the economy and to also ensure that these resources are distributed across the economy in the most productive way.

From this neo-classical perspective, therefore, anything that is done to interfere with the free operation of labour markets is economically harmful – whether the action concerned, for example, involves the laying down of minimum rates of pay, statutory provisions on maternity leave and pay, or support for the activities of trade unions that serves to increase their capacity to affect how employers utilise the labour they employ or the terms and conditions on which it is employed. In each of these cases the view, typically taken, is that such regulatory provisions will increase labour costs above 'market clearing' ones and consequently lead to higher levels of unemployment.

Not all economists, however, accept the central tenets of neo-classical theory or, more specifically, the proposition that employment regulation is inevitably economically harmful. In particular, critics of the neo-classical approach argue that labour markets, in fact, operate for a number of reasons, in an imperfect way, with the result that the distribution of bargaining power between employers and workers is not, as assumed in the neo-classical model, equal. What therefore follows from this is that employers, because of their superior (monopsonistic) bargaining power, are able to employ workers on terms and conditions below those that would be provided in a fully competitive labour market and therefore on a basis that works against the efficient utilisation of labour (and other) resources in the economy (Manning 2003; Turnbull 2003).

Those holding this alternative view consequently argue that, at least in certain circumstances, employment regulation can be economically beneficial, both directly and indirectly, by strengthening the coverage and strength of trade union organisation and by countering the monopsonistic bargaining power of employers (Deakin and Wilkinson 2005; Kaufman 2009). In addition, and more specifically, it has been argued that such regulation can yield a number of economic benefits through such means as: (1) enhancing the purchasing power of workers and hence aggregate economic demand; (2) prompting firms to use labour more productively because of its increased cost (Rubery and Edwards 2003); and (3) creating fairer employment relations that result in higher levels of worker motivation and better employer–worker relationships (Edwards 2007).

REGULATION AND SOCIAL WELFARE

A key rationale underlying neo-classical economic theory is that the autonomous, market-based activities of economic actors, by maximising economic efficiency at the individual firm level, simultaneously have the same effect on social welfare at society level. Indeed, at root, this social welfare effect provides the central rationale for those who advocate such neo-liberal, and neo-classically informed, policies. These views became more influential among governments as they were developed by an increasingly influential group of economists. Notable among these were Hayek (1944), who first popularised the notion that state intervention is both economically inefficient and also an attack upon individual liberty; Friedman (1968), who extended this by linking price inflation to wages being kept 'artificially' high by the raised expectations of unions and protective regulations; and by Olson (1971), who linked the logic of collective action (through unions) as the prime mechanism for creating this situation.

Again, however, not everybody supports the view that social welfare is best enhanced by the operation of market forces. For those who don't, two main lines of 'counter analysis' can be distinguished.

The first of these counterarguments essentially mirrors the counterargument at firm level, arguing that labour markets do not, in reality, operate in accordance with neo-classical theory and that, rather, they produce outcomes rather different from those anticipated. Such outcomes could, for example, encompass a dynamic involving a transfer of income away from low-paid workers to shareholders and consumers via reduced prices (Kaufman 2009).

As regards the second line of argument, this draws attention to evidence that highlights the fact that societies marked by relatively high levels of income inequality tend to also be characterised by a range of adverse social outcomes, including higher levels of poverty, marital breakdowns, more crime, greater health inequalities (World Health Organisation 2008; Wilkinson and Pickett 2009) and lower life expectancy. Evidence, therefore, seems to provide a justification for regulatory actions aimed at constraining or reducing such inequality, for example through the laying down of minimum (and maximum) pay rates, legislative provisions to protect the employment security of vulnerable groups of workers and action to support the recognition and collective bargaining role of unions (for example see TUC 2008). This view, it should be noted, receives support from other evidence pointing to a strong linkage between the rise in male wage inequality, which has occurred over the last three decades in the UK, and the decline in union membership that occurred during this period (Card et al 2004).

THE POST-WAR EVOLUTION OF BRITISH EMPLOYMENT LAW

Until the 1960s it was common to describe the post-war British system of industrial relations as a voluntaristic one, that is, one marked by a low level of legal intervention and a strong reliance on 'social regulation' by employers and workers and their unions, with this regulation most notably occurring through the process of national-level, multi-employer, collective bargaining, or, in the terminology coined in the 1950s by eminent employment lawyer Sir Otto Kahn-Freund (1954), 'collective laissez-faire'.

Under this system, few statutory individual employment rights existed. Individual employment relationships were governed, for the most part, by rights and duties that had evolved through common law-based judicial decisions and collective agreements (through unions) were not legally enforceable. No legal obligations relating to the recognition of trade unions or the establishment of other 'collective voice' arrangement, such as works councils, existed, and the law governing industrial conflict and, in particular, strikes, comprised a set of 'negative statutory immunities' to a range of common law liabilities that would otherwise confront unions organising industrial action.

At the same time, however, as is the case with all attempts to succinctly describe the essential nature of complex social phenomena, aspects of the then prevailing industrial relations system sat uncomfortably with the above depiction (Davies and Freedland 1993). Statutory provisions on health and safety at work, although incomplete in their coverage, had, for example, been in place from the early part of the nineteenth century and evolved considerably over the period since then, while provisions also existed governing the working hours of women and young people, and the Truck Acts regulated the way in which pay was provided and the deductions that could be made from it. Similarly, the role of 'collective laissez-faire' was qualified by the existence of a statutory, tripartite-based system of wages councils which, as well as laying down minimum terms and conditions of employment in low-paying sectors of the economy, marked by an absence of voluntary collective bargaining arrangements, had the (unfulfilled) objective of stimulating the establishment of such arrangements, and both the Fair Wages Resolution and the Terms and Conditions of Employment Act 1959 provided mechanisms for enforcing the application of relevant 'collectively agreed', or 'recognised', terms and conditions of employment.

Beginning in the 1960s, however, changes to this picture of voluntarism began to occur in the area of individual employment law. This shift started with the Contracts of Employment Act 1963 – which laid down provisions concerning minimum notice periods and the giving by employers of certain written particulars of employment in situations where no written contract existed – the Redundancy Payments Act 1965 and the Race Relations Act 1968. It continued during the 1970s with the Equal Pay Act 1970, the introduction of unfair dismissal legislation in 1971, and the Sex Discrimination Act 1975, as well as the reform and expansion of coverage of health and safety legislation via the Health and Safety at Work Act 1974.

This general trajectory of growth in individual employment rights in the 1960s and 1970s, however, occurred alongside much more mixed, and contradictory, legislative developments in the area of collective employment law. Thus, they initially encompassed the introduction of a completely new framework of collective employment law, via the Industrial Relations Act 1971, under Edward Heath's Conservative Government of 1970–74, which introduced both new legal rights and liabilities for unions, and then the repeal of this Act and the establishment of a framework of law that acted to marry together the key elements of the previously existing voluntaristic one with the provision of new rights supporting trade union and collective bargaining activity under the Labour Governments of 1974–79.

The overall outcome of these developments, therefore, were, on the one hand, that the previously existing reliance on negative statutory immunities to set the legal framework on industrial conflict had been reinstated and, on the other, the existence alongside this non-interventionist approach of an array of more interventionist statutory measures. These measures included the right for recognised unions to appoint workplace safety representatives, the presence of a statutory procedure through which unions could seek recognition from employers, and the provision of rights, where recognition existed, for trade union officials to receive paid time off to perform duties in connection with the conduct of industrial relations between employer and union, and for unions to obtain certain information from employers that was relevant to collective bargaining, and to be consulted over collective redundancies. They also further encompassed the provision of protection to employees from discriminatory action by employers on the grounds that they had joined or taken part in the activities of independent trade unions, and an ability on the part of unions to seek to extend the provisions of collective agreements to other relevant employers through, rather more wide-ranging, provisions akin to those that had previously existed in the Terms and Conditions Act 1959.

Conservative reforms 1979–1997

In considering the reforms brought in during the Conservative Governments of 1979–1997, a few important statements need to be made to understand this period of reform in some context. The first point is that this was the first government that fully bought into the neo-classical prescription of regulating individual employment rights and restricting the influence that unions would be able to have on the labour market. The second point of significance is that, despite the broad economic policy agenda being pursued being defined as 'laissez-faire' (and therefore "non-interventionist"), in terms of trade unions, the government launched the largest legislative programme of state intervention of any government – probably anywhere in the world.

The broad approach of this government was to shift the balance of power significantly in favour of employers through the restriction of union activity and the reduction of individual employee rights, all to the end of creating greater labour market flexibility.

The most notable individual employment rights reduction was action to remove those with less than two years' service from the coverage of unfair dismissal law, increasing the power of employers to make deductions from pay under the Wages Act 1986, and the removal of restrictions on the working hours and employment of women and young people. It also, however, saw the passing of the Disability Discrimination Act 1995 and a number of new laws introduced to address failures to comply with the requirements of European directives in some existing laws and to transpose those of new ones.

In the case of the former area, for example, important changes were made to sex discrimination legislation, via the Sex Discrimination Act 1986 and provisions on equal pay for work of equal value were introduced. Meanwhile, in the case of the latter one, the period saw the making of the Transfer of Undertakings (Protection of Employment) Regulations 1981, and a number of new sets of health and safety regulations introduced, including the Management of Health and Safety at Work Regulations 1992 (as amended) and the Health and Safety (Consultation with Employees) Regulations 1996.

This rather mixed set of developments in the area of individual employment rights occurred alongside, however, the undertaking of a range, in terms of their nature, of more consistent set of actions to reduce the power and influence of trade unions. This set of actions had three main, but inevitably interrelated, targets: a reduction in the regulatory role of collective bargaining; the greater encouragement of non-union membership; and the placing of greater constraints on workplace union activities and the ability of unions to lawfully undertake industrial action.

The primary actions taken to support the first of these aspirations encompassed the abolition of the statutory union recognition procedure, the repeal of the statutory support that existed to extend the provisions of collective agreements to 'other employers', as well as the rescinding of the Fair Wages Resolution, and the abolition of wages councils. Those undertaken to further the second, meanwhile, included the outlawing of compulsory union membership (closed shop) agreements, the requirement that written consent be obtained every three years to authorise the deduction of union subscriptions 'at source' and a reduction in the protection provided against employers taking discriminatory action on grounds of union membership. Finally, with regard to the third, they encompassed a reduction in the existing rights relating to time off for trade union duties, an increase in the ability of employers to selectively dismiss those on strike, the making of unions liable to damages for 'authorising or endorsing' unlawful industrial action, and a number of changes that served to increase substantially the vulnerability of unions to actions in tort while undertaking strikes and other forms of collective action.

This last increase was achieved through four areas of reform. Firstly, legal immunity was removed from certain types of action, such as picketing away from a picket's own workplace, undertaking secondary action against an employer not party to a dispute, and the carrying out of action aimed at ensuring that contracted-out work was done by unionised companies or workers. Secondly, a narrower definition of a lawfully protected 'trade dispute' was adopted that limited such disputes to ones involving workers and their own employer and required such disputes to not just be merely connected to at least one of the issues specified in the definition, but to relate 'wholly or mainly' to them. Thirdly, the application of the immunities were made dependent on majority support for action having been obtained from the workers concerned through a secret ballot conducted in accordance with a complex set of laid-down rules. Fourthly, provisions were introduced that provided 'citizens' and union members with the ability to pursue litigation against unions on the grounds that they had undertaken unlawful industrial action.

Post-1997 developments: the New Labour years

When Labour returned to government after the long period of Conservative ascendancy, it had significantly shifted in a number of key areas that informed its approach to employment regulation. First, it had made some conscious efforts to weaken its links with trade unions and consciously realigned its core appeal beyond its traditional class base. Labour had also reappraised its position on Europe. Taking advantage of deep divisions among the Conservatives on this issue, Labour went from its 1970s hostility to the EU to its pro-Social Chapter stance in 1997, to a more qualified support by the 2000s when, on employment as other issues, Labour was attempting to position itself as a bridge between US approaches (flexible labour markets) and Europe (social partnership). Overall the 'New Labour' approach was one that incrementally enhanced areas of individual employment rights, while resisting demands to radically overhaul its Conservative predecessors' trade union reforms. A poignant example of this sentiment was in the phrasing of the Prime Minister's foreword to its early flagship White Paper 'Fairness at Work', which seems to be written more with a mind to its potential opponents than to those who were intended to benefit:

> There will be no going back. The days of strikes without ballots, mass picketing, closed shops and secondary action are over. Even after the changes we propose, Britain will have the most lightly regulated labour market of any leading economy in the world. But it cannot be just to deny British citizens basic canons of fairness... (Tony Blair: Foreword to Fairness at Work White Paper: HMSO 1998)

With regard to individual employment law, this period can be seen, when compared with the period of Conservative rule discussed above, to have been marked by a wide range of legislative action that stemmed from a combination of purely domestic initiatives and ones driven by the need to transpose the requirements of European directives.

A number of significant domestic innovations occurred early in the period of New Labour rule. During 1998, for example, the National Minimum Wage Act was passed, as was legislation to protect 'whistleblowers' following the Government's decision to support a Private Member's Bill on the issue. The following year also saw the passing of an Employment Relations Act, which acted to reduce the qualifying period for making an unfair dismissal claim from two years to one, thus partially reducing the increase that had occurred over the period of Conservative rule, increased the maximum compensatory award that could be made in such cases, and made agreements to waive the right to make claims in fixed-term contracts void.

Subsequent domestically inspired developments encompassed the provision of a right to unpaid time off to deal with certain 'domestic emergencies', and measures on paternity leave and pay, adoption leave, and maternity leave and pay, which in some respects went beyond what was required by the European Parental Leave Directive (see below).

In addition, while not neatly falling under the umbrella of 'individual employment law' and not serving to directly enhance the employment rights of workers, two other sets of measures were taken that had potentially important beneficial consequences for both the treatment of workers and for employer compliance with existing employment rights. The first of these involved the passing, as a result again of government support for a Private Member's Bill, of the Gangmasters Licencing Act 2004 – a statute that, in conjunction with supporting regulations, requires agencies supplying labour to work in the food processing and production sectors to be licensed, obliges relevant users of such labour to only obtain it from agencies holding a licence, requires agencies, as a condition of both obtaining and retaining such a licence, to ensure that workers so supplied receive their statutory employment entitlements, and additionally created an inspectorate to enforce its requirements. Meanwhile, the second involved the incorporation into the Race Relations Amendment Act 2000, the Disability Discrimination Act 2005 and the Equality Act 2006 of duties on public authorities to work towards the elimination of unlawful discrimination and the promotion of equality of opportunity – provisions that at the time of writing were proposed to, in turn, be incorporated into a new Equality Act, an Act that it was further proposed would make a number of other important changes to existing equality law.

Meanwhile, a range of further measures were introduced in response to the requirements of European directives. These included the introduction of a completely revised set of transfer of undertakings regulations, as well as new regulatory provisions on working time (and paid holidays), part-time and fixed-term workers, parental leave, as already noted, and discrimination on the grounds of disability, sexual orientation, religion and belief, and age. These provisions, however, like those similarly introduced by the post-1979 governments, often complied with the relevant European requirements in a minimalist, and at times incomplete, way.

As regards collective employment law, under the Employment Relations Act 1999, and supporting regulations, the first post-1997 Labour Government honoured the promise it had made to the union movement to introduce a statutory union recognition procedure. It then, via the Employment Act 2002, provided recognised unions with the right to appoint learning representatives possessing certain consultative rights.

Action was also been taken to provide employees with a right to be accompanied by a trade union official in formal disciplinary and grievance hearings, regardless of whether the union concerned is recognised, abolished the need for check-off arrangements to be periodically authorised, and, albeit only after it had been ruled to be in breach of the European Convention on Human Rights by the

European Court of Human Rights, restricted the scope for employers to take discriminatory action on grounds of union membership by making it unlawful for them to offer inducements intended to induce (1) a worker not to become a member of a union or take part in its activities or use its services and (2) a member of a recognised union, or one seeking recognition, not to have their terms and conditions determined by collective bargaining.

New, time-limited protection against unfair dismissal was also introduced to those engaged in undertaking lawful industrial action and some simplification of industrial action balloting requirements made. No other action was, however, taken to change the legal restrictions on industrial action introduced by the previous Conservative Governments.

Finally, in the area of collective employment law, regulations were made to transpose the European Works Council Directive and European Framework Directive on (national level) worker consultation into domestic law. In both cases, though, the regulations concerned – the Transnational Information and Consultation of Employees Regulations 1999 and the Information and Consultation of Employees (ICE) Regulations 2004 – embodied an essentially minimalist approach to transposition. For example, in the case of the ICE ones, the Government chose not to accord any priority to trade union representation, expand the issues over which employers were required to consult, extend their coverage to employers with fewer than 50 employees or make them apply 'automatically' to relevant employers. These choices can be seen to be consistent with the fact that the UK Government actively opposed the Framework Directive's adoption.

CONCLUSION

Earlier in the chapter it was noted that governments promote policies based on balancing competing objectives (for example economic efficiency and social cohesion), and that in the context of the employment relationship, this inevitably is reduced to the conflicting interests of 'capital' and 'labour'. It was further observed that, because political parties define what is acceptable through the lens of ideology, markedly different perspectives can be held concerning the economic and social desirability of using the law to regulate relationships between employers and workers and their unions.

The preceding outline of the evolution of employment law over the post-war period illustrates this last point clearly. With regard to the provision of legislative support to trade unions and the role of collective bargaining, for example, marked differences are apparent in the approaches adopted by the 1974–79 Labour Governments, the 1979–97 Conservative ones, and the post-1997 New Labour ones. The governments during the first of these periods took the view that it was both socially and economically desirable to provide such additional support. Those during the second adopted a contrary approach based on the view that unions and collective bargaining served to unjustifiably impede the operation of market forces. And those since 1997 steered a 'third way' path that encompassed a similar hesitancy to interfere with market forces through the enhancement of the rights of unions and the role of collective bargaining but one that was qualified, to a relatively limited degree, by a perceived need to increase labour market 'fairness'.

Similarly, notable differences can be identified in the extent to which governments during these three periods sought to extend individual employment rights. Differences can be seen to be particularly apparent in the actions taken by those in power during the post-1979 and 1997 periods of Conservative and Labour rule. And these can, again, be linked to the adoption of markedly different perspectives regarding the social and economic desirability of extending such rights.

In terms of 'where we are now' and 'where we may go', this clearly becomes speculative. However, there are some clear patterns that can be observed to indicate likely possibilities. Two conflicting issues emerge. The first is where the balance of party political consensus on the issue of employment regulation will settle and the second is the extent to which the deregulatory consensus of the previous period has been broken by the aftermath of the financial crisis of 2008.

In terms of a 'new consensus' there were, by 2008, signs that the Conservatives were making a qualified move to dissociate themselves with their image as being merely the 'mouthpiece of big business' (*Observer* 2005) and closer to the New Labour agenda. To this end it attempted to 'detoxify' its image associated with opposing all measures towards equality in employment and was, in the period leading up to the 2010 general election, claiming its endorsement of measures to strengthen gender equality and work–life balance.

After the 2010 election, the Conservatives – by this time in a coalition government with the Liberal Democrats – would seem to be in further hybridisation of the New Labour mould. The Coalition's early promises were to promote work–life balance through some enhanced employee rights, to promote greater gender pay equity, to support existing measures protecting employees from discrimination on race, gender, sexuality and disability. On the other hand, there was a renewed desire to make further incremental tightening of strike regulations and of seeking opt-outs from EU employment regulations. But perhaps the greater impact is going to be in the Coalition's role in the state as employer: The Conservatives' 'Big Society' idea (Conservative Party 2010) saw some convergence with the Liberal Democrats' own more recent shift towards a smaller state (Laws and Marshall 2004) and the employees in the public sector were promised large-scale retrenchment, involving redundancy, pay restraint and a significant curtailing of 'gold-plated pensions' as a response to the financial crisis. The extent to which this agenda will be wholly realised, and the extent to which this new agenda will permeate beyond the public sector, is yet to be seen.

HRM IN THE MEDIA

CRITICAL REFLECTIONS

In relation to the first question, the Labour Government's motives for trying to influence employers' work–life balance policies was to further embed the acceptability of such working arrangements as being normal – which would have benefits for working families and, as a side issue, for making returning to work after the birth of a child more acceptable and potentially reduce certain welfare costs of the state. The regulations potentially enhanced employees' sense of entitlement in this area while leaving final discretion with employers where they felt a 'business case' to refuse.

The second question demonstrates the difficulty in objectively assessing the legitimate limits and direction of state intervention in the area of employment. At a very basic level, it is clearly incorrect to say that all governments intervene in favour of employees: the explicit policy agenda of the Conservatives in the 1980s and 1990s was to deregulate in the area of individual employment rights and regulate heavily in relation to the rights of unions. The New Labour policy agenda was subject to criticism from employer lobby groups who argued that it introduced too much and from employee rights advocates who argued that it chose to introduce EU regulations in too weak a fashion.

In relation to the third question, there are no absolute guarantees. However, it could be comfortably predicted that the Coalition Government of 2010 would be hostile to collective employment rights and sceptical about individual rights. They were hinting at further restricting strike laws. They seemed comfortable with some measures to enhance a 'living wage' and equal pay, though were not clear about any particular measures.

EXPLORE FURTHER

HOWELL, C. (2005) *Trade unions and the state: the construction of industrial relations institutions in Britain 1890–2000.* Princeton: Princeton University Press.

This is a provocative, but very well-argued, overview of the big changes in the British employment system – especially Chapters 6 and 7.

SMITH, P. and MORTON, G. (2005) Nine years of New Labour: neoliberalism and workers' rights. *British Journal of Industrial Relations.* Vol 44, No 3. pp401–420.

Critical account of the New Labour approach to employment.

BLYTON, P. and TURNBULL, P. (2005) *The dynamics of employee relations.* 3rd ed. New York: Palgrave Macmillan.

Chapter 6 of this is a good guide to the role of the state applied primarily to trade unions.

CHAPTER 8

HRM and Socio-demographics: Age Diversity and the Future Workforce

Matt Flynn and Michael Muller-Camen

OVERVIEW

This chapter considers the impact of an ageing population on the workplace. It examines the experience and expectations of older workers and the extent to which these are met by employers. It discusses how HR policies in the areas of recruitment and selection, flexible working and retirement can be age-neutral and can make organisations employers of choice. It also considers the role played by important stakeholders such as line managers, trade unions and supporting organisations in disseminating good practice and points to international differences.

LEARNING OBJECTIVES

Reading this chapter will enable the reader to:

- critically examine how older workers experience work and what they expect from it
- critically examine good practices in relation to the employment of older workers
- critically examine the role played by line managers and trade unions in dissemination of age diversity policies
- critically analyse the international differences in the area of managing an ageing workforce.

HRM IN THE MEDIA

'OLDER TEACHERS WARN OF AGEISM'

BBC News (2010) reported that older teachers feel they are being pushed aside and treated unfairly, based on a survey from the teachers' union NASUWT. The survey found that one in five older teachers have faced discrimination and marginalisation because of their age, instead of having their experience valued. The union's general secretary noted that abuse on the grounds of age is as serious as all other forms of bullying. The teachers' conference heard that prejudice against older workers is not as much publicly condemned as other forms of discrimination.

The union's survey of 3,525 teachers found that anti-bullying policies relating to age discrimination are only present in 1 in 10 schools. In addition, 1 in 3 older teachers believed that they have been made to feel 'less capable' than younger colleagues, 1 in 5 have felt that their 'professional

capabilities had been marginalised or undermined due to their age', and some of the older teachers expressed fears that they were seen by head teachers as being too expensive.

The union demanded greater protection for older teachers as they approach retirement, such as fair access to professional development and promotion and a career exit strategy as they get closer to retirement age (Coughlan 2010).

Questions

1 What is older teachers' experience of work?

2 What HR policies could local authorities adopt that would help older teachers?

3 Which other stakeholders play a role and what could they do?

INTRODUCTION

The UK, like many parts of the world, is facing an ageing population. By 2031, the 65 and older population will outnumber those under 20. The UK is not unique: according to EUROSTAT data, for the European Union as a whole, the proportion of the population over 65 will roughly double by 2050. And ageing demographics is not exclusive to developed countries. Rapidly expanding economies, such as China and India, are facing ageing populations in the short to medium term, which will impact on economic growth and productivity. They face what has been termed a 'demographic window': a period in which employers and government should prepare for older populations.

The fact that the UK is ageing is not necessarily bad news. After all, it simply reflects that people are living longer and more healthily. However, it does pose a dilemma for employers. Because populations are ageing, fewer younger people will be available and people will be expected to work longer. The State Pension Age is due to rise to 68 by 2044, and there is some speculation it may be sooner. In the past, employers have managed changing work demands by getting rid of older workers. However, such a youth-centric approach is no longer viable. In the future, employers will need to look to workers across the life course, including older ones.

Older people have many of the same expectations from work as younger people; and for employers, new approaches to managing people across the life course can be found within existing HR policies. The challenge for HR professionals lies in challenging preconceived assumptions of how best to manage people of different ages. In the UK context, it is particularly important that workplace-level managers adopt age-neutral approaches to managing people. Line managers hold a significant amount of responsibility in day-to-day management; and personal age biases can often get in the way of implementing organisational-level HR policies.

In this chapter, we will discuss approaches that employers are taking to better manage people of all ages. It is based on a number of research projects carried out on behalf of the UK Government, the Economic and Social Research Council and European Union, as well as an age diversity good practice guide for managers published jointly by the CIPD and Trades Union Congress (Flynn and McNair 2007). The research looked at work in later life from both the employees' and employers' perspectives. This chapter seeks to answer three questions:

- What do older workers want from work?

- How are employers meeting older workers' expectations?

- How are age-neutral HR policies being implemented at the workplace level?

WHAT DO OLDER WORKERS WANT FROM WORK?

In 2004 and 2006, two surveys were conducted to look at people's experience of and expectations from work. The first study (McNair et al 2004) surveyed people aged 20–70 about their job transitions over the previous five years. Job transitions (such as taking a promotion, changing working hours or leaving the labour market altogether) are good indications of people's work orientations and experiences since they show how people are 'pulled' (that is, persuaded) or 'pushed' (that is, forced) into making job changes. The study also asked people to describe the support that they received from their managers, colleagues and others when making their last job transitions, as well as their willingness to stay in work past their normal retirement ages. In 2006, a follow-up survey (Flynn and McNair 2008) was conducted of participants of the first survey who were between 50 and 70 years old. This survey looked at what older people value from work as well as perceptions of the quality of their current jobs, and relationship with their managers and colleagues.

As people age, the frequency of job transitions reduces. Figure 8.1 shows the proportion of people who have made a job transition in the past five years. As people enter middle age, their job transitions become fewer. This may, in part, reflect the fact that young people move about employers seeking the right kind of job. By their thirties, many people have settled into work that suits them. The prospects for promotion also decrease, as opportunities for progression grow fewer the further one goes up the organisational hierarchy. By the time people reach their mid-to-late fifties, the main transition is retirement. However, a person who is hired in their fifties is likely to stay longer with the organisation than one in their twenties.

Reasons for career transitions also change over time. People in their twenties tend
to move jobs for career reasons or to make more money. However, the frequency
of such job transitions steadily decreases. By their early sixties, people still in
work are more likely to change jobs to reduce work pressure than to seek a job
with greater responsibility.

Figure 8.1 Reasons for job change

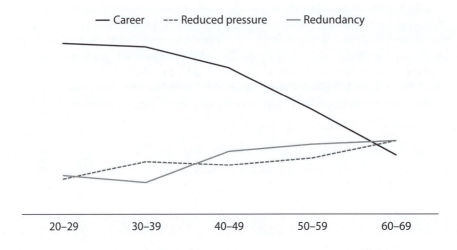

Nineteen per cent of people aged 60–64 who were still in work said that their last
job transition resulted in more work responsibility, while 26% said it resulted in
less.

Figure 8.2 Outcomes of job transitions

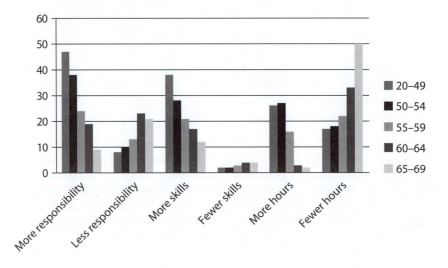

The survey asked people what type of support they received (such as, for example, employer-sponsored training or help from workmates). Two-thirds of people over 50 had received no support in their last job transition compared with 56% of job-changers aged 20–49 years old. Even among older workers who had transitioned into jobs with greater responsibility or requiring more skills, over half had received no help. Such figures may indicate in part that employers are discriminating against older people in the provision of workplace learning. However, a project for the European Union (McNair and Flynn 2005a) presented a more nuanced picture. Older workers who said they could have benefited from additional training in the performance of their current jobs said that neither they nor their employers had considered the benefit of such training.

The 2006 follow-up survey asked older workers how they feel about their jobs, workplaces, colleagues and managers. It also asked whether they would like to stay in work beyond their normal retirement age. It should be noted here that what is considered normal retirement age is not necessarily the national default retirement age of 65. Only 9% of people cited the company or state mandatory retirement age as their own retirement age. Thirty per cent listed their retirement age as when they can start to draw a full pension; and 34% said that their retirement dates are timings of their own choosing.

Older people's views on work are generally positive. Seventy per cent said that their work is enjoyable; 79% said that they enjoy working with their colleagues; 64% feel valued by their employer; and 78% said that work suited their personal circumstances. Sixty-nine per cent said that they would miss work if they retired today.

A majority (53%) of older people who were still in work said that they would definitely (27%) or probably (26%) like to stay in work after retirement age. Seventy-six per cent of those who said they would like to work past retirement age said that they would want to do so on a part-time basis, against 6% who would prefer to continue working full-time. Only 17% of people who had already retired said they would consider returning to work. However, 54% of retired people said that, had they had the opportunity to work part-time, they would have delayed when they retired.

It has often been suggested that older workers would consider working longer if they have the opportunity to work flexibly, combining work and retirement activities (Joseph Rowntree Foundation 2003; Phillipson 2004; Watson Wyatt Worldwide 2004). However, flexible work opportunities for older people tend to be rare (Loretto et al 2005; Naegele 1999). Older workers tend more than younger ones to allow pressures from combining full-time work and home responsibilities to mount up until the stress forces them out of the labour market (Mooney and Stratham 2002; Vickerstaff 2006). Employer interventions through flexible working options can help older people stay economically active and, as can be seen by the survey data, are more effective than measures to draw retired people back into work.

The survey also gave a picture of the type of older person who would be amenable to extending working life. Not surprisingly, those who are already working part-time, or those who identified themselves as 'retired but still in paid work', are more likely than full-time workers to want to carry on working. Workers who said that their jobs were enjoyable or that they would miss working if they retired today were also more willing to stay in work. Financial considerations also played a role in work and retirement decisions, as people who said that they either need to stay in work to top up their pensions or to keep employment benefits were also more likely to want to delay retirement. In other words, older people (like younger ones) are driven by both extrinsic and intrinsic work values.

Finally, it is worth noting that the 'older workforce' is not a homogeneous group. Like all age groups, social class, gender, skills and occupation influence perceptions of work. As people age, experiences in work grow more different rather than more similar. Various studies have sought to identify older workers according to their work and retirement patterns (Barnes et al 2004; Vickerstaff 2006). A common theme from these studies is the role that skills (not only formal qualifications, but also experiential knowledge, social networks and generativity) play in buttressing older workers' ability to choose career and retirement paths (Flynn 2010b). People with high skills tend to also be able to shape end-of-career work to suit their expectations. Those with low skills are more likely to be either pushed out of work early through redundancy or ill-health; or be pulled into work for financial reasons. In terms of 'active ageing' HR interventions, it may be those on the lower end of the labour market who would be most in need of support in staying economically active.

In summary, older workers' views on work in later life tend to be positive. Why then do media stories such as 'Grim Britain: work till you drop' (*Daily Express* 5 September 2008) have such resonance? The answer lies not so much in older workers' attitudes, but in employer practices. While older workers would be willing to delay retirement, they want work that is high quality and suits their needs. Such support for older workers is more rare than for their younger colleagues. However, in recent years, some employers have been responding to the age demographic challenge by adopting new policies to increase their employees' work longevity. In the next section, we will discuss some innovative new practices.

EMPLOYERS' AGE MANAGEMENT PRACTICES

Although age-related HR policies are still relatively uncommon, employers are starting to pay attention to the impact of changing age demographics on their organisations. In 2006, the Government passed the Employment Equality (Age) Regulations (known as the Age Discrimination Regulations), which focused employers' attention on how people across all ages are managed. Many employers adopted age-neutral policies not only to comply with the new law, but also to meet labour shortages, demonstrate socially responsible management practices and become 'employers of choice'. Indeed, both the UK Government and European Union have online databases of examples of good age management practices that have been adopted by organisations. HR policies that can have an age dimension include health and safety (mitigating the impact of age-related health problems), career development (providing promotion opportunities to people of all ages), training (eliminating age barriers to organisation-provided training), pay systems (limiting the use of age or years of service in determining pay), and redundancy (selecting workers for redundancy on the basis of organisational need rather than age). This chapter will focus on three policy areas that are particularly affected by age: recruitment and selection; access to flexible working opportunities; and retirement.

RECRUITMENT AND SELECTION

The UK, unlike many European countries, features an external labour market. This means that people working in the UK do not necessarily expect to be employed for life by one employer. Compared with countries such as Germany or France, job security both in terms of employment law and employer practices is low. However, in the UK, there should be more opportunities for British workers to change employers throughout their careers.

For people wishing or needing to, opportunities to find new jobs decline with age (Itzin et al 1993; McNair et al 2007; Taylor and Walker 2003). In recent years, employers have shown increasing willingness to retain their own older workers. An older employee may have a 'proven track record' with the employer, or may possess important company-specific skills or knowledge that the employer is eager to retain. However, employers' willingness to retain older workers has not yet been matched by a willingness to recruit them.

The reasons behind employers' reluctance to recruit older workers are complex. Employers may believe, for example, that a younger recruit will stay with the organisation longer than an older one, and therefore the employer would have a longer period in which to benefit from its investment in recruiting, inducting and training the employee. As noted above, that assumption is mostly false. An employer might also be reluctant to recruit an older worker who is perceived to be overqualified for the job. On the other hand, the current generation of older workers is more likely than their younger equivalents to have gained their skills on the job rather than through formal education, and lack of qualifications is often a barrier to work. Finally, people who have been out of the labour market for a long time, for example due to unemployment or ill-health, face particular challenges when trying to return to work, as employers may be reluctant to hire job applicants with career gaps.

Since the Age Regulations became law, an increasing number of employers have adopted practices to mitigate the potential for age discrimination in recruitment decisions. For example, some employers have used a wide range of media (for example, newspapers, trade journals, company websites, and so on) in advertising jobs to a wide range of potential candidates. Many employers have also stopped requesting CVs, which can provide unsolicited information, such as the job applicant's date of birth, and have instead relied on their own application forms from which the organisation can limit the information solicited and received.

Changes to the selection process have also been shown to reduce the chances of age discrimination. Interview panel members can unintentionally be influenced by information that infers the job applicant's age, such as when she graduated from university. In many organisations, HR professionals with short-listing responsibilities (that is, selecting candidates for interview) have also played a role in removing age-related information. Some particularly innovative employers have completely abolished traditional application forms in favour of forms focused exclusively on skills and competencies.

Of course, barriers to work for older unemployed people may not only be in the recruitment and selection processes, but also of needed skills or confidence. A retail company that the authors investigated was piloting an innovative approach to helping older people into work. It had opened a large shop in an urban regeneration area in which a large number of residents had been either long-term unemployed or inactive. The company had set a target of employing at least 50% of the shop's staff from the local community's displaced workers. To achieve this, it partnered with a jobs agency to provide job applicants with skills, as well as guarantee a job interview. The job agency provided on-site staff to help employees with problems they face in staying employed, such as access to further skills.

According to the shop's managers, the advantages from the recruitment scheme for the company were threefold. First, it added to the company's credentials as an employer of choice. Second, the recruitment of older people and those who had been hitherto long-term unemployed helped the company fill labour and skills shortages. Third, the scheme was part of a broader effort of the company to build a relationship with the local community from which it draws its customers.

FLEXIBLE WORKING

In many organisations, provision of flexible working arrangements, such as part-time work, job-sharing, alternating work patterns or part-year employment is restricted to workers with childcare responsibilities. Indeed, the statutory 'right to request' flexible working arrangements is limited to workers with children under eight (although in 2007, this right was extended to people who are caring for an elderly relative). However, people often desire flexible working arrangements for a variety of reasons beyond childcare. This could include wanting to pursue an educational qualification or an interest, or, for older workers, wanting to balance work and retirement activities. Although the right to request flexible working was extended to people with eldercare responsibilities, some evidence suggests that older carers are less likely than young parents to ask for or receive flexible working arrangements to help them balance work and retirement (Mooney and Stratham 2002).

As noted above, most older workers would be willing to delay retirement if they could reduce their working hours towards the end of their careers. Figure 8.3 shows that, for those who stay in work beyond 65 (roughly one in five workers, rapidly declining with age), the majority do so on a part-time basis.

Figure 8.3 Working part-time, by age

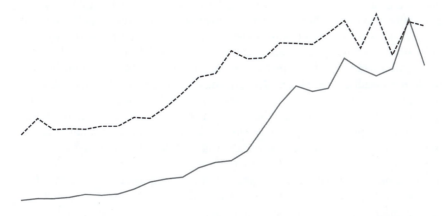

50 51 52 53 54 55 56 57 58 59 60 61 62 63 64 65 66 67 68 69 70 71 72 73 74 75

—— Male   --- Female

Many older workers who want flexibility in their work patterns decide to work on a consultancy basis. In other words, they establish their own businesses, selling their skills and services to the wider market. Employers may also provide support for older workers who want to pursue entrepreneurship in retirement in the form of training. Consultancy work can work well for some older workers, particularly those with highly sought after or specialised skills, or those with some experience in running a business. However, for others, there is a risk that the older worker's business is overly reliant on one client (usually the former employer) or a few; and, as time goes on and the older consultant's skills become obsolete, the number of contracts diminishes (Platman 2003).

According to a large national survey (Metcalf and Meadows 2006), most employers are conditionally willing to consider requests from older employees to stay in work. Seventy-eight per cent say they would be willing to consider requests from employees to work part-time in the run up to retirement. However, managers were twice as likely to say that a delay of retirement would only be granted 'where there is a business need which would be difficult to otherwise meet' as those who granted flexible work arrangements 'if possible to meet the employees' preferences'. In sectors such as health, social services, retail and hospitality, flexible working patterns are more common than in the economy as a whole. Because HR systems are in place to manage flexible working, line managers tend to find accommodating older workers' requests to reduce working hours easier than their equivalents in other sectors (McNair et al 2007). Large public sector organisations, such as the National Health Service and London Metropolitan Police, also have policies on providing flexible working to all employees. On the other hand, small employers often use networks to find part-time employment for older employees whom they themselves cannot accommodate (Arrowsmith and McGoldrick 1997).

A particularly interesting approach to flexible working found by the authors was operated by a construction sector firm. Many jobs in this sector are not only physically demanding, but also involve a great amount of travel, both of which could make work unattractive for older workers. However, the sector involves a great amount of intergenerational skills transfer. One HR manager with whom we spoke described the technology his company used as, 'not changed much since the Roman viaducts were built'. Recognising that, on the one hand, existing work had become unattractive to older workers, and, on the other, the older workers had high-value skills that would be lost to the organisation once the employees retire, the company developed a mentoring scheme as part of its apprenticeship programme. Older construction workers were employed on reduced working hours, closer to home, supporting apprentices through their training programme. The scheme was described as a benefit to both the employer (which was able to retain in-house experiential knowledge) and the older worker (who not only could work flexibly, but could also make use of their skills for a mentally rather than physically challenging job).

RETIREMENT

The third and final policy area we want to focus on is retirement. In 2006, under the Age Regulations, the UK Government set a default retirement age of 65, after which an employer can compulsorily retire an employee. The CIPD, as well as the TUC and Age UK's predecessors, lobbied the Government to abolish mandatory retirement completely. Such a move would have followed the USA, Australia and parts of Canada, which have not had mandatory retirement for a long time. Instead the Age Discrimination Regulations placed a duty on employers to consider requests from employees who want to continue in work beyond 65, which is discussed below.

At the time of writing (summer 2010), the Government ruled that the default retirement age in the UK would be scrapped from October 2011. Under this ruling, employers will not be allowed to dismiss staff because they have reached the age of 65. An employer will, therefore, need to be able to justify a decision to dismiss an employee that does not depend on age. Few people rely on reaching their employer's retirement age as the basis of deciding when to retire (Meadows 2004), so this change in the Government's retirement policy is unlikely to lead to a massive and immediate change in older workers' retirement patterns. However, the focus on retirement as a public policy issue has led employers to review their practices.

Even before the Government began reviewing the default retirement age, employers were doing away with their own mandatory retirement ages. Some large retailers have abolished their retirement ages as ways to attract older people to front-line jobs. The DIY shop B&Q is perhaps best known for employing older tradespeople. Other retailers are taking the same approach to meet labour shortages. Small organisations are also considering the benefits of living without retirement ages. For example, a family firm we investigated had abolished its retirement age, and soon afterwards hired an experienced finance manager who was over 65. The business owner noted that, because of the size of the firm, it only needed (and could only afford) a part-time finance manager. This arrangement suited the manager who was appointed, as he wanted time off for retirement activities.

Since 2006, although employers could mandatorily retire people at 65, they were obliged to consider requests from employees who wanted to delay retirement. Normally, a decision on whether to allow an employee to delay retirement is made by their immediate line manager. It may be felt that the line manager has the best perspective of the employee's performance and ability to continue to be productive. Line managers tend to be relatively sympathetic to employees' requests to delay retirement (McNair and Flynn 2005b). However, they are often not provided the support nor direction from senior managers in finding ways to retain older workers who want to continue working (Flynn 2010a). For example, a line manager may not be aware of their organisation's retirement policy or whether it has a mandatory retirement age. Prior to the Age Regulations, over half of employers had no mandatory retirement policy (Metcalf and Meadows 2006).

One of the main themes of this chapter is that older workers may not necessarily want to continue with their existing work routines after reaching retirement age. Many older worker do, and employers need to take care not to 'push' older workers into less demanding job roles, as this could constitute constructive dismissal. However, because older workers request to stay in work beyond 65, managers, especially immediate line managers, need to have the resources with which to discuss career options. For example, line managers need to be aware of the employer's policies on flexible working, job change, training and mentoring in order to identify options for employees who want to continue working.

A university that we investigated has developed an innovative approach to advising line managers of options available to workers who want to delay retirement. Members of its HR team have been given roles that the organisation has termed 'age champions'. When an employee makes a request to delay retirement, an age champion organises a meeting with the employee, their line manager and an employee representative to discuss work options that would suit both the employee and organisation. According to the HR specialist with whom we spoke, the role of the age champion is to expand the range of choices and to encourage both the line manager and employee to think creatively about how work can be designed to provide a good alternative to retirement. The age champion is also responsible for feeding back to the HR team the outcome of the agreement. For example, if the employee and line manager agree that the employee would take a mentoring role, the age champion takes details of the arrangement in order to disseminate the approach between schools in the university.

DISSEMINATING AGE DIVERSITY POLICIES

The case study mentioned above highlights the main challenge organisations face when implementing new approaches to age diversity. As noted in the first section, older people who are in work would be willing to delay retirement if work could be designed to suit their circumstances. Managers, as mentioned in the second section, are not generally averse to allowing older workers to delay retirement. Particularly in times of economic uncertainty, employers may be eager to retain skilled workers. During the 2009 economic recession, in fact, the proportion of the post-65 population in work actually increased. The key challenge for businesses seeking to change age management practices is not so much changing hearts and minds, but raising awareness of how work can be better designed for older workers.

Implementing HR policies can be particularly difficult in a UK context where HR responsibilities are often devolved to the local level. Line managers are usually not focused on people management issues and are unaware of good practice. On the other hand, line managers are often seen by employers as having the best day-to-day knowledge of their employees and as being best positioned to maximise their productivity. Devolution is also seen as a way to 'empower' local managers.

The university case study mentioned above is a good example of an HR department taking a 'light touch' approach to implementing change in workplace-level practices. Age champions with whom we spoke emphasised their roles were not to impose HR policies on line managers, but to present the range of options available to them. This represents a top–down approach to disseminating age management policies.

Other organisations are facilitating the development of employee networks for groups of workers who are underrepresented in the workplace, such as older workers. Employee networks are usually informal groups of workers focused on an employment policy issue and which may give recommendations to the organisation. For example, workers with eldercare responsibilities may form a network to discuss some of the challenges that they face in balancing home and work responsibilities. The network can then make recommendations to the employer on how to extend flexible work arrangements as well as other ways to support employees with caring responsibilities. In order to facilitate employment policy recommendations, employers often provide support for employee networks through room and IT facilities.

In workplaces in which they are recognised, trade unions can also play an important role in disseminating good age management practices. Some organisations are using trade union learning representatives (workplace union representatives tasked with talking to employees about their training and skills needs) as a model for championing age management practices. Union learning representatives have played an important role in opening up communication channels between managers and employees who are reluctant to discuss their learning needs. Some organisations are working with unions to adopt 'equality representatives' who work with line managers in identifying and eliminating barriers to work.

Like people with training needs, older workers may often be reluctant to ask for support from their managers to improve their employability. For example, an older worker who would like to reduce their working hours may worry that such a request would indicate to their manager that their commitment to the organisation has diminished. The trade union representative can therefore play an important role in articulating to management the demand for HR support at not only an individual but also organisational level. Both employee networks and trade union equality representatives reflect a bottom–up approach to reforming HR practices.

In Germany, trade unions have a much stronger institutional role in organisations compared with the UK (Muller-Camen et al 2010). At the national level, collective bargaining agreements between employers and unions on age management have been reached in two industries: chemicals and steel. Both sectors are facing similar challenges. Over the past decades, job attrition has been managed to a large extent by curtailing recruitment. Skills shortages exist in key occupations such as engineers. Most importantly, many employers in both sectors expect a large proportion of their workforces to reach retirement age within the next 10 years. Consequently, from the employer's perspective, there is a strong demand to keep older workers productive. From the employee's perspective, routes to early retirement, such as the so-called 'block retirement' scheme (a state-financed pension scheme that allows workers to retire as early as 58) are being closed, and the State Pension Age is rising to 67 by 2023. Unions are therefore facing pressure from their members to secure high-quality work for them in later life, when many older workers encounter health issues such as musculo-skeletal problems, heart disease and health problems associated with sedentary lifestyles that may have a negative impact on productivity.

The collective bargaining agreements in the German steel and chemical industries have three major elements. Firstly, employers are required to do an analysis of the age and qualification structure of all units of the organisation. Secondly, firms are encouraged to adopt a range of age-positive HR practices. This includes awareness-raising about the implications of demographic change for the workforce; job design and work organisation that takes into account age and ageing; working hours flexibility for older workers; continuous professional qualification; as well as knowledge and experience transfer. Thirdly, employers and employees pay into a demographic fund to alleviate a demographic challenge that includes options such as additional pension, long-term working hours account or incapacity insurance.

Finally, many organisations are incorporating age diversity into their management training programmes. As an HR manager of a multinational company explained to us, her organisation is accustomed to training managers on diversity issues – managing international work teams, for instance. Age is one more dimension that can be managed through existing diversity tools.

One particularly innovative approach to training is to task line managers with conducting an 'age audit' of their workplaces. Age audits are a useful tool that managers can be asked to complete as part of their training. The purpose of an audit is to investigate current workplace attitudes, assumptions and practices with a view towards identifying and eliminating explicit and implicit discrimination. Such an audit would involve gathering information in the workplace, for example:

- the age profile of the manager's workplace, matched against the company as a whole or equivalent workplaces

- calibration of employees' views on working conditions and career paths through an anonymised survey

- benchmarking of the workplace against practices in the sector as a whole

- identification of good age management practices through case studies of organisations that have faced similar challenges in managing age-related issues.

A wealth of tools available from sources such as the Department for Work and Pensions, Acas, Business Link, the CIPD, TUC and EUROFOUND can be used to age audit. For example, EUROFOUND provides a database of organisational age management practices that have been adopted by employers across the European Union. The database is organised by country, sector and policy area, and is a useful tool for disseminating good practice.

Like employee networks and equality representatives, age audits provide participants (in this case, line managers) lines of communication to impact on HR policies. Findings from audits can be used to change practice organisation-wide. They are also useful for managers to challenge their own preconceptions. As one manager noted to us, before conducting an audit, he had been aware that managers in his workplace tended to be young. He had assumed that older workers did not want to take jobs with higher responsibilities. On talking with his older employees, he found that many had not put themselves forward for promotion because they assumed their skills were not valued by the organisation. Consequently, he took new approaches to appraisal that value the range of taught and experiential skills that his employees possess.

CONCLUSION

The impact of changing age demographics on both economic development and social welfare has been identified as a priority issue for the United Nations, the World Health Organization and the International Labour Organization. Ignoring the fact that populations are ageing can have significant consequences to productivity, labour supply and the availability of skills. However, managing age does not need to be a daunting issue for employers. Good age management practices not only can ensure a good supply of workers into the future, but also aid in knowledge retention, acquisition and retention of important skills, improving working conditions, promoting equality and attracting talent.

This chapter suggested that on average older workers have positive views on work and many of them want to work beyond the retirement age. However, at least to some extent this depends on the opportunities offered to them by employers. In particular they are interested in flexible working opportunities.

By now there are a number of best practice organisations both in the UK and in other countries that have introduced age-neutral HR practices. In terms of recruitment and selection this not only means that organisations encourage older workers to apply, but also that they reduce the chances of age discrimination in the selection process. A second important policy area is flexible working. This means opening up opportunities for part-time work, job-sharing and other flexible arrangements for all employees and not restricting them to those with childcare responsibilities. The third policy area discussed in this chapter was retirement, where many older employees would prefer flexible retirement options and/or the opportunity to work beyond retirement on a part-time basis.

Examples of organisations provided throughout the text suggest that there is a business case for such age-neutral HR policies. However, how can an organisation assure that such initiatives at the strategic level are disseminating throughout the organisation? Here the final part of the chapter pointed to the importance of securing the commitment of line managers, as in many organisations they are the ones that create or restrict opportunities for older workers. Also trade unions can play an important role. In this context we pointed to two innovative collective bargaining agreements on demographic change that have been concluded in Germany which provide incentives for organisations to implement age-neutral HR policies. However, we also pointed out that by now there are many tools available to organisations that want to go down this route.

HRM IN THE MEDIA

CRITICAL REFLECTIONS

The mini case study presented at the beginning of this chapter raises questions about the work experience of older teachers and what organisations could do to support them.

First of all, it suggests that at least a significant minority of older teachers have a negative work experience. They feel under pressure from pupils, younger colleagues and head teachers. This has to be seen in the general context of the teaching profession. On the one hand, shortages of teachers and the funding of pension funds will make it necessary to retire teachers at a later age or to find more retired teachers who are willing to continue on a part-time basis. On the other hand, teaching is a high-stress occupation. Higher work demands by more difficult people, new technology and more regulations have caused stress-related health issues for many teachers.

At the local authority and national level a number of HR policies can be introduced that could help older teachers. Among these are the better use of the experience of older teachers (for example, in teacher training and mentoring) and more opportunities for part-time retirement.

However, an important role is also played by head teachers, who are the line managers of teachers. They have, for example, the authority to provide part-time options for older teachers or not. Nevertheless, a potential problem might be that older teachers are not comfortable with discussing work-related issues with their manager. Here unions may be able to play a stronger role by creating awareness for age discrimination and by supporting their members to improve their working situation.

EXPLORE FURTHER

CHIVA, A. and MANTHORPE, J. (eds) (2008) *Older workers in Europe*. London: Open University Press.

This book, which has a strong focus on the UK, contains a diverse collection of examples of innovative practice in working with individuals, employers and intermediaries.

The EUROFOUND database is available online at www.eurofound.europa.eu/areas/ populationandsociety/ageingworkforce.htm

This database contains about 200 case studies of organisations known for best practices in the area of age management from 27 countries. It documents good practice in relation to such issues as recruitment, training and development, flexible working, health and ergonomics.

FLYNN, M. and MCNAIR, S. (2007) *Managing age: a guide to good employment practice*. London: CIPD.

This guide, available online at www.tuc.org.uk/extras/managingage.pdf, helps to develop good practice to meet the requirements of the age discrimination law that was introduced in October 2006.

MULLER-CAMEN, M., CROUCHER, R., FLYNN, M. and SCHRODER, H. (2010) National institutions and employers' age management practices in Britain and Germany: 'path dependence' and option creation. *Human Relations*, in press.

This article provides a good overview of international differences in age diversity and how they can be explained by different national institutional contexts.

PARRY, E. and TYSON, S. (2010) *Managing an age-diverse workforce*. Basingstoke: Palgrave Macmillan, in print.

This edited book contains contributions on a whole range of age management practices and has authors from around the world.

CHAPTER 9

Critical Issues in Managing the Business Environment

Anne Daguerre

OVERVIEW

This chapter begins with a short case study – the announcement of the Emergency Budget by the Coalition Government in June 2010 – and its impact on pay structures in the financial sector. This case study illustrates how changes in the political and legal environment impact managerial policies. Second, an overview of the influential models of strategic human resource management will be outlined, examining the influence of the 'resource-based view of the firm'. Third, the explanatory framework for monitoring changes in the external environment – the PESTLED (political, economic, social, technological, legal, ecological[1] and demographic) model – is integrated into the general understanding of HR strategy. Finally, the chapter applies the PEST model to the original case study, showing how changes are interrelated in a variety of ways. As a result the managerial decision-making process is often incomplete and intrinsically complex. The chapter concludes by emphasising the difficulties in monitoring change. In practice, information must be made organisation-specific to be useful to managers. As a result, extremely generic and static monitoring systems such as the PEST model and its derivatives have serious limitations.

---

1 The term 'ecological' is used in this chapter in order to differentiate between the term 'environment' (as in 'environmentalism') and 'external environment'.

LEARNING OBJECTIVES

Reading this chapter will enable the reader to:

- critically understand how human resource management integrates into the broader issue of strategic management in an organisation

- identify the main external factors used in the PEST model and use this to investigate appropriate derivative indicators in the context of HRM decision-making scenarios

- articulate the complex interactions between various contextual factors and how they can impact HRM strategies

- use the PEST model in a critical way to analyse a variety of business case studies.

HRM IN THE MEDIA

'THE 2010 EMERGENCY BUDGET'

Following the general election of May 2010, the Chancellor of the new Coalition Government announced an Emergency Budget. This followed a period of great economic and political uncertainty that followed the global economic crisis of 2008 and led to a number of competing pressures and proposed remedies. The recession itself was due to the global credit crunch following the collapse in confidence of the international financial system, based on bad lending. The solutions ranged from co-ordinated responses to restimulating the economy through the G20 group of nations, to the restructuring of the banks and containment of the salary structures said to be partly responsible for incentivising short-term risk leading to the crisis, to the retrenchment of government spending to allay fears about the threat of financial markets downgrading government finances with the consequent effects on interest rates hitting 'the real economy'.

The Emergency Budget – as long predicted by the Conservative election campaign – prioritised the latter of these approaches. An increase to personal and corporate taxation was announced and larger-scale cuts – up to 25% over four years – were trailed for the public spending review in October 2010. In addition, a levy on bank profits was also announced.

Commentators writing in the *Financial Times* (23 June 2010) could not agree on the merits of the Chancellor's approach: while all agreed that it was the boldest and most dramatic budget in living memory, there was disagreement over whether this would lead to a permanent rebalancing of the economy away from the public sector, or a risky contraction that would lead to a contraction of the economy, harming a fragile recovery.

In May 2010, the public deficit reached a peak. Public sector net debt, expressed as a percentage of gross domestic product (GDP), was 63.9% at the end of June 2010 compared with 57.3% at end of June 2009. When the Labour Government bailed out a large proportion of failing UK banks in October 2008, the then Chancellor Alistair Darling insisted that the bailout was not a blank cheque. Bank executives were asked to show restraint, especially in relation to bonuses. By the summer of 2010 it was clear, however, that bonuses in the City were back to pre-crash levels, increasing the public moral outrage with the banks, and challenging the new government to tax or regulate them – against the normal political instincts of the Conservatives.

Questions

1   What kind of planning could HR do if they were advising a public sector organisation?

2   What kind of planning could HR do if they were advising a bank?

3   What kind of planning could HR do if they were in a large contractor supplying services to public sector organisations and banks?

INTRODUCTION

This chapter discusses an issue of strategic importance for HRM practitioners: how to manage uncertainty in the global business environment. Managers make crucial HR-related decisions relating to issues of recruitment, pay structure, employee retention, how work should be organised and how to engage employees with any or all of these decisions. All of these judgements must be informed on managers' perceptions of the current and future business context. For instance, if they expect to experience difficulties in recruiting due to tight labour market conditions, they are more likely to adopt extensive and expensive recruitment methods. Good information and monitoring systems are therefore crucial in helping managers to make sense of a constantly changing business context.

The media story in the introductory case study illustrates how political decisions affect the economic environment of public and private sector organisations. In the wake of the major global financial crisis in September 2008 and the government rescue of the financial sector, a watershed seemed to have taken place that would have not have been predicted just two years previously: the Government intervening – by means of taking ownership – into the financial services sector. Conversely, the incoming government in 2010 were pledging a major and permanent contraction in the scale and scope of the public sector.

All this demonstrates how a change in the immediate external environment of the firm can impact managerial decisions. Managers in public sector organisations are faced with a severe dilemma as budget cuts unavoidably lead to recruitment freezes and job losses. Managing redundancies raises all sorts of challenges, especially as remaining employees must remain committed to the organisation. Managers in the private sector may also want to wait until the economy is fully recovered before taking on new staff. As a result, changes in the political environment represent the first dimension of the PEST model, as we shall explore in more depth in the next section.

The strategic aspect of human resource management is based on the idea that people represent the firm's best competitive advantage (Allen and Wright 2007, pp88–101). Managers should be aiming to maximise employees' skills and aptitudes in order to compete in the external environment. This, in turn, is based on the notion of the 'resource-based view' (RBV) of the firm.

RBV was developed by Penrose (1959) and focuses on the factors giving organisations a distinctive edge in comparison with competitors. In contrast to traditional economic models of the firm, which focus on basic factors of production, Priem and Butler (2001, p23) argue that 'competitive advantage is secured through the organisation developing and mobilising specific internal resources', rather than 'responding primarily to external stimuli' (Rubery et al 2003, p268). Wernerfelt (1997, p119) defines resources as 'those (tangible and intangible) assets which are tied semi-permanently to the firm'. So brand names, in-house knowledge of technology, skilled personnel, trade contracts, machinery, efficient procedures, and so on, are all considered to be a firm's resources. Barney (1991, p105) argues that firms can hold the potential of sustained competitive advantage if resources (a) are valuable (in the sense of exploiting opportunities and/or neutralising threats in a firm's environment), (b) are rare among a firm's current and potential competition, (c) are imperfectly imitable, and (d) strategically equivalent substitutes do not exist for these resources.

If it is assumed that the goal of HRM is to build organisational and individual performance, Boxall and Purcell (2007, pp5–7) contend that individual performance (P) is determined by three factors: ability (A), motivation (M) and opportunity (O). The resultant formula, $P = f(A,M,O)$, indicates that performance is a function of the combined interaction of workers who are skilled and capable of doing useful work, are motivated to work well and co-operatively and that they are given the opportunity to succeed. Individual performance must be related to organisational strategy, so that there is a goodness of fit between the organisation and its employees. While HRM practices will tend to differ across organisations, depending on factors such as size, sector, labour market and demographic characteristics of the workforce and the nature of goods and services produced, there are, nonetheless, also common features. For example, a legal firm highly dependent on the skills and knowledge of its employees will seek to attract and retain the best lawyers in a particular area of law, and will adopt a high-skill, high-commitment strategy including high pay and extensive internal development. This is because its business model turns on providing excellent service standards based on highly motivated and knowledgeable staff. This virtuous scenario, though, would not insulate such a firm from being complacent about changes in, for example, equality legislation. By contrast, while a fast-food restaurant is more likely to adopt a low-road HR strategy as its business model, being low-cost and relying on providing standardised levels of routinised relatively unskilled service and being comfortable with high labour turnover (Royle and Towers 2002), a change in employment law would, despite the differences with the legal firm, still need to consider its own policies.

The essential HR challenges for managers are to recruit and retain the appropriate number of capable, motivated employees at a competitive rate of remuneration in a constantly changing business environment. Predicting future demand for the service or goods provided and analysis of competitors is clearly important. For HR issues, however, there is a clear rationale for applying the PESTLED model to measure other elements.

THE PEST MODEL AND ITS DERIVATIVES

The PEST model has been widely used since the 1980s. It proposes a taxonomy of the factors (political, economical, sociological and technological) that shape the environment of the firm. To understand the external environment is absolutely crucial, especially as the economy is likely to remain instable in the foreseeable future. A globalised economy tends to be highly competitive, particularly with the advent of the emergence of new powers such as the so-called BRIC nations (Brazil, Russia, India and China). It can also be extremely volatile due to pre-eminence of financial markets. The financial markets tend to operate to short-term developments and, when unexpected external shocks take the financial markets by surprise, can overreact to economic and political events, thus adding further confusion to an already complex picture.

Research on the wider meso- and macro-economic environment in which organisations operate started to develop in the 1950s in the United States. This work emphasised the importance of understanding the external environment in order to make sound strategic decisions. To understand long-term trends and analyse the position of the organisation vis-à-vis these long-term trends was crucial for identifying scenarios for growth and challenges. In very simple terms, it was stressed that firms operate in a changing context, which in turn affects their potential for growth (opportunities) and weaknesses. Francis J. Aguilar (1967) was the first scholar to use a model of this kind.

We now consider each factor in turn, although because of the more logical links between some of these, we will consider them in a different order.

THE POLITICAL ENVIRONMENT

The political environment includes *the state* and, within the state, *government* in various tiers, *political parties* and *party politics*, and *interest* and *lobby groups*.

The state and the government: the state comprises the various institutions of government: the bureaucracy, the police, the courts, and in general all recognisable public state institutions, by contrast to private institutions of civil society, such as trade unions, businesses and the family. The state is an autonomous entity that enforces collective decisions that apply to all members of a given nation state. While many functions of the state are enduring and fairly consistent between nations (the legal system, the mechanisms used to enforce order) some aspects, while still remaining fairly consistent over time (the mechanisms used to regulate the economy) do vary between nations (see Chapter 4 by Wood). The aspects of the state that are most liable to uncertainty for the HR planning process are the more overtly political factors associated with government itself. The government is part of the state but is only temporary; governments come and go depending on election results; forms of government may also change or evolve. Traditionally, right-wing governments are more likely to promote business-friendly legislation (low corporate tax, less 'red tape'), than their left-wing counterparts, the latter being more inclined to favour redistribution of revenues to the advantage of labour and in general to promote a form of regulated capitalism. But, once again, what matters is the impact of political and regulatory decisions on a particular sector, which explains the interest of business associations like the Confederation of British Industry (CBI) or the interests represented by particular sectoral interests within the economy – the influence of financial capital in the City of London has long been regarded as having a particularly powerful influence over governments in the UK with the potential to change or block what it would consider to be undesirable political outcomes (Michie 2004).

The form of governments can also differ, ranging from a Westminster-style parliamentary democracy such as in the UK, with a first-past-the-post system and a concentration of power in the hands of the governing party, to a presidential system with a strict division of power between the executive, the legislature and the judiciary, to the extent that the legislature can actually paralyse the actions of the executive and vice versa, as can be the case between Congress and the Presidency in the United States.

The geographical distribution of power also differs across nations. Power can be located in the centre, as in the UK, with traditionally little power for local authorities and regions – or delegated to regions with legislative decision-making prerogatives (as in Spain, with extremely large powers for autonomous communities) and states, as in the US, where states draw their own constitutions.

The organisation and the localisation of power have far-reaching implications for society at large. For instance, if power is traditionally concentrated in the hands of the prime minister, as in the UK, interest groups and lobbies will concentrate their efforts on forging links with the Government. Of course, they will try to influence members of Parliament as well but for the most part will focus on the governing party. By contrast, in the US, Congress is a crucial political player, which enjoys many more resources than the White House. This explains why lobbyists devote tremendous efforts to forge special links with Congressional representatives.

Supranational institutions must also be taken into account when analysing the political environment, as national governments are increasingly adapting their domestic legislative frameworks in response to supranational pressures, notably from the European Union (EU). The EU and its main institutions, such as the European Commission, the Council of Ministers, the European Parliament and the European Court of Justice, have played a crucial role in shaping the domestic political agenda of all European countries. This is the reason why a range of special interest groups such as financial institutions, industry and non-profit organisations are involved in lobbying business at the EU level, in the context of increasing power transfer to Brussels (Mazey and Richardson 1993).

In contemporary democracies, political programmes emanate from the mandate secured by an incoming government by way of the *political party* (and sometimes *coalitions* of political parties) which won the national election. Party manifestos and political platforms spell out specific proposals in relation to the degree of economic regulation and labour market co-ordination, level and type of taxation, which will in turn impact the economic environment of the firm. Although political parties have distinct values and ideologies about the utility of business, for instance, political affiliation is no longer as reliable a factor for predicting the extent to which a particular party will implement a range of seeping changes. In the developed world there is far less ideological difference between the main left-wing and right-wing parties than there has been in the past. It may be equally instructive to consider the particular parameters that both left and right parties agree about in a liberal market economy such as Britain (for example, on labour market flexibility) and what particular parameters that both left and right parties agree about in a liberal market economy such as Germany (for example, on the issue of protecting strategic industries from foreign takeover).

THE ECONOMIC ENVIRONMENT

The economic environment refers to a society's economic structures and such variables as the movements in the global financial markets, the levels of economic growth (generally measured in terms of gross domestic product – GDP), the public deficit, interest and inflation rates, and unemployment rates. Changes to these factors, in combination, affect the behaviour of economic actors – consumers, businesses, financiers, governments, trade unions – and affect decisions made in relation to wages, hiring, redundancy, outsourcing, training, and so on. Further factors influencing such decisions are partly affected by political factors and include the degree of openness of the economy, the degree of state control and regulation of the economy. For instance, the degree to which the labour market is regulated, as in co-ordinated market economies, or the degree to which employers are free to hire and fire at will, as in liberal market economies such as the United States, will have direct implications for the HR function in firms when they plan their recruitment strategy (see Chapter 4 by Wood). HR professionals will also need to be aware of the degree of openness of the economy – are some sectors of the economy protected by the state, as in the case of agriculture in the EU or in the United States? These variables impact differently on different industries. Indeed, generic economic factors will be of little relevance to HRM departments, as senior managers cannot utilise excessively general and abundant information on the state of the economy. In other words, the analysis has to be sector-specific in order to forecast possible scenarios for a particular organisation. What is also clear is that political and economic factors constantly interplay and interconnect in complex and often unexpected ways: the economic environment is shaped by regulatory and political decisions that can be located in the political environment, but equally such decisions are not made in an economic vacuum and are shaped by perceived economic constraints.

THE SOCIAL ENVIRONMENT

The social environment refers to cultural attitudes, ethical beliefs, shared values, level of differentiation in lifestyle, demographics, education levels, and so on. Of direct interest here are shifts in values and lifestyles. For instance, increased female participation in the labour market since the late 1960s, with tremendous acceleration in the late 1980s, is a major sociological and demographic change that has had a series of repercussions on organisations. In the 1990s, as employers became aware that they were losing a skilled labour force that either stopped working or worked part-time once they became mothers, HR practitioners began to be interested in work–life balance policies in order to accommodate the specific childcare needs of their female employees – where such employees were in hard-to-recruit positions. Over the past 20 years, the workforce has become increasingly diverse, which raises specific challenges for HRM departments. In general, until the late 1970s, managers were dealing with a relatively homogeneous workforce, with a relatively predictable set of attitudes towards work, leisure and the family. The typical production worker displayed a strong degree of loyalty towards their workplace, was respectful of hierarchies and expected to have clearly identifiable tasks, though they were also more likely to be unionised and more willing to engage in industrial action to further their terms and conditions of employment. In exchange, the employer was expected to provide job security and incremental career progression within the same organisation. This formed the basis of the employment contract in developed countries between the 1950s and the early 1970s. In the early twenty-first century, this stable employment contract no longer exists, especially for low-skilled employees who are at the periphery of the labour market.

In contemporary society, where the world of work is becoming more unstable, global and uncertain, employees have changed their expectations towards their employers. Although the workplace remains a major source of socialisation, it is no longer the only source of identity formation and self-gratification, especially for the so-called Y Generation, which is discussed more below. In the UK, immigration has played an important role too. Immigrants make up a large proportion of the 'new' workforce entrants in the context of an ageing population. With such migration (see Chapter 17), there are increasing risks of clashes in cultural values in the workplace, notably in relation to religious beliefs. Organisations have had to put in place anti-discrimination policies, as the law has adjusted to deal with the changing demands for equal treatment for all. But it is not merely compliance with the law that is important here. Migration has become commonplace in the twenty-first century. Managing an increasingly mobile and diverse workforce raises specific challenges for HR specialists, as Chapter 17 illustrates.

DEMOGRAPHIC FACTORS

Closely related to the social environment, demographic changes, although not originally included as a separate category in the PEST model, affect in crucial ways HRM departments, who need to know the age profile of their workforce in order to devise effective recruitment and retention strategies. Lower birth rates coupled with an ageing workforce have resulted in a shrinking labour pool in all major developed economies. In the UK, there will be a rapid increase in the number of people aged 50 and over in the near future. The number of people aged 50 and over is expected to rise from 19.8 million in 2005 to 24.5 million in 2020. The number of prime age people – aged 25–49 – is projected to rise until 2011 and then decline from 2012 onwards, mainly due to the Baby Boom generation leaving the 25–49 age group (ONS 2006). As people aged 50 and over have lower activity rates than the prime age population, activity rates of the working age population – 16–64 – is projected to fall by 1.4 percentage points from 63.1% in 2005 to 61.7% in 2020. The activity rate for men in this age group is projected to fall to 67% in 2020 from 70.5% in 2005, while for women it is projected to increase to 56.6% in 2020 from 56.1% in 2005. Migration is projected to partially offset the decline in activity rates for the working age population. A higher level of migration is associated with a higher activity rate because the majority of migrants are between the ages of 15 and 34, thus pushing activity rates higher. Although there are many uncertainties attached to these projections, it is nevertheless clear that the diversity of the workforce is set to increase, with specific challenges in terms of managing age diversity (Brooke and Taylor 2005; see also Chapter 8 in this volume).

It has also been suggested that demographic changes can be reflected in different generations' attitudes. Thus it has been asserted that 'Baby Boomers' (roughly those born between 1945 and 1964), 'Generation X' (1965–1980) and Generation Y, or 'millennials' (1980 onwards) have to co-operate in the workplace despite their different attitudes to work, managing change and perception of organisational hierarchy (Howe and Strauss 1991; 2000). For instance, it is asserted that Generation Y cohort workers are results-oriented and do not care much about the methods used to achieve the outcomes, while Baby Boomers tend to value traditional working methods, as opposed to working from remote locations. Moreover, while Baby Boomers and Generation X prefer face-to-face conversations and direct communication, younger millennials favour text-messaging and emails. In sum, managing different generations within an organisation raises additional challenges for HRM managers (Glass 2007). However, HR specialists should be wary of these Generation X and Y stereotypes, which can be prone to oversimplification, overlooking factors such as class, gender and ethnicity, and of the fact that these generational cohorts are models based on demographic and socio-political events in the United States and may not be universally applicable.

THE TECHNOLOGICAL ENVIRONMENT

Technological factors refer to changes in technology that can alter the firm's competitive position. Development of automation has resulted in the elimination of workers, especially in the manufacturing and production sectors. Innovation has also dramatically altered some forms of skilled work. As organisations have become leaner and more efficient, they have also emphasised the ability to perform multiple tasks. Employees are increasingly expected to work on team-based projects, to work in an autonomous fashion, with little guidance from their line managers. In this context, job specification has become less important as employees are expected to perform a new set of tasks whenever this is required.

Innovation plays an important role in the economic cycle. Fluctuations in the economy can follow long, predictable patterns – these are the long waves identified by the economist Kondratiev at the beginning of the twentieth century – or, on the contrary, follow short-term, unpredictable patterns. According to Schumpeter (1975), innovation, the process of 'creative destruction', characterises the development of capitalism. Indeed, constant economic competition between firms obliges them to innovate: 'The fundamental impulse that sets and keeps the capitalist engine in motion comes from the new consumers, goods, the new methods of transportation or markets, and the new forms of industrial organisations that capitalism creates.... This process of creative destruction is the essential fact about capitalism' (Schumpeter 1975, pp82–85). The introduction of technologies in the workplace also means that employees are required to constantly retrain in order to acquire the skills to use these new technologies. Those who are unwilling or unable to keep up risk losing their jobs, as pointed out by Burke and Ng (2006, p90). Indeed, a major risk is skills obsolescence, which can happen extremely quickly given the rapid acceleration and diffusion of new information technologies and their applications. Information technology represents a major technological revolution that has given rise to the creation of knowledge workers, who expect employers to provide them with constant creative opportunities and challenges. Technological inventions such as mobile phones, BlackBerrys and Wi-Fi connections have facilitated new forms of work arrangements, with an increasing number of employees working from home. Information technologies have introduced a change in working patterns, with the frontiers between life and work being increasingly blurred as workers are connected 24/7.

THE LEGAL ENVIRONMENT

Employment law represents one of the major constraints for HRM departments because it has a direct impact on the way in which HR practitioners can negotiate the employment relationship. Employment law and practices vary across nations as they stem from different legal systems and traditions. Scholars have identified two clusters of legal traditions in industrialised countries: the common law system and the codified law system.

Common law systems are dominant in English-speaking countries (England and Wales) and former British colonies such as the United States, Canada, Ireland, New Zealand, Australia, South Africa, Hong Kong, Singapore and Malaysia. In this system 'the law is made by judges building on custom and tradition' (Taylor and Lucas 2006, p260). Parliament passes statutes that adapt common law principles but statutes are quite short. Statutes are then interpreted by judges and once a statute has been interpreted in a higher court (in England the Supreme Court is the House of Lords), this becomes common law. In English-speaking countries, employment law is not very detailed; employment law statutes tend to be much less detailed than labour codes predominant in civil law systems. Although there have been a move towards codification in common law systems, in general employers and employees remain freer to establish their own terms and conditions than in civil systems. National collective agreements, when they exist, are not always legally binding, in contrast to collective agreements in continental Europe.

Codified law systems (or civil law systems) are based on Roman law and, more recently, on the French Napoleonic codes (Taylor and Lucas 2006, p261). Here the interpretation of the law plays a much less important role than in the common law system. Indeed, codes spell out in great detail what the law is and how it should be interpreted. Employment law is spelled out in labour codes and the judge refers to the relevant codes when issuing a judgment. Employment law is quite rigid, legally binding and there is much less room for interpretation. Codified law systems are dominant in continental and southern Europe (France, Germany, Austria, Italy, Spain, Portugal), and in those countries' former colonies.

The interpretation of the law continues to play an extremely important role in the UK context, especially because statutory employment law does not spell out in great detail what the law is supposed to mean. As a result, the law is constituted of many grey areas that can be open to interpretation. This is a source of potential conflict and litigation between employers and employees. In the standard employment relationship, the employer has residual rights over the labour of their employee and may change the terms of the employment contract without this necessarily constituting a breach of contract. The key word here is that the employer is required by law to make reasonable changes within the terms of the existing agreement as defined either explicitly by flexibility clauses in the employment contract, or implicitly by so-called implied terms.

If an employee brings a claim for breach of contract to an employment tribunal because they do not agree with the changes of terms and conditions set out by the employer, the tribunal may well decide that flexibility clauses/implied terms allow the employer to make reasonable changes to the employment contract. In general, the term 'reasonable' means that these are not drastic changes, and that the employer has followed the consultative procedures required by law when changing the terms and conditions of an employment contract. But, ultimately, what may appear as reasonable to the judge or the employer may not seem at all reasonable to the employee.

Another difficulty may occur when employers overestimate the extent of their power in the employment relationship. Although UK employment law reflects the fundamental power imbalance between the employer and the employee, this imbalance can never be absolute; otherwise the employment contract, in theory freely negotiated by two parties, would be akin to forced labour or slavery. Unfortunately, some HRM departments are not always aware of the niceties of the law and may wrongly advise employers to arbitrarily change the terms of the employment contract. Yet the law stipulates that a series of steps must be taken by the employer, and if such steps are not properly followed, the employer may be liable to a claim of a breach of contract and/or unfair dismissal.

Such 'miscalculations' on the part of overzealous HRM departments are more likely to occur in a situation of conflict and/or uncertainty regarding the rules of the game of the organisation, its long-term goals and strategic direction. Such difficulties have been reported when public organisations such as NHS trusts are given permission to set new terms of the employment contract as part of the transition process away from a public service ethos towards a more managerial, target-driven ethos. In general, transition periods are especially difficult to manage in public organisations and can result in a series of legal disputes.

UK employment law has been subjected to tremendous changes since the mid-1990s, especially as a result of EU influence. The traditional model of employment relationships in the UK was that of laissez-faire (Marchington and Wilkinson 2008), whereby employers and employees were left to sort out their disputes. The law was seen as an instrument of last resort, when disputes could not be solved through collective bargaining. This is no longer the case and a series of statutory requirements – set out by the legislator, in other words the government of the day – now regulate the employment contract. Moreover, UK employment law is becoming increasingly complex as it is subjected to two sets of contradictory legal and political influences. Traditionally the UK has been characterised by a highly flexible labour market with minimum employment rights for employees. Since the 1990s Conservative and Labour Governments have taken active steps to ensure that increasingly precise and demanding statutory requirements do not constrain employers in an excessive fashion. Indeed, there is a political consensus according to which flexibility represents a key competitive advantage for the UK economy. Yet British policy-makers are also required to translate EU directives into domestic law, that is, statutory requirements. The problem is that in general EU legislators take a much less benevolent stance than UK policy-makers in relation to employers' rights, and are more likely to impose limits on labour market flexibility. To preserve employers' rights and operational flexibility, the legislator has taken advantage of a range of opt-out clauses that allow employers to set the terms of the employment contract without being subjected to new EU-inspired statutory requirements, as illustrated by the ongoing controversy regarding the opt-out from the 48-hour limit on the working week.

The EC Working Time Directive (93/104/EC of 23 November 1993), implemented in the UK by the Working Time Regulations 1998, imposed a general limit of 48 hours on the working week. It allowed member states to let individuals opt out of this limit if both employer and employee agreed. At the time the UK was the only EU country that took advantage of this opt-out. Employees can agree to work longer than the 48-hour limit provided that they sign a written agreement to that effect. Workers can cancel the opt-out agreement whenever they want, although they must give their employer at least seven days' notice, or longer if this has been agreed. Several attempts have been made at the EU level to oblige the UK to cancel the opt-out, but they have been fiercely opposed by the Government and employers' representatives. The Confederation of British Industry (CBI) – in common with other business lobby groups – broadly approved of the opt-out. However, as pointed out by Keter (2009, p21), 'there is evidence that the opt out is being abused by employers'. A survey by the CIPD, reported by the *Financial Times*, found that 'more than one in five people who signed the hotly-debated opt-out clause, said they did so under employer compulsion' (compare Keter 2009, p21).

To recap, UK employment law is both complex and ambiguous as it attempts to reconcile fundamentally contradictory political and ideological pressures, that is, on the one hand a minimalist stance towards employees' rights in the name of flexibility and social partners' freedom to define the terms of the employment contract, and a much more demanding EU stance towards employers' obligations and employees' rights, especially those who work atypical hours or are in non-standard forms of employment, such as agency workers, on the other hand.

ECOLOGICAL FACTORS

Little will be said about this factor here. In other areas of management planning, such considerations – the effects of pollution – are more directly relevant. However, this is an area that has been identified as being the factor behind some of the most momentous political, economic, social, technological, legal and demographic changes of the twenty-first century, in that the global issue of climate change is set to be a dominant feature of planning issues worldwide. Even if one were to acknowledge the complaints made by 'climate sceptics', it will not prevent this issue from being close to the top of agendas. There are, at this point, few obvious HR policy implications. It is likely to feed into staff terms and conditions via working practices – particularly relating to travel. Beyond this it is difficult to predict, but it is a growing area.

CONCLUSION

A core assertion in modern HRM is that people (who work in an organisation) are an organisation's most important asset. While this assertion can appear trite in some circumstances, such as when redundancies are occurring, it also points to a vital truth. The skills, knowledge, aptitudes, attitudes and – crucially – effort of workers is the key determinant of the quality and quantity of the organisation's output, whether the organisation is a private manufacturer, bank or public service provider. Understanding how to ensure the most appropriate people are brought in, how they are treated within the organisation and how indispensible any one individual may be considered to be in any organisational circumstance requires planning. HR planning requires taking a strategic view of the external environment. The influences on future environments can occur as shocks to the existing norms, but more commonly follow trends already occurring. A sound understanding of the external environment is essential for this. The PEST model is a useful heuristic tool that helps make sense of the business environment.

CRITICAL REFLECTIONS

Before considering each scenario individually, let us consider the broad climate described. The 2008 global economic crisis was expected to adversely affect unemployment for some years to follow. In addition, the 2010 Emergency Budget of the new Coalition Government promised severe cuts to public sector budgets, affecting employment directly in this sector and also those parts of the private sector working closely with the public sector. Add to this the effect of dampening spending by more cautious consumers more fearful of their own jobs, and this was also predicted to affect retail. Employment prospects were therefore predicted to remain quite bleak for new entrants to the labour market – including graduates – in the following three to five years, unless there was a significant growth in export-led private sector organisations. In such circumstances employers would be able to 'cherry pick' and offer relatively unattractive employment conditions to new job-seekers. However, HR planners also need to be aware of the interaction between global and domestic labour markets: as the workforce is highly mobile, the best graduates could be driven away from the UK and seek better employment opportunities elsewhere, especially in the US. This was already the case by the end of the twentieth century: indeed, 'European-born immigrants in the US labour market have considerably higher skills levels than in Europe, and they compare favourably to Americans of similar educational levels in terms. European expatriates are several times more likely to have a PhD than the average US labour market participants' (Saint-Paul 2004, p15). In other words, employers would have to ensure that their employees remain committed to the organisation in a context of stagnant growth and limited opportunity structures, so HR managers will have to be exceptionally creative in order to keep their employees motivated.

In relation to public sector organisations, then, the situation would be likely to be a challenge for organisations that rely on a highly skilled workforce, such as the NHS with the spending constraints in place for the longer term. A key question for HR planners in UK-based banks would be how to ensure that they continue to attract talented individuals, given the negative reputation they have received. However, if the bonuses are really back, planners could take solace in the thought that young graduates, the so-called Y Generation, may be more attracted by short-term financial gain than reputation – though this has not been tested before: City jobs were seen not only as lucrative, but also as being at the vanguard of the UK economy. However, the fact remains that in the banking sector individual value is very much measured by salaries and bonuses, and that the stress and long-working-hours culture that prevails in the City of London are considered to be a price worth paying only if compensated by tremendous financial gains. Managers will have to keep a balancing act between attractive pay awards and increased government and/or media scrutiny as a result of public moral outrage with the banks.

Perhaps the most difficult scenario to predict would be those organisations supplying these sectors. For the public sector contractor industry, a potential boom has been predicted, following the austerity years, as part of the public sector are expected to be hived off to outside providers as part of the 'Big Society' restructuring of the state. Early indications were, however, that the scale of the cutbacks were affecting contractors first and hardest as public bodies sought quick savings by cancelling projects – and where the costs of redundancy would be borne by contractors, not the public services themselves.

EXPLORE FURTHER

BOXALL, P. and PURCELL, J. (2007) *Strategy and human resource management.* 2nd edition. Basingstoke: Palgrave.

Full coverage of the issue of strategic HRM covering all the major definitions.

STOREY, J. (2007) What is strategic HRM? In: STOREY, J. (ed.). *Human resource management: a critical text.* London: Thomson Learning.

Useful overview – with case study – of the main aspects of SHRM.

BOXALL, P., PURCELL, J. and WRIGHT, P. (eds) (2007) *Oxford handbook of human resource management.* Oxford: Oxford University Press.

Chapter 3 by Boxall and Chapter 5 by Allen and Wright provide good overviews of the role of strategy in HRM.

LEGGE, K. (2004) *Human resource management: rhetorics and realities.* Basingstoke: Palgrave Macmillan.

This definitive critical text on HRM remains a very good text. Especially useful are Chapters 1, 3 and 4.

PART TWO

HR PROCESSES AND PRACTICES

Critical Issues in People Resourcing (1): Reconceptualising Employee Performance

Sebastian Fuchs

OVERVIEW

The shift from personnel management to the more contemporary and strategically oriented human resource management paradigm led many organisations to introduce performance management systems in order to enhance job and, ultimately, organisational performance. This chapter sets out to discuss and question traditional and commonly held views on employee job performance in organisations by arguing that employee performance can also be seen as behaviours, actions and activities as opposed to results and mere job outcomes in organisational life. Further, it identifies and suggests a number of facets, triggers and predictors of different job performance elements on the individual, group and organisational level of analysis.

LEARNING OBJECTIVES

Reading this chapter will enable the reader to:

- critically examine the concept of job performance
- critically analyse the distinction between functional and dysfunctional work behaviour
- critically examine the elements and triggers of task-oriented work behaviour and context-oriented work behaviour
- critically examine the elements and triggers of counterproductive work behaviour and withdrawal work behaviour.

HRM IN THE MEDIA

'EMPLOYEE SABOTAGES BAKERY'

BBC News (2009) reported that a Nottingham food company lost more than £1 million after an employee allegedly sabotaged its industrial bakery by sprinkling peanuts in nine places with the intention to contaminate goods. A peanut contamination meant that the company could have found itself liable to prosecution should a customer with a nut allergy have been taken seriously ill or died. The bakery had to close down for three days in order to be decontaminated. The alleged sabotage took place after an incident in which the factory manager discovered an inappropriate calendar in the employee's room during an inspection. The employee was questioned in relation to the calendar, but no disciplinary action was taken at the time. It was claimed in this case that traces of nuts were found on the employee's work clothes and he was suspended. A few months after the incident he was paid £11,000 and his contract was terminated. The employee denied the allegations.

Questions

1   If the employee did contaminate the bakery, how would you categorise this type of employee behaviour?

2   What could be done to reduce the possibility that the same situation would not occur in the future?

INTRODUCTION

This chapter discusses the different elements of the notion of job performance in organisations. It highlights both the need to understand job performance in terms of behaviours and actions and the critical consideration of functional and dysfunctional work behaviour in the concept of job performance. Based on this distinction, the chapter suggests that functional work behaviour consists of organisationally desired behaviours related both towards job tasks and job contexts, and that dysfunctional work behaviour consists of a range of organisationally undesired behaviours. In arguing this line of reasoning, the chapter offers a fresh and comprehensive evidence-based multifaceted conceptualisation of the different types of employee behaviour that constitute job performance. The analysis is structured around the triggers of each type of behaviour based on different organisational levels.

JOB PERFORMANCE IN ORGANISATIONS

The shift from personnel management to the more contemporary and strategically oriented human resource management paradigm has given way to the introduction of performance management systems that aim to enhance job and ultimately organisational performance (Godard 2004). In order to fully utilise performance management systems in the management of human resources (HR), however, it is important to understand the concept of performance in organisations. Performance, commonly referred to as job performance, is employees' 'actions or behaviours relevant to the organization's goals' (Landy and

Conte 2010, p2175). Accordingly, it incorporates employee activities that help the organisation to attain previously determined goals and objectives such as the acquisition of new clients and customers, an increase in market share through increased sales or the development of new and innovative products and services, among others. One way both practitioners and researchers often understand and conceptualise job performance is based on the use of a number of outcome measures or performance indicators in order to determine employees' individual job performance. This, for instance, includes things such as the number of pieces produced, total days of absence, the overall value of sales or the acquisition of new customers. This is an approach often found in organisations as it links performance management directly to organisationally desired outcomes.

While this appears to be a logical way of assessing employees' job performance, two important elements are overlooked by such an approach. Firstly, a number of related variables are likely to be beyond the control of an employee. For instance, the quality and price of products and services offered, the competition, the equipment and technology used, potential budget constraints, supervision and co-workers are all uncontrollable factors for employees and henceforth potentially confounding variables in the assessment of their job performance using a mere outcome-related approach. In other words, an employee can work very hard but does not deliver the desired results based on factors that are beyond their control. Secondly, and of equal importance, a mere results-oriented approach to job performance is unlikely to provide the employee and the organisation with feedback on how to improve job performance at a later stage as the sheer results do not necessarily indicate areas for improvement of actual employee behaviour. As a result of these two limitations, job performance may alternatively be seen as a set of employee behaviours and actions as opposed to mere results or outcomes attained by employees (Colquitt et al 2009).

CONCEPTUALISING JOB PERFORMANCE IN ORGANISATIONS

The formalisation of job performance adopted above suggests that it incorporates all actions and behaviours of employees that are relevant to the attainment of organisational goals. Such employee behaviours and actions can contribute either positively or negatively to organisational goal attainment and performance (Jex and Britt 2008). This chapter, as such, distinguishes between functional and dysfunctional work behaviours respectively.

FUNCTIONAL WORK BEHAVIOUR

Here, functional work behaviour is defined as a set of employee behaviours exhibited inside and outside the workplace that contributes positively towards the attainment of organisational goals and objectives. The two main types of functional work behaviour constitute of task-oriented work behaviour (T-OWB) and context-oriented work behaviour (C-OWB).

Task-oriented work behaviour

Most employees in organisations are employed in order to engage in predetermined specific tasks and roles or are hired to solve a particular problem. As such, employees usually have a set of tasks and duties to fulfil for which they have been employed. Such tasks and duties are usually formalised in a job description, which differs significantly between various jobs, occupations and professions. A job description for a fire fighter, for instance, usually includes T-OWB related to searching for fire victims in burning buildings and the operation of fire fighter equipment in order to put out fires. For an accountant, however, T-OWB is likely to include the preparation, examination and analysis of accounting records and tax returns for their accurateness and completeness. Despite the vast range of diverse T-OWB in different organisational roles and occupations, T-OWB can also be understood in terms of how frequently the content and context of a job changes. Routine T-OWB, for instance, involves known and familiar responses to job demands that occur in a predictable and foreseeable way. For instance, a flight attendant giving routine safety instructions or distributing beverages and snacks is one example of routine T-OWB. The flight attendant would, when exhibiting such behaviours, act in a programmed and, over time, almost habitual way. In more-rare organisational situations, however, there may be instances in which adaptive T-OWB is required in order to fulfil one's job duties. This is sometimes referred to as 'adaptability' and involves the response of employees to task demands that are unusual, novel and to some extent hard to predict for both the employee and the organisation. One example of such adaptive T-OWB is that of flight attendants working on a commercial aeroplane that has to perform a forced landing on a meadow due to technical problems. Flight attendants, in such a situation, would need to evacuate the aeroplane quickly as there is often a danger of fire and explosion on board soon after the forced landing. As such, T-OWB shifts from less routine behaviours to more novel and unfamiliar behaviours even though it is still considered part of a flight attendant's overall job. Despite this being an extreme example, many employees find themselves increasingly often in situations in which they have to perform more adaptive T-OWB due to the changing nature of many organisational contexts forced through an increase in globalisation, technological advances and knowledge-intensive jobs (Hulin 1991).

One important assumption needs to be addressed explicitly, however, in relation to T-OWB at this stage. Even though plausible and logical in itself, the question remains if there really is such a strong link between T-OWB exhibited by employees and overall organisational goal attainment. In other words, what is the evidence that T-OWB actually predicts and positively affects organisational goal attainment? There is some empirical evidence that T-OWB contributes positively towards overall organisational functioning and performance. For instance, Gratton et al (1999) provide both qualitative and quantitative evidence based on a selection of US and UK organisations that a close link between employee T-OWB and overall organisational performance (as measured by organisational profitability and growth rates among others) in fact exists and that a focused and constantly adapted management of people potentially strengthens this link. In other words, the more aligned tasks and employees' exhibited work behaviours of a job (job alignment) are, the stronger the link between job performance and high levels of overall organisational performance (see also Boxall and Purcell 2003).

The underlying issue of the above-discussed considerations of T-OWB and the link to overall organisational goal attainment, however, refers to the factors that foster and increase individuals' engagement in such types of behaviour, given its importance for overall organisational goal attainment. This chapter distinguishes between three different organisational layers when analysing the triggers, or antecedents, of T-OWB, namely the individual level, the group level and the organisational level.

Individual-level antecedents of T-OWB

There is some empirical evidence that certain individual factors are associated with T-OWB. In other words, the extent to which individuals engage in T-OWB lies, to some degree, with the person as opposed to factors in their work environment. An individual's age, organisational tenure and the related idea of job experience have been investigated by organisational scholars in greater detail in terms of an existing connection to higher levels of T-OWB. This work fits into a wider attempt of countering the stereotype of the non-productive older worker. A meta-analysis presented by Sturman (2003) presents interesting findings in this respect. His study finds support that age, organisational tenure and job experience all exhibit an inverted u-shaped relationship with T-OWB (both measured by supervisors and by more objective task-based results). In other words, over time, individuals in fact seem to engage to a lesser extent in T-OWB. This, he qualifies, however, is more so in jobs that lack complexity such as simple manufacturing or service-related positions. For knowledge work and jobs with high complexity, job experience becomes a stronger predictor of T-OWB over time. As such, a certain degree of job experience is likely to positively influence individuals' levels of T-OWB. Here, the argument goes, an increase in experience counters physical abilities, which may decline over time, and compensates with more effective and efficient task strategies and better time management (Spector 2008).

The construct of general mental ability (GMA) has also been looked at in terms of a relationship between individual factors and T-OWB. GMA is defined by Jex and Britt (2008, pp111–112) as 'an individual's capacity to process and comprehend information'. Meta-analytical evidence presented by Schmidt and Hunter (2004) and further conceptual evidence presented by Motowidlo et al (1997) suggests that GMA is in fact positively associated with T-OWB. Overall, one's individual mental ability seems to predict, to some extent, T-OWB through the psychological mechanism of a more efficient and effective acquisition of job knowledge. In other words, one's GMA is directly linked to a rapid attainment of knowledge and skills that are required for a particular task, and these are directly related to overall higher levels of T-OWB.

There is also evidence that certain personality traits positively affect individuals' T-OWB. For instance, Stewart (1999) provides empirical evidence that conscientious individuals, or people who are generally dependable, responsible and achievement-oriented, tend to display higher levels of T-OWB both when they were newly hired and after considerable organisational tenure. In other studies, Barrick et al (1993) and Barrick et al (2002) provide empirical evidence that conscientiousness is positively related to salespeoples' T-OWB. This, the authors argue, is explained by a heightened desire for accomplishment and status-striving of conscientious individuals, and the capacity to set realistic goals and stay committed to them over time. Further, meta-analytic evidence presented by Hurtz and Donovan (2000) suggests that there is a moderate positive relationship between conscientiousness and T-OWB, which is stable across different occupations and jobs. It is important to note at this point, however, that conscientiousness is one of the few personality types that is moderately associated with T-OWB across different jobs and occupations in a timely stable manner. Other, more narrowly defined personality traits such as one's ability to influence other people or a strong work orientation have stronger effects on T-OWB contingent upon the type of task and job at hand. In other words, the more relevant the respective personality trait for the job, the stronger the positive association between that trait and the level of T-OWB (for empirical evidence see Tett et al 2003).

Group-level antecedents of T-OWB

There are, in addition to the individual-level antecedents presented above, group-level antecedents that are associated with T-OWB. Group-level antecedents are factors to do with organisational groups such as one's department or immediate work group. The Hawthorne studies conducted by Mayo (1933) and colleagues were one of the first systematic studies that looked at groups in organisations. Mayo (1933) found that workers restricted other workers on the assembly line from working too fast or too slow. This was done through a number of different visual, verbal and physical influencing tactics. Based on this early evidence, one can argue that group norms or expected behaviours and beliefs directly influence individuals' engagement in T-OWB, either positively or negatively.

Even though the literature does not provide abundant conceptual and empirical support for the role of co-worker support and T-OWB, one may nonetheless argue that the ability and willingness of co-workers to support and assist others in job tasks is related to overall T-OWB. In other words, some tasks occasionally require the help of others and this may be an important antecedent of actually exhibiting high levels of T-OWB.

Organisational-level antecedents of T-OWB

There are also predictors of T-OWB at the organisational level. For instance, the job-related information employees receive from their organisation and their immediate organisational agents is associated with high levels of T-OWB. This is linked to Campbell et al's (1993) notion of declarative knowledge and the extent to which employees have all the relevant information they need in order to perform a set of tasks. Organisations can increase levels of such knowledge through managers and supervisors, peers, company rules and policies, learning and development initiatives and job-related induction programmes.

The tools, machinery and equipment employees have at their disposal are also of crucial importance for high levels of T-OWB (Peters and O'Connor 1980). For instance, a plumber needs to have all the tools required for changing sinks and toilets while being at the client's site and these tools need to be up to standard and reasonably well maintained as this otherwise inhibits the plumber from fully engaging into the core parts of the job. As such, organisations need to constantly assess both the suitability and the state of tools, machinery and equipment in operation.

This is directly linked to the materials and supplies needed in order to exhibit T-OWB. Peters and O'Connor (1980) argue that a lack of materials and supplies can prevent employees from engaging in tasks of a job and, if missing or available insufficiently only, reduces levels of T-OWB. Therefore, organisations should incorporate an assessment of materials and supplies needed for a job into ongoing job analyses.

Other factors that influence T-OWB proposed by Peters and O'Connor (1980) refer to sufficient budgetary support, which is required to carry out an assigned job – this includes financial resources for things such as travelling or off-the-job training – and necessary help and support from organisational agents in order to carry out the tasks as required.

Finally, there is some evidence that incentive and reward schemes can have a positive effect on T-OWB, especially on performance quantity (Spector 2008). Often, organisations try to reward specifically for behaviours and outcomes that are highly desirable from their point of view – salespeople receiving a commission for the number of sales closed is one such example. Despite the argument that rewards and incentives can increase the outcome produced by employees (but not necessarily the quality), they are not necessarily a universally successful tool to increase levels of T-OWB. For instance, Yukl and Latham (1975) argue that incentives do not instinctively work universally among different groups of individuals when tested in a laboratory setting and in an industrial setting, and Coch and French, Jr (1948) document how peer pressure within work groups can undermine the effects of incentives and rewards.

Context-oriented work behaviour

The second type of functional work behaviour differs from T-OWB in the sense that it is not directly related to behaviours and actions exhibited within the scope of one's job. Context-oriented work behaviour (C-OWB) – sometimes also referred to as organisational citizenship behaviour, contextual performance, pro-social organisational behaviour or extra-role behaviour – has been defined by Organ et al (2006, p3) as 'individual behaviour that is discretionary, not directly or explicitly recognized by the formal reward system, and in the aggregate promotes the efficient and effective functioning of the organization'. There are many different ways in which employees can exhibit C-OWB. For instance, a bricklayer who helps a colleague to fix a door into a doorframe even though this is not part of their role on the construction site, a lorry driver who assists a colleague to establish the quickest route to a location driving around a traffic jam they have just been stuck in, or a tax accountant who develops a new and improved way of handling tax requests of clients, are all activities commonly referred to as C-OWB. These are activities that are not necessarily officially part of one's job, yet in the aggregate help the organisation to achieve its goals. This concept has been subject to substantive quantitative and qualitative research in the organisational sciences and much is known about the different types of C-OWB today. For instance, Podsakoff et al (2000) identified almost 30 different dimensions and forms of C-OWB and LePine et al (2002) detected over 40 measures of behaviour that organisational scientists have referred to as C-OWB. The main dimensions or common themes of C-OWB are helping behaviour, sportsmanship, organisational loyalty, organisational compliance, individual initiative, civic virtue and self-development (for a detailed discussion on dimensions of C-OWB, see Organ et al 2006).

One important issue needs to be addressed at this point, however. If there are so many ways in which employees' engagement in C-OWB is conceivable, what is the link to overall organisational goal attainment? In other words, does C-OWB actually impact on the overall performance of an organisation? There is sound conceptual and empirical evidence that suggests that C-OWB in fact contributes positively to the quantity and quality of work group productivity, sales performance, profitability and operating efficiency, among other things. For instance, Podsakoff et al (1997) provide empirical evidence that helping behaviour in a US-based paper mill positively affects both the quantity and quality of outcomes and that sportsmanship has a positive effect on the quantity produced. Other studies confirm these results and link a variety of C-OWB dimensions to other organisational performance indicators (see for instance meta-analytical evidence provided by Podsakoff et al 2009). Consequently, there is a real business case as to why organisations need to better understand the reasons individuals engage in C-OWB.

Individual-level antecedents of C-OWB

Many studies tried to establish a connection between certain personality traits and C-OWB in the belief that one's willingness to engage in organisationally desired discretionary behaviour lies with a person as opposed to the context. A number of meta-analyses and extensive research projects, however, found only a moderate relationship between merely one broad personality trait and C-OWB. Organ and Ryan (1995) among others argue that conscientiousness is only moderately associated with C-OWB across a number of samples of different organisations and contexts. This is surprising as one might intuitively predict that some people are just more likely to go beyond their normal job requirements than others do. However, antecedents originating in the work context are seen as stronger predictors for C-OWB than personality traits are (Organ et al 2006). This, to some extent, is good news for organisations as they henceforth can amend and change the work conditions and context in order to elicit higher levels of C-OWB.

Group-level antecedents of C-OWB

One way of influencing the work context and conditions is to make amendments at the group level of an organisation. There is evidence that, for instance, the degree of group cohesiveness or group members' individual liking and affinity towards each other and the adherence to group norms are associated with higher levels of C-OWB, especially those directed towards other group members (Podsakoff et al 1996). This is because a heightened degree of liking influences one's willingness to help out when needed (helping behaviour), a strong desire to remain a group member, which is more likely if others value the contribution made to the group (individual initiative), an adherence to what is accepted within a work group and exhibited consequent behaviour (organisational compliance), and a shared group identity, which increases the chances to defend and promote the organisation to outsiders (organisational loyalty and civic virtue) – all constitute elements of C-OWB. Bommer et al (2003), for instance, provide empirical evidence that the degree to which work group members exhibit C-OWB is linked to C-OWB through some of these processes. As such, in the attempt to foster C-OWB, organisations could try to develop work group norms receptive to C-OWB and increase levels of group cohesiveness through the introduction of overall work group goals, fairness of rewards between group members, stable group memberships and a heightened opportunity to interact with each other (Huczynski and Buchanan 2007).

There is also conceptual and empirical evidence that work group support and positive interactions and relationships with other group members (often captured in the concept of team-member exchange) are associated with higher levels of C-OWB (Organ et al 2006). For instance, Chiaburu and Harrison (2008) provide meta-analytical evidence that team and group member support is linked to C-OWB, both directed at the organisation and certain individuals within the organisation. This suggests that organisations should seek to assist employees in developing positive and meaningful relationships with other group members in order to increase overall levels of C-OWB. This could be achieved through team-building exercises, group socialisation efforts, proactive management of dealing with conflict and increased levels of mutual respect and appreciation in a work group, among others.

Organisational-level antecedents of C-OWB

There are also a number of C-OWB antecedents that are best explained at the organisational level of analysis. The organisational task characteristics of a job, for instance, predict one's willingness to engage in C-OWB. In their meta-analysis, Podsakoff et al (1996) find empirical evidence that task feedback, or the information one receives on task performance and task variety, or the degree to which routine tasks need to be carried out in a job, are related to various forms of C-OWB. Further, the degree to which individuals have the opportunity to engage in C-OWB and task interdependencies between individuals and groups are likely to positively predict C-OWB. This, the argument goes, is due to a heightened sense of co-operation norms in work settings with high task interdependencies, a felt ownership and responsibility for the task and the subsequent willingness to 'get the work done somehow' even though it falls outside a job description, and a perceived greater worthiness of jobs with such characteristics and from there derived job satisfaction, which in turn predicts C-OWB (Organ et al 2006). Based on these empirical findings, consequently, organisations could seek to redesign their jobs and work practices and increase levels of feedback, variety and task interdependencies when seeking to increase levels of C-OWB.

Organisational justice perceptions, or the extent to which an individual feels treated fairly by the organisation in terms of outcomes, procedures and interactions with organisational actors, are another important set of antecedents of C-OWB. Conceptual and empirical evidence provided by Conlon et al (2005), Fassina et al (2008) and Lavelle et al (2009) suggests that perceived fair treatment is often reciprocated by employees with an engagement in C-OWB. Further, Ertürk (2007) and Karriker and Williams (2009) suggest that these relationships are mediated by trust and positive perceptions of interactions and relationships with supervisors and other organisational agents, highlighting the crucial role of individuals located higher up in the organisational hierarchy. In other words, organisations need to implement fair reward and incentive schemes, transparent and just procedures concerning all areas of human resource management, and train organisational actors in managerial positions in the significance and rules of organisational justice in order to increase levels of C-OWB. In fact, studies by Skarlicki and Latham (1996; 1997) suggest that training in organisational justice is likely to increase levels of justice perceptions, which in turn increase levels of C-OWB.

DYSFUNCTIONAL WORK BEHAVIOUR

Having presented the notion of functional work behaviour and its two main elements, T-OWB and C-OWB, and a significant even though not exhaustive range of antecedents on different organisational levels, this chapter now moves on to discuss the organisationally undesired side of job performance, here referred to as dysfunctional work behaviour. Dysfunctional work behaviour can be defined as a set of employee behaviours exhibited inside and outside the workplace that contributes negatively to the attainment of organisational goals and objectives. Dysfunctional work behaviour consists of both counterproductive work behaviour (CWB) and withdrawal work behaviour (WWB).

Counterproductive work behaviour

Here, CWB is defined as 'motivated behaviour by an employee or group of employees that has negative consequences for an individual within the organization, a group of individuals within the organization, and/or the organization itself' (Griffin et al 1998, p67). In other words, CWB is behaviour exhibited by individuals within organisations that intentionally harms other organisational actors or the organisation as a whole. The CWB literature suggests a number of different labels for this type of behaviour, such as organisational misbehaviour, workplace deviance, anti-social behaviour or organisational retaliatory behaviour, among others. A classical typology of CWB proposed by Robinson and Bennett (1995) and further conceptually substantiated by Vardi and Weitz (2004) includes interpersonal CWB, referring to behaviours such as violence and aggression, discrimination, bullying and sexual harassment. Production-oriented CWB, on the other hand, refers to wasting resources, intentionally working slow and social loafing. The third type of CWB refers to property-oriented CWB, which is concerned with issues such as theft, sabotage and vandalism, and industrial espionage. Finally, political CWB constitutes favouritism, impression management, blaming colleagues for errors and the misuse of organisational power. There are, henceforth, a number of different types of CWB in which employees may engage.

It is difficult to exactly establish a figure for the financial burden CWB causes organisations. There is, however, some evidence on property-oriented CWB that has been investigated both by academics and professional organisations. For instance, Bamfield (2008) and colleagues from the Centre for Retail Research in Nottingham argue that shrinkage (typically used as a label for theft in organisations) only created by employees accumulated to costs of £17,464 million across 32 countries in North America, the Asia-Pacific and Europe in 2008. This excluded other shrinkages caused by customers and vendors and does not entail costs for prevention means, such as security staff. Given the existence of other types of CWB and their conceivable impact on organisational financial performance, CWB is a real problem and causes significant financial and functional burdens on many organisations. Various theories as to why CWB occurs help explain the prevalence of such organisationally undesired behaviour exhibited by individuals.

Individual-level antecedents of CWB

A number of personality factors have been found to be associated with greater levels of individual engagement in CWB. For instance, Fox and Spector (1999) provide empirical evidence that trait anger and trait anxiety are predictors of CWB. In other words, individuals who tend to constantly react angrily and furiously towards events happening in their social environment and who are chronically anxious tend to engage more frequently in CWB. This, Fox and Spector (1999) argue, is partly explained by the mediating force of affective responses such as low job satisfaction levels and greater frustration at work for individuals scoring high on these traits.

In another study, Raelin (1986) provides empirical support that age, across different professions and disciplines, is negatively related to CWB. In other words, as employees get older, they tend to be less likely to engage in CWB. There is an interesting parallel here with the aforementioned stereotype of the older non-productive worker and how this argument is not fully scientifically substantiated.

Group-level antecedents of CWB

In addition to predictors of CWB found on the individual level of analysis in organisations, group-level antecedents also help explain why individuals engage in such organisationally undesired behaviour. This is mainly explained through social information processing theory (see for instance Bouckenooghe et al 2006) and social learning theory (Bandura 1977). Social information processing theory suggests that individuals acquire and use information from their immediate social environment in order to make sense of events around them. Based on this sense-making process, individuals develop appropriate attitudes and an understanding of expectations within that social context. They further tend to exhibit behaviour that is in line with the formerly acquired knowledge, information and expectations of others. As such, the social environment, according to this theory, explains a great deal of individual behaviour. This is, to some extent, linked to social learning theory. Social learning theory argues that individuals identify role models in their immediate social environment and, through a number of different processes, seek to adopt and copy the behaviour exhibited by such role models. Transferring this line of reasoning to organisations, other colleagues and workmates form one's immediate social environment in an organisation and henceforth individuals seek to make sense of such environments and are likely to seek role models in such contexts. If the role models exhibit CWB themselves, individuals are more likely to copy and exhibit such behaviour over time. Robinson and O'Leary-Kelly (1998) conducted an empirical study in order to shed light on the likelihood of these processes in organisations with respect to CWB. They found, based on a varied sample, that individual levels of CWB are positively associated with levels of CWB exhibited by others in one's work group. In other words, the extent to which co-workers engage in CWB is directly associated with individual levels of CWB.

Organisational-level antecedents of CWB

There are also a number of antecedents that can be discussed at the organisational level of analysis. For instance, organisational task characteristics such as autonomy, variety and challenges may help to explain the occurrence of CWB. Vardi and Weitz (2004) suggest that most jobs allow for some scope to engage in many of the above-outlined different types of CWB. Jobs with less autonomy and task variety, however, are often more strictly controlled by internal and external agencies or by technology and henceforth CWB may be less frequently encountered there. Overall, however, higher skill variety and challenging tasks are in fact solid predictors of lower levels of CWB. For instance, an empirical study by Raelin (1986) finds strong support that a certain degree of job variety and challenging tasks negatively predicts CWB across different professions and disciplines. As such, the way jobs are designed seems to play an important role in explaining the occurrence of CWB.

The concept of organisational justice has also been studied with regard to CWB. A significant body of research suggests that individuals tend to reciprocate for unfair treatment with an increase in CWB. For instance, Skarlicki and Folger

(1997) provide evidence that different types of organisational justice predict CWB based on an individual's desire to retaliate for unfair treatment. More recent research by Jones (2009) confirms these findings and further argues that individuals, out of a revenge motive, direct their CWB towards either the organisation or individuals within the organisation, depending upon the respective source of perceived injustice. Yang and Diefendorff's (2009) findings extend this line of reasoning even further and provide empirical evidence that interpersonal mistreatment and unfairness experienced from customers creates heightened negative emotions and that individuals henceforth engage in CWB, possibly as a relief function for the perceived unfairness.

There is also some evidence that control and disciplinary systems are related to CWB (Vardi and Weitz 2004). To be more precise, Fox and Spector (1999) provide empirical evidence that an individual's perception of not getting punishment after deliberately harming the organisation is strongly linked to CWB. Further, Robinson and O'Leary-Kelly (1998) report empirical findings that potential punishment and sanctions from management reduce individuals' engagement in CWB caused by group dynamics inclined to such behaviour. These findings provide the basis for a strong case that tight employee control and disciplinary systems can, to some extent, reduce employees' engagement in CWB.

Withdrawal work behaviour

As opposed to CWB, which is commonly seen as behaviour that intentionally harms the organisation or hinders organisational goal attainment, WWB can be seen as types of employee behaviour that allow individuals to escape psychologically or physically from their work environment (Colquitt et al 2009). In other words, it is organisationally undesired work behaviour that is displayed by employees who appear disengaged and disenchanted in their jobs. Such behaviour is often due to unfavourable work contexts and conditions. Research suggests that there are four main types of WWB individuals may engage in as a response to such unfavourable work contexts (Farrell 1983). Individuals may either leave the organisation and seek organisational membership elsewhere or put up with the situation and display a certain degree of loyalty. Alternatively, they may increase their voice in the organisation and try to change things or react in a negative way and disengage and withdraw their psychological stake in the organisation.

All of these behaviours are seen as problematic and widely undesirable for organisations as they are associated with an increase in costs of recruitment, selection and induction for new employees, lower job performance and greater levels of fatigue in organisations (Spector 2008). Despite the wide acknowledgement of potential detriments of WWB, it remains a problem in many industrial societies. For instance, MacLeod and Clarke (2009) draw together evidence from a wide-ranging selection of UK organisations and argue, based on a recent CIPD report presented by Truss et al (2006), that only three in ten UK employees were actively engaged in their jobs. Other figures suggest that almost half of all employee working time is used up for late starts and early departures, long coffee breaks and personal matters, among others (Colquitt et al

2009). This, arguably, is however highly dependent on the types of jobs and other factors, which are discussed below. Quintessentially, WWB is a costly, undesired yet frequently encountered type of behaviour in many organisations (Furnham and Taylor 2004).

Individual-level antecedents of WWB

Some of the most important individual antecedents of WWB have been highlighted with regard to absenteeism and lateness. For instance, Farrell and Stamm (1988) provide meta-analytical evidence that employees' absence history is one of the strongest absence predictors, and Koslowsky (2000) and Iverson and Deery (2001) argue that job dissatisfaction is likely to trigger employee lateness, early departure from work and absenteeism.

Family responsibilities have also been studied with regard to WWB. Here, a number of scholars found that primary responsibilities for childcare predicted absenteeism and lateness (Spector 2008). As such, childcare facilities and flexible working hours could be introduced by organisations in order to remedy this trigger of WWB.

It is also conceivable that certain personality types are associated with WWB. For instance, Type B personalities are associated with a number of traits centred on relaxation, such as a general lack of urgency, a low focus on achievement and the ability and desire to enjoy leisure (Chamorro-Premuzic 2007). Arguably, individuals with such personality traits may be less inclined to exhibit loyalty and as such easily switch into a neglect mode. Type A personalities, characterised by ambition, impatience and a general sense of urgency, on the other hand, would arguably be more likely to try and change the work context and engage in voice activities (Huczynski and Buchanan 2007). There is, overall, only limited empirical evidence on personality traits and their impact on WWB. One study by Iverson and Deery (2001), however, argues that positive affectivity or one's natural propensity to see things in a positive way is positively related to tardiness and negatively to absenteeism. Employees' early departure from work is additionally predicted by positive as well as negative affectivity in their study.

Group-level antecedents of WWB

There are also a number of potential WWB antecedents operating at the group level in organisations. The argument that job dissatisfaction is a likely predictor of various types of WWB has been raised above already (Iverson and Deery 2001). Arguably, employees' personal relationships with each other may play an important role in determining levels of job dissatisfaction and WWB explained at the group level. For example, employees who dislike their colleagues and find it hard to relate to them are likely to take particularly long breaks away from the organisation, miss meetings, come late and leave early and are likely to be absent on a number of occasions.

Further, perceived interpersonal aggression, sexual harassment and abuse from work group members has the potential to act as a predictor of WWB as well. Here, WWB is defined as a psychological or physical escape from the organisation. Assuming that an immediate work colleague abuses and harasses another employee, heightened levels of WWB may well operate as an escape and relief function for that employee (Paetzold 2004). As such, the relationship with colleagues and within work groups can be seen as a key trigger of WWB on the group level of analysis.

One can additionally speculate that group cohesiveness is related towards WWB. When group members like each other and have affective and meaningful mutual relationships, WWB such as tardiness and absenteeism should be less likely to occur, as employees would want to spend time with other colleagues. Conversely, a lack of cohesiveness in a work group may operate as an antecedent of WWB as individuals may not feel the desire to totally commit to the work group.

Organisational-level antecedents of WWB

Finally, a number of organisational-level antecedents of WWB have been identified by organisational scholars. Potentially the most crucial factor refers to organisational task characteristics of a job. Jobs that lack skill variety, autonomy, task identity and significance, and feedback on job performance, based on Hackman et al's (1975) job characteristics model, are likely to result in high levels of WWB such as absenteeism, lateness and excessive socialising, among others.

Justice perceptions held by employees have also been linked to WWB. For instance, Iverson and Deery (2001) provide empirical evidence that distributive justice perceptions, or the extent to which individuals feel resources are distributed fairly in an organisation, are negatively associated with employee tardiness. This, arguably, may be because employees reciprocate for fair distributive treatment with coming to work on time.

Absence and lateness cultures are also seen as important organisational-level antecedents of WWB. For instance, conceptual evidence by Nicholson and Johns (1985) suggests that there are different types of absence cultures in organisations. Empirical evidence presented by Iverson and Deery (2001) confirms the existence of such absence cultures and suggests that their occurrence is positively associated with early departure from work. Further, absence permissiveness or the extent to which management lets people 'get away' with not coming to work is also positively associated with tardiness and early departure from work. As such, strict absence and lateness policies and guidelines may remedy these triggers of WWB.

A MULTIFACETED CONCEPTUALISATION OF JOB PERFORMANCE IN ORGANISATIONS

The chapter has discussed and highlighted two different types of work behaviour that constitute overall job performance, namely functional and dysfunctional work behaviour. Both types of behaviour consist of two subcategories that predict overall levels of the respective type of work behaviour. T-OWB and C-OWB are types of functional work behaviour that relate positively towards overall job performance. CWB and WWB, on the other hand, are types of dysfunctional work behaviour that contribute negatively towards overall job performance. Figure 10.1 depicts the relationships between these concepts. Further, as discussed above, Figure 10.1 also argues that the link between employees' overall job performance and organisational performance is contingent upon the degree to which a job is aligned with the aims and objectives of the organisation. In other words, even exceptionally high job performances of employees may not necessarily contribute significantly towards overall organisational goal attainment if the jobs are not in line with what the organisation seeks to achieve as a whole (Boxall and Purcell 2003). As such, ongoing job evaluations and assessments are needed to constantly adjust and improve the alignment of jobs in organisations.

Figure 10.1 Multifaceted conceptualisation of job performance

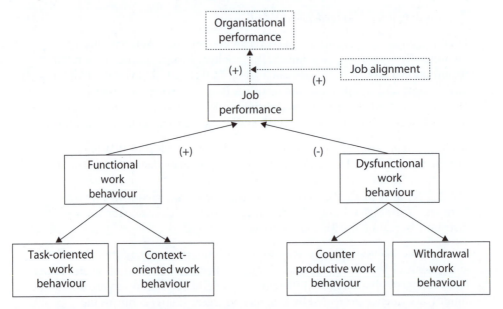

CONCLUSION

This chapter offers a fresh and comprehensive multifaceted conceptualisation of job performance based on the suggestion that job performance should be seen as employee behaviours, actions and activities as opposed to mere job-related outcomes. It further argues that job performance consists of both functional work behaviour and dysfunctional work behaviour, each comprising different types of more concrete behaviours that relate either positively (such as T-OWB and C-OWB) or negatively (such as CWB and WWB) to overall job performance in organisations. A selection of the most prominent triggers of either facet of functional and dysfunctional work behaviour was presented and structured around individual-, group- and organisational-level antecedents.

HRM IN THE MEDIA

CRITICAL REFLECTIONS

In relation to the first question, the employee, if he did deliberately contaminate the food, could be said to have exhibited dysfunctional work behaviour in that his intentions were motivated by a desire to inflict damage to the organisation's reputation. This type of behaviour can be categorised, according to the literature presented in this chapter, as property-oriented counterproductive work behaviour (CWB). This type of behaviour is associated with issues such as theft, vandalism and industrial sabotage.

Relating to the second question, it is very important for the organisation to have internal communication processes regarding matters such as this one. It is the organisation's responsibility to effectively communicate acceptable practices to employees. For example, in this case, the organisation would need to have clarified the consequences of having inappropriate decorations in employees' offices. Furthermore, disciplinary procedures should be made clear and always followed. In this case, although an informal chat took place, no formal disciplinary procedure was followed. Perhaps if the employee was clear about the expectations of the organisation and, moreover, if the organisation had followed appropriate disciplinary procedures, the situation could have been avoided. However, one must also note that in some cases where even communication of issues effectively takes place in an organisation, employees do decide to act in their own ways. It is then the organisation's responsibility to deal with such actions appropriately.

EXPLORE FURTHER

FURNHAM, A. and TAYLOR, J. (2004) *The dark side of behaviour at work: understanding and avoiding employees leaving, thieving and deceiving.* Basingstoke: Palgrave Macmillan.

This book provides an overview of CWB and WWB in organisations and suggests ways of measuring and minimising such types of behaviour.

LIEVENS, F., CONWAY, J.M. and DE CORTE, W. (2008) The relative importance of task, citizenship and counterproductive performance to job performance ratings: do rater source and team-based culture matter? *Journal of Occupational and Organizational Psychology.* Vol 81. pp11–27.

This journal article sheds light on potential rater biases in the assessment of T-OWB, C-OWB and CWB in organisational life and discusses the main implications for performance management appraisal systems.

MOTOWIDLO, S.J. and VAN SCOTTER, J.R. (1994) Evidence that task performance should be distinguished from contextual performance. *Journal of Applied Psychology.* Vol 79. pp475–480.

This journal article provides empirical evidence that both task performance, or T-OWB, and contextual performance, or C-OWB, are two distinct elements of job performance and that both have unique antecedents and triggers.

ORGAN, D.W., PODSAKOFF, P.M. and MACKENZIE, S.B. (2006) *Organizational citizenship behaviour: its nature, antecedents, and consequences*. Thousand Oaks, CA: Sage Publications.

This book summarises the concept of organisational citizenship behaviour, or C-OWB, and discusses its different conceptualisations, antecedents, outcomes and measurement issues for both researchers and practitioners.

VARDI, Y. and WEITZ, E. (2004) *Misbehavior in organizations: theory, research, and management*. Mahwah, NJ: Lawrence Erlbaum Associates.

This book provides a detailed overview of misbehaviour, or CWB and WWB, in organisational life based on a levels-of-analysis framework.

CHAPTER 11

Critical Issues in People Resourcing (2): The Dilemmas with Outsourcing and Offshoring

Rea Prouska

OVERVIEW

This chapter explores outsourcing and offshoring strategies as a means of resourcing the organisation. Definitions of outsourcing and offshoring will be explored and the rationale for and against such strategies will be examined. Although such strategies are often justified on short-run cost benefits, the discussion will raise issues relating to the long-term implications associated with, among other things, declining employer-funded training, skills losses, and reduction of organisational and national competitiveness. The discussion will use current examples of HR outsourcing and offshoring and explore their impact on the UK economy.

LEARNING OBJECTIVES

Reading this chapter will enable the reader to:

- critically examine the meaning of outsourcing and offshoring
- critically evaluate the rationale for outsourcing and offshoring decisions
- critically analyse the potential implications of outsourcing and offshoring decisions
- critically analyse the complexities of managing HR when outsourcing and offshoring is taking place.

'FEARS FOR JOBS AT BISCUIT COMPANY'

In 2009 fears for jobs was reported at United Biscuits, a well-known biscuit company producing brands such as McVitie's and Jacob's biscuits. The company announced plans to move 125 jobs from its Liverpool factory to India as part of a restructuring programme. The planned move involved work in the administrative and financial department of the company. Overall, approximately 750 people were employed at the Liverpool site. Union leaders called for talks with the company's management based on the argument that since the firm had made healthy profits the previous year, staff should be rewarded, not threatened with redundancy. A management official commented that no decisions had yet been made about the restructuring programme while the union official assured employees of the Liverpool factory that they would do everything in their power to ensure that these jobs were not offshored (BBC News 2009).

Questions

1 What HR processes are involved in 'offshoring' jobs to India?

2 What reasons does United Biscuits have to offshore these jobs?

3 What grounds does the union have in objecting to this plan?

4 How would you advise on the relative benefits and risks of offshoring?

INTRODUCTION

The opening case study illustrates the practice of offshoring jobs to a foreign location. Offshoring is considered by many a special form of outsourcing, a concept that is far from new. In the late 1930s, Coase (1937) was one of the first academics to consider the question of why firms adopted their chosen structure and to discuss the boundaries of the firm. Coase's (1937) insights were not taken up until the 1970s, when the transaction cost economics school emerged, an important figure of which was Williamson (1975). According to this school of thought, the decision as to whether to provide goods and services internally or to outsource rests upon the relative costs of production and transaction. In other words, if the cost of supplying the goods or services internally is greater than the cost of managing the outsourcing relationship, then an outsourcing strategy should be used.

Organisations started implementing outsourcing strategies in the late 1980s and early 1990s, when the 'core competency' model started gaining ground (Lonsdale and Cox 2000). One of the most influential people in the development of this model was Tom Peters (Peters and Waterman 1982), while later on in the decade the work of Prahalad and Hamel (1990) greatly influenced this approach. Their work on 'the core competence of the organisation' developed an inside–out corporate strategy model that starts the strategy process by focusing on the core strengths of an organisation, instead of using an outside–in approach focusing on the market, the competition and the customer as a starting point. In other words, by analysing their business processes and identifying which ones are core (strategic) and which non-core (non-strategic), organisations could decide to outsource the non-core ones while focusing on the core ones that contribute to their competitive advantage. From that point on, organisations started outsourcing various business processes, for example information technology, financial planning, housing benefits services, human resources, road transport, maintenance, standard production equipment and semi-/non-skilled labouring work (Cooke 2001a).

Overall, three main factors influenced the gradually increasing use of outsourcing by organisations since the 1970s (Corbett 2004). Firstly, the continuous increase in the number and capabilities of outsourcing service providers made them superior in service provision than any internal service provision process. Secondly, the constant change of technology made internal technology investments a high-risk path, compared with buying provider services, which were considered a lower-risk path. Thirdly, competitive pressures placed on organisations drove them towards the buy decision, that is, in order for an organisation to continue to perform an activity internally, it must be better at it than its direct competitors *and* the best outsourcing providers its competitors can hire. Especially in the 1990s, the fast advancement in information technology and the rapid growth of the Internet was the leading factor that caused a huge increase in business process outsourcing (BPO).

Offshoring is also not a new concept. Firms in industrial nations such as the USA, UK and Germany have offshored many operations since the Second World War, for example steel, shipbuilding, automobiles, manufacturing, textiles and apparel, consumer electronics, tool making, and others (Carmel and Tjia 2005). However, there is currently a new turn in offshoring of services (Carmel and Tjia 2005), for example IT functions (for example software development) or IT-enabled business services (for example call centres, back-office processing) (Atkinson 2004). Trade liberalisations have made it possible to move many information processing and business service jobs offshore to low-wage, but increasingly higher-skilled, countries (Atkinson 2004), for example India and China. Offshoring is also feasible because of technological advancements, for example due to the growth of the Internet, the benefits of digital storage and the exchange of information quickly, cheaply and securely (Skipper 2006).

But what exactly is meant by 'outsourcing' and 'offshoring'? Are these two concepts similar or different, and in what ways? Even today, there is great debate surrounding the definitions of outsourcing and offshoring. The following discussion provides a range of definitions to illustrate the complexity of these terms and explains the commonalities and differences between these two concepts.

DEFINING OUTSOURCING AND OFFSHORING

OUTSOURCING DEFINITIONS

The definitions supplied in the literature for the concept of outsourcing, in its traditional form, tend to be similar to one another. They all describe a make or buy decision (Woodall et al 2002) by using a different angle in defining this concept. For example, Domberger (1998, p12) defines outsourcing as the 'process whereby activities traditionally carried out internally are contracted out to external providers'. Or, in other words, it is 'the practice of handing over the planning, management and operation of certain functions to an independent third party' (Rothery and Robertson 1995, p4). This is done, as Hesketh (2005, p21) puts it, by a 'complete redesign of organisational processes and structures to achieve profound cultural change in your people so they can fulfil the strategic mission of your organisation'. Other definitions of outsourcing include, 'the transfer of whole activities to external control' (Reilly and Tamkin 1996, cited in Woodall et al 2002, p50), 'long term contractual relations for business services from an external provider' (Lever 1997, p37), and 'the use of external agents to perform one or more specific functions of importance to a business' (Maul and Krauss 1996, cited in Woodall et al 2002, p50).

The definition of outsourcing is further complicated by the various other terms that have evolved over the years for more specialised cases of outsourcing, but basically come down to describe what we can generally term 'outsourcing'. Such terms include subcontracting, contracting-out, flexible staffing, employee leasing, professional services, contract programming, facilities management, contract manufacturing and contract services (Johnson 1997). For example, contracting-out describes the situation where 'one organisation contracts with another for the provision of a particular good or service... in the private sector, contracting-out is a common and growing phenomenon and is sometimes referred to as "outsourcing"' (Ascher 1987, p7). Summing up from the above discussion, we can create a broad definition of outsourcing as follows: outsourcing is a process by which an internal activity, operation or function is handed over to an external provider.

OFFSHORING DEFINITIONS

Outsourcing can occur within the country where the organisation is located, otherwise called 'domestic outsourcing', or abroad, otherwise called 'outsourcing abroad' or 'offshoring' (OECD 2007). Or, as Hunter (2006, p2) puts it, offshoring can be defined as 'the act of transferring some of a company's recurring internal activities to outside providers who are located in a different country and market economy, under a formal service contract. As is a matter of common practice in outsourcing generally, both the activities and the factors of production (people, facilities, equipment, and technology) and decision rights over how certain processes are performed are often transferred to the new provider.' This practice of partial or total transfer of the production of goods or services to a non-affiliated enterprise is often termed 'offshore outsourcing' (OECD 2007). However, it might be the case that the production of goods or services is partially or totally transferred abroad within the same group of enterprises (that is, the organisation's foreign affiliates), termed 'offshore in-house sourcing' (OECD 2007). In other words, organisations are faced with the decision of whether to produce their products or services internally domestically (domestic in-house production), externally domestically (domestic outsourcing), internally abroad (offshore in-house), or externally abroad (offshore outsourcing) (OECD 2007).

From the above discussion, it is clear that the concepts of outsourcing and offshoring are far from clear, due to the variety of definitions provided in the literature used to describe the various forms of outsourcing and offshoring. However, the difference between the two is nicely captured by Catchpowle et al (2007, p29): 'Outsourcing…refers to the transfer of operations from internal provision to purchase from an external party. In contrast, offshoring represents the transfer of operations to another country regardless of whether it remains provided within the corporation or not.' But why would an organisation decide to outsource/offshore or not a business activity? The next two sections elaborate on the rationales for and against outsourcing and offshoring decisions.

RATIONALE FOR OUTSOURCING

There are various reasons for which organisations decide to outsource one or more of their business activities and these reasons can be divided into strategic and operational reasons.

The flexibility rationale

Outsourcing can be considered as a response to organisations' need for flexibility. Especially during the 1990s, when outsourcing particularly gained ground, the constantly increasing competitiveness on national and global levels, the continuous advancements of technology, and the changes in labour demand and supply were all contributing factors to the increasing need for flexibility. Organisations started implementing strategies, such as flattening and downsizing, business process re-engineering, subcontracting and outsourcing, in an attempt to address these issues and to create flexible firms able to rapidly adapt to changes in the external environment (Volberda 1998). The theory of 'the flexible firm' was introduced by Atkinson and others (Atkinson 1984; Atkinson and Meager 1986; NEDO 1986) in the 1980s and provides a framework for understanding the strategy of outsourcing.

Atkinson's research suggested that there are three kinds of organisational flexibility: functional, numerical and financial (Atkinson 1984, p28). Functional flexibility refers to quickly redeploying employees between activities. Numerical flexibility refers to quickly increasing or decreasing the number of employees as needed. Financial flexibility refers to the ability of firms to easily adjust pay and other employment costs in order to reflect the supply and demand in the external labour market and to shift to new pay and remuneration systems that facilitate either numerical or functional flexibility.

Atkinson (1984) argues that the workforce can be divided into two basic groups: core workers and peripheral workers (see Figure 11.1). Core workers conduct the organisation's key activities and offer functional flexibility to the firm. Peripheral workers offer numerical flexibility to the firm and are divided into the first and second peripheral groups. The first peripheral group is characterised by full-time employees enjoying a lower level of job security and performing 'plug-in' rather than key activities. These jobs are less skilled, while training required is little to none. If the numerical flexibility offered to the organisation by the first peripheral group needs to be supplemented by functional flexibility, then a second peripheral group can be distinguished. This group is characterised by subcontracted staff, self-employed workers, temporary staff, staff on short-term contracts, part-time staff or staff that are job-sharing, all of which are performing

Figure 11.1 The flexible firm (Atkinson 1984, p29)

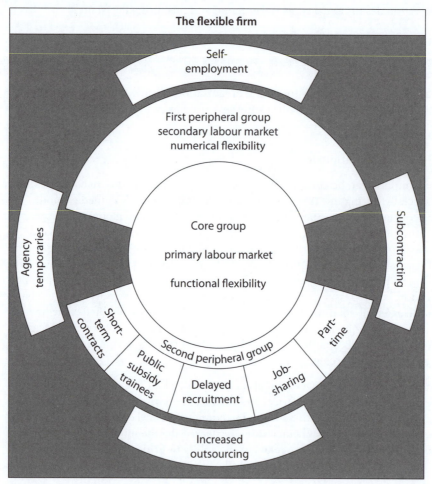

activities that are either very specialised or very mundane. These readily available human resources maximise organisational flexibility while minimising the firm's commitment to offer job security, pay prospects and career development to employed staff.

Outsourcing can, therefore, lead to increased organisational flexibility, enabling the firm to cover fluctuations in labour demand (Davis-Blake and Uzzi 1993; Cooke 2001b; Conklin 2005), as well as fluctuations in production demand (Nooteboom 1999; Greene 2000; Jennings 2002). In the first case, organisations facing fluctuations in labour demand use outsourcing as a way to gain access to external sources of skills. These skills can readily be acquired when the organisation has a need for them and quickly be disposed when they are not needed any more (Carroll et al 2002). In the second case, outsourcing gives firms the opportunity to overcome constraints of their own production capacity in meeting product demand fluctuations and can therefore enable organisations to adapt their products and services to changing business conditions (Oates 1998; Nooteboom 1999).

Other strategic rationales

On the strategic side, there are several other reasons for outsourcing further to increase organisational flexibility. Organisations may outsource activities or functions in order to focus on core competencies (Quinn et al 1990; Oates 1998; Carroll et al 2002; Jennings 2002; Conklin 2005). There is also the possibility for an organisation to outsource in order to learn the latest techniques and then bring them back internally without having to invest money in learning these techniques on its own. This is also referred to as capacity-building associated with organisational learning (Osland and Yaprak 1995; Carroll et al 2002) since outsourcing is a form of strategic alliance or organisational network. As two firms (organisation and contractor) work together, learning and knowledge can be transferred across organisational boundaries (Rubery et al 2002).

Furthermore, outsourcing can help an organisation transfer the risk from the business to the supplier, as for example in cases of investment in new technologies and experimentation with new techniques. Business risks can also be reduced, since the experts hired can anticipate problems and handle them before they develop (Curson 1986; NEDO 1986; Domberger 1998; Das and Teng 2001; Bachmann 2003). However, in cases where the outsourced activity is, or comprises part of, a strategic function, increased risk may be involved, since the organisation is now lacking internal control over critical resources (Nooteboom 1999; Das and Teng 2001; Zineldin and Bredenlow 2003).

OPERATIONAL RATIONALES

From an operational point of view, one reason for outsourcing is the possibility for cost reduction, although this point is highly disputed in the outsourcing literature. Cost is considered under different aspects while evaluating outsourcing decisions and this fact is what makes this point complex in its analysis.

Outsourcing user firms may be able to achieve economies of scale (Davis-Blake and Uzzi 1993; Nooteboom 1999; Greene 2000; Carroll et al 2002). Externalising work or labour has been widely reported as being cost-effective (for example Davis-Blake and Uzzi 1993; Lonsdale and Cox 1997; Greene 2000) in that it reduces many types of employment and administrative costs. Employment costs are reduced, since externalisation does not require the organisations to pay for direct employment costs (Greene 2000), such as health insurance costs, employer-funded pension plans, or unemployment insurance, as well as some other employee-related costs originating from employment legislation and rights such as leave (special leave, parental leave, work-related injury leave), dismissal complexities and risk and liability (as for example in cases of occupational injuries). Health insurance costs, costs relating to employer-funded pension plans and unemployment insurance costs are also reduced by the use of externalised workers (Davis-Blake and Uzzi 1993). Administrative costs are also reduced, since the supplier is responsible for managing their own work and training for skills, thus making the firm responsible for only few administrative resources in the daily management of employees (Davis-Blake and Uzzi 1993; Greene 2000). In addition, Carroll et al (2002, p329) argue that this 'just-in-time' deployment of human resources also brings other advantages of saving direct cost (for example reducing headcount and overtime working) and indirect cost (for example cutting administration and backup cost, saving recruitment and training costs, saving absence cost, and reduced industrial relations problems). Linking to the abovementioned point is the advantage of paying lower wages (Carroll et al 2002), in that even though independent contractors may be paid at a higher rate than employees, they do not represent an ongoing cost, since 'wages' are replaced with contractor 'fees' (Greene 2000). In addition, another advantage of outsourcing is the predictability of contractual performance, while organisations also have the flexibility to change contractors or contracts and may also be able to reduce future costs by 'selecting the most competitive tender for renewing the contract' (Carroll et al 2002, p329).

Furthermore, outsourcing enables organisations to have access to external expertise (Conklin 2005). In many cases, organisational downsizing has been responsible for loss in expertise that can only be regained through the use of service providers. Through outsourcing, organisations can gain access to external expertise (Carroll et al 2002; Oates 1998), being able to 'profit from the rising comparative advantage of specialised service providers who may have expertise in the areas concerned' (Carroll et al 2002, p329). For example, organisations can gain access to technology without having to purchase or continuously upgrade this technology, thus avoiding risk of technological or skill obsolescence (Conklin 2005). Access to expertise may also mean that organisations can gain access to superior quality for the particular component they are outsourcing (Jennings 2002).

Another advantage of outsourcing is the efficiency in the use of resources by the contractor (Greene 2000). Contractors are more likely to tender more for their own resources (that is, vehicles, machinery, tools, and so on) in comparison with how an employee would treat organisational resources. In addition, a 'reduction of capital tied up in plant and equipment' (Greene 2000, p189) may be achieved in cases where contractors do not work on the organisation's premises using its resources, but work on their own premises using their own equipment.

The use of independent contractors may also minimise or lead to avoidance of resistance from trade unions (Pfeffer and Baron 1988; Reilly and Tamkin 1996; Greene 2000). In general, trade unions respond differently to the use of independent contractors. Although some trade unions may resist the use of contractors (Davis-Blake and Uzzi 1993), others may see it as a way to secure core employees within the organisation (Greene 2000).

The above discussion summarises the main reasons for which an organisation might decide to outsource business activities or functions. The following section will explore the possible drawbacks of such a decision.

CHALLENGES AND LIMITATIONS OF OUTSOURCING

It was argued earlier in this chapter that outsourcing can lead to increased organisational flexibility, enabling the firm to cover fluctuations in labour demand (for example Davis-Blake and Uzzi 1993; Cooke 2001b) by using outsourcing as a way to gain access to external sources of skills. However, it might be the case that an organisation is incapable of maintaining the continuity of skill supply through its outsourcing agreement (Carroll et al 2002). Skills and knowledge are argued by Porter (1990) to be key factors in creating and sustaining competitive advantage. Outsourcing can decrease the levels of in-house skills, since the skills needed are acquired by the service provider (Cooke 2001a). In addition, many firms outsource in order to reduce training costs, assuming that training for key skills will be carried out by the contractor. However, the levels of training that the provider undertakes to upgrade these skills are questionable. This poses questions on the quality of services provided. It is well known that service providers, as independent business entities, are mostly interested in making a profit, thus not really investing in training for acquiring new skills or upgrading existing skills (Cooke 2001a). Since the organisation is not tendering for these skills (this is the reason for hiring the provider), and the provider is not investing in training to acquire or upgrade skills, exactly how the organisation will achieve organisational competitiveness remains questionable. However, Cooke (2001a) argues that outsourcing may not be an ill-judged strategy, but greater risks may be incurred when it is deployed as a cheap substitute for investment in building in-house skills, where skill plays an important role in production activities.

Furthermore, Nooteboom argues that outsourcing can increase the cost of assets, since firms can produce them more cheaply internally due to scale, scope and experience. Competencies may be undermined as suppliers may not have the technical, or other, competence needed for handling the firm's resources, while at the same time, the use of suppliers may increase the risk of spill-over of a firm's core competencies to its competitors, thus jeopardising its competitive advantage. Nooteboom also argues that a firm's positional advantage may be undermined by its increased dependence on the supplier, making the organisation vulnerable to interruptions of production, quality, availability and risk of 'hold-up', as well as making a firm unable to maintain its competencies in order to have the possibility for entry into novel markets.

Another drawback of outsourcing is the potential loss of quality (Carroll et al 2002), due to 'lower standards of quality control, inferior technology and engineering/craft skills' (Carroll et al 2002, p30), which are often found to be major causes for the poor quality of products produced by contracting firms. Jennings (2002) also notes that, since quality depends on the supplier's expertise and the way the outsourced component is handled, firms may experience a decrease in quality, leading to a need to redevelop the activity in-house.

This point is further connected to the lack of control over the product or service, quality standards, performance or standards monitoring, and skill levels required (Greene 2000). The issue of control links to the employer–contractor relationship and is a function between relative bargaining power and dependence between the two parties. Greene (2000, p191) argues that, 'the employer is likely to be able to exert more control over an independent contractor when market forces are in the employer's favour, and/or the contractor is dependent on that employer'. However, in cases where the employer is dependent upon a contractor for a product or service, then the contractor can exert more power over the employer. In both cases, this unbalanced relationship of power and control between the two parties is seen as a drawback of outsourcing (Greene 2000).

Further to this, there may also be issues with the strategic alignment between the outsourcing and corporate strategies. Contractors may require information on the corporate and HR strategies in order to design the service provision and this may lead to confidentiality issues. Moreover, differences between the contractor and organisation in management styles and corporate cultures may result in such a non-alignment of strategies.

In addition, Oates (1998) evaluates the outsourcing decision in respect to the transfer of knowledge between the employer and the contractor. Employees working in an organisation have accumulated knowledge on the specific activity, thus a first point for concern relates to the time needed for the contractor to acquire this knowledge. The second issue concerns the adaptation period needed when a contractual relationship begins. Especially in cases of an employer–contractor culture gap, an adaptation period is needed for the cultural characteristics to be absorbed by both parties (Oates 1998; Khatri and Budhwar 2001). A final issue in the outsourcing relationship concerns the number of contractors used by an organisation. In cases where an organisation uses multiple outsourcing providers, issues arise on the way it will manage relationships between all parties involved. Particularly in cases where the independent contractors are working in the same project, the organisation is faced with difficulties of co-operation and trust between the parties.

Another important area of concern is the impact of outsourcing decisions on employees (Greene 2000). Outsourcing may lead to job insecurity, lower motivation and reduced employee commitment, resulting in decreased productivity and performance (Davis-Blake and Uzzi 1993; Greene 2000). The effect an outsourcing decision might have on employees depends on various factors, such as the type of outsourced activity or function, the extent of outsourcing, and the place where the contractors will work (that is, within the organisation or on their own premises) (Greene 2000). A common result of outsourcing is employee job insecurity, which is caused by the presence of subcontractors or service providers (Cooke 2001a). Studies have shown that job insecurity is related to poorer physical and mental health (that is, psychosomatic complaints, depression), lower job satisfaction and organisational commitment (for example Hartley et al 1991; Nelson et al 1995; Kennedy et al 2002), and decreased motivation and morale (Burchell et al 1999). Another case for consideration concerns the possibility of employees willingly leaving the organisation while an outsourcing initiative takes place. Valued employees may decide to leave the organisation once an outsourcing initiative has been put in effect, as their roles are redefined and the organisation is realigned. Kennedy et al's research (2002) on the influence of outsourcing on job satisfaction and turnover intentions of technical managers suggests that outsourcing negatively affected the employees' job satisfaction and subsequently negatively influenced turnover intentions. Regardless of the negative impact that outsourcing might have on employees, some organisations consider independent contractors as a disciplinary tool for employees (Pfeffer and Baron 1988; Davis-Blake and

Table 11.1 Reasons for and against outsourcing

Reasons for outsourcing	
Strategic rationales • increase organisational flexibility • focus on core competencies • cross-organisational learning • transfer risk to the supplier • reduce business risks	*Operational rationales* • cost reduction • access to external expertise • efficiency in the use of resources by the contractor • minimise resistance from trade unions
Reasons against outsourcing	
• increased risk in case of strategic activity • lack of control over internal resources • inability to maintain continuity of skill supply • increased cost of assets • undermined competencies • jeopardising organisational competitive advantage • increased dependence on the supplier • potential loss of quality • lack of control over the product/service • time needed for the contractor to acquire organisational knowledge • long adaptation period when a contractual relationship begins • issues in managing multiple contractors • impact on employees	

Uzzi 1993), or as a tool for direct threat in order to force cost reduction and productivity improvement (O'Connell-Davidson 1991).

This section has explored the rationale for and against outsourcing and the main discussion points are summarised in Table 11.1. The next section looks into the rationale for offshoring.

RATIONALE FOR OFFSHORING

Although it is quite difficult to exactly measure the extent of offshoring projects (Catchpowle et al 2007), the most well-known ones are the banking sector's offshore IT and call-centre activities (for example HSBC, JP Morgan, Aviva), the utilities sector's offshore customer billing and service contact work (for example Thames Water), as well as offshoring projects in the pharmaceutical sector (for example GlaxoSmithKline), and retail sector (for example Sainsbury's, Tesco, Lastminute.com, Thomas Cook). But why do these organisations decide to offshore work to foreign locations?

The reasons that organisations decide to offshore vary depending on the business sector and the form of offshoring. However, a primary reason for offshoring concerns the reduction of costs. This includes, firstly, labour costs (the difference between wages and benefits of comparably qualified employees in developed and developing countries) (Skipper 2006; Brewster et al 2007; OECD 2007). For example, Indian graduates are prepared to work for salaries that are 80% lower than those of their Western counterparts (Dowling et al 2008). And secondly, costs involved in the production process are lower, for example financial, management, advertising, communication, transportation costs, and so on (Skipper 2006; Brewster et al 2007; OECD 2007).

Another indirect benefit of offshoring is that employees from the home country affected by the offshoring decision can be re-employed in higher-value jobs (Brewster et al 2007). As Atkinson (2004) argues, if jobs lost to offshoring are low-wage, low-skill, the country can benefit as laid-off workers can move up to higher-wage, higher-skilled jobs, especially if they receive training and support. However, such an outcome can only be achieved if the home country is close to full employment, if most of the offshored jobs are not higher-wage, higher-skill jobs, and if the country moves up the ladder to higher value-added work. But if this is not the case, offshoring can threaten particular groups of workers, or entire communities (Atkinson 2004). It may also reduce a country's competitiveness in particular fields. For example, in the case of the US, the offshoring of service jobs has led to the movement of a significant number of high-tech, IT and other research and development and engineering positions to developing nations (Skipper 2006). This movement has weakened the US's position as a 'world leader' in technological innovation.

Other reasons for offshoring include proximity to clients, improved productivity, accessing a foreign market, improving service quality, reducing the process cycle, avoiding capacity constraints, extending the scope of services, strengthening an existing affiliate, accessing technology and infrastructure, and increasing focus on core competencies (Brewster et al 2007; OECD 2007).

Further to the above reasons for which an organisation might decide to offshore work to a foreign location, there are several other reasons against such a decision. The next section explores these reasons.

CHALLENGES AND LIMITATIONS OF OFFSHORING

One of the main concerns relating to the negative implications of offshoring is its effect on the economy, particularly employment. In the case of the UK, offshoring jobs to a variety of destinations, with India and China being two major ones, may affect the total number of jobs in the UK since many jobs will be moved to a foreign location (Abramovsky et al 2004). It may also affect the type of jobs available in the UK, the skills needed to do these jobs and the distribution of these jobs across regions and across people (Abramovsky et al 2004). The type and composition of the offshore labour market also has the potential to change the demand for skills and thus the relative market position of the UK labour (Catchpowle et al 2007). For example, if UK companies offshore highly skilled technical work (for example work performed by research and development professionals), the country as a whole will be left with lower-skilled technological jobs. This will have implications not only for the type of skills required to do these jobs, but will also raise questions relating to what types of jobs the employees who used to be employed in those highly skilled technological jobs (but who are now left unemployed) will perform.

The use of information and communication technologies (ICT) is especially associated with new patterns of job creation and loss (Catchpowle et al 2007). For example, such technologies automate old occupations (for example telephone switchboard operators) and at the same time create new occupations (for example call-centre workers). This has positive implications for developing countries as new jobs are created, while at the same time negative implications for developed nations who are observing massive moves of jobs to offshore locations.

Furthermore, according to Atkinson (2004), offshoring can worsen the erosion of middle-class jobs. Jobs that pay middle-class wages (for example manufacturing jobs and information-based services) are growing more slowly than higher-paid 'knowledge' jobs at the top and lower-paid 'service' jobs at the bottom. Therefore, if the jobs offshored are mostly the ones performed by middle-class workers, then such offshoring can be the source of a middle-class job squeeze.

Another concern relates to the uncertainty over the outsourcer's ability to ensure the appropriate quality and performance of labour (Catchpowle et al 2007). Organisations need to evaluate the effectiveness and productivity of the foreign labour in relation to the UK labour in order to ensure quality of the product or service. However, some main problems that often occur with the use of foreign labour relate to the flexibility and speed of service delivery due to language, time difference, cultural subtleties, and the level of face-to-face interaction (Catchpowle et al 2007).

Offshoring also has major implications for the employment relationship, especially the relationship to trade unions, which are now pushing for greater protection for local labour markets (Catchpowle et al 2007). For example, in the UK the union Connect obtained an agreement with BT to protect staff whose jobs were outsourced by promising voluntary redundancies and redeployment (Catchpowle et al 2007), and the union Amicus-Unifi negotiated an offshoring agreement with Barclays to protect affected staff by helping them find new work by giving them three months' advance notice and three months' paid leave (Pitt 2005).

Other shortcomings include a loss of organisational control over its business and its immediate access to expertise due to the geographical distance, inadequate quality of goods and services supplied (which can have serious consequences especially in the case of defective spare parts in transport or in the case of medicines not complying with health regulations), higher costs than anticipated (for example quality control costs, transport costs, and so on), failure to meet delivery times on the supplier's part, failure to respect intellectual property in

Table 11.2 Reasons for and against offshoring

Reasons for offshoring	
<ul><li>reduce labour costs</li><li>re-employ employees from the home country affected by offshoring in higher-value jobs</li><li>proximity to clients</li><li>improve productivity</li><li>access a foreign market</li><li>improve service quality</li><li>reduce process cycle</li><li>avoid capacity constraints</li><li>extend scope of services</li></ul>	<ul><li>strengthen an existing affiliate</li><li>access technology and infrastructure</li><li>increase focus on core competencies</li><li>can create new occupations (especially through the use of information and communication technologies)</li></ul>
Reasons against offshoring	
<ul><li>negative effect on home country's employment</li><li>affect types of jobs available, skills needed to perform these jobs and the distribution of these jobs across regions and across people</li><li>affect demand for skills and thus the relative market position of the home country's labour</li><li>can threaten particular groups of workers or entire communities</li><li>can reduce a country's competitiveness in particular fields</li><li>can lead to job loss (especially through the use of information and communication technologies)</li><li>can worsen the erosion of middle-class jobs</li><li>uncertainty over the outsourcer's ability to ensure quality and performance of labour</li><li>can cause tensions in the employment relationship as trade unions push for greater protection of local labour markets</li></ul>	<ul><li>loss of organisational control over the business and access to expertise due to geographical distance</li><li>inadequate quality of goods/ services supplied</li><li>increased transaction costs</li><li>failure to meet delivery times on the supplier's part</li><li>failure to respect intellectual property in the foreign location</li><li>inability to adapt to technological change</li><li>difficulties in managing communication issues between the home enterprise and foreign location</li></ul>

the foreign location (which exposes organisations to the risk of being copied and of experiencing unfair competition), inability to adapt to technological change (which assumes that the local workforce in the country of relocation are skilled and able to meet the changes), and difficulties in managing communication issues between the home enterprise and foreign location due to language and cultural differences (Catchpowle et al 2007; OECD 2007).

This section has explored the main reasons for and against offshoring business activities (see Table 11.2). The next section concludes this chapter.

CONCLUSION

This chapter has raised several issues surrounding the concepts of outsourcing and offshoring. Firstly, the definition of these two concepts is not as clear as one might expect. Outsourcing describes a make or buy decision, or, in other words, a process by which an internal activity, operation or function is handed over to an external provider, although the variety of terms used make this concept more complicated to understand. Some say that offshoring is a form of outsourcing, while others say that it is a completely different concept. This chapter has distinguished between outsourcing (the transfer of operations from internal provision to purchase from an external party) and offshoring (the transfer of operations to another country) and has further acknowledged the variety of terms used to describe the concept of offshoring (for example domestic outsourcing, outsourcing abroad, offshore outsourcing, and offshore in-house sourcing). In addition, it has explored the various options with which organisations are faced when deciding to produce their products or services (for example internally domestically [domestic in-house production], externally domestically [domestic outsourcing], internally abroad [offshore in-house], or externally abroad [offshore outsourcing]).

Secondly, there are many and conflicting rationales for and against outsourcing and offshoring. Some main strategic and operational reasons for outsourcing include increased organisational flexibility, cost reduction, focus on core competencies, cross-organisational learning, transfer of risk from the business to the supplier, access to external expertise, efficiency in the use of resources by the contractor, and avoidance of resistance from trade unions. However, many of these points are debatable. For example, it was argued that outsourcing increases organisational flexibility. The theory of 'the flexible firm' that this chapter explored provides a framework for understanding the strategy of outsourcing under which it can enable the firm to cover fluctuations in labour and production demand. Specifically in the first case, outsourcing can be used as a way to gain access to external sources of skills which can readily be acquired and disposed according to the organisation's needs. However, this raises concerns about the continuity of skill supply in the organisation and how this will affect the quality of services provided and the overall competitiveness of the business. It was also argued that outsourcing can lead to cost reductions. This is another point heavily debated in the outsourcing literature, since cost is considered under different aspects (for example employment costs, administrative costs, and so on) and hence makes an evaluation highly complex. In addition, many argue that outsourcing can increase the cost of assets, since firms can produce them more cheaply internally due to scale, scope and experience.

Some of the reasons for which organisations decide to offshore business activities include cost reduction (for example labour costs, production costs), and re-employment of home country employees into higher-skilled occupations. However, these points are also highly debatable. Labour and production costs do increase in time and favoured offshoring destinations will be replaced by new destinations. In addition, if jobs lost to offshoring are higher-wage, higher-skill jobs, and the country does not move up the ladder to higher value-added work, it can result in serious implications for the labour market in the home country. Further to the points above, the chapter explored many reasons that make offshoring not an attractive option, as, for example, it can lead to loss of organisational control over the business and immediate access to expertise due to the geographical distance, inadequate quality of goods and services, inability to adapt to technological change, and difficulties in managing communication issues.

HRM IN THE MEDIA

CRITICAL REFLECTIONS

The mini case study presented at the beginning of this chapter raises the question of whether United Biscuits should offshore the administrative and financial department jobs to India and what the possible implications of such an action would be. In this case, offshoring these jobs to India would mean a closure of the current department and, consequently, job losses.

United Biscuits could have been considering this offshoring option for various reasons, but the most likely reason was to take advantage of the relatively low cost and high availability of skilled administrative labour in India. The union's objections are based solely on the basis of protecting existing and future jobs. Offshoring decisions result in job losses and the HR function will be left, effectively, with the scenario of managing redundancies: the new offshored services will invariably be considered a supplier with little or no HR input. This could have negative implications: it could lead to skill loss, reduced service quality and thereby jeopardise competitive advantage. In addition, it would reduce the remaining employees' job security, motivation, commitment, and this could affect productivity and performance. Furthermore, given that it is not uncommon for problems to occur in managing the relationship of the new provider of administrative and financial services, United Biscuits needs to also consider the possibility of having to in-source back these jobs and the cost that this will incur. Furthermore, United Biscuits might not be able to revert this procedure easily, given that by offshoring jobs and closing down the relevant internal department means that the organisation will no longer have the expertise, skills and knowledge to perform the activities of this department.

This chapter has highlighted the main rationales for and against offshoring (see Table 11.2). However, the course of action that United Biscuits should take is not so clear. Management should carefully consider the pros and cons of such an offshoring decision and evaluate possible courses of action against their short- and long-term gains or losses. It is certain, however, that given the dissatisfaction already caused among its employees, United Biscuits should plan a clear communication and consultation strategy with the union in place.

EXPLORE FURTHER

GUPTA, A. (2008) *Outsourcing and offshoring of professional services: business optimization in a global economy.* US: Information Science Reference.

This book discusses the considerations and implications surrounding the outsourcing and offshoring of professional services, such as software development, computer-aided design and healthcare, from multiple global perspectives.

LAWLER, E.E., ULRICH, D., FITZ-ENZ, J. and MADDEN, J.C. (2004) *Human resources business process outsourcing: transforming how HR gets its work done.* San Francisco: Jossey-Bass.

This book focuses on new approaches organisations can take to improve HR administration and to best organise HR functions.

OSHRI, I., KOTLARSKY, J. and WILLCOCKS, L.P. (2009) *The handbook of global outsourcing and offshoring.* Basingstoke: Palgrave Macmillan.

This book offers a broad perspective on various issues relating to the sourcing of systems and business processes in a national and global context.

The Outsourcing Institute—Gateway to the Outsourcing Marketplace, available online at www.outsourcing.com

This website provides a resource tool for outsourcing information, consulting and networking opportunities.

WINKLER, D. (2009) *Services offshoring and its impact on the labour market.* Germany: Physica-Verlag Heidelberg.

Focusing on the case of Germany, this book shows how services offshoring has grown, who is most affected and what policy-makers can do.

PERMISSIONS

'The Flexible Firm' diagram, p29 in ATKINSON, J. (1984) Manpower strategies for flexible organisations. *Personnel Management.* August. pp28–31. CIPD Publishing. Permission granted on 14 August 2009.

Critical Issues in Employee Relations (1): From Employee Consent to Employee Engagement

Susie Leigh and Ian Roper

OVERVIEW

This chapter examines the perplexing problem organisations face when trying to 'manage' employees into being proactively engaged in the activities of their employer. In the past it has been said that the means by which employees' loyalties have been sought was distinguished by two opposing approaches: the first being the view that employees should be assumed to be naturally loyal and that opposing competing employee loyalties (particularly unions) would ensure engagement; the second being that employees should be assumed to naturally hold competing loyalties (particularly to a union) and that engagement would be best achieved by management engaging with these competing interests to achieve optimum outcomes. More recently the emphasis on employee engagement has shifted. The decline in the influence of unions has led to, on the one hand, a questioning of the relevance of engaging with unions and, on the other hand, a realisation that the absence of a union does not seem to lead to a more loyal workforce. With this in mind, a consideration of some more recent attempts to explain employee engagement is undertaken, ranging from concepts such as the 'psychological contract' and 'employee engagement' to 'organisational citizenship behaviour' and a renewed interest in the broad issue of 'trust'.

LEARNING OBJECTIVES

Reading this chapter will enable the reader to:

- critically compare and contrast the assumptions behind 'unitarist' and 'pluralist' views of the employment relationship

- critically evaluate the advantages and disadvantages of the decollectivisation of employment relations

- critically evaluate the extent to which employee engagement may be able to enhance the employment relationship in an increasingly individualised employment relationship.

HRM IN THE MEDIA

'CABIN CREW SACKED FOR POSTING COMMENTS ABOUT CUSTOMERS ON A SOCIAL NETWORKING WEBSITE'

In October 2008 it was reported that 13 cabin crew working for Virgin Atlantic were sacked for posting comments about customers onto a social networking website (BBC News 31 October 2008). Disciplinary action was taken against the staff after it was revealed that they had posted comments referring to passengers as 'chavs'. It was also alleged that they also made comments about the condition of the aircraft that they were working on.

Similar issues had been reported in recent years: similarly disruptive comments were posted by ex-workers of phone directory company 'the Number' in 2007 (*Guardian* 2007) and in 2009 a young woman was sacked for commenting that she thought her job 'boring' (BBC News 27 February 2009).

This form of 'disloyalty' using new social networking media is relatively new, and in some ways the common story here may seem to apply to the use of new technology as a form of employee 'resistance'. However, while this is an important aspect of these stories, the technology merely provided the means of expression for acts of employee discontent and a new form by which this form of 'voice' is being expressed. It could be that all these employees were pathologically disruptive. However, there is also the possibility that it may indicate gaps in management–employee relations that have led to a feeling of disenfranchisement.

Questions

1 To what extent may the presence or lack of a union in the workplace make the management of such situations easier or more difficult for management?

2 In what ways could management engage with employees to reduce the likelihood of such situations arising in the future?

3 To what extent are such acts of employee disloyalty more common, less common or just 'different' now than they were in the past?

INTRODUCTION

The story above could be said to be a case of 'service sabotage' (Noon and Blyton 2007) whereby dissatisfied staff take out their frustrations about aspects of their work in a way that damages the reputation of the company they work for. Historically a common means for expressing discontent has been through formal collective mechanisms of employee voice – principally through a union. This could take the form of employee representatives negotiating changes to aspects of the working environment or – *in extremis* – through a 'temporary stoppage of work by a group of workers in order to express a grievance or to enforce a demand' (Griffin 1939, p20) – that is, a strike. In many ways, a strike, while clearly disruptive to an organisation, may be easier to resolve than less formal, more individualistic forms of dissent: a strike will inevitably end through some form of agreed terms (however begrudgingly on one side's point of view); and managers also have a focal point of whom they could talk to to reach any such resolution. When employees resort to unorganised, unmediated forms of conflict – such as the case above – there is no such source of resolving underlying causes, beyond firing the culprits. Such individualised and (usually) unorganised conflict is generally acknowledged to range from forms of sabotage (including new forms such as the social networking version mentioned above), absenteeism, high labour turnover and acts of petty theft. It can also include a range of behaviours more difficult to pin down and involves a lack of something, rather than a proactive action: a 'poor attitude', a lack of commitment. In differing circumstances this has been associated with coping strategies for situations at work: the actions of 'making out' and general misbehaviour associated with boring work (Ackroyd and Thompson 1999), and the more recently observed forms of resistance to the pressures of emotional stress in workplaces involving direct customer interaction – notably this has been identified in airline cabin crew (Hothschild 2003) and call centre work (Taylor et al 2002).

Clearly all of this is problematic for management. Indeed it can be linked to anxieties reported by employer lobby groups such as the Confederation of British Industry, which regularly reports that there are more days lost due to absence from work than days lost to strikes: in 2007, for example, it is claimed that 172 million days were lost to sickness absence at a cost of £13.2 billion (CBI 2008). More generally, there is a perception by some that business is afflicted by a tendency towards 'compensation culture' whereby employees are increasingly likely to take their employers to an employment tribunal, thereby seeking external legal intervention into their workplace grievances. Not all of this stands up to serious analysis. However, the perception is certainly there, and it does indicate that underlying problems remain in workplaces long after the root cause of what was termed Britain's 'industrial relations problem' was thought to have been solved.

The chapter is structured in two main parts. The first section provides a critical overview of the state of employee relations since 1979. It considers the broad situation in terms: (1) a summary of the developments leading up to 2010; (2) a snapshot of key indicators (levels and influence of unionisation broken down by organisational and demographic factors); and (3) the main employee relations challenges facing organisations when dealing with a more decollectivised employee relations environment. The second section provides an overview of recent developments in the notion of 'employee engagement', which arguably offers a solution to the problems identified in the first section.

UNITARISM, PLURALISM, COLLECTIVISM AND INDIVIDUALISM

Historically the management of employee (or employment or industrial) relations has concerned managing the relationship that exists between management and the representatives of employees – almost exclusively trade unions in the UK. In its heyday this focus was not only important for understanding the dynamics of employee behaviour with regard to the issue of 'procedural justice' – that is, the extent to which managers are able to establish 'the rules' within an organisation unilaterally and the extent to which it could be considered legitimate to involve employees via their representatives to participate in establishing rules – but also in the issues of 'distributive justice' – that is, the extent to which employee representatives participate in decisions affecting the distribution of the proceeds of the business: 'how do we share the spoils?' This inevitably meant that understanding the institutions and processes of employee relations was key to understanding the other key areas of HR practice: reward, resourcing, and learning and development. As a principle for understanding the basis of the dynamics existing between management and employees, in all organisational settings, this remains the case – a point clearly put by Blyton and Turnbull (2005) in their highly influential text on the subject and a point strongly made in a recent defence of the discipline (Darlington 2009).

Nevertheless, a cursory review of the trends in the basic institutions studied in employee relations shows that significant changes have occurred that could lead one to conclude that the traditional 'problem' of industrial relations has now gone. Let us reconsider what the traditional 'problem' of industrial relations in Britain was thought to be and what happened.

As is explained in Chapter 7, the incoming Thatcher Government of 1979 placed 'the union problem' at the centre of its strategy for improving business in general. As such the intention was to curb the ability of unions to challenge management in workplaces through a long list of regulatory restrictions to union activity and over the entire length of Conservative ascendency in government (1979–1997). Key restrictions here include: removing a union's right to statutory recognition by an employer where substantial membership existed; the significant curtailing of the ability to organise industrial action (that is, strikes); the restriction of a union's ability to set and enforce its own rules upon its members; and the removal of the ability of a union to make membership compulsory among workers in certain workplaces (the 'closed shop'). The intention of these measures was to aid in the creation of greater numerical and functional flexibility: that is, reducing union power increases management's ability to hire and fire (numerical flexibility) and to increase the scope and quantity of tasks performed by workers (functional flexibility). By definition, this series of government interventions was also a reform agenda seeking to shift the basis of employee relations from a pluralist outlook to a unitarist one.

The pluralist/unitarist typology of management orientation towards employee relations returns us to Alan Fox's classic typology (Fox 1966). Fox identified two basic types of management ideology in relation to their employees. The unitarist employer assumes that because employees join the organisation out of choice, they have thereby accepted the terms on which they entered. Authority, within the company, is derived exclusively from the management appointed by the owners. Employees are – given the right leadership – assumed to be basically loyal and committed to the unified entity of the business. Any cases of employees contesting management decisions are considered, by the unitarist, to be aberrant and caused by either pathological motives by an individual employee or by the influence of unwelcome 'third party' intervention offering alternative sources of loyalty. Preventing such problems from arising, under this view, requires careful recruitment and selection of employees – stopping potential 'trouble-makers' from gaining employment; appropriate and firm leadership; and resisting any attempts to introduce a 'third party' into the organisation. The 'third party' under this definition, is of course a trade union. This view is exemplified well by the following view from a chief executive who was commenting on proposals in 1998 to reintroduce statutory union recognition under the Employment Relations Act 1999: 'We pride ourselves on our ability to recruit, train and educate our staff to offer customers a higher quality of service. A third party that comes between employer and employee can only interfere with that and harm our drive for quality', (Clive Thompson, Chief Executive of Rentokil Initial, quoted in the *Observer* 31 May 1998).

In contrast to the unitarist view, the classical pluralist view asserts that legitimate conflicts of interest exist within the employment relationship – just as conflicts of interest exist in wider society. The principal basis for this conflict of interest lies in the employment relationship itself. If both parties are assumed to be 'rational', employers will require workers with appropriate abilities to do the maximum amount of work over a fixed period of time for the lowest level of wages that can be obtained when taking account of labour market conditions; for their part, employees require rewarding work for the highest pay possible. For the pluralist there will always be a potential gap between these sets of expectations and that because the power imbalance between any individual employee and their employer will be so great, employees will quite rationally seek to act collectively to enhance their bargaining position. Unions are therefore, for the pluralist, a quite legitimate manifestation of employee interests and, as such, 'good' management deals with employee relations through the process of collective bargaining: distributive and procedural justice are optimised and legitimised through the creation of formal mechanisms to allow unions and management to reach agreements (Walton and McKersie 1991).

UNION INFLUENCE ON HR IN THE UK: FROM HIGH WATERMARK TO STEEP DECLINE (1979–1998)

A number of writers have highlighted the scale and scope of the decline in union influence from its peak (in terms of public visibility) in the 1970s to the 2000s. It has led some to question the continued need for HR employee relations specialists to be preoccupied with union-related issues (Emmott 2006). As an indicator, the strike statistics for 2008 show that there were 758,900 days lost to strikes in the UK, involving 511,200 workers (Hale 2009, p27), a figure roughly in line with recent years. While at first sight this appears high – and indeed it is evidence that the strike will never fully disappear as a form of conflict in the workplace – it also looks low when compared with figures from previous periods: Blyton and Turnbull (2005, pp334–5) have derived averages from national statistics indicating that the average number of days lost to strikes per year in the period 1969–74 was nearly 13 million and in the period 1975–79 was over 11.5 million.

The story of the changing influence of unions in organisations in the UK is complex, but the basic facts are well known. At the end of the 1970s unions had record levels of membership and membership densities (union density being the more important figure as it indicates the proportion of union membership across the workforce as a whole). Union influence was further indicated by the high proportion of workplaces covered by collective agreements brokered by unions. From this high point, union density and membership declined year on year throughout the 1980s and 1990s: at the high point in 1980, unions were present in 73% of workplaces and had densities of 65% in 1998 (Millward et al 2000, pp85, 87), while in 1998 were present in only 54% of workplaces with densities of only 36%. With this decline came steep decline in union influence in their primary activity of collective bargaining: from being formally 'recognised' for the purposes of negotiating terms and conditions of employment in 64% of workplaces in 1980 to 42% in 1998 (Millward et al 2000, p96). The precise reasons for such a steep decline have been the focus of some debate over the years (see Kelly 1998; Pencavel 2004; Howell 2005). Regardless of the particular combinations of cause and effect on union decline during this period, the factors involved are known: the role of the state in restricting union activity during the Thatcher and Major governments (see Chapter 7), economic circumstances (particularly the disproportionate effects of recession and unemployment in the unionised sectors of the economy), changes to the labour market (particularly the growth of temporary, part-time and self-employed work), and the associated changes to organisational structures and mobility (outsourcing, offshoring and the influence of the 'flexible firm' model) (Pollert 1991). A final factor was, of course, unions' own inability to successfully adapt to the circumstances that they found themselves in – something that the Trades Union Congress began actively pursuing through its 'New Unionism' project in the late 1990s (Heery 2002).

UNION INFLUENCE ON HR IN 1998–2009

The picture between 1998 and 2009 was one of much greater stability. While some modest decline over the entire period did take place, it was not on the catastrophic scale seen in the previous period. In 2008 average union density in the UK was 27.4%, with membership at 6.9 million; 49.6% of employees worked in an establishment that had some form of union presence. There are differences between organisational types, however. The most obvious distinction is that larger organisations remain much more likely to have a union presence than small workplaces; that public sector workplaces remain much more likely to have a union presence than not; that the private services sector continues to have a very low union presence (for example only 5.3% density in hotels and catering). The most dramatic shift has been in the manufacturing sector, where union density fell from 68% in 1980 (Millward et al 2000) to just 20.4% in 2008 (Barratt 2009).

There are differences in individual characteristics of workers who are likely to be a union member, too. The traditional image of the average union member being a white older male in a semi-skilled manufacturing job have not held true for decades. It does remain true that the average union member is significantly older than the average worker – and this has been true for years. In 2008, while 29.2% of those in the 35–49 age group were union members, only 5.4% of those in the 16–24 age group were. Even counting for the fact that this age group is the one most likely to spend a high proportion in full-time education and training, the reasons for younger workers not joining unions are not simple to identify. It would be easy to suggest that union membership is merely not considered as 'relevant' for an aspiring 'Generation Y' cohort. It could also be claimed that younger workers are deterred from union membership through fear of the consequences of employer backlash. In neither case is there compelling evidence to back up such claims. Nevertheless, some differences in the structure of the labour market may explain some aspects of union membership among younger workers. For example, union membership rises consistently with the time spent in the same job (only 11% of those in post less than a year are union members compared with 56.3% of those in post more than 20 years). So age cohort may be less of an issue than job stability.

Apart from age, the other aspects of the 'pale, male and stale' stereotype no longer hold, however. In terms of the 'white' image of union membership, Black-British people were the most likely ethnic group to be union members in 2008 at 30.3%. As for the male image, there are now more female union members – in absolute terms – than male (29.2% of all women in the workforce compared with 25.6% for men).

Union membership is also now associated with higher skills and academic qualifications than their non-union counterparts. If these are combined it can be seen that the skills gap polarises among women more than men: thus while union membership among unskilled males is 20.8% and 26.6% of males with a degree qualification, only 17.2% of unskilled females are union members compared with 42.8% of females with a degree. Cross-comparing between gender and different types of work, some other striking differences emerge. For example, 57.8% of female professionals are union members compared with only 12.3% of males working in sales and customer services (Barratt 2009).

In terms of personal circumstances, permanent employees (28.1%) were more likely to be union members than temporary workers (16.8%); and of those using some form of flexible working hours – which one could have assumed some unanimity in aspiration – an astonishing 71% of full-time employees using term-time working arrangements were union members compared with only 9.1% using some form of home-working arrangements (Barratt 2009).

Overall, then, the relevance of union influence in the modern workplace can be seen to have diminished significantly from its pre-eminent position in the 1970s. But union presence in UK organisations remains significant and is likely to remain so. The final indication of this is to compare the UK experience internationally. It would not be seen as surprising to any student of international employment relations to discover that the UK's 28% average union membership is lower than in Scandinavian countries (for example, Sweden was 70.8% in 2007) and higher than in the US (11.6%). What does surprise some is to learn that the UK has higher union membership levels than Germany (19.9%) – where union influence has much greater institutional support – and significantly higher than in France (7.8%) – where the reputation of unions' capacity for mobilisation (strikes) is disproportionate to its 'official' membership.

THE UNITARIST DILEMMA: WITH WEAKENED UNIONS, WHY ARE EMPLOYEES STILL NOT LOYAL?

Despite all the above a significant fact remains the same: in most British workplaces, employee relations take place without the presence of a union. If, in the past, the dilemma for managers was trying to get local union representatives to match the agreements made at industry level, or to put it another way, to match the difference between the 'official' industrial relations system with that of the workplace-level reality, the dilemma now facing HR – particularly those who still seek the unitarist ideal of the loyal, committed and 'engaged' worker not being diverted by rival 'third party' loyalties – is: why are employees not more loyal? Arguably this is not entirely new. Certainly much work has been done in the past indicating that certain individualistic forms of 'misbehaviour at work' have been reported on going back some decades (Mars 1982; Ackroyd and Thompson 1999). Conversely, there are also signs that may indicate that individualised worker discontent may be positively associated with union membership (Kersley et al 2005). It is also true to say that, in practice, employees can hold multiple loyalties (employer, co-workers, profession) where a unitarism was the formal governing frame of reference.

Nevertheless, if commentaries by employer and management groups are true, rather than 'moral panic', there would appear to be 'a problem' associated with the decollectivised employee relations climate of the early twenty-first century that directly contradicts the ideology of unitarism. Part of this lies in the issue of conflict at work. It has long been argued that reducing the levels of strike activity by coercive means, that is, suppressing the union's ability to strike and/or suppressing the worker's ability to act collectively through a union, will displace, rather than reduce, underlying conflict (Edwards and Scullion 1984). Statistics on the number of employment tribunals lodged is a clear indication of this. During the 1970s the number of cases rose from under 20,000 per year to over 40,000 by 1980. From here, the figures rise further and reach over 100,000 by 1995. In Figure 12.1, the figures for the 2000s are presented, showing that the annual number seems doggedly fixed at this higher rate.

Figure 12.1 Employment tribunal cases accepted, 1998–2008

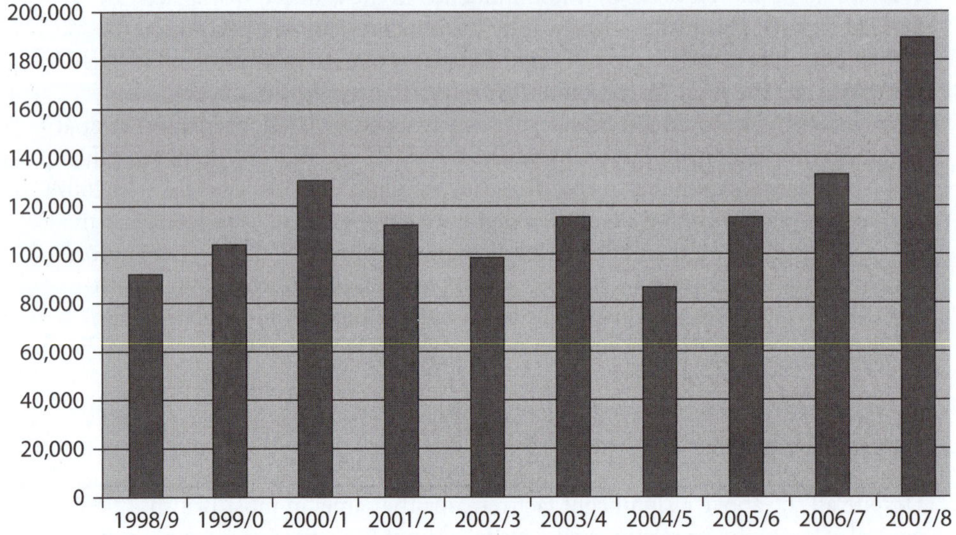

Source: derived from Employment Tribunal Service annual reports 1999–2009

Other measures of discontent also reflect this broad picture. It is interesting to note, for example, that problems that employers face, as reported in CIPD annual reports on absence and labour turnover. On absence, the annual average number of working days lost to absence per employee is reported as varying between 3.5 and 4.4 days per year, per employee between the years 2000 and 2008 (CIPD 2008a, p4). There are also differences between organisational types that are persistent. In general, higher absence is reported in public sector organisations than private. What is not clear is the extent to which this relates to more general employee relations climate and what is related to workplace conditions: are workplaces with high unionisation more tolerant of higher absence levels or are such workplaces – for example the NHS – inherently more prone to illness, injury and stress?

Turnover figures suggest an equal and opposite relationship to the absence figures. In a separate survey the CIPD reports that average labour turnover in the years 2004–08 ranges between 15.7% per year and 18.3% per year (CIPD 2008b, p20). Broken down by organisation type, turnover seems inversely proportionate to union influence: so while there was only a 6.4% annual (voluntary) turnover rate in transport, where union membership is relatively high, it was 30% in hotels and catering, where union membership is very low – see above (CIPD 2008 b, p21).

Arguably, this 'problem' is at least partly related to the very mechanisms by which employment relations were 'decollectivised' in the 1980s and 1990s. While the central thrust of management thinking and government policy during this period was to 'restore management's right to manage' (the unitarist principle), it did so not just with the variety of legislative restrictions (explained in Chapter 7) but also with the prevailing dominance of the ideology of individualism. Yet individualism, despite its antipathy to the collectivism associated with unions, is not compatible with unitarism. If, in the then prime minister's terms, 'there is no such thing as society', and if part of the ethos of the age was being self-reliant, rather than being dependent on the state or on the false protections offered by unions, then why would workers submit loyalty to the collective interests of their employer?

Of course, in reality it is not quite as straightforward as this. But something is going on here. In a report for the Government, Dix et al (2008) suggest that while individualised forms of conflict are not a direct substitute for collective forms, it does seem that the lower the opportunities for employee voice (for example via unions), the greater the incidence of employee 'exit' as a means of expressing discontent. Recent years have seen attention shift towards a more individualised approach to managing the employment relationship and, in particular, the focus on 'employee engagement'.

TOWARDS A NOTION OF EMPLOYEE ENGAGEMENT

The essence of the employment relationship is more complex than other exchange relationships. However, within the sub-discipline of industrial relations, the nature of the employment relationship has often been assumed to be reducible to 'the effort bargain' (Behrend 1957), that is, the implicitly or explicitly agreed amount of work done at the agreed wage. Beyond this elemental set of bilateral expectations, however, a range of other, less tangible expectations exist. Employers want highly competent employees who will do their best work going beyond the formal expectations of their contract. Equally, employees want good work: jobs that are interesting, secure, have a high degree of autonomy, good prospects for progression and pay well. Some of this (pay, working time) falls within the formal contract of employment. Other aspects ('attitude', 'job security', 'empowerment') are much more nebulous and subjective. With a more decollectivised employee relations climate, these come more to the fore and, as a result, there has been a growth in interest in the notion of the related concepts of the 'psychological contract' and its place in the notion of 'employee engagement'.

WHAT IS EMPLOYEE ENGAGEMENT?

There are a number of definitions of employee engagement. MacLeod and Clarke (2009) identify 56 different definitions in their comprehensive review. Most of the definitions include some references to 'organisational commitment' where employees buy into the values of their employer and demonstrate a willingness to go beyond the contractual requirements of their stated terms and conditions of employment. Examples include being helpful to colleagues, working effectively in teams and providing extra levels of customer service, and there are a number of cross-references to the notion of organisational citizenship (see Chapter 10). Engagement would seem to be more than job satisfaction or motivation. Whatever the exact definition, it is generally considered to have something to do with the related concept of the psychological contract.

The psychological contract is subjective in that each employee and employer has their own view of what is expected of each other. It is a unique combination of beliefs held by an individual and their employer about what they expect of each other. This is in contrast to the written, legal contract, the statement of terms, which is likely to be the same for groups of employees.

The concept of the psychological contract has been around for some time but was developed more fully by researchers such as Denise Rousseau (1996) and, with some important reservations about where psychological contracts can fail in the employment relationship, is probably most associated in the UK with David Guest and colleagues (Guest 1998, 2009; Guest and Conway 2002a, 2002b, 2004). There are a number of definitions of the psychological contract but the following is a useful summary of the essential features:

> Psychological contracts refer to beliefs that individuals hold regarding promises made, accepted and relied upon between themselves and another. (In the case of organizations, these parties include an employee, client, manager, and/or organization as a whole.) Because psychological contracts represent how people interpret promises and commitments, both parties in the same employment relationship can have differing views about specific terms. (Rousseau and Wade-Benzoni 1994, cited in Armstrong 2007, p226)

What is broadly agreed is that the psychological contract is developed between employee and employer over an extended period of time. It begins with the experiences that a job candidate has when applying for the job, develops during the recruitment and selection process and continues during induction. It then continues to be developed throughout the period of employment. For management the most important aspect of obtaining a 'positive' psychological contract is in ensuring that this constant process of revision and adjustment is well managed.

A poor psychological contract occurs where employee expectations are not being met. The task of management, then, is in being clear what expectations are realistic in any particular set of circumstances, how expectations can be managed and how these managed expectations can be met. This 'state of the psychological contract' has implications for motivation, performance, attendance and retention. Guest's model of the state of the psychological contract is determined by both personal and individual factors and by organisational policies and practices. In particular it is influenced by 'fairness', 'trust' and 'delivery of the deal' (Guest and Conway 2002a). Outcomes of the state of the psychological contract are the behaviours and attitudes that contribute to employee engagement.

The psychological contract is based on the idea of mutuality and exchange between employers and workers. As students of employment relations are aware, one can never assume that the signing of a contract of employment allows either side to be able to guarantee the outcomes of this because the employment contract, unlike any other conventional contract, is one where the employee is invariably faced with an unequal bargaining position, where the contract is open-ended and where it does not specify a guaranteed quantity or quality of work output to be achieved.

Other things being equal, then, we could assume that when employers meet those commitments expected from employees, this reinforces employees' sense of fairness and trust in the organisation and generates loyalty from the employee, hence fulfilling a positive psychological contract between employer and employee (Guest and Conway 2004).

In reality it is unrealistic to be able to expect *all* expectations of *all* employees to be fulfilled *all the time*. However, providing that an optimal amount of the most important issues are perceived to be met, balance is achieved. Where these expectations are perceived by employees not to be met, the psychological contract is considered to be 'violated'. This happens when one party makes a significant change without first getting the agreement of the other party. Such scenarios tend to be most frequently experienced in times of rapid organisation change. 'Managing change' in such a way that does not alienate employees through a perceived lack of adequate involvement in the process or in increased fears about job security are classic examples of such a violation.

A related attribute of employee engagement is in its link with the notion of 'going with the flow' – the term used by psychologists to describe the state of mind in which people become immersed in an activity that they lose track of time. Since engagement is intended to be getting workers to work 'smarter not harder', it is associated with enhancing the potentially positive benefits of enhancing employees' discretionary behaviour through greater 'empowerment'. This does require an honest delegation of authority for employers, however, and this is not always fully understood or practised (Cunningham et al 1996). 'Going with the flow' is also argued to be more likely in environments where a healthy work–life balance can be achieved. Much of this is in line with the so-called 'high performance' management paradigm (Purcell et al 2003) whereby line managers – not HR departments – create the conditions under which employees will offer 'discretionary behaviour'.

The idea of the psychological contract has great appeal both for managers and students of HR and organisational behaviour because it offers a way of trying to understand the relationship that forms between an employee and their organisation. However, a number of serious conceptual and theoretical limitations to the concept of the psychological contract have been identified. Cullinane and Dundon (2006) critically analyse the concept of the psychological contract from a number of perspectives. Firstly, they are critical of the way that the different theorists described the make-up of the psychological contract resulting in a wide variety of both objective and subjective variables. There are some theorists who talk about 'obligations', some about 'promises' and others who talk about 'expectations'. Some stress that there is both an employer perspective and an employee perspective, while other theorists put the majority of the emphasis on the employee's perspective. In addition, the relationships between the different variables are hard to measure. Cullinane and Dundon (2006) also query whether the psychological contract can actually be called 'a contract' because such a notion implies that there is at least an appearance of an agreement about the content. They argue that something that is as subjective as the psychological contract cannot therefore be called 'a contract'. They also point out the difficulties in making a contract with an organisation given that employment relationships are becoming increasingly complex. Another major obstacle is the issue of violation of the contract. If employees perceive that their psychological contract has been violated or breached, is it because managers have failed to deliver on an expectation or promise or is it because the employee had erroneous or false expectations? In addition, some protagonists of the psychological contract do not take into account the wide range of people and practices that influence an employee's psychological contract. These go far beyond the employee's line manager and begin even before the employee starts working for the organisation.

CHARACTERISTICS OF AN 'ENGAGED WORKFORCE'

Many large organisations increasingly recognise the importance of having a strong 'employer brand'. The promotion of a strongly engaged workforce is therefore seen as being part of a virtuous circle of performance: engaged employees provide the basis for the employer to promote this brand when recruiting new staff and these engaged staff work better, protecting the employer from the problems associated with poor service levels or product quality associated with less engaged staff (see Chapter 10).

However, achieving this scenario requires, as an essential first stage, some means of assessing the extent of employee engagement on a regular basis. Most large employers in the private and public sectors conduct some form of staff attitude survey (Kersley et al 2005) and calibrating such surveys to measure employee engagement is increasingly common. Done correctly, the findings from consecutive surveys could be used to inform decision-making about HR policies and practices. The dimensions measured may vary from organisation to organisation. However, common features include the issues of pay and benefits, communications, learning and development, line management and work–life balance. The results of such surveys would be able to give a picture of the staff satisfaction levels on the dimensions measured and areas for improvement can be identified as a result. The surveys can be designed especially for the organisation or an 'off the shelf' survey can be used. Overall, the CIPD (Alfes et al 2010) has a broad model for what could be considered as essential drivers for employee engagement, and these could be reduced to: (1) giving employees opportunities to express their opinions to senior managers; (2) keeping employees well informed about what is happening; and (3) having managers who the employees perceive as being committed to the organisation: all themes familiar to employee relations specialists. However, while perceptions of managerial fairness are critically important in creating a positive psychological contract, it is interesting to note that this research did not find that this was related to employee engagement.

Robinson et al (2004) conclude that a sense of feeling valued and involved is a major driver of employee engagement. In order to feel valued and involved employees need to believe that they are:

- involved in decision-making
- have the freedom to voice ideas, and managers listen to those ideas
- given the skills, tools and knowledge to perform well
- given opportunities to develop the job
- working for an organisation that is concerned for employees' health and well-being.

All in all, Robinson et al (2004) show how levels of engagement are influenced by personal characteristics. While a minority of employees will remain resistant to becoming engaged at work, the study shows how important the ways managers communicate with and behave towards their employees are in influencing the levels of engagement: issues of task flexibility, work intensity and levels of autonomy have a major influence on whether work is perceived as being meaningful and engaging.

Given the association between engagement, job satisfaction, advocacy and performance, there would seem to be a clear case to introduce employee engagement initiatives in organisations. To achieve this, proponents of engagement recommend a series of important principles – which are remarkably similar to some traditional 'industrial relations' principles relating to procedural justice and employee voice. These are (CIPD 2009):

- allowing people the opportunity to feed their views and opinions upwards
- keeping employees informed about what is going on in the organisation
- showing employees that managers are committed to the organisation
- having fair and just management processes for dealing with problems
- recognising that different groups of employees are influenced by different combinations of factors.

Drawing on studies of a wide range of organisations in both private and public sectors, MacLeod and Clarke (2009, p69) conclude that leadership, line management, employee voice and integrity are key enablers of engagement and that 'the correlation between engagement, well-being and performance is repeated too often for it to be a coincidence'. They argue that if the principles and practices associated with employee engagement were more widely taken up by employers, then the associated benefits in employee well-being and, in turn, employee performance could be realised, leading to a positive impact on

UK competitiveness and performance overall. However, while examples of good employee engagement are identified, they also identify a series of barriers to its likely uptake, particularly among smaller businesses. These barriers are lack of awareness of employee engagement, not knowing how to address the issue in their organisations, the attitudes of managers and organisational culture, and underestimating the importance of engagement (MacLeod and Clarke 2009).

In order to promote a greater diffusion of best practice in employee engagement, MacLeod and Clarke (2009) argue that the whole concept should be led by a sponsoring group consisting of representatives from business, the public sector, not-for-profit sector and unions; and that support for organisations be tailored to the needs of specific sectors and be practical.

CONCLUSION

Employee relations in most organisations differs greatly from the scenario in previous decades. Declining union membership among workers has led to declining union influence. This should not be overstated, however. Unions remain significant in many workplaces. Most large organisations and all public sector workplaces continue to see union influence, so understanding the processes and motivation involved in collective bargaining will continue to be an important skill and knowledge base for HR practitioners.

For the non-union workplace, however, a different set of employee relations dilemmas exist. As the case study at the beginning of the chapter indicated, and as the statistics describing trends in absence and employment tribunals demonstrate, the unitarist vision of the harmonious union-free workplace has not occurred as a result of the decollectivisation of employee relations. Indeed, the ideology of individualism harnessed from the 1980s onwards against unions has now brought its own problems for management.

Can a renewed focus on employee engagement bring about a shift here? Advocates of this approach emphasise the need for HR to ensure that, in its desire to be proactively engaged in a transformational role at a strategic business level, it does not neglect its vital role as employee advocate (Ulrich and Brockbank 2005). In many ways, the aims of employee engagement involve an attempt to duplicate the missing role of the union (employee voice, procedural justice) and there may be a paradox that – as is often the case for 'best practice' HR initiatives – that the take-up of employee engagement may well be higher among pluralist employers and ignored completely by a swathe of workplaces identified as occupying what Guest and Conway (1999) termed the 'black hole' in employee relations.

HRM IN THE MEDIA

CRITICAL REFLECTIONS

Relating to the first question, from management's point of view, the relative merits of a union being able to mediate in such circumstances will depend partly on management ideology. If management are unitarist, they would not be able to see beyond the principle of management's absolute right to command loyalty among staff – and that a union would be seen as an interference. The pluralist, however, would see the union as a means of engaging with employees and attempting to tackle underlying reasons for employee 'misbehaviour'. This would not be straightforward, though. While the union would not nominally endorse individual acts of 'sabotage' and would be willing to negotiate measures aimed at reducing employee alienation, it would also be obliged to act on behalf of any of its members individually subjected to disciplinary action resulting from the original incident.

Regarding the second question, pluralist management would engage with the union. Unitarist management would not. In either case, management could consider the whole issue of employee engagement and consider how issues such as job satisfaction, mechanisms for voicing general issues of concern to management and the extent to which employees feel that 'management is listening' are addressed.

Finally, relating to the third question, it is impossible to make exact comparisons. However, there are some clear patterns in like-by-like indicators. Collective forms of conflict – most notably strikes – have declined significantly. While this could partly be explained by changes to the law, making striking more difficult, it may also indicate some shift in worker attitude over the period. Parallel trends, however, indicate an almost equal rise in individual forms of conflict, most evidently the figures relating to employment tribunal claims. It would seem, then, that patterns of 'disloyalty' are 'different' rather than 'less'.

EXPLORE FURTHER

BLYTON, P. and TURNBULL, P. (2005) *The dynamics of employee relations*. 3rd ed. Basingstoke: Palgrave.

This book provides a critical assessment of employee relations within contemporary organisations.

COLLING, T. and TERRY, M. (eds) (2010) *Industrial relations: theory and practice*. Chichester: Wiley.

This book explores industrial relations in Britain within a comparative perspective and discusses employment relations actors, contexts, processes and outcomes.

GUEST, D.E., ISAKSSON, K. and DE WITTE, H. (eds) (2010) *Employment contracts, psychological contracts, and employee well-being: an international study*. Oxford: Oxford University Press.

This book focuses on the relationship between temporary employment contracts and employee well-being using an analytic framework of the psychological contract.

ALBRECHT, S. (ed.) (2010) *Handbook of employee engagement: perspectives, issues, research and practice.* London: Edward Elgar Publishing.

This book contains cutting-edge contributions from a wide range of scholars and consultants on essential topics to the science and the practice of employee engagement.

CHAPTER 13

Critical Issues in Employee Relations (2): Global Unions

Richard Croucher

OVERVIEW

This chapter discusses an issue of strategic importance for senior managers in multinational companies: how to manage global employment relations. HR managers in multinationals are expected to be expert and to play a key role in deciding strategy in this field, where mistakes can be extremely costly.

The chapter begins with a short case study showing some problems that can occur. Next, the global regulatory framework is introduced. Following this, a picture of trade unionism worldwide is made showing how companies are talking to global union organisations to help them deal with the problems. A case study of how one of these global labour organisations helped a large multinational deal with HIV/AIDS among employees in Africa, saving many union members' lives, rounds off the chapter's core. The conclusion summarises the main argument made in this chapter, which is that working with global union bodies in a constructive way is most likely to provide sustainable solutions to the issues.

LEARNING OBJECTIVES

Reading this chapter will enable the reader to:

- make a considered critique of why employment relations issues in a host country are important to a multinational company in its country of origin
- critically evaluate the principal roles of the actors in global employment relations
- critically evaluate the importance of what global-level agreements can mean at local level.

'BRITISH AND AMERICAN UNIONS TO MERGE'

Britain's biggest union, Unite, announced that it was to merge with the US-based United Steelworkers union (USW) to create a new 'global' union called 'Workers Uniting' (BBC News 2008).

The leaders from both unions said that this was an inevitable consequence of globalisation and that the future aim would be for the new union group to synchronise pay negotiations with multinationals that were currently done separately in different countries. In the present situation, the unions, operating independently from each other, felt the pressure from global businesses able to play unionised workers in one country off against workers in another. The union said that it was concerned that this would lead to deteriorating pay and conditions for workers in Europe and the US, and that the new union would look to tackle an increase in the 'casualisation' of employment.

Derek Simpson (Unite) also urged other unions, from Poland to Australia, to join Workers Uniting.

Questions

1 How does Workers Uniting, described above, compare with conventional unions and with global union federations (GUFs)?

2 What implications could the existence of Workers Uniting have for HR planning processes at a multinational firm?

INTRODUCTION

Most coverage of employee relations is focused at workplace, organisation, sector or national level. This is quite logical. The core issues involved in employee relations – communication between managers and workers, negotiating, bargaining, workplace conflict – all occur at workplace level, are defined by sectoral influences and are legally constrained and regulated at national level. However, it is also commonly agreed that influences on HR trends and practices at workplace, sectoral and national level are affected by global trends. This chapter considers how these global issues affect employee relations and, in particular, the key actors involved: international regulatory institutions, multinational corporations and the global union federations (GUFs).

GLOBAL LABOUR STANDARDS: THE ILO CONVENTIONS

A set of interlocking guidelines exists suggesting how workers should be treated in all global situations. There is a wide range of advisory documentation, including the longstanding Organisation for Economic Cooperation and Development's (OECD) guidelines for multinational companies and the International Labour Organization's (ILO) Conventions. All of this merely constitutes guidance, and Hyman suggests that taken collectively they are 'weak and largely tokenistic' (Hyman 2002, p1). Companies are therefore in a more uncertain situation, with more potential hazards than at national level where 'hard' law exists. They need help from experts.

The most comprehensive and widely recognised set of guidelines is those issued by the ILO, based in Geneva. The ILO sets labour standards that represent a 'floor' of fundamental rights. The ILO is a very longstanding global tripartite body, comprising representatives of governments, employers and workers, who together agree conventions. Governments can choose to sign up to its conventions or not. If they do so, they agree to ensure that reality in their countries conforms to certain principles. The ILO in 1998 adopted a small set of 'core' labour standards that it regards as human rights; these are standards that all ILO members have decided are basic rights to be applied even if they have not signed the relevant conventions. These have passed into customary international law and cover the following matters (in practice there is often more than one convention dealing with any given subject):

- eradication of child labour (Conventions 138 and 182)

- ending forced and compulsory labour (Conventions 29 and 105)

- elimination of discrimination (Conventions 100 and 111)

- trade union rights ('Freedom of Association' Convention 87).

- right to bargain collectively (Convention 98).

There are hundreds of other ILO conventions including, for example, those on health and safety, the right to strike, women's rights, access to decision-makers and conventions designed to protect migrant workers. The countries that have signed up to the different conventions are also shown in a set of useful global maps produced by the International Centre for Trade Union Rights (ICTUR), based in London. It cannot be considered excellent labour practice simply to follow ILO standards; rather, it indicates a bare minimum. Best practice, after all, demands much more than simply not being associated with child, forced or slave labour.

'Soft guidance' of this sort may appear meaningless, but breaking it can have hard consequences for companies. The world's development banks use ILO core labour standards in the design and allocation of loans. Campaigners can and do pick up on them to criticise multinationals, affecting companies' relations with the many governments they have to deal with, as well as their international images and brands. They may find themselves the target of the kind of 'anti-corporate' campaigning described by Naomi Klein (2010) in which activists target and contaminate valuable brands with the so-called 'brand boomerang' effect. The well-known example of Nike is enough to remind us of how this can work. Put another way: 'where were your trainers made?'

MULTINATIONALS AND THE REGULATION OF GLOBAL LABOUR

Companies have two types of method for dealing with these issues. One is to develop their own policies and internal controls; the second is to find help from outside organisations. Normally, they do both simultaneously but for clarity the two types of method will be considered in turn.

COMPANY POLICIES AND INTERNAL CONTROLS

In recent years, most large companies have developed corporate social responsibility (CSR) policies. CSR is discussed elsewhere in this book by Elizabeth Cotton (Chapter 3), who argues that it does not provide a robust framework for ensuring labour rights. The most widespread tool is company codes of practice, and thousands of these exist (Holdcroft 2006).

These codes are simple statements of what a company's practices should be. They are framed in a very general way and are rarely concerned with labour issues: most do not even mention employees' rights as workers. They normally contain a range of general statements about the company's respect for the environment and for all of its stakeholders. Only a few mention the ILO's Core Labour Standards (Schömann et al 2008). These statements may sometimes be used by consultants or 'independent' monitors employed by companies to check how they correspond to reality.

Multinationals vary greatly in the extent to which they even try to have global policies at all: in some cases, they simply have 'values' (such as the company's own interpretation of CSR), so in reality the subjects considered in this chapter are often left largely to local managers to interpret. Multinational companies can have global policies about matters such as reward, equality of opportunity and employee representation. These vary widely between companies. American-based companies, for example, tend to have performance-related pay principles (practically impossible to apply across the world because of widely varying institutional frameworks in different countries). They tend also to have statements about equality of opportunity and to favour company-based forms of employee representation. European-based companies, on the other hand, normally have more open views about forms of employee representation.

Increasingly, multinational companies employ fewer people directly, preferring, instead, to 'externalise' employment either by creating subsidiary companies or supply chains with very small contractors. As a result, employment practices in these subsidiaries are likely to be very different from those in the parent company. In such circumstances the multinational is likely to disclaim all responsibility for what is happening at the end of the supply chain. However, this may not hold up in the court of consumer opinion in developed countries, or in the views of developing countries' governments. For these reasons, outside organisations may also be used to help.

HELP FROM OUTSIDE ORGANISATIONS

There are many systems of 'independent' certification available to companies to show that they follow labour standards. An example is the Social Accountability International (SAI) auditing programme, which audits and certifies workplaces. This system focuses on International Labour Organization standards and a wide and sometimes bewildering range of other such monitoring systems exist.

The first problem is whether any of these systems are independent in any real sense: companies pay fees for audit and are therefore customers of the auditing bodies. Secondly, even if they are independent, how effective can outside auditors be? Visits to workplaces by outsiders are necessarily isolated events that look at the situation at just one point in time.

Auditing solutions are designed as permanent ones, but there are others that can be used either together with or instead of them, on a more 'as required' basis. Non-governmental organisations (NGOs) such as War on Want or Oxfam may on occasions offer companies advice, but they are more commonly critics of company practice and generally refer companies to others for detailed advice on how to proceed. The first instinct of companies is to involve consultants and/or lawyers with whom they already have a relationship and therefore trust. Consultants very rarely have real expertise in this field, often offer off-the-shelf solutions and, unlike union bodies, cannot be held publicly responsible for their advice. Lawyers are even less likely to be helpful, because the issues involved are only partly legal.

There are real problems for companies and their HR specialists in relying on any of the methods described above. Companies ultimately have to take responsibility for the practices of both their own subsidiaries and their suppliers, and for taking effective measures to ensure that they are not merely legally compliant but also will satisfy those looking critically at the situation from the outside. It is HR who has to take a lead on this, as they are the specialists in the field. They have probably already correctly decided that this is demanding. They therefore need reliable partners.

For these reasons, companies have begun to adopt a second solution: to sign labour agreements with global union federations (GUFs). As is explained below, the GUFs are global union organisations. They are independent, they have huge expertise and their affiliates have the capacity to monitor conditions from hour to hour on the ground through their workplace representatives. Different forms of employee representation – and how they fit with the global union federations (GUFs) – will now be explained.

EMPLOYEE REPRESENTATION AT LOCAL AND GLOBAL LEVELS

In this section, the main forms of employee representation that exist in the world are briefly outlined. This begins with works councils and then moves on to discuss trade unions. Global union organisations (including GUFs) are dealt with later in the section.

WORKS COUNCILS

What is a works council? In the English-speaking world, where they have long existed with little or no legal support, they are usually called 'joint consultative committees'. The term is used here to mean an enterprise-based employee representative body without comprehensive bargaining rights that represents all employees to management. Unlike trade unions, which only represent their (subscription-paying) members, they normally represent all employees. They discuss issues that are not likely to be major sources of conflict between managers and employees. Typically, these include employee welfare, training, work organisation, hours of work and the wide range of lower-level subjects that have to be dealt with in workplaces if they are not to become serious issues. Works councils do not normally negotiate wages.

In many European countries (including eastern Europe) and in Taiwan, South Korea and Singapore, works councils have their functions defined in national law. How strong their powers are depends on the national law in which they operate. In the 'stronger' forms of co-determination common in western Europe, works councils have considerable bargaining power because their agreement to certain changes is required by law. This is called co-determination (meaning that their agreement must be obtained before certain sorts of changes, for example in Germany to working time, can happen), to be consulted and to receive information from management. Weaker legal support for works councils is more common in eastern Europe and Asia. An extreme contrast, right at the other end of the spectrum from Germany, is the Singaporean form of works council. These are essentially simply consultative bodies with no mechanisms for compulsion. A European directive has also encouraged the establishment of works councils in multinational companies operating in the EU. There are now hundreds of these European works councils operating in Europe. They are also consultative bodies and do not have the strong co-determination powers of works councils in Germany.

At the workplace level, there is good evidence that local managers find works councils useful for sorting out low-level problems with employees before they grow into larger issues. They also find them helpful consultative bodies where they can try out new ideas. US-based companies tend to prefer these enterprise-based bodies to dealing with trade unions. Some large European companies (Volkswagen for example) have established world works councils. This underlines how useful managers can find them. The relationship between unions and works councils is complex, but in general works councils are most common where trade unionism is also strong (Brewster et al 2007). This suggests that works councils and trade unions are in practice closely associated, that is, they are to be found in the same companies.

It is important to note that for employers to establish a works council does not meet the ILO requirements either for freedom of association nor for collective bargaining. They cannot be seen as suitable substitutes for trade unions and are not capable of helping to solve major global labour issues.

TRADE UNIONS

In this section the great diversity in the world's unions is demonstrated. Trade unions worldwide cannot be understood from the experience of one country. Assumptions based on unions in the developed world are not transferable to the developing world since most of the world's unions do not have the same level of bargaining power. Later, it will be shown that unions may have potential as partners for management but also warn that unions that are reduced to being simple tools of management are not only no use to workers, but are also no use to management.

A trade union is defined here as a continuous association of wage earners dedicated to the advancement of its members' interests. National union federations that are recognised as free and independent are generally members of the International Trade Union Confederation (ITUC: until recently called the International Confederation of Free Trade Unions). They are also frequently members of a global union federation, organisations open to unions operating in particular industries.

The proportion of workers who are members of trade unions has declined over the last 20 years, because of massive restructuring of work in the world economy, the dominance of neo-liberal ideas and the effects of the international financial institutions' 'structural adjustment' policies. As a result, in many countries, the great majority of workers are not employed at all, but work in the 'informal' economy. They grow crops, sell small goods and services and live on the edge of survival. They have little possibility of joining unions.

The proportion of unionised workers varies widely between countries. Statistics are often unreliable. In Scandinavian countries 85–90% of employees are unionised, in the Russian-speaking world over 50% are union members, but in Africa (outside South Africa) only around 10% are. There are exceptions. In Ghana, for example, unions play an important role in the formal economy and membership levels are higher. Importantly, union membership is normally concentrated in large employers, and is much higher in multinational corporations than in national economies as a whole. For example, in the UK, while only about a quarter of all companies have a union presence, 48 of the UK's FTSE 50 companies (all multinationals) have some union presence. All Japanese-based multinationals have unions somewhere within them.

Simplistic assumptions about what a trade union is, and what it does, are dangerous for HR managers operating on a global level. The definition given above helps us to understand why, because it is a wide one that allows for many different functions and approaches by unions. The definition includes the phrase 'dedicated to the advancement of its members' interests'. In some countries, unions have been subordinated to political parties or the interests of the state in such a way that they cannot be called 'free' or 'independent'. This is arguably the case, for example, in Belarus, China and Egypt, to give just three examples. An important reservation should be made here, however, because even in these countries trade unions have a 'legal watchdog' role. This means that these unions, in common with the great majority of unions in the world, are likely to keep management aware of local labour laws. The function is extremely useful to multinationals' managements who invariably wish to stay legally compliant.

Many millions of Chinese workers are registered as union members. In China, unions are essentially Communist Party organisations, tools of control rather than democratic bodies with elected officials. They are not currently recognised by the ITUC as members of the free trade union movement. Therefore, although 'bargaining' takes place there, this is called by many 'sweetheart bargaining' and never results in formal conflicts such as strikes. The very large number of strikes in China have all been carried on outside of the official trade unions.

The Chinese example shows how important unions that are little more than the tools of government or employers are in terms of the number of members that they have. For multinationals, they serve only limited purposes, because they will not represent the legitimate voice of employees. In short, they will resemble ineffective works councils.

Elsewhere, companies themselves sometimes establish a union that is insufficiently independent of management to be considered 'free'. This commonly happens in parts of eastern Europe and the Russian-speaking world. Generally speaking, if union officers and workplace representatives are not subject to regular, free and democratic election without management interference, then they cannot be considered independent. This is not in management interests, because it means that there can be no legitimate collective employee voice and so management cannot ascertain employees' views accurately. Nor does it help companies to defend themselves against accusations of poor labour practice.

Free trade unions have very different structures, functions and approaches across the world and a few examples follow.

Union structures

Unions are normally based either on workplaces, companies or industrial sectors and may also have political affiliations. In Japan, the Russian-speaking world and Mexico, most unions are essentially workplace organisations, based in one company. In the Russian-speaking world, almost all members' subscriptions are held at the workplace and only small amounts are passed on to regional and national federations, which have relatively little power. These structures are favoured by US-based multinationals because they feel that they are more concerned with the company itself than with 'outside interests'. By contrast, in many other countries unions are national, industry-based organisations with no clear role in most workplaces; in Europe they mainly exercise influence in workplaces by having their members operating as works councillors. In many countries, such as those of Francophone Africa, unions are very much politically based. This means that different union confederations exist according to their political rather than their industrial orientation.

Union functions

Union functions differ widely. Many do little collective bargaining over wages and conditions. In the Russian-speaking world, although efforts are being made to change them, many unions are basically welfare organisations, distributing holiday and other vouchers to their members. They organise visits to sanitoria, distribute funds to members in difficulties and sign 'collective agreements' that are rarely bargained over and represent standard terms and conditions. Similarly, many African unions have strong welfare functions. In some other countries, unions have become major lifelong learning facilitators.

Union approaches

Union approaches are also very varied across the world. In Latin American countries, trade unionism is often a broad, community-based phenomenon. These unions are 'social movement' bodies and are sometimes capable of mobilising whole communities on a large scale. On the other hand, in the Russian-speaking world this is rarely the case. In western Europe, unions have become largely institutionalised and they tend to be less politicised than their Latin American counterparts.

It will now be clear that what a trade union is and what people assume it to be in different countries both vary enormously. Managers need to understand how unions operate. Unions can play an important role for companies by providing some protection to individual employees wishing to raise issues; individual employees do not always express their discontents openly or fully to managers because they fear that this may be seen as 'disloyal'. Managers may have reservations about unions for fear that they will raise the cost of labour or reduce managerial control. But, as Geoff Wood explains in Chapter 4 of this book, the highly successful German model is based on high labour costs and co-determination, which many argue are the essential bases for high-quality products. Increased labour costs need not mean increased total costs, since co-operative policies can create important efficiencies such as reduced employee turnover (Rizov and Croucher 2009). Moreover, as suggested above, many of the world's unions may be free unions but also more closely resemble works councils than they do the collective-bargaining-oriented unions of the developed world. They are therefore more likely to operate in co-operative ways. In short, managers need to develop an approach that develops co-operation and partnership but does not try to reduce them to the point at which they become mere tools of management.

It is very difficult for managers in multinationals to become expert in all of the different situations internationally. Therefore they need a global partner with strong understanding of these complex issues, who will also remind managers of the value of free trade unionism. Global union federations provide this possibility.

GLOBAL UNION FEDERATIONS

Global union federations (GUFs) have existed for over a century. Each is based on a group of industries and they are centres of great expertise in global labour issues in their industrial sectors. They are international organisations to which national trade unions may choose to affiliate on payment of a fee.

National union centres (such as the Ghana Trades Union Congress, for example) are also usually affiliated to the International Trade Union Confederation (ITUC). The ITUC has less direct dealings with companies than the GUFs do, because the ITUC is a co-ordinating, political and campaigning body that does not unite unions in any particular industry. Some examples of important GUFs covering the private sector are:

- International Union of Food and Agricultural Workers' Unions (IUF), based in Geneva

- International Union of Chemical, Energy, Mineworkers' and General Unions (ICEM), also based in Geneva

- International Transport Workers' Federation (ITF), based in London

- International Metalworkers' Federation (IMF), based in Brussels.

The GUFs have many roles in relation both to their affiliated unions and to employers. In other words, like their affiliates at national level, they perform many different functions. Thus, the ITF itself actually bargains collectively with employers in the international shipping industry to fix wages in a large part of merchant shipping. The others do not have this function but are very active in building exchanges of information, as their websites illustrate. All the GUFs frequently campaign against companies infringing basic human rights such as the right to freedom of association. GUFs, along with the ITUC, have also been very active in campaigning around important matters such as child labour, something engaged in by some 200 million children worldwide. The proportion of children working worldwide has therefore been falling in recent years.

INTERNATIONAL FRAMEWORK AGREEMENTS

In recent years, GUFs have been heavily involved in developing international framework agreements (IFAs) with companies, which provide a basis on which their activists can operate within them. Examples of these agreements can be viewed on the International Metalworkers' Federation website, and they are fully discussed in Croucher and Cotton (2009). A growing number of major employers have signed these agreements, and indeed companies have in recent years themselves begun proactively to approach the GUFs to ask to negotiate them. The first IFA was signed by the French food manufacturer Danone, with the IUF, in 1988. In 2000 just nine agreements existed, but by 2004 there were 32, and by mid-2008 there were 59, mainly in the metalworking, chemical and energy, building and wood, and services sectors (Schömann et al 2008). These 59 companies include some of the world's largest multinationals.

Most of the multinational companies that have signed IFAs are European-based. American-based companies (an exception is Chiquita, which has an IFA) rely more on internal company mechanisms and CSR. There are three main reasons for companies signing:

1 They are interested in building on the co-operative relations that they have in their European headquarters countries, analysed elsewhere in this book by Geoff Wood (see Chapter 4).

2 They want to improve market perceptions of them.

3 Finally, and importantly, they also wish to protect themselves from accusations of social irresponsibility in subsidiary or supplier organisations. By reaching an agreement with a GUF, they establish a formal relationship with a global partner that is expert in labour matters and which can be expected to monitor, through its affiliates, labour practices wherever it operates. Where problems arise, they have a partner who is, along with themselves, also to some extent responsible for dealing with them.

IFAs frequently do little more than reiterate the company's commitment to ensuring that the basic rights contained in the ILO conventions are in fact observed. Typically, they contain the following elements:

● general statements about the company's commitment to human rights and good employment practice

● a statement of in which workplaces the agreement will operate

● provision for a periodic review of the agreement's operation in practice

● a list of the ILO Conventions and other guidelines that the company agrees to observe

● the period for which the agreement will be in force

● signatories, who are usually the GUF general secretary, the company CEO and the relevant leader of a national trade union.

The main function of the agreements from the GUF viewpoint is that they give national unions possibilities to organise and extend union membership, since the company has agreed to observe the right to freedom of association. They can – and probably should – be part of a wider dialogue.

COMPANY–GUF DIALOGUES: A CASE STUDY

BACKGROUND

It has been shown above how formal agreements at the global level can help companies to ensure that they have in a sense 'covered themselves' in relation to international labour rights. As is also suggested, there can ultimately be no guarantees unless the companies themselves take vigorous action to ensure that local managers actually live up to the agreements and indeed embrace their spirit as well as their letter.

The discussion now moves a stage further, to argue that these agreements should be seen as just one part of a wider picture. This needs to be one of partnership with the GUF, meaning that there is regular, meaningful and honest dialogue between both parties. Dialogue can help to build trust and co-operation so that conflicts, disagreements and problems can be handled constructively. In this way, the relationship can go beyond one in which companies 'cover themselves' to one in which important benefits can be reaped.

To show in detail how this has worked in one large multinational, a case study of relations between it and a major GUF is now presented. Space only allows a short version of the case to be presented, but the full case is available in Croucher and Cotton (2009).

THE COMPANY, THE GUF AND HIV/AIDS

Anglo American (AA) is one of the world's largest corporations, ranked 88 in the *Financial Times* Stock Exchange index of the world's largest companies and employing 162,000 people worldwide in 2006. Its operations are focused on mining.

The company, owned mainly by British financial institutions, operates in many countries but its main mining operations are in sub-Saharan Africa and Latin America. It was for some time South Africa's largest conglomerate and a key corporate player in negotiating the post-apartheid employment settlement (Von Holdt 2004). It has a complex and highly devolved structure, claiming in response to criticisms of the activities of companies in which it has an interest (War on Want 2007) that it does not have 'management control' of them (Anglo American 2007).

Company relations with stakeholders have to be built on a long-term basis, Sir Mark Moody-Stuart, Company Chairman, argued to shareholders at the April 2008 AGM. The mining industry cannot move production sites. Fixed sites and high front-end expenditure mean 'that we have to live with the judgements we make about our ability to operate ethically in particular locations' (Anglo American 2008). 'Resource nationalism' in the developing world, whereby countries resent the control exercised over their natural resources by foreign-based companies, increasingly means the company has to attend to its wider political profile throughout its operations.

HIV/AIDS is a central labour management concern for multinationals invested in Africa and eastern Europe. In sub-Saharan mining, infection rates are approximately double national averages and frequently higher. In Zambia the BBC reports a national infection rate of 14%, and an estimated 50% in mining communities. These high rates are explained by four factors. The first is the remoteness of mining operations and the communities surrounding them. Second, single-sex workers' hostels, although reducing in number, are normal. Third, many male migrant and contract workers are away from their partners, further stimulating high levels of prostitution and 'second families'. Fourth, stigma and denial around sexual practice and prevention of infection is widespread.

AA has taken a 'business case' approach to HIV/AIDS provision, although business and CSR rationales are in this case very close. Research carried out by the company showed in 2006 that it was economic to provide private medical insurance, including treatment, for all employees and their dependants rather than to provide nothing. After the first year, the costs of providing drugs would decline relative to savings from absenteeism and health care. This calculation accompanied a move beyond the classic position taken by companies, whereby they deny any legal responsibility for workers' sexual health. The latter position clearly rejects any real responsibility for reducing risk in order to limit potential legal liabilities.

The company has reasons for improving both its health and safety record and its public image: in 2007 it reported that 44 people were killed in its mining operations, and its practices in relation to indigenous communities have been sharply criticised (War on Want 2007). Part of its reply to War on Want's criticisms was to point to its record in publicly insisting that the Colombian government attend to the physical defence of trade unionists. Like many mining employers, AA is reconciled to trade unionism and almost all of its mining sites have a major union presence. The company has sought to construct positive relations with unions, including them in efforts to improve efficiency by cost reduction; union co-operation in health and safety has brought major benefits to the rate of return on capital employed. The links between trade unionism, health and safety and profitability are well recognised at the top of the company.

The company has robust long-term relations with the South African National Union of Mineworkers (NUM), based on AA's progressive positions on recognising black unions in South Africa, and its part in the transition to democracy. The NUM itself had a central role in ending apartheid and enjoys great prestige within the trade union movement, both in Africa and internationally, with high-profile participation in the ICEM and the IMF. The NUM has long emphasised HIV/AIDS as an issue. It has had a long-term relationship with the Ghana Mineworkers Union (GMWU) based on personal contacts developed through the ICEM Regional Committee. The GMWU is itself a strong union within the well-developed Ghanaian trade union movement and is therefore a relatively equal partner for the NUM. It is a highly politicised organisation, focused on dialogue with the state, which until recently ran the mines. It was only therefore relatively recently that the GMWU had to negotiate with private management and it stood to learn from a relationship with the NUM.

Exchanges between the ICEM and AA were partly based on the longstanding relationship between Fred Higgs (then ICEM General Secretary) and Sir Mark Moody-Stuart. There was also a long-term and complex web of relationships between the ICEM, its key affiliate the NUM and of both with the CEO of the AA company Anglo Gold Ashanti, Bobby Godsell. In west Africa, long-term relationships also existed between AGA management and medical staff, the ICEM and the GMWU.

THE ICEM'S HIV/AIDS PROJECTS

The ICEM was one of the first GUFs to take a lead on promoting HIV/AIDS action by unions since workers in these sectors are disproportionately affected.

Following six months of consultation with affiliates already active around the issue and experienced HIV/AIDS activists, the ICEM and these affiliates decided to promote medical provision and prevention programmes, and to negotiate anti-discrimination policies through pilot schemes that could later be adopted elsewhere in the world. The agenda was therefore more ambitious than the earlier common union practice of simply carrying out awareness campaigns. It entailed developing core expertise, raising funds from new sources and dialogue with both employers and government. Companies play a considerable role in the diagnosis of HIV/AIDS and in providing access to treatment as well as in health care more broadly.

If a worker with HIV/AIDS is threatened with dismissal, this raises fundamental issues about that worker's future. Workers' fear of losing their jobs demands strong workplace representation by the union, since local management may take action against them despite statements by senior company staff in London. Workers must be convinced that testing will not lead to dismissal and, to a lesser degree, they also must be confident that it will lead to treatment. The role of trade unions is important in negotiating, verifying and policing any assurances by securing anti-discrimination and anti-victimisation protections in collective agreements, promoting and monitoring voluntary counselling and testing (VCT) provision and by convincing workers that they will not suffer if tested.

Most workers, even in highly infected areas, do not present themselves for testing. Only tiny percentages of workers will normally volunteer, particularly if testing is offered by company doctors in company facilities. They require credible guarantees of protection from management action against them that only union involvement can offer.

In September 2002, at ICEM initiative, an International Framework Agreement was signed between Anglo Gold, ICEM and the NUM. This was the first such agreement signed with a company operating in Africa. The agreement was signed in public after the UN's World Summit in South Africa, and promoted as part of the company's sustainable development work. It had essentially symbolic rather than substantive significance in tackling HIV/AIDS, because it contains no clause on the subject. It nevertheless cemented the relations between the three signatories and was relevant background to their co-operation in the HIV/AIDS field.

By 2004 the ICEM had launched an international HIV/AIDS initiative, designed to identify pilot workplaces where the GUF and its affiliates could develop workplace provision, with the support of employers, local hospitals and international funding. It was decided to work in two Ghanaian mining regions, Obuasi and Tarkwa. Overall, the project worked within the comprehensive guidance offered by the ILO Code of Practice on HIV/AIDS in the Workplace; the immediate objective was to implement a strategy based on the code. The pilot project aimed to secure, through negotiations with key employers, the establishment or development of dedicated medical facilities for VCT and treatment and adequate anti-discrimination and non-victimisation clauses in agreements. The pilots would in due course identify other important needs, including a need for trained peer counsellors from union cadres to support miners diagnosed positive. These counsel people before and after testing, helping them to make lifestyle changes and to manage their treatment.

AA felt that union involvement could have a major positive effect by raising workers' take-up of testing. The massive influence of charismatic union leaders in influencing workers' perceptions is difficult to understand outside of the African mining context. Their role is highly significant since they are seen as community, and not simply as workplace, leaders. Senzeni Zokwana, the president of the NUM (elected president of the ICEM at its Bangkok Congress in 2007), personally took the issue of HIV/AIDS to mines. He carried out awareness-raising activities and encouraged testing. He publicly submitted himself for personal testing at each mine, paving the way for successful testing drives. The union also undertook a wider educational effort to train peer educators and negotiators to bargain for protections for people living with HIV/AIDS.

PROJECT RESULTS

The results were major. In the AA subsidiary Anglo Gold Ashanti in 2004, 10% of employees were being tested; in the company's 2006 annual report, 75% were reported as having been tested. By June 2006, 34% of AA's workers had been tested: of an estimated positive workforce of 28,294, just under 10,000 were enrolled in the company's HIV/AIDS programme, 3,772 of whom were taking up antiretroviral treatment. In comparative terms, these are high take-up rates and a very significant improvement on previous levels.

CASE STUDY CONCLUSION

Prior to the GUF initiative, the company had made little progress in dealing with HIV/AIDS. The case shows how GUF involvement, based on long-term dialogue, changed this situation and was beneficial to both parties. For the unions and the GUF, members' lives were saved. For the company, huge losses from sickness and death were reduced, raising efficiency. Its CSR reputation was enhanced.

CONCLUSION

The chapter has shown the value of a partnership approach to unions at both local and global levels. In this way, companies win partners who can help them minimise risk and build defensible labour practices. An increasing number of companies work constructively with GUFs. The alternative is for them to face accusations of corporate social irresponsibility not only from unions, but also from other, often more hostile, anti-globalisation activists.

This conclusion has real implications for skills development for both international managers and employee representatives, since representation, consultation, negotiation and the development of mutually beneficial dialogue are complex arts. As well as excellent skills, 'best practice' in international employment relations must be based on detailed understanding. HR professionals need a good grasp of the different institutional environments that their companies operate in and the risks that they pose. That is very difficult for a multinational, because of the sheer range of environments they operate in. For this reason, opening dialogues with global union federations, experts in their sectors and the very varied trade unions within them, offers the best prospect for companies to ensure that major problems are avoided. The alternatives (certification systems, internal experts and self-monitoring schemes) are all built on inherently inadequate models that do not stand up to scrutiny by increasingly critical consumers and governments. A constructive approach to GUFs, as the Anglo American case shows, can on the other hand not only help defend companies, but can go further and bring positive benefits of value to multinationals and their employees.

HRM IN THE MEDIA

CRITICAL REFLECTIONS

In relation to the first question, it should be clear, after reading this chapter, that Workers Uniting is an attempt to combine two national unions in a form of alliance in order to co-ordinate their bargaining activities with multinational employers. If successful, such an alliance would offer some useful benefits to the members of each national union who are often at a disadvantage when facing an employer who has options of relocating work as a sanction against overdemanding unions. Workers Uniting is not the same as a global union federation, however. GUFs may facilitate dialogue between affiliated national unions and multinational corporations about core labour standards, set up around framework agreements, and apply them locally.

In relation to the second question, the merger, if successful, could reduce a multinational's key advantage – that of being able to use a global position to affect different local negotiations. When negotiating with unions in one country, a multinational is able to, either overtly or tacitly, threaten to move work away from the countries with higher wage costs to those with lower wage costs – as those unions in lower-cost countries may be better able to try to match terms and conditions upwards. A merged cross-national union would be better placed to offset this advantage held by the employer.

CROUCHER, R. and COTTON, E. (2009) *Global unions, global business: global union federations and international business.* London: Middlesex University Press.

This book provides the only detailed and up-to-date account of global union federations.

ELLIOTT, K.A. and FREEMAN, R.B. (2003) *Can labour standards improve under globalization?* Washington DC: Institute for International Economics.

A very useful book on the issue of labour standards and 'development' by two Harvard economists.

BOGNANNO, M.F., KEANE, M.P. and YANG, D. (2005) The influence of wages and industrial relations environments on the production location decisions of US multinational companies. *Industrial and Labour Relations Review.* Vol 58. pp171–200.

A useful discussion of how American-based multinational companies take decisions on where production is located in the world shows how these are not simply taken on a labour cost basis.

Important sources on international labour standards may be found on the International Labour Organization's website (www.ilo.org/global/lang--en/index.htm). This huge site contains a wealth of information, including a large range of working papers and publications dealing with many complex labour issues in different countries. Especially useful is *Rules of the Game: A brief introduction to international labour standards* (revised edition 2009).

The Global Work and Employment Project (GWEP) website, part of Middlesex University's website, also contains free access to a number of papers relevant to the subject, available online at www.mdx.ac.uk/research/areas/enterprise/gwep/index.aspx

EXPLORE FURTHER

CHAPTER 14

Critical Issues in Learning and Development: Beyond 'the Learning Organisation'

Mary Hartog

OVERVIEW

This chapter discusses the idea of the learning organisation and offers a critical review of what it means. The chapter begins with a case study, 'The run on the Rock', which tells the story of the Northern Rock Building Society and how its dealings in the sub-prime mortgage market and the events of 2007 made it synonymous with *the credit crunch*. This case study illustrates how events can shape an organisation and its business agenda for learning today. Secondly, the chapter provides an introduction to the learning organisation followed by a critique. It concludes by returning to the agenda for organisational learning today and critically analyses the way in which knowledge of the learning organisation has evolved and how it might inform our practice today.objectives

LEARNING OBJECTIVES

Reading this chapter will enable the reader to:

- critically examine what is meant by 'the learning organisation' and 'organisational learning'
- critically examine how critical incidents and events in the wider business environment influence and shape the learning agenda for business and organisations
- critically analyse the way in which knowledge of the learning organisation has evolved and how it might inform our practice today.

HRM IN THE MEDIA

'THE RUN ON THE ROCK'

For Northern Rock, in 2008 the UK's fifth largest mortgage lender, the sub-prime panic created such fear in the banking system that commercial credit lines dried up, causing the Rock to go to the Bank of England (BoE), the bank of last resort, to borrow money. In an attempt to calm the situation and bring stability to the banking system, on 13 September 2007, Alistair Darling, the Chancellor of the Exchequer, stepped and made the BoE facilities available to Northern Rock. Panic ensued, with customers queuing around the block to withdraw funds (BBC News 2007a).

Northern Rock had 18.9% of UK lending loans and assets at the time of this bailout of £113 billion and it had retail customer deposits of £24 billion. In the first six months of 2007, Northern Rock announced pre-tax profits of £300 million, on par with the previous year, yet share values in the year were to fall by half. In the first six months of 2007 lending at Northern Rock rose by 47% to just under £11 billion. By

June it had added £6.2 billion customer loans into the pipeline, which were arguably late in the day as interest rates had already turned (BBC News 2007b).

Northern Rock's pioneer product was the 'Together' loan, which allowed young couples to borrow six times' their annual income rather than the much safer and *traditional* multiple of three (Rawnsley 2010, p489). Adam Applegarth (the CEO) was a marketing man, with no banking qualification to his name.

Questions

1 What HRD advice would you give the top management team to help stop this type of incident from occurring again?

2 What type of learning interventions might you recommend for individual and collective learning at Northern Rock?

3 What might a sustainable organisational learning strategy for Northern Rock look like?

INTRODUCTION

The idea of 'the learning organisation' was an academic invention that in turn helped place the agenda for organisational learning on the map both in terms of theory and practice. 'The learning organisation may be defined as one in which learning is not restricted to discrete "hunks" of training activity, either fragmented or systematic, but is one where it has become a continuous process, and where on the job learning has become a way of life' (Barham et al 1988, p50).

Bob Garratt wrote *The Learning Organisation* (1987, 1994) and *Creating a Learning Organisation: A guide to leadership learning and development* (1990). Significantly he is renowned for the emphasis he placed on the role of directors and the leadership team as the 'organisational brain', whose job it was to lead the way in growing a learning organisation.

Building on a speech in early 1986 made by Geoffrey Holland, then Director of the Manpower Services Commission, which called for a new management development initiative in the UK, the idea of the learning company was born. He had argued that for individuals and companies to survive we needed to create learning companies. This idea was picked up by Pedler et al in the UK in *The Learning Company: A strategy for sustainable development* (1991) and by Burgoyne et al in *Towards the Learning Company: Concepts and practices* (1994). Their work stirred the imagination of the corporate world and encouraged practitioners to share the ambitions of this learning strategy.

'A learning company is an organisation which facilitates the learning of all its members and continuously transforms itself in order to meet its strategic goals' (Pedler et al 1989, p91). Their dream was that we can design and create organisations capable of adapting, changing, developing and transforming themselves in response to the needs, wishes and aspirations of people both in and outside of the organisation (including employees, customers and suppliers). They preferred the language of 'the learning company', as opposed to 'the learning organisation' (which they regarded as mechanical by contrast) and emphasised the importance of collective endeavour and joint enterprise.

In the United States, Senge (1990), in *The Fifth Discipline* and later in *The Fifth Discipline Fieldbook* (Senge et al 1996), created a model that sought to capture a systematic approach to organisational learning, based on five disciplines, which also offered practitioners a framework for practice.

The aim of these authors was to encourage organisations to transform themselves into top-class players in an increasingly competitive and changing global economy. While the ideas served to provide frameworks and models for enabling organisations to harness learning as a tool for improving organisational performance fell out of fashion, the agenda and need for sustainable high-performing organisations remains. Indeed, one might argue in addressing the current economic global crisis that the agenda for organisational learning is ever more prescient.

THE IDEA OF THE LEARNING ORGANISATION

The idea of the learning organisation emerged in the context of change that occurred in the 1980s and 1990s. Manufacturing was in decline (see Chapter 19) and a new service economy was in the ascendency. The stability of the post-1945 business world, it was argued, had given way to a world in flux. At the same time came the paradigm-changing nature of information and communications technology. White-collar workers were adapting to a changing work environment based on computers and the paper-based systems of business were changing rapidly. Boundaries of the business world had shifted; businesses had to look beyond local markets. China had opened its doors to worldwide trade in 1978. There was, at this point in time, a new emphasis on the need for greater competitive awareness and strategic thinking. It was in this context that the *learning organisation* found its place. A strategic approach to learning was essential to any business that wished to be successful and achieve its business goals in this rapidly changing and turbulent world.

In 1988 the Management for the Future project (MFF) was launched by the Foundation for Management Education and Ashridge Management College and was disseminated as a report. It aimed to help managers face an increasingly turbulent world, by seeking to uncover what made successful companies different from their competitors. Barham et al (1998) looked at the visions successful companies had for their futures, the skills needed by managers and how they were planning to prepare their managers for the task ahead. Their research was twofold: first, a literature search with the aim of identifying organisations that had been cited as innovative or excellent was conducted; and second, research was conducted in companies identified in the first phase and who were considered worthy of further investigation. Benchmarks for measuring success were a successful and consistent record of financial performance, identified as innovative or excellent, so that best practice might be shared. A cross-section of companies, including manufacturing, service and finance in the UK and Europe, were included.

The findings from this report included an examination of the role of training and development. It suggested that organisations tended to exhibit three different approaches to training and development:

1 *A fragmented approach* in which training may be offered but was provided often on the whim of a manager. It would, likely as not, fail to be linked to the needs or goals of the business, for example, a training course might be offered to an employee as a 'reward' or perk. While this approach was in the minority, it was still worthy of reporting.

2 *A formalised approach,* by contrast, involved a planned and systematic approach to training and development that was linked to the needs of the business. Training was usually the domain of a training function, trainers designed and delivered training courses, selected from a menu of training to be offered in-house or in some cases off-site. This approach was much more common and what you would expect to find in the majority of organisations at that time.

3 *A focused approach,* which, they suggested, 'may also be called the "learning organisation". This phase is described as "focussed" because training and development activities are driven both by the strategic goals of the organization as well as the needs of individuals' (Barham et al 1988, p50). By contrast, this was a strategic use of learning and development, considered to be an appropriate way forward for business in the future. Their report offered some examples of companies who had put this approach into practice.

The authors cite an example given by a manager at BMW, who describes the difference between 'an offer' and 'a problem-oriented approach', whereby the traditional training course takes second place to learning on the job or a work-based learning solution. This approach emphasised the importance of personal development. It was learner-centred as opposed to trainer-centred and included learning in respect of being a manager as well as how to do management. Coupled with work-based learning, this approach was regarded as the best way of developing managers for the future.

In another example from Norsk Data, the manager alludes to a key element of a successful learning organisation, including a learning environment in which individuals are both empowered to learn new things while learning about the process of learning itself. Barham et al (1988) asserted that the learning organisation would be the pattern of management education and development for the future. Freedom to be proactive and taking early responsibility were hallmarks of this performance culture for managers, where individuals would be committed to hard work and long hours. The latter could be noted as potentially problematic, drawing our attention to the potential dark side of the learning organisation agenda.

In another example, ACCOR is cited as using training to reinforce the business strategy: 'the ability of training to influence strategy is a natural extension of the role of training in a learning organisation' (Barham et al 1988, p53). New skills of facilitation were needed to support this learner-centred approach. MFF echoed the beliefs of Garratt, that development should be targeted at managers who were, in his words, 'the corporate brain'. He believed the best way to develop them was by a form of work-based learning known as *action learning*, where managers learn to resolve 'real' work problems. In *action learning* managers come together in small groups known as *action learning sets* where these work problems are explored. Managers support and challenge each other as learners through a process of questioning insight (see Revans 1982; Hartog 2004a).

Development for 'high flyers' was identified as imperative to ensure that companies benefited from the best talent. Business schools were urged to deliver more MBAs, and in-company programmes and 'corporate universities' were seen as one solution to develop middle managers who were viewed as the 'backbone' of organisational business life. *Networking* was regarded as important as the formal curriculum. In addition, the development needs of international managers was also highlighted. Finally, *learning to learn* was regarded as the imperative for success.

IMPACT OF THE LEARNING ORGANISATION

In the UK, Pedler et al (1991) created the *learning company* project. Their research began in 1986 in support of a government initiative that believed organisations needed to become learning companies if they were to survive as companies and if the UK was to survive as a country. Their research spawned books and other publications, a decade of conferences, a consultancy project and resources.

They built on the work of learning theorists such as Argyris and Schön (1978, 1990) on organisational learning, and Peters and Waterman (1982), whose work *In Search of Excellence* was credited with first using the term 'the learning organisation'. Additionally, they drew on the work of Revans (1982), giving renewed emphasis to action learning as a tool for developing managers.

As previously mentioned, Pedler et al (1989, p91) defined the learning company as 'an organisation which facilitates the learning of all its members and continuously transforms itself in order to meet its strategic goals'. The three elements of this definition speak directly to the ambition and vision of what becoming a learning company entailed. What was significant was threefold. Firstly, the emphasis was on learning for everyone, not just the privileged few. Secondly, inherent in the definition was the *transformational potential* definition – that organisations were capable of influencing and taking hold of their own future. Thirdly, a core idea was that it was possible to shape the business environment context, as much as being shaped by it. In their attempt to model the learning company from their research with organisations, Pedler et al identified 11 characteristics of a learning company:

1 a learning approach to strategy

2 participative policy-making

3 'informating'

4 formative accounting and control

5 internal exchange

6 reward flexibility

7 enabling structures

8 boundary workers as environmental scanners

9 inter-company learning

10 a learning climate

11 self-development opportunities for all.

These practices provided practitioners with a diagnostic tool to assess where an organisation was weak and where it needed to plug the gap(s) in helping it become a learning company. A *learning approach* to strategy required attention to be paid to the process of formulating and implementing a strategy, and moreover checking and testing if it was working and weighing the risk of moving in any particular direction. Managers were encouraged to adopt an experimental attitude to learning. *Participative policy-making* sought to involve all members of an organisation to contribute to policy and ideas with commitment and ownership for the direction and actions shared by all concerned. *'Informating'* concerned the marriage of management information and technology to make that information accessible and inform decision-making. *Formative accounting and control* was used in a learning company to assist everyone to learn about how money works in the business and encourage people to take responsibility for their part of the business and provide access to key information that would help them do this. *Internal exchange* to encourage internal customer-focused relationships. *Reward flexibility* was encouraged to reward learning. Companies were urged to make transparent what it was they valued and were rewarding. It was also seen to be beneficial to give people some control in determining what type of rewards they wanted. *Enabling structures* were regarded as those that were able to adapt and change to the needs of the business. *Boundary workers as environmental scanners* involved people learning from the external business environment, including listening to customers and stakeholders. *Inter-company learning* involves how companies can learn from one another. For example, HR practitioners set up breakfast clubs to exchange good practice and networking became commonplace among business professionals. *A learning climate* aimed to foster a culture of learning, which included the ethos that mistakes were also a learning opportunity. Managers were encouraged to lead by example and embrace their learning too, making time for reflection, both individual and collective. The learning of managers was significant because hitherto many managers had taken the view that they did not need learning; after all, they had already got to the top! *Self-development opportunities for all* was emphasised as critical to the learning company. Learning was no longer seen as being just for the privileged few but for everyone. Companies were encouraged to make resources available and individuals were encouraged to take responsibility for their own learning and development.

Behind these 11 characteristics lay an 'e' – energy model. Pedler et al (1989) argued that the learning company required an uninterrupted flow of energy between four domains: policy, operations, actions and ideas. This was depicted in a figure, showing how the four domains interacted with one another. By paying attention to where energy flowed freely between these four domains or where it was blocked, organisations could monitor and refresh their learning environment and organisational effectiveness.

Meanwhile in the USA, at MIT another team was working on ideas that came into the public domain through the work of Senge et al (1990, 1994) in *The Fifth Discipline* and later in the fieldbook of the same name for practitioners. This work also spawned an industry of conferences and a Society for Organisational Learning in the US, UK and Europe. The learning organisation was seen as both capable of adaptive learning to the changing environment and of generative learning. Senge et al's framework of five disciplines were presented as strategies and tools for building a learning organisation:

1 *Personal mastery*: learning to expand our personal capacity to create the results we most desire, and creating an organisational environment that encourages all its members to develop themselves towards the goals and purposes they choose

2 *Mental models*: reflecting upon, continually clarifying and improving our internal pictures of the world, and seeing how they shape our actions and decisions

3 *Shared vision*: building a sense of commitment in a group, by developing shared images of the future we seek to create and the principles and guiding practices by which we hope to get there

4 *Team learning*: transforming conversational and collective thinking skills, so that groups of people can reliably develop intelligence and ability greater than the sum of individual members' talents

5 *Systems thinking*: a way of thinking about, and a language for describing and understanding, the forces and interrelationships that shape the behaviour of systems. This discipline helps us see how to change systems more effectively, and to act more in tune with larger processes of the natural and economic world.

In addition, three skills and capabilities were required to underpin these disciplines; they were:

- *aspiration*, including the desire to change and move in the right direction, not just changing as a requirement to comply

- *reflection* and conversation, in other words, the art of dialogue and the capacity to hold *learningful* conversations

- *conceptualisation*, being able to see the relationship or connection, of one part of a system to the whole.

A CRITIQUE OF THE LEARNING ORGANISATION

The goals of the learning organisation have as much currency in today's economic climate as they did at its inception. In the learning organisation collective learning is assumed to be the chief vehicle for achieving learning leverage in the organisation. Shared learning is believed to increase an organisation's 'learning intelligence', leveraging its capability to be competitive. Learning to learn remains a challenge: 'the ability to learn faster than your competitors may be the only source of competitive advantage' (DeGeus 1988, p71).

Is it individuals who learn, or is it the organisation? Indeed, we have to ask: can an organisation 'learn' and, if so, what does organisational learning look like? Some assumptions behind the learning organisation phenomenon are:

- To be a successful organisation you need to become a learning organisation.

- Increased knowledge will improve action.

- The organisation needs to manage its relationship to its environment.

- Collective thinking and collective learning are key points of leverage.

- An organisation and its people must be proactive in respect of learning and change.

- Organisational learning will enhance the bottom line.

Dibella and Nevis (1998) identify three perspectives in learning organisation practice:

1 *A normative perspective:* the learning organisation exists as a product of design, intervention and strategies serve to constrain barriers to learning

2 *A development perspective:* 'a life cycle lens', as with the Ashridge Model (Barham et al 1988), where learning moves from an ad hoc approach to training, to a planned/formalised approach and, finally, to a strategic stage of development, where learning is a continuous cycle of improvement

3 *A capability perspective:* all organisations have intrinsic capabilities and there is no one best way for an organisation to learn.

Shipton (2006) and Shipton and Zhou (2008) provide a typology of organisational learning research in which two types of literature are described: prescriptive/

normative (which focuses on how to become a learning organisation) and descriptive/explanatory (which explores how organisational learning happens). The latter is characterised by the notion that a positive relationship exists between organisational learning and performance (see Senge 2006; Pedler et al 2000). Proponents of the learning organisation offer prescriptions for learning to achieve the goal of becoming a learning organisation.

KNOWLEDGE AND THE LEARNING ORGANISATION

Knowledge management or *knowledge transfer* is implicit in the learning organisation model, with learning interventions designed to manage, harness and generate new knowledge. Therefore, some understanding of how knowledge is held, accessed and flows through an organisation is essential to understand how it contributes to corporate intelligence and competitive advantage. Sligo (1996) suggests that knowledge may be viewed as intelligence or as power. Access to knowledge may not be equal in an organisation, yet if we are attempting to create a more intelligent organisation, staff need to be able to access a broader field of data, especially in times of change when organisational responses to external changing conditions matter the most (Sligo 1996).

It is commonly asserted that we are all knowledge workers now, since all organisations operate within a knowledge economy. If we accept this argument, we must accept that all levels of employees need access to some strategic knowledge. Sligo suggests that workers need an overview of how their job fits into an overall scheme. His example of workers making bricks or building a cathedral offers a clear perspective on how different information and knowledge can enhance the capacity of a worker to know what their contribution is all about. In his research with a New Zealand processing plant he discovered that information guiding management decision-making was divided between supervisors and their subordinates and middle and senior managers. The implications of this for organisational learning are clear. If information and knowledge is constrained by hierarchical management structures and traditional systems of control, then the ability and opportunity for employees to contribute to making their firm more intelligent is constrained. What Sligo's study enables us to see is that organisation structures and cultures are potentially barriers to learning.

DEFINING THE 'LEARNING ORGANISATION' AND 'ORGANISATIONAL LEARNING'

The learning organisation and organisational learning are frequently used interchangeably and can lead to confusion. Leitch (1996) suggests that the learning organisation excels at collective learning, while organisational learning describes the *methods used* to achieve collective learning. Tsang (1997) similarly differentiates these terms by suggesting that the learning organisation is a type of company that is good at organisational learning and that the term organisational learning refers to the learning activities that take place in the company. While these definitions are helpful, they are by no means definitive. Organisational learning is, for example, as much about the processes of learning as it is about activities and this is because learning itself is complex, involving both tangible and intangibles. Organisational learning may be best understood as a metaphor and the learning organisation a form of shorthand that describes a prescription of an ideal vision or destination.

Shipton's (2006) analysis of the prescriptive normative literature of the learning organisation suggests that its inspirational and emotive language masks the difficulties associated with learning. Easterby-Smith and Lyles (2003) suggest that the field has divided into two camps, practitioner and academic, each with differing agendas in terms of theory and practice. Walton (1999) describes the ultimate goal of practitioner-based human resource development (HRD) as the achievement of the learning organisation. This rationale serves to elevate HRD to the strategic agenda. It is attractive to practitioners because it offers a framework and methods for ways of thinking and integrating learning with business imperatives. It is attractive to the firm because it promises to unlock the potential of individuals and groups who can contribute to the sustainable and competitive advantage of the firm, while enhancing the organisation's capacity and readiness for change.

WHAT CAN A CRITICAL PERSPECTIVE OFFER?

A critical perspective aims to interrogate the rhetoric and reveal the reality of organisational experience. Walton (1999) suggests that, while fashionable, the learning organisation tends to be vague. He cites work by Prothero (1997) and found that the learning organisation was found to be seen as 'fluffy' or as an 'experiential concept'.

Walton (1999) also highlights the problematic nature of continuous transformation (common in learning organisation rhetoric). He suggests that organisations need to consolidate what they are trying to achieve before embarking on further transformative endeavours.

To date, there remains a dearth of robust empirical evidence about the learning organisation, not least because accounts of real organisations' efforts to become a learning organisation are often written by consultants. A recent study by Marshall et al (2009) provides a case study of the learning organisation that is suggested to bridge the academic–practitioner divide. Nonetheless, we need to be cautious, since organisational learning is such an idiosyncratic and complex concept that is difficult to imitate (Lopez et al 2005) and, therefore, difficult to transfer learning from one organisation to another.

WHAT DO WE UNDERSTAND BY LEARNING?

What we understand by learning is important if we are to make sense of the conundrum of organisational learning. The achievement of the learning organisation is usually held to be a manifestation of 'organisational learning'. But the idea of organisation learning is contentious. Organisations do not or cannot learn. Rather, only individuals have the capacity to learn. However, it is the knowledge outcome of individual learning that has the potential to raise the collective wisdom of the organisation:

> ...the only resource capable of learning within an organisation is the people who comprise it. The very diversity of the experience of these people is a valuable asset, if one can only learn to harness the experience and use it. (Walton 1999, p386)

Organisational learning occurs because individuals act as learning agents for the organisation, scanning and monitoring the external environment and detecting and correcting errors (Argyris and Schön 1978). Individual learning therefore is only one part of the equation and thus theories of individual learning serve only to highlight half of the picture. In addition, individual theories of learning tend to emphasise behavioural and cognitive theories – the latter is concerned with changing routine behaviours and the former with thinking processes. Shipton (2006, p241) tells us that literature which takes a normative perspective towards organisational learning, though offering a more critical perspective than the prescriptive literature, nonetheless tends to focus on processes whereby individuals transfer their learning to the organisation, and less on how individuals learn. Suffice to say that individual learning is the first stage of the organisational learning cycle. To understand collective learning we need to consider social theories of learning. This can help us understand collective learning processes and consider what we mean by organisational learning.

LEARNING AS A SOCIAL PROCESS

Social learning is both a consequence of everyday interactions in the organisation and of planned learning interventions, designed to bring employees together to share their experience, knowledge and understanding of events and processes in their work. Learning can therefore be understood to be socially constructed. Lave and Wenger's work on social learning theory has helped us understand this phenomenon. They tell us that 'learning is situated in a participation framework, not in an individual mind' (Lave and Wenger 1991, p15). For example, historically, 'apprentices' are involved in a social process of learning from a 'master craftsman' over a number of years. This begins with what Lave and Wenger call 'legitimate peripheral participation'. Over time as their training progresses and they become more skilful and knowledgeable they move beyond the periphery. *Communities of learning* and *communities of practice* have been identified as a site for social learning and as such have received considerable attention in respect of social and collective learning in the learning organisation and organisational learning literature. Communities of practice build up repertoires of appropriate practice knowledge, and the socialisation process of newcomers ensures that this learning is transferred from one generation to the next and it is through this process that tacit knowledge is learned and embedded.

Transferring learning from individuals to the organisation shifts learning from the individual to the collective and from a passive to an active undertaking.

DeGeus (1988, p70) defines institutional learning as 'the process whereby management teams change their shared mental models of their company, their markets and their competitors'.

LEVELS OF LEARNING

According to Argyris and Schön (1978), three levels of learning can take place in organisations. Level 1, also known as *single loop learning*, is concerned with maintenance of an organisation's operating systems and seeks to identify and correct errors accordingly. It is a reactive process. In other words, there is a problem and we resolve it. Burgoyne (1995) describes this as habitual learning; in other words, this is what we do when things go wrong and, as such, we do not need to think too hard about it. Level 2, also known as *double loop learning*, involves challenging the organisational orthodoxies: the 'otherwise', the 'whys and wherefores' of what we are doing. For example, this type of learning may lead us to redefine our organisational mission or values. Burgoyne (1995) defines this as an adaptive form of learning. Level 3, known as *deutero learning*, is concerned with learning to learn. It is a higher level of learning that involves enquiry and reflection, for example, looking back at past events and asking what worked and what didn't. It is a process of deep learning that can lead to new discoveries and transformative practices. Burgoyne (1995) describes this as learning for the sustainable organisation. While many organisations lay claim to being a learning organisation, the reality is that most organisations achieve little more than learning at level one.

BARRIERS TO LEARNING

There are a range of factors that can enable or inhibit an organisation's ability to learn. Barriers to learning can include structural issues in the organisation; and associated contradictions, which may mean, on the one hand, the organisation wants to become a learning organisation, while on the other restricting access to information that limits the flow and use of knowledge in the organisation. Reviewing the literature on organisational learning, Marshall et al (2009) identify four contextual factors for organisational learning, namely: culture, strategy, structure and the business environment. Similarly, Popper and Lipshitz (2000) identify structure and culture to be significant, with strong leadership and continuous learning key to enabling effective organisational learning to occur.

Anxiety is also a significant barrier to learning, both for individual and organisational learning. It manifests itself in a form of defence or resistance. At the organisational level, Argyris and Schön (1990) point to defensive routines and defensive reasoning, which they suggest may be explained by the gap between espoused theory and theory in use, in other words, the difference between what an organisation says and what it does. Similarly, defensive routines at the individual level are designed to protect the ego (through self-defence), serving to counter embarrassment and threat. Rowan (2001) suggests that the development of a mature ego involves a process of learning akin to a developmental step change.

In the learning organisation the team is identified by Senge et al as the key unit of learning in the organisation and dialogue as the vehicle to foster team learning. Team learning and shared thinking is assumed to facilitate understanding and lead to more effective decision-making and action. It is suggested that in this context employees can come together to discuss issues openly. Subordinates and managers alike are assumed to be able to engage in this process, as long as they abide by the 'rules' of dialogue. The rules of dialogue include listening, equality of participation and equal opportunity to speak, enquire and not jump to conclusions. However, Shipton (2006) highlights the fact that it is an assumption that people will speak openly and honestly about the concerns and anxieties they hold. For example, subordinates may hesitate to share their views with their managers and managers may not be in a position to reveal all. There may indeed be a contradiction in that the company genuinely aspires to empower employees through team learning and yet information may be deemed too sensitive to share. Personal motives, company secrets, power and politics may all contrive to limit the effectiveness of otherwise well-intentioned learning interventions. Additionally, individuals may not want to share their knowledge with others, they may not be motivated to, or they may regard their knowledge as their own intellectual property. Walton (1999), referring to the 'ICL model' (Mayo and Lank 1994), points out that where knowledge is viewed as a commodity there is danger that people become human *resources*, rather than being seen and treated as resourceful *human beings* (Walton 1999, pp405–6). Overcoming barriers to learning is thus a complex undertaking, as Hartog and Frame (2004) indicate in their study.

WHAT DO WE NEED FROM THE HRD AND OD PRACTITIONER?

According to Walton (1999), HRD practitioners need to have the skills to be able to unpack organisational realities and be ready for change. HRD refers to a strategic framework for aiding employees to develop their personal and organisational skills, knowledge and abilities. As such, it incorporates different HRM elements, such as training, career development, performance management and development, coaching, mentoring and succession planning (Walton 1999). Harrison and Kessels (2004) found that the skills of learning and development practitioners had failed to keep up with changes that the learning organisation and knowledge economy demand. They discuss the trend to push responsibility for learning and development to the line and point out that this is a flawed strategy, since the line manager often does not have the skills to do the work (see also Chapter 19). HRD is a specialist skill-set involving the strategic management of learning and development in the organisation. Harrison and Kessels (2004) describe the role of HRD as knowledge-productive work, not training. HRD practitioners need the intellectual skills to understand the complexities of this work and the practical skills to take on new roles as facilitators and reflective educators for the organisation. Skilled HRD practice is a lifetime's work and therefore commitment to one's own continuous professional development is essential (Hartog 2004b).

Similarly the organisational development (OD) practitioner uses diagnostic tools to examine the links between the corporate environment, the organisation's work (its strategic imperative), its customer experience and employee satisfaction in order to make judgements about the health and effectiveness of the organisation and to identify where intervention may be required. OD is concerned with 'attempts to improve the overall performance and effectiveness of the organisation...it is an applied behavioural science approach to planned change and development of an organisation' (Mullins 2007, p719). Holbeche and Cheung-Judge (2009) argue that OD goes beyond organisation learning and development in that its aim is to build capacity in the organisation, to enable its internal capacity to match its strategic ambition. The role and skill-set of the OD practitioner includes the ability to work well with groups and understand what works in bringing out the best in people. Additionally, OD practitioners must be skilful politicians to be able to influence internal politics and the organisation's shadow system.

It can often be difficult for organisations to see beyond their immediate economic situation. Nonetheless, organisations need to think and act beyond the limits of short-term survival if they are to thrive. Holbeche (2010) argues that organisation development strategies can play an important role in this, helping to build resilient organisational cultures, enabling organisational responsiveness to cope with the uncertainties and turbulence of the market and supporting the development of high-performance teams and organisational leadership.

MEASUREMENT AND EVALUATION OF LEARNING

The 'bottom line' is the assumed relationship between organisational learning, improved performance and competitive success and return on investment (RoI). But direct correlations between investment in learning and RoI are problematic. Hard measures cannot capture the subtleties of learning processes such as improved relationships or a greater flow of information and knowledge in a firm, so it behoves HRD practitioners to understand and explain the learning processes that are intended to facilitate particular learning and performance outcomes. In difficult economic times employers want evidence of tangible benefits if they are to continue to invest in learning and, if this cannot be provided, history has shown that investment in learning activity is often the first to be cut when times are tough.

In view of the complex nature of learning described in this chapter, evaluation of learning organisation interventions and thus organisational learning needs to address not only organisational-level outcomes in respect of profit, competitive advantage and success, but also it must consider the wider social and ethical agenda facing business today. Furthermore it must take account of the fact that learning interventions (activities) and strategies are themselves complex and not without difficulties.

CONCLUSION

In conclusion, the learning organisation offers a vision with tools and models, such as those offered by Senge et al and Pedler et al. The journey to the learning organisation is a visionary ideal and while embarking on that journey is compelling (in that success brings with it potentially greater organisational intelligence and competitive advantage), we must be wary of the sometimes overblown rhetoric within this narrative. One organisation's prescription does not necessarily translate into suitable treatment or a guaranteed cure for all. We must keep in mind that all organisations are unique and that the organisational context for learning is of prime importance.

Furthermore, we must keep in mind that knowledge itself is subject to change and our capacity to learn both as individuals and as an organisation is also variable. Could staff at Northern Rock have prevented the crisis or predicted the 'fracture lines' (Morgan 1988) in the business environment? Possibly not: the problem was systemic, with the entire financial sector operating in a mode of normative deviance in which critical reflection on practice was wholly absent.

Knowledge changes and people come and go in organisations. Therefore we need to realise that organisational memory may lapse and shift too, unless we build strong communities of practice to reinforce learning and identify tacit knowledge crucial to organisations' survival. Like a car, an organisation needs a regular service. The HRD practitioner (like a Formula 1 engineer) needs to ensure that learning strategies and activities are fit for purpose and that learning for individuals and the organisation addresses future as well as current needs. HRD practitioners have a duty to monitor and evidence their learning interventions and ensure that learning adds value and offers a wise and sound investment.

Commenting on the CIPD's Shaping the Future research and engagement agenda, Holbeche and Cheung-Judge (2009) note that OD programmes are intended to advance HR and management practice and lead to sustainable organisational improvement. Finally, Shipton (2006) identifies two areas of research for the learning organisation: (1) how does individual learning promotes organisational learning; and (2) how do particular learning activities lead to learning outcomes?

CRITICAL REFLECTIONS

Critical incidents provide excellent opportunities for learning both at the individual and organisational level. From a learning perspective, what is important is that no one saw it coming and there is a risk that it could happen again. Trust in leaders and managers, from politicians to bankers, is at an all-time low. It is in this context that the learning agenda needs to be revisited. 'HR leaders support and challenge business leaders, not only to deliver today's business agenda but also to lay firm foundations for tomorrow's success' (Holbeche 2010, p7). Writing about the crisis, Holbeche argues that there is a need to build resilient organisation cultures and to create strategies that are more anticipatory, facilitating flexibility and responsiveness. She points out that a performance-driven culture is 'characterised by learning, collaboration and team working across boundaries' (Holbeche 2010, p7). Moreover Holbeche (2010) argues that organisations need to become 'change-able', in other words, to be capable of being innovative, flexible and agile at the same time and be able to manage the paradox of innovation and risk simultaneously.

One challenge is for HR to address some of the issues that nearly brought down our economic system, including overemphasis on financial incentives to motivate employees and their top managers and the consequent need to explore alternatives. As Holbeche (2010, p9) points out: 'No wonder then that the UK government has sought to discourage the big bonus culture in banking which is thought to be responsible at least in part for the rash and even unethical behaviour which led to the current crisis.' Among these alternatives is to encourage employees to give greater priority to ethical considerations in their work. These might include professional ethics but could also be much wider, including societal and moral concerns.

The scale of this crisis requires an organisational development and learning approach. A new learning strategy is needed to support the development of a new business model based on values of stakeholder accountability, which include shareholders and the wider community, and a back-to-basics, prudent policy of business practice and product development. The strategy and learning interventions must provide a learning orientation to the problem and future of the business. A corporate learning event that looks backwards and forwards is a good start. The strategy requires renewal. The event must invite reflection on the problem, draw what is known and understood about it, and identify what has worked well in the past. 'What business are we in?' is a good question to facilitate thinking and enquiry about what the future of our customer base, product development and customer orientation might look like. The aim is to create a culture of learning to learn and to clarify and communicate through participation a clear vision with new – operational – business values going forward.

A sustainable learning plan then can be designed around the needs of the business and identify gaps in organisational capability going forward (thus informing reorganisation, recruitment and retention for new roles and skills).

To develop current staff, a renewed learning needs assessment and personal and professional development plans are required. Priorities for the business probably would include risk and audit, new sales programmes and emergent sustainable product development. Management learning and development is likely to be a priority, perhaps with some emphasis on reflective learning and business ethics. In addition, the development needs of potential high-performers need to be addressed.

EXPLORE FURTHER

EASTERBY-SMITH, M., BURGOYNE, J. and ARAUJO, L. (1999) *Organizational learning and the learning organization: developments in theory and practice.* London: Sage.

This book provides a synthesis of the debates surrounding the two different concepts of 'organisational learning' and the 'learning organisation' and offers an advanced perspective on these issues.

HOLBECHE, L. (2010) *HR leadership.* Oxford: Butterworth-Heinemann.

This book provides insights into HR leadership, its meaning and application in organisations. It addresses some of the really critical issues of today for HRM leadership.

REYNOLDS, M. and VINCE, R. (eds) (2004) *Organizing reflection.* Aldershot: Ashgate Publishing.

This edited book includes a collection of writings focusing on the development of the concepts of public reflection, collective reflection and critical reflection, and provides insights into new approaches to the role of reflection in organisations.

HARTOG, M., MORTON, C. and MULLER-CAMEN, M. (2008) Corporate social responsibility and sustainable HRM. In: MULLER-CAMEN, M., CROUCHER, R. and LEIGH, S. (eds). *Human resource management: a case study approach.* London: CIPD. pp470–477.

This chapter looks at the agenda of CSR and sustainable HRM and it offers a good grounding for organisations to understand that agenda and to see what initiatives are taking place.

CHAPTER 15

Critical Issues in Reward Management: Is the 'New Pay' Still New?

Geoff White

OVERVIEW

Following the presentation of a media-based case study, this chapter will critically review the 'new pay' paradigm, considering its various elements: a fall in collective mechanisms for employees to co-determine wages, a rise in the link between individual and collective 'performance' in how pay is determined and a shift from internal equity to external competitiveness. It will then go on to consider some emerging – or re-emerging – issues in reward: the relationship between low pay and top pay in organisations, the rise of contingent pay and the dilemmas posed by making reward 'strategic'.

LEARNING OBJECTIVES

Reading this chapter will enable the reader to:

- critically evaluate the relative influences and trends in collectively negotiated versus individually negotiated reward systems
- compare and contrast the relative importance of internal equity and external equity on pay
- compare and contrast the relative importance of market pressures versus regulatory pressures on pay.

HRM IN THE MEDIA

'ANGER OVER "EXCESSIVE" PAY'

Following announcements of large-scale redundancies and pay freezes across the public sector, a row emerged over the pay package of an Inner London head teacher – reportedly being paid over £200,000 in the current year (BBC News 2010). The pay package, which included special payments for additional work done, was said to be good value considering the important work done in transforming the school and the money was needed to attract top talent, as would be the case in the private sector. However, it was also questioned whether the gap between top pay and average pay was justified.

Questions

1 What processes should be involved in setting the pay of this head teacher?

2 What considerations need to be made to ensure that the level set is fair to the individual, to the organisation and to other colleagues working at the school?

3 Who should be consulted about pay?

INTRODUCTION

The last three decades have witnessed major changes in approaches to remunerating employees. In the 1970s remuneration systems in most large organisations in the UK were largely based on the traditional divide between pay systems for manual or 'blue-collar' workers, which emphasised contingency and payment by results, and those for staff or 'white-collar' workers, which emphasised stability, status, loyalty and seniority. It was also a world in which a majority of the UK workforce had its pay determined through collective negotiations with trade unions. Pay management was seen as 'pay administration' and the concept of strategic alignment of remuneration with business objectives was unheard of. Reward was simply a business risk to be managed as best as it could be. By the end of the 1980s, however, this picture had begun to change dramatically. In making sense of the changes, academics and other commentators have increasingly sought broader management theory for explanations. Where once the study of pay policy and practice was rooted in economics, sociology and industrial relations, the influence of psychology and organisational behaviour have become increasingly important as well as the broader business strategy literature. In the UK the subject has also become increasingly influenced by a substantial North American literature, partly reflecting the growth of both US company influence in the UK and the rise of US-based management consultancy within Europe. Nonetheless, the employment relationship remains fundamental to reward management and many of the insights about remuneration gained from the industrial relations and sociology literature of the past are as relevant today as in the past. The reward management relationship remains rooted in the employment relationship between the employer and the employee and the 'effort bargain' between the parties that this entails (Behrend 1957).

THE RISE OF THE REWARD MANAGEMENT PARADIGM

The relatively stable and settled picture of pay determination in the 1970s began to change with the major changes in the global economic system of the 1980s. In the UK this led to a major decline in manufacturing industry, as international competition drove more and more jobs offshore, and with it a major decline in the work opportunities for unskilled and skilled wage workers. This was largely a male phenomenon and contrasted with the growth of new service sector jobs in retail, hospitality, business and financial services, where many of the new jobs were part-time and taken by females. Employment in sectors such as retail and hospitality have a history of poor pay and poor unionisation with protection by statutory wages councils to set minimum pay and conditions. The growth in the proportion of female workers within the workforce also led to new concerns about employment discrimination and equal pay. The decline of the manufacturing and extractive industries also hit trade union organisation badly and with it the use of collective bargaining as the major method of determining pay. Alongside these economic changes there were also changes in the management of employment with the rise of the 'human resource management' paradigm that emphasised the strategic use of human resources to meet organisational objectives (see Guest 1990; Storey 1992; Sisson 1994; Legge 1995).

The development of the 'reward management' paradigm among personnel practitioners was the result of these changes. Its development was closely linked to the emergence of what became known as the 'new pay' literature in the USA. The term 'new pay' was first used by the US management writer Edward Lawler in 1990 (Lawler 1990) and later developed by others such as Schuster and Zingheim (1992) and Gomez-Mejia and Balkin (1992). The 'new pay' writers argued that remuneration needed to become part of business strategy and linked to corporate objectives. As Lawler (1995, p14) stated:

> The new pay argues in favour of a pay-design process that starts with business strategy and organisational design. It argues against an assumption that certain best practices must be incorporated into a company's approach to pay.

The new employee–organisation relationship that had developed in the less predictable economic environment of the 1980s meant changes were needed in 'attitudes, plans and approaches to both how we work and how we are paid' (Schuster and Zingheim 1992, p4). The 'new pay' was intended to encourage a more contingent and strategically focused approach to reward, which challenged traditional approaches such as job evaluation, cost-of-living pay rises and external referencing (Schuster and Zingheim 1992). The 'new pay', in contrast, starts from the premise that pay should vary in line with individual, group and organisational performance. In other words, reward systems should be contingent on business needs and risks should be shared between employer and worker through the reward system. The key concept of the 'new pay' was the shift from traditional 'job-related' pay structures to new 'person-related' structures. This implied much more emphasis upon variable forms of remuneration. Mahoney (1992, p338–9) argued that 'the concept of job was the unifying concept in the

Scientific Management approach to organisation and management', which in turn led to 'the development and application of a concept of job ownership expressed in the labor movement and collective bargaining'. The new pay literature therefore takes a fundamentally unitarist and normative view of the employment relationship (see Chapter 12). The importance of the shift to 'person-related' pay was explained by Lawler (1990, p153) as follows:

> Paying people according to their value in the market pays…. After all, it is people who move from job to job and from company to company, it is people who develop skills, and it is people who are the important organisational assets.

Another facet of the new pay is emphasised by Gomez-Mejia (1993, p14), who argues that it is based on a strategic orientation 'where issues of internal equity and external equity are viewed as secondary to the firm's need to use pay as an essential integrating and signalling mechanism to achieve over-arching business objectives'. In other words, the new pay is about using reward as a key ingredient of cultural change in organisations.

Heery (1996) identified three important aspects of the new pay paradigm. First, the ratio of variable pay to guaranteed basic pay should be increased. As the CBI argued in 1994, the great attraction of variable pay is that it 'can go up and, crucially, down in line with individual, group and company performance' (CBI/Wyatt 1994, p5). Linked to this was a reduction in indirect remuneration to free up more cash for incentive pay. The second aspect identified by Heery was that the scope of variable pay should be expanded to reflect a range of measures of corporate performance – at individual, group and organisational levels. The third aspect was that base pay should reflect individual market value rather than the content of the job done. Instead of what were seen as rigid, narrow-graded, job-evaluated pay structures, employers were encouraged to introduce simpler, broadbanded grading within which managers would have much more discretion over where to appoint and progress individual workers. It was this erosion of employee collective voice within the new reward relationship and the increased transfer of organisational risks to the employee that Heery identified as having strong ethical implications for employers.

It has also been argued, by Thomson (2009, p121), that: 'Because of the concept of the new pay elides two ideas (that of thinking strategically and the introduction of new pay practices), the new pay can be criticised for lacking clarity and precision. This, in turn, can create problems in researching the nature, purpose and impact of adopting a so-called "new pay" approach.' However, as Thomson accepts, Lawler recognised this dilemma, stating that: 'New pay is not a set of compensation practices at all but rather a way of thinking about the role of reward systems in a complex organisation' (Lawler 1995, p15, cited in Thomson 2009).

MANAGEMENT DISCRETION VERSUS EMPLOYEE VOICE

A key change in reward policy and practice has been the rise of management discretion in the determination of pay and the decline of joint regulation of pay and conditions through collective mechanisms. This, it has been argued, has led to the decline of 'employee voice' in the process of pay determination (Lindop 2009). As Heery (2009) argues, trade unions remain 'the prime institution of worker voice' but other forms have emerged in recent times. Sometimes these new forms sit alongside or augment traditional employer–union arrangements but in other cases they have replaced collective bargaining. What is clear from the evidence is that management discretion is now the main method by which an individual employee's rewards are determined. As Brown et al (2009, p22) state: 'Possibly the most remarkable feature of the period after 1980 in Britain was the collapse of collectivism as the main way of regulating employment.' According to the Workplace Employee Relations Survey (WERS), by 2004 non-union-only voice was the most common voice regime, being found in 46% of workplaces, three times the figure in 1984. 'The inevitable implication to emerge…is that, by 2004, voice at the workplace was predominately an employer-generated phenomenon' (Willman et al 2009, p103). In contrast, the legal regulation of remuneration policy, as with other aspects of employment policy, has grown stronger with the introduction of a National Minimum Wage, minimum holiday entitlement, equal pay for men and women and statutory minima for family-friendly benefits such as paid maternity leave. Voluntary regulation through collective agreements between employers and unions has been gradually replaced by increasing statutory regulation.

Thus, two major changes in pay determination have occurred over the last 25 years. First, the coverage of collective bargaining has diminished and second, where collective bargaining is not present, the major form of pay determination is now through unilateral management discretion (Kersley et al 2006, p179). The locus of pay decisions has also changed. According to Brown et al (2009, p34): 'There has been a clear trend after 1984 for firms to continue to bring pay determination in-house.' This was evident whether pay was fixed by collective bargaining or unilaterally by management. However, there have been different trends between workplaces which are independent employers and those that are part of multi-site employing organisations. In most single-site, independent private sector workplaces the fixing of pay has become almost entirely done by on-site management, whereas in multi-site private organisations it appears that, from the 1990s, there was a shift towards pay being increasingly determined centrally at a higher level in the organisation. According to Brown et al (2009, p35), 'Freed from trade union constraints and old worries about their "comparability claims", employers have become more able to respond to the opportunities and pressures of local labour markets, but also more able to follow wider corporate strategies.'

But what about employee voice in the reward relationship? Without trade unions to act as a collective voice in the process, how do employees ensure that their interests are considered in the 'effort bargain'? Heery (2009, p50) argues that of five identifiable ways in which employee voice can affect reward management, unions continue to have a beneficial impact from the point of view of the employee. One key union influence is that of the effect on pay levels – the so-called 'union mark-up' or union wage premium gained by those in trade unions. While some research has indicated that this union premium has been declining, there continues to remain a pay advantage for those workers who are union members. Indeed, the work of Blanchflower and Bryson (2009, p63), using 2004 WERS data, has revealed that this is particularly important in very small workplaces where the 'relatively rare presence of union influence in small private sector workplaces was particularly beneficial to the wages of the employees concerned'. While Lindop (2009, p56) might argue that 'employee voice is changing its form rather than fading away', the empirical evidence seems to indicate that in the key areas of reward – pay levels and benefits provision – organised workers still appear to have an advantage over the unorganised. It is hard to see how alternative forms of employee voice will ever have the influence over reward in concrete economic advantage that trade unions do.

EQUITY VERSUS MARKET

The twin demands of any reward system have traditionally been, on the one hand, a method of allocating rewards that is seen internally as fair and equitable in its distribution by employers and employees (internal equity) and, on the other hand, a method for keeping pay at a sufficient level to attract and retain recruits from the external market for labour (external equity). There is a dynamic tension between these two demands because the price at which labour can be purchased from the external market may vary, reflecting the value of the different occupations at any particular point in time (White 2009). Thus occupations which might have the same 'job weight' under a job evaluation scheme, for instance, may have very different values in the external market. While in reality these two demands are rarely in balance, the state of the labour market will tend to have a profound influence. When the labour market is tight and recruitment difficulties are to the fore, employers will seek to follow the market whereas when labour is in abundance employers may worry less about market factors and concentrate more upon internal equity.

However, during the 1990s it was argued by the new pay writers that a third demand had emerged, the corporate strategy of the organisation. According to Gomez-Mejia (1993, p4): 'The emerging paradigm of the field is based on a strategic orientation where issues of internal and external equity are viewed as secondary to the firm's need to use pay as an essential integrating and signalling mechanism to achieve overarching business objectives.' As Kessler (2007) has commented, this 'strategic' approach assumes that three fundamental principles underpin pay systems – business strategy, internal equity and external equity – and that these are competing and alternative principles that organisations might choose to weight in different ways. Lastly, it assumes that organisations are abandoning internal and external equity issues in favour of some more defined corporate reward strategy.

While it is relatively easy to identify reward practices that typify approaches to internal and external equity, it is perhaps less easy to identify a set of practices that indicate linkage to business strategy. Kessler (2007, p161) makes a useful observation that 'the relationship between business strategy and pay can be seen to equate more directly to person and performance than to job', which in turn relates more to the method of progression through the pay structure, rather than the allocation of value and place in the social order that comes from internal and external equity. In other words, internal and external equity are primarily about pay structures and establishing the value of a particular job within the market. In contrast, progression or additional reward – such as the various forms of variable pay – relates more to the individual person and their individual contribution to the business. While we consider the prevalence of 'strategic reward' in more detail later in this chapter, here we are concerned to examine the degree to which approaches to pay determination have shifted between the three principles laid out by Gomez-Mejia.

Internal equity has been a cornerstone of reward practice ever since the creation of 'grades' for different levels of employee. In the past, these grading structures were relatively simple and largely reflected levels of skill (for example skilled, semi-skilled or unskilled) and related primarily to male manual workers. With the development of the non-manual workforce, grading became more complex and increasingly related to responsibilities as well as skill levels. The development of job evaluation in the period between the two world wars, which in turn related to the development of strong internal labour markets, codified these levels and sought to provide some quasi-scientific rationale for ascertaining the worth of individual jobs (Figart 2001). Pritchard and Murlis (1992) note that concerns about internal equity rather than external market competitiveness, and hence job evaluation, became particularly prominent in the UK in the 1960s and 1970s under the limitations of government incomes policies.

We can trace the growth of job evaluation in the UK through the periodic WIRS/WERS surveys. Between 1980 and 1990 the prevalence of job evaluation in workplaces with 25 or more employees rose from 21% to 26%. By 2004 the figure had fallen back to 20%. But in public sector workplaces job evaluation increased from 27% of workplaces in 1990 to 44% in 2004. In contrast, in private sector workplaces there was a decline in the use of job evaluation, perhaps indicating a waning interest in internal equity.

The key driver of internal equity in the 1990s was the increasing risk from 'equal pay for work of equal value' legislation (Corby 2009). The gender pay gap in the UK remains one of the widest in the European Union and the gap remains over 20% (ONS 2009), even after 35 years of equal pay legislation. While the Equal Pay Act of 1970 had outlawed unequal pay for men and women doing the same jobs, this measure did not take account of the fact that women's employment tends to be concentrated in particular industries and occupations and hence that their pay was usually lower than for jobs of the equivalent value for men. This was because their pay was often seen as 'women's work' and therefore innately inferior to men's work, rather than based on any rigorous assessment of the comparative value of the work. The concept of 'equal pay for work of equal value' had been part of EU employment legislation since the original Treaty of Rome in 1957 but the UK equal pay law in 1970 was domestic legislation. When the UK joined the EU in 1973, UK law had to be brought into line with EU law. The result was the Equal Pay (Amendment) Regulations 1983. These regulations require employers to demonstrate that their pay structures do not discriminate on the basis of equal value.

Contrary to Gomez-Mejia's view that equity, both internal and external, has become secondary to strategic intention, Kessler (2007) argues that both may be central to strategic imperatives. The effect of equal pay legislation has been profound but the impact upon pay structures has been most clearly seen in the public sector, where the increasing risk of legal action by both trade unions and individual workers led to major reform of existing pay determination arrangements. Equal pay is a particularly important issue for the public services for three reasons: (1) because reward practices tend to be more transparent than in the private sector; (2) because the Government has encouraged the public services to set an example of good practice; and (3) because there have clearly identified cases of gender discrimination in pay practices. Such reforms have been evident in local government, the NHS and the higher education sector where separate bargaining groups have been brought together on to single pay spines (Bach et al 2009; Perkins and White 2010). These so-called 'pay modernisation' agreements have also had other objectives – not least increased flexibility in pay determination at local level – but the major driver has been equal pay considerations. Such agreements also involved greater equity in terms of bringing different levels and types of worker onto single pay structures. Indeed, the first of these agreements – in local government in 1997 – was called the 'single status' agreement. These agreements have come under increasing challenge from 'no win, no fee' lawyers where the requirement for backdating the effect of any proven case of pay discrimination has caused major problems in local government and to a lesser extent in the NHS.

In contrast, in the private sector there is much less evidence that the law has impinged on existing practices (Corby et al 2005). The major development in the private sector in the 2000s, rather, was increasing reliance on external equity or so-called 'market rates'. In the very tight labour market of the economic boom years from the mid-1990s to the crash in 2008, recruitment and retention became the major priority of private sector organisations in the 'war for talent'. Under such arrangements, individual jobs or groups of jobs are benchmarked against the external pay rates for similar jobs in similar industries. This normally involves the use of salary surveys and other comparative data. The CIPD claims that some 75% of UK organisations share information through such surveys (CIPD 2005). In order to compare whether internal pay levels are in line with the market, employers may calculate a 'compa-ratio' (IDS 2004). The advantages of market-based pay are that it allows employers to respond flexibly to changes in the labour market and to target pay costs according to external value. However, there may be problems in linking pay too closely to market comparisons. It can undermine internal relativities and teamworking across different jobs. It can also break down harmonised pay structures and can lack transparency. As IDS (2004) has argued, employees must take on trust the benchmark estimate of the value of their job in the external market. Most importantly, following the market can lead to an upward spiral in pay as employers seek to stay ahead of the pack, and not least, such systems can simply reinforce traditional gender pay discrimination.

The most recent CIPD annual survey of reward management indicates that the most common salary structure practices are to use individual pay rates/ranges/ spot rates (36%) and broad bands (26%) (CIPD 2010). For setting salary levels the most important methods are market rates (either alone or linked to a job evaluation database) and ability to pay.

EMERGING ISSUES

The previous section considered the influences and trends that have influenced reward management to the present. This section now considers emerging issues that may influence reward management in the future.

LOW PAY VERSUS TOP PAY

Another aspect of equity concerns the distribution of earnings within the workforce. As Machin (2003, p191) argues:

> A striking feature of the UK labour market of the recent past has been the rapidly increasing wage gaps between higher paid and lower paid workers. In fact levels of wage inequality are higher than at any point since the Second World War and probably since representative statistics were first collected at the end of the nineteenth century.

In general, the distribution of earnings has continued to widen since 1975, with the most rapid widening of the gap between the lowest and highest paid occurring in the 1980s (Machin 2003). Income inequality continued to widen, but at a slower rate, in the 1990s. Between 1994/5 and 2002/3 real income growth across the distribution remained fairly stable, with similar increases for those at the bottom and top of the income distribution, but there was a fall in inequality between 2001/2 and 2004/5 (ONS 2004).

The scale of this change is shown in more recent research. The report of the National Equality Panel, commissioned by the Government Equalities Office and chaired by John Hills, indicates that for men at the 90th percentile of earners, full-time weekly earnings doubled between 1977 and 2002 while those at the median saw an increase of 56%. In contrast, the earnings of those at the bottom, the 10th percentile, only grew by 27% (National Equality Panel 2010). For women, however, the 10th percentile of earnings rose by 56%, the median by 84% and the 90th percentile by 114%. The figures also show that 'there was very little change at all in real earnings across the distribution for men or women between 2002 and 2008, even before the recession started' (National Equality Panel 2010, p28).

In the mid-2000s, however, wage inequality began to increase again and it remains high by historical standards. The ratio of the highest to the lowest decile for gross weekly earnings was 3.6 in April 2006, largely unchanged from 3.5 in 1997 (Dobbs 2007). While the UK is not the only country with widening wage differentials over the last 30 years – in terms of the ratio between the 10th and 90th percentiles of earnings – only the USA exceeds the UK in the widening of the gap (National Equality Panel 2010, p30).

A major legal intervention to tackle income inequality was introduced in 1999 – the National Minimum Wage. Coupled to government changes in taxation, with the introduction of tax credits, the minimum wage has had some effect. Between 1998 and 2003 there was a clear impact from the minimum wage, with hourly wages of the lowest paid increasing by more than the median (Butcher 2005). There was also a marked impact upon the gender pay gap. Warnings of dire negative economic effects before the NMW's introduction have not been manifested (Dickens and Manning 2003). Indeed, apart from the clothing industry, all of the economic sectors most affected by the NMW saw sustained employment growth after the NMW's introduction. This partly reflects the fact that the NMW was introduced at the beginning of a 10-year period of sustained economic growth from 1998 but may also indicate that the level of wage was set at such a prudent level that its effect has been limited. In fact the minimum wage has been gradually increased over time by more than the general increase in earnings to increase the 'bite' of the wage (that is, its ratio to the median hourly wage) (Arrowsmith 2009). At the time of writing, the adult rate of the NMW was £5.70 per hour from October 2009, up from £3.60 in 1999 when it was introduced (a 58% increase).

The debate has now shifted to enforcement issues (Arrowsmith 2009). The system is designed to rely on self-enforcement through two routes – either workers can take a case against their employer through an employment tribunal or they can contact the HMRC compliance officers, who can investigate on their behalf. Research by Croucher and White (2007), who conducted interviews with both employers and employees who had been through the enforcement process, identified a number of problems with the process, and the Low Pay Commission stated in their 2007 report that there remains 'no effective deterrent to non-compliance and no real disincentive for firms contemplating evading the minimum wage requirements' (Low Pay Commission 2007, pp215–16).

Similarly, at the other end of the earnings distribution, there has been mounting concern about the rapid rise in the pay levels of the highest paid. According to the National Equality Panel report, the top 5% of full-time employees earned more than £1,100 per week and the top 1% £1,900. Those at the 90th percentile had hourly earnings of £21.30 in 2008, compared with £5.50 at the bottom 10th percentile (LFS data cited in National Equality Panel 2010, p24). The panel stated: 'It is right at the top of the distribution that there have been the fastest increases in earnings in the last 30 years' (National Equality Panel 2010, p29).

Various voluntary codes to ensure that executive remuneration was fair and transparent were published in the 1990s and 2000s (Cadbury 1992; Greenbury

1995; Hampel 1998; Higgs 2003), but these failed to allay public concerns. Research by IDS revealed that just over half of the CEOs of the FTSE 350 companies earned over £1 million, with five receiving total packages worth more than £10 million (IDS 2006). In the same survey, IDS found that FTSE 100 CEOs earned on average 98 times more than all full-time UK employees in 2006, which it judged the biggest gap since the start of the decade. Between 2000 and 2006, FTSE 100 CEO earnings had increased by 102.2%, compared with 28.6% for all UK full-time employees.

The banking crisis of 2008/09 brought these matters to a head and led to the very real possibility of government legislation to limit the size of bonuses. While public concern was about the absolute levels of earnings of chief executives and bankers, there was also concern among shareholders and other corporate stakeholders about the methods by which such staff were paid and the composition of their pay packages. In particular there was concern at the increasing use of short- and medium-term incentives to reward staff, especially when there appeared to be little linkage of bonuses to actual performance of the organisations. There were also concerns, following the 2008 international banking crisis, about the perverse effects of some of these incentives. In tandem with this public anxiety about the level of senior staff pay in the private sector was rising concern about rising pay differentials for public sector chief executives (House of Commons PAC report 2009).

The Walker Review of Corporate Governance, set up by the Chancellor of the Exchequer in February 2009, reported in July 2009 and made a number of recommendations regarding remuneration practices. These included proposals for more power for remuneration committees to scrutinise firm-wide pay; extending the remit of remuneration committees to oversee pay of high-paid executives not on the board; a significant deferred element in bonus schemes for all high-paid executives; and increased public disclosure about the pay of higher-paid executives. The review commented that bonus schemes contributed to excessive risk-taking by rewarding short-term performance (Walker 2009). Sir David Walker, the chair of the review, commented that: 'Taken alongside the arrangements being proposed by the Financial Services Authority, the recommendations on remuneration are as tough or tougher than anything to be found elsewhere in the world. An important and urgent challenge is to promote adoption of similar approaches internationally' (HM Treasury Press Release 16 July 2009).

THE RISE OF INDIVIDUAL CONTINGENT PAY?

Linked to the growth of the wage gap between the lowest and highest paid employees has been the growth of contingent pay. A key aspect of the new pay paradigm was its advocacy of more contingent or 'at risk' elements within reward systems. Contingent pay covers a number of types of reward, including individual, team and corporate level, but all of these forms of reward are 'variable' and hence not guaranteed to the employee. Armstrong and Murlis (2007, p348) define contingent pay as 'payments related to individual performance, competence, or skill or to team and the organisation'. A number of employer objectives for contingent forms of remuneration have been identified: to elicit greater work effort or output from workers; to enhance employee commitment to the employer; to attract better quality employees; to retain workers when labour is in short supply; to achieve equity by targeting reward at those who work hardest or most effectively; and to act as a substitute for direct monitoring of worker performance (Pendelton et al 2009, pp257–8).

While there is nothing new about contingent pay, defined as pay linked to measures of input, output or behaviours, the 'nature and use of contingent pay systems in Britain has changed markedly' over the last 25 years (Pendleton et al 2009, p256). Research by the Office for National Statistics (ONS), using data from the New Earnings Survey, found that incentive pay declined as a proportion of total pay between 1987 and 1990 but has remained fairly constant since. In 2002 one in seven employees received some incentive pay compared with one in five in 1992. These 'payments by results' contributed an average 22% of gross pay (Grabham 2003, p398) but were much more likely to be received by men than by women. There is some indication that individual payment by results has diminished in its traditional arena of manufacturing industry but has increased in service sector employment. For example, the ONS research found that incentive pay accounted for a quarter of gross pay in the financial services sector in 2002.

The 2004 WERS survey indicates significant growth: 32% of workplaces had performance-related pay in 2004, compared with 20% in 1998 (Kersley et al 2006). The WERS 2004 data also indicated that incentive pay was much more likely to be found in the private sector (44% of workplaces) than in the public sector (19%). Analysis of the WERS data reveals that the overall incidence of contingent pay grew considerably in the economy as a whole between 1984 and 1990 (up from 41% of workplaces in 1984 to 56% in 1990) but fell slightly in 2004 (to 55%). In the private sector the incidence of variable pay grew from 52% in 1984 to 72% of workplaces in 1990, falling back to 67% in 2004 (Pendleton et al 2009).

WERS identifies four forms of contingent pay: individual payment by results; collective payment by results; profit-related payments; and employee share ownership schemes. Despite the prevailing view that individual performance-related pay systems have become the major form of contingent reward, the major change between 1984 and 2004 has been a shift from individual payment-by-results to more collective forms of contingent pay. Between 1984 and 2004 around a fifth of all workplaces had some form of individual payment by results. Within this overall picture, however, there are variations. The use of individual payment by results appears to have diminished in the public sector and private manufacturing but to have grown in private services. In contrast the use of collective payment by results has grown substantially (from 15% in 1984 to 25% in 2004) (Pendleton et al 2009).

The development of organisation-wide variable pay systems – profit-related pay and employee share ownership schemes – was actively encouraged by government tax concessions in the 1980s and 1990s. Profit-related pay increased from 20% of private sector workplaces in 1984 to 45% in 2004. Employee share ownership increased from 24% of workplaces in 1984 to a peak in 1990 of 31% before falling back slightly in 2004.

Despite the WERS findings, the most recent CIPD annual survey of reward management (CIPD 2010) continues to show individual performance as being the key factor used to manage pay progression (68% of respondents), followed by market rates (48%). Similarly, the survey finds that individual-based bonuses and incentive plans remain by far the most common (58% of respondents).

CAN REWARD BE STRATEGIC?

A key tenet of the new pay paradigm is that reward must be strategically driven and linked to business needs. Lawler, a key writer in the new pay literature, states that: 'The starting point for any pay system design process needs to be the strategic agenda of the organisation' (Lawler 1990, p15). Moreover, as Trevor (2009, p21) has suggested, 'never before in post-war Britain have private sector employers enjoyed so much unilateral freedom to determine the basis of employee pay, and in the interest of achieving purely managerial ends.' A major question is, therefore, whether reward management has become more strategic.

The most recent CIPD annual survey of reward management indicates that only 35% of respondents have a written reward strategy and only 33% have adopted a 'total reward' approach, an indication that reward is being managed strategically. On the other hand, 52% of respondents state that their total reward priority for 2010 is to ensure alignment with the business strategy (CIPD 2010). It is interesting to note that the figure of 35% for those claiming to have a formal reward strategy is unchanged from 2007 and the number planning to introduce one has actually reduced (from 40% in 2007 to 31% in 2010).

Recent research by Trevor (2008) on organisations' implementation of reward strategies found that 'many organizations experience profound managerial difficulties when attempting to use compensation strategically' and as a result actual practice reflects neither espoused strategy nor policy. Negative outcomes from such attempts at strategic reward include high costs, greater administration and industrial conflict manifested in employee disengagement and demotivation. Trevor argues that strategic reward systems may not be the value-creating mechanism advocated by the new pay writers but 'rather a business risk that requires careful management and good governance to ensure that it does not diminish or consume more value than it creates' (Trevor 2008, p1). He also argues that, while the philosophy underpinning the employment relationship has been transformed through the demise of collective pay determination, 'many of the features of old pay continue in practice to pervade the operational management of pay'. Despite the underlying ideology of unitarism within the new pay paradigm, in reality the management of pay operationally continues to be 'characterised by pluralist relations between employer and employee, and by pluralism within the management structure itself' (Trevor 2009, p38).

CONCLUSION

This chapter has sought to review the major changes in reward management practice over the last three decades. Over this time, both the context and the content of remuneration policy and practice have changed significantly. Central to this change has been the decline of employee voice in the reward process, leaving employers in a much stronger position to impose a strategic vision on reward policy and practice. However, attempts to develop a more strategic approach to reward have been challenged by other developments. Far from a retreat from concerns about equity in the UK, both internal and external equity have become more important. Both have in effect undermined employer attempts to concentrate on reward policies driven purely by strategic business objectives.

At the same time, reward practices at organisational level have been partly responsible for the growing divide between the lowest- and highest-paid members of society, with the wider social implications that that development has created. While attempts have been made to limit the worst excesses of a completely market-driven approach to pay levels through the imposition of a statutory floor to wages in a minimum wage, as yet no attempts have been made to curb the pay of those at the top of the earnings distribution, even though it now appears that there is wide public appetite for such action. Whether we will see new curbs on executive pay remains uncertain. At the time of writing political concern about pay restraint appears to have shifted more to public servants.

A key aspect of the growth of executive pay has been the increasing use of variable pay in the form of short-, medium- and long-term incentives. While this has been associated with 'City bonus culture', the growth of variable pay has not been limited to the highest paid. It is interesting, however, to note that the WERS data indicates that this growth has been more in collective, rather than individual, incentives, contradicting the widely held view that individual performance-related pay is now the norm.

Lastly, drawing on the work of Trevor (2008, 2009), it has been argued that the core theme of the new pay writers, that new pay is by its very nature strategic pay, may be problematic in operational terms. The evidence to date does not indicate either a wide acceptance among managers that reward should be strategic or that this is a necessarily desirable objective for businesses. Reward remains a risk that has to be managed. Trevor's work confirms that reward remains contested terrain between employers and employees and that much can be learned from the history of *traditional* or *old* pay on how the effort bargain can be managed.

HRM IN THE MEDIA

CRITICAL REFLECTIONS

This scenario does not offer easy solutions. In relation to the first question, it should be noted that the overall package included an element of 'normal' salary, plus payment for additional activities. It would be difficult to retrospectively renege on the additional payments if they were agreed in advance and were for specific work carried out beyond the normal contract; and the 'normal' element would have been within the national pay-scale band for a head teacher. The dilemma posed is the balance between *internal* and *external* equity. External equity relates to the pressure to find a suitably generous pay package to attract the best candidates for the post, when compared with similar positions elsewhere. Internal equity is the perception of fairness, in relation to top pay and average pay: in this case, whether this one individual deserves such a large differential when compared with the other staff at the school, who, it can be assumed, also contributed to its success.

In relation to the second question, pay would be agreed by the school's governing body, but may well have been advised by external advice. A large element would be benchmarked against national pay surveys.

In relation to the third question, it has to be said that the process involved appears to be relatively transparent. It is generally agreed that secrecy in pay settlements is the most significant barrier to achieving pay equity. Assuming that the pay package was approved by the school's board of governors, parents and staff representatives would be likely to have been involved. For other staff, unions would be involved in the process: at national level via consultation from the Pay Review Body for teachers and through collective bargaining for support staff.

EXPLORE FURTHER

WHITE, G. and DRUKER, J. (eds) (2009) *Reward management: a critical text*. 2nd ed. Abingdon: Routledge.

This edited collection covers a range of reward dilemmas in contemporary context.

CORBY, S., PALMER, S. and LINDOP, E. (eds) (2008) *Rethinking reward*. Basingstoke: Palgrave Macmillan.

An edited collection providing a critical look at recent trends in reward.

ARMSTRONG, M. and BROWN, D. (2001) *New dimensions in pay management*. London: CIPD.

While not new, this text provides the rationale for the new pay paradigm in the UK.

Critical Issues in Equality and Diversity (1): Gender Equity and the Myths of the Work–life Balance Narrative

Uracha Chatrakul Na Ayudhya and Suzan Lewis

OVERVIEW

Work–life balance (WLB) is a hot topic for HRM nowadays. However, it tends to be applied uncritically, which can severely limit the scope and impact of current so-called WLB policies implemented by HRM. In this chapter, we consider some of the critical aspects of 'WLB' as a narrative by drawing on the theory of 'gendered organisations' (for example Acker 1990). We describe and challenge assumptions underpinning the WLB narrative, which tend to ignore deep-seated diversity issues, particularly related to gender and the life course.

We then move on to critique the current WLB narrative by considering how it limits the implementation of HRM initiatives that aim to address employees' needs to harmonise work and personal life. We argue that taking a dual-agenda approach, through the lens of gender equity (as opposed to gender equality), can lead to more innovative and effective approaches to these issues. We draw on case studies of organisations to illustrate the limitation of traditional WLB approaches as well as key processes for broadening the focus and closing the gap between policy and actual practice.

LEARNING OBJECTIVES

Reading this chapter will enable the reader to:

- compare and contrast notions of 'gender equality' and 'gender equity'

- critically evaluate WLB as a contested term through an appreciation of the theory of 'gendered organisations'

- critically examine the complex relationships between HRM policy implementation and actual practice in relation to WLB issues

- critically apply a dual-agenda approach and processes to move beyond the HRM implementation gap between policy and practice.

HRM IN THE MEDIA

'BRITISH AIRWAYS "EXCLUDES MOTHERS AS PILOTS"'

It was reported in 2005 that a 26-year-old woman pilot was taking her employer, British Airways (BA), to an employment tribunal for indirect sex discrimination after the airline refused her request to work 50% part-time to look after her one-year-old daughter (BBC News 2005a).

She told the tribunal that she and her husband, also a BA pilot, worked 'extremely irregular' shift patterns, allocated by a computerised bidding system based on seniority, making it difficult for the couple to arrange their shifts so someone was always free to care for their child.

By law, employers have a duty to seriously consider employees' requests to work flexible hours and should only reject such a request if there are good business reasons for doing so. In this case, the employer argued that their decision to refuse the request was unreasonable given the nature of the job and the effect on other pilots: that it was based on safety, not sex discrimination (BBC News 2005b).

The employee told the hearing that her employer's lack of accommodation for working mothers works to exclude females from its pilots and to reinforce, rather than reform, the traditional male dominance in its workforce.

Questions

1 To what extent do you think the employee's request to work 50% part-time was reasonable?

2 How good a case do you think the employee had for accusing her employer of indirect sex discrimination?

3 Who do you think won the case and why?

INTRODUCTION: WLB AS A NARRATIVE

To define WLB in a straightforward way is problematic. This is because WLB is not one single reality or truth. Rather, there are multiple perspectives and levels of analysis of WLB in the current literature (Gambles et al 2006; Fleetwood 2007).

We begin this chapter with the main argument that WLB is a narrative. In other words, it is a way of talking (that is, a discourse) about time pressures experienced by women and men due to the increasing demands of work and other areas of life. However, there is a tendency to forget that it is just a discourse and to think that there is some universal achievable goal, whereby work and personal life are in balance. Yet work is part of life, not something to be balanced with it. Positioning work and life as separate and conflicting is unhelpful. Moreover, the balance people need or ways that people want to harmonise their work and personal life change as they move through the various phases of the life course, such as transitions into adulthood, employment, parenthood or retirement (for example, see Chatrakul Na Ayudhya and Lewis 2010).

In a critical examination of the WLB debate, Lewis et al (2007) point to at least two overlapping but distinct WLB discourses. The first is 'personal control of time WLB discourse', based on an assumption that individual workers (particularly knowledge workers) have a choice and a personal responsibility to get the right balance between paid work and other areas of life. The second is 'workplace flexibility WLB discourse', which assumes that WLB is a characteristic of the workplace and is manifested in the existence of organisational WLB policies. These policies are framed as a way of offering employees choices in how they implement flexibility in their working arrangements. Yet, both discourses overemphasise the role of individual responsibility by assuming that individuals are able to achieve WLB as long as they make a series of right choices to either work harder or longer or to prioritise their non-work (that is, 'life') commitments (Lewis et al 2007). At the same time, they underplay the role of structural constraints (for example, the socially constrained nature of gender norms and gendered organisations on individuals). In reality, both individuals and social structures play a part in shaping experiences of WLB of women and men across the life course. We argue that the main problem with this narrative is that it focuses on individual responsibility to 'get the balance right' and overlooks the role of social structures in shaping people's experiences of managing their work and personal lives in different ways.

GENDER AND EMPLOYMENT IN THE UK

The news story introduced at the start of the chapter illustrates the complex ways in which the issue of gender is crucial to debates on how women and men combine employment and personal life. Such debates must be contextualised within the current situation relating to gender and employment in the UK.

According to the Office for National Statistics (ONS 2010b), there has been a marked increase over the past three decades (1985–2008) in the number of employee jobs performed by women in the UK. In 1985, men filled 2 million more jobs than women. In March 2008, the numbers for women and men were similar, with each performing around 13.6 million jobs.

At first reading, these figures appear encouraging, as they indicate that the gender gap in the rate of labour force participation is narrowing. However, almost half the women's jobs were part-time compared with around one in six of the men's. These figures suggest that women are more likely than men to work part-time, particularly if they have dependent children. In 2008, 38% of women with dependent children worked part-time compared with 22% of those without dependent children and only 4% of men with dependent children and 7% of men without dependent children worked part-time. All these indicate that the presence of a dependent child has a substantial impact on employment for women, but not for men (ONS 2010a).

In addition to differences between women and men in the rates of full-time and part-time employment, there is still a clear sex segregation of occupations. Men are ten times more likely than women to be employed in skilled trades (19% compared with 2%) and are also more likely to be managers and senior officials. A fifth of women in employment do administrative or secretarial work compared with 4% of men. Women are also more likely than men to be employed in the personal services and in sales and customer services. Similar proportions of men and women work in professional, associate professional and elementary occupations, such as labourers and catering assistants (ONS 2010b).

Finally, all of these trends contribute to the ongoing gender inequality in pay, where men tend to earn more than women (see the Government Equalities Office (GEO) 2010). In 2008, the gender pay gap for all employees (in full- and part-time employment) was 22.5%. The gap narrowed in 2009 to 22% (ONS 2010c). According to research into the causes of the gender pay gap conducted by the GEO, the following factors were key in explaining the pay gap:

- 10% of the overall pay gap can be attributed to occupational sex segregation
- 12% of the gap is due to the industries in which women work
- 21% of the gap is due to differences in years of full-time work
- 16% of the gap is due to the negative effect on wages of having previously worked part-time or of having taken time out of the labour market to look after family
- 5% of the gap is due to formal education levels.

Interestingly, the research suggests that a significant proportion (36%) of the pay gap could not be explained by any of these factors, suggesting sex discrimination may be an important factor (GEO 2010).

WLB, GENDER EQUITY AND GENDERED ORGANISATIONS

The WLB narrative tends to focus on gender as an individual characteristic rather than looking at existing assumptions and norms about gender that underpin (outdated) notions of the ideal worker and ideal careers. For example, there is a tendency to see women 'choosing' not to conform to normative workplace expectations and behaviours (for example, 'choosing' to work part-time to raise dependent children) rather than challenging these existing norms as being based on an outdated 'male model of work'.

Before discussing the role of gender issues in critical approaches to WLB, we explain the ways in which we use some key terms. Firstly, we make a broad but important distinction between the terms sex and gender. *Gender* is a social category, which means that there are social expectations attached to notions of 'masculine' and 'feminine', unlike *sex*, which is a biological category. Secondly, it is important to distinguish between notions of gender equality and gender equity. *Gender equality* in the context of work refers to equal opportunities for women and men. Yet in practice, it tends to be interpreted as equal opportunities for women to work in the way men do. For example, it is about women having the opportunity to progress in their careers by acting in the traditional way that men do, but not necessarily changing the nature of work and careers (for example by not taking parental leave and working long hours, which are often inefficient). *Gender equity*, on the other hand, is about fairness. It has been defined as equal opportunities and constraints for women and men, which implies that both women and men are involved family care and in careers. For this to happen, we need to be aware of and challenge the gendered nature of organisations, which is explained below.

GENDERED ORGANISATIONS

Theory of gendered organisations (Acker 1990; Britton 2000; Martin and Collinson 2002; Rapoport et al 2002; Swanberg 2004; Bailyn 2006; Gambles et al 2006) contends that women's secondary position in the labour market in many contexts can be attributed to the gendered nature of organisations. That is to say, it is not due to overt discrimination or to women's characteristics or patterns of labour market participation *per se*, but to the unintended effects of daily working practices and assumptions that can appear to be gender-neutral but are grounded in a male model of work (see below).

The myth of separate (gendered) spheres

These everyday working practices and the assumptions on which they are based can be traced to the ideology of separate, gendered spheres, that is, the public sphere of work as a man's world and the private sphere of the family as women's domain and responsibility (Rapoport et al 2002; Bailyn 2006; Haas and Hwang 2007). This separation of family and working life that began with industrialisation has produced gendered structures that are remarkably resilient despite changing gender roles and relationships (Crompton et al 2007). This model contrasts with the twenty-first-century reality in which both women and men are in the workforce and also involved in family care, and where boundaries between work and family are increasingly blurred (see Figure 16.1).

Figure 16.1 Gendered spheres

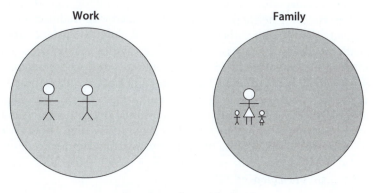

Separate spheres ideology

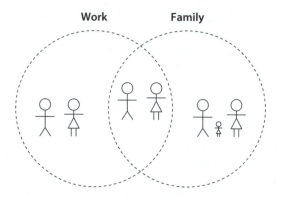

21st Century blurred boundaries

In the context of the separate spheres ideology, organisational structures tend to be built around a cultural picture of the ideal worker as someone who can work as though they have no social or caring obligations outside work. This is referred to as *a male model of work*. This affects how commitment is defined and competences of workers are valued (Lewis 1997, 2001; Rapoport et al 2002; Rees and Garnsey 2003; Swanberg 2004). Commitment is widely constructed in terms of work primacy, which assumes that work comes first and above other commitments, such that time to spend at work is unlimited, and the demands of family, community and personal life are secondary.

The myth of separate and gendered spheres also leads to the valuing of certain types of behaviour more than others. There is often an assumption that stereotypically masculine characteristics are necessary to be effective in the workplace. Thus, traditionally masculine values and behaviours, such as competitiveness and the ability to work long hours, come to be associated with the ideal worker, while more traditionally feminine characteristics and skills such as interpersonal skills and collaboration are often undervalued in workplace settings. Ideas of competence thus become associated with traditional ideas of masculinity (Bailyn 2006). That is, assumptions about competence are so linked with the idealised images of men and masculinity that it makes it difficult for women's achievements to be recognised unless women work in masculine ways (Bailyn 2006; Rapoport et al 2002; Rees and Garnsey 2003). These gendered expectations are deeply embedded in workplace structures but are counterproductive. The deconstruction of structures and cultural norms at work and their underlying assumptions is the first step in analysing a workplace using a gender theory lens, which bring to the fore gendered assumptions of the ideal worker and the ideal career that are typically not recognised or articulated and therefore remain unchallenged.

'MYTHS' ABOUT WLB

We now turn to examining three fundamental assumptions about WLB. We refer to these assumptions as 'myths', as they fail to adequately acknowledge the diverse nature of WLB needs and experiences, and therefore limit the way we think about the issues.

MYTH 1: THE ASSUMPTION THAT WLB IS GENDER-NEUTRAL

WLB as a terminology was developed initially to counter the focus on women, particularly mothers of young children, evident in initial 'work–family' research and practice. It is positioned as gender-neutral and therefore purports to challenge assumptions about separate, gendered spheres. Furthermore, it was expected that it would help to broaden the issues considered from work and family to other aspects of personal life, such as the desire to pursue personal development opportunities. For example, in the case of young workers, this includes time for leisure, learning new skills (including new languages) and social groups (Chatrakul Na Ayudhya 2009). However, changing the language from 'work–family' or 'family-friendly' to 'work–life' does not, in itself, change the reality of gendered assumptions in organisations.

This is clear when it comes to examining the effectiveness of WLB policies. The impact of policies is not gender-neutral. For example, part-time work may be seen as a solution for working parents and others who do not conform to the male model of work pattern. But unless the gendered notion of the ideal worker is challenged, part-time workers will be marginalised and undervalued. For example, in a study by Lewis and Humbert (2010) of a French pharmaceutical company (PharmaCo), both women and (in theory) men have the option of working four days a week in order to have more time for non-work activities. In reality, only women scientists in PharmaCo have taken up this option. In fact, they do not reduce their workloads but condense their work into four days and lose one-fifth of their salary (Lewis and Humbert 2010). Most feel that this is a fair trade-off. They know that they are 'buying' flexibility but do not feel entitled to full pay because visibility is highly valued at this company (in keeping with the male model of work).

Therefore, the company fails to recognise that the women who do a full workload in less time and for less pay are actually more efficient than those who spread their work over five days. Moreover, many of these women are not promoted or offered development experiences. Instead, it is those who spread their work out over five days for full pay (and are thus less efficient) who advance. Good women workers are not realising their potential, which perpetuates gender inequity and is a poor HRM talent management strategy. Most of the managers say that this is the women's choice and the women themselves usually agree, but choices are always socially constrained. These women do not have certain other choices such as to work a four-day week *and* have their efforts recognised and rewarded or to cut their workload as well as number of days and salary down to four-fifths. This illustrates how the gender-neutral assumptions of WLB can and do obscure wider ongoing gendered discourses and practices that serve to reinforce and reproduce gender inequities. Gendered practices such as rewarding inefficient working practices including taking longer to do work that can be accomplished more quickly by those working reduced hours are bad for organisations as well as individual employee.

MYTH 2: THE ASSUMPTION THAT WLB IS ABOUT INDIVIDUAL CHOICE

Earlier in this chapter, we introduced the personal control of time WLB discourse (Lewis et al 2007), which focuses on the individual rather than workplace and wider social norms that may constrain individual choice. Another myth about WLB is that it is an individual choice. It is often said that women with children *choose* not to work full-time and therefore want to be different (as in the PharmaCo case discussed above). This implies that they choose to deviate from the male model of the ideal worker. However, choices are always socially constrained by what is available, not only at the workplace but also in wider social contexts (for example what support do working mothers and fathers have for childcare? Can parents find good affordable childcare if they both work full-time? Do women earn the same income as their spouses or do they earn more or less so that men's careers are prioritised?). In the case of PharmaCo, women make trade-offs, which are detrimental to their career progression, not just out of preference, but because there are few realistic alternatives. A focus on individual choice in the WLB narrative firmly places the blame on the individual and not on the way work is typically organised and valued. While women and men clearly have some control in these processes, ignoring structural constraints when explaining their behaviours can lead to a blaming of those who do not conform to the traditional male model, rather than challenging the adequacy of this model.

MYTH 3: THE ASSUMPTION THAT WLB IS ONLY FOR WORKING PARENTS

We have made a strong case for why narratives of WLB should not just be about women. We also argue that it should not just relate to working mothers and fathers, but should be more inclusive. It is important to recognise that there are diverse WLB needs, for example, at various phases of the life course (for example, transitions from education to employment or from employment to retirement). While some progress has been made in some organisations towards recognising that these issues are not confined to parents, in practice, WLB is often still regarded as primarily a woman's issue or a parents' issue.

Insofar as organisations continue to assume that WLB is mainly about work and family, then this limits the impact of policies to enable more people to manage their work and private lives. Other groups such as young people (Chatrakul Na Ayudhya and Lewis 2010) and single people (Casper et al 2007) also have work–life needs, which should not be overlooked. In light of age discrimination law and the removal of the retirement age in some organisations, older workers may also need flexible working arrangements as they remain in the workforce for longer. If policies are perceived as focusing only on parents of young children (especially mothers), this can be experienced as unfair. It can lead to resentment and backlash among non-parents (Young 1999).

In the UK, the right to request flexible working legislation applies to both parents with children under the age of 16 (or 18 if the child is disabled) and carers of adults, but at the time of writing the Government has so far resisted extending this to all workers. This can perpetuate these perceptions of unfairness. Focusing on the needs of specific groups, rather than the way work is organised, marginalises those who use the policies and provokes feelings of unfairness among those whose diverse needs are neglected. This ultimately fails to challenge traditional models of work, which were designed for workers with a full-time homemaker, which is no longer the norm.

THE 'DUAL AGENDA'

One way of challenging these myths is through the adoption of a *dual-agenda approach*, which guides initiatives and processes that affect both equity issues and effectiveness concerns. This approach serves to simultaneously address and enhance both the interests of employees (women and men from all phases of the life course) and the employer. As discussed in Lewis and Roper (2008), a dual-agenda approach involves changes being implemented to meet the needs of both employer and employees, with both given equal weight. Initiatives based only on just the needs of employers or of employees will be less effective (Rapoport et al 2002). This approach stresses the importance of going beyond policy development to start a process that first challenges (gendered) assumptions that sustain ineffective practices and then involves collaboration to develop more appropriate and effective norms and practices.

It must be emphasised at this point that the goal of the dual-agenda approach is not the identification of good practices as such, as these so-called good practices are dynamic and will vary across time and place. Rather, we argue that it is about the principles of effective processes to achieve innovations that are appropriate to specific contexts.

We have seen that WLB issues are complex. Work–personal life dilemmas are the consequences of workplace practices that are rooted in deep-seated gendered assumptions about what makes an ideal worker and an ideal working trajectory. The ideal worker in many workplaces is expected to work long hours and/or intensively, to put in 'face time', be constantly available and visible and to work full-time and often rigid working hours across their working life course. The overvaluing of these behaviours can obscure diverse ways of working, which may be equally or often more effective.

HRM clearly has a role to play in addressing these issues. However, there is a tendency for HRM departments to respond to WLB challenges through the implementation of regulation and development of policies. These are, of course, important, not least for the following reasons:

- Regulation provides employees with a floor of entitlements, for example, protection for part-time workers and the right for some employees to request flexible work.

- HRM policies such as flexible working arrangements can, if well implemented, meet the dual agenda by helping employees to manage their work and personal lives and helping employers to recruit and retain a wider pool of labour.

- Childcare or assistance with the costs of childcare, whether provided in the community or in the workplace, is essential to enable employees with young children to sustain employment.

However, regulatory and HRM policies tend to be based on an uncritical approach to WLB. We have argued that there is no ideal state of work–life balance but that the ways in which diverse employees want or need to harmonise their work and non-work activities are dynamic and fluid across the life course. Currently policies are usually developed to help employees with particular needs and responsibilities to adapt to current ways of working rather than challenging workplace cultures and practices for a diverse workforce. For example, flexible working arrangements such as reduced working hours or flexitime can help people to fit in work and personal life demands. Yet, if there is no attempt to change values and assumptions of how work should be done, then those who take up these options are often stigmatised as second-rate employees (Lewis 1997, 2001). Moreover, some forms of flexible working, particularly using technology-assisted communication, enable and encourage people to work more, for example taking work home or responding to email during leisure activities. For this reason, flexible working initiatives are no panacea for WLB issues.

While policies are crucial and can be a first step towards deeper change, they should not be regarded as an end in themselves. Attention is also needed to good implementation of these policies, including initiatives designed to bring about changes in workplace beliefs and practices. Before discussing wider initiatives for change, we focus below on the ways in which WLB policies are implemented and reasons for the widely reported gap between policy and actual practice.

POLICY VERSUS PRACTICES: THE HRM IMPLEMENTATION GAP

Research shows that there is often a gap between policies, however well intentioned, and the way they are implemented in practice (Gambles et al 2006; Haas et al 2002). This does not only apply to workplace policy. The outcomes of government policy also depend upon how they are implemented at the workplace level. For example:

- Parental leave may be a statutory entitlement for all, but take-up, by men in particular, is often restricted by gendered organisational beliefs that ideal workers do not modify work for family reasons and hence fear of the career consequences of taking leave, even in the Nordic countries where these initiatives are highly developed and have a long history (Brandt and Kvande 2002; Haas et al 2002).

- The right to request flexible working legislation tends to have gendered outcomes. More women than men make such requests and proportionately more men have their requests turned down. Again, this illustrates the impact of gendered beliefs and assumptions on the practice of a policy that is intended to apply to both men and women equally.

Even if requests for flexible working are made and accepted, recent European research shows that workers who make use of formal HRM flexible working policies (specifically flexitime, working from home and reduced hours working) do not necessarily report greater satisfaction with their jobs or WLB. In some cases they are even more dissatisfied than those who do not take up such policies. There are a number of possible explanations for these findings, for example: flexible workers are not valued; formal flexible working arrangements do not really provide the autonomy and control that employees need; and they blur the boundaries between work and personal life, enabling people to work more. There is some evidence to support all these explanations.

In Lewis and Roper (2008), a case study of the case of Proffco was described. This was a professional services firm with an impressive raft of work–life policies, but only on paper. Although there were some favourable outcomes such as an increase in the rate of return from maternity leave, the take-up of these policies remained low and confined to women, and those who did take up the policies were often stigmatised. Those working flexibly often worked more efficiently, but again this was not recognised because of a dominant long-hours culture, so their career advancement was curtailed. Below we discuss in detail some of the factors and processes that undermine WLB policies if they are introduced without initiatives to change organisational norms and beliefs and other aspects of culture. All these factors can be traced back to the prevailing model of the ideal worker as well as a lack of understanding of the dual agenda. That is, they are based on the outdated belief that enabling people to work in different ways will be a cost to the organisation rather than potentially benefiting employers and employees.

FACTORS THAT UNDERMINE EFFECTIVE IMPLEMENTATION OF WLB POLICIES

On a practical level, a range of obstacles commonly act to undermine effective and sustainable WLB.

Poor communication

For policies to be effective in addressing the dual agenda, they must be well communicated so that employees are aware of their entitlements and managers are aware of the potential advantages. Often the employees who would most benefit from policies are not aware of what is available. Policies are not always well communicated. In some cases this is a deliberate attempt by management to limit take-up because policies are regarded as costs and not as opportunities to innovate to meet a dual agenda for change. Flexible working arrangements may be regarded as a favour and an inconvenience if they are perceived to be one-sided rather than in terms of mutual flexibility with give and take on both sides.

The PrintCo case discussed below illustrates the benefits of communication that emphasises the rights and responsibilities of employees and managers to work together to establish mutual trust and flexibility. It suggests that if flexible working arrangements are treated in this way more employees will experience a sense of entitlement to use them and do so in a responsible way.

Intensification of work

Employees often report that they are reluctant to take up flexible working options or even to take full holiday entitlements. Reducing work or taking time off for any reason, in the context of high workloads and lean workforces, often involves returning to a huge backlog of work. Intense workloads also undermine the capacity of autonomous working teams to enhance flexibility as employees know that if they are not at work they will further overload colleagues, who are already working at the height of their capacity (Back-Wiklund and Plantin 2007).

Policies are not inclusive

Even when work–family policies are well established, gendered organisational norms can undermine the dual agenda and gender equity. For example, in Denmark, almost every employer will state that they pay special attention to the needs of parents (Rosenstock et al 2008) and gender equity (Holt et al 2006). However, a study of two Danish workplaces reveals that in both organisations women and men began with equivalent qualifications but men progressed more quickly than women (Holt and Lewis 2010). Gender inequity was perpetuated in a number of subtle ways, based on ideal worker assumptions. These practices included allocating interesting work to those who are most visible and do not take up parental leave or flexible working entitlements.

The idealisation of those who work long and inflexible hours can obscure the value of more diverse and often more effective ways of working, which was illustrated in the case of PharmaCo (see Myth 1). One manager at PharmaCo was unusual in recognising how illogical this is. He explained that one woman in his team has asked to finish on time every day although it was usual for the team to work much longer hours. To enable this, the manager had to look at different ways of getting the work done. The result was that not only was the woman who had requested this able to finish on time, but so was the rest of the team, including the manager. The work was still finished to a high standard and everyone benefited.

Management discretion and perceived fairness

We have argued that if the use of policies is not regarded as a core workplace practice but is only allowed for certain workers, then it can lead to stigmatisation of flexible workers and resentment or backlash among those who do not work flexibly. Lack of management support and management inconsistency in the implementation of policies are major factors sustaining the implementation gap between policy and practice. There is often an emphasis on management decision-making rather than on encouraging collaboration, trust and creativity to work out how best to meet organisational and employee needs. Moreover, if some managers are more convinced of the potential benefits of the dual agenda than others, inconsistency in implementation of policies across an organisation can result. Those employees who are not supported by their managers then feel unfairly treated and resentful. This can lower morale and be linked with turnover intentions, undermining the purpose of work–life policies.

A quick-fix approach

The development of a policy is much easier and quicker than trying to achieve culture change, but quick-fixes produce superficial solutions and sustain the policy–practice gap. Moreover, there is evidence that more fundamental changes can save time in the long term and with real bottom-line benefits (Rapoport et al 2002). The case of PrintCo, below, illustrates the impact of an organisational change approach that challenges assumptions and addresses diversity of WLB needs.

MOVING BEYOND THE HRM IMPLEMENTATION GAP

We have seen that the focus on flexible policies in WLB approach is no more than a first step. What is needed is an integrated approach to ensure that such policies are integrated and, thus, sustainable. To illustrate this as a possibility, a case study may be useful. In Lewis and Cooper (2005) the example of PrintCo was used to indicate how this could be possible. At PrintCo, the new managing director had bought into the idea of cultural change to support sustainable working patterns. He found ways of involving and collaborating with the workforce that included holding briefing sessions on the state of the business and the need for change. He also talked to staff about their jobs and about their lives generally, bringing in personal as well as job-related matters. He asked about working practices, teasing out taken-for-granted assumptions about the ways in which work was carried out. Two crucial points about implementation were: (1) employees were encouraged to come to the managing director not with requests, but with solutions, usually negotiated with teams; (2) policies were not implemented until practices had been established and shown to work.

Working methods were therefore adjusted to enable WLB, but were done in such a way that integrated organisational needs with those of individual employees. Central to this was the benefits associated with the functional flexibility and multi-skilling that were enabled by a more flexible approach to working time.

Workplace values and assumptions can undermine the potential effectiveness of policies and, therefore, need to be examined and challenged. Such values and assumptions link back to earlier discussions of the theory of gendered organisations and the male model of work and include:

- Ideal workers work full-time and long hours.
- Part-time workers are neither committed nor valuable.
- Those working in non-standard ways cannot be trusted to get their work done.

Giving people the right to, for example, work flexible hours alongside intensified workloads or without tackling cultures in which only those who work long and inflexible hours are fully valued is clearly not sufficient. More fundamental structural and cultural changes are necessary to challenge such assumptions if organisations and employees are to derive the full benefits from the work–life initiatives through a dual-agenda approach. Much remains to be done to foster increased mainstreaming of work–life initiatives as 'core' human resource and management strategies. For fundamental change, more attention needs to be given to 1) cultural support and 2) value change.

CULTURAL SUPPORT

Cultural work–life support refers to informal workplace social and relational support, for example support from supervisors and co-workers. Such support helps to communicate to employees that those who work flexibly to be involved in family or other personal roles are fully valued. This should ideally be the case for men as well as women. This type of support is a critical factor influencing whether or not workers make use of work–life policies (Hammer et al 2009).

Initiatives to foster such support include change efforts such as training to increase social support from supervisors and co-workers for employees' non-work demands, and to foster positive group and organisational norms (Hammer et al 2010; Kossek and Hammer 2008).

VALUE CHANGES

To move beyond the policy–practice implementation gap and take account of age and other forms of diversity in work–life needs, it is important to ask different questions. The main question usually asked in developing policies is, 'how can the organisation support working parents (or sometimes just working mothers) to enhance recruitment and retention and other workplace outcomes?' Given the widespread implementation gap and mounting evidence of diversity of work–life needs, a more important question is, 'how can workplace culture and practice support diverse workers in managing their personal lives and enhance their work engagement?' Instead of asking how women (and in some cases men) with family responsibilities can be enabled to adapt to current workplace practices, the question is, 'how can the organisation challenge unrealistic expectations at work and value diverse ways of working?'

CHANGE PROCESSES

This more radical approach would entail a focus on the nature of work and job design using a dual-agenda lens. The specific WLB needs of individuals would become irrelevant if all jobs were designed on the assumption that all employees have multidimensional and dynamic lives and that recognising this, as in the case of PrintCo, can enhance effectiveness and productivity.

Sustainable systemic change requires a focus on process. The specific nature of the process and the outcomes will vary according to organisational needs and we do not wish to be prescriptive. Nevertheless, there are a number of generalisable principles, based on action research studies (Bailyn 2006; Lewis and Cooper 2005; Rapoport et al 2002). Many of these aspects of the process are exemplified in the PrintCo case above. They include:

- linking changes to a pressing business issue, such as recruitment and/or retention problems or, as in the PrintoCo case, absenteeism, lack of trust and flexibility, or poor performance

- examination of the way that work is done and the assumptions on which this is based

- challenging entrenched organisational norms and assumptions about ideal workers and ideal ways of doing work to highlight the ways in which they undermine workplace effectiveness and WLB

- collaborating teams (comprising workers and managers) in designing appropriate innovations in order to engage the workforce.

Of course, some resistance to any change process is inevitable and this cannot be ignored. Resistance can be conceived as something negative that has to be overcome, but it can also be understood as a positive force for change. For example, Rapoport et al (2002) treat resistance as useful and important. Where tension exists, it can be worked with to bring about change. The aim is to challenge underlying assumptions about working practices in order to move resistance from a desire to block constructive changes towards resistance against current systems that undermine work–personal life integration and workplace effectiveness (Rapoport et al 2002).

Again, it is important to emphasise that these are basic principles and the exact process will depend on the specific organisational context. This is very different from the popular idea of 'best practices', which assumes that the answer to WLB issues lies in certain policies and practices without taking account of the nature of the organisation, the work being done and workplace cultures.

CONCLUSION

In this chapter, we have argued that the WLB narrative has led to HRM solutions in terms of policies, which are an important first step. However, these policies rarely lead to changes in workplace structures, cultures and practices because underlying and outdated assumptions about ideal workers and the way that paid work should be carried out are not challenged (Lewis et al 2007). Currently, WLB in the organisational flexibility sense is often regarded as a (short-term) cost, even if it is recognised that there may be long-term benefits. This contrasts with a dual-agenda approach that addresses both workplace effectiveness and opportunities for equitable strategies for combining paid work and personal life, where both are given equal importance.

We have provided examples of organisations that have adopted a dual-agenda approach to change, which involved a collaborative process for surfacing prevailing assumptions about how work is done, considering the impact of these assumptions on both effectiveness and employees' work and personal lives and developing innovations to meet this dual agenda. There is mounting evidence that this approach, for example using action research, can be successful in meeting a dual agenda in a range of contexts (Rapoport et al 2002; Lewis and Cooper 2005; Lewis et al 2007). It requires more effort than simple policy initiatives but can result in important next steps towards sustainable gender-equitable, inclusive and effective working practices.

HRM IN THE MEDIA

CRITICAL REFLECTIONS

The news story at the start of the chapter presents a clear illustration of how discussions of WLB cannot be disentangled from the issue of gender equity. As a mother of a one-year-old daughter, the employee requesting flexible working hours recognised that the airline's shift patterns for pilots made it difficult for her and her husband to care for their child. From the employee's perspective, then, her request was reasonable and justified, given her dual responsibility as a worker and as a parent. By making the request, she was challenging the airline's existing norms of how the work of pilots should be done, which were based on the male model of work discussed throughout this chapter. The employer's initially persuasive argument, that disrupting the rostering system was not possible, proportionate or fair on other pilots, was less convincing when it became apparent that the seniority basis of the system was biased against newer staff, rather than on genuine need.

This brings us to the second question raised. We would argue that she had a good case against her employer for indirect sex discrimination. This is because BA's system of allocating shift patterns for pilots is based on seniority, which may seem 'fair' and gender-neutral at the surface. However, when we stop to reflect on how many men and women are employed as pilots at BA (2,828 men and 152 women in 2005), we see how the gendered nature of organisations is played out in this case. Considering the glaring gender gap in the employment rate of pilots, it is questionable how many women in comparison with men actually progress to senior positions if they 'deviate' from the male model of the ideal worker (due to their constrained choices, such as the employee in question).

In relation to the last question, the tribunal ruled in favour of the employee and again at the Employment Appeal Tribunal in July 2005. BA had planned to take the case to the Court of Appeal, but dropped it in 2007. The airline later stated that they '...recognise the need for flexibility on the part of employers to enable parents to balance the needs of a demanding career and family life'. This outcome is encouraging, because it enables good women workers to realise their potential and has implications for effective HRM talent management strategy.

EXPLORE FURTHER

GAMBLES, R., LEWIS, S. and RAPOPORT, R. (2006) *The myth of work–life balance: the challenge of our time for men, women and societies.* Chichester: Wiley.

This critical and comprehensive book, based on research conducted in seven diverse countries, explores the multiple difficulties in combining paid work with other parts of life and challenges the myth of achieving WLB through 'quick-fixes'.

LEWIS, S. and COOPER, C. (2005) *Work–life integration: case studies of organisational change.* London: Wiley.

A book of case studies using a work–life integration approach to bring about organisational change and flexibility. This provides a range of practical examples and has learning points at the end of each chapter.

RAPOPORT, R., BAILYN, L., FLETCHER, J. and PRUITT, B. (2002) *Beyond work–family balance: advancing gender equity and workplace performance.* London: Jossey-Bass Wiley.

A very detailed but readable account of an action research model of organisational change using a work–life balance lens.

Critical Issues in Equality and Diversity (2): Defining and Challenging Institutional Racism

Doirean Wilson

OVERVIEW

This chapter examines issues regarding institutional racism, while identifying how it can be addressed. The chapter begins with a news story on a recent claim of racial discrimination lodged against the Metropolitan Police Service. The main body of the chapter discusses the importance of race and culture in context with migration, as a prelude to exploring the benefits of diversity in the workplace. An exploration of the meaning of the terms racism and institutional racism precedes discussions regarding their differences. The chapter concludes with an overview of the main points of debate. This chapter draws on theories that underpin the understanding of workplace racism as a form of discrimination, how this concept is extending through the notion of institutional racism and the issues involved in challenging institutional racism.

LEARNING OBJECTIVES

Reading this chapter will enable the reader to:

- critically examine the dimensions and origins of racism in the workplace
- critically compare and contrast how the concept of institutional racism extends a general understanding of racism
- critically evaluate the impact of racism in the workplace
- critically evaluate equitable approaches for promoting diversity within the workplace as a means of tackling racism.

HRM IN THE MEDIA

'INSTITUTIONAL RACISM IN THE MET?'

According to the *Guardian* (Gray 2008), in August 2008, Tarique Ghaffur, Assistant Commissioner for the Metropolitan Police, accused Scotland Yard of being racially discriminatory. Ghaffur was at the time the most senior Asian officer in the UK. He was later suspended when he gave a press conference, claiming that he had been humiliated, sidelined and discriminated against while in his role as Chief of Security, in charge of planning for the London 2012 Olympics.

Ghaffur's claim of institutional racism prompted the Metropolitan Black Police Association to boycott the recruitment of ethnic minorities to the Metropolitan Police Force. The outcome of this case was not conclusive. While an out-of-court settlement had been reached, Mr Ghaffur had signed a 'gagging clause' as part of the agreement, but was said to have settled for £300,000. The inconclusiveness of this case is further highlighted in a commentary in *Prospect Magazine* (Gilligan 2008). Here, it is claimed that the Metropolitan Police has not dealt with the issues of racism well. On the one hand, at senior level, it is overly sensitive to the issue of race, reacting to external lobbies and a variety of internal pressure groups within the service to demonstrate its commitment to diversity. On the other hand, reports of a corrosive 'canteen culture' of racism still permeates the lower ranks, thereby preventing talented black, Asian and minority ethnic (BAME) officers from progressing.

Questions

1 The outcome of the case was inconclusive. Nonetheless, what do you think the Metropolitan Police Force could have done to prevent this claim of race discrimination?

2 Was the Metropolitan Black Police Association's decision to boycott the recruitment of ethnic minorities to the Metropolitan Police Force a good decision?

3 Do you think this case – centred on very senior-level officers – is likely to be reflective of the experiences of lower-ranking officers in the organisation?

INTRODUCTION

The term institutionalised racism was coined by American civil rights leader Stokely Carmichael in the 1960s and is concerned with an indirect and possibly invisible series of assumptions and practices that can lead to unintentional barriers and selection/promotion procedures that serve to disadvantage members of ethnic minority groups (Price 2007). The term was resurrected three decades later by Sir William Macpherson in his report into the murder of Stephen Lawrence in 1993. Macpherson's committee concluded that the Metropolitan Police was to blame for the lack of a conviction of those responsible for Stephen's murder, due to the catalogue of blunders made that the committee believed was based on prejudices held against black citizens, something the Metropolitan Police later accepted.

There were many barriers to development endured by members of the black, Asian and minority ethnic (BAME) community rendering them disadvantaged. Heightened hostilities between the black community and the police led to a catalogue of riots across the UK during the 1980s. In 1981 a series of riots erupted in Manchester, Liverpool, Bristol, Birmingham, Leeds and Brixton, London, the latter causing £6.5 million worth of damage. Further riots occurred in Handsworth four years later and in 1985, after police shot and killed Cherry Groce when they stormed her flat in search of her son, led to the Broadwater Farm riots resulting in the death of PC Keith Blakelock. While it would be wrong to call these 'race riots', they all took place within communities that had sizeable Afro-Caribbean communities, and a significant element of the grievances – as concluded in the Scarman Report (1981) – was a combination of chronic lack of employment opportunities and the overtly discriminatory treatment by the police.

So the issue of racism was not new when the more recent definition of institutional racism was raised. Before we move to this, though, some background to the broader issues is required.

RACE, MIGRATION AND DEMOGRAPHY

The history of racist atrocities serves as a constant reminder of why the topic of race and culture remain relevant in society today. In its most extreme, one could consider crimes such as the slave trade, the Holocaust and the series of genocides and 'ethnic cleansing' from Armenia to Rwanda to Bosnia as being based on the issue of race. As a political and civil rights issue, race was the basis of the apartheid regime in South Africa and the semi-official system of segregation in the southern US – as well as the social movements that displaced them: from the National Association for the Advancement of Coloured People (NAACP) and the civil rights movement in the USA to the African National Congress (ANC) and the global anti-apartheid movement in the case of South Africa.

The UK has not been exempt from these cases of overt race discrimination, albeit less extreme. The issue in the UK has centred on the patterns of inward migration and has, for the most part, been tied to Britain's adaptation to post-colonialism. Local and national politicians and public servants have worked to fight overt racism. In practice, however, the issue has been a permanent feature of life for many migrants.

In the 2000s new waves of immigration into the UK from eastern Europe caused a new 'moral panic' from the popular press about the displacement of British workers by foreigners. This phenomenon was neither new nor exclusive to the UK. Castles (2002, p1) notes:

> International migration suddenly became a key issue in international politics at the beginning of the 1990s, when the breakdown of the bi-polar power constellation of the Cold War seemed to have opened the floodgates for vast new population flows [and that] the effects of migration on both sending and receiving societies remain prominent in political and academic discourse.

Migration is therefore a key feature of globalisation, which has resulted in a more diverse workforce. This is likely to be a major challenge for HR practitioners in the future (see Chapter 23). In the UK, though, the issue is not entirely new. Hence a need for closer attention to ensure that organisations are compliant with equality and diversity legislation – such as, for example, that outlined in the Equality Act 2010 (p59) regarding further and higher education courses. The specification is that responsible bodies have a duty of care to ensure that they do not discriminate (unwittingly or otherwise) against a person enrolled on a course in the services that it provides or offers to provide. The need for closer scrutiny is probably an approach that would be worthy for other organisations to consider. Migration to the UK since the mid 1940s was born of either push factors, that is, lack of employment in the home country and poor health; or pull factors, such as perception of a high standard of living in the host country (Shultz et al 1998). As previously acknowledged, migration has resulted in a more diverse workforce and labour market, which Miyazake (1977, p1) described as being 'a market for labour contracts. A firm is identified as having an internal labour market if the efficient mode of production requires that it employ heterogeneous worker types by offering a wage structure as a set of subsidizing contracts.' However, 'economic discrimination in labour markets is conventionally defined as the presence of different pay for workers of the same ability' based on, for instance, their race (Aigner and Cain 1977, p175).

Between 1945 and 1959, approximately 126,000 workers arrived and settled in Britain from the Caribbean. Many came with the intention of staying temporarily to earn enough money in order to return to the Caribbean in elevated social status. The majority of these workers were from Jamaica. Phrases such as, 'land of milk and honey' were popularly used to entice them to Britain with promises of better jobs, pay and living conditions. A second wave, this time from the Indian sub-continent and also from the south Asian diaspora in east Africa and elsewhere, began in the 1960s and continued into the 1970s. There were no major patterns from then until the accession of eight new European Union member countries in central and eastern Europe in 2004 (Czech Republic, Estonia, Hungary, Latvia, Lithuania, Poland, Slovakia and Slovenia), whereby a remarkably large number of migrants – by any previous comparison – entered the UK seeking employment. As an issue of 'race', if not culture, this last group provides an interesting situation, as they are almost exclusively white.

Government figures (National Statistics 2002; Annual Population Survey 2004a, 2004b) showed that people from a minority ethnic background totalled 4.5 million, or 7.6%, of the population. Within this broader picture some interesting local trends emerge. It was reported, for example, that by 2019, no single ethnic group – including white – would constitute the majority of the population of the city of Leicester and that Birmingham would reach a similar state by 2024 (BBC News 2007). Many places already have populations where BAME communities constitute a majority. This is particularly the case in many parts of London, arguably the most cosmopolitan city in the world. For example in 2001, the population of BAME residents in the London boroughs of Brent and Newham was more than 50%. By 2026, it is anticipated that other London boroughs such as Harrow, Redbridge, Tower Hamlets, Hounslow, Croydon and Ealing will also have a BAME population of more than 50% (Bains 2007).

The growth in the numbers of BAME communities in these boroughs suggests they are becoming less white and as such more diverse. While this might be viewed as a positive development by the BAME community and by those keen to promote cosmopolitanism, there are those who see the issue around 'white flight' and about degeneration. The same GLA report (Bains 2007) that highlights the changing composition of populations acknowledges the influences that the media has on stereotypical beliefs about racial groups. This results in a tendency to relate property with perceptions of services, accessing jobs, security and safety and an assumption that when white people leave an area, income levels are likely to drop, and crime escalates, which means the area would not be the best place to do business.

RACISM IN EMPLOYMENT

The central concern within this chapter is in identifying the dynamics of racism in employment. Firstly, it is important to identify what racism is in general, before moving on to identify how it manifests itself.

Racism, as an individual psychological form of prejudice, can be understood to be the belief in the superiority of one ethnic group over others; or the inferiority of a particular ethnic or cultural group. Van Dijk (2002, p145) further asserts that 'racism is understood as a complex societal system of ethnically or "racially" based domination and its resulting inequality'. The Commission for Racial Equality (2007) states that the term racism 'is used to justify placing a particular racial group/s in an inferior position to another'. According to Sivanandan (2001, p1) 'racism has always been both an instrument of discrimination and a tool of exploitation'. But it manifests itself as a cultural phenomenon. Zavala et al (1987, p81) also believe 'racism, and more generally, ethnicism, are partly reproduced through various forms of discourse, such as everyday conversations, parent–child discourse, textbooks, official discourse of the authorities, and various types of media discourse, such as news reports, movies, TV programs, and advertising'.

So why are people racist? There are wider social and historical dimensions to this: a collective view perpetrated by a legacy of colonialism. That is, as Grosfoguel (1999) put it, 'postwar Caribbean colonial migration, to the metropoles provide an important experience for the examination of racial discrimination in core zones' and that 'they were part of a colonial labour migration to supply cheap labour'. Then 'with the contraction of the capitalist world-economy after 1973, first and second generation Caribbean colonial migrants began to be excluded from the labour market' and 'have been the target of the "new racist" discourses that attempt to keep them in a subordinated position within the core zones by using "cultural racist" discourses'. But with such colonial folk memories being increasingly distant, it may be worthwhile considering individual reasons for such behaviours.

Negative perceptions of those of difference is likely to be inextricably linked with negative stereotypes held about them. These stereotypes can influence beliefs that govern expectations of minority groups and, as such, are unlikely to lead to favourable outcomes. Jussim et al (1996, p281) acknowledge a similar school of thought when referring to social scientists who they believe 'have a longstanding interest in one particular source of expectation which they state were stereotypes [and that this is] largely because stereotypes may contribute to social inequalities and injustices', such as a belief that members of a particular ethnic group are workshy, therefore employers might avoid recruiting them thus giving credence to this belief. They raise interesting questions in this regard. The first question is: 'Are people so malleable that they readily fulfil others' inaccurate expectations?' This suggests a defeatist self-perception of the group that happens to be in the minority. An implication of this first question is that people in the minority are often willing participants, eager to 'fulfil others' inaccurate' and speculatively 'stereotypical expectations' of them. However, it would be wise not to assume that the behaviour displayed by those of difference means acceptance, willingness to comply or need to conform to inaccuracies. Instead, we should be reminded that racism, institutional or otherwise, restricts, demoralises and suppresses development, which in itself is a manifestation of disrespect. It is a widely held view that a core British value is one of 'tolerance'. Yet it may be more universal than this. A two-phase study (2007–2008 and 2008–2009) conducted by Wilson (2010) with groups of final-year undergraduate students from a wide range of nationalities and cultures suggested that respect was a 'core value' for all 'irrespective of culture or ethnicity'. This said, attitudes and expectations of minority groups, based on negative stereotypes, could be perceived as disrespectful and, as such, would challenge respect as a common core value. All of this suggests a need to identify a common value of mutual respect in organisations to nurture awareness of those of difference and foster harmonious working relationships.

Many victims of discrimination fear repercussions that they believe they would endure if they were to complain, so instead might opt for what they regard as expedient, less painful options, such as deciding to resign from their positions, or to tolerate the behaviour. Others might assume that to invoke a formal grievance as the first stage of the disciplinary procedure would be a last resort for addressing racism at work. To resign or tolerate racism, however, does not resolve the problem, nor does it encourage perpetrators to correct or reflect on the impact that their behaviour might have on others. As such, this scenario is likely to be ongoing albeit more complicated than previously thought. One possible reason for this is the growth in race legislation, thus driving racism underground and making it less overt and more covert and not as easy to eradicate.

The second question that Jussim et al (1996) ask is how accurate interpersonal expectations are as they can lead to biases and self-fulfilling prophecies. The accuracy of interpersonal expectations would depend on the accuracy of the stereotypical perceptions held about those of difference. That is, whether these stereotypes are based on fact or fiction; and, equally, whether they are negative or positive. For example, a common perception of black people is that they are good at sports and, as such, there might be a tendency to assume either that they would be willing participants in sporting events or that they would be better at it than anyone else. Equally, black individuals, especially black men, might perceive such a stereotype as providing them with the opportunity to prove and be accepted as being worthy, although such stereotypes might not be one of choice. As noted in this regard by Majors (2001, p213), 'sports play an important and – in some limited ways – a positive role in many black males lives'. Majors (2001, p213) points out that 'the sports establishment does not operate as an apolitical, asocial enterprise, but as part of the larger society'. Nevertheless, 'sports often appears to be one of the few arenas that provides true opportunity', albeit in a limited way. What is also recognised is that 'this distortion of reality draws young black males into athletic careers into disproportionately high numbers', thus giving the impression as intimated by Jussim et al (1996) of an eagerness to fulfil others' inaccurate expectations of them – when in fact the motivation was based on a need to seize a socially acceptable opportunity, where there was likely to be more positive interactive expectations of black men as achievers, something they would otherwise not have been afforded had they been competing in, for instance, an academic arena.

Jussim et al's (1996) final question is, 'to what extent do stereotypes bias person perception and lead to self-fulfilling prophesies?' (1996, p281). Extent is a measure that is not easy to gauge. Nevertheless, research evidence suggests it is safe to assume that stereotypes can influence and can bias a person's perception of others and as such can be limiting. According to Niemeyer (2004), 'stereotypes are essential for basic functions of perception and human perception'; however, he also warned that 'stereotypes also introduce significant limitations on human experience'. This suggests a tendency to see the behaviour displayed by those of difference, only in context with perceived stereotypes, while being close-minded to factors that might reveal what in essence is real and true, and not what is believed to be the reality. This might be because these truths deviate from the stereotypes. Nonetheless, it is acknowledged that 'social perception is a major force in the creation (construction) of social reality' (Jussim 1991, p54).

Smith and Mackie (2010) explain that stereotypes include many types of characteristics, which can be positive or negative, accurate or inaccurate, and that they can be learned through personal experience. However, this process can create bias, as people often associate particular extreme characteristics as being 'normal' characteristics for that group. This can be far from the truth, as these experiences might not reflect the majority of those who belong to these particular groups. In addition, social roles, emotions generated by group interactions and social learning contribute to stereotypes (Smith and Mackie 2010). More worryingly, 'stereotypes and discrimination are often accepted and endorsed as right and proper by members of a particular group, becoming social norms', therefore making it more difficult to deconstruct social learning about particular cultural groups. 'Motives to form stereotyping mastery, connectedness' and, as such, 'justifying existing social inequalities', thus giving birth to discriminatory practices, suggesting further that racism is a complex issue that has existed in the UK for some time.

PATTERNS OF RACE DISCRIMINATION IN EMPLOYMENT

The impact of racism differs in different aspects of life. In employment, racism manifests itself through its impact on access to jobs and through inequalities in progression within organisations.

During economically prosperous years, government figures indicate some differences in unemployment rates among different ethnic groups, with white ethnic groups tending to have lower rates (Annual Population Survey 2004b). In particular, unemployment rates for black Caribbean (9%), Indian (8%) and Chinese (7%) women were around twice the rates for white British and white Irish women. Among men, those from black Caribbean, black African, Bangladeshi and mixed ethnic groups had the highest unemployment rates (between 13 and 14%). These rates were around three times the rates for white British and white Irish men (5% in each case).

According to the Commission for Racial Equality (CRE), people from ethnic minorities were far less likely (13.6%) than white people (24.7%) to work in production industries, with over a third of them (35.1% compared with 26.1% of white workers) working in hotels and catering, distribution and transport and communications. It was also noted that similar percentages of ethnic minorities were employed in private services such as finance, business and the public services. This, in itself, should not be significant except for the increased prevalence of low-status, low-paid and insecure work in many of these industries.

Evidence drawn from statistical sources show that people from non-white ethnic groups fare worse in employment, earnings and career progress than their white counterparts, even after taking into account other factors known to affect performance. Such factors include age, sex and educational qualifications. Ethnic minority workers in public sector services in the UK also tend to be concentrated in lower-grade positions. In the Civil Service, for example, ethnic minority staff made up 8.2% of civil servants overall (3.8% Asian, 2.5% black, 0.9% mixed parentage and 0.2% Chinese), but only 3.3% were in senior grades – a figure that constituted a grand total of just 120 employees nationwide (CRE 2007, p6).

According to Willey (2003, pp199–200), political initiatives taken against discrimination can be either 'minimalist' or 'maximalist', and in Britain it is tending towards the latter position in recent years. Amendments to the Race Relations Act (2000) and the accompanying Statutory Code of Practice (2002) are attempts to rectify some of the shortcomings, particularly in respect of public authorities and the exercise of their functions. Sargeant and Lewis (2008, p191) warned, however, that 'any consideration of the Race Relations Act must take into account the fact that race discrimination (as with sex discrimination) continues to exist'. Nevertheless, the criminal law on racially motivated harassment and violence has been improved in recent years. The Crime and Disorder Act (1998) and the Criminal and Security Act (2001) have created a new criminal offence of religiously aggravated harassment (Willey 2003, p200), which is directly relevant to employment as well as to civil society as a whole.

INSTITUTIONAL RACISM

To gain a clearer understanding of the significance and impact of institutional racism in the workplace, it is crucial to distinguish what it is and how it differs from racism *per se*. According to Henry et al (2004, p517), institutional racism '…refers to the ways in which racist beliefs or values have been built into the operations of social institutions, in such a way as to discriminate against, control and oppress various minority groups'. The Commission for Racial Equality (CRE 2007) describes institutional racism as being 'concerned with racial discrimination that has been incorporated into structures, processes and procedures of organisations, either because of racial prejudice or because of failure to take in to account the particular needs of black and ethnic minority people'.

Sivanandan (1976) is regarded as a pioneer in articulating a paradigm shift in race thinking from the hard-done-by black people to the race-suppressing white institutions. He argued that discrimination was taken 'out of the market place' and given 'the sanction of the state. They made racism respectable and clinical by institutionalising it. But in so doing they also increased the social and political consequences of racism.' For Sivanandan (1976), institutional racism in the UK is in essence 'laissez-faire discrimination' that is structurally bound and systemic in nature.

The aforementioned definition for institutional racism helps to distinguish how institutional racism differs from racism. That is, the term racism suggests negative personal biases born of societal perceptions, assumptions, stereotypes and beliefs about those of racial and cultural difference that govern behaviour, attitudes and expectations of 'them'. In comparison, institutional racism could be deemed derivative of racism as it refers to the intent to design organisational policies, procedures and systems that are wittingly or unwittingly influenced by personal negative biases. This is reflected by the CRE (2007), which states that institutional racism is 'concerned with racial discrimination that has been incorporated into structures, processes and procedures of organisations'. As such, these organisational policies could be seen as more detrimental than racism *per se*. This is because they tend to be long term, are inextricably linked to in-company approaches and operations, and often create a covert culture that suggests racism in the workplace is not just acceptable but an expectation. Institutional racism is therefore likely to be entrenched and difficult to eradicate, thus creating a restrictive cordon around black and minority ethnic staff, making it difficult for them to be recognised and be treated in the same way as their white co-workers.

A shift in emphasis from racism to institutional racism suggests the latter is not as easy to address and is therefore more difficult to eradicate. Racism is the manifestation of individuals, therefore the outcome of racist behaviour makes it easy to identify and deal with the cause. On the other hand, the malevolence of institutional racism could be described as an endemic nuance of discriminatory practices guised in the 'fabric' of organisational policies and procedures. As such, institutional racism is more complex, less obvious and not as easy to tackle. It is reputed that 'the concept of institutional racism was developed in the 1960s primarily to serve the purpose of moving our gaze from individual attitudes to the collective impact large organisations have in maintaining white privilege' (Law et al 2004, pviii). In some instances, the root cause of discriminatory practices derives from policies that do not afford minority ethnic employees the same opportunities of fairness and equality given to, for example, initiatives that promote gender equality.

CHALLENGING INSTITUTIONAL RACISM: PROMOTING WORKPLACE DIVERSITY

While 'diversity' is a phrase used as a positive way of promoting the benefits of inclusion for all categories relating to inequality, it is in the area of race and culture that this approach may have the most obvious benefits: while there remains some debate on the issue of gender equity whether women will benefit from a 'diversity' approach in comparison to an 'equality' approach, on the issue of race there are very few arguing for socio-cultural homogeneity as a route to an equitable and harmonious workplace.

Prior to exploring the benefits of diversity in the workplace, it would be worthwhile to define what the term 'diversity' means. According to McGrath et al (1995, p2), 'diversity is a characteristic of groups of two or more people and typically refers to demographic differences of one sort or another among group members.'

Grieve and French (2000) believe it is important to be objective and transparent about these issues. These thoughts reflect Wilson's (2010) research, based on an exploration of the relationship between respect and culture. The research volunteers comprised final-year undergraduate male and female students of mixed ethnicity and cultures and with varying experiences of work. The students were encouraged to share and discuss their stories of respect and disrespect and the impact that their experiences had on them emotionally, the majority of which were work-related. The storytelling process helped to promote greater awareness and understanding of those of difference, which had a positive impact on attitudes and interactive behaviour as displayed among the volunteers.

Institutional racism constitutes 'contempt', 'hostility', 'conflict' and a 'breach of equal opportunities', which can lead to serious negative consequences for an organisation. What is widely acknowledged is that to combat racism in the workplace, employers, practitioners and, indeed, HR policy-makers need to ensure that they have a clear understanding of what the term 'institutional racism' means and its implications not just from their standpoint, but from the position of those of difference. According to Price (2007, p420) 'institutional racism is an indirect and largely invisible process which can be compared with cloning and the glass ceiling'. When interpreted this suggests an act, intentional or otherwise, that ensures that those of a particular background (white, male, middle-class) are treated more favourably and, as such, often excel to positions of authority and seniority. In comparison an organisation might treat others (those of black and minority ethnic origin, those with seen disabilities, women) in a less advantageous way irrespective of their competencies. Price (2007, p420) stated that the term institutional racism encompasses 'the often unintentional, barriers and selection/promotion procedures which serve to disadvantage members of ethnic minority groups'. The need for institutions to nurture and uphold a culture that embraces equality and fairness is paramount if they intend to remain sustainable. The following seven steps for preventing and addressing institutional racism suggest how this can be achieved:

1 Employers need to ensure that they are conversant with current equality legislation to ascertain the impact on their organisation.

2 Employers need to conduct regular assessments to identify the 'true' diversity of their workforce, to update staff demographic profiles.

3 Employers need to conduct in-house equality and diversity health-check audits. This can be an online activity that incorporates feedback from staff in order to ascertain whether the organisation is able to comply with equal opportunities legislative requirements.

4 Employers need to implement suitable diversity and equal opportunities policies and procedures that are 'best' fit for the workforce and, in turn, the organisation.

5 Employers should make it their duty to review the organisation's diversity and equal opportunities policies and procedures to ensure that they are able to appropriately meet the needs of the workforce.

6 Employers need to appraise the effectiveness of the methodology adopted for monitoring the organisation's equality and diversity policies/procedures.

7 Employers should incorporate diversity and equality contingency measures that are specific, measureable, achievable, realistic and time-bound (SMART).

CONCLUSION

The universal message that institutional racism is unacceptable needs to be disseminated across all sectors of industry to ensure that employers do not breach race relations law. At the moment, some improvements have been made relating to the conduct of organisations and how these have affected some ethnic groups (Ogbonna and Harris 2006).

Several key points were discussed in this chapter with regard to the meaning of institutional racism: namely, the impact of migration in Britain and the xenophobic response of the indigenous community to the influx of those of difference. The terms racism and institutional racism were defined and compared to give greater insight to the consequences of racism in the workplace, while discussing the benefits and ways in which to promote workplace diversity.

Institutional racism and its counterpart racism are serious issues that have devastating effects and, as such, are worthy of being remembered. This is described quite graphically by Acuna (2010) in his paper, where he states that 'racism resembles bacteria' and that it 'has an uncanny ability to resist cures. Like bacteria, racism includes variants with unusual traits which have the ability to withstand antibiotic attack on a microbe.' He continues by stating that 'for the moment the drug or law kills the defenceless bacteria, leaving behind or selecting in biological terms those that can't resist it. These renegade bacteria then multiply, increasing their numbers a million-fold in a day, becoming the predominant microorganism.' Acuna emphasised his point, which was his perception 'that we once believed that racism had been defined and that we were on our way to eradicate this ugly social disease only to find it active and well but in another form'. This suggests that racism has mutated into a less visible and more covert form than it used to be. But what, we may ask, are the implications of this transformation? Going undercover would render the proof of burden regarding acts of discrimination, such as institutional racism, not as easy as it once was to evidence or 'root' out. Employers should take heed that being 'ignorant' of the fact, in this regard, 'is not bliss', as organisations could be rendered being in breach of equality laws.

HRM IN THE MEDIA

CRITICAL REFLECTIONS

The news story at the beginning of this chapter, which considered the complaint of race discrimination lodged against the Metropolitan Police Service by one of its senior officers, raises several important issues, including the extent to which a claim of race discrimination can impact on morale and harmonious working relationships in the workplace. The perception of the public would also need to be considered, especially when bearing in mind that the role of the Metropolitan Police is to act as enforcers of the law for the community in which it serves. If there is a vote of no confidence from the wider community, then this would make the Met's job somewhat more difficult. Limitation strategies would also need to be considered to address negative perceptions of the police that might emerge or be reignited as a result of such complaints of racism. Nevertheless, there are several issues that would need to be considered in order to answer each of the mini case study questions.

For example, the first question asks whether there was anything that the Met Police could have done to prevent the claim of race discrimination. A claim of race discrimination is generally governed by a claimant's belief that, for example, negative perceptions of their race have resulted in them being treated less favourably or unfairly in the workplace in comparison with those in the majority, or those who they might assume believe they are superior. This said, it could be argued that it would be worthy for the Met to acknowledge that in general members of the BAME community are probably more inclined to be portrayed negatively in the media. If so, perhaps this could influence perceptions and attitudes towards them at work. If indeed this was the case then this might result in an assumption that certain behaviours, decisions and attitudes could be racially motivated, which might or might not be the case. Therefore the need for greater awareness and understanding of BAME needs and expectations with regard to their perception of fair treatment in the workplace might be both a preventative measure and a potential solution.

The second case study question asks whether the Met Black Police Association's decision to boycott the recruitment of ethnic minorities to the Met Police was a good decision. One could argue that this would depend on whether this decision was made in response to the allegation prior to, or after the case had been fully investigated.

The final question was whether the case is likely to be reflective of the experiences of lower-ranking Met officers. This would depend on whether there is evidence to suggest that claims of a similar kind have been lodged by junior Met officers.

Readers are encouraged to reflect throughout this chapter on their own experiences of discrimination at work or on those with which they are familiar as an aide for considering the key things learned as a result.

EXPLORE FURTHER

BETTER, S.J. (2008) *Institutional racism: a primer on theories and strategies for social change.* UK: Rowman and Littlefield.

This book focuses on the social phenomenon of institutional racism.

PENKETH, L. (2000) *Tackling institutional racism: anti racist policies and social work education and training.* Bristol: Policy Press.

This book explores why the challenges to institutional racism face hostility in state organisations.

EZORSKY, G. (1991) *Racism and justice: the case for affirmative action.* Ithaca, NY: Cornell University Press.

This book discusses institutional racism in context with a review of the impact of neutral procedures on employment and selection.

SANDERS, C.L. (1973) *Black professionals' perceptions of institutional racism in health and welfare organisations.* Fair Lawn, NJ: R.E. Burdick.

This book is reputed to provide the most definitive discussions for institutional racism.

JACKSON, J.P. and WEIDMAN, N.M. (2004) *Race, racism and science: social impact and interactions.* Santa Barbara, CA: ABC-Clio Ltd.

This book discusses institutional racism from a historical scientific study of race and colonialism.

Equality and Human Rights Commission website: www.equalityhumanrights.com/

This website covers all aspects of equality and diversity, since it was merged in 2010.

CHAPTER 18

Equality and Diversity (3): Disability Discrimination and the Modern Workplace

Asiya Siddiquee and Uracha Chatrakul Na Ayudhya

OVERVIEW

This chapter explores the issue of disability discrimination within the modern workplace. It begins with an overview of the broad trends of the employment of disabled people in the UK and introduces two prominent models of disability: medical and social. The two models are critically compared in brief. The remainder of the chapter is framed around the 1995 and 2005 Disability Discrimination Act (DDA). The Act's definition of disability and discrimination are firstly critically explored. The chapter then focuses on how the legislation is being implemented and enforced to ensure disability equality. In terms of implementation, various HR practices and procedures are outlined and particular detail is given to measures taken to ensure equality for disabled people in terms of recruitment and conditions of employment. The chapter then moves to a discussion of how the Act is enforced and an evaluation of its success. Areas of critical discussion will be highlighted throughout the chapter and reference will be made where relevant to the perspective of employers and employees. The chapter concludes with an exploration of future developments or progression for the disability equality movement in terms of employment.

LEARNING OBJECTIVES

Reading this chapter will enable the reader to:

● critically compare the medical model and social model of disability

● critically evaluate government legislation towards disability discrimination and its implications in the modern workplace, including employers' duty to make 'reasonable adjustments'

● critically explore practices and procedures related to recruitment and terms of employment that are meant to promote equality for disabled people

● consider key issues relating to disability in the workplace and critically evaluate the implementation of policy into practice.

HRM IN THE MEDIA

'DISABLED WOMAN SUES IMAGE-CONSCIOUS MULTI-NATIONAL CLOTHING COMPANY FOR DISCRIMINATION'

It was reported in 2009 that a 22-year-old woman, who was born with a missing forearm, was taking her employer, Abercrombie & Fitch (A&F), to an employment tribunal for disability discrimination after she was forced to work in the stockroom after wearing a cardigan to cover her prosthetic arm (BBC News 2009a).

The employee told the tribunal that when she told A&F about her disability after getting the job, the firm agreed she could wear a white cardigan to cover the link between her prosthesis and her upper arm. But shortly afterwards she was told she could not work on the shop floor unless she took off the cardigan, citing that she was breaking the firm's 'look policy'. The policy stipulates that all employees 'represent A&F with natural, classic American style consistent with the company's brand' and 'look great while exhibiting individuality'.

At the tribunal, she stated that someone in the A&F head office suggested she stayed in the stockroom 'until the winter uniform arrives'. She argued, 'I had been bullied out of my job. It was the lowest point I had ever been in my life' (Pidd 2009).

After the case was ruled, counsel for A&F said the findings of the tribunal were based 'on the events of a single day' and that these were not representative of the employee's overall employment with the firm. 'We continue to believe that these events resulted from a misunderstanding that could have been avoided by better communication on the part of both parties,' said the counsel, who added that the company continued to support the rights of disabled individuals (BBC News 2009b).

Questions

1 Do you think it was fair for the firm to enforce its 'look policy' to all its shop floor employees, regardless of their disability or non-disability statuses? Why or why not?

2 To what extent do you agree that the employee had a good case for taking the company to the employment tribunal on the grounds of disability discrimination?

3 To what extent do you think that the Disability Discrimination Act (DDA 1995 and 2005) is sufficient in ensuring that disabled employees are not unjustifiably treated less favourably than non-disabled employees?

INTRODUCTION

The news story above illustrates some of the sensitive and complex issues pertinent to disability within the modern workplace for both employers and employees. Outlining the context of disability within the UK, Stevens (2002) suggests that disabled people are under-represented within the UK labour market. Statistics and figures from the Office for Disability Issues (ODI) further support this. For instance, using data from national surveys (that is, Labour Force Surveys and the Family Resources Survey), the ODI states that there are approximately 10 million disabled adults in Great Britain; this includes sensory impairments, physical impairments, mental health illnesses and learning difficulties. Using figures from the 2007/08 Labour Force Survey, the ODI (2010) suggest an employment rate of 48.4% for working age disabled individuals (that is, males aged 16–60 and females aged 16–59) – which is comparable with an approximately 80% overall employment rate. Looking at the differences between full-time and part-time employment, figures for 2008 suggest 34.3% of disabled people are in full-time employment, compared with a figure of 61.3% for non-disabled people, while 14% of disabled people are in part-time employment compared with 18.3% non-disabled people. These figures suggest that disabled people are under-represented in the labour market and are more likely to engage in part-time work.

TWO MODELS OF DISABILITY: MEDICAL VERSUS SOCIAL

Before we consider key issues in the employment of disabled people and their implications for HRM, it is important to acknowledge that there is more than one way of looking at 'disability' as a construct. Broadly speaking, there are two main models of disability: the medical model and the social model. *The medical model of disability* adopts the view that disability is a result of 'individual pathology and is something that can be "rectified" (to a greater or lesser extent) through the intervention of medical and quasi-medical expertise' (Goss et al 2000, p807). In contrast to this, *the social model of disability* rejects the idea that disability is solely an individual problem of incapacity. Instead, the social model 'directs the analytical focus away from individual functional limitations to the barriers to social inclusion created by disabling environments, attitudes, and cultures' (Barnes and Mercer 2005, p531). In other words, disability is regarded as a social construct that occurs 'within a social environment which devalues difference' (Woodhams and Danieli 2000, p403). It can be argued that the medical model tends to perceive disability as a negative experience, whereas the social model prefers to focus on the positive aspects of being disabled (Woodhams and Danieli 2000).

In the context of employment, the two models interpret 'disability' differently. Such contrasting interpretations have implications for the equal treatment of disabled people at work and the role of HRM in ensuring equality for all workers. The following description by Berthoud (2008) provides a precise depiction of the broad distinction between the two approaches:

> The medical model focuses on impairment – that is, the limitation on the tasks that disabled people can perform. These limitations reduce their

potential productivity, and so restrict their job opportunities. This model is commonly assumed by doctors (it is a 'medical' model), as well as by many economists who perceive impairments as a form of negative human capital reducing disabled people's value to employers...

The social model assumes that the problem lies in the relationship between impaired people and the labour market: employers will not hire them, either out of ignorance of their capabilities, or to avoid adapting their working practices to accommodate the varying needs of potential employees... it is strongly endorsed by organizations of disabled people, who argue that they are 'unable to get a job' because of discrimination. (Berthoud 2007, p132)

Having outlined the basic distinctions between the two models above, it is important to point out that it is beyond the scope of this chapter to provide a critical discussion of the strengths and weaknesses of the two models (for examples of such critiques, see Barnes and Mercer 2005 and Foster 2007). Nonetheless, this brief introduction to the two models provides a platform for further considerations and debates of existing policies and practice in relation to the employment of disabled people. Indeed, such debates are essential as it is the medical model that still tends to dominate the 'popular consciousness' in how society regards disabled people and the issue of disability (Woodhams and Danieli 2000). Furthermore, it has been argued that the current legislation that purports to protect the employment rights of disabled people reflects the medical definition rather than the social view of disability (Barnes and Mercer 2005; Foster 2007). In order to advance the equal treatment of workers (both disabled and non-disabled) in the modern workplace, it is important to be aware of and challenge outdated (yet persistent) assumptions about disability through the adoption of alternative models such as the social model.

EMPLOYMENT RIGHTS OF DISABLED PEOPLE

Legislation covering the employment rights of disabled individuals was established in 1995 with the Disabled Discrimination Act (DDA) (1995), which came into operation on 2 December 1996 (Goss et al 2000). This Act sought to protect disabled individuals' employment rights and to increase their chances of obtaining and remaining in employment (Bell and Heitmueller 2009). In particular, section 4 of the Act states that it is unlawful for a potential employer to discriminate on the basis of disability during various stages of employment – including arrangements made for determining whom the offer is made to (for example application and interview), terms of employment offered to the person, conditions provided during employment (such as transfer, training or promotion) and reason for terminating employment (Chandler 2003). Furthermore, the Act made it a duty upon the employers to provide 'reasonable adjustment' to accommodate the needs of the disabled employee by, for example, making adjustments to the premises, providing specialist equipment, altering work hours or allocating the disabled person's duties to another worker.

The following sections in this chapter will explore the DDA in detail and will critically evaluate its implications in terms of practice in the British employment context. Key terms will be defined throughout and areas for discussion will be included in order to critically explore what disability discrimination means in the modern workplace. For the remainder of this chapter, the reader is invited to consider and evaluate the influences of both the medical model and the social model in the current legislation and in how the legislation is implemented at organisational level through policy and practice.

EXPLORING THE DISABILITY DISCRIMINATION ACT AND DEFINING KEY TERMS

DEFINING DISABILITY

Section 1 of the 1995 DDA makes it clear that disability is considered to be a physical or mental impairment that has long-term adverse effects on an individual's ability to carry out day-to-day activities. Unpicking the various components of this definition, in terms of types of disabilities this includes individuals who have sensory, physical or mental impairments. The Act was revised in 2005 (Disability Discrimination Act 2005) to include individuals with HIV, cancer or multiple sclerosis. The phrase 'long-term' generally refers to conditions that have either lasted or will last for 12 months or for the rest of the person's life (Bell and Heitmueller 2009; Woodhams and Corby 2003); while the aspect referring to affecting 'day-to-day' activities is described as pertaining to: mobility, manual dexterity, physical co-ordination, continence, ability to lift, hearing or eyesight, memory, ability to concentrate, or perceive the risk of danger (Woodhams and Corby 2003, p163).

Critically evaluating the definition of disability proposed by the Act, Goss et al (2000) argue that this is both theoretically and practically problematic. Theoretically, the 1995 Act's definition provides no new understanding of disability (Goss et al 2000). Indeed, the 2005 alterations, which included other types of disabilities, would indicate that the concept of disability is one that evolves over time and is socially constructed.

Furthermore, they argue:

> ...before a complainant can claim unfair treatment they must first prove that they fall within the definition of a disabled person. The inclusion in the Act's definition of the terms 'substantial', 'long term', and 'normal' makes this a difficult and contentious task... the definition of disability is drawn so restrictively that... UK cases may fall on the question of whether a person can be recognized as disabled (and thus entitled to protection) rather than on the nature of discrimination or the employment practices of the discriminator.... (Goss et al 2000, p812)

Adding to this, various authors (Berthoud 2008; Woodhams and Corby 2007; Woodhams and Danieli 2000) argue that the term 'disability' is far too broad a grouping and is not representative of the diversity of disability and experiences of employment within this group. Berthoud (2008, p130) emphasises this point by stating that:

> It is standard practice to quote an overall statistic for the proportion of disabled people in employment. This single figure implicitly discourages a view that disability is a complex construct with a variable influence on employment chances.

Furthermore, Woodhams and Corby (2003), who explore in depth the problematic nature of this definition of disability, claim that the definition creates numerous issues and problems. This includes in terms of providing medical evidence about a disability (that is, how does one prove that they are disabled according to this definition); the incongruence between the legal definition and its interpretation by employers; its portrayal of disability in a negative manner; and the fact that often disability is hidden. This illustrates some of the tensions that exist between policy and practice and will be explored further in the chapter when considering the enforcement of the Disability Discrimination Act and critically evaluating its success.

DEFINING DISCRIMINATION

Section 5 of the 1995 DDA focuses its attention on defining the term 'discrimination'. In summary, discrimination is described as unjustifiably treating a disabled person (either before, during or after employment) less favourably than others and for failing to make the necessary (and reasonable) adjustments to support disabled individuals in their application, recruitment and in facilitating them to fulfil their employment duties.

Looking in detail at the actual experiences of discrimination for disabled individuals, Grewal et al (2002) found that 17% of their disabled participants (out of a sample of approximately 970) expressed that they had experienced actual workplace discrimination, while 37% experienced prejudice or unfair treatment. Grewal et al (2002, p6) also found that:

> …there was evidence that disabled people frequently believed they had encountered prejudice in the application process, and many people (46 per cent) believed that employers were not as likely to employ people with disabilities as people without them.

Stalker and Lerpiniere's (2009) study also identified examples of disability discrimination for individuals with learning difficulties, which included being treated without respect and courtesy and employers failing to make reasonable adjustments. Their research found that this particular disabled group expressed a strong sense of injustice and experienced unfair treatment (not only within employment but also in terms of access to services). A recurrent theme was the desire to be treated with the same respect, to have the same opportunities and rights as non-disabled individuals and to use the same facilities.

While this highlights some of the forms of discrimination faced by disabled employees, looking in further detail at the notion of 'disability discrimination', Deal (2007) argues that the hardest aspect to tackle is a more subtle form of prejudice, which he terms 'aversive disablism'. This form of prejudice is one that is not necessarily as strong or overt as previously held notions of discrimination, whereby disabled individuals are considered lesser than able-bodied individuals, but is instead rooted in more subtle attitudes that in fact inhibit disabled employees from progressing. Providing a concrete example of this, Deal (2007, p100) writes:

> Aversive disablism may have an influence whereby an employer, through good intentions, could decide not to put a disabled employee under additional pressure by exposing them to a new function or requiring them to attend a stressful training event, but doing so inadvertently limits career development and thus places the employee in a more vulnerable position with respect to his/her career.

Consequently, Deal (2007) calls for greater measures to challenge both subtle and blatant prejudice in order to actualise a vision of equality for disabled employees.

IMPLEMENTATION AND ENFORCEMENT OF THE DISABILITY DISCRIMINATION ACT (1995)

So far, the chapter has presented the context of employment for disabled people and has outlined and critically challenged some of the terms used in the DDA. This section will now explore the ways in which the DDA has been implemented in the modern workplace. An aspect related to this is the disability symbol of 'two ticks', which refers to those organisations that are 'positive about disabled people'. This symbol was initiated by the Government in 1990 as an indication that an employer is working towards good practice in recruitment and is committed to equality for disabled employees (Dibben et al 2002). Since its development, the symbol has evolved and currently the symbol is awarded to organisations (in England, Wales or Scotland) by Jobcentre Plus (2010) as a symbol of five commitments, which are:

- to interview all disabled applicants who meet the minimum criteria for a job vacancy and to consider them on their abilities

- to discuss with disabled employees, at any time but at least once a year, what both parties can do to make sure disabled employees can develop and use their abilities

- to make every effort when employees become disabled to make sure they stay in employment

- to take action to ensure that all employees develop the appropriate level of disability awareness needed to make these commitments work

- to review these commitments each year and assess what has been achieved, plan ways to improve on them and let employees and Jobcentre Plus know about progress and future plans (Directgov 2010).

While these commitments are quite broad, the following section will focus on some of these aspects in detail by examining firstly current practices and procedures associated with recruitment and secondly adjustments related to employment.

ADJUSTMENTS TO RECRUITMENT PRACTICES AND PROCEDURES

One aspect covered by the DDA is to ensure that employers do not discriminate against disabled applicants during the recruitment stage. Breaking this down into various aspects, this includes from application through to interview and also the process of being offered the position being applied for. Exploring the variety of practices surrounding recruitment within the modern workplace, Simm et al (2007) used both qualitative and quantitative methodologies to explore employers' attitudes, knowledge and practices surrounding disability and employment. The research found that organisations typically made the following 'adjustments' related to recruitment (Simm et al 2007, p4):

- providing disability awareness training to staff involved in recruitment (45%)

- guaranteeing disabled job applicants an interview (41%)

- checking at interview whether the applicant would need any adjustments (38%).

Other specific examples included organisations holding interviews in an alternative location (for example if the building was inaccessible for wheelchair users), ensuring all application documents were in easy-to-read and audio formats, providing the vacancy information and application forms in large print and Braille and also displaying the 'two ticks' symbol on their vacancy advertisement. This demonstrates some of the means by which employers can ensure that disabled people are treated equitably during the application stage of recruitment. Other innovative practices (though these were not necessarily in place by the majority) included organisations that focused on networking and building partnerships with disabled charities or organisations to advertise positions.

Critically evaluating this adjustment to recruitment practices by organisations, Simm et al (2007) used their research to try to understand which factors predicted whether or not organisations were more likely to implement such adjustments during the recruitment stage. They found that larger organisations were more likely to implement recruitment adjustments – though they suggest this may be linked to the wider number of posts, which may lead to more interest from disabled applicants, and also the fact that larger organisations may have more dedicated HR facilities (for example an HR department or HR advisers) who can track the legislation and dedicate resources to pursuing these practices. Other factors they identified as predicting whether or not an organisation was more likely to use recruitment adjustments included those that employ or employed a disabled person within the past 10 years and those that had more awareness and knowledge about the Act. This would indicate that in terms of adopting practices that are compliant with the DDA, there are various contextual factors that influence the extent to which organisations will endeavour to achieve equality for disabled individuals.

ADJUSTMENTS RELATED TO EMPLOYMENT

Exploring the variety of 'adjustments' once employment has commenced, Simm et al (2007) found that at least 84% of the employers participating in their research (and who had employed disabled staff within the past 10 years) stated that they had made adjustments. Common adjustments included firstly providing flexible working time (56%) – for example shorter working hours, allowing time for regular breaks, allowing time for medical appointments, and so on. The second most common adjustment (53%) was making physical adjustments to the workplace (including workstation or the work environment) – for example voice recognition software, display screen equipment (for example magnifiers), changing the design of machinery (for example adapting handles), chairs ergonomically designed for back problems, and so on. Finally, the third most common (50%) was flexible work organisation – for example changing job duties, moving staff to other areas of work if their disability prevented them from carrying out their current role, and so on. Other adjustments identified as good practice but not necessarily corresponding with any of the previous categories included:

- Adjustment to pay and/or remuneration benefits – one establishment had given a disabled employee a car allowance, rather than a standard company car, to enable them to keep their own vehicle, which had been modified for their disability.

- New health and safety procedures or equipment – there were several examples of adjustments to health and safety including evacuee chairs and equipping diabetic staff with medical 'bleepers' to be used in emergencies.

A small number of establishments also provided access to counselling or employee assistance services that could help staff deal with issues such as stress (Simm et al 2007, p66).

Furthermore, Simm et al (2007) found that when making these adjustments, most organisations expressed that changes were relatively straightforward to make and most did not have any cost implications. Good practice identified in terms of overcoming problems associated with making adjustments included 'having effective systems in place to monitor the need for adjustments and assess what might be required, looking at the adjustment in terms of cost effectiveness, rather than cost, and disability awareness training among line managers' (Simm et al 2007, p4).

Critically evaluating the implementation of 'adjustments', Simm et al (2007) found that of those organisations in their research who had made no reasonable adjustments, the main reason stated was because of no disabled employees – though Simm et al (2007) argue that this may actually be because of non-disclosure of a disability by employees. Other reasons (in small numbers) included 'lack of perceived need and practical issues such as health and safety, planning constraints, and shortage of space' (Simm et al 2007, p83). In contrast, Foster (2007), who explored the 'negotiation process' surrounding adjustments from a disabled employee's perspective, found that for disabled staff, negotiations around adjustments were often extremely individualised and depended on the attitude, knowledge and the goodwill of 'poorly trained line managers'. Foster's (2007) research, which involved in-depth interviews with 20 disabled employees, found that as a result of the negotiation process disabled staff often experienced bullying from managers that resulted in stress and ill-health. Thus the process of negotiating adjustments does not necessarily result in a positive outcome, regardless of the requirements by government legislation. Furthermore, from a legal standpoint the notion of 'reasonable' when considering an adjustment can become a point of contention. As Woodhams and Corby (2003, p161) point out, 'the employer can justify a failure to accommodate a disabled person specifically because of the financial costs that could be incurred...'. This refers to the fact that the DDA calls for 'reasonable' adjustment, and often organisations can claim that the adjustment is not cost-effective and therefore they are not legally bound to make such changes.

ENFORCEMENT

While the previous sections have presented and critically examined the various practices and procedures used by employers to ensure they are not subjecting individuals to disability discrimination, this section will look at the way in which the DDA is enforced and the implications for being in breach of the Act. It must also be noted that while the original 1995 Act was applicable to employers with more than 15 employees, one of the additions to the revised 2005 Act (as well as widening the definition of disability as previously mentioned) was to remove this exemption and to include all employers regardless of the size of their workforce (Bell and Heitmueller 2009).

In terms of the way the Act is enforced, according to the 1995 DDA, section 8 states that if an individual complains that they have been discriminated against (based on the remits provided within the Act and as detailed previously in this chapter), the case is to be referred to employment tribunals (for specific details regarding the process for making a complaint, refer to the employment tribunal website at www.employmenttribunals.gov.uk). Employment tribunals are defined as 'independent judicial bodies who determine disputes between employers and employees over employment rights' (Tribunals Service: Employment 2010). The Act continues further to state that if a tribunal finds that the complaint is 'well-founded' and that the employer is in breach of their statutory duty (that is, they are found to be discriminating on the grounds of disability), then the employer will be liable to compensate the complainant and will be provided with a specific time limit by which to remove the factor or circumstance causing the discrimination. Furthermore, if an employer should fail to deliver on the stated requirements of the tribunal, then they may be subject to an increase in the amount of compensation payable.

Providing some insight into the outcome of disability discrimination tribunal cases, Williams (2008) reviewed a total of 2,497 cases, which were over an 18-month period from January 2005 to the end of June 2006. Summarising this review, Williams (2008, p1) found that:

> Of a total of 2497 cases, 2271 (91 percent) were withdrawn or settled before going to tribunal. Of the remaining 226 cases, 38 were default judgements [where the respondent failed to send in their response on time and as a result the claimant automatically won the case]. In total, 188 cases were actually heard and only 65 judgements were recorded. Of these, 50 (2 percent of all cases) were full hearings.

While Williams' (2008) review fails to comment on the total number of cases where claims of discrimination were upheld (in part due to unrecorded or partial information), the review provides a good indication of the magnitude of cases during a specific time frame and how many progressed to a full hearing.

Taking a critical approach towards the outcome of employment tribunals based on disability discrimination, Konur (2007) undertook an outcome analysis of decisions made in relation to disability discrimination claims. The study (which reviewed the outcome of around 176 cases from 1996–2004) found that a major stumbling point for cases heard by tribunals was related to the procedures associated with the process (for example in terms of submitting forms and evidence within deadlines) and in terms of the claimant or employee being judged to be 'disabled'. Furthermore, Konur (2007, pp200–1) states:

> In the UK, employees have additionally little incentive in filing a DDA claim because:
>
> • there is limited access to legal advice and representation, especially at the tribunal level;
>
> • compensatory awards are low…
>
> …[also in the UK] the average dismissal case award is in the £10,000s whilst court costs are in the range of £100,000s.

Konur (2007) also argues that the high success rate of employers at 63% is indicative of a bias within the rules and procedures surrounding claims. Gooding's (2000) review of the implementation of the Act using various sources of data taken from tribunal cases provides additional evidence for the existence of bias in the process. Examining the points of detail within cases, she argues that (as per Konur's 2007 review) one of the major stumbling blocks facing claimants is to prove that they are disabled as per the terms set out by the Act. Citing figures from *Monitoring the DDA*, Gooding (2000) states that of all cases in the first 18 months of the 1995 Act, 18% failed on the definition of disability. She argues that:

> The difficulties have partly been caused by a poor understanding of the law by tribunals, but seem more fundamentally to stem from the complex and restrictive definition in the DDA. (Gooding 2000, p535)

An additional hurdle in tribunals is described as being due to the 'narrow interpretation' of the Act's reference to 'less favourable treatment'. Gooding (2000) uses the example of an actual case (*Clarke v. Novacold* in May 1999) in which Mr Clarke was dismissed after taking four months' absence due to sick leave related to his disability. In terms of the legality of this case, the issue that was disputed was whether or not the treatment towards Mr Clarke was 'less favourable' than that of other non-disabled employees. As Gooding (2000, p537) contends, the tribunal 'argued that if a non-disabled employee would have been dismissed after a similar absence then the employer could not be said to have treated the disabled employee less favourably'. The outcome of this trial, however, was in favour of the claimant, with the court ruling that the correct comparison needed to be made with someone who did not take any time off. This case is interesting as it illustrates how employers could in theory subject all their employees to the same 'less favourable' treatment and therefore justify why they are not in breach of the Act. This point of technicality demonstrates how the law can be manipulated and, thus, while the DDA seeks to ensure equal treatment for all, in practice this vision is not necessarily carried forward in the procedures and regulations of employment tribunals (for details regarding a variety of other disability discrimination cases, see Gooding 2000; Petts 2008; and Woodhams and Corby 2003).

While this covers the legal implications of being in breach of the Act, it must be noted that in terms of 'enforcement' other factors (rather than just the legality of disability discrimination) also play a part in determining employers' adherence to the Act. Uncovering such factors, Jackson et al (2000) surveyed a sample of approximately 80 personnel directors and managers (this number represents a 38.5% response rate) about attitudes towards people with disabilities. The overall result of their survey illustrated that willingness to comply with the DDA was likely to be as a result of both knowledge of the Act and positive attitudes towards people with disability. Furthermore, there was a willingness to make 'reasonable adjustments' based on cost implications and the level of disruption caused. Thus, Jackson et al (2000, p126) conclude that:

> ...although employers are legally required to take such steps, whether they might actually do so is more directly influenced by attitudes and knowledge of the appropriate legislation. Failure to comply with the DDA's requirements may therefore at least partly be because of negative attitudes towards PDs [people with disability] and poor knowledge of the Act.

Calling for further research into this area, Jackson et al (2000) suggest other factors that may play a role in whether or not the Act is implemented include the state and nature of the job market (for example unemployment rates or flexible short-term contracts). This therefore indicates that rather than just the legal ramifications, other factors play a role in the implementation of policies regarding disability equality in the modern workplace.

CRITICALLY EVALUATING DISABILITY DISCRIMINATION IN THE MODERN WORKPLACE

The chapter thus far has critically discussed various aspects of disability discrimination in the workplace, using the DDA as a focal point and exploring various employment practices relating to fulfilling the legal requirements. As stated previously, the aim of the DDA is to promote equality for disabled people in the workplace and to ensure there is equal treatment. This section will evaluate how successful the Act has been in achieving this, using a variety of evaluation indicators. These indicators can be used as a way to measure whether or not the Act is achieving all it sets out to achieve. This includes whether or not the Act has resulted in more disabled people entering the workforce; the consistency of experiences across various types of disability; and to question whether or not policies are useful in tackling disability discrimination in the workplace.

Considering in detail whether or not as a result of the Act more disabled people are entering employment, Bell and Heitmueller (2009) argue that the Act has not had an impact on the employment rate, but may have actually worsened it. Some of the possible reasons for this have been discussed throughout this chapter, though Bell and Heitmueller (2009) suggest lack of awareness about the Act among employers as well as disabled people, a lack of financial support, and uncertainty around the cost of sending a case to an employment tribunal. Adding to this, Jones and Jones (2008, p305) state that:

> the evidence suggests it [a positive impact of the DDA] is through creating a more favourable climate for all disabled workers, such as through raising awareness of the employment potential of the disabled.

Thus, rather than the actual legislation itself, it is the awareness-raising or bringing to the consciousness of employers issues around disability and equality that have resulted in more positive effects.

Another indicator used to evaluate the success of the DDA is to consider the variety of experiences within the disabled community. It can be argued that for the Act to be considered 'successful' this would ensure consistency of experience across a diverse range of disabilities – though Berthoud (2008, p130) argues that 'quantitative research in this area has overlooked potential variations in experience between disabled people'. Nevertheless, some of the research tackles this issue and indicates that employment experiences vary according to the disability type. For example, Jacoby et al (2005) found employers' attitudes towards people with epilepsy had not changed; and Stuart (2006) found evidence of stigma towards disabled employees suffering from mental health problems.

In evaluating the Act, it is also useful to critically consider whether or not policies are indeed an effective means of tackling inequality in the workplace. Some of these aspects have been implicitly discussed through this chapter, though summarising this explicitly, Bambra and Pope (2007, pp425–6) state that:

> Our research suggests therefore that anti-discriminatory legislation, at least in the UK context, may not be the most effective way of overcoming the

social consequences of ill health and disability, nor a particularly useful policy tool in terms of reducing inequalities.

Gooding (2000) adds to this by arguing that one of the flaws within the Act is that it provides a 'disincentive' to employers not to discriminate, rather than providing incentives to promote equality. Thus it can be argued that for some employers, protocols to improve the experience of disabled people and employment is geared towards preventing litigation rather than embracing the values of equality and diversity. This sentiment is expressed by Deal (2007), who highlights that the law is useful in changing 'behaviour' but not necessarily 'attitude', while Woodhams and Corby (2003, p175) surmise: 'There should be a positive duty to promote equality.' Nevertheless, providing a balanced view, Woodhams and Corby (2007, p574) highlight that although inequality still persists there are indications that:

> ...anecdotal evidence suggests that in this case, the DDA has stimulated changes to both the quantity and type of HR measures that employers adopted and that some of these measures were effective.

This is also supported by Simm et al (2007), who found that awareness of the DDA led to more positive views around disabled employees. Simm et al (2007, p5) also suggest that:

> The fact that awareness of the DDA was a significant factor in the likelihood of making either recruitment, employment, or service-related adjustments also suggests that the legislation had a strong influence.

This suggests that although there are many shortcomings within the legislation, some changes within the employment sector indicate some success in promoting equality for disabled people within the workplace.

CONCLUSION

This chapter has presented the complex issue of disability discrimination in the workplace, using the DDA as a focal point. In critically evaluating its terminology, implementation and enforcement, the chapter has illustrated the varying ways in which policies affect practice and their legal implications. The chapter has also presented the perspective of the employer and disabled employee to illustrate the different perspectives surrounding disability and the workplace.

In concluding this chapter, it is useful to present some future directions and developments for disability and employment, and to suggest possible ways forward to benefit the continued inclusion of disabled individuals in the workplace. For example, Berthoud (2008) makes the valid point that the legal system is one that continually evolves, and optimistically suggests that over time, landmark legal cases may set a precedent for future cases. Therefore, it is still too early to fully grasp the full extent of the impact of the DDA on disability in the workplace. Dibben et al (2002), however, call for more awareness-raising to increase the impact of the DDA and suggest that one possible way to increase compliance with the legislation is to promote a 'business case for employing people with disabilities' (Dibben et al 2002, p466).

Other future directions can be gleaned from the Office for Disability Issues Annual Report (2009), which describes certain developments and goals for achieving disability equality by 2025. One particular aspect of interest is the development of an Equality Act (or a Single Equality Bill), which is currently being developed and aims to 'streamline discrimination law'. This Act will build on existing provision of the DDA and, although currently being finalised, changes could mean different ways to claim for disability discrimination and requesting reasonable adjustments. Other aspects affecting employment include the Department for Work and Pensions (DWP) investing an extra £8 million into the Access to Work scheme (which is a scheme whereby grants are awarded towards the cost of any support needed that is disability related). Another scheme recently launched is 'Valuing Employment Now', which is aimed at increasing the employment rate of people with learning disabilities. Finally, other schemes that have been launched or are being piloted include 'Project Search', which provides internships for people with learning disabilities, and an 'Access to Volunteering Fund', which funds the additional costs involved in disabled individuals undertaking voluntary activities. Such innovative programmes, projects and activities are indicative of a government commitment to progressing disability equality. The issue of the success of such initiatives in pushing towards disability equality in the employment sector will have to be continually addressed and evaluated.

HRM IN THE MEDIA

CRITICAL REFLECTIONS

The case study presented at the start of the chapter raised questions relating to the sensitive and complex issues surrounding disability discrimination within the modern workplace that are pertinent for both employers and employees.

Before we reflect on the questions raised, it is important to consider the tribunal's ruling. In August 2009, the ruling stated: 'The tribunal is satisfied the reason for the claimant's dismissal was her breach of the look policy in wearing a cardigan. Whilst the tribunal is satisfied the claimant's dismissal was a consequence of her unlawful harassment, it cannot be characterised direct disability discrimination' (BBC News 13 August 2009).

Reflecting on the first question, the firm could argue that it was right to enforce its 'look policy' to all its shop floor employees despite their disability or non-disability statuses. From the firm's perspective, it could contend that the policy should be applied to everyone on the basis of equal treatment of all employees. Thus, if all employees are expected to adhere to the store's look policy, then any special exceptions made could be seen as inconsistent to the image of the brand that employees are expected to portray. It could be argued that the fact that the employee's refusal to remove her cardigan while on the shop floor means that it was her, not the firm, who had a problem with her prosthetic forearm and that it was ultimately her choice not to work on the shop floor by failing to comply.

The second question asked the extent to which the employee had a good case against her employer for disability discrimination. Despite the tribunal ruling (see above), we would argue that A&F did not provide reasonable adjustment to accommodate the employee's needs by not allowing her to wear a cardigan on the shop floor. Based on the social model of disability, the company's look policy is an example of a social environment that devalues difference (Woodhams and Danieli 2000) that has led to the unfair treatment of an employee. As a consequence (and arguably a penalty) of her personal preference to wear her cardigan, the firm relegated her to work in the stockroom.

Finally, the last question encouraged the reader to critically evaluate the DDA in terms of its effectiveness in ensuring that disabled employees are not unjustifiably treated less favourably than non-disabled employees. Throughout this chapter, we have highlighted how definitions of 'disability' and 'discrimination' as proposed by the DDA are both theoretically and practically problematic. Both definitions outlined by the Act are open to interpretation and, therefore, claims of unfair treatment by disabled employees are subject to challenge. Referring back to the *Clarke v. Novacold* case in 1999, a similar argument could be made in this case that the employee was subjected to the same 'less favourable' treatment as all her colleagues (through the look policy) and, therefore, A&F was not in breach of the Act. The tribunal's ruling that her claim of direct disability discrimination was 'not well founded' (BBC News 13 August 2009) could be construed as an example of how the law can be interpreted in a way that is insufficient to ensure equal treatment for all. In such cases, existing legislation has the potential to become a barrier instead of enabling the promotion of equal employment opportunities for disabled people.

EXPLORE FURTHER

CIPD Disability and Employment factsheet. Available online at www.cipd.co.uk/subjects/dvsequl/disability/disandemp.htm.

This is a good starting point for readers who are unfamiliar with the topic of disability and employment from the perspective of HRM practitioners.

Employers' Forum on Disability website. Available at www.efd.org.uk

The organisation describes itself as 'the world's leading employers' organisation focused on disability as it affects business. Our mission is to enable companies to become disability confident by making it easier to recruit and retain disabled employees and to serve disabled customers.' Further resources can also be found on the website.

Jobs not Charity website. Available at www.shef.ac.uk/jobsnotcharity/index.html

This website is the home of the European Union-funded project 'Jobs not Charity: Promoting Disabled People's Access to the Labour Market and the Role of Organisations of Disabled People' and is a valuable resource for finding out more about disabled people's experience of work and external barriers that inhibit equal employment opportunities of disabled people. A copy of the final research report can be downloaded free of charge from the website.

BARNES, C. and MERCER, G. (2010) *Exploring disability: a sociological introduction.* 2nd ed. Cambridge: Polity.

This book provides an up-to-date resource for readers looking for a critical and cutting-edge overview in the area of disability studies, including a chapter that critically examines competing models of disability and a chapter on exploring employment as a social barrier for disabled people to fully participate and be valued in society.

PRIESTLEY, M. (2000) Adults only: disability, social policy and the life course. *Journal of Social Policy.* Vol 29, No 3. pp421–439.

This article provides a relevant and thought-provoking perspective to understanding society's treatment of disabled people as being different from social norms of 'adulthood'. It is highly recommended for readers who wish to learn more about taking a social model towards understanding disability as a social construct.

PART THREE

CONTEXTUALISING HRM – SECTORAL VIEW OF HR PRACTICE

CHAPTER 19

HRM in Manufacturing

Lola-Peach Martins and Geoff Wood

OVERVIEW

This chapter starts with an overview of the broad trends in employment in UK manufacturing and a profile of the workforce. It then considers the issue of strategic choice in HR policy and the HR policies that are associated with 'high-road', 'hi-tech' manufacturing versus the policies and practices associated with low-cost manufacturing. The chapter then moves on to consider organisational structure and leadership issues in manufacturing and, in particular, the inter-relationship of roles played by workers, line managers and the HR function.

LEARNING OBJECTIVES

Reading this chapter will enable the reader to:

- critically examine the trends in UK manufacturing employment
- critically analyse the relationship between context and competitiveness in manufacturing
- critically compare and contrast the HRM policies and practices commonly associated with 'hi-tech' and 'sweatshop' manufacturing
- critically examine the HR role of line managers in the context of management and leadership.

HRM IN THE MEDIA

'MANUFACTURING EXPERIENCES JOB GROWTH'

It was reported in May 2010 that, in spite of the recession elsewhere in the economy, and despite previous gloom in the sector, British manufacturing appeared to be experiencing a revival (*Independent* 2010). Results from a recent survey by the Chartered Institute for Purchasing and Supply (CIPS) indicated an upsurge in levels of confidence although confidence was tempered by fears of contraction in the eurozone – by far Britain's biggest export market – and by the risk that government austerity measures may cool demand. The boost was said to be stretching existing capacity leading to backlogs in uncompleted orders. This, in turn, was predicted to increase the demand for staff and investment.

Questions

1   What initiatives could UK manufacturers undertake to take maximum advantage of the upturn in the context of sustaining and developing the workforce?

2   What could be achieved by a strategic review of the role that line managers play in HR decision-making?

INTRODUCTION

Within the HR literature, a common distinction in terms of practice is that of hard and soft HRM (Storey 2007). Hard HRM is taken to assume that people are a resource, just as is the case with any other resources, and should be sourced, deployed and disposed of, as and when the strategic aims of the firm change. It is assumed that any resources devoted to a firm's people – other than that devoted to securing and maximising short-term returns – is money diverted from the rightful recipients, a firm's owners. In short, hard HRM is associated with a shareholder view of the firm – as explained in Chapter 2 – where employers and employees are in a zero-sum relationship. Any additional gains by workers beyond what is immediately necessary to maximise returns is a loss to owners (Botero et al 2004). An alternative approach is that of soft HRM, which has emphasised the human side of HRM, and which suggests that through involving and nurturing people, a win–win situation is possible (Gooderham et al 2006). However, the most recent literature has pointed to a diversity of HR practice, and that different types of HR practice are encountered in different sectors (and, for that matter, regions). Indeed, specific types of HR are particularly conducive to particular types of organisational activity (Collings and Wood 2009). In this chapter, the diversity of HR practice in manufacturing is explored, particularly in relation to practices associated with hi-tech and low-cost manufacturing. It then considers the roles played by key HR actors in the sector and, in particular, that of the delegated role of line managers in HR decision-making: this is seen as crucially transformed through waves of managerial initiatives over the past 30 years.

THE MANUFACTURING SECTOR IN THE UK

The manufacturing sector is a strategically important sector to the UK economy. However, manufacturing has declined in terms of its significance to the UK economy, relative to other sectors. Employment in manufacturing has declined, as a proportion of the total workforce, even more than the sector's contribution to GDP – suggesting that productivity is proportionately higher in this sector compared with others. Again, however, manufacturing has shrunk in importance more in the UK than in other comparable industrial economies. Three notable observations are important here. First, the shrinkage of the size and importance of manufacturing is particularly evident in historical terms given the pre-eminent position of British manufacturing as being at the vanguard of the Industrial Revolution some 200 years ago. Second, and relatedly, the shrinkage in manufacturing is not new. Arguments about the relative decline of manufacturing stem back at least to 1945, but arguably as far back as 1870. The third issue is that there has, for most of the timescale outlined, been concern – from within the sector and beyond – about this relative decline. More recently there has been more dissent in official circles about the importance of this relative decline. Indeed, it could be argued that leading up to the 2008 financial crisis, it was consensus to consider that the relative losses experienced in manufacturing were more than offset by the relative gains enjoyed by the proportionate strength in the financial services sector. Such a view was not taken in other countries. Germany, for example, while also experiencing a net decline in the proportion of its national economy and the share of employment, has adhered firmly to the notion that manufacturing remains of strategic national importance as its main engine of export potential.

In 2008 the UK was the sixth largest manufacturing economy in the world (BERR 2008), accounted for £154.9 billion in gross value added (GVA) in 2007 which, while seeming impressive, accounts for just 12.4% of the total economy. As a comparison, manufacturing share of GVA in 1977 was 26.5% (HC 2009). To some extent this has been due to increased productivity where UK performance, in terms of productivity *growth*, has enabled some catch-up with other nations. Nonetheless, at the base of increased services and major decline of manufacturing, economic restructuring towards higher value-added, knowledge-intensive sectors presents a much more interesting picture. That is, growth in high-technology sub-sectors such as aerospace, pharmaceuticals and computer manufacturing has outstripped growth in low-technology sectors. With regard to high-cost economies, such as the UK, the activities that are likely to thrive are those that by their nature are complex and high value-added, and those that act as a key part of the global value chain.

In terms of employment the 2004 Workplace Employment Relations Survey (WERS) shows that manufacturing industry made a significant contribution to the number of workplace SMEs in the UK, at 19%. At the same time, the survey revealed that the number of workplace manufacturing organisations involved with wholesale and retail was significant. Compared with workplaces belonging to larger firms, those belonging to SMEs are more likely to be engaged in manufacturing, that is, 18% SMEs compared with 5% large manufacturing workplaces. The pattern of SME employment by industry sector was broadly in line with workplace distribution. Regarding large firms, while manufacturing sites comprised only 5% of all workplaces in large firms, they accounted for almost one-fifth of all employees. In contrast, the two-fifths of workplaces engaged in wholesale and retail accounted for only one-quarter of all employees. Overall, regarding large firms, this implies that manufacturing sites had a significantly large number of employees, while wholesale and retail firms spread their activities across smaller sites.

HRM AND THE NATURE OF EMPLOYMENT SYSTEMS

There are many limits to the hard/soft dichotomy and its value in understanding HR practice. Firstly, it assumes that there are only two viable ways of managing people. It is held that all firms are likely to ultimately drift towards one of these two paradigms. However, implicit in this literature is that it is somehow better to practise soft HRM, on the basis that this is likely to prove more sustainable, and is ultimately more ethical; people should not be treated as a disposable and infinitely malleable asset. However, comparative evidence of HR practice – for example, that provided by the Cranet (www.cranet.org) and the 2004 WERS – points to somewhat greater diversity. Indeed, a look at changes in practice over the years would reveal no drift to a single set of common ways of managing people (Brewster et al 2007). But, by the same measure, both Cranet and WERS results do not point to what may be termed 'diffuse diversity'; there are recognisable clusters of practice encountered in different times, places and, central to this chapter, according to sector. This mixing and matching of practices also reveals a lot of complexity and ambiguities in people management.

But, what does this suggest in terms of sector and, more specifically sectoral performance? It depends on the underlying assumptions as to how we understand people management. What almost all the HR literature has in common is that it is in agreement with the empirical evidence alluded to above: what types of HR are adopted and retained tend to share common features with similar firms in a particular sector and region (Gooderham et al 2006; Storey 2007; Collings and Wood 2009). Three reasons have been advanced for this. There is some merit in each account and they are not mutually exclusive. Firstly, as Marsden (1999) notes, common practices reduce transaction costs. No written employment contract can ever be complete and both parties to the employment relationship bring to the table preconceptions as to what is acceptable practice in the sector and region; cross-reference to other employees and employers allows for adjustments to be made and unrealistic behaviour to be recognised. After a period of time, the employment system becomes entrenched, even if features may alter or evolve over time (Marsden 1999). Secondly, practices represent both responses to external informal rules and formal regulations (Boyer 2006). Thirdly, there is the manner in which actors harness their knowledge and understanding to identify and build on complementarities, that is, sets of rules and practices that work together better than they do on their own (Crouch 2005). For example, greater job security under the law may encourage firms to spread training costs over a longer time frame, as staff turnover is lower, while, given their greater security, employees have greater incentives to acquire organisation-specific skills (Harcourt et al 2007). So, incremental human capital development works better in a climate of greater job security; the converse is also true.

NATIONAL CONTEXT AND INCREMENTALLY INNOVATIVE MANUFACTURING

If differences in employment and work relations are compared from context to context, a number of differences become immediately apparent. If a comparison of differences between the most advanced societies is made, it can be found that a major distinction is between the liberal market (or shareholder-orientated) economies, such as the United States, the United Kingdom, and the co-ordinated market (or stakeholder-orientated) economies of continental north-western Europe and Scandinavia (Dore 2000; Hall and Soskice 2001). In terms of work and employment relations, the key differences are as follows. First, there is the law. Despite a global decline in union membership, in some settings unions have fared very much worse than in others and, indeed, enjoy fewer rights under the law. In general unions are very much weaker in liberal market economies and enjoy weaker organisational rights in such settings. Such legal rights are much more explicit and extensive in co-ordinated market economies and include the right to conduct basic organisational activities in the workplace, the right to formal recognition for the purposes of collective bargaining and protection of union activists against victimisation (Hall and Soskice 2001).

Again, in co-ordinated markets, individual workers enjoy greater and more explicit protection as individuals under the law as well. This would include job security and the right to be treated fairly and equally (Hall and Soskice 2001; Harcourt et al 2007). Social protection in co-ordinated market economies is also greater. This would include more generous unemployment and retirement benefits (Botero et al 2004). All of this has the effect of increasing the bargaining power of individual workers and mitigating the costs of exit from an organisation that seeks to impose particularly poor terms and conditions of work and employment. In addition, labour inspectorates tend to be more active in co-ordinated markets, reining in rogue employers and ensuring that what is enshrined in the law is followed by practice. Finally, in many co-ordinated contexts, works councils are compulsory. Here elected worker representatives (often from the relevant union) negotiate with management around changes to work organisation (Brewster et al 2007). In turn, this means that worker understanding of, and buy-in into, changes in technology and the social organisation of work is greater; this would be of particular value in terms of manufacturing (Dore 2000).

If the first dimension is labour law, the second is the relative power of shareholders. Shareholder rights in liberal markets – both in terms of the law and precedent – are generally stronger than in co-ordinated ones (Botero et al

2004). The former serves to shift the managerial agenda towards short-term returns, even if this means a reduced investment in people, and less job security. Conversely, in co-ordinated markets, more patient investors allow for a longer-term view; firms are hence freer to invest in their people and equipment, even if returns are not immediately visible.

A third dimension is the national training context. Liberal markets have generally been associated with good generic tertiary education systems, but poor vocational training (Thelen 2001). This makes for a workforce of which segments are well equipped for careers in the service and the high-technology sector, but there are great shortfalls in the technical skills required for incrementally innovative manufacturing. In contrast, co-ordinated markets have been generally associated with very much stronger vocational training systems, significantly more conducive to incrementally innovative manufacturing (Thelen 2001; Goergen et al 2009). While in practice there is some diversity between co-ordinated market economies in terms of the actual provision of vocational training, a variety of training schemes provide workers with access to needed technical skills, depending on the context, at various points of their careers.

In terms of actual firm practice, greater employee involvement and participation is commonly encountered in co-ordinated markets, reflecting the above-mentioned rights and ways of doing things (Brewster et al 2007). This is matched by stronger expectations of security of tenure. In turn, as noted above, this means firms can spread training costs over many years, particularly important in areas of manufacturing requiring workforces with high levels of skills specific to both the firm and the industry.

But, how do these national differences translate into differences in the performance of manufacturing? In general, co-ordinated markets are very much stronger in terms of high value-added incrementally innovative manufactured products, ranging from motor cars to white goods. Indeed, three of the most successful exporters in the world, Germany, Japan and Italy, are co-ordinated markets. In contrast, liberal markets have generally underperformed in these areas, running chronic balance of payments deficits; notoriously, much of the growth in Britain and the US over the past 30 years can be ascribed to debt-fuelled consumption and financial speculation (Pollin 2007).

We can conclude this section by reiterating that success in manufacturing in the developed world is contingent on a favourable institutional setting. However, the relationship is an indirect one: much of the interface between formal rules and successful practice is in terms of HRM. Incrementally innovative manufacturing (that is, developing and refining both process and product on a high value-added basis) is greatly facilitated through HR policies that encompass a relatively secure workforce with a good skills base that can be built on in the light of changing organisational needs (Harcourt et al 2007). It is also about having mechanisms in place that allow for the insider-knowledge employees have of the production process to be harnessed. And, a stronger employee voice ensures that any concerns are likely to be taken more seriously.

NATIONAL CONTEXT AND LOW-COST MANUFACTURING

Of course, not all manufacturing is incrementally innovative. A large proportion of manufactured goods in the world are produced on an extremely low-cost basis. This would include many clothes, cheaper consumer electronics, everyday household items, many toys, and so on (MacEwan 1997; Moody 1997). Much of this is produced in countries where labour costs are very low, which would include large areas of China, India, Bangladesh, Vietnam, Thailand and Indonesia. In such contexts, the management of labour is focused on extracting the maximum amount of labour power; this is done through tried and trusted methods of control. The latter would include deskilling – reducing the amount of skilled input required by workers – through the usage of automated production lines, and/or dividing jobs up into their smallest component parts (Thompson and Smith 2010). Where firms lack the capital to invest in automation, jobs are further subdivided, with immediate visual monitoring by an army of only marginally less poorly paid supervisors (Moody 1997). Any inefficiencies that result from low staff morale may be partially compensated for by extending the hours worked for the amount of pay awarded (Moody 1997). In turn, the latter may be determined either through piecework (that is, simply linking pay to production) or through paying the bare minimum necessary for the workforce to physically survive and, in some notorious instances, even less. Fatalities are being readily filled by an army of unemployed. In many cases, workers employed are from more vulnerable or easily exploited categories of labour, namely women and children. Furthermore, low-cost production paradigms are often characterised by extremely poor health and safety.

On the one hand, such extremely low-cost production paradigms have been able to drive out not only many higher-wage producers in the developed world, but even firms in the developing world that have not been able or willing to squeeze labour quite so ruthlessly. On the other hand, the sweatshop model brings with it costs and risks of its own. There is the omnipresent threat of even lower-cost producers emerging elsewhere, in countries where the cost of reproducing labour power is even lower (in other words, where it is possible to pay workers even less to physically survive and reproduce) and/or the cost of inputs (raw materials, energy, water, plant and estate, and so on) is even cheaper.

A further problem is that countries that rely too much on extremely low-cost manufacturing face persistent crises of domestic demand. What happens is that employees are paid too little to consume much more than basic foodstuffs and discarded clothing, forcing firms to largely rely on export markets. This brings risks of its own: currency fluctuations making one's exports potentially more expensive; the risk of protective tariffs; and a lack of intimate awareness of the tastes of target consumers. In turn, the latter forces many low-cost manufacturers in the developing world into the role of subcontractors, supplying goods to order for Western brand names; the latter have many potential suppliers and may readily switch orders according to short-term changes in demand and costs. It may prove very hard for subcontracting firms to break from such dependency on their contractors, making for low returns and ever-downward pressures on costs. All this means that industries – and entire nations – may be locked into a sweatshop trap (Moody 1997). Only determined government action, including co-ordinating firms and domestic markets, active industrial policy and picking winners that have the potential to move beyond low-cost production, can break such a cycle. And, for every country that has done so – for example, Taiwan, South Korea and Malaysia – there are many others that have failed – for example, Thailand, Indonesia and Vietnam. Workers themselves can play a role in breaking out of the sweatshop trap, with waves of strike action in developing nations such as South Korea and South Africa – and, more recently, China – forcing firms to rethink the basis of their production paradigms and wage policies.

NATIONAL CONTEXT AND HI-TECH MANUFACTURING

We have seen that in co-ordinated markets, manufacturing tends to be most successful in the production of incrementally innovative goods, associated with highly co-operative HR paradigms, while a number of developing countries have staked their fortunes on very low-cost manufacturing, predicated on squeezing their employees. We have also seen that liberal market economies have tended underperform in manufacturing, at least since the 1970s. Are there any areas where liberal markets have been successful in this area? And, what kind of HRM is encountered there?

Good tertiary educational systems in such countries make for a pool of generic (non-industry-specific) skills that may be conducive to high-technology activity. Insecure jobs are, in most instances, bad for employees and impose costs on companies. However, highly skilled labour may have highly marketable skills and rapid movement between jobs may diffuse knowledge and ideas across an industry; this has helped underpin the competitiveness of hi-tech industry clusters, such as in Silicon Valley (Thelen 2001). In such contexts, the primary source of skilled labour is the external labour market. While investors may be more fickle and short-termist, they may be more willing to take the risks associated with start-ups, again conducive to innovation. HR in high-technology industry is associated with pay linked to performance (backed up by appraisals) and the frequent use of share option schemes (Thelen 2001). The latter ensures that employees share the risks – and rewards – in the case of start-ups, and allow for potentially more attractive packages than the organisation could immediately afford to pay (Wood and Wright 2009). Of course, hi-tech industry is to a large extent about ideas: many good or great ones, such as the iPod and the iPhone, require a lot of skilled input and ideas to bring the production from conception to production, but then readily lend themselves to outsourcing the latter to low-wage subcontractors. In other words, hi-tech industry may support – and even need – low-cost manufacturers, rather than being a substitute for them (Wright and Dwyer 2006).

Manufacturing in liberal markets is not just about the hi-tech sector (Wright and Dwyer 2006). There persist many more traditional manufacturing enterprises, ranging from motor cars to steel, in both the US and the UK. However, in recent years they have been undermined by more successful incrementally innovative manufacturing firms in co-ordinated markets and, indeed, low-cost producers. But, there is also a significant sweatshop sector as well: firms that locate low-cost production in such markets to escape protective tariffs and/or where products (for example, convenience and fast foods) are not easily transportable across long distances. Some notorious examples of sweatshops have been identified in the clothes finishing and sandwich manufacturing sectors (see Cooke 2009; NowPublic 2009).

CHANGING PARADIGMS

As Grugulis (2009, p228) notes, it should be possible for a firm in manufacturing, or elsewhere for that matter 'to change the way it uses labour, but very few firms prioritize this'. Even if products change (or indeed, if a firm shifts to a greater or lesser emphasis on actual production), knowledge may remain concentrated in the hands of management. Indeed, changes in products may allow for greater automation that promotes deskilling and forcing employees to work at the pace set by machines (Grugulis 2009). Although a wide range of authors (for example, Kochan and Osterman 2002; Appelbaum et al 2000) have argued that firms can indeed be more successful if they switch to higher value-added production paradigms – characterised by upskilling, greater participation in terms of organising work and determining employment conditions, and better communication – many firms have simply not risen to the bait. The reason is simple: many firms make a great deal of money founded on sweatshop manufacturing. Even if this is not sustainable, short-term competitive pressures and the need to placate investors may make managers reluctant to consider a switch.

THE HR FUNCTION AND LINE MANAGEMENT IN MANUFACTURING

The discussion above highlights the choices potentially available for either 'high-road' or 'low-road' approaches to HRM in a manufacturing context. This section now addresses the problem of the relative roles of the HR function in relation to the shop floor and to line management. If the previous discussion considers strategic HR choices, this section considers the means by which any HR paradigm is delivered.

REAPPRAISING THE LINE MANAGER'S HR ROLE

A recurring theme in management literature has been the interrelated issues of management structure, the role of HR and the role of line management. While this relates to all sectors, it has the longest history in manufacturing, where most of these issues were first addressed as central issues in the pioneering work on 'scientific management' and later with the human relations school of thought.

Hales (2005) in his empirical study, which aimed to clarify whether the role of line manager has changed, and how, as well as the extent of the changes, addresses two claims in order to shed some light on the alleged 'new role'. That is, the shift from an operational supervision (traditional forms of control and authority) to a more strategic business management role, which requires leadership qualities and strategic management competencies, including excellence in championing leadership throughout the organisation (Rayner and Adam-Smith 2009).

From the beginning of the 1980s, aside from the decline of shop floor trade union power, three main factors led to the reappraisal of line managers in manufacturing industry and the crucial role they played in managing shop floor/ front-line staff. These factors were:

- the globalisation of product market competition acting in conjunction with
- increased interest in Japanese production techniques such as total quality management (TQM), just-in-time (JIT) and business process re-engineering (BPR) and
- the emergence of new managerial philosophies – decentralisation, de-layering and devolution.

In general, the changes to the line manager's role were introduced in the expectation that they would serve to engender improved workforce performance – ensuring quality products to meet customer demands. In the event, however, the existing evidence suggests that they have met with very mixed success, both within and across organisations.

Perhaps the common feature with TQM, JIT and BPR was the reconfiguration of the line manager's role in a way that sought to re-emphasise its authority component and at the same time encourage line managers to move to a more facilitative and empowering type of leadership role. This role encompassed greater responsibility for HR tasks such as training, recruitment, discipline, absence management and, critically, managing their team's performance.

From a historical perspective it can be argued that this reconfiguration is not 'new' *per se*, but rather cyclical, with elements of the previous role still required or at least refined. For example, in some organisations, the role is regarded as more strategic, perhaps depending on the stage of organisational change. In some manufacturing organisations, the idea of line managers undertaking core HRM activities has also been identified as being more rhetorical than real (Hales 2005).

It is common in manufacturing to find a plethora of titles used for line managers. Typically, the titles include supervisor, first-line manager, team leader, middle manager, or even senior manager, which tend to overlap in meaning. Table 19.1 presents a series of definitions of roles over time. Earlier studies, such as Child and Partridge (1982) and Thurley and Wirdenius (1973), pointed out that problems with defining who line managers are stem from problems with determining the role itself – based on the degree of decision-making powers actually held (Hale 1986). By no means is the list of definitions presented an exhaustive one, but it clearly illustrates some issues worth paying attention to at this stage. Generally, while the definitions can clearly be seen to vary in one way or another, there are some common features.

Table 19.1 Defining the term 'line manager'

1950s to 1960s	1970s to 1980s	1990s to twenty-first century
• 'A supervisor is a person in constant control of a definite section of a labour force in an undertaking, exercising it either directly or through subordinates; and responsible for this to a higher level of management' **Ministry of Committee of Training of Supervisors (1954)**	• '…it might be easier to define supervision as being composed of common "supervisory tasks". In particular, in many studies, supervision has been identified with "man management" or leadership tasks and the actual process of getting workers to do what management wish them to do' **Thurley and Wirdenius (1973)**	• 'First line (supervisory) management are responsible for the production of goods and services, and are the point of interface with non-managerial employees' **Woodall and Winstanley (1998)**
• 'Supervisor is the person who has received the commission to carry out the intentions of top management through direct leadership of a workgroup in the company organisationally subordinate to him. Thereby he has taken over the responsibility for carrying out these intentions as concerns this organisational unit. He is supposed to do work for the same kind as his subordinates only in emergencies or for training purposes' **Grabe and Siltberer (1956)**	• 'A supervisor is an assistant to a full manager who performs certain delegated functions without serving the manager's direct authority over employees' **Jaques (1976)**	• 'A first line supervisor or team leader…having responsibility for a team of people… Team leaders are the people that "make the people make the systems work" and their performance is key to business success' **Gwent TEC (1999)**
• 'The definition of "supervisor" …is based on the theory that the purpose of management is to control the operatives and operations on the shop floor. Thus, a supervisor (as distinct from a purely administrative manager) is someone who exercises control by "overseeing" inspection and direction in the area of operations' **Thurley and Hamblin (1964)**	• '…the role of line manager is usually claimed by British companies to be a managerial one, the person who has direct and undisputed authority over shopfloor, office, or service operations' **Child and Partridge (1982)**	• 'First-level managers are those managers to whom those workers report to have no subordinates themselves. They are in charge of a small unit, department, or section, coordinating the activities of a local work team.' **Jong et al (1999)**
	• 'The supervisor's role…responsible for the smooth running and production of goods and services under their control, through the resources available to them' **Industrial Society, cited in IDS (1987)**	• 'A member of the first line of management responsible for work groups to a higher level of management' **IRS Employment Review (2000) taken from the Advisory, Conciliation and Arbitration Service (ACAS)**
		• 'A supervisor is considered to be a manager because he or she is directly accountable for obtaining results through people in his or her organisation in comparison to the individual worker, who does not have the same level of accountability and responsibility to senior management for the work of others' **MacNeil (2003)**

DEVOLUTION, DECENTRALISATION, DE-LAYERING

Generally, changing views on roles and their implied impact on the decision-making process has been accompanied by structural change in the form of decentralisation, de-layering and devolution (Kirkpatrick et al 1992). From this, HR functions were pushed down to various business unit and profit centre managers. Some believed that organisations were moving away from the practice of being functionally organised.

Authors such as Storey (1992) had argued that in order for change initiatives (such as devolution) to be successful, they had to rely on line managers to carry out HRM tasks such as team briefings, lead quality circles, train and monitor workers; and recruit the most suitable candidate for jobs, as well as administer discipline and grievance. However, as highlighted above, without the necessary partnerships through which support for undertaking these tasks are gained, the handling of such tasks would be difficult.

Many had accepted that the line manager's HRM role was crucial not just for productivity, but more importantly for the quality of production. By 1993, for example, the Institute of Supervisory Management was reporting that the role of the supervisor was growing from that of a 'traditional foreman' to that of a first-line manager, whose duties included production-scheduling, quality control, employee selection, training, and so on. Despite this, almost a decade later, further studies were revealing that the role of line managers still tended to be nebulous in some organisations (Martins 2008, 2009).

PERFORMANCE BARRIERS

Various researchers and authors have drawn attention to the HRM competencies line managers are required to have for the efficient and effective performance of their HRM role. In so doing they allude to the evidence which suggests that in the absence of key HRM competencies the line manager's performance would be mediocre, and discordant with organisational and business objectives. While this is true, other evidence shows that even where they have gained such competencies they have still been hindered when it comes to performing their HRM duties, hence drawn between rhetoric and reality.

Aside from difficulties line managers encounter in managing absence, other studies have revealed that line managers have found it difficult to adopt a 'hands-off approach' to managing their staff (Child and Partridge 1982; Buchanan and Preston 1992). This still seems to be apparent in manufacturing companies today as similar findings are revealed in McGovern et al (1997) and Martins (2007, 2009).

Guest (1987) states that HRM policies should be adopted in order to achieve employees' commitment to the organisation with the aim of making the employees concerned more satisfied, more productive and more adaptable. In a more general sense, it has been argued that adopting such HRM policies may not always be possible as a number of issues may work against the intended outcome, for example, where factors such as high competencies or stakeholders' interest determines what an organisation does (particularly one in its growth stage).

Lowe (1992) has also pointed out that, where a considerable amount of responsibility is placed on line managers but there is a lack of support for the supervisors, this is likely to impede rather than facilitate any 'transformation' to more effective HRM. While line managers are sometimes aware of their HRM role, some still had the preconceived idea that HRM and personnel management is the same thing. As a result they were unclear about their roles and were reluctant to take on people management activities. This lack of clarity is pervasive and testifies to the interrelationships that need to exist between the factors influencing the HRM of line managers and the radical nature of the underlying organisational changes in this regard.

A MODEL FOR ENHANCING LINE MANAGEMENT HR CAPACITY

An effective strategy for the enhanced performance of line managers requires the integration of their role into wider business strategies, structures and systems on the one hand, and HR policies, activities and resources on the other. One of the core reasons for this is because the integration of HRM policies and business goals is inevitable for enhanced performance (Rayner and Adam-Smith 2009).

Overall, the research concerned with the strategic management of line managers shows that the key factors influencing the line manager's HRM performance are the definition of the line manager's role, their training/development, the perceptions and attitudes of primary stakeholders, and the provision of broader organisational support of HRM performance.

To achieve a better integration of the sometimes disparate array of skills and attributes that the line manager needs, the following approach has been proposed (Martins 2007). The broader areas concerned with the complex social, political and economic factors that shaped the line manager's people management role during disparate phases, hence, the four phases in the nature of the changing role of line managers to date, are illustrated in 'The 4M Cycle/Five Factors Conceptual framework', which is represented in Figure 19.1.

The framework also highlights the congruent systems of production and the main characteristics of the role. Importantly, it draws attention to the fact that there are major complexities associated with the role, particularly in the context of the management of line managers given the devolution of core HRM activities to them. Since the complex bureaucracies associated with the other three phases are still prevalent in the current phase, in this chapter attention has been paid to the trends in the nature of their changing role – that is, the cyclical nature of the role, and the challenges those responsible for the strategic management of line managers face.

Figure 19.1 A four factor framework

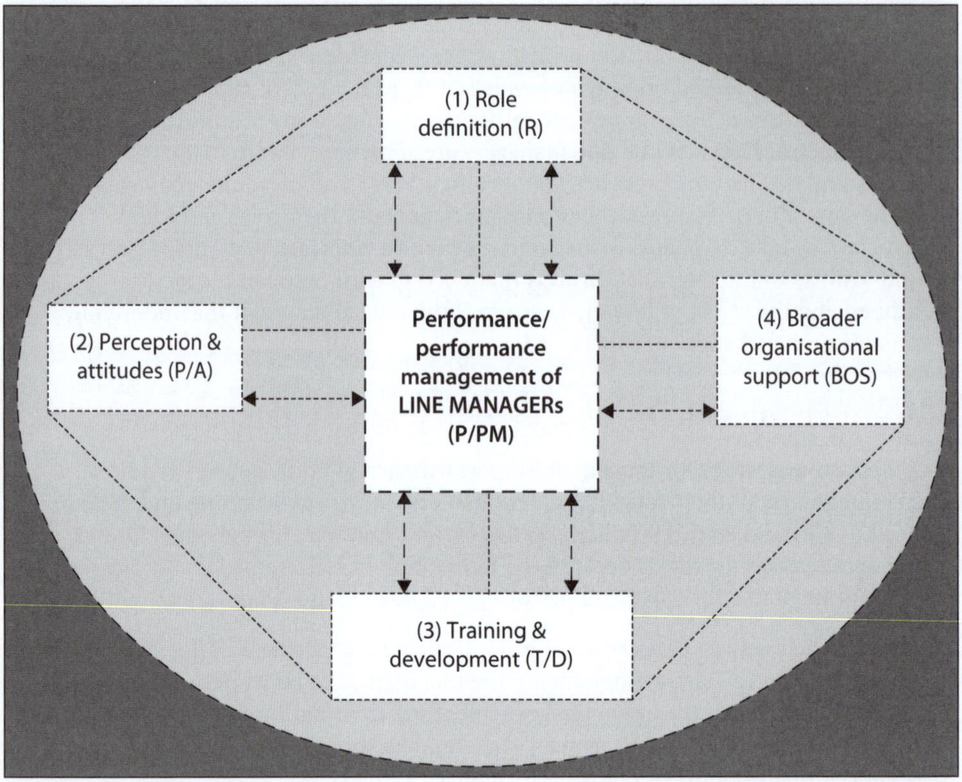

Employment in manufacturing in the UK has been in decline for most of the twentieth century – though the decline has sharpened in more recent years as more low-cost manufacturing has migrated to the developing low-wage economies. Hi-tech manufacturing in the UK could be said to be better able to compete globally than low-cost manufacturing. Notwithstanding the existence of some internationally renowned UK manufacturers, there is a problem for such organisations associated with the liberal market approach to developing organisational capacity, where longer-term HR development would generally be seen to be better supported by employment practices associated with a co-ordinated market approach.

The implementation of any strategic reorientation of HR policy is also tied to implementation of policies and practices at the shop floor. This is tied to the orientation of the relationship between the HR function and the line management function. Following a range of initiatives and influences from the 1980s onwards, line management has evolved to take on more of these functions. However, this has not been without its problems. Line management is hampered by the range of definitions used for the function and the associated ambiguity about its role. This is combined with the skills and attributes that are reasonable to expect from people working in this position.

CRITICAL REFLECTIONS

In relation to the first question, the image and reputation of manufacturing could be said to have been revived, with the 'old economy' stereotypes portrayed during the boom in the service economy – above all financial services – during the 1990s and 2000s increasingly seeming misplaced. Manufacturing, in 2010, had once again become recognised as a major source of sustainable growth, as a provider of 'good' jobs and a means of alleviating the UK's chronic balance of trade deficit. However, if HR strategies are driven merely on the basis of short-term trading conditions (the low value of the British pound compared with other currencies – making UK manufacturing cheaper) – then this may mean that the focus will be on low-cost, low-road manufacturing, where the UK could not realistically compete with the emerging economies. Unfortunately, the official discourse remains dominated by the ideology of deregulation and the need for a highly flexible labour market, which, in practice, translates to insecure jobs, low commitment and interdependence between the firm and employee, and low pay (the latter, in turn, undermining the basis of consumer demand).

In relation to the second question, a review of the relationship between shop floor workers, line management and the HR function could benefit from a consideration of what functions are best achieved by empowerment and delegation. More high-trust relations between shop floor workers and line management facilitated by clearer lines of accountability between the line manager's HR role on day-to-day activities could be promoted.

BREWSTER, C. and SODERSTROM, M. (1994) Human resources and line management. Chapter 4 in: BREWSTER, C. and HEGEWISCH, A. (eds). *Policy and practice in European human resource management: the PriceWaterhouse Cranfield survey.* London: Routledge. pp51–67.

This chapter explores decentralisation and devolvement of responsibility for HRM to line managers and explores the resultant changes in the relationship of HR specialists and line managers.

MACDUFFIE, J.P. (1995) Human resource bundles and manufacturing performance: organizational logic and flexible production systems in the world auto industry. *Industrial and Labor Relations Review.* Vol 48, No 2. pp 197–221.

This journal article tests two hypotheses: that innovative HR practices affect performance when implemented as part of a 'bundle' and that these 'bundles' contribute most to assembly plant productivity and quality when they are integrated with manufacturing policies.

BUDHWAR, P.S. (2000) Evaluating levels of strategic integration and devolvement of human resource management in the UK. *Personnel Review*. Vol 29, No 2. p141–157.

This journal article evaluates the levels of strategic integration of HRM into the corporate strategy and devolvement of responsibility for HRM to line managers in the UK manufacturing sector.

INSTITUTE FOR MANUFACTURING. (2010) IfM Management Technology Policy and University of Cambridge. Available online at www.ifm.eng.cam.ac.uk

The Institute for Manufacturing (IfM) is the public face of the Department of Engineering's Manufacturing and Management Division. The IfM brings together expertise in management, technology and policy to address the full spectrum of industrial issues. This website offers latest manufacturing industry statistics.

CHAPTER 20

HRM in Private Services

Sebastian Fuchs

OVERVIEW

This chapter discusses the role of human resource management (HRM) in private services by determining the main idiosyncrasies of services and their impact on perceptions of service quality and customer satisfaction. Further, the chapter aims to integrate the concepts of service climate, perceived service quality, customer-oriented behaviour, customer satisfaction and organisational outcomes into a conceptual framework for the study of human resources in service organisations.

LEARNING OBJECTIVES

Reading this chapter will enable the reader to:

- critically examine the main idiosyncrasies of services
- critically evaluate the concept of perceived service quality
- critically analyse the concept of service climate with its different dimensions
- conceptually integrate the notions of service climate, perceived service quality, customer-oriented behaviour, customer satisfaction and organisational outcomes.

'CALL CENTRE COMPLAINTS AT A BRITISH BANK'

A big London-based newspaper recently reported that a British bank with global operations has been singled out for particular poor service quality and customer complaints about the bank's call centres. For example, a customer had arranged a mortgage advance of £25,000 with the call centre but when coming to the bank branch it was not approved after all. Branch employees apologised for this unfortunate incident and admitted that the call centres were often very inefficient. Unfortunately, this was not an isolated incident of poor customer service at the bank. The newspaper collected a fair amount of such customer complaints and forwarded them to the bank's general manager. The manager argued that the amount of complaints had to be seen against the backdrop of all the successfully completed customer requests and more

than 80 million calls a year. He insisted that most of these calls were handled in a very efficient and professional way. He did, however, acknowledge that the bank would not 'always get everything right' and that they do make mistakes. The general manager further assured that the call centres have been improved as a result of the reader's comments.

Questions

1   What are the main problems of the service delivery in this story?

2   What could the bank do in order to rectify these problems?

3   Based on the response from the bank's general manager, how do you evaluate the chances that these problems will be reduced in the future?

INTRODUCTION

This chapter sets out to discuss the role of HRM in private services. Given the vast array of different classifications of services, the main focus of this chapter is on labour-intensive services that rely significantly on human resources and the individual behaviour of service providers (for different classifications, see for instance Korczynski 2002). The chapter first outlines the main service idiosyncrasies and their significance for the management of services and then integrates the concepts of perceived service quality, customer satisfaction and organisational outcomes and argues that the HRM-related concepts of service-climate and customer-oriented behaviour are instrumental in order to trigger this chain of events.

CHARACTERISTICS OF THE PRIVATE SERVICE INDUSTRY

While many different classifications of economic divisions exist in the literature, the three classical types of economic sectors in economies refer to the agricultural sector, the manufacturing sector and the service sector (Palmer 2008). There is much evidence that services, in particular in the private sector, are on the rise in many advanced economies. For instance, within the 27 European Union (EU) member states of 2009, services accounted for 71.6% (including public administration, health and education) of the total value added to the

EU economy (EUROSTAT 2009). A number of private service industries have been, in fact, growing exceptionally fast between 1995 and 2005. For instance, distribution, communication and transport services grew by approximately 32% with respect to economic value added and 12% in terms of employment. In contrast, manufacturing increased in the same time period by only 18% in terms of value added to the economies of the (back then) 25 EU member states but employment in manufacturing declined by 12%. In other words, there seems to be a general shift away from manufacturing towards services in more advanced economies (Palmer 2008). In fact, figures from the ILO (International Labour Organization 2006) confirm these trends. Over three-quarters of employees in most Western developed economies are employed in service jobs in the service industry (for example United States of America 75.3%, United Kingdom 72.6%, Germany 69.2% and Japan 68.1%). In more developing countries, however, lower figures can be found. For instance, in the Philippines 53.2%, in India 51.2% and in Indonesia 39.9% of the overall workforce are employed in service roles. Lower levels of service workers with respect to the overall working population can be found in less developed economies such as Mexico (30%), Bangladesh (28%) and Ethiopia (9%). These figures, to some extent, confirm the often stated correlation that the more advanced an economy becomes, the lower the level of agriculture and manufacturing in terms of employment and economic value added becomes in turn (see for instance Palmer 2008).

Some of the main reasons for this growth, according to Baron et al (2009), refer to the general deregulation in many advanced economies and with this the associated surge of private providers offering services such as legal advice, financial management, education and transport among others. Further, an increase in individuals' spending power associated with the economic development of many advanced economies often signifies greater levels of disposable income which can be spent on services that substitute previously self-managed activities such as cooking, ironing, cleaning and the organisation of parties and social events among others. The level of economic development of a country, to some extent linked to an increase in free time and disposable income in many advanced economies, also resulted in citizens' general desire to fill their leisure time with activities such as travelling or health club pursuits. This, the argument goes, has also contributed to the growth of service sectors in many advanced economies and contributed to the mushrooming of private leisure and recreation providers (Baron et al 2009).

Despite the general trend in more advanced economies towards greater service sectors and away from traditional agriculture and manufacturing as economic value generators, one needs to be cautious in interpreting the figures presented by economists and fiscal statisticians. Firstly, the way in which national statistics are compiled on service sector indicators such as labour force and gross domestic product varies from country to country and has not been harmonised throughout the world. As such, statistical variation may lie, to some extent, in the way the data is compiled and presented as opposed to an actual variation of indicators (Palmer 2008). Secondly, an increase in outsourcing of peripheral services by many manufacturers in advanced economies has led statisticians and economists to classify these services (such as call centres, cleaning or catering) as pure services even though they still serve similar purposes as they did when they were classified as manufacturing-based economic activity. Third and finally, the system of Standard Industrial Classifications traditionally puts a greater emphasis on products and manufactured goods and henceforth did not classify and measure services with similar accuracy in the past. As such, economists using this indicator ultimately create more detailed and fine-tuned information about products than about services that may bias some of the existing statistics on service sectors and their growth in advanced economies (Palmer 2008).

With regard to the service sector in the United Kingdom, the growth of employment is in line with those of many other European economies, and recent figures suggest that 72.6% of employees are employed in service roles (ILO 2006). There are some gender biases depending on the service type in this sector. For instance, in wholesale and retail, hotels and restaurants, financial services, education, health and social work, and general community services 55%, 62%, 57%, 75%, 81% and 52% of all employees are female respectively. The lowest percentage of female employees in the British service sector can be found, on the other hand, in transport and communication (29%) and electricity, gas and water (36%) (Kersley et al 2006). As such, the service sector in the United Kingdom seems to have a gender bias towards female employees in certain industries. Further, with regard to age distribution in the British service sector, there also seems to be some variation. For instance, 47% of hotels and restaurants and 35% of wholesale and retail organisations employ over one-quarter of employees aged between 16 and 21, indicating the relatively young and with this potentially lower qualified (or still in the process of generating academic or professional qualifications) workforce in this sector (Kersley et al 2006). In contrast, 36% of transport and communication, 45% of education and 58% of health and social work organisations employ more than one-quarter of employees older than 50 years (Kersley et al 2006). This information is important with respect to labour turnover in some service sectors. In particular, hotels and restaurants (39%) and wholesale and retail (27%) experience high levels of annual labour turnover (Kersley et al 2006).

There is also evidence that the global financial crisis, which as such was initially acknowledged by commentators in 2007, had and still has an impact on the British service sector. For instance, Guest et al (2009) and Clinton and Woollard (2010) provide empirical evidence collected from a range of senior HRM professionals that professional services, media and entertainment, general business and financial services, utilities, retail and leisure, and transport and communication service providers experienced negative effects of the recession on their organisations. While only the retail and leisure sector (12%) reported an increase in employment among the private service organisations surveyed at the end of 2009 (respondents were asked to indicate figures based on the last 12 months), business services reduced their workforce by 3%, financial services by 4%, professional services by 6%, media and entertainment by 10%, transport and communications by 11% and utilities by 12% in the same period. As such, the impact of the global financial crisis on service sector employment in the United

Kingdom has been predominantly negative, with the exception of the retail and leisure services.

IDIOSYNCRASIES OF SERVICES

While much research in the fields of marketing, operations, management and HRM is concerned with organisations that produce physical goods, less research has been done on these business functions in terms of services. A clear theoretical and practical distinction between these two broad categories of organisational outcomes relates to the idiosyncrasies, or special characteristics, of services. Brassington and Pettitt (2003), Jobber (2007) and Kotler et al (2002) suggest that services differ from physical goods in five distinct ways, which all hold important implications for the management of services. Firstly, services are intangible, that is, they cannot usually be seen, felt, tasted, heard or smelled before they are actually consumed. As such, a service is typically a deed, performance or effort exerted by an employee and it is difficult for the consumer to evaluate the service before the purchase. Organisations can apply a number of techniques to increase the level of tangibility by, for instance, introducing tangible cues. Tangible cues are communication means that aim to bring the actual service experience closer to the customer. For instance, a hotel can produce leaflets with pictures and guest comments in order to indicate to potential guests what a stay at the hotel would actually be like. Many of these tangible cues involve employees' behaviour and appearance, creating a real need for organisations to carefully consider the role of staff in service settings.

A second idiosyncrasy of services refers to the inseparability of their production and consumption. While physical goods are usually produced, stored, sold and then consumed, services are usually first sold and then produced and consumed at the same time. For instance, tickets for a theatre play are purchased and then consumed while the actors perform the play. Again, this bears a number of important considerations for organisations, as the production cannot be separated from the consumption. The service employee or, for some services, a technology, is likely to be part of the service offering. Consider the role of a seminar tutor at university: he or she can only give the seminar if students are present and interact with the tutor. As such, the inseparability of services often also includes the presence of other consumers. This is important as the attitudes and behaviours of co-service consumers can impact on the satisfaction levels of all present consumers. Hence, service organisations not only need to manage their staff effectively while producing a service, but also must carefully manage the relationships between the consumers.

A further important idiosyncrasy of services refers to their variability. This means that the quality of a service is linked to the person who performs it, the time of performance and the location of performance. For instance, a key challenge for many hairdressers is to consistently provide the exact same haircut for customers even though on one occasion they may be under more time pressure (due to many customers waiting) than on other occasions. Hence, on the busier occasions they have less time to essentially produce the same outcome for the customer. Many organisations react to such variability with strict codes of conduct and practices, extended training and development or the reduction of staff through technology (Kotler et al 2002).

A fourth service idiosyncrasy refers to the perishability of services. While physical goods can usually be stored and thereby saved for later consumption, services often perish if not consumed. For instance, a flight ticket is only valid for the exact date it was booked for. If nobody purchases the seat on the plane, the service value perishes. This is usually not problematic for the organisation as long as the demand for a service is steady, but when it fluctuates organisations need to buffer this effect. Some organisations fully charge for unused flight tickets and in some countries dentists and general practitioners charge patients for missed appointments. In order to match supply and demand for a service, however, organisations can use additional part-time staff at peak times, multi-skill their existing staff, reduce the price for off-peak times and introduce reservation systems, among other things.

Finally, services lack the quality of ownership. Physical goods can be purchased, used and even sold if desired by the owner. Services, on the other hand, are not usually owned by anybody and are restricted for a certain period of time. For instance, an insurance policy is only active when constantly renewed and paid for, but if not continued the consumer loses the right to rely on assistance associated with the insurance. Because services lack the quality of ownership, service providers ought to reinforce its benefits and advantages. This can be done by offering incentive schemes for reusing a service or the introduction of membership cards and associations that transmit an impression of ownership. These five idiosyncrasies have important implications not only for the management and operations of services, but more specifically for customers' service quality perceptions, customer satisfaction and a number of organisational outcomes.

PERCEIVED SERVICE QUALITY, CUSTOMER SATISFACTION AND ORGANISATIONAL OUTCOMES

PERCEIVED SERVICE QUALITY

It is important to conceptually understand what perceived service quality means when discussing the role of HRM in private service organisations. A well-established conceptualisation of service quality perceptions that considers different service quality elements is that put forward by Parasuraman et al (1985), which was subsequently tested on a number of different occasions (see for instance Zeithaml et al 1996). These scholars conducted focus groups, interviews and a number of quantitative surveys in a wide range of service organisations to determine global dimensions of service quality perceptions, often referred to as SERVQUAL (short for service quality). The dimensions refer to assurance, empathy, reliability, responsiveness and tangibles. Such global dimensions of service quality are important for the majority of services given their above-discussed specific characteristics and idiosyncrasies and can be used by organisations and scholars to determine specific elements of service quality perceptions of customers (Parasuraman and Zeithaml 2002). Table 20.1 provides the definitions of the different service quality perception dimensions presented by Parasuraman et al (1985).

Table 20.1 Service quality perception dimensions

Service quality perception dimension	Definition
Assurance	Knowledge and courtesy of employees and their ability to inspire trust and confidence (incorporates the original dimensions of competence, courtesy, credibility and security)
Empathy	Caring, individualised attention the organisation provides to its customers (incorporates the original dimensions of access, communication and understanding the customer)
Reliability	Ability to perform the promised service dependably and accurately
Responsiveness	Willingness to help customers and provide prompt service
Tangibles	Appearance of physical facilities, equipment, personnel and communication materials

Source: Adapted from Parasuraman et al (1985) and Parasuraman and Zeithaml (2002).

A point to note at this stage is that a number of other global service quality perception conceptualisations have also been presented by other service scholars (for a comprehensive overview, see Schneider and White 2004). Additionally, more industry-specific measures are available for scholars and practitioners with a special interest in, for instance, the lodging industry (Knutson et al 1990), hospitals (Reidenbach and Sandifer-Smallwood 1990) and restaurants (Stevens et al 1995) among others. As such, a number of tools to measure service quality perceptions are available for application in different service industries.

PERCEIVED SERVICE QUALITY, CUSTOMER SATISFACTION AND ORGANISATIONAL OUTCOMES

The measurement of service quality is not only important in order to determine service quality perception levels of service users, but has also been linked to customer satisfaction with a service. Customer satisfaction, as opposed to service quality perceptions, refers to a more evaluative and emotionally laden judgement about the satisfaction levels (as opposed to more descriptive and factually based evaluations) during or after a service encounter (Schneider and White 2004). As such, customer satisfaction is a distinct yet related concept of service quality perceptions. There is strong evidence that customer satisfaction is an outcome of high service quality perceptions. For instance, Loveman (1998), Reidenbach and Sandifer-Smallwood (1990) and Woodside et al (1989) among others provide empirical evidence that service quality is positively associated with customer satisfaction in retail banking and hospitals. In line with these research findings and Schneider and White (2004), then, customer satisfaction is seen as an outcome of positive perceptions of service quality in these areas.

This is an important conclusion, as high customer satisfaction levels have in turn been linked to a number of organisationally desired outcomes. For instance, Woodside et al (1989) provide empirical evidence that overall satisfaction with a hospital stay is associated with the behavioural intention to receive care from the same hospital in the future, and Reidenbach and Sandifer-Smallwood (1990) report that patient satisfaction is positively associated with recommending a hospital to others in the future. Similar results were reported by Zeithaml et al (1996) for private and corporate clients operating in a number of different industries. In more explicit financial terms, Loveman (1998) provides empirical evidence that customer satisfaction is associated with customer loyalty, which in turn is associated with higher levels of revenue growth and profitability in retail banking. In another study, Schneider et al (2005) report empirical evidence that customer satisfaction with a specific supermarket is associated with higher levels of sales of that very supermarket. As a consequence, then, customer satisfaction – often triggered through positive perceptions of service quality (Schneider and White 2004) – serves as an important mediating variable between service quality perceptions and organisationally desired outcomes. This poses the question as to how organisations can create positive perceptions of service quality and thereby trigger the associated advantageous outcomes of such perceptions. The following section offers a number of HRM concepts and considerations on how to trigger this beneficial chain of events in service organisations.

THE CONCEPT OF SERVICE CLIMATE

One of the most promising and effective ways of providing high service quality, and thereby creating high levels of customers satisfaction, refers to the introduction and establishment of a service climate. A service climate refers to 'the shared employee perceptions of the policies, practices, and procedures and the behaviours that get rewarded, supported, and expected with regard to customer service and customer service quality' (Schneider and White 2004, p100). In other words, a service climate is an all-encapsulating, deeply rooted construct of management, operations and HRM that places service quality at the heart of the organisation. It tangibly acknowledges the central role of service providers in its operations. A number of different conceptualisations of service climates have been presented ever since Schneider et al (1980) delivered their seminal paper on the construct. Schneider et al (1980) conducted focus groups and interviews with many different organisational constituencies in several branches of a large US-based bank and proposed a number of different service climate dimensions such as managerial functions, service effort rewarded, retaining customers, personnel support, central processing support, marketing support and equipment, and supply support. Further statistical analysis performed by Schneider and Bowen (1985) suggested the reduction of these seven dimensions to four dimensions, namely branch management, customer attention and retention, systems support and logistics support. One of the main limitations of these service climate constructs is that they have been developed only in the banking industry and hence may carry some bias towards financial services with them. A conceptualisation that overcomes this weakness of industry-specific data is that of Lytle et al (1998), which was developed in a number of different industries. Lytle et al (1998) provide 10 global service climate dimensions that were, as Schneider et al's (1980) and Schneider and Bowen's (1985) constructs, measured at the individual level of analysis (for a discussion of the suitability of such aggregation approaches, see for instance Schneider and White 2004). These dimensions refer to servant leadership, service vision, customer treatment, employee empowerment, service training, service rewards, service failure prevention, service failure recovery, service technology and service standards communication. Table 20.2 provides the definitions of Lytle et al's (1998) different service climate dimensions.

Table 20.2 Service climate dimensions

	Service climate dimensions	Definition
Proximal–individual	Customer treatment	Degree to which organisation and employees treat customers in ways that will enhance service quality
	Employee empowerment	Degree to which employees have responsibility and authority to meet customer needs
	Service training	Training in teamwork, problem-solving and interpersonal skills among others that contribute to the delivery of service quality
	Service rewards	Extent to which employees are recognised, rewarded and compensated to deliver quality service
	Service standards communication	Extent to which service standards or benchmarks are communicated to and understood by employees
Distal–structural	Servant leadership	Extent to which leaders of organisation display service-oriented behaviours in their leading
	Service vision	Extent to which leaders have and espouse a vision for being a service-oriented organisation
	Service failure prevention	Practices that proactively prevent service failures
	Service failure recovery	Practices that function to respond effectively to customer complaints or service failures
	Service technology	Organisation's use of technology and technology-based systems to serve customers

Source: Adapted from Lytle et al (1998).

Although not fully developed and tested by Lytle et al (1998), the different dimensions of their service climate conceptualisation may be further classified according to their proximity to service providers (note that Lytle et al (1998) conceptually suggest four different areas of dimensions). For instance, the elements of customer treatment, employee empowerment, service training, service rewards and service standards communication are arguably more proximal to the individual service provider as they influence perceptions of service quality directly based on the service provider. For instance, ongoing and service-related technical and interpersonal training is likely to have a positive effect on consumers' perceptions of reliability and assurance on a daily basis. Conversely, then, the elements servant leadership, service vision, service failure prevention, service failure recovery and service technology are more distal and of structural nature for the service process. Establishing a system that actively prevents service failure or tries to recover failures with minimal disruption and inconvenience for the customer is arguably less frequently encountered and thereby more distal for service users' day-to-day activities. In fact, they can also be seen as more hidden service climate dimensions from a service user's perspective. As such, this distinction allows us to separate more operations and management-based issues from more HRM-related matters in service organisations or, to use different terminology, more proximal–individual versus more distal–structural dimensions. The effects of these more proximal and distal service climate dimensions on service quality perceptions and customer-oriented behaviour and ultimately customer satisfaction have been studied by service scholars on an ongoing basis and are further discussed in the next section.

SERVICE CLIMATE, CUSTOMER-ORIENTED BEHAVIOUR AND LINKAGES TO PERCEIVED SERVICE QUALITY

Some of the most frequently cited studies that link and discuss global measures of service climate, that is, an aggregation of different service climate dimensions, to global perceptions of service quality, are those presented by Schneider et al (1980), Schneider (1990) and Schneider et al (1998). All studies suggest a strong link between the existence of a service climate and more positive perceptions of service quality among customers. In other words, implementing and executing the different service climate dimensions in service organisations positively affects customers' perceptions of service quality and this, the argument goes, is ultimately related to customer satisfaction and positive organisational outcomes (Schneider and White 2004). Fewer studies on service climate and perceived service quality, however, looked systematically at specific service climate dimensions and their link to specific dimensions of perceived service quality.

CUSTOMER-ORIENTED BEHAVIOUR, PERCEIVED SERVICE QUALITY AND CUSTOMER SATISFACTION

Service climate and more specific service climate dimensions may be linked to pro-social service providers' behaviour, which is associated with higher levels of customer satisfaction. For instance, Peccei and Rosenthal (2001) suggest that a number of HRM practices such as the perception of supportive management or service-related training account for an increased level of service provider empowerment, that is, the internalisation of training content, greater job competence and job autonomy, which acts as a mechanism to trigger customer-oriented behaviour. Other research presented by Liao et al (2009) confirms this line of reasoning in a different service setting. Customer-oriented behaviour, more specifically, refers to employee behaviour that is in nature 'more personalized, flexible and receptive to individual customer demands' (Peccei and Rosenthal 2001, p837) and is as such related to service quality dimensions. To some degree, one may argue, these are the types of employee behaviours that are captured in Parasuraman et al's (1985) assurance, empathy and responsiveness service quality dimensions when transferred directly onto the individual service provider (see for instance appendix in Peccei and Rosenthal 2001 for comparison). In other words, there seems to be a conceptual and empirical overlap between certain service quality dimensions and customer-oriented behaviour. As such, the establishment of a service climate is likely to have a positive effect on both service providers' customer-oriented behaviour and certain service quality dimensions. And this, as ample conceptual and empirical evidence reported by for instance Anderson et al (2008), Liao and Chuang (2004), Loveman (1998), Mayer et al (2009), Schmit and Allscheid (1995), Schneider et al (2005) and Susskind et al (2003) suggests, in turn is linked to higher levels of customer satisfaction, which is associated with a number of organisationally desired behavioural and financial outcomes (Schneider and White 2004).

SERVICE CLIMATE AND PERCEIVED SERVICE QUALITY

Having established a global link between service climate and service quality perceptions and the conceptual and empirical overlap with customer-oriented behaviour, this section now identifies and discusses specific service climate dimensions and connects them with service quality perceptions based on the distinction of proximal–individual and distal–structural service climate dimensions.

Proximal–individual service climate dimensions

Empirical evidence presented by Schneider and Bowen (1993) suggests that a reduction of work stressors and an increase in work facilitation through abandoning organisational and job attributes that hinder task attainment is positively related to high levels of service quality perceptions. In other words, by empowering service providers and reducing their autonomy constraints, organisations can increase positive perceptions of service quality of customers. As such, employee empowerment seems to positively contribute towards a service climate and this in turn to service quality perceptions.

There is also empirical evidence that service training, another proximal–individual service climate dimension, positively affects service quality perceptions. For instance, Schneider and Bowen (1993) argue that employee socialisation and induction programmes with a focus on service quality are linked to customers' overall service quality perceptions. In another study, Hausknecht et al (2009) argue that voluntary employee turnover rates are negatively related to service quality perceptions and that greater concentration of newcomers in service units strengthen this negative relationship. As a consequence, then, the use of induction and service training programmes seems to be of great importance for the customers' service quality perceptions and may, to some extent, remedy this potential source of negative influences of perceptions of service quality. There is also empirical evidence presented by Giardini and Frese (2008) that emotional intelligence and competence is positively related to customers' positive effect and emotional state, which in turn relates to more positive service quality perceptions. This, the argument goes, suggests the need to introduce and offer emotional intelligence and competence training courses for employees operating in service roles. Evidence presented by Nelis et al (2009) argues that emotional intelligence, at least certain elements of it, can be learned and acquired by individuals in specifically designed training courses. As such, there is ample evidence for the crucial role of service training as a component of service climate and its link to service quality perceptions.

In addition to service training, specific rewards for service excellence form part of the more proximal–individual service climate dimensions. Conceptual evidence for nursing homes put forward by Eaton (2000) suggests that wages and benefits for excellent service provision can positively influence residents' service quality perceptions. Vroom's (1964) expectancy theory and other extrinsic reward theories further substantiate this line of reasoning.

Finally, there is also evidence that service standards communication, one of the proximal–individual service climate dimensions as well, is linked to the service quality perceptions of responsiveness and empathy. For instance, Susskind et al (2003) provide empirical evidence from US-based first-line service providers that the existence and communication of service standards predicts employees' levels of responsiveness, assurance and empathy (referred to as customer orientation in Susskind et al's 2003 study) and that this in turn predicts customer satisfaction. The line of reasoning here is that the relationship between service standards communication and customer orientation is fully mediated by perceptions of co-worker support. In other words, service providers' perception of being valued and appreciated by colleagues is what seems to explain the relationship between service standards and service quality dimensions. The implication for service organisations, then, is to create high levels of morale and good interpersonal relationships between service providers in order to increase the efficacy levels of service standards communication.

Distal–structural service climate dimensions

With regards to the more distal–structural servant leadership service climate dimension, Salvaggio et al (2007) provide empirical evidence from a US-based supermarket chain that manager personality, more precisely managers' core self-evaluations such as levels of self-esteem, self-efficacy, locus of control and neuroticism, predict managers' service quality orientation, which in turn predicts service providers' perceptions of service climate. As such, certain personality traits of managerial staff may in fact be a predictor of a service climate in service organisations. In another study, Schneider and Bowen (1993) suggest that management behaviour and supervision, including the provision of feedback, information-sharing and setting clear service standards, are positively associated with overall perceptions of service quality. Moreover, Schneider et al (2005) argue that unit service leadership behaviour contributes positively to a service climate in a sample of US-based supermarkets. This link was, to some extent, supported by Schmit and Allscheid (1995) in a security systems company. Further, qualitative evidence presented by Dean and Rainnie (2009) suggests that managerial attitudes such as being approachable and accessible when needed affect employees' service climate perceptions. In sum, then, the way supervisors and management behave and the extent to which they exhibit service-oriented behaviours towards their own employees can be seen as an important element of the more distal–structural service climate dimensions.

In terms of a service vision, Borucki and Burke (1999) provide empirical evidence that the importance of service for top management and store management is positively related to assurance and empathy, which in turn predicts higher individual service provider performance and store financial performance. Hence, there is some evidence for the service climate dimension of service vision and its link to service quality perceptions.

SERVICE CLIMATE AND CUSTOMER-ORIENTED BEHAVIOUR

Our distinction of service climate elements also has important implications for the creation of customer-oriented behaviour. In particular, the more proximal–individual service climate dimensions seem to have a strong effect on employees' customer-oriented behaviour. For instance, Peccei and Rosenthal (2001) argue that employee empowerment operates as a psychological mechanism as to why service providers engage in customer-oriented behaviour. Similar results were found by Peccei and Rosenthal (1997) that job competence (arguably an element of empowerment) was positively, and job routinisation negatively, related to commitment to service (a related concept of customer-oriented behaviour). Further, Liao and Chuang (2004) argue that psychological empowerment (in their study part of a high-performance work system) is positively associated with employees' customer-oriented behaviour. As such, then, employee empowerment in fact seems to be an important ingredient of service climates and can be directly linked to customer-oriented behaviour.

Service training, another proximal–individual service climate dimension, has also been linked to customer-oriented behaviour. For instance, Peccei and Rosenthal (2001) provide empirical evidence that participation at service value-based training, mediated through the internalisation of such values and job competence (see also Peccei and Rosenthal 1997 for similar findings), predicts customer-oriented behaviour. Arguably, then, the efficacy and applicability of service training explains the link between service training and an increase in customer-oriented behaviour in service organisations.

Figure 20.1 An integration of service climate, perceived service quality, customer-oriented behaviour, customer satisfaction and organisational outcomes

Note: The service climate dimensions are adapted from Lytle et al (1998).

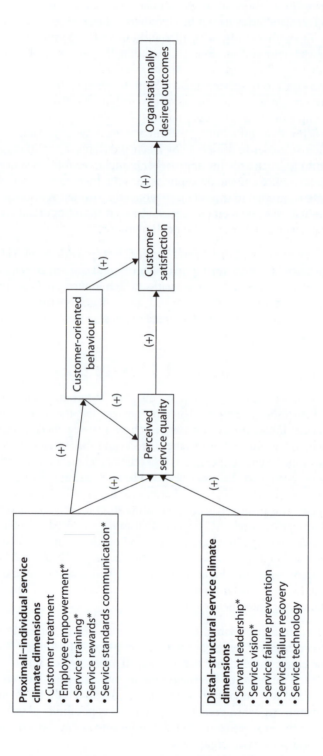

*Empirical/conceptual evidence presented for link between service climate dimensions and perceived service quality/customer-oriented behaviour. For further non-directly HRM-related evidence see, for instance, Lytle et al (1998).

Finally, the proximal–individual service climate dimension of service standards communication has also been liked to customer-oriented behaviour. Susskind et al (2003), for instance, suggest that service standards and their communication and internalisation on behalf of the service providers positively predicts customer-oriented behaviour. This relationship, the scholars argue, is fully mediated by co-worker support and perceived appreciation from colleagues. In fact, this links in well with the above-outlined definition of service climate as a perception shared by all employees with regard to the significance of service quality for the entire organisation.

INTEGRATING SERVICE CLIMATE, PERCEIVED SERVICE QUALITY, CUSTOMER-ORIENTED BEHAVIOUR, CUSTOMER SATISFACTION AND ORGANISATIONAL OUTCOMES

The discussion above suggests the efficacy of many of the service climate dimensions in order to increase levels of positive service quality perceptions and customer-oriented behaviour. Moreover, the discussion argues for a strong link between both customers' perceptions of service quality and customer-oriented behaviour and customer satisfaction. These are in turn related to a number of organisationally desired outcomes such as customer loyalty, intent to recommend the service to others and more direct financial outcomes such as an increase in sales and profitability. The evidence presented herein, as such, provides a strong case for the establishment and implementation of various service climate dimensions in order to increase overall performance of service organisations. Many of the service climate dimensions are either embedded in the HRM function in organisations or are, at least, related to it. This, in line with Schneider and Bowen (1993), the argument goes, highlights the crucial yet not unique role of HRM for service organisations. Figure 20.1 depicts the conception presented above and integrates the concepts of service climate, perceived service quality, customer-oriented behaviour, customer satisfaction and organisational outcomes.

CONCLUSION

This chapter outlined the main service idiosyncrasies – intangibility, inseparability, variability, perishability and non-ownership – and discussed evidence that service climate, conceptualised in accordance to more proximal–individual and distal–structural service climate dimensions, positively influences customers' perceptions of service quality and service providers' customer-oriented behaviour. This is argued to be related to greater customer satisfaction, which in turn predicts a number of organisationally desired outcomes such as greater customer loyalty, higher sales and superior profitability among others.

CRITICAL REFLECTIONS

After considering some of the main theoretical perspectives on service quality and HRM in private services, the answers to the news story can now be addressed from a more scientific point of view. For instance, the first question might now include a more structured answer in which Parasuraman et al's (1985) five different service quality dimensions are incorporated. The bank needs to improve in terms of the reliability dimension, as the customer reported having received mixed messages and could not access her mortgage advance even though finalised with the call centre. One could think about all of these dimensions in more detail and could also conclude that low perceptions of service quality have an impact on customer satisfaction and ultimately on organisational performance.

With regard to the second question, the bank first would need to establish a clear set of problem areas based on such evidence presented by the newspaper in order to systemically change and improve the service delivery of the call centres. Parasuraman et al's (1985) conceptualisation of service quality perceptions could be one way of structuring the set of action points. More precisely, the bank would need to address all elements and determine what could be done internally to address the issues. This may include the creation and establishment of a service climate as outlined by Lytle et al (1998) in the call centres. For example this could include empowering employees, offering extensive training on how to conduct oneself properly over the phone, rewarding service excellence as potentially based on the number of customers having to follow up a problem after their first call, the training and recruitment of supervisors and managers that exhibited servant leadership in the past or have the potential to do so in the future, the systematic documentation and use of such customer complaints in order to prevent service failures from happening again and an improvement in the technology used by the call centres among others.

In terms of how likely it is that these problems will be reduced in the future, one could argue that no commitment or reference was made by the bank's general manager in terms of how to rectify these problems or what is generally done in order to prevent such service failures from happening again. In fact, the bank had a real opportunity here to not only rectify these problems but to also get some potential media exposure from the newspaper for their service recovery function. Further, the statement that only relatively few service failures occur, and that an organisation cannot deliver service constantly without problems, suggests that there is no real service vision in place and that top management's priority lies somewhere else. In fact there is no strong argument that the situation is actually going to improve for the bank's customers in the future.

GILMORE, A. (2003) *Services marketing and management.* London: Sage Publications.

This book summarises many of the different conceptualisations and current issues of the management and marketing of services.

GRÖNFELDT, S. and STROTHER, J. (2006) *Service leadership: the quest for competitive advantage.* Thousand Oaks, CA: Sage Publications.

This book provides a comprehensive framework for the management of services and illustrates many real-life service issues from leading international service providers.

LUCAS, R.W. (2005) *Customer service: building successful skills for the twenty-first century.* 3rd ed. New York: McGraw-Hill Irwin.

This book offers many practical examples and activities to students (and professionals) to improve and fine-tune their service skills.

SCHNEIDER, B. and BOWEN, D.E. (1993) The service organization: human resources management is crucial. *Organizational Dynamics.* Vol 21, No 4. pp39–52.

This article provides quantitative and qualitative evidence that HRM practices of service organisations need to fit the market niche in which they operate in order to create a competitive advantage.

SCHNEIDER, B. and WHITE, S.S. (2004) *Service quality: research perspectives.* Thousand Oaks, CA: Sage Publications.

This book discusses the main research streams and current developments in service quality research and service management.

TEBOUL, J. (2006) *Service is front stage: positioning services for value advantage.* Basingstoke: Palgrave Macmillan.

This book suggests that service operations can be distinguished according to front-stage and back-stage activities and discusses several managerial implications of such a distinction.

CHAPTER 21

HRM in Public Services

Miguel Martínez Lucio and Ian Roper

OVERVIEW

This chapter considers the factors shaping HR decision-making in public service. Following a news story example that highlights specific dilemmas in this sector, the chapter provides a contextual overview of public services and the public sector. It then considers the external and internal factors shaping change in the sector and examines some of the complexities and tensions that exist.

LEARNING OBJECTIVES

Reading this chapter will enable the reader to:

- critically evaluate the features defining HR issues in public services
- compare and contrast what distinguishes HR in public services from other sectors
- critically evaluate the internal and external factors that shape HR decision-making in public services.

HRM IN THE MEDIA

'HOSPITAL STAFFING LEVELS LEAD TO PATIENT DEATHS'

On 24 February 2010 an independent inquiry into the failings of an NHS trust hospital in Staffordshire reported back its key findings. Its conclusions – which were the main news item of the day (for example BBC 2010) – were that the hospital was 'in breach of NHS values'. The scandal was first identified in 2009 when it was revealed by the Healthcare Commission that the hospital had an unacceptable fatality rate in the years between 2005 and 2008, which was directly linked to the hospital's mismanagement. A significant part of this failure was linked to management's pursuit of key financial targets to enable it to gain the coveted 'foundation trust' status. One consequence of this was chronic under-recruitment of key front-line staff. Another issue – possibly related – was the culture of neglect permeating staff throughout the hospital. The political fallout from this controversy was huge. Inevitably the Minister of Health blamed the management; opposition parties blamed the perverse incentives created by a 'target culture'

brought in by the Government. Union critics blamed the commercial imperative involved in the drive to gain foundation trust status. Others asked why professionals working at the hospital did not 'blow the whistle' on the malpractices.

Questions

1 What is the role of HR in this? Is its first duty, when advising on staff planning, to senior management's strategic objective of obtaining its financial targets?

2 Would HR have been capable of advising of possible consequences of understaffing?

3 With myriad unions present representing staff from senior medical professionals to nursing staff, manual staff and administrative staff, why did no one raise the alarm about this from the staff side, especially as it is not uncommon for unions to do this?

INTRODUCTION

The aim of this chapter is to outline some of general dynamics and developments in public sector human resource management (HRM) and employment relations. The sector remains a substantial part of the UK economy as an employer and provider of services. The sector is integral to the functioning of the country in terms of social order, social justice, infrastructure and economic development. It covers a wide range of activities ranging from education, health, personal social services and emergency services to the armed forces. They are areas with high profiles in terms of their public awareness and newsworthiness. These areas have been subjected to a range of influences and pressures in the past few decades but they remain relatively regulated and centrally managed in terms of their work and employment relations in a curiously unique way that balances traditional and modern forms of HRM and employment relations. Indeed, this distinction of terminology is important in this sector and a consideration of terminology may be useful here. Developments in the study of HRM over many years have led to a gradual supplanting of the term 'HRM' in place of 'personnel management' and 'industrial relations'. This was due to a range of factors discussed by many academics over the years. However, a large part of this has been the trend towards 'decollectivisation', discussed in Chapter 12. The one exception to this trend has been the public sector, where unions remain – and will continue to remain – a significant influence and therefore a significant aspect of HR decision-making. For this reason this chapter will frequently use the term HRM when referring to the management side, Industrial Relations (IR) when referring to the union/staff side and employment relations when referring to the processes and outcomes of the intersections of the two.

The chapter aims to explain the background to the public sector employment relations and its uniqueness and differences when compared with other sectors. It also aims to outline the pressures for change and the way in which the management of work and workers in the public sector has evolved since the early 1980s. A range of different forces for change are considered and the way they have shaped change at different times is discussed. When discussing such forces for change it is important that we differentiate between them and understand that they do not always have a straightforward effect on the way management changes (Martínez Lucio and Noon 1994). Having looked at these competing imperatives, the chapter will then examine two general themes that are shaping the character of contemporary employment relations in the sector. Firstly, continuities are outlined in terms of the way it remains regulated through collective mechanisms and political influences (or *political contingencies*, as Batstone et al 1984 called them). If anything, IR activity appears to be active and political. Secondly, the chapter then focuses on developments in HRM in relation to these pressures and continuities. The chapter ends with a brief outline of some of the pressures of balancing individual and collective dimensions of employment relations within an increasingly fragmented and boundaryless environment (Grimshaw et al 2000) where public and private interests and views engage. Managing or representing workers in the public sector is, therefore, an area that requires knowledge of the forces and context that shape its characteristics and the tensions, both old and new, in its employment systems.

THE PUBLIC SECTOR AND PUBLIC SERVICES

Most people have a good understanding of what is meant by 'the public sector' or by 'public services'. However, it is worth providing an overview as to what is involved. Firstly, we definine what may distinguish public services from 'the public sector', which are broadly interchangeable. One distinction is that the public sector is wider than the specific areas of public services. In the past 'the public sector' may have activities ranging from nationalised industries (ranging from car manufacturing and shipbuilding), to public utilities, public transport, aspects of the public infrastructure through to the military. To these we would add the activities more commonly associated as being 'public services': the emergency services, health, education, employment and welfare services, personal social services and the various activities of local government (planning, street cleaning, environmental health, household waste and recycling). As a public service there are some overlaps and exceptions. Public transport would seem to have many characteristics associated with a public service, and shares many IR features, though, is now predominantly privately owned and normally treated separately. Conversely, the police is broadly considered a public service but in the case of uniformed services it remains a fairly specific situation with regard to employment status, union rights and joint consultation. A second issue that should be considered is the 'mixed economy' that now exists in public services. The implications and development of this will be considered further, below (and also in Chapter 22), but some basic information is required here. The key point is that what are popularly thought of as 'public' services are often delivered by a hybrid of arrangements involving aspects that are contracted out or delivered with non-public 'partners' involved. This aspect is significant. Public services now constitute a significant amount of business for a growing (and internationalising) array of private companies almost completely dependent on public services for their survival (Pollock 2005). As an indicator of this, the Department for Business, Enterprise and Regulatory Reform (BERR 2008) estimates the value of public service contracts as being worth £44 billion per year, making it bigger than automobiles and pharmaceuticals.

In terms of the workforce, in 2008 there were 2,479,000 people working in central government activities (ONS 2009), which, because of the fairly high number working part-time, equates to a full-time equivalent (FTE) of 2,156,000 (ONS 2009). In local government there were 2,938,000 people working (ONS 2009) or 2,178,000 FTE (ONS 2009). Table 21.1 provides an indication of the breakdown of the public sector workforce in more detail.

In terms of the demographic profile, in 2004 65% of workers in the public sector were women, compared with 40.8% in the private sector (ONS 2005). There is no real difference in terms of ethnicity – about 7% non-white in both public and private sectors (ONS 2005). Employees with a long-term disability accounted for 13.1% – slightly higher than in the private sector (ONS 2005). More workers in the public sector worked part-time hours (29.9% compared with 24.4% in

Table 21.1 The public sector workforce in 2008

Sector	Headcount
Armed forces	193,000
Police (including civilians)	285,000
Public administration	1,230,000
Education	1,389,000
National Health Service	1,499,000
Other health and social work	379,000
Construction	56,000
Other	732,000

Derived from ONS (2009) based on employment in 2008 Q1.

the private sector) (ONS 2005). This probably accounted for the shorter average hours worked (the statistics measure hours worked, but do not indicate hours worked above contracted hours). Another contrast is length of service: workers in the public sector stay in post longer than the private sector – for example, 24.2% of employees have stayed with the same employer between 10 and 20 years compared with 17.2% of employees in the private sector (ONS 2005).

Before moving on to the detailed discussion of employment relations in public services, we emphasise the importance of the role of the state (Chapter 7) and the influence of political factors on HR policy (Chapter 9). Nowhere is this more significant than when managing in the public sector. Not only do changes to general employment policy need to be considered, but the public sector is also the place where government policy is played out. HR can be impacted by, for example, aspects of social policy and by government attempts to reform the working practices of public sector workers. Consider the scenario for HR managers in the spring of 2010. The situation was one of a very large public accounts deficit as a result of government spending to deal with the effects of the recession, and the money pledged to support state bailouts of failing banks in 2008. It was also a period where a general election was certain and all political parties were pledging their intention to make very large cuts in public spending. The planning scenario for HR managers in such a situation is not enviable. They are anticipating a period of large-scale cutbacks to jobs. Unlike in a private sector scenario of job cuts, however, they are anticipating, on average, a stable and, in many instances, an increase in the demand for the services that their remaining employees will be expected to provide.

THE TRADITIONS OF PUBLIC SECTOR EMPLOYMENT RELATIONS

There is a need to appreciate that public sector personnel administration and IR differed from their private sector counterparts to a great extent during much of the twentieth century (see Bach and Winchester 2003). The public sector was not as exposed to the pressures of market relations compared with private firms, although this depended on the market in question. The basis of public sector employment systems was bureaucratic decision-making and formal procedures. Within this context the role of political factors – political contingencies – was significant given that the Government was the final point for decisions on a range of relevant issues (see Batstone et al 1984). Yet this relative importance of hierarchy and bureaucracy – while making for a less voluntarist system of IR – was influenced by systems of worker representation that were, in the main (since the early to mid-twentieth century), based on national councils and committees that oversaw the establishment of the basic working conditions and terms of employment. These had emerged since the First World War through the recommendations of the Whitley Commission. In turn the public sector emphasised the need for the state to be a 'good employer' (Winchester 1983): that is to say, it was meant to attract and retain workers to key service jobs in teaching or nursing, for example, by offering good employment conditions (something that was not always that clear at times – see Bach and Winchester

2003). This notion of the good employer, in turn, was politically important for setting standards to private sector employers, benchmarks for their own employment practices (although this would not be the language used then). The reasons for this interest in the notion of good employment were linked to the importance of the services that were delivered and the need to limit social disorder and bad practices in employment that could become politicised in the longer term through more militant worker activists, for example. Hence, the public sector was known for experimenting with good employment practices related to work–life balance and health and safety standards and, for some (Boyne et al 1999), this has in great part remained the case. These were in turn underpinned by strong union engagement across a range of issues through forms of bargaining or, on occasions, through industrial conflict if benefits and conditions of work were deemed to be eroded by management or government. The public sector has also been known for strong internal labour markets and clear career progression (see MacKenzie 2002 on the public sector tradition in telecommunications before it was privatised in the 1980s, for example). This legacy of expectations and rules has changed, but they are still visible in the public sector and are central to its different features of organisation.

PRESSURE FOR CHANGE: THE RESHAPING OF THE PUBLIC SECTOR SINCE THE EARLY 1980s

There is a range of imperatives for change that vary from the market-led to the politically directed and the technologically facilitated. Kirkpatrick (2006) identifies three main aspects of organisational change in the public sector, which dovetail with the development of organisational forms in the private sector: first, a departure from vertical integration; second, the move to fragment and decentralise the management of public services; and finally, the trend towards more flexible service delivery and employment. The nature of marketisation in the public sector takes various forms according to the dominant imperatives for change and their specific national and subsectoral contexts. However, we can outline a series of salient developments in relation to work and employment matters in the public sector. These have confronted, either directly or indirectly, the existing nature of collective bargaining and the role of joint regulation of employment through trade unions (Martínez Lucio 2007).

In terms of form there are a range of factors. First, there is the policy of privatisation. This challenges IR by providing a new co-ordinated employer who is sometimes even co-ordinated at a transnational level. New attitudes may emerge in relation to trade unions and collective forms of representation and bargaining with these 'new' employers. Within such a context, market pressures are more clearly articulated vis-à-vis the workforce. The dimension of external competition is referenced more explicitly, even if the market remains monopolised (Martínez Lucio et al 1997). Second, within this context there is a decentralisation of the organisation. Increasingly, there are attempts to divisionalise organisational processes and to develop a greater emphasis on cost centres and financially accountable units. This decentralisation might involve no more than a formal separation and reorganisation of units, or it might involve the subcontracting of these to the external business environment. Decentralisation means that the process of bargaining and negotiation may be stretched across different entities within and beyond the organisation, testing the resources and co-ordinating ability of trade unions and worker representatives as they try to represent interests of the workers who are more widely dispersed.

There is also the question of content in the employment relationship and at work. The development of a more market-oriented approach, and a more decentralised pattern of organisation, can lead to a greater emphasis on performance management and measurement within the public sector and its employment relations. There is an attempt at a greater alignment of pay and labour activity to determined outputs. This is not always a very clear development but it is increasingly visible. The cult of surveillance becomes a common feature of many organisations along with a greater propensity to measure performance. This is facilitated by the use of new forms of information technology and more elaborate forms of financial accounting. This development links remuneration and activity more closely, challenging external reference points within bargaining processes. Moreover, the development of performance measurement parallels an increasing reference to the role of customer interests. 'Customers' of public services have been the subject of much academic concern since the early 1990s (Kirkpatrick and Martínez Lucio 1995). The invoking of an external interest in the form of the customer may align itself to employer interests and performance targets, although, as we explain below, this is not necessarily the case. Martínez Lucio and MacKenzie (1999) argue that there may be tensions between the measurement project and the customer dimension. Even so, a new age of the customer has underpinned employment relations in the public sector, especially in countries such as the UK and the US, where we have seen a greater degree of litigation from public service customers. Bach (2004) argues that the privatisation of aspects of the public sector has to an extent led to Taylorist-style employment mechanisms being implemented in the British National Health Service (NHS). Finally, these developments have underpinned the use of labour in a more 'flexible' and 'individualised' manner. There is an increasing questioning of the culture of lifetime employment. Temporary contracting is increasing within public services, as is agency work. Many speak of a greater individualisation of employment as workers fall outside the remit of collective regulation in terms of collective bargaining, and are influenced by distinct points of reference and arrangements of an individual or agency-based nature.

These developments need to be understood in terms of the way different points and approaches are emphasised at different times. For example, in the 1970s the reforms were mainly in cost terms, given the crisis of expenditure and the crisis of the welfare state approach. The 1980s saw the continuation of these types of strategies but the then Conservative government emphasised a tighter managing of resources and a fondness for outsourcing and privatisation. Those aspects that were not systematically outsourced or privatised were reorganised around competitive relations whereby schools and hospitals, for example, competed to an extent for funds and 'customers' (Colling 1995). These features defined the later years of the Conservative administration (1979–1997) and – in common with similar developments in other Anglo-Saxon countries – is broadly defined as 'new public management' (Dibben et al 2004; Hood 1991). The Labour governments (1997–2010) continued aspects of this policy, but with a continued focus on efficiency, managerialism and commercially led 'modernisation' (Finlayson 2003), by limiting privatisation to an extent but emphasising performance measurement and controls. The way in which these developments operate varied enormously. There is no clear development that ensures that the above are starkly realised within employment relations. However, their impact is increasingly observable within a range of studies (Bach et al 1999). In terms of employment relations, the shift to a marketised approach is linked to a more co-operative and conciliatory shift in terms of union–management relations (Stuart and Martínez Lucio 2005), even if the reality is different (Prowse and Prowse 2007).

However, while there are significant continuities in relation to the way that Labour governments had followed the Conservatives in terms of 'new public management', it was applied with differences to how the workforce should be treated within this. As noted in Chapter 7, the emphasis under New Labour was on strengthening aspects of individual employment law while sidelining collective rights (Smith and Morton 2001, 2006). In public services this has led to a paradoxical position (Roper et al 2007): being strengthened by national-level initiatives (equality, job harmonisation) while being more marginalised by local initiatives (especially outsourcing).

Overall, Ackroyd (1995) and Bach (1999) have questioned the stability and cohesiveness of the reforms in the United Kingdom; but the cult of the private sector, and of the entrepreneurial and the political belief in managerialism are factors that link the post-1979 Thatcher and Major Conservative governments with the post-1997 Blair and Brown Labour governments.

CONTINUITIES AND CHANGE IN THE IR ENVIRONMENT

Irrespective of these developments the IR system has managed to exert a considerable influence on the management of human resources in the public sector. While membership of unions in the public sector has fallen from 80% in 1989 to just over half by 2005 (Cunningham and James 2007), unions play a considerable role in terms of bargaining, the establishment of conditions of employment through various bodies and in the day-to-day representation of workers when compared with the private sector. Union recognition remains ubiquitous in the public sector, unlike other sectors.

The challenges to the system of joint regulation and trade union roles have come in the form of new management and organisational pressures outlined above. In terms of changes to IR systems, two particular developments are notable that have placed further burdens on the pattern of worker representation and activism. There has been a tendency to use pay review bodies in the setting of pay in various sectors within public services. While bargaining remains the dominant pattern in terms of establishing agreements, these bodies develop advice and recommendations on pay and various related issues – they use a range of experts and representatives from the organisation and workers represented. They are subject to influence and bargaining dynamics but present themselves as independent and expert-based review bodies. They have established themselves steadily since the early 1980s and can be at odds with the logic of collective bargaining by providing a range of 'independent' recommendations that can influence the conduct of collective bargaining. They cover approximately a quarter of public service employees (ONS 2005). Secondly, there has been a steady decentralisation of bargaining in terms of the use of performance-related pay and attention to local issues around local consultative committees in some cases, which take the form of bargaining relations at times. These begin to erode the co-ordination of bargaining and the manner in which it is effectively supported by union structures. It also places new and detailed pressures on local management as they take on more of the regulation of employment relations.

Yet, regardless of these developments in relation to regulation and collectivism, broadly defined, trade unions continue to exert a range of pressures on the system of public sector management. Firstly, the bargaining function and role remains largely intact and unions continue to work through the formal arenas of bargaining, the informal lobbying of governments and the development of campaigns and marketing campaigns to further their cause. In the case of teachers, the National Union of Teachers prepares its bargaining campaigns with the development of studies and materials on the case for increasing pay and on the changing conditions of teachers in relation to such issues as workloads. UNISON, as a leading union for a range of public services, has developed a range of campaign materials and studies to shore up the arguments on various issues. It has developed a series of business information systems that collate agreements within public sector employers such as local councils and NHS trusts that allow it to evaluate and monitor developments. Secondly, much of this activity in terms of campaigning and negotiations is focused on a whole new range of individually oriented worker issues such as absenteeism (Perrett et al 2007), bullying (Beale 2005) and racism (Corby 2007), for example. Unions are addressing a whole new range of 'individual' issues emerging from greater workloads, new forms of management control and greater uncertainty at work. Hence, union engagement on individual grievances against management, management-initiated disciplinary hearings and legal cases through employment tribunals are increasing and forming a vital part of their work. This has prompted some to suggest that a much stronger 'workplace-based' orientation for unions would be much more productive for them than their often disembodied presence at national level. Trade unions are increasingly engaging with the new dimensions of IR. Thirdly, while there is a degree of 'institutional stability' regardless of the limits of their 'regulatory reach', according to Cunningham and James (2007), in terms of their organisational and broader character and identity, trade unions in the public sector have reflected the new politics of workplace change. Questions of equality, health and safety, and fairness are more central and integral to their work. These themes are located within a strong public service ethic and a greater shift (in broad terms) to the left of the political spectrum in the form of a new leadership (the so-called 'awkward squad' (Smith 2003)). This is followed by the seemingly significant, but in practice little-acted-upon, 'Warwick Agreement' between the Labour government and unions in 2005 (Bewley 2006). This means that the notion of a more commercialised and business-oriented public sector environment in terms of HRM and IR needs to be approached and viewed with an element of caution. What we see instead is a new range of issues and challenges within the public sector.

MANAGEMENT STRATEGIES AND CHANGE IN A FRAGMENTED ENVIRONMENT

Faced with these general dynamics the role of management has changed within the public sector. Not least, there are greater calls for its professionalisation and development, given a more fragmented and commercialised operational environment on the one hand and continuing regulatory dynamics through bargaining and unions on the other. Management has to cope with increasing formalisation and controls from central government, which require greater transparency. These pressures do not necessarily move public sector HRM to a private sector model, but create a curious hybrid and set of dual arrangements similar to what are understood to be the case in the unionised parts of the private sector, except that in the public sector case the political contingencies are greater.

HRM PRACTICES

It is acknowledged that the public sector has seen the development of high-commitment approaches to HRM. Gould-Williams (2004, p67) has argued that the evidence suggests that 'public managers have been using a form of "high commitment" management with staff training, "model" working practices and job security regarded as the norm..., based on normative theories of HRM, [and that] these practices should lead to highly committed and motivated workers'. However, attempts to imitate private sector practice have been described as limited, piecemeal, opportunist and ad hoc (Bach and Winchester 2003; Farnham and Giles 1996; Lupton and Shaw 2001). According to Oswick and Grant (1996) such attempts are simply a 'knee-jerk' response to financial constraints. Gould-Williams' own research proved slightly more positive, seeing various new practices as being important to a better climate of HRM, such as teamworking. However, the core thrust of his work and research suggests that the engagement with the model of high commitment-practices lacked a systematic and strategic integration.

HRM AND PERFORMANCE

These types of practices are steered and introduced in context where one can see twin pressures for change that do not necessarily push in a uniform direction. On the one hand, there is the general push to enhance control and management prerogative. A central part of the development of management strategy has been its reliance on control and measurement (Martínez Lucio and MacKenzie 1999). This has been a feature that tries to refocus worker behaviour onto particular market-facing and customer-facing tasks, which in turn reinforce a more numeric and quantifiable view of work. Yet such developments, along with new private–public partnerships, lead to a more instrumental worker view (Grimshaw and Roper 2007). The fascination with measurement through customer satisfaction surveys, unit cost budgeting and throughput operational measures aims to provide organisations with the information required to reprofile staff and their activity and manage their relations with suppliers and their respective staff. Yet this more directed system of performance measurement since the 1990s has emerged through the development of a range of audits and political levels of control. As Brignall and Modell (2000) have shown, there are a range of agents involved in the question of performance measurement: professional groups within the provider organisation focus on innovation and quality; purchasers focus on quality, resource utilisation and competitiveness; funding bodies focus on financial results and resource. Under the 1997–2010 Labour Government's audits of local government, for example, there has been an increasing focus on a range of management and organisational activities, including HRM activity and employee roles. Yet managing performance measurement has become a major bureaucratic challenge for middle- and lower-level management in the public sector and has seen a significant expansion in the remit and power of the range of regulatory bodies overseeing the activities of public service (the Audit Commission, OFSTED and the QAA among others). In the university sector, managing central and local performance management systems is a major bureaucratic task that involves real as well as knowledge capital. This creates a set of training initiatives linked to this bureaucratic exercise that highlights a need to constantly manage the measurements and explain them.

HRM AND COMMUNICATION

This dimension of management has been paralleled by the emergence of a new employee communication paradigm in the public sector that has in part facilitated the move to the management of performance but at the same time created new tensions and challenges. The use of new forms of performance management and measurement in the form of emails, circulars, briefings and general internal marketing materials on a range of developments has meant that we are seeing a new management of direct communication. This has in part been spurred on by the ease of communication facilitated by information and communication technology. As in the manner in which the move to using and manipulating customer interest creates a new set of bureaucracies in the public sector focused on this role, so does the move to continuous and focused communication create its own management function and costs. This is now one of the dominant features of current management roles, and in the public sector it is exacerbated by the amount and regularity of performance measurement. Managing such direct forms of communication and more direct forms of employee involvement and participation (EIP) is a challenge. Grey (2009), in a study of a local college, noted how the desire for greater EIP led to the ongoing development of different approaches that varied from a 'Dragons' Den' approach to more traditional suggestion schemes. This led to a need to be constantly innovative with regard to EIP in relation to flagging and overwhelmed employee interest and concerns.

HRM AND THE BYPASSING OF REGULATION

Balancing performance measurement and new forms of direct communication in the context of continuing collective bargaining and union arrangements gives rise to a range of strategies in the face of the latter. These vary from circumvention to inclusion. The strategy of management at various levels can involve a complex set of 'games' involving working around the rules and regulations of employment established through collective processes. Within universities, the fast-tracking of particular staff in terms of promotion, quickly recruiting staff without consultation, using performance payment systems to dismiss staff, and the increasing use of external advisers normally from business to legitimate commercialisation is normally one of the ways different channels and relations are established without union involvement and even knowledge. This is visible in the way line management deploys staff, and, for some, it shows a new form of assertive or aggressive management that can test and undermine the fabric of IR and collective agreements. In the case of the Royal Mail, this has been seen to be a major cause of management bullying (Beale 2005), where the speeding-up of decision-making or the forcing through of decisions in the realisation that trade unions and workers may not be able to impede them or force discussion on them is becoming a major issue in the public sector, or in health as has been identified by Lewis and Gunn (2007). Hoel and Beale (2006) argue that this is systemic rather than individualised.

HRM AND THE RENEWAL OF COLLECTIVE PARTICIPATION?

Irrespective of such developments, we see the politics of circumventing regulation – dual arrangement and game-playing – still having to confront the reality of collectivist processes. Within the public sector, there has been a major drive to support the need for specific and fast decisions by trying to construct new forms of partnership arrangements and flexible joint decision-making. The work of Upchurch et al (2008) on the remaking of consultation within the public sector suggests that it is likely to be linked to an attempt to limit union opposition and engagement on a range of issues, thus incorporating them into a new managerial agenda. Throughout the NHS, partnership arrangements have been supported by government with the assistance of ACAS, which has tried to facilitate new forums and more flexible dialogue between management and unions on a range of issues such as staff rosters and deployment (Stuart and Martínez Lucio 2008). In local government, employers have used such arrangements to develop new forms of grievance procedures and mentoring mechanisms, for example, to dissolve conflict (Martínez Lucio and Stuart 2007). Hence we see that in the realm of consultation there are initiatives to support changes in terms of work and the regulation of work. This represents an attempt to remould aspects of collective IR in relation to the new challenges facing the public sector. However, while there are risks that unions may be steered away from an independent position, there are also problems due to the resources and sustainability issues related to these new forms of participation. In fact, one could argue that with the high turnover of management and union staff, along with the complexity and resources required by such partnership processes, it is a major effort to sustain such developments and trust-based systems, especially in a context where public sector organisations are increasingly fragmented and decentralised (Martínez Lucio and Stuart 2007). The challenge of recalling agreements, sustaining informal relations between union representatives and managers, and seeing through long-term projects of change in HRM is undermined by this greater volatility and fragmentation. Some maintain that the public sector retains many of its virtues as a good employer, yet the pressures on the system of management and regulation make the organisational monitoring and support of fairness at work a considerable organisational task.

HRM AND LEADERSHIP SOLUTIONS TO PARADOXES

It is for this reason that we have seen central government try to resolve these challenges by focusing on management development and in particular leadership development. The focus on the social, communication and strategic features of managers in the public sector – head teachers, department heads in universities, local social service centre managers and others – means that the solutions to many of the tensions outlined above are viewed in terms of improving management competency. This has led to a variety of training schemes of variable quality. These aim to develop the general management skills of individuals but also provide an ideological dimension in terms of their perspective and market orientation. The presence of such leadership courses aims to create a more direct, durable and innovative set of leaders. However, much of this is contested owing to the reliance on North American and commercialised views of management, which have more to do with 'evangelical' visions – the idea of unfettered and less restrained management. This is arguably inappropriate for successfully managing a workforce consisting of a high proportion of workers who consider themselves to be autonomous professionals (Lawler 2009). Such developments are an indication of the political desire to create a new hierarchy within the public sector capable of managing the tensions of the new imperatives and developments of change in the face of a continuing public service and collective ethos at the level of the customer and worker. Research indicates that the link between innovation and leadership requires a series of sophisticated HRM approaches based on recognition, staff consultation, an emphasis on autonomy, and supporting local and 'bottom–up' approaches (Borins 2002). Leadership is therefore more closely linked to HRM and people management for innovation to occur, and this raises issues of how, in the UK, leadership is viewed and used more for political purposes than genuinely participative ones. In the UK public sector there remains 'a privileging of masculine behaviours and norm as the basis for defining effective leadership' (Ford 2006, p97). Therefore a challenge in HRM terms is how such disruptive views of leadership will fit with a more regulated and socially oriented public sector. The remit and form of leadership is a salient issue in the public sector (Terry 1998), as government increasingly views its role as essential in bypassing 'traditional' cultures. Yet this will give rise to new issues and tensions, given what it is that the public sector does and how it is regulated in terms of employment and service delivery.

CONCLUSION

There is a need to understand the public sector as consisting of a combination of different characteristics. On the one hand, it still provides universal public services to one extent or another and it also consists of a collective dimension in terms of its IR. On the other, it is subject to change in terms of its structure through outsourcing and decentralisation around cost units, and a greater attention to performance management in part due to the risks of this fragmentation. HR managers, therefore, face an environment that brings together competing challenges and that gives rise to new forms of tensions. The public sector is also a high-profile set of services that have great impact in media terms. The attempt to recreate collective participation and dialogue around these new organisational pressures while maintaining the legacy of being a fair employer creates a particular environment for public sector workers, their representatives and their managers.

The traditional way management is developed and supported is questioned. In large part the problem is increasingly one of an under-resourced HRM function and constituency having to engage directly with operational imperatives and questions of delivery. Governments have increasingly stood on the sidelines, alongside the customer, setting objectives and expectations as if it was not integral to the chain of command. The current challenge is one of a new populism within governments as they align themselves with students, patients and others in their desire for more and better services – something that emerged in the 1980s (Hall 1988) – while downplaying their role in determining the resource frameworks for public services.

In the face of this, the challenge of the 2010s is going to be how a more fragmented public service context can actually link unions, workers and local managers together in a proactive dialogue around employment and delivery issues. How this is supported by national regulations on such issues and national resources will be another question. The HRM function is, therefore, unlikely to look like that of the private sector beyond a symbolic adoption of the gestures and language of the latter. It will remain subject to political factors, social pressures, the daunting media hysteria and a greater concern for fairness and equality at work. One suspects that participation will continue to be a centre of attention and the capacities of managers and trade unionists a focus for development programmes, but there are limits to these in the face of external political realities.

HRM IN THE MEDIA

CRITICAL REFLECTIONS

In relation to the first question, HR managers in this situation are in a difficult dilemma. On the one hand, there would seem to be a professional duty to advise on strategic decisions regarding appropriate staffing levels. On the other hand, HR has established its position, over recent decades, to emphasise that the modern HR professional should be a 'strategic business partner' and involved at senior level. There is, then, a tension. Should HR have acted as an independent 'critical friend' and advised senior management on appropriate staffing levels – the broader public interest or should its role be confined to advising senior management on how to achieve whatever staffing policy they wish to pursue?

However, in relation to the second question, HR may well not have had the capacity to advise on such issues. Other trends in HR best practice have involved the HR function stepping away from day-to-day decisions relating to departmental issues in favour of devolving such decisions to those managers who run the service directly.

In relation to the third question, it is unclear what unions were doing on this issue, although the investigation report did refer to widely held views from staff of the problems of understaffing. This is not a straightforward issue for unions either. The primary role of unions with management is to negotiate on the interests of their members. It is not immediately obvious how a union – beyond protesting at a principle – could mobilise a mandate on a lack of staff, unless it related directly to the effects of work intensification of the remaining staff coping with the understaffing problem.

EXPLORE FURTHER

DIBBEN, P., JAMES, P., ROPER, I. and WOOD, G. (2007) *Modernising work in public services: redefining roles and relationships in Britain's changing workplace.* Basingstoke: Palgrave.

A number of chapters in this book explore the broad context of employment relations in public services as they were during the New Labour period.

BEATTIE, R. and OSBORNE, S. (eds) (2008) *Human resource management in the public sector.* London: Routledge.

Coverage of some fundamental public sector HR issues, plus chapters dedicated to particular public service areas.

FLYNN, N. (2007) *Public sector management.* 5th ed. London: Sage.

Good overview of all major public sector management change initiatives underpinning HR practice.

LEGRAND, J. (2005) *Motivation, agency and public policy: of knights and knaves.* Oxford: Oxford University Press.

This explains the rationale for much of the reform agenda from one of the most influential proponents of change.

CHAPTER 22

HRM in the Not-for-profit Sector

Ian Cunningham

OVERVIEW

This chapter explores issues in the management of human resources in the UK voluntary sector. It focuses its analysis on one particular subsector of the voluntary sector, that is, its largest employer of paid labour, the part of its workforce responsible for delivering personal social services to vulnerable groups. It highlights the key role the state increasingly plays in shaping and determining employment policies within voluntary organisations. Moreover, it highlights how this state influence, although bringing real benefits, such as employment growth, the spread of good employment policies and practices and the accreditation of the workforce, is leading to tensions in the voluntary sector employment relationship. These tensions are caused by intensifying resource constraints imposed by central and local governments leading to problems funding workforce accreditation, the undermining of pay and conditions and an intensification of work. Moreover, recent developments such as increased retendering of services provided by the sector and the personalisation agenda in care promise to make these resource constraints more pronounced. It concludes that, combined, these pressures threaten one of the key characteristics of the sector, the high commitment of its workforce.

LEARNING OBJECTIVES

Reading this chapter will enable the reader to:

- critically explore what is meant by the not-for-profit (herein called the voluntary) sector, its activities and size, and its increasing role in providing services to vulnerable groups in society

- critically evaluate how the sector's relationship with the state helps shape employment outcomes in voluntary organisations

- critically analyse the positive outcomes from this relationship, such as employment growth, the introduction of good HR practice and accreditation of the workforce

- critically explore tensions arising from this relationship that impact on HR policies, such as difficulties in meeting accreditation standards, recruitment problems, downward pressures on pay and conditions and industrial relations problems.

HRM IN THE MEDIA

'VOLUNTARY ORGANISATION FACING VOTE FOR STRIKE ACTION OVER PAY'

In 2007, a large voluntary organisation delivering services to a range of vulnerable adults and children in Scotland faced a vote for strike action over pay, in which union members voted two to one in favour. The dispute was over a management pay offer to staff of 2.5% and efforts by the union to target rises on the lowest-paid staff members. The union wanted a 3.4% rise in line with local authorities. The strike action is highly unusual in a sector noted for its commitment to the care of vulnerable people such as the elderly and those with disabilities, and the first in this organisation's history. The union targeted this organisation as part of a wider campaign to improve pay in the sector and ensure that wages for voluntary sector workers were broadly comparable to those in the public sector. Further talks failed to resolve the dispute, with the employer citing income from local authority funding falling short of that needed to pay the increase the union demanded. A number of services for vulnerable adults and young people were affected by the strike (Tinning 2010).

Questions

1 What particular aspects of this case study make it different from other similar cases in the private sector?

2 What options can management consider to reduce vulnerability of their organisation to financial pressures from external funders?

3 How can the specific pay deal be resolved?

INTRODUCTION

This chapter explores key issues in the management of human resources in the UK voluntary sector. Compared with private and public sector organisations, the study of HR in voluntary organisations remains in its infancy. This is surprising given its workforce totals over 600,000 paid employees and relies on the contributions of millions of volunteers (National Council for Voluntary Organisations (NCVO) 2007). The chapter focuses on one particular subsector of the sector, that is, its largest employer of paid labour, organisations delivering personal social services to vulnerable groups, such as the elderly, disabled, homeless and disadvantaged young people.

The chapter highlights the key role the state plays in shaping employment within this sector. This influence stems from increasing levels of resource dependence by voluntary organisations on state funding as governments contract out social services to the sector. The chapter argues that state influence, although bringing benefits, such as employment growth, good employment policies and practices and the accreditation of the workforce, leads to tensions in voluntary sector employment relationships. These tensions are caused by intensifying resource constraints imposed by central and local government leading to problems in funding workforce accreditation, the undermining of pay and conditions and intensification of work. The chapter argues that these pressures threaten one of the key characteristics of the sector, the high commitment of its workforce.

Divided into five sections, the chapter begins by outlining what is meant by the voluntary sector and its diverse pattern of activity. The second section outlines the increasing degree of resource dependency by the sector on state funding. The third explores the impact of this dependency on workforce levels, HR policies and practices, training, pay and conditions, and industrial relations. The fourth then identifies several key issues that will increasingly shape the future development of HR in the sector – the personalisation of care and employee commitment. The final section presents concluding comments.

WHAT IS MEANT BY THE 'VOLUNTARY' SECTOR?

For students approaching the study of HR in the voluntary sector, they may feel confused when attempting to find a single sector definition. Indeed, there remains no internationally accepted definition of the sector, and in the UK this definitional issue is a continuing source of debate (see Vincent and Harrow 2005). For the purposes of this chapter, and in line with influential UK scholars (Kendall and Almond 1998), the *narrow definition* of the sector is utilised, that is, voluntary organisations are referred to as constitutionally independent and self-governing organisations that are non-profit-distributing and include a degree of voluntarism (Kendall and Knapp 1996; Kendall and Almond 1998). This covers a vast number of established national charities, with large budgets, and thousands of volunteers and paid staff.

To gain an understanding of the management of HR within the sector it is equally difficult as organisations differ in activity, size and income. Activities include the environment, education and training, religion, overseas aid, social services, health, advocacy, leisure activities and the protection of animals, but exclude schools, universities, trade unions and business associations (Vincent and Harrow 2005). Given such diverse activities, there is unlikely to be one common sector-wide style or approach to the management of HR.

The sector also has a unique workforce as it can involve the management of paid and unpaid staff. It is estimated that 21.4 million people in the UK volunteer at least once a year and 14.1 million at least once a month – bringing value estimated at the equivalent of 1.2 million full-time UK workers, at a cost of approximately £27.5 billion (based on the national average wage), demonstrating the continuing role of volunteering in underpinning the sector's activities (NCVO 2007).

However, because of space limitations, this chapter focuses on issues surrounding the management of paid workers in that part of the voluntary sector that provides social services/social care to various vulnerable groups. This subsector represents the major source of paid employment among voluntary organisations and has, in recent years, been subject to increasing sector-level and academic scrutiny, which has expanded our knowledge concerning HR in voluntary organisations beyond traditional, anecdotal generalisations.

A TRADITIONAL VIEW OF HR IN THE VOLUNTARY SECTOR

Until recently, assessments of HR management in voluntary organisations presented a traditional unitary view characterised by relatively harmonious and reciprocal employer–employee relationships. This perspective identified a distinctive culture where paid employees and management shared values linked to the cause/mission of organisations. Consequently, it was presumed that employees were highly committed to their employer's cause, resulting, if necessary, in an acceptance of lower pay, less personal advancement and job insecurity (Paton and Cornforth 1992; Zimmeck 1998). For management, the perceived advantages from this high commitment were that it could be used to encourage employees to work longer hours, and go some way in meeting the gap between organisational missions that address the needs of the most vulnerable in society without adequate resources (Orlans 1992).

This unitary, reciprocal relationship was also seen to characterise the sector's approach to employee participation. Here, employee commitment and attachment to organisational missions led to an environment that allowed high involvement in decisions regarding work organisation and service delivery (Paton and Cornforth 1992). This harmonious employment relationship with employees benefiting from a participative culture was held partly accountable for the low level of unionisation in the sector. This is coupled with reports of management hostility to efforts by unions to organise (Ball 1992).

There is little or no evidence to accurately test whether the above scenario was an ideal or a reality. Recently, however, work has emerged that recognises that managing HR in voluntary organisations is more complex than this idealistic unitary view. In particular, there is growing recognition of how, in different ways, HR specialists in the sector have to introduce policies and practices that fit with the specific values and mission of voluntary organisations, but also co-ordinate these with organisational responses to diverse and contradictory external funding and regulatory constraints (Ridder and McCandless 2008), while balancing myriad work orientations among their staff. This chapter argues that this complex HR environment represents the reality of managing employment in voluntary organisations as governments of all political persuasions outsource public services to the sector.

THE CHANGING STATE: VOLUNTARY SECTOR RELATIONSHIP IN THE UK

Most Western industrialised economies have contracted out public services to voluntary organisations (Kendall 2003). In the UK, this began following the election of the Thatcher governments and the acceptance of 'New Right' critiques that the welfare state was poorly managed, unaccountable, professionally dominated and lacking client involvement due to an absence of market incentives and pressures (Walsh 1995; Osborne 1997). Successive Conservative governments, therefore, sought to create a mixed economy of welfare where local and health authorities changed from being monopoly providers of care to becoming the planners, commissioners and monitors of services contracted out to non-statutory providers in the private and voluntary sectors (Harris et al 2001).

This 'enabling' role for local and health authorities was further encouraged by successive Labour governments from 1997 to 2010. New Labour advanced arguments that voluntary organisations possessed attributes that made it desirable to accord them a greater role in delivering public services. These virtues included their greater closeness to service users, specialist skills, expertise and capacity for innovation and reduced cost (Taylor and Bassi 1998; Whelan 1999; Davies 2007).

Within this climate, public bodies have increasingly regulated voluntary organisations with which they had contracts by establishing precise, measurable and binding performance criteria and output controls in exchange for funding. Moreover, these resources from the state were also delivered to the sector using increasingly legalistic and enforceable contracts rather than grants. Commercial private sector practices also emerged as the preferred approach to management for the sector, with voluntary organisations compelled to demonstrate that they are 'business-like' in order to secure funding (Perri and Kendall 1997; Tonkiss and Passey 1999; Harris et al 2001). The origins of this greater scrutiny and managerialism came from the application of the principles of new public management (NPM), the underpinning philosophy of which was to encourage continuous increases in efficiency, professional management and a labour force disciplined to productivity in the provision of public services (Pollit 1995).

These changes have led to significant resource dependence by the sector on government funding. The NCVO's annual analysis (2007) shows the sector's income during 2006/07 standing at £33.2 billion, a 3.3% increase on the previous year. Income from statutory sources accounted for £12 billion, or one-third of the total. The state's contribution to sector income is linked to the aforementioned outsourcing of public services by central and local government, the highest proportion of which is received by voluntary social care organisations, totalling £4.2 billion (2006/07).

Despite this increasing income, much of this funding is insecure and has been based on one- or two-year contracts, rather than three-year funding as recommended in New Labour's Voluntary Sector Compact and its policy of best value. Available evidence suggests that, at best, the application of three-year contracts is not common and that funding insecurity persists (Cunningham 2008). It is now useful to turn to some of the implications for HR in voluntary organisations in this environment.

IMPLICATIONS FOR THE MANAGEMENT OF HR IN THE VOLUNTARY SECTOR

WORKFORCE TRENDS

HR practitioners have overseen significant employment growth in voluntary organisations as state funding has increased. In 2004, the UK voluntary sector workforce stood at 608,000 (approximately 488,000 full-time equivalents), or 2.2% of the total UK workforce, compared with 408,000 employees in 1995. The majority of employees in the sector are situated in larger organisations that are more likely to secure government funding, with women accounting for over two-thirds of the workforce (415,000), half of whom are part-timers (Wainwright et al 2006; Wilding et al 2004).

Social care has seen a significant employment growth over this period. In 2004 social work accounted for over half of the UK voluntary sector workforce (51.6%), or 313,000 employees. This has increased steadily, with a rise of around 110,000 from 1995 to 2004 (Wainwright et al 2006). More recent figures show that between 1997 and 2006 there was a significant rise in the number of voluntary sector workers employed in social work activities, rising from 222,000 to 350,000, an increase of 58%, reflecting the transfer of social care services from the public sector (NCVO 2007).

The character of HR policies to manage this growing and diverse workforce in social services will be to a significant degree determined by the type of relationship voluntary organisations have with funders. Research from private organisations reveals how commissioning organisations in supply chain/ contractual relations do, in reality, directly or indirectly intervene to shape employment policies of organisations with which they have contractual relations (Hunter et al 1996; Rubery et al 2002; Truss 2004). These outcomes, however, depend on the nature of the relationship, that is, 'obligational' or 'arm's length'. Under obligational contracts, because of synergy and interdependence between the parties, positive consequences for employment policies in supplier organisations emerge. In contrast, under arm's-length contracts, the relationship between the parties is distant, short term and cost-based, implying far from positive outcomes for employees in supplier organisations (Sako 1992).

The same literature, however, also acknowledges the complexity of contractual relationships (see Marchington et al 2005; Bresnan 1996; Hunter et al 1996). Multiple outcomes are shaped by management in supplier organisations exercising varying levels of strategic choice with their external environment (Child 1972). Suppliers establish diverse relations with a variety of purchasers characterised by varying degrees of dependency and autonomy (Bresnan 1996; Hunter et al 1996). Here, the likelihood is that there will be differing outcomes regarding HRM policy among supplier organisations that reflect multiple forms of contracts along an obligational–arm's-length continuum, shifting according to changes in power relations between purchasers and providers (Truss 2004).

HR IN THE VOLUNTARY SECTOR: TAKING THE HIGH OR LOW ROAD?

In attempting to understand how these interorganisational dynamics of the state–voluntary sector relationship shape the roles and responsibilities of HR practitioners, Legge (2007) presents useful scenarios that utilise the aforementioned obligational–arm's-length continuum (Sako 1992). Under obligational contracts, positive roles such as facilitating employee secondments across organisational boundaries, performance management and career development, the sustaining of trust among the workforce are anticipated for HR practitioners. Moreover, the reduced emphasis on cost between the parties implies less external pressure on wages and conditions, as in examples of exploitative supply chain relations. Consequently HR can potentially adopt a role akin to 'employee champion', maintaining or improving working conditions (Legge 2007) .

Under arm's-length contracts, purchasers/customers can dictate HR policies and practices. Moreover, if resources are tight, customers can force HR specialists in supplier organisations to implement detrimental changes to pay structures, undermining efforts to maintain high commitment among staff. This leads to industrial relations problems as control over pay is taken out of the employer's hands despite agreements with unions (Marchington et al 2005). Within this scenario, the HR function becomes marginalised and struggles to manage and resolve such tensions.

In applying these principles to the voluntary sector where organisations have a strong funding relationship with state agencies, HR practitioners will operate across a spectrum of 'high' and 'low' road employment strategies in an effort to co-ordinate organisational responses to diverse and contradictory external funding and regulatory constraints and relationships (Ridder and McCandless 2008), while at the same time attempting to exercise degrees of strategic freedom from the influence of funding bodies (Johnson et al, 1998; Brandl and Guttel 2007). Moreover, recognition has to be given to how these external factors will interact with internal characteristics of voluntary organisations to shape the HR function and its policies, such as the need to retain high employee commitment.

At this juncture it is useful to review available evidence of the trajectory of HR policies in voluntary organisations within this complex environment. In doing so, the next section looks at the areas of HR policies and practices, including recruitment and workforce development, pay and conditions, and industrial relations.

HR POLICIES AND PRACTICES

In exploring the impact of the state–voluntary sector relationship on HR policies and practices, the state is a key source of *coercive* isomorphic pressure responsible for ensuring conformity and similarity in management practices across organisations through rules, processes and resources (Meyer and Rowan 1977). *Coercive isomorphism* (DiMaggio and Powell 1983), involves the state, through force and persuasion, imposing structures, working practices and rules on organisations. The voluntary sector is vulnerable to coercive isomorphic pressure because of its need to attain legitimacy in the eyes of the state to maintain funding (Osborne 1998).

Recent research presents a positive picture of how this isomorphic influence shapes modern people management in the sector (Parry et al 2005). With regard to recruitment it has been found that voluntary organisations now comply with the statutory requirements for criminal disclosure among applicants in order to protect vulnerable clients from potential abuse. Similarly, isomorphic pressure has led to policies such as discipline and grievance, health and safety, and equality policies within the sector being brought up to the standard of those common in public organisations. This process of upgrading policies and procedures was seen as, again, a way to secure legitimacy for voluntary organisations in the eyes of funders (Cunningham 2008).

Another study examined the state's influence on HRM policies in the sector through exploring the implementation of government quality marks such as Investors in People. This research illustrated how isomorphic pressure led to voluntary organisations investing resources to reach the standards expected of such quality marks and revealed a deep integration of the values of such awards into their training practices and HR policies (Paton and Foot 2000).

Further analysis of training within the sector highlights the state's influence. Care workers across public, private and voluntary organisations are required to undertake tasks of complexity, involving high levels of sensitivity, interpersonal skills and flexibility, mixed with a wider range of personal care functions and the ability to apply medical procedures. In recent years the UK government has sought to extend workforce accreditation to ensure that the care workforce possesses such skills. As a consequence, new care standards and specific requirements for workforce accreditation through NVQ/SVQ qualifications have been placed on all care providers. These requirements placed specific responsibilities on voluntary sector organisations to have 50% of their workforce trained to NVQ 2 and SVQ 2 standards by 2005, and an expectancy that all managers of registered homes should be qualified to NVQ/SVQ 4 standard (Cunningham 2008).

However, evidence suggests that the difficult financial environment faced by the sector has led to problems for HR practitioners in achieving these targets, through the poaching of qualified staff (Cunningham 2008). Many voluntary organisations have also faced severe recruitment problems, because the sector is perceived to be an unattractive place to work with uncompetitive pay that can be more than matched by retail employers, but without the associated stress of caring for individuals with challenging behaviour (Nickson et al 2008; Wilding et al 2004).

Funders also consistently fail to pass on the necessary finance to resource training in the sector. The Scottish Social Services Council (SSSC) reports how sector employers have access to far lower sums of money for training than local authority counterparts (SSSC 2008). Another study has found that among major voluntary sector providers in Scotland, 64% of the workforce are neither fully nor partially qualified to the required standards of the SSSC (Community Care Providers Scotland 2007).

PAY AND WORKING CONDITIONS

Prior to the quasi-market, pay scales in voluntary organisations were in many cases aligned to local authority terms and conditions (Ball 1992). This began to unravel during the 1979–1997 Conservative era as voluntary organisations came under pressure from government calls for 'efficiency savings', and 'value for money' (Cunningham 2001; Knapp et al 2001). Ford et al (1998) found that in comparison with care workers in local authorities and the private sector, employees in voluntary organisations had the widest range of pay in the community care sector, with evidence of comparability only for those staff in specialist care roles. Other studies revealed pay gaps between the private and public sectors of around 20%, with a gap in London of up to 25% (Remuneration Economics 2002; Incomes Data Services (IDS) 2001; 2002). Pay rises also consistently fell behind that of public sector increases (Barnard et al 2004; Shah 2004), with voluntary organisations less likely to pay their staff higher rates of pay for skill acquisition (IDS 2005).

Other studies have pointed towards the influence of statutory regulation of pay, with the National Minimum Wage acting as a floor for the lowest starting rates in social care generally, which would include the voluntary sector (IDS 2007). There remains, however, a possibility that the pay gap will remain in comparison with other sectors given voluntary organisations have less capacity to award bonus schemes or London weighting (Remuneration Economics 2006). Moreover, it is worth highlighting how average weekly earnings in the Scottish voluntary sector are 13% lower than in the private sector, and have fallen even further behind in comparison with those in the public sector (20%) (Shah 2004).

Research exploring the implications of outsourcing has highlighted how 'arm's-length' contracts are prevalent and are exerting downward pressure on terms and conditions of employment in voluntary organisations. A study of 58 large organisations revealed how approximately three-quarters reported how pay was below that of local authorities (Barnard et al 2004). A study of 24 voluntary organisations revealed how many had moved away from public sector pay comparability, and among those that retained the link, pressure remained on this and other aspects of their reward package. To further control costs, management intensified work through altering skill mixes so that lowest grade front-line workers were given more responsibilities, with fewer higher paid workers recruited (Cunningham 2008). In addition, cuts and reconfigurations to specific government funding schemes, such as Supporting People, have led to organisations implementing pay freezes and recruiting new staff on inferior terms and conditions (Cunningham and James 2007).

Additional pressures on the sector's pay include those arising from the application of European Union procurement legislation, specifically the Public Contracts Regulations 2006, introduced as a consequence of the Public Contracts Directive (2004/18/EC). Voluntary organisations subjected to retendering under this directive by local authorities have had to adopt more 'business-like', competitive cultures; experienced a breakdown in previously co-operative relationships with other sector providers and funders; lost income and staff when losing retenders; employed workers on multiple terms and conditions of employment when winning retenders; imposed further cuts in terms and conditions to achieve competitiveness; and experienced problems with demotivated staff as a consequence of heightened perceptions of insecurity (Cunningham and Nickson 2009).

We cannot assume, however, that all voluntary organisations suffer financial pressures from the state to the same degree, nor that they all take an increasingly 'low road' approach to HR. Much depends on the type of relationship with local authorities, that is, obligational or arm's-length (Sako 1992). Indeed, one study indicates how some voluntary organisations deploy a series of methods to increase their ability to exercise strategic choice and offset financial pressure. Methods include organisations positioning themselves as part of a group of a few select 'approved providers' in niche services. Others offset shortages in funding in one area through subsidies from more generous contracts secured elsewhere. Larger voluntary organisations, because of their national profile, turn down 'arm's-length' contracts because of a surplus of work. A minority of organisations draw from their own resources (financial reserves) to give them a stronger voice in their relations with funders. Moreover, combining several of these strategies was likely to lead to voluntary organisations being able to protect their financial status and retain comparability with public sector terms and conditions (Cunningham 2008).

INDUSTRIAL RELATIONS IMPLICATIONS

The voluntary sector presents a promising but challenging environment for union growth. The Labour Force Survey highlighted how during the 1990s, membership had failed to keep pace with the rise in voluntary sector employment, so maintaining low levels of union density (Passey et al 2000). Latest estimates of density place it at around 25% (Unison 2006). There are, as yet, no reliable figures pertaining to recognition in the sector, so information is patchy. Contracting out means that people entering from the public sector involuntarily from local authorities will also transfer their union membership and recognition into the sector. Unison has reported how a substantial proportion of its membership comes from this source, especially from transfers of housing stock from local authorities (Unison 2006).

The growth of outsourcing has also led to an increase in campaigns for and recognition of trade unions in voluntary organisations. This partly reflects a desire among some employers to have more sophisticated approaches to employee relations and communication as workforces grow as a consequence of taking on state contracts. Legislative measures such as the collective recognition procedures under the Employment Relations Act 1999 (Amended by Employment Act 2004) and the Information and Consultation measures have also directly and indirectly led to voluntary sector employers recognising unions for the first time (Cunningham 2000, 2008).

Despite some of these agreements being established under the heading of 'partnership', union recognition has not come without tensions for voluntary sector HR specialists. Union recognition drives have been based on employee concerns regarding their terms and conditions and job insecurity (Cunningham 2000; Simms 2003, 2007; Cunningham and James 2010). Among employers with long-established recognition agreements, previously stable collective bargaining arrangements have also been strained as decisions by purchasers threaten employee terms and conditions and, in response, unions have resisted, leading to pay disputes and industrial action. Where unions have had a weak or no presence, discontent has emerged through increases in employee turnover and absence (Simms 2003; Cunningham 2008).

It is, however, likely that the sector will continue to be a challenging environment for unionisation for the foreseeable future. Unions face a number of difficulties including organising a diverse and geographically spread workforce working unsocial hours; continued hostility and negative tactics from some employers; difficulties in recruiting sufficient union activists; a lack of tradition among the workforce of unionisation; and competition for internal union resources to devote to organising the sector (Simms 2007; Cunningham and James 2010).

LOOKING TO THE FUTURE

The final part of the chapter looks at two important future issues facing those managing HR in the voluntary sector – the personalisation agenda and sustaining commitment among the workforce.

IMPLICATIONS FROM THE PERSONALISATION AGENDA

Personalisation has been described as central to the future of social care. Its principles embody notions of self-determination by service users, rather than the service-based and prescriptive approach that has individuals as passive recipients of care. Service users are empowered to make their own choices about when, how and from whom they receive care. Personalisation is common to most developed European states, where it has often been implemented through allowing people to hold and spend their own budgets. In the UK this has been done through the mechanisms of means-tested 'direct payments', where service users are given control of their care budget by a local authority and pay the service provider direct for social care (Help the Aged 2008; Yeandle and Stiell 2007).

The other arm of the personalisation agenda in the UK is through 'individual budgets', introduced in 2003. Here, individuals are not compelled to be wholly responsible for managing their care, but can direct a local authority with regard to how to spend the budget allocated to them and which particular agency should provide it. Service users can also decide whether their budget is given to them in the form of cash, services or a mixture of both. Moreover, these budgets can be used to stream a series of separate funding packages rather than one specific fund, as under direct payments (Help the Aged 2008).

Voluntary sector involvement in providing personalised social services will have great significance for HR practitioners. For example, personalisation implies a programme of change that fundamentally alters recruitment and selection procedures so that advertised job roles individually cater for, and include in the selection process, each service user (Carr 2008; Social Care Institute for Excellence (SCIE) 2009).

Voluntary organisations will also need to ensure there is sufficient capacity within their workforce to deliver on the aspirations of the personalisation agenda and to identify the functions, skills and behaviours to meet these aspirations, so that staff training plans are shaped by the needs of service users (SCIE 2009). Estimates of the range of skills for HR to develop to facilitate personalisation include workers increasingly involved in roles that focus on prevention; dealing with multiple agencies; personal advocacy, counselling and risk assessment; and navigating service users to the type of services they require (Leadbetter and Lownsbrough 2005). Other studies highlight the need to develop multi-skilled workers at all levels to create 'hybrid roles' where they undertake tasks previously done by other professions concerning issues such as health, housing, leisure and employment. In addition, there is a need for agencies to enable workers to get their qualifications quickly to meet these challenges (Carr 2008).

There are, however, concerns with the personalisation agenda. Studies reveal that the use of direct payments is characterised by cost containment, with estimates of savings of 30–40% for local authorities that participate. This emphasis on cost containment, again, raises questions regarding whether there will be sufficient resources available to the sector to fund the further necessary workforce development (Yeandle and Steill 2007; Carr 2008). Indeed, in the current climate of dramatic cuts in public expenditure, an obvious fear from the drive to personalisation from funders will be that they are more concerned with the lure of budget savings rather than workforce development and improved services.

In this context, the implications for sector terms and conditions of employment are alarming (Help the Aged 2008). Voluntary organisations securing contracts through individual budgets may receive financial resources that are smaller than offered through conventional contracts. This means voluntary agencies, again constrained by what is affordable within the contract price set by public commissioners, perhaps will have to look at either drawing additional funds from their own reserves or fundraising to supplement worker pay or offer inferior employment packages to employees who are providing personalised services.

SUSTAINING HIGH COMMITMENT IN THE VOLUNTARY SECTOR

Once we understand the complex nature of worker orientations in the sector and how they differ from the aforementioned traditional view of the employment relationship, the threat to the stability of employee commitment is a real issue for HR practitioners in voluntary organisations. High commitment to a cause/mission is a central worker orientation in the sector, but one that is also influenced by career aspirations development, training, pay and conditions, and other more instrumental considerations (Ford et al 1998; Nickson et al 2008; Cunningham 2008).

The implication for HR practitioners is that reductions in terms and conditions due to cuts in funding could lead to significant employee discontent. Studies from overseas show how public sector funding cuts and declining terms and conditions lead to problems with employee morale (Singer and Yankey 1991; Mirvis 1992; Onyx and Maclean 1996; McMullen and Brisbois 2003; Saunders 2004; Baines 2004). Evidence from the UK voluntary sector confirms these trends as employees, in the face of continued pressure on living standards, and irrespective of their commitment to the organisation and service user, have been found to experience problems with morale and even quit (Cunningham 2008; Ford et al 1998). It is unsurprising, therefore, that analysis of employee turnover in the voluntary sector reveals figures averaging around 23%, which are higher than the public sector (12%) (Scottish Council for Voluntary Organisations 2004).

CONCLUSION

The growth of the voluntary sector and its role in the provision of public services makes its approach to HR an increasingly important area of study. The relationship with the state is key to understanding the management of HR in the voluntary sector. Our understanding of the nature of HR within the sector has advanced from that outlined in the traditional view of employment relations in voluntary organisations.

Although many of the changes to employment policies in the sector as a consequence of outsourcing from the state have been positive, this relationship ensures the sector is under-resourced; it struggles to meet workforce accreditation targets; and its pay and conditions are slipping behind that of the public sector. Employment relations in the sector to a large degree exhibit those most associated with 'arm's-length' contracting with public sector funding bodies, contradicting rhetoric by successive governments that advocate 'partnership' with voluntary organisations. Employees, in turn, struggle to retain their standard of living, suffering 'burnout' through work intensification, which challenges their commitment. Worker voice is also limited to non-unionised, informal participatory processes, or to unionised forums, where the prospect for the emergence of strong collective bargaining is constrained.

Financial pressures on the sector will persist, if not intensify, given the current climate of public sector expenditure retrenchment brought on by the 'credit crunch' and deficit reduction programmes by the new Conservative/Liberal Democrat Coalition Government. This raises fears regarding jobs and the future for employment policies in voluntary organisations. These fears are exacerbated by the influence of EU procurement regulations that intensify competition between voluntary organisations and an agenda promoting personalisation, which itself may fall victim to the call for cost savings. This presents an increasingly complex and challenging environment for practitioners to construct an HR climate that contributes to fulfilling voluntary sector missions and delivering on public service commitments, while at the same time sustaining employee morale. The chapter concludes by claiming that although one of the benefits of outsourcing public services to voluntary organisations is cost savings, governments of all political persuasions must be aware that goodwill and commitment among the voluntary sector workforce is not a bottomless well.

HRM IN THE MEDIA

CRITICAL REFLECTIONS

Relating to the first question, voluntary organisations are different from private sector organisations in that they do not produce marketable products or services. In addition, people who work in the voluntary sector are more likely to be motivated by a public service ethos, rather than a commercial one.

As far as the second question is concerned, an increasing number of voluntary organisations find themselves working on a contractual basis for public sector organisations with tight budgetary constraints. To resolve the issues in the opening case study, management may consider options designed to reduce the vulnerability of their organisation to financial pressures from external funders highlighted in the chapter. These include diversifying their funding to reduce resource dependence and developing expertise, a niche in services to build reputation and interdependence through obligational contracts with funders.

Regarding the third question, the specific pay deal was resolved by agreeing to a flat-rate increase for lower-paid staff and a review of their salary grading.

EXPLORE FURTHER

CUNNINGHAM, I. (2008) *Employment relations in the voluntary sector.* London: Routledge.

This book provides an in-depth exploration of state–voluntary sector relationship and impact on employment.

KENDALL, J. (2003) *The voluntary sector.* London: Routledge.

This book introduces key issues in the UK voluntary sector.

MARCHINGTON, M., GRIMSHAW, D., RUBERY, J. and WILMOTT, H. (2005) *Fragmenting work: blurring organisational boundaries and disordering hierarchies.* Oxford: Oxford University Press.

This book is a key source to understanding broader debates around interorganisational relationships and impact on employment.

NICKSON, D., WARHURST, C., DUTTON, E. and HURRELL, S. (2008) A job to believe in: recruitment in the Scottish voluntary sector. *Human Resource Management Journal.* Vol 18, No 1. pp20–35.

This journal article studies recruitment in the voluntary sector.

RIDDER, H.G. and MCCANDLESS, A. (2008) Influences on the architecture of human resource management in nonprofit organisations: an analytical framework. *Nonprofit and Voluntary Sector Quarterly.* Vol 20, No 10. pp1–18.

This journal article presents a recent effort to link HRM and voluntary sector literatures.

Students interested in this topic are also encouraged to visit the websites of the National Council for Voluntary Organisations (NCVO) and the Scottish Council for Voluntary Organisations (SCVO), as well as the websites of unions organising the sector, such as Unison and Unite.

PART FOUR

CONCLUSIONS

CHAPTER 23

Global Challenges for Development of Human Resources

Anil Verma and Qian He

The strange buoyancy of hominids is in us, a hopeful heritage of response to novel environmental dilemmas…. Our genetic blueprint enables our brains and societies to live creatively in an uncertain world. (Rick Potts 1996, p277)

INTRODUCTION

Constant change and growing complexity are two imperatives of the evolution of human civilisation. Strides in human ingenuity have allowed us to not only cope with new and complex problems that arise over time, but to also prosper as a *species*. Rick Potts, a scholar of evolutionary biology, suggests that this ability of humans to learn and adapt in response to environmental threats and opportunities is deeply embedded in our DNA. In this chapter, we draw attention to some key challenges facing the development of human resources globally. The ascendance of these issues is a direct result of two trends: *globalisation* and *knowledgisation* of our societies. *Knowledgisation*, to coin a term, refers to the trend of increasing emphasis on applying knowledge using one's judgement as opposed to repetitive application of a narrow range of skills that characterises mass production. Increasingly, the work we do in our own homes and workplaces affects the work of people in other countries, be it through trade, innovation or terrorism. New products, services and ideas are changing human life from the remotest jungle or desert to the slums of large cities.

The human resource challenge in the global knowledge-driven context is to develop our human resources in such a way that our collective ingenuity not only keeps pace with our problems but exceeds them. We cannot accomplish our goal to survive and prosper unless we develop every individual's capability to their potential. The current state of human resources in the world is characterised by missed human potential, great inequalities and lack of fairness. Some of these inequalities and unfairness can be attributed to historical developments but others are a result of the more recent trends in globalisation and knowledgisation. Inequality and unfairness are problems that need to be addressed if we have to outpace the growing complexity of problems. In this respect, the status quo is not an option for the world today. Ignoring these problems can reverse the march of civilisation by making most, if not all, of us worse off.

In this chapter we highlight several challenges and choices facing policy-makers in developing talent for a globalising, knowledge-driven world. From a human resource point of view, the biggest problem is the extreme poverty in which a large number of people live today. According to the International Labour Organization (ILO), nearly half the world's workers live on less than US$2 a day (ILO 2004a). Their lot can be improved in a sustainable way only by giving them access to better skills through education and training. Former US President Bill Clinton was fond of the saying, 'earn what you learn', an adage that is more valid in the global knowledge-driven economy than at any other time in the past. Extreme poverty in some areas, even as prosperity grows in other areas, leads to a host of problems. The Declaration of Philadelphia in 1944, an annexure to the ILO's Constitution, states, 'poverty anywhere constitutes a danger to prosperity everywhere'.

One major consequence of uneven prosperity is migration, both legal and illegal. Migration within national boundaries and across international borders has been given a boost by increasing integration of our national economies and societies. Immigration and emigration tend to increase diversity in national labour forces. The nature of growing diversity can vary by place and time. It can be race, ethnicity, language, gender, religion, age, physical ability, nationality, sexual orientation or a combination of these or other attributes. Even as diversity is increasing all across the globe, the legal and social standards for treating people with dignity and respect are rising everywhere as well. These challenges apply equally to internal migrants as well as to immigrants from another country. As a group, immigrants have a common identity but their make-up is anything but homogeneous. They can be legal immigrants based on skills, family connections or business purposes. Or, they can be illegal immigrants in search of economic opportunities. Moreover, internal conflicts, wars, natural disasters, intolerant regimes, and so on, often threaten life and liberty, forcing people to seek refuge elsewhere. All of this adds to the challenge of integrating these people into the workforce and into host societies. Given current trends, this will remain a key challenge for policy-makers to address in the foreseeable future.

As mentioned earlier, some of our current problems have historical origins but others emanate from the effects of globalisation and knowledgisation. Growth in informality in the labour market and the related growth in precarious employment are two such examples of human resource challenges. This trend is similar across the globe irrespective of whether one looks at developed or developing economies. While informality in and precariousness of employment are not new phenomena, their occurrence in the contemporary context is laden with implications for reconsidering human resource policy, both public and private. First, this trend is associated with growth in low-wage jobs, particularly in the private services sector. Second, these jobs are taken disproportionately by workers who are vulnerable already: women, immigrants, ethnic minorities, people with disabilities, and so on. Third, these workers remain beyond the ambit of union representation for a variety of reasons. Thus, a growing segment of the global workforce remains unprotected by either markets or by institutions, such as collective bargaining and trade unions. The challenge for HRM is to find ways to integrate this segment of the workforce into the mainstream of society and economy by offering them opportunities to develop their skills so that they can aspire to the same levels of economic security enjoyed by the mainstream. If a large segment of the workforce remains excluded from the benefits of globalisation, it will eventually lead to pressures to scale back global trade and investment. Any pull back from the free movement of capital and ideas across borders would crimp innovation and lead to fewer economic opportunities for the very same people who need better opportunities to develop their skills so that they may contribute to the global economy.

There are other challenges at the workplace and personal levels. While a full discussion of the range of challenges is beyond the scope of this chapter, two other issues are discussed here because they define the workplace context in which the global workforce must perform: work–life balance and lifelong learning. Both of these issues have acquired a new significance in the globalising economy.

Lifelong learning is an essential coping mechanism in a global economy that has shortened product half-cycles. Many technologies in use today would likely not be in use beyond this decade. The paradigm of lifelong learning provides a key methodology for human resource development in a rapidly changing world. Similarly, work–life balance is an essential ingredient for developing human resources for knowledge creation and innovation. Human resource policies of most organisations around the globe were developed in response to the needs of mass production, which is characterised by repetitive work. However, the need of the future is to develop a workforce for innovation and creativity. Work–life balance policies would be a key tool for organisations that move towards knowledge work and innovation.

Each of these challenges is elaborated upon and discussed in the rest of this chapter with the intent to challenge students and policy-makers alike to engage in a constructive debate that will lead to creative solutions. Nothing less than the future prosperity of all the citizens of the world depends on it.

INTERNATIONAL MOVEMENT OF LABOUR AND GROWING DIVERSITY

The United Nations Convention on the 'Protection of the Rights of All Migrant Workers and Members of Their Families' defines a migrant worker as a person who is engaged or has been engaged in a remunerated activity in a state of which he or she is not a national. But it can also be used to describe someone who migrates within a country, possibly their own, in order to pursue work (OHCHR 2010). For example, migrant workers from China's rural areas move to urban areas in search of work opportunities. The number of migrants within and across countries has grown rapidly since the 1970s. According to recent UN estimates,

Figure 23.1 Global migration problems

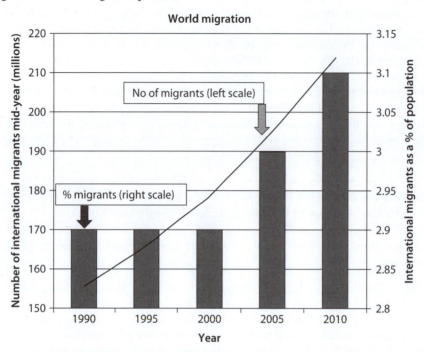

Note: Chart made by authors with data obtained from UNDP website, accessed 10 August 2010.

there were roughly 214 million migrant workers in 2010, up from 155 million in 1990, who had moved across national boundaries, or 3.1% (2% in 1990) of the global population (Figure 23.1). This represents an increase in the number of international immigrants by 38% in the last 20 years. These numbers do not include migrant workers within national boundaries, for which global estimates are harder to obtain. The size of this workforce worldwide is huge. According to official statistics, there were 120 million migrant workers (9% of the population) in China alone. China's urban migrants send home an estimated US$65.4 billion (Wang 2005).

Similarly, increases in inflow of immigrants as well as in the number of internal migrants can be observed in the EU. According to a recent report, migration has played a significant role in increasing the population within the EU (Vasileva 2009). Approximately 56% of the non-nationals living in the EU-27 member states have European citizenship; 37% are citizens of another EU member state and 19% are citizens of a non-EU country. Around 40% of the EU-27 foreigners come from countries outside Europe and most (75%) of the foreigners in the EU-27 live in Germany, Spain, the UK, France and Italy. At the same time, citizens of these countries are among the most numerous EU foreigners living in another member state.

Similar patterns can be seen in Asia and North America, where migrants (including refugees) as a share of the population were estimated at 29% and 23%

respectively (ILO 2004b).[1] The vast majority of these migrants, internationally or within national boundaries, end up staying in distant lands. Most do not return home even when conditions worsen. Evidence shows that under economic downturns, new outflows from some countries of origin have slowed down, but no mass returns of migrant workers have been observed (ILO 2010b). This suggests that the need to address their situation through specific and directed policy measures is necessary to ensure peace, progress and prosperity of both receiving and sending jurisdictions.

Although anti-immigrant sentiments are expressed frequently by receiving populations, the evidence suggests that migrant workers contribute positively to the growth and development of both home and host societies.

Receiving countries with full-employment policies need workers for meeting excess demand for labour that often arises from low rates of internal population growth. Immigration flows can meet general labour shortages and stimulate growth without inflation. While this is a positive outcome during periods of growth, immigration may cause higher unemployment among natives during periods of slower growth. Countries with highest levels of immigration are among the most successful economically: the US, Canada, Australia and the UK are good examples. Increasing diversity also leads to increasing social tensions. Immigrants who are not fully productive can be a burden on host societies since they extract more from public services and welfare payments when they first arrive than they contribute in terms of taxes and social security contributions. Migrants may also contribute to fragmentation of the working classes and segmentation of the labour market (ILO 2004b).

There are many benefits to origin countries from emigration. They receive remittances from migrant workers, which in many cases becomes a significant source of income and investment. Flows of remittances are a reliable and stable source of income that tend to fluctuate less with economic cycles. Migrant families and their communities are better off as their incomes rise with remittances. Migrants also contribute to trade by establishing stronger links between the source and destination countries. Returning migrant workers bring back new ideas, new ways of doing things and new networks with the outside world to enrich their home countries or regions. In some cases, emigration reduces population pressure on scarce land and jobs, although these effects are moderate. Of course, there is a social cost of emigration in terms of fractured family and community (ILO 2004b).

Emigration of more skilled workers has additional consequences for the sending country. Traditionally, people decide to emigrate if the receiving countries offer higher returns to their education. However, more recent evidence shows that people may decide to emigrate even if the returns to education in the receiving country are below those in the sending country (Brücker and Defoort 2009).

---

[1] Africa, Latin America and Caribbean, and Oceania had significantly lower shares of migrants in their population at 9%, 3% and 3% respectively (ILO 2004b).

In such cases, other factors may dominate the pure economic returns for the emigrant, for example quality of life, prospects for children's education and career, future potential for upgrading their own skills, and so on.

Moving to a labour market with potentially better opportunities offers some benefits but also other challenges at the individual level, as we shall now elaborate.

UNDEREMPLOYMENT

Migrants are less likely to find jobs commensurate with their education and experience: the bias that immigrants face in host labour markets may induce them to adopt some behaviours or signals to modify employers' beliefs. Some migrants would build up a personal reputation, exploit ethnic networks rooted in the hosting country, and attain higher educational levels. The immigrant worker generally needs to send a stronger signal about their skills and productivity compared with the native-born worker. Often this bias, perceived or real, leads the immigrant to accept jobs that require a much lower educational and skill level compared with what they possess (Mancinelli et al 2010). Migrant workers are generally over-represented in jobs with poor working conditions and/or in the informal economy (ILO 2010b).

LOWER EARNINGS

One robust research finding is that recent migrants earn less than their native-born counterparts in relation to their human capital endowments such as education and experience. These findings, consistent over time and across countries, have been reported in many countries including Canada, Australia, the US and the UK among others. Because recent migrants in some countries have relatively high levels of education, a number of explanations have been suggested for the earnings gap, such as lack of host-country-specific skills (ILO 2004b; Reitz 2007a, 2007b; Clark and Drinkwater 2008).

LOWER HUMAN CAPITAL ACCUMULATION

There are other groups of migrants who tend to have lower levels of human capital and hence predictably they are unlikely to do well in the receiving labour market. This is particularly true of rural migrants in China where earnings differences between urban residents and rural migrants can be attributed not so much to an exclusionary bias but to lower human capital endowments. Rural migrants tend to be younger, much less experienced and much less educated than urban residents (Démurger et al 2009).

Returning to the broad issue, international and domestic migration is occurring on a large scale and at times the problems arising from it may appear overwhelming. But these flows of human resources can be viewed also as opportunities for a globalising economy. The problems need to be addressed through targeted policies at various levels: international, regional, national, employer and workplace levels. A full discussion of these policy responses is beyond the scope of this chapter. However, it is important to outline the implications for human resource policies of governments and employers. In its report on migration, the ILO recommends that member states strengthen their laws to protect and recognise the important role of migration labour. Governments, employers and unions can work together in countries of origin and destination to improve international labour standards and apply them equally to all workers, including migrant labour (ILO 2004a).

PRECARIOUS WORK AND NON-STANDARD EMPLOYMENT

Precarious work often refers to a non-standard employment situation that is poorly paid, insecure, unprotected and cannot support a household. It differs from the norm of a full-time, full-year, permanent paid job through five categories of work status: *part-time* employment; *temporary* employment (including term-time or contract, seasonal, casual, temporary agency and all other jobs with a specific predetermined end date); own-account *self-employment*; *multiple job-holding* and *shift work*.

Gerry Rodgers (1989, p35) indentified four dimensions central to establishing whether a job is precarious: firstly, degree of certainty of continuing employment, where time horizons and risk of job loss are emphasised; secondly, control over the labour process – this dimension is linked to the presence or absence of a trade union and, hence, control over working conditions, wages and pace of work; thirdly, the degree of regulatory protection – that is, whether the worker has access to an equivalent level of regulatory protection through union representation or the law; finally, income level, a critical element since a given job may be secure in the sense that it is stable and long term but precarious in that the wage may still be insufficient for the worker to maintain themselves as well as dependants. Among these four dimensions, the first one has become more and more important under the circumstances of a global recession. For example, the Towers Watson's 2010 *Global Workforce Study* found that employees' desire for security trumps everything; mobility is at a decade-long low point, and many are sacrificing career growth for a secure job. Employees understand they are responsible for their long-term financial and physical health but they doubt their ability to take on this role.

Young employees, females, visible minorities and immigrants are more likely to be in precarious employment than those at the peak of their careers, males and natives. For example, in Canada, the share of employed women aged 15 to 24 with a full-time permanent job fell from 53% in 1989 to 35% in 2002; for young men, the percentage fell from 58% to 45%. During this period, participation in post-secondary education increased markedly among 15- to 24-year-olds (Cranford et al 2003). In the US, non-standard work makes up about one-third of the total labour force. In Australia, casual employees represent 27.6% of total employees (Campbell 2004). This rate is as high as 37% in Japan, and 40% to 50% in some EU countries (Broschak et al 2008).

The rapid increase in precarious work is being driven both by corporations and governments. From the corporate side, the popularity of precarious employment is associated with many benefits. First, it offers flexibility in the size of workforce to be maintained and/or types of skills required to deal with fluctuations in demand. Second, it allows an organisation to reduce costs by avoiding employment protection and benefits. Third, it brings expertise or knowledge that would be otherwise unavailable to the organisation. Lastly, it helps reduce the risk of hiring the wrong persons in full-time positions by allowing the organisation to observe their performance as non-standard workers and then using that information to effectively screen workers for permanent full-time jobs (Boyce et al 2007; Houseman 1997, 2001).

Its benefits notwithstanding, there are many disadvantages of holding a non-standard, precarious job. First, research suggests that precarious jobs are associated with worse health and safety conditions. Precarious workers are often exposed to strenuous and tiring positions, intense noise and repetitive movements, have less freedom to choose when to take personal leave and are seldom represented in health and safety committees. They are more likely to work extremely long or extremely short hours. There is also evidence that they have less information about their work environment and enjoy less job autonomy and control over schedules than workers on permanent contracts (Benach and Muntaner 2007; Bohle et al 2004). Further, precarious employment was found to be associated with deterioration in occupational health and safety (OHS) in terms of injury rates, disease risk, hazard exposures or worker (and manager) knowledge of OHS and regulatory responsibilities (Quinlan et al 2001). Second, pay is generally lower and benefits are limited in such jobs. Their pay rates were often below those of permanent workers who performed the same job, or even below minimum wage (Burgess et al 2005). Third, growing shares of non-standard workers may be unprotected or less protected either because they are excluded by law or de facto because they are less likely to meet contribution requirements or satisfy other relevant eligibility criteria (OECD 2009). Lastly, although some precarious jobs have been touted as a way to reconcile work and family duties, it is likely that the precarious nature of the job contributes to increased conflict and strain for families. These jobs come with higher levels of insecure employment and the attendant lack of predictability and control over their working schedules and income. Such insecurity would make it difficult to plan social and family activities, as well as to budget family expenditures and savings. For example, one study found that temporary employees are less likely to intend to have children in the future, to have relatively less spare time for their family and to experience a higher level of conflict with their partner. Furthermore, general life satisfaction and well-being was clearly lower and the perceived household income situation was worse. Health-related issues reported to arise from work–life conflict included sleep disturbance, fatigue and disrupted exercise and dietary regimes (Scherer 2009; Bohle et al 2004).

In terms of public policy, across the world national labour laws are being amended to better enable employers to create yet more precarious jobs at the expense of stable employment. For example, in 2006, the Australian Government introduced new labour laws that immediately plunged millions of workers into precarious employment by taking away their right to protection from unfair dismissal. The laws also encourage contract and temporary work.

It has been suggested that better access to skills training is needed and that government intervention is needed to improve access (MacDonald and Holm 2002). Some possible interventions could include: stronger provisions for study leave and income support to allow for the training while still at work, career development loans, learning credits or accounts. Other mandatory provisions that could benefit temporary workers are: equal rights regardless of employment status, policies to increase the portability of entitlements (such as sick leave, parental leave, study leave, long service leave and redundancy pay) through industry-wide bodies, socially responsible labour hire arrangements and requirements for employers to provide minimum and maximum work during a certain period (Connell and Burgess 2006).

Contrary to precarious employment is the concept of decent work, referring to work that is productive and delivers a fair income, security in the workplace and social protection for families, better prospects for personal development and social integration, freedom for people to express their concerns, organise and participate in the decisions that affect their lives and equality of opportunity and treatment for all women and men. So what we need is not only more jobs, but more, better jobs.

The ILO recommends a multipronged approach to decent work: promote and realise fundamental principles and rights at work; create greater opportunities for women and men to secure decent employment and income; enhance the coverage and effectiveness of social protection for all; and strengthen tripartism and social dialogue (ILO 2006).

WORK–LIFE BALANCE

The pace of globalisation and knowledgisation has had a huge impact at the individual level in terms of increased work demands that eventually leads to conflict between work and family. Although it is difficult to measure this conflict on a scale that could be generalised across the world, most attempts to quantify conflicts between work and family (or life in general) point to the trend of increasing demands at work. In knowledge industries, these demands are manifest in the long hours put in by managers and professionals. In lower-paid, lower-skill work these pressures are felt by workers who need to work the extra hours to increase their earnings. Very long hours at work lead predictably to greater stress, lower productivity, higher absenteeism and higher rates of injury and illness. But even if the hours are not very long people can suffer from stress if they are unable to find a balance between work and their personal lives. In this section, we draw attention to the important need to pursue human resource policies that can help people attain better work–life balance. We discuss two situations: one at the individual level – the example of young workers and their preference for work–life balance; and the other at the national level – the case of South Korea. Both of these situations illustrate the need to emphasise work–life balance in a global economy characterised by innovation and creativity.

There are several theories used to explain the interplay between work and life. *Spillover theory* asserts that the relationship between work life and family life can influence each other in a positive or negative way (Guest 2001). For instance, job stress at work may lead to an increase in the number of negative family interactions or result in the family needing to expend personal resources in helping the worker manage their stress (Zedeck and Mosier 1990). Another explanation comes from *segmentation theory*, which posits that work and family spheres are separable and that people can segment these two environments using differences in function, space and time. In this view, family life can be seen as a source of affectivity, intimacy and signification relationships, whereas work life is viewed as impersonal and competitive (Piotrkowski 1979; Zedeck and Mosier 1990).

Compensation theory of work and life postulates that where there is a void in one environment, the other environment will substitute (Guest 2001). It can be broken down into its component parts of *supplemental compensation* (which occurs when desirable experiences, behaviours and psychological states are insufficient in one sphere and actively sought out in the other sphere), and *reactive compensation*, where deprivations in one area are made up for in the other (Zedeck and Mosier 1990).

Instrumental theory posits that success in one realm facilitates success in the other realm (Guest 2001). For instance, doing well at work will lead to greater income, which allows one to engage in extravagant vacations with the family. Finally, *conflict theory* suggests that there is a trade-off between the two worlds (Guest 2001). Success and satisfaction in one entails a sacrifice in the other world due to an inherent incompatibility between the two environments. These theoretical explanations help us understand why imbalance between work and life can be problematic. These explanations also suggest that it is possible to attain better work–life balance under certain conditions. A sound basis for policy intervention can be developed from these explanations.

Previous research has found that younger workers express a stronger desire for work–life balance than do older workers (Lewis et al 2002; Smola and Sutton 2002; Sturges and Guest 2004; McDonald and Hite 2008).[2] This preference for work–life balance is evident in younger workers' conceptions of achievement. Work–life balance was cited as a central concern when assessing employment options. One study found that within young individuals' definitions of career success, work–life balance was paramount; while individuals' expressed interest in obtaining sufficient income and appropriate advancement, those factors would not alone determine career success (McDonald and Hite 2008).

---

[2] The authors are grateful to Geoffrey Ho for assistance with this discussion.

Similarly, high- and low-skilled young workers were found to be increasingly willing to make an exchange between less optimal conditions, such as lower pay in exchange for reasonable hours and flexibility in attempts to achieve work–life balance. Likewise, Lewis et al (2002) found in a qualitative study of young workers (aged 18–30) across five European countries that balancing work and life outside of the workplace was of particular concern, more so than was the case with older workers. Young workers were willing to accept reduced opportunities or rewards in exchange for better balance between work and life. The preference for work–life balance was expressed by both men and women irrespective of family obligations. Smola and Sutton (2002) found that young workers were less likely than those of the same age a generation earlier to view work as the most important aspect of the their lives. Moreover, they expressed less loyalty to their organisation than older workers. It is possible that this lack of loyalty may be a response to the perceived lack of loyalty that employers exhibit towards employees. If employees feel disposable within the organisation, they are likely to place greater priority on achieving their personal goals to balance between work and life.

Despite the emphasis placed on work–life balance by young workers, Sturges and Guest (2004) report that as people gain more work experience the number of hours at work increases, which causes employees to experience unsatisfactory work–life balance. This trend simply captures the fact that over time, workers gain experience and are likely to be promoted to positions of greater responsibility, which in turn will likely upset the work–life balance they may have aspired to initially. These workers will tolerate some of the pressures, because they would stand to reap the rewards of their hard work. However, employers who ignore such preferences and develop corporate cultures that undervalue balance are likely to face higher turnover, particularly during periods of talent shortages. Employers who determine advancement based on an imbalanced lifestyle are likely to face the wrath of younger generations.

The case of South Korea is a case in point (Verma et al 2009). The Korean economy has grown tremendously in recent decades thanks to great advancements in technology and capital. Despite Korea's growing economic prosperity in recent years, the conditions for Korean workers do not reflect the same success story because of inadequate attention paid to work–life balance issues. Workers' dreams of reasonable work hours, safe workplaces and comfortable family lives have not been realised. There are five significant issues impeding the achievement of positive outcomes for Korean workers. The first is long work hours. Korean employees work, on average, significantly longer hours compared with other OECD countries. The second is the growth of non-regular workers. By 2005, 29% of all employees in Korea were temporary workers, typically earning significantly less and receiving fewer benefits compared with regular workers. The third is high occupational accident rates. The fourth is a very low birth rate. Korean birth rates are the lowest among OECD countries, at 1.1 children per woman. The final issue for Korean workers is the lack of women in the labour force. The female employment rate in Korea is lower than the OECD average, partly due to a Korean culture that supports the notion that women will discontinue employment once they have children and also due to a lack of family-friendly work policies. Essentially, there is a gap between the economic success of Korea and the quality of work and life for workers. Employers and public policy initiatives can help Korean workers realise their dream.

The nature of the workforce today is generally very different from the workforce of decades past. The male breadwinner in a full-time permanent job with one company for his career is no longer the prevailing description of a worker. Throughout the world, there is an increase in self-employment, contract work, temporary work, periodic career changes, educational endeavours, relocation, female participation in the workforce and non-traditional family structures. The issue of work–life balance has become increasingly important for individuals and organisations. Finding a better balance between work and family for Korean workers is intricately linked to the country's development and productivity. There are three predominant initiatives towards which workers, employers, the government and non-governmental organisations need to tune their agendas. Firstly, working hours need to be reduced, through various public and private policy initiatives. Secondly, non-regular employment needs to be better regulated so that these workers are afforded comparable pay and benefits to regular workers. Finally, more family-friendly policies are needed to promote the status of women both at home and at work.

LIFELONG LEARNING

Lifelong learning has become a key operative concept in the development of individuals, organisations and economies (Johnson and Sharman 1998). Human endeavour and ingenuity has brought knowledge to a level where the pace of change in a globalising, knowledge-driven world is faster than ever before (Smith 2004). This means that current organisational systems and procedures need to respond to a changing marketplace, changing technology and newer products and services. Thus, learning, a very personal activity, has become a part of our strategy to deal with growing complexity in our external environment (Portwood 1993). The dynamics of learning in a post-industrial economy involve motivating people to learn new skills on a continuous basis and to give people the skills to find out what is relevant to learn. Lifelong learning is a personal tool that gives us the ability and the confidence to interact with the world at large. Organisations can play a vital role in promoting learning although they cannot fully control it because lifelong learning is only a concept unless it is incorporated in the way people relate to their work.

At a practical level, it must be operationalised in steps that individuals and organisations can follow. Corporations, governments, community organisations and individuals all play a role in helping us implement the ideas of lifelong learning into our jobs, careers and personal growth. One view of lifelong learning is that it is a partnership between individuals and organisations (Pate et al 2000). Individuals possess specialised knowledge of their aptitudes and learning capacities (Allen and Hart 1998). Individuals also have better knowledge of their own motivation (Thite 2001). Organisations, on the other hand, have better knowledge of technology trends, market shifts and the business opportunities offered by markets. Thus, each party brings something unique to the partnership. Lifelong learning can take place when these two parties to the employment relationship join hands in a series of mutually rewarding behaviours (*Human Resource Management International Digest* 2001; Petridou and Chatzipanagiotou 2004).

There is great variation in ways in which the lifelong learning concept is operationalised in various organisations. At the level of the firm, effective and continuous learning depends on many policies and practices. Although training is at the core of it, other policies such as selection and recruitment, performance appraisal, reward systems and mentoring also contribute in a significant way (Rubinstein and Ryan 1996). For example, job-specific training may be undertaken with the expectation of an immediate promotion. On the other hand, basic learning in a field may not yield immediate benefits but may lead to a more flexible future for the individual and the organisation. For example, employer policies can encourage people to take courses on their own time as opposed to learning on employer-paid time (Sambrook and Stewart 2000).

Within the performance management process there are three ways to facilitate learning: formal training programmes, work assignments and learning on one's own time lead to effective lifelong learning in organisations (Verma et al 2005). The three avenues of learning can be mutually reinforcing. For instance, formal training programmes may provide an employee with the requisite skills to participate in a work assignment in an alternative department. Similarly, a work assignment may encourage employees to take the opportunity to learn on their own time in order to fulfil their new obligations and feel competent in a different department. Taking courses on one's own time may also highlight the need to take on more formal training. In sum, they are mutually reinforcing and directed by the performance management system to ensure that learning is focused on organisational objectives.

Noe and Wilk (1993) found that the most important factor in learning was the individual motivation to learn, which had a consistent, significant and positive influence on different outcomes related to development activity. Hicks and Klimoski (1987) suggested that motivation to learn could be enhanced when employees are provided with realistic information regarding the benefits of development opportunities. Noe and Wilk (1993) also found that employees' perception of the work environment influenced development activity. Specifically, they found that social support from managers and peers for development activity and the type of working conditions positively influence development activity. Another aspect of the work environment that may impact an individual's willingness to engage in learning activities is the availability of resources. Employees with insufficient resources to complete work assignments, such as lack of time or poor equipment, may experience frustration and devote most of their time, attention and energy towards daily work, while neglecting development opportunities (Peters and O'Connor 1980; Peters et al 1980).

Individual characteristics, which determine how personal and work-related goals are set and how they can be achieved, are brought into the performance management system whereby the manager and employee meet in a participative forum to discuss performance and developmental goals. Bevan and Thompson (1991) suggested that performance management could be conceived as a place to discuss rewards and recognition and one that emphasises training and development. They argue that an effective development-driven integration is necessary for long-term success.

An important feature of the performance management process is goal-setting. Goal-setting has been linked to individual and organisational success (Locke and Latham 2002). Some of the goals are learning goals whereby the employee desires to branch into a new area within the organisation, gain a promotion or upgrade their existing skill set for the current job. The manager is required to facilitate this learning by showing ways that the employee can reach those goals through formal training, work assignments or learning on one's own time.

Formal training has long been regarded as imperative to organisational success. Read and Kleiner (1996) presented the most commonly used formal training methods across non-industry-specific companies in the US as videotapes, lectures, one-on-one instruction, role-plays, games/simulation, case studies, slides, computer-based training, audiotapes and films. Another avenue for learning is through work assignments. The provision of work assignments can be initiated by the employee or by their manager for the purpose of upgrading their skills through a work assignment. Work assignments may provide employees with the opportunity to try a different role within the organisation. A final route to learning that organisations can supply is learning on one's own time. Here, employees are provided with the resources to learn after working hours. This may include e-learning courses, weekend courses, 'lunch and learn' sessions, bursaries or temporary leave allowances to take on more formalised education.

In a fast-paced, global economy, there is a strong case for a learning partnership between organisations and individuals. The three methods of learning, that is, formal training, work assignments and learning on one's own time, can be best operationalised if there is concerted action by both employees and employers. It requires a combination of the three types of learning to maintain an integrated and effective learning system.

The evidence suggests that effective lifelong learning is a multidimensional process. It builds on the traditional forms of employer-paid, employer-sponsored training for job skills in two directions. First, it engages individuals in self-initiated and self-motivated learning activities. The employer can abet this process but it is the individual who is in charge of their own personal and career development through learning. Second, lifelong learning happens when the learning processes are closely integrated with work itself. It is the work assignments, stints on taskforces and time spent on projects that make lifelong learning both possible and effective by creating a synergy between work and learning.

Looking to the future, the principal policy issue for organisations is not whether lifelong learning is necessary for creativity and innovation in a globalising economy but rather how best to operationalise it. The challenge ahead is to make full use of lifelong learning in finding creative solutions in a fast-paced economy driven by knowledge and innovation.

CONCLUSION

The problems and challenges facing human resource management in a globalising economy are too numerous to receive full treatment within the span of this chapter. However, it is possible to apply the lens of globalisation and knowledge-driven innovation to the traditional concerns of developing human resources. Foremost, policy-makers and educators alike need to develop and subscribe to a global vision of human resource development needs of the world. This vision would include raising the global floor for labour standards and conditions of work. To flourish, trade and development need to be inclusive, which implies that globalisation must offer an opportunity for advancement to *all* the citizens of this planet, not just a privileged minority. In this spirit, we have highlighted two labour market issues – conditions of migrant workers and non-standard workers – as issues of global concern. Two other issues at a more disaggregated level have been highlighted, namely, work–life balance and lifelong learning. Both of these issues, familiar to human resource students and practitioners within the domestic context, it is argued, have acquired greater significance within a knowledge-driven, global economy.

References

CHAPTER 1

BHASKAR, R. (1986) *Scientific realism and human emancipation*. London: Verso.

BOUD, D. and FELETTI, G. (1991) Introduction. In: BOUD, D. and FELETTI, G. (eds). *The challenge of problem based learning*. London: Kogan Page.

BRAVERMAN, H. (1974) *Labour and monopoly capital*. New York: Monthly Review Press.

CURRIE, G., KNIGHTS, D. and STARKEY, K. (2010) Making the business school more critical. *British Journal of Management*. Vol 21. S1–S5.

DEVINE, J. and EGGER-SIDER, F. (2009) *Going beyond Google: the invisible web in learning and teaching*. London: Facet.

ELDRIDGE, J. (1993) News, truth and power. In: ELDRIDGE, J. (ed.). *Getting the message: news, truth and power*. London: Routledge. pp3–28.

FLEETWOOD, S. and ACKROYD, S. (2004) *Critical realist applications in organisation and management studies*. London: Routledge.

GLASGOW UNIVERSITY MEDIA GROUP. (1976) *Bad news*. London: Routledge.

HABERMAS, J. (1984) *The theory of communicative action*. Cambridge: Polity Press.

KNIGHTS, D. and WILLMOTT, H. (1989) Power and subjectivity at work: from degradation to subjugation in social relations. *Sociology*. Vol 23, No 4. pp535–558.

THOMPSON, P. and VINCENT, S. (2010) Labour process theory and critical realism. In: THOMPSON, P. and SMITH, C. (eds). *Working life: renewing labour process analysis*. Basingstoke: Palgrave Macmillan. pp47–69.

WALLACE, M. and WRAY, A. (2006) *Critical reading and writing for postgraduates*. London: Sage.

CHAPTER 2

AOKI, M. (2001) *Toward a comparative institutional analysis*. Cambridge, MA: MIT Press.

ARGYRIS, C. (1964) *Integrating the individual and the organization*. New York: Wiley.

ARMSTRONG, M. (2006) *A handbook of human resource management practice.* London: Kogan Page.

BERLE, A.A. and MEANS, G.C. (1932) *The modern corporation and private property.* New York: Macmillan.

BEYER, J. and HASSEL, A. (2002) The effects of convergence: internationalisation and the changing distribution of net value added in large German firms. *Economy and Society.* Vol 31, No 3. pp309–332.

BIRCH, A. (1967) *The economic history of the British iron and steel industry – 1784–1879.* London: Frank Cass.

BLAIR, M. (1995) *Ownership and control: rethinking corporate governance for the 21st century.* Washington DC: The Brookings Institution.

BLAIR, M.M. and ROE, M.J. (1999) *Employees and corporate governance.* Washington, D.C.: The Brookings Institution.

BOXALL, P. and PURCELL, J. (2008) *Strategy and human resource management.* 2nd ed. Basingstoke: Palgrave Macmillan.

BURCHELL, G., GORDON, C. and MILLER, P. (1991) *The Foucault effect: studies in governmentality.* Hemel Hempstead: Harvester Wheatsheaf.

CAMPBELL, J.P., MCCLOY, R., OPPLER, S. and SAGER, C. (1993) A theory of performance. In: SCHMITT, N. and BORMAN, W. (eds) *Personnel selection in organizations.* San Francisco: Jossey-Bass.

CAPPELLI, P. and SINGH, H. (1992) Integrating strategic human resources are firms' core competencies. *Organizational Dynamics.* Winter. pp7–22.

CLARKE, T. (2007) *International corporate governance: a comparative approach.* Oxford: Routledge.

COMBINED CODE. (1998) *The London Stock Exchange Limited.* June. London.

COMBINED CODE. (2003) *The Financial Reporting Council.* July. London.

COMMITTEE ON CORPORATE GOVERNANCE. (1998) *Committee on Corporate Governance: Final report.* Hampel Report. London: Gee.

COMMITTEE ON CORPORATE GOVERNANCE. (2003) *Review of the role and effectiveness of non-executive directors.* The Department for Trade and Industry, Higgs Report. London: Gee.

COMMITTEE ON THE FINANCIAL ASPECTS OF CORPORATE GOVERNANCE. (1992) *The financial aspects of corporate governance.* Cadbury Report. London: Gee.

DAILY, C.M., DALTON, D. and CANNELLA, A. (2003) Corporate governance: decades of dialogue and Data. *Academy of Management Review.* Vol 28. pp371–82.

DAVIES, P.L. (2000) Board structure in the UK and Germany: convergence or continuing divergence? *International and Comparative Corporate Law Journal.* Vol 2, No 4. pp435–456.

DAVIS, J.H., SCHOORMAN, F.D. and DONALDSON, L. (1997) Toward a stewardship theory of management. *Academy of Management Review.* Vol 22, No 1. pp20–47.

DENIS, D.K. and MCCONNELL, J.J. (2003) International corporate governance. *Journal of Financial and Quantitative Analysis.* Vol 38, No 1. pp1–36.

DONALDSON, L. and DAVIS, J.H. (1991) Stewardship theory or agency theory: CEO governance and shareholder returns. *Australian Journal of Management.* Vol 16, No 1. pp49–56.

DORE, R. (2000) *Stock market capitalism: welfare capitalism: Japan and Germany versus Anglo-Saxon.* Oxford: Oxford University Press.

EEC. (1975) Employee participation in company structures in the E-European Community. *Bulletin of the European Communities.* European Economic Community, COM (75) 570 final, 12 November (Supplement 8/75).

FREEMAN, R.E. (1984) *Strategic management: a stakeholder approach.* Boston: Pitman Press.

GREENBURY COMMITTEE. (1995) *Study group on directors' remuneration (final report).* London: Gee.

HEALY, C.N. and PALEPU, K. (2001) Information asymmetry, corporate disclosure, and the capital markets: a review of the empirical disclosure literature. *Journal of Accounting and Economics.* Vol 31. pp405–440.

HENDRY, K. and KIEL, G.C. (2004) The role of the board on firm strategy: integrating agency and organizational control perspectives. *Corporate Governance: An International Review.* Vol 12, No 4. pp500–520.

HILLMAN, A.J., CANNELLA, A.A. and PAETZOLD, R.L. (2000) The resource dependence role of corporate directors: strategic adaptation of board composition in response to environmental change. *Journal of Management Studies.* Vol 37. pp325–254.

JACKSON, G. (2003) Corporate governance in Germany and Japan: liberalization pressures and responses. In: YAMAMURA, K. and STREECK, W. (eds). *The end of diversity? Prospects of German and Japanese capitalism.* Ithaca, NY: Cornell University Press. pp.261–305.

JACKSON, G. and MIYAJIMA, H. (2007) Introduction: the diversity and change of corporate governance in China. In: AOKI, M., JACKSON, G. and MIYAJIMA, H. (eds). *Corporate governance in Japan: institutional change and organizational diversity.* Oxford: Oxford University Press.

JACKSON, G., HOPNER, M. and KURDLEBUSCH, A. (2004) Corporate governance and employees in Germany: changing linkages, complementarities, and tensions. Discussion paper, RIETI.

JENSEN, M.C. and MECKLING, W.H. (1976) Theory of the firm: managerial behaviour, agency costs and ownership structure. *Journal of Financial Economics.* Vol 3. pp305–360.

KEASEY, K., THOMPSON, S. and WRIGHT, M. (1997) *Corporate governance: economic, management and financial issues.* New York: Oxford University Press.

KERSLEY, B., ALPIN, C., FORTH, J., BRYSON, A., BEWLEY, H., DIX, G. and OXENBRIDGE, S. (2005) *Inside the workplace: first findings from the 2004 Workplace Employment Relations Survey.* London: DTI.

KIEL, G.C. and NICHOLSON, G.J. (2003) *Boards that work: a new guide for directors.* Sydney: McGraw-Hill.

KIRKBRIDE, J. and LETZA, S. (2003) Establishing the boundaries of regulation in corporate governance: is the UK moving toward a process of collaboration? *Business and Society Review.* Vol 108, No 4. pp463–485.

LAING, D. and WEIR, C.M. (1999) Governance structures, size and corporate performance in UK firms. *Management Decision.* Vol 37, No 5. pp457–464.

MALLIN, C. (2007) *Corporate governance.* Oxford: Oxford University Press.

MARCHINGTON, M. and WILKINSON, A. (2008) *Human resource management at work: people management and development.* London: CIPD.

MUTH, M.M. and DONALDSON, L. (1998) Stewardship theory and board structure: a contingency approach. *Corporate Governance.* Vol 6, No 1. pp5–28.

OECD. (2004) *OECD principles of corporate governance.* Paris: OECD Publications Service.

PASS, C. (2006) The revised combined code and corporate governance: an empirical survey of 50 large UK companies. *Managerial Law.* Vol 48, No 5. pp18–27.

PFEFFER, J. and COHEN, Y. (1984) Determinants of internal labour markets in organizations. *Administrative Science Quarterly.* Vol 29. pp550–572.

SCHULER, R.S. and JACKSON, S.E. (2007) *Strategic human resource management.* London: Blackwell Publishing.

SHEIK, S. and REES, W. (1995) *Corporate governance and corporate control.* London: Cavendish Publishing Limited.

SHERIDAN, T. and KENDALL, N. (1998) *Corporate governance: an action plan for profitability and business success.* London: Pitman Publishing.

SHISHIDO, Z. (2000) Japanese corporate governance: the hidden problems of the corporate law and their solutions. *Delaware Journal of Corporate Law.* Vol 25, No 2. pp189–233.

SHLEIFER, A. and VISHNY, R.W. (1997) A survey of corporate governance. *The Journal of Finance*. Vol LII, No 2. pp737–783.

SIKKA, P. (2008) Corporate governance: what about the workers? *Accounting, Auditing and Accountability Journal*. Vol 21, No 7. pp955–977.

SMALLMAN, C. (2004) Exploring theoretical paradigms in corporate governance. *International Journal of Business Governance and Ethics*. Vol 1, No 1. pp78–94.

SOLOMON, J. (2007) *Corporate governance and accountability*. Chichester: John Wiley.

SPIRA, L.F. (2001) Enterprise and accountability: striking a balance. *Management Decision*. Vol 39, No 9. pp739–748.

STARKEY, K. (1995) Opening up corporate governance. *Human Relations*. Vol 48, No 8. pp837–884.

STERNBERG, E. (1997) The defects of stakeholder theory. *Corporate Governance: An International Review*. Vol 5, No 1. pp3–10.

STILES, P. and TAYLOR, B. (2001) *Boards at work: how directors view their roles and responsibilities*. Oxford: Oxford University Press.

SUNDARAMURTHY, C. and LEWIS, M. (2003) Control and collaboration: paradoxes of governance. *Academy of Management Review*. Vol 28, No 3. pp397–415.

THOMPSON, S. (2005) The impact of corporate governance reforms on the remuneration of executives in the UK. *Corporate Governance: An International Review*. Vol 13, No 1. pp19–25.

TRICKER, R.I. (1984) *Corporate governance*. Aldershot: Gower.

WALTON, R.E. (1985) From control to commitment in the workplace. *Harvard Business Review*. Vol 63. pp77–84.

WEDDERBURN, B. (2004) *The future of company law: fat cats, corporate governance and workers*. Liverpool: The Institute of Employment Rights.

WEINBERG, J.A. (2003) Accounting for corporate behaviour. *Economic Quarterly*. Vol 89, No 3. pp1–20.

ZAHRA, S.A. and PEARCE, J.A. (1989) Boards of directors and corporate financial performance: a review and integrative model. *Journal of Management*. Vol 15, No 2. pp291–334.

CHAPTER 3

BACKHAUS, K. and TIKOO, S. (2004) Conceptualizing and researching employer branding. *Career Development International*. Vol 9, No 5. pp501–517.

CRANE, A., MATTEN, D. and SPENCE, L.J. (2008) *Corporate social responsibility: readings and cases in a global context.* London and New York: Routledge.

CROUCHER, R. and COTTON, E. (2009) *Global unions, global business: global union federations and international business.* London: Middlesex University Press.

GLOBAL UNIONS. (2009) *Getting the world to work: global union strategies for recovery.* Geneva: ITUC.

GODFREY, P.C, MERRILL, C.B. and HANSEN, J.M. (2009) The relationship between corporate social responsibility and shareholder value: an empirical test of the risk management hypothesis. *Strategic Management Journal.* Vol 30. pp425–445.

GREENFIELD, G. (2006) *The impact of financialization on transnational production systems: the role of new financial imperatives in the restructuring strategies of Nestlé, Kraft and Unilever.* Paper delivered to the International Workshop, 'The Impact of Global Production Systems on Trade Union Strategies'. 10–11 May, Institute of Social Studies, The Hague, Netherlands.

HELD, D. (2006) Reframing global governance: apocalypse soon or reform! *New Political Economy.* Vol 11, No 2. June.

HUSTED, B.W. (2003) Governance choices for corporate social responsibility: to contribute, collaborate or internalize. *Long Range Planning.* Vol 36. pp481–98.

ICEM ONLINE NEWS. (2008) Thailand: Thai industrial gas workers win through striking, engagement in earnest bargaining table talks. 25 August. Available online at http://cal.icem.org/index.php/en/icem-cal-news/26-thai-industrial-gas-workers-win-through-striking-engagement-in-earnest-bargaining-table-talks.

INTERNATIONAL FEDERATION OF CHEMICAL, ENERGY, MINING AND GENERAL WORKERS UNIONS (ICEM). (2008) *Guide to contract and agency labour.* Geneva: ICEM.

INTERNATIONAL LABOUR ORGANIZATION. (2003) *Information note on corporate social responsibility and international labour standards.* Geneva: International Labour Organization.

INTERNATIONAL LABOUR ORGANIZATION. (2007) *The employment relationship: an annotated guide to the ILO Recommendation 198.* Geneva: International Labour Organization.

INTERNATIONAL LABOUR ORGANIZATION. (2010) International Labour Standards. Available at: www.ilo.org/global/What_we_do/InternationalLabourStandards/lang--en/index.htm.

INTERNATIONAL METALWORKERS' FEDERATION. (2008) *Survey on changing employment practices and precarious work.* Geneva: IMF.

KOÇER, R.G. and FRANSEN, L. (2009) Codes of conduct and the promise of a change of climate in worker organization. *European Journal of Industrial Relations.* Vol 15. p237.

LINDE AG. (2008) *Staying on track: the Linde annual report.* Munich: Linde AG.

RUGGIE, J.G. (1993) Multilateralism: the anatomy of an institution. In: RUGGIE, J.G. (ed.). *Multilateralism matters: the theory and praxis of an institutional form.* New York: Columbia University Press. pp3–48.

RUGGIE, J. (2008) *Promotion and protection of all human rights, civil, political, economic, social and cultural rights, including the right to development.* New York: United Nations, Human Rights Council 8ᵗʰ Session.

SACHS, J.D. (2005) *The end of poverty: economic possibilities for our time.* New York: Penguin Press.

THERON, J. (2005) Employment is not what it used to be: the nature and impact of work re-structuring in South Africa. In VON HOLDT, K. and WEBSTER, E. (eds). *Beyond the Apartheid workplace: studies in transition.* Scottsville: University of Kwa Zulu-Natal Press. pp293–316.

WERTHER, W. and CHANDLER, D. (2005) Strategic corporate social responsibility as global brand insurance. *Business Horizons.* Vol 48, No 4. pp317–324.

CHAPTER 4

AMABLE, B. (2003) *The diversity of modern capitalism.* Oxford: Oxford University Press.

ASHLEY, D. and ORENSTEIN, D. (1995) *Sociological theory: classical statements.* Boston, MA: Allyn and Bacon.

BBC NEWS. (2009) General Motors cancels Opel sale. Available online at http://news.bbc.co.uk/1/hi/8341485.stm.

BOTERO, J., DJANKOV, S., LA PORTA, R. and LOPEZ-DE-SILANES, F. (2004) The regulation of labor. *The Quarterly Journal of Economics.* November. pp1339–1382.

BOYER, R. (2006) How do institutions cohere and change? In: WOOD, G. and JAMES, P. (eds). *Institutions and working life.* Oxford: Oxford University Press.

BREWSTER, C., WOOD, G., CROUCHER, R. and BROOKES, M. (2007) Collective and individual voice: convergence in Europe? *International Journal of Human Resource Management.* Vol 18, No 7. pp1246–1262.

BUDHWAR, P. and SPARROW, P. (2002) Strategic HRM through the cultural looking glass. *Organization Studies.* Vol 23, No 4. 599–638.

DORE, R. (2000) *Stock market capitalism: welfare capitalism.* Cambridge: Cambridge University Press.

FANG, T. (2007) Asian management research needs more self-confidence: reflections on Hofstede (2007) and beyond. *Asia Pacific Journal of Management.* Published online: 19 February 2009.

FRIEDMAN, M. (1997) The social responsibility of business is to increase its profits. In: BEAUCHAMP, T. and BOWIE, N. (eds). *Ethical theory and business.* Upper Saddle River, NJ: Prentice Hall.

FUKUYAMA, F. (2000) The end of history. In: BURNS, R. and RAYMENT-PICKARD, H. (eds). *Philosophies of history.* Oxford: Blackwell.

GELB, S. (1989) *The economic crisis in South Africa.* Cape Town: David Philip.

GOERGEN, M., BREWSTER, C. and WOOD, G. (2009) Corporate governance and training. *Journal of Industrial Relations.* Vol 51, No 4. pp459–487.

HALL, P. and SOSKICE, D. (2001) An introduction to varieties of capitalism. In: HALL, P. and SOSKICE, D. (eds). (2001) *Varieties of capitalism: the institutional foundations of competitive advantage.* Oxford: Oxford University Press.

HARCOURT, M. and WOOD, G. (2004) Do unions affect employer compliance with the law? *British Journal of Industrial Relations* Vol 42, No 3. pp527–541.

HARCOURT, M. and WOOD, G. (2007) The importance of employment protection for skill development in coordinated market economies. *European Journal of Industrial Relations.* Vol 13, No 2. pp141–159.

HOFSTEDE, G. (1991) *Culture and organizations.* London: McGraw Hill.

HOLLINGSWORTH, J.R. (2006) Advancing our understanding of capitalism with Niels Bohr's thinking about complementarity. In: WOOD, G.T. and JAMES, P. (eds). *Institutions, production and working life.* Oxford: Oxford University Press. pp62–82.

HOLLINGSWORTH, J.R. and BOYER, R. (1997) Coordination of economic actors and social systems of production. In: HOLLINGSWORTH, J.R. and BOYER, R. (eds). *Contemporary capitalism: the embeddedness of institutions.* Cambridge: Cambridge University Press. pp1–47.

HUDSON, R. (2006) The production of institutional complementarity. In: WOOD, G.T. and JAMES, P. (eds). *Institutions, production and working life.* Oxford: Oxford University Press. pp104–122.

JACKSON, T. (2002) The management of people across cultures: valuing people differently. *Human Resource Management.* Vol 41, No 4. pp455–475.

JESSOP, B. (ed.) (2001) *Regulation theory and the crisis of capitalism – volume 1.* London: Edward Elgar.

JOHNSON, J.P., LENARTOWICZ, T. and APUD, S. (2006) Cross-cultural competence in international business: toward a definition and a model. *Journal of International Business Studies.* Vol 37, No 4. pp525–543.

LANE, C. and WOOD, G. (2009) Introducing diversity in capitalism and capitalist diversity. *Economy and Society.* Vol 38, No 4. pp531–551.

LA PORTA, R., LOPEZ-DE-SILANES, F. and SHLEIFER, A. (1999) Corporate ownership around the world. *The Journal of Finance.* Vol 54, No 2. pp471–517.

LINCOLN, J. and KALLEBERG, A. (1990) *Culture, control and commitment: a study of work organization in the United States and Japan.* Cambridge: Cambridge University Press.

MCSWEENEY, B. (2002) Hofstede's model of national cultural differences and their consequences: a triumph of faith – a failure of analysis. *Human Relations.* Vol 55, No 1. pp89–118.

MOODY, K. (1997) *Workers in a lean world: unions in the international economy.* London: Verso.

NORTH, D.C. (1990) *Institutions, institutional change and economic performance.* Cambridge: Cambridge University Press.

OECD. (2007) *Country statistical profiles.* Paris: OECD.

PAGANO, M. and VOLPIN, P. (2005) The political economy of corporate governance. *American Economic Review.* Vol 95. pp1005–1030.

PARSONS, T. (1951) *The social system.* Glencoe: Free Press.

PSYCHOGIOS, A. and WOOD, G. (forthcoming 2010) Human resource management in comparative perspective: alternative institutionalist perspectives and empirical realities. *International Journal of Human Resource Management.*

REDER, E. (1980) Industrial relations and organizational theory. In: BARRETT, B., BEISHON, J. and RHODEE, E. (eds). *Industrial relations and wider society.* Harmondsworth: Collier Macmillan.

RITZER, G. (1992) *Classical sociological theory.* New York: McGraw Hill.

ROE, M. (2003) *Political determinants of corporate governance.* Oxford: Oxford University Press.

SIMMEL, G. (1980) *Essays on interpretation in social science.* Manchester: Manchester University Press.

SORGE, A. (2005) *The global and the local.* Oxford: Oxford University Press.

THELEN, K. (2004) *How institutions evolve: the political economy of skills in Germany, Britain, Japan and the United States.* Cambridge: Cambridge University Press.

THOMPSON, P. and SMITH, C. (2010) Introduction: labour process theory in retrospect and prospect. In: THOMPSON, P. and SMITH, C. (eds). *Working life: renewing labour process analysis.* London: Palgrave. pp1–10.

TOYNBEE, P. (2003) *Hard work.* London: Bloomsbury.

TUNG, R.L. (2008) The cross-cultural research imperative: the need to balance cross-national and intra-national diversity. *Journal of International Business Studies.* Vol 39, No 1. pp41–46.

TURNER, J. (1998) *The structure of sociological theory.* New York: Wadsworth.

WALLACE, R. and WOLF, A. (1995) *Contemporary sociological theory: continuing the classical tradition.* New York: Prentice Hall.

WHITLEY, R. (1999) *Divergent capitalisms: the social structuring and change of business systems.* Oxford: Oxford University Press.

WÖCKE, A., BENDIXEN, M. and RIJAMAMPIANINA, R. (2007) Building flexibility into multi-national human resource strategy: a study of four South African multi-national enterprises. *The International Journal of Human Resource Management.* Vol 18, No 5. pp829–844.

WOLDU, H., BUDHWAR, P. and PARKES, C. (2006) A cross-national comparison of cultural value orientations of Indian, Polish, Russian and American employees. *International Journal of Cross-Cultural Management.* Vol 17, No 6. pp1076–1094.

WOOD, G. and FRYNAS, G. (2006) The institutional basis of economic failure: anatomy of the segmented business system. *Socio-Economic Review.* Vol 4, No 2. pp239–277.

WOOD, N. (2003) *Tyranny in America.* London: Verso.

CHAPTER 5

APPELBAUM, S., GREWAL, K. and MOUSSEAU, H. (2006) Whistleblowing: international implications and critical case I. *The Journal of the American Academy of Business.* Vol 10, No 1. pp7–13.

BELL, D. (1973) *The coming of post-industrial society.* New York: Basic Books.

BLACKLER, F. (1995) Knowledge, knowledge work and organizations. *Organization Studies.* Vol 16, No 6. pp1021–46.

CASTELLS, M. (2001) *The rise of the network society.* Oxford: Wiley-Blackwell.

CIPD. (2002) *Training in the knowledge economy.* Research report. London: CIPD.

CIPD. (2005) *Technology and people management: the opportunity and the challenge.* London: CIPD.

CIPD. (2009) Why only Twits would ignore the potential (and pitfalls) of Twitter. *People Management.* 23 April. p36.

DANFORD, A., RICHARDSON, M. and UPCHURCH, M. (2003) *New unions, new workplaces: a study of union resilience in the restructured workplace.* London: Routledge.

EVANS, A. (2008) Dealing with dissent: whistleblowing, egalitarianism, and the republic of the firm. *Innovation: the European Journal of Social Science Research.* Vol 21, No 3. pp267–279.

FERNIE, S. and METCALF, D. (1997) *(Not) hanging on the telephone: payment systems in the new sweatshops.* London: Centre for Economic Performance, London School of Economics.

FOUCAULT, M. (1995) *Discipline and punish: the birth of the prison.* Translated from the French by Alan Sheridan. New York: Vintage Books.

GOVERNMENT COMMUNICATION NETWORK. (2007) *A review of the government's use of social media.* London: Government Communication Network.

GREENE, A.M., HOGAN, J. and GRIECO, M. (2003) Commentary: e-collectivism and distributed discourse: new opportunities for trade union democracy. *Industrial Relations Journal.* Vol 34. pp282–289.

GUARDIAN. (2005) Ocado gets Big Brother tag. Available online at: www. guardian.co.uk/business/2005/jun/11/supermarkets.jobsandmoney.

KAROLY, L. and PANIS, C. (2004) *The 21st century at work: forces shaping the future workforce and workplace in the United States.* Santa Monica, CA: Rand.

LENHART, A. and FOX, S. (2006) *Bloggers: a portrait of the internet's new storytellers.* Washington, D.C.: Pew Internet Project.

LEWIS, D. (2002) Whistleblowing procedures at work: what are the implications for human resource practitioners? *Business Ethics: A European Review.* Vol 11, No 3. pp202–209.

MARTIN, G., REDDINGTON, M. and KNEAFSEY, M. (n.d.) *Web 2.0 and HR: a discussion paper.* London: CIPD.

MATHIESON, T. (1997) The viewer society: Michel Foucault's panopticon revisited. *Theoretical Criminology.* Vol 1, No 2. pp215–234.

NOLAN, P. and WOOD, S. (2003) Mapping the future of work. *British Journal of Industrial Relations.* Vol 41, No 2. pp165–174.

RIFKIN, J. (1996) *The end of work: the decline of the global labour force and the dawn of a post-market era.* New York: G.P. Putnam.

SEMLER, R. (2003) *The seven-day weekend: a better way to work in the twenty-first century.* London: Arrow Books.

TAYLOR, P. and BAIN, P. (1997) An assembly line in the head: work and employee relations in a call centre. *Industrial Relations Journal.* Vol 30, No 2. pp101–117.

TAYLOR, R. (2002) *Britain's world of work: myths and realities.* Leeds: ESRC Future of Work Programme – Leeds University.

TAYLOR, P. and BAIN, P. (2003) Subterranean worksick blues: humour as subversion in two call centres. *Organization Studies*. Vol 24, No 9. pp1487–1509.

THOMPSON, M., ELLIS, R. and WILDAVSKY, A. (1990) *Cultural theory*. Jackson, TN: Westview Press.

THOMPSON, P. and ACKROYD, S. (1995) All quiet on the workplace front? A critique of recent trends in British industrial sociology. *Sociology*. Vol 29, No 4. pp615–633.

WENGER, E. (1998) *Communities of practice: learning, meaning and identity*. Cambridge: Cambridge University Press.

ZOHAR, D. and MARSHALL, I. (2005) *Spiritual capital: wealth we can live by*. London: Bloomsbury.

ZUBOFF, S. (1988) *In the age of the smart machine: the future of work and power*. Oxford: Heinemann.

CHAPTER 6

AGLIETTA, M. and REBÉRIOUX, A. (2005) *Corporate governance adrift: a critique of shareholder value*. Cheltenham: Edward Elgar.

ALCHIAN, A. and DEMSETZ, H. (1972) Production, information costs and economic organization. *American Economic Review*. Vol 62. pp777–795.

BARAN, P.A. and SWEEZY, P.M. (1966) *Monopoly capital: an essay on the American economic and social order*. New York: Monthly Review Press.

BAUMOL, W.J. (1962) On the theory of expansion of the firm. *American Economic Review*. Vol 52, No 5. pp1078–1087.

BBC NEWS. (2009) Cadbury fights back in bid battle. 14 December. Available online at http://news.bbc.co.uk/1/hi/business/8411233.stm

BERLE, A.A. and MEANS, G.C. (1992) *The modern corporation and private property*, originally published 1932, new edition edited by M. Weidenbaum and M. Jensen. London: Transaction Publishers.

BLANKENBURG, S. and PLESCH, D. (2007) *Corporate rights and responsibilities: restoring legal accountability*. London: RSA.

BLOWFIELD, M. and MURRAY, A. (2008) *Corporate responsibility: a critical introduction*. Oxford: Oxford University Press.

BOWLES, S. and GINTIS, H. (1990) Contested exchange: new microfoundations for the political economy of capitalism. *Politics and Society*. Vol 18, No 2. pp165–222.

BRYNJOLFSSON, E., HITT, L.M. and YANG, S. (2002) Intangible assets: computers and organizational capital. *Brookings Papers on Economic Activity*. No 1. pp137–181.

COASE, R. (1937) The nature of the firm. *Economica*. Vol 4. pp386–405.

DEAKIN, S. (2004) *Renewing labour market institutions*. Geneva: International Institute for Labour Studies.

FAMA, E.F. and JENSEN, M.C. (1983) Agency problems and residual claims. *Journal of Law and Economics*. Vol 26, No 2. pp327–349.

GALBRAITH, J.K. (1967) *The new industrial state*. Princeton: Princeton University Press.

GRAHL, J. (2006) Financial change and European employment relations. In: JAMES, P. and WOOD, G. (eds). *Institutions, production and working life*. Oxford: Oxford University Press.

GRAHL, J. (2009) The impact of financial change on European employment relations. In: GRAHL, J. (ed.). *Global finance and social Europe*. Cheltenham: Edward Elgar.

GRANOVETTER, M. (1985) Economic action and social structure: the problem of embeddedness. *American Journal of Sociology*. Vol 91, No 3. pp481–510.

GROSSMAN, S. and HART, O. (1986) The costs and the benefits of ownership: a theory of vertical and lateral integration. *Journal of Political Economy*. Vol 94. pp691–719.

JACOBY, S.M. (2004) *Employing bureaucracy: managers, unions and the transformation of work in the 20th century*. London: Lawrence Erlbaum.

JENSEN, M.C. (1986) Agency cost of free cash flow, corporate finance and takeovers. *American Economic Review*. Vol 76, No 2. pp323–329.

JENSEN, M.C. (2004) Agency costs of overvalued equity. *ECGI Finance Working Paper*, 39, May.

PUTTERMAN, L. and KROSZNER, R.S. (eds) (1996) *The economic nature of the firm*, 2nd ed. Cambridge: Cambridge University Press.

STIGLER, G. (1962) *The intellectual and the marketplace*. Chicago: University of Chicago Press.

WHYTE, W.H. (1956) *The organization man*. New York: Simon & Schuster.

WILLIAMS, K. (ed.) (2000) Symposium on shareholder value. Special issue of *Economy and Society*. Vol 29, No 1.

WILLIAMSON, O. (1985) The governance of contractual relations. In: WILLIAMSON, O.E. (ed.). *The economic institutions of capitalism: firms, markets and relational contracting*. London: Simon & Schuster.

WRIGHT MILLS, C. (1951) *White collar: the American middle classes*. New York: OUP.

ZINGALES, L. (2000) *In search of new foundations.* University of Chicago, Center for Research in Security Prices, Working Paper 515, University of Chicago.

CHAPTER 7

BBC NEWS. (2008) Flexible work changes 'reviewed'. 20 October. Available online at http://news.bbc.co.uk/1/hi/uk_politics/7679802.stm

CARD, D., LEMIEUX, T. and RIDDELL, W. (2004) Unions and wage inequality. *Journal of Labour Research.* Vol 25. pp519–562.

CONSERVATIVE PARTY. (2010) *An invitation to join the government of Britain. The Conservative Party manifesto.* London: Conservative Party.

CREWE, I., SÄRLVIK, B. and ALT, J. (1977) Partisan dealignment in Britain 1964–1974. *British Journal of Political Science.* Vol 7. pp129–190.

DAVIES, P. and FREEDLAND, M. (1993) *Labour legislation and public policy.* Oxford: Oxford University Press.

DAVIES, P. and FREEDLAND, M. (2007) *Towards a flexible labour market: labour legislation and regulation since the 1970s.* Oxford: Oxford University Press.

DEAKIN, S. and WILKINSON, F. (2005) *The law of the labour market: industrialization, employment and legal evolution.* Oxford: Oxford University Press.

EDWARDS, P. (2007) *Justice in the workplace: why it is important and why a new public policy initiative is needed.* London: The Work Foundation.

FREEMAN, R. and MEDOFF, J. (1984) *What do unions do?* New York: Basic.

FRIEDMAN, M. (1968) The role of monetary policy. *The American Economic Review.* Vol 58, No 1. pp1–17.

GAMBLE, A. (2003) *Between Europe and America: the future of British politics.* Basingstoke: Palgrave Macmillan.

GIDDENS, A. (1998) *The third way: the renewal of social democracy.* Cambridge: Polity Press.

GOLDTHORPE, J., LOCKWOOD, D., BECHHOFER, F. and PLATT, J. (1969) *The affluent worker in the class structure.* Cambridge: Cambridge University Press.

HALSEY, A. (1978) *Change in British society.* Oxford: Oxford University Press.

HAYEK, F. (1944) *The road to serfdom.* London: Routledge.

HINSLIFF, G. (2009) Bosses to be told to offer more part-time work for parents. *Observer.* 25 October.

HMSO. (1998) *Fairness at work.* London: HMSO.

KAHN-FREUND, O. (1954) Legal framework. In: FLANDERS, A. and CLEGG,

H. (eds). *The system of industrial relations in Great Britain.* Oxford: Oxford University Press.

KAUFMAN, B. (2009) Promoting labour market efficiency and fairness through a legal minimum wage: the Webbs and the social cost of labour. *British Journal of Industrial Relations.* Vol 47, No 2. pp306–326.

LAWS, D. and MARSHALL, D. (eds) (2004) *The orange book: reclaiming liberalism.* UK: Profile Books.

MANNING, A. (2003) *Monopsony in motion: imperfect competition in labour markets.* Princeton: Princeton University Press.

OBSERVER. (2005) 'I'm not a deeply ideological person. I'm a practical one.' David Cameron interviewed by Andrew Rawnsley. 18 December.

OLSON, M. (1971) *The logic of collective action.* Cambridge, MA.: Harvard University Press.

RUBERY, J. and EDWARDS, P. (2003) Low pay and the National Minimum Wage. In: EDWARDS, P. (ed.). *Industrial relations: theory and practice*, 2nd ed. Oxford: Blackwell.

TUC. (2008) Closing the gender pay gap: an update report for the TUC Women's Conference 2008. London: Trades Union Congress.

TURNBULL, P. (2003) What do unions do now? *Journal of Labour Research.* Vol 24. pp491–527.

WEBER, M. (1964) *Theory of social and economic organization.* London: Collier Macmillan.

WILKINSON, R. and PICKETT, K. (2009) *The spirit level: why equality is better for everyone.* London: Allen Lane.

WORLD HEALTH ORGANIZATION. (2008) *Closing the gap in a generation: health equity through action on the social determinants of health.* Geneva: WHO.

CHAPTER 8

ARROWSMITH, J. and MCGOLDRICK, A.E. (1997) A flexible future for older workers? *Personnel Review.* Vol 26, No 4. pp258–273.

BARNES, H., PARRY, J. and TAYLOR, R. (2004) *Working after state pension age: qualitative research.* London: DWP.

COUGHLAN, S. (2010) Older teachers warn of 'ageism', NASUWT conference told. BBC News. 3 April. Available online at http://news.bbc.co.uk/1/hi/education/8601867.stm

FLYNN, M. (2010a) The United Kingdom government's 'business case' approach to the regulation of retirement. *Ageing and Society.* Vol 30, No 4. pp308–324.

FLYNN, M. (2010b) Who is motivated to extend working life beyond retirement age? Typologies of older workers. *Personnel Review.* Vol 39, No 5. pp421–443.

FLYNN, M. and MCNAIR, S. (2007) *Managing age: a guide to good employment practice.* Department for Trade and Industry. London: Chartered Institute of Personnel Development and Trades Union Congress.

FLYNN, M. and MCNAIR, S. (2008) What would persuade older people to stay longer in work? In: CHIVA, A. and MANTHORPE, J. (eds). *Older workers in Europe.* Miton Keynes: Open University Press.

ITZIN, C., PHILLIPSON, C. and LACZKO, F. (1993) *Age barriers at work – maximising the potential of mature and older workers.* Solihull: Metropolitan Authorities Recruitment Agency.

JOSEPH ROWNTREE FOUNDATION. (2003) *The role of flexible employment for older workers.* York: Joseph Rowntree Foundation.

LORETTO, W., VICKERSTAFF, S. and WHITE, P. (2005) *Older workers and options for flexible work.* Manchester: Equal Opportunities Commission.

MCNAIR, S. and FLYNN, M. (2005a) *Age management in the automotive industry: a baseline analysis.* Report sent to ESF Article 6: not yet in the public domain, Brussels.

MCNAIR, S. and FLYNN, M. (2005b) *The age dimension of employment practices: employer case studies.* London: Department of Trade and Industry.

MCNAIR, S., FLYNN, M. and DUTTON, Y. (2007) *Employer responses to an ageing workforce: a qualitative study.* London: DWP.

MCNAIR, S., FLYNN, M., OWEN, L., HUMPHREYS, C. and WOODFIELD, S. (2004) *Changing work in later life: a study of job transitions.* Guildford: CROW-University of Surrey.

MEADOWS, P. (2004) *Retirement ages in the UK: a review of the literature.* London: DTI.

METCALF, H. and MEADOWS, P. (2006) *Survey of employers' policies, practices and preferences relating to age.* London: DWP.

MOONEY, A. and STRATHAM, S. (2002) *The pivot generation: informal care and work after 50.* Bristol: The Policy Press.

MULLER-CAMEN, M., CROUCHER, R., FLYNN, M. and SCHRODER, H. (2010) National institutions and employers' age management practices in Britain and Germany: 'path dependence' and option creation. *Human Relations,* in press.

NAEGELE, G. (1999) Gradual retirement in Germany. *Journal of Aging and Social Policy.* Vol 10, No 3. pp83–102.

PHILLIPSON, C. (2004) Work and retirement transitions – changing sociological and social policy contexts. *Social Policy & Society.* Vol 3, No 2. pp155–162.

PLATMAN, K. (2003) The self-designed career in later life: a study of older portfolio workers in the United Kingdom. *Ageing and Society.* Vol 23. pp281–302.

TAYLOR, P. and WALKER, A. (2003) Age discrimination in the labour market and policy responses: the situation in the United Kingdom. *Geneva Papers on Risk and Insurance – Issues and Practice.* Vol 28, No 4. pp612–624.

UN OFFICE ON AGEING AND INTERNATIONAL ASSOCIATION OF GERONTOLOGY. (2006) *Research agenda on ageing for the 21st century.* Madrid: Valencia Forum.

VICKERSTAFF, S. (2006) 'I'd rather keep running to the end and then jump off the cliff': retirement decisions: who decides? *Journal of Social Policy.* Vol 35, No 3. pp455–472.

WATSON WYATT WORLDWIDE. (2004) *Phased retirement: aligning employer programs with worker preferences – 2004 survey report.* Watson Wyatt Worldwide.

CHAPTER 9

AGUILAR, J. (1967) *Scanning the business environment.* New York: Macmillan.

ALLEN, M. and WRIGHT, P. (2007) Strategic management and HRM. In: BOXALL, P., PURCELL, J. and WRIGHT, P. (eds). *Oxford handbook of human resource management.* Oxford: Oxford University Press. pp88–107.

BARNEY, J. (1991) Firm resources and sustained competitive advantage. *Journal of Management.* Vol 17, No 1. pp99–120.

BOXALL, P. and PURCELL, J. (2007) *Strategy and human resource management.* 2nd edition. Basingstoke: Palgrave.

BROOKE, L. and TAYLOR, P. (2005) Managing age relations. *Ageing and Society.* Vol 25. pp415–429.

BURKE, R.J. and NG, E. (2006) The changing nature of work and organizations: implications for human resource management. *Human Resource Management Review.* Vol 16. pp86–94.

GLASS, A. (2007) Understanding generational differences for competitive success. *Industrial and Commercial Training.* Vol 39, No 2. pp98–103.

HOWE, N. and STRAUSS, W. (1991) *Generations: the history of America's future, 1584 to 2069.* London: William Morrow.

HOWE, N. and STRAUSS, W. (2000) *Millennials rising: the next great generation.* New York: Vintage Books.

KETER, V. (2009) Working time directive: opt-out from 48-hour limit on working week. House of Commons Library Standard Note, SN/BT/2073.

MARCHINGTON, M. and WILKINSON, A. (2008) Forces shaping HRM at work. In: MARCHINGTON, M. and WILKINSON, A. (eds). *Human resource management at work.* London: CIPD.

MAZEY, S. and RICHARDSON, J. (1993) *Lobbying in the European Community.* Oxford: Oxford University Press.

MICHIE, R.C. (2004) The City of London and the British government: the changing relationship. In: *The British government and the City of London in the twentieth century.* Cambridge: Cambridge University Press, pp31–55.

ONS. (2006) *Projections of the UK labour force, 2006 to 2020.* London: The Stationery Office.

PENROSE, E.T. (1959) *The theory of the growth of the firm.* Oxford: Basil Blackwell.

PRIEM, R. and BUTLER, J. (2001) Is the resource-based 'view' a useful perspective for strategic management research? *Academy of Management Review.* Vol 26, No 1. pp22–40.

ROYLE, T. and TOWERS, B. (eds) (2002) *Labour relations in the global fast food industry.* London: Routledge.

RUBERY, J., COOKE, F.L., EARNSHAW, J. and MARCHINGTON, M. (2003) Inter-organisational relations and employment in a multi-employer environment. *British Journal of Industrial Relations.* Vol 41, No 2. pp265–289.

SAINT-PAUL, G. (2004) *The brain drain: some evidence from European expatriates in the US.* CEPR Discussion Papers 4680, Centre for Economic Policy Research, London.

SCHUMPETER, J.A. (1975) *Capitalism, socialism and democracy.* New York: Harper. pp82–85.

TAYLOR, S. and LUCAS, R. (2006) Employment law. In: LUCAS, R., LUPTON, B. and MATHIESON, H. (eds). *Human resource management in an international context.* London: CIPD. pp259–282.

WERNERFELT, B. (1997) A resource-based view of the firm. In: FOSS, N.J. (ed.). *Resources, firms and strategies.* Oxford: Oxford University Press. pp117–130.

CHAPTER 10

BAKKER, A.B. and LEITER, M.P. (eds) (2010) *Work engagement: a handbook of essential theory and research.* Hove: Psychology Press.

BAMFIELD, J. (2008) *The global retail theft barometer 2008.* Nottingham: Centre for Retail Research/Checkpoint Systems.

BANDURA, A. (1977) *Social learning theory.* Englewood Cliffs, NJ: Prentice-Hall Publishers.

BARRICK, M.R., MOUNT, M.K. and STRAUSS, J.P. (1993) Conscientiousness and performance of sales representatives: test of the mediating effects of goal setting. *Journal of Applied Psychology.* Vol 78, No 5. pp715–722.

BARRICK, M.R., STEWART, G.L. and PIOTROWSKI, M. (2002) Personality and job performance: test of the mediating effects of motivation among sales representatives. *Journal of Applied Psychology.* Vol 87, No 1. pp43–51.

BBC NEWS. (2009) Man denies peanut sabotage plan. Available online at http:// news.bbc.co.uk/1/hi/england/nottinghamshire/7843310.stm.

BOMMER, W.H., MILES, E.W. and GROVER, S.L. (2003) Does one good turn deserve another? Coworker influences on employee citizenship. *Journal of Organizational Behavior.* Vol 24. pp181–196.

BOUCKENOOGHE, D., DEBUSSCHE, F. and WARMOES, V. (2006) Perception and diversity. In: BUELENS, M., VAN DEN BROECK, H., VANDERHEYDEN, K., KREITNER, R. and KINICKI, A. (eds). *Organisational behaviour.* 3rd ed. Maidenhead: McGraw-Hill Education. pp126–170.

BOXALL, P. and PURCELL, J. (2003) *Strategy and human resource management.* Basingstoke: Palgrave Macmillan.

CAMPBELL, J.P., MCCLOY, R.A., OPPLER, S.H. and SAGER, C.E. (1993) A theory of performance. In: SCHMITT, N., BORMAN, W.C. and ASSOCIATES (eds). *Personnel selection in organizations.* San Francisco, CA: Jossey-Bass. pp35–70.

CHAMORRO-PREMUZIC, T. (2007) *Personality and individual differences.* Oxford: The British Psychological Society/Blackwell Publishing.

CHIABURU, D.S. and HARRISON, D.A. (2008) Do peers make the place? Conceptual synthesis and meta-analysis of coworker effects on perceptions, attitudes, OCBs, and performance. *Journal of Applied Psychology.* Vol 93, No 5. pp1082–1103.

COCH, L. and FRENCH, Jr, J.R.P. (1948) Overcoming resistance to change. *Human Relations.* Vol 1, No 4. pp512–532.

COLQUITT, J.A., LEPINE, J.A. and WESSON, M.J. (2009) *Organizational behavior: essentials for improving performance and commitment in the workplace.* New York: McGraw-Hill, Irwin.

CONLON, D.E., MEYER, C.J. and NOWAKOWSKI, J.M. (2005) How does organizational justice affect performance, withdrawal, and counterproductive behavior? In GREENBERG, J. and COLQUITT, J.A. (eds). *Handbook of organizational justice.* Mahwah, NJ: Lawrence Erlbaum Associates. pp301–327.

ERTÜRK, A. (2007) Increasing organizational citizenship behaviours of Turkish academicians: mediating role of trust in supervisor on the relationship between organizational justice and citizenship behaviours. *Journal of Managerial Psychology.* Vol 22, No 3. pp257–270.

FARRELL, D. (1983) Exit, voice, loyalty, and neglect as responses to job dissatisfaction: a multidimensional scaling study. *Academy of Management Journal.* Vol 26, No 4. pp596–607.

FARRELL, D. and STAMM, C.L. (1988) Meta-analysis of the correlates of employee absence. *Human Relations.* Vol 41, No 3. pp211–227.

FASSINA, N.E., JONES, D.A. and UGGERSLEV, K.L. (2008) Meta-analytic tests of relationships between organizational justice and citizenship behaviour: testing agent-system and shared-variance models. *Journal of Organizational Behavior.* Vol 29. pp805–828.

FOX, S. and SPECTOR, P.E. (1999) A model of work frustration-aggression. *Journal of Organizational Behavior.* Vol 20. pp915–931.

FURNHAM, A. and TAYLOR, J. (2004) *The dark side of behaviour at work: understanding and avoiding employees leaving, thieving and deceiving.* Basingstoke: Palgrave Macmillan.

GODARD, J. (2004) A critical assessment of the high-performance paradigm. *British Journal of Industrial Relations.* Vol 42, No 2. pp349–378.

GRATTON, L., HOPE-HAILEY, V., STILES, P. and TRUSS, C. (1999) Linking individual performance to business strategy: the people process model. In: SCHULER, R.S. and JACKSON, S.E. (eds). *Strategic human resource management.* Oxford: Blackwell Publishing.

GRIFFIN, R.W., O'LEARY-KELLY, A. and COLLINS, J. (1998) Dysfunctional work behaviours in organizations. In COOPER, C.L. and ROUSSEAU, D.M. (eds). *Trends in organizational behaviour.* Chichester: John Wiley and Sons. pp65–82.

HACKMAN, J.R., OLDHAM, G., JANSON, R. and PURDY, K. (1975) A new strategy for job enrichment. *California Management Review.* Vol 17, No 4. pp57–71.

HUCZYNSKI, A.A. and BUCHANAN, D.A. (2007) *Organizational behaviour.* 6th ed. Harlow: Pearson Education.

HULIN, C. (1991) Adaptation, persistence and commitment in organizations. In: DUNNETTE, M.D. and HOUGH, L.M. (eds). *Handbook of industrial and organizational psychology.* Palo Alto, CA: Consulting Psychologists Press. pp445–505.

HURTZ, G.M. and DONOVAN, J.J. (2000) Personality and performance: the big five revisited. *Journal of Applied Psychology.* Vol 85, No 6. pp869–879.

IVERSON, R.D. and DEERY, S.J. (2001) Understanding the personological basis of employee withdrawal: the influence of affective disposition on employee tardiness, early departure, and absenteeism. *Journal of Applied Psychology.* Vol 86, No 5. pp856–866.

JEX, S.M. and BRITT, T.W. (2008) *Organizational psychology: a scientist-practitioner approach*. 2nd ed. Hoboken, NJ: John Wiley and Sons.

JONES, D.A. (2009) Getting even with one's supervisor and one's organization: relationships among types of injustice, desires for revenge, and counterproductive work behaviors. *Journal of Organizational Behaviour*. Vol 30. pp525–542.

KARRIKER, J.H. and WILLIAMS, M.L. (2009) Organizational justice and organizational citizenship behaviour: a mediated multifoci model. *Journal of Management*. Vol 35, No 1. pp112–135.

KOSLOWSKY, M. (2000) A new perspective on employee lateness. *Applied Psychology: An International Review*. Vol 49, No 3. pp390–407.

LANDY, F.J. and CONTE, J.M. (2010) *Work in the 21st century: an introduction to industrial and organizational psychology*. 3rd ed. Hoboken, NJ: John Wiley and Sons.

LAVELLE, J.J., BROCKNER, J., KONOVSKY, M.A., PRICE, K.H., HENLEY, A.B., TANEJA, A. and VINEKAR, V. (2009) Commitment, procedural fairness and organizational citizenship behaviour: a multifoci analysis. *Journal of Organizational Behavior*. Vol 30. pp337–357.

LEPINE, J.A., EREZ, A. and JOHNSON, D.E. (2002) The nature and dimensionality of organizational citizenship behaviour: a critical review and meta-analysis. *Journal of Applied Psychology*. Vol 87, No 1. pp52–65.

MACLEOD, D. and CLARKE, N. (2009) *Engaging for success: enhancing performance through employee engagement*. London: Department for Business, Innovation and Skills.

MAYO, G.E. (1933) *The human problems of an industrial civilization*. New York: Macmillan Publishing.

MOTOWIDLO, S.J., BORMAN, W.C. and SCHMIT, M.J. (1997) A theory of individual differences in task and contextual performance. *Human Performance*. Vol 10, No 2. pp71–83.

NICHOLSON, N. and JOHNS, G. (1985) The absence culture and the psychological contract – who's in control of absence? *Academy of Management Review*. Vol 10, No 3. pp397–407.

ORGAN, D.W. and RYAN, K. (1995) A meta-analytic review of attitudinal and dispositional predictors of organizational citizenship behaviour. *Personnel Psychology*. Vol 48. pp775–802.

ORGAN, D.W., PODSAKOFF, P.M. and MACKENZIE, S.B. (2006) *Organizational citizenship behaviour: its nature, antecedents, and consequences*. Thousand Oaks, CA: Sage Publications.

PAETZOLD, R.L. (2004) Sexual harassment as dysfunctional behaviour in organizations. In: GRIFFIN, R.W. and O'LEARY-KELLY, A.M. (eds). *The dark side of organizational behaviour*. San Francisco, CA: Jossey-Bass. pp159–186.

PETERS, L.H. and O'CONNOR, E.J. (1980) Situational constraints and work outcomes: the influences of a frequently overlooked construct. *Academy of Management Review.* Vol 5, No 3. pp391–397.

PODSAKOFF, N.P., WHITING, S.W., PODSAKOFF, P.M. and BLUME, B.D. (2009) Individual- and organizational-level consequences of organizational citizenship behaviours: a meta-analysis. *Journal of Applied Psychology.* Vol 94, No 1. pp122–141.

PODSAKOFF, P.M., AHEARNE, M. and MACKENZIE, S.B. (1997) Organizational citizenship behaviour and the quantity and quality of work group performance. *Journal of Applied Psychology.* Vol 82, No 2. pp262–270.

PODSAKOFF, P.M., MACKENZIE, S.B. and BOMMER, W.H. (1996) Meta-analysis of the relationships between Kerr and Jermier's substitutes for leadership and employee job attitudes, role perceptions and performance. *Journal of Applied Psychology.* Vol 81, No 4. pp380–399.

PODSAKOFF, P.M., MACKENZIE, S.B., PAINE, J.B. and BACHRACH, D.G. (2000) Organizational citizenship behaviours: a critical review of the theoretical and empirical literature and suggestions for future research. *Journal of Management.* Vol 26, No 3. pp513–563.

RAELIN, J.A. (1986) An analysis of professional deviance within organisations. *Human Relations.* Vol 39, No 12. pp1103–1129.

ROBINSON, S.L. and BENNETT, R.J. (1995) A typology of deviant workplace behaviours: a multidimensional scaling study. *Academy of Management Journal.* Vol 38, No 2. pp555–572.

ROBINSON, S.L. and O'LEARY-KELLY, A.M. (1998) Monkey see, monkey do: the influence of work groups on the antisocial behaviour of employees. *Academy of Management Journal.* Vol 41, No 6. pp658–672.

SCHMIDT, F.L. and HUNTER, J. (2004) General mental ability in the world of work: occupational attainment and job performance. *Journal of Personality and Social Psychology.* Vol 86, No 1. pp162–173.

SIEBERT, W.S. and ZUBANOV, N. (2009) Searching for the optimal level of employee turnover: a study of a large UK retail organization. *Academy of Management Journal.* Vol 52, No 2. pp294–313.

SKARLICKI, D.P. and FOLGER, R. (1997) Retaliation in the workplace: the roles of distributive, procedural and interactional justice. *Journal of Applied Psychology.* Vol 82, No 3. pp434–443.

SKARLICKI, D.P. and LATHAM, G.P. (1996) Increasing citizenship behaviour within a labour union: a test of organizational justice theory. *Journal of Applied Psychology.* Vol 81, No 2. pp161–169.

SKARLICKI, D.P. and LATHAM, G.P. (1997) Leadership training in organizational justice to increase citizenship behaviour within a labour union: a replication. *Personnel Psychology.* Vol 50. pp617–633.

SPECTOR, P.E. (2008) *Industrial and organizational psychology: research and practice*. 5th ed. Hoboken, NJ: John Wiley and Sons.

STEWART, G.L. (1999) Trait bandwidth and stages of job performance: assessing differential effects for conscientiousness and its subtraits. *Journal of Applied Psychology*. Vol 84, No 6. pp959–968.

STURMAN, M.C. (2003) Searching for the inverted u-shaped relationship between time and performance: meta-analyses of the experience/performance, tenure/performance, and age/performance relationships. *Journal of Management*. Vol 29, No 5. pp609–640.

TETT, R.P., STEELE, J.R. and BEAUREGARD, R.S. (2003) Broad and narrow measures on both sides of the personality-job performance relationship. *Journal of Organizational Behavior*. Vol 24. pp335–356.

TRUSS, C., SOANE, E., EDWARDS, C.Y.L., WISDOM, K., CROLL, A. and BURNETT, J. (2006) *Working life: employee attitudes and engagement 2006*. London: Chartered Institute of Personnel and Development.

VARDI, Y. and WEITZ, E. (2004) *Misbehaviour in organizations: theory, research, and management*. Mahwah, NJ: Lawrence Erlbaum Associates.

WEFALD, A.J. and DOWNEY, R.G. (2009) Job engagement in organisations: fad, fashion, or folderol? *Journal of Organizational Behavior*. Vol 30. pp141–145.

YANG, J. and DIEFENDORFF, J.M. (2009) The relations of daily counterproductive workplace behaviour with emotions, situational antecedents and personality moderators: a diary study in Hong Kong. *Personnel Psychology*. Vol 62. pp259–295.

YUKL, G.A. and LATHAM, G.P. (1975) Consequences of reinforcement schedules and incentive magnitudes for employee performance: problems encountered in an industrial setting. *Journal of Applied Psychology*. Vol 60, No 3. pp294–298.

CHAPTER 11

ABRAMOVSKY, L., GRIFFITH, R. and SAKO, M. (2004) *Offshoring of business services and its impact on the UK economy*. Advanced Institute of Management Research. Available online at www.ifs.org.uk/bns/bnoffshoring.pdf

ASCHER, K. (1987) *The politics of privatisation – contracting out public services*. Basingstoke: Macmillan Education.

ATKINSON, J. (1984) Manpower strategies for flexible organisations. *Personnel Management*. August. pp28–31.

ATKINSON, R.D. (2004) *Understanding the offshoring challenge*. Policy report. May. Progressive Policy Institute. Available online at www.ppionline.org/documents/Offshoring_0504.pdf

ATKINSON, J. and MEAGER, N. (1986) Is flexibility just a flash in the pan? *Personnel Management.* September. pp26–29.

BACHMANN, R. (2003) The coordination of relations across organisational boundaries. *International Studies of Management and Organisations.* Vol 33, No 2. pp7–21.

BBC NEWS. (2009) Fears for jobs at biscuit company. BBC News Channel, 13 March. Available online at http://news.bbc.co.uk/1/hi/england/merseyside/7942709.stm

BREWSTER, C., SPARROW, P. and VERNON, G. (2007) *International human resource management.* 2nd ed. London: CIPD.

BURCHELL, B.J., DAY, D., HUDSON, M., LAPIDO, D., MANKELEW, R., NOLAN, J.P., REED, H., WICHERT, C.I. and WILKINSON, F. (1999) *Job insecurity and work intensification: flexibility and the changing boundaries of work.* Work and Opportunity series No11. York: York Publishing Services.

CARMEL, E. and TJIA, P. (2005) *Offshoring information technology: sourcing and outsourcing to a global workforce.* Cambridge: Cambridge University Press.

CARROLL, M., COOKE, F.L., HASSARD, J. and MARCHINGTON, M. (2002) The strategic management of outsourcing in the UK ceramic tableware industry. *Competition and Change.* Vol 6, No 4. pp327–343.

CATCHPOWLE, L., CRONIN, B. and HALL, D. (2007) Offshoring and its consequences for the employment relationship in the service sector. *International Journal of Employment Studies.* Vol 15, No 1. pp25–47.

COASE, R. (1937) The nature of the firm. *Economica.* Vol 4, No 16. pp386–405.

CONKLIN, D.W. (2005) Risks and rewards in HR business process outsourcing. *Long Range Planning.* Vol 38. pp579–598.

COOKE, F.L. (2001a) Maintaining change: the maintenance function and the change process. *New Technology, Work and Employment.* Vol 18, No 1. pp35–49.

COOKE, F.L. (2001b) Human resource strategy to improve organisational performance: a route for British firms? *International Journal of Management Reviews.* Vol 3, No 4. pp321–339.

CORBETT, M.F. (2004) *The outsourcing revolution: why it makes sense and how to do it right.* Chicago: Dearborn Trade Publishing.

CURSON, C. (ed.) (1986) *Flexible patterns of work.* London: Institute of Personnel Management.

DAS, T.K. and TENG, B.S. (2001) Trust, control and risk in strategic alliances: an integrated framework. *Organisation Studies.* Vol 22, No 2. pp251–283.

DAVIS-BLAKE, A. and UZZI, B. (1993) Determinants of employment externalisation: a study of temporary workers and independent contractors. *Administrative Science Quarterly.* Vol 38. pp195–223.

DOMBERGER, S. (1998) *The contracting organisation: a strategic guide to outsourcing.* Oxford: Oxford University Press.

DOWLING, P.J., FESTING, M. and ENGLE, A.D. (2008) *International human resource management.* 5th ed. London: Thompson Learning.

GREENE, B. (2000) Independent contractors: an attractive option? *New Zealand Journal of Industrial Relations.* Vol 25, No 2. pp183–204.

HARTLEY, J., JACOBSON, D., KLANDERMANS, B. and VAN VUUREN, T. (1991) *Job insecurity.* London: Sage Publications.

HESKETH, A. (2005) Focus on your core skills. *Personnel Today.* September. p21.

HUNTER, I. (2006) *The Indian offshore advantage: how offshoring is changing the face of HR.* Aldershot: Gower.

JENNINGS, D. (2002) Strategic sourcing: benefits, problems and a contextual model. *Management Decision.* Vol 40, No 1–2. pp26–34.

JOHNSON, M. (1997) *Outsourcing in brief.* London: Butterworth-Heinemann.

KENNEDY, J.F., HOLT, D.T., WARD, A.W. and REHG, M.T. (2002) The influence of outsourcing on job satisfaction and turnover intentions of technical managers. *Human Resource Planning.* Vol 25, No 1. pp23–31.

KHATRI, N. and BUDHWAR, P.S. (2001) A study of strategic HR issues in an Asian context. *Personnel Review.* Vol 31, No 2. pp166–188.

LEVER, S. (1997) An analysis of managerial motivations behind outsourcing practices in human resources. *Human Resource Planning.* Vol 20, No 2. pp37–47.

LONSDALE, C. and COX, A. (1997) Outsourcing: risks and rewards. *Supply Management.* Vol 2, No 14. pp32–34.

LONSDALE, C. and COX, A. (2000) The historical development of outsourcing: the latest fad? *Industrial Management.* Vol 100, No 9. pp444–450.

MAUL, J.P. and KRAUSS, J.D. (1996) Outsourcing in training and education. In CRAIG, R.L. (ed.). *The ASTD training and development handbook.* New York: McGraw-Hill. pp1008–1030.

NEDO. (1986) *Changing working patterns: how companies achieve flexibility to meet new needs.* London: National Economic Development Office.

NELSON, A., COOPER, C.L. and JACKSON, P.R. (1995) Uncertainty amidst change: the impact of privatisation on employee job satisfaction and well-being. *Journal of Occupational and Organisational Psychology.* Vol 68, No 1. pp57–71.

NOOTEBOOM, B. (1999) *Inter-firm alliances: analysis and design.* London: Routledge.

OATES, D. (1998) *Outsourcing and the virtual organisation.* London: Century Ltd.

O'CONNELL-DAVIDSON, J. (1991) Subcontract, flexibility and changing employment relations in the water industry. In: BLYTON, P. and MORRIS, J. (eds). *A flexible future? Prospects of employment and organisation.* Berlin: Walter de Gruyter. pp241–258.

OECD. (2007) *Offshoring and employment: trends and impacts.* Paris: OECD Publishing.

OSLAND, G.E. and YAPRAK, A. (1995) Learning through strategic alliances. *European Journal of Marketing.* Vol 29, No 3. pp52–66.

PETERS, T. and WATERMAN, R. (1982) *In search of excellence.* New York: Harper & Row.

PFEFFER, J. and BARON, J. (1988) Taking the workers back out: recent trends in the structuring of employment. *Research in Organisational Behaviour.* Vol 10. pp257–303.

PITT, P. (2005) Staff newsletter: partnership, pay and offshoring. *Globe.* pp18–21.

PORTER, M.E. (1990) *The competitive advantage of nations.* Basingstoke: Macmillan.

PRAHALAD, C.K. and HAMEL, G. (1990) The core competence of the corporation. *Harvard Business Review.* Vol 68, No 3. pp79–91.

QUINN, J.B., DOORELY, T.L. and PAQUETTE, P.C. (1990) Technology in services: rethinking strategic focus. *Sloan Management Review.* Winter. pp79–87.

REILLY, P. and TAMKIN, P. (1996) *Outsourcing: a flexible option for the future?* Report No320. Brighton: Institute of Employment Studies.

ROTHERY, B. and ROBERTSON, I. (1995) *The truth about outsourcing.* Aldershot: Gower Publishing.

RUBERY, J., EARNSHAW, J., MARCHINGTON, M., COOKE, F.L. and VINCENT, S. (2002) Changing organisational forms and the employment relationship. *Journal of Management Studies.* Vol 39. pp645–672.

SKIPPER, W. (2006) Services offshoring: an overview. *Anthropology of Work Review.* Vol 27, No 2. pp9–17.

VOLBERDA, W.H. (1998) *Building the flexible firm: how to remain competitive.* Oxford: Oxford University Press.

WILLIAMSON, O.E. (1975) *Markets and hierarchies: analysis and antitrust implications.* New York: Free Press.

WOODALL, J., GOURLAY, S. and SHORT, D. (2002) Trends in outsourcing HRD in the UK: the implications for strategic HRD. *International Journal of Human Resource Development and Management.* Vol 2, No 1–2. pp50–66.

ZINELDIN, M. and BREDENLOW, T. (2003) Strategic alliance: synergies and challenges: a case of strategic outsourcing relationship SOUR. *International*

Journal of Physical Distribution & Logistics Management. Vol 33, No 5. pp449–464.

CHAPTER 12

ACKROYD, P. and THOMPSON, P. (1999) *Misbehaviour at work.* London: Sage.

ALFES, K., TRUSS, K., SOANE, E., REES, C. and GATENBY, M. (2010) *Creating an engaged workforce.* Research report. London: Chartered Institute of Personnel and Development.

ARMSTRONG, M. (2007) *A handbook of human resource management.* London: Kogan Page.

BARRATT, C. (2009) *Trade union membership 2008.* London: BERR/National Statistics.

BBC NEWS. (2008) Crew sacked over Facebook posts. Available online at http://news.bbc.co.uk/go/pr/fr/-/1/hi/uk/7703129.stm

BEHREND, H. (1957) The effort bargain. *Industrial and Labour Relations Review.* July. pp503–515.

BLYTON, P. and TURNBULL, P. (2005) *The dynamics of employee relations.* 3rd ed. Basingstoke: Palgrave.

CBI. (2008) Sickies and long term absence give employers a headache. Confederation of British Industry Press Release, 14 May.

CIPD. (2008a) *Absence management.* Annual survey report. London: Chartered Institute of Personnel and Development.

CIPD. (2008b) *Recruitment, retention and turnover.* Annual survey report. London: Chartered Institute of Personnel and Development.

CIPD. (2009) *Employee engagement.* London: Chartered Institute of Personnel and Development.

CULLINANE, N. and DUNDON, T. (2006) The psychological contract: a critical review. *International Journal of Management Reviews.* Vol 8, No 2. pp113–129.

CUNNINGHAM, I., HYMAN, J. and BALDRY, C. (1996) Empowerment: the power to do what? *Industrial Relations Journal.* Vol 27, No 2. pp143–154.

DARLINGTON, R. (ed.) (2009) *What's the point of industrial relations? In defence of critical social science.* Manchester: British Universities Industrial Relations Association.

DIX, G., FORTH, J. and SISSON, K. (2008) *Conflict at work: the pattern of disputes in Britain since 1980.* NIESR Discussion Paper 316.

EDWARDS, P. and SCULLION, H. (1984) *The social organization of industrial conflict.* Oxford: Blackwell.

EMMOTT, M. (2006) *What is employee relations?* London: Chartered Institute of Personnel and Development.

FOX, A. (1966) *Industrial sociology and industrial relations.* Royal Commission Research Paper No 3. London: HMSO.

GRIFFIN, J.I. (1939) *Strikes.* New York: Columbia University Press.

GUARDIAN. (2007) Directory firm wants ex-workers' Facebook page shut down. 7 August.

GUEST, D. (1998) Is the psychological contract worth taking seriously? *Journal of Organizational Behaviour.* Special Issue: The Psychological Contract at Work. Vol 19. pp649–664.

GUEST, D. (2009) *Public and private sector perspectives on the psychological contract: results of the 2001 CIPD survey.* London: Chartered Institute of Personnel and Development.

GUEST, D. and CONWAY, N. (1999) Peering into the black hole: the downside of the new employment relations in the UK. *British Journal of Industrial Relations.* Vol 37, No 3. pp367–389.

GUEST, D. and CONWAY, N. (2002a) Communicating the psychological contract: an employer perspective. *Human Resource Management Journal.* Vol 12, No 2. pp22–38.

GUEST, D. and CONWAY, N. (2002b) *Employee well-being and the psychological contract.* Research report. London: Chartered Institute of Personnel and Development.

GUEST, D. and CONWAY, N. (2004) *Employee well-being and the psychological contract.* Research report. London: Chartered Institute of Personnel and Development.

HALE, D. (2009) Labour disputes in 2008. *Economic and Labour Market Review.* Vol 3, No 6. pp26–38.

HEERY, E. (2002) Partnership versus organising: alternative futures for British trade unionism. *Industrial Relations Journal.* Vol 33, No 1. pp20–33.

HOTHSCHILD, A. (2003) *The managed heart: commercialization of human feeling.* Berkeley: University of California Press.

HOWELL, C. (2005) *Trade unions and the state: the construction of industrial relations institutions in Britain 1890–2000.* Princeton: Princeton University Press.

KELLY, J. (1998) *Rethinking industrial relations: mobilization, collectivism and long waves.* London: Routledge.

KERSLEY, B., ALPIN, C., FORTH, J., BRYSON, A., BEWLEY, H., DIX, G. and OXENBRIDGE, S. (2005) *Inside the workplace: findings from the 2004 Workplace Employment Relations Survey.* London: Routledge.

MACLEOD, D. (2009) Interview in view. No 22. Summer. NHS Institute for Innovation and Improvement.

MACLEOD, D. and CLARKE, N. (2009) *Engaging for success: enhancing performance through employee engagement*. London: Department for Business, Innovation and Skills.

MARS, G. (1982) *Cheats at work: an anthropology of workplace crime*. London: Counterpoint.

MILLWARD, N., BRYSON, A. and FORTH, J. (2000) *All change at work? – British employment relations 1980–1998 as portrayed by the Workplace Industrial Relations Survey series*. London: Routledge.

NOON, M. and BLYTON, P. (2007) *The realities of work*. 3rd ed. Basingstoke: Palgrave.

PENCAVEL, J. (2004) The surprising retreat of union Britain. In: CARD, D., BLUNDELL, R. and FREEMAN, R. (eds). *Seeking a premier economy: the economic effects of British economic reforms 1980–2000*. Chicago: University of Chicago Press.

POLLERT, A. (1991) The orthodoxy of flexibility. In: POLLERT, A. (ed.). *A farewell to flexibility*. Oxford: Blackwell.

PURCELL, J., KINNIE, N., HUTCHINSON, S., RAYTON, B. and SWART, J. (2003) *Understanding the people and performance link: unlocking the black box*. Research report. London: Chartered Institute of Personnel and Development.

ROBINSON, D., PERRYMAN, S. and HAYDAY, S. (2004) *The drivers of employee engagement*. Brighton: Institute for Employment Studies.

ROUSSEAU, D. (1996) *Psychological contracts in organizations: understanding written and unwritten agreements*. Newbury Park, CA: Sage.

TAYLOR, P., MULVEY, G., HYMAN, J. and BAIN, P. (2002) Work organisation, control and the experience of work in call centres. *Work, Employment & Society*. Vol 16, No 1. pp133–150.

TRUSS, K., SOANE, E., EDWARDS, C., WISDOM, K., CROLL, A. and BURNETT, J. (2006) *Working life: employee attitudes and engagement*. London: Chartered Institute of Personnel and Development.

ULRICH, D. and BROCKBANK, W. (2005) *The HR value proposition*. Boston, MA: Harvard Business School Press.

WALTON, W. and MCKERSIE, R. (1991) *A behavioural theory of labour negotiations*. 2nd ed. New York: McGraw-Hill.

CHAPTER 13

ANGLO AMERICAN. (2007) *Response to allegations made in War on Want's 'Anglo American: the alternative report'*. London: Anglo American.

ANGLO AMERICAN. (2008) *AGM 2008 – chairman's speech*. AngloAmerican

Plc. Available online at www.angloamerican.com/aal/investors/meetings/agm2008/chairman2008/?t=print&set=low

BBC NEWS. (2008) Merger forms transatlantic union. 2 July. Available online at http://news.bbc.co.uk/1/hi/business/7484639.stm

BREWSTER, C., WOOD, G., CROUCHER, R. and BROOKES, M. (2007) Are works councils a threat to trade unions? *Economic and Industrial Democracy*. Vol 28, No 1. pp49–77.

CROUCHER, R. and COTTON, E. (2009) *Global unions, global business: global union federations and international business*. London: Middlesex University Press.

HOLDCROFT, J. (2006) International framework agreements: a progress report. *Metalworld*. Vol 3. pp18–22.

HYMAN, R. (2002) *The international labour movement on the threshold of two centuries: agitation, organisation, bureaucracy, diplomacy*. Available online at www.arbarkiv.nu/pdf_wri/Hyman_int.pdf

KLEIN, N. (2010) *No logo*. New York: Picador.

RIZOV, M. and CROUCHER, R. (2009) Human resource management and performance in European firms. *Cambridge Journal of Economics*. Vol 33, No 2. pp253–272.

SCHÖMANN, I., SOBCZAK, A., VOSS, E. and WILKE, P. (2008) *Codes of conduct and international framework agreements: new forms of governance at company level*. Dublin: European Foundation for the Improvement of Living and Working Conditions.

VON HOLDT, K. (2004) Political transition and the changing workplace order in a South African steelworks. In: WEBSTER, E. and VON HOLDT, K. (eds). *Beyond the apartheid workplace: studies in transition*. Scottsville: University of Kwa-Zulu Natal Press. pp45–72.

WAR ON WANT. (2007) *Anglo American: the alternative report*. London: War on Want.

CHAPTER 14

ARGYRIS, C. and SCHÖN, D. (1978) *Organizational learning: a theory of action perspective*. Reading, MA.: Addison Wesley.

ARGYRIS, C. and SCHÖN, D. (1990) *Overcoming organizational defenses: facilitating organizational learning*. Upper Saddle River, NJ: Prentice Hall.

BARHAM, K., FRASER, J. and HEATH, L. (1988) *Management for the future*. London: Ashridge Management Research Group.

BBC NEWS. (2007a) Northern Rock shares plunge 32 percent. Available online at http://news.bbc.co.uk/1/hi/business/6994328.stm

BBC NEWS. (2007b) Rush on Northern Rock continues. Available online at http://news.bbc.co.uk/1/hi/business/6996136.stm

BURGOYNE, J.G. (1995) Learning from experience: from individual discovery to meta-dialogue via the evolution of transitional myths. *Personnel Review*. Vol 24, No 6. pp61–72.

BURGOYNE, J., PEDLER, M. and BOYDELL, T. (1994) *Towards the learning company: concepts and practices*. London: McGraw-Hill.

DEGEUS, A. (1988) Planning as learning. *Harvard Business Review*. Vol 66, No 2. pp70–74.

DIBELLA, A.J. and NEVIS, E.C. (1998) *How organisations learn: an integrated strategy for building learning capacity*. San Francisco: Jossey Bass.

DIXON, N. (1994) *The organisational learning cycle: how can we learn collectively*. London: McGraw-Hill.

EASTERBY-SMITH, M. and LYLES, M. (2003) Watersheds of organizational learning and knowledge management. In: EASTERBY-SMITH, M. and LYLES, M. (eds). *Blackwell handbook of organizational learning and knowledge management*. Oxford: Blackwell. pp1–16.

FIOL, C. and LYLES, M. (1985) Organisational learning. *Academy of Management Review*. Vol 10, No 4. pp803–813.

GARRALT, B. (1987) *The learning organisation*. London: Fontana.

GARRALT, B. (1990) *Creating a learning organisation: a guide to leadership, learning and development*. Cambridge: Director Books.

HARRISON, R. and KESSELS, J. (2004) *Human resource development in a knowledge economy: an organisational view*. London: Palgrave Macmillan.

HARTOG, M. (2004a) Critical action learning: teaching business ethics. *Reflective Practice*. Vol 5, No 3. pp395–40.

HARTOG, M. (2004b) Educating the reflective educator. In: REYNOLDS, M. and VINCE, R. (eds). *Organizing reflection*. Aldershot: Ashgate Publishing. pp156–171.

HARTOG, M. and FRAME, P. (2004) Business ethics in the curriculum: integrating ethics through work experience. *Journal of Business Ethics*. Vol 54. pp399–409.

HOLBECHE, L. (2010) *HR leadership*. Oxford: Butterworth-Heinemann.

HOLBECHE, L. and CHEUNG-JUDGE, M.Y. (2009) Organisational development – what's in a name? *IMPACT: Quarterly Update on CIPD Policy and Research*, No 26, February.

LAVE, J. and WENGER, E. (1991) *Situated learning: legitimate peripheral participation*. Cambridge: Cambridge University Press.

LEITCH, C. (1996) Learning organisations – the measurement of company performance. *Journal of European Industrial Training*. Vol 20, No 1. pp31–44.

LOPEZ, S.P., PEON, J.M.M. and ORDAS, C.J.V. (2005) Organisational learning as a determining factor in business performance. *The Learning Organisation: An International Journal*. Vol 12, No 3. pp227–245.

MARSHALL, J., SMITH, S. and BUXTON, S. (2009) Learning organisations and organisational learning: what have we learned? *Management Services*. Summer. pp36–44.

MAYO, A. and LANK, E. (1994) *The power of learning: a guide to gaining competitive advantage*. London: IPD.

MORGAN, G. (1988) *Riding the waves of change*. London: Jossey Bass.

MULLINS, L.J. (2007) *Management and organisational behaviour*. 8th ed. Harlow: Prentice Hall.

PEDLER, M., BOYDELL, T. and BURGOYNE, J. (1989) The learning company. *Studies in Continuing Education*. Vol 11, No 2. pp91–101.

PEDLER, M., BURGOYNE, J. and BOYDELL, T. (1991) *The learning company: a strategy for sustainable development*. Maidenhead: McGraw-Hill.

PEDLER, M., BURGOYNE, J. and BOYDELL, T. (2000) *The learning company toolkit*. Maidenhead: Peter Honey.

PESTON, R. (2007) Northern Rock gets bank bailout. BBC News, 13 September. Available online at http://news.bbc.co.uk/1/hi/6994099.stm

PETERS, T. and WATERMAN, R.H. (1982) *In search of excellence*. New York: Harper & Row.

POPPER, M. and LIPSHITZ, R. (2000) Organisational learning in a hospital. *Journal of Applied Behavioural Science*. Vol 36, No 3. pp345–361.

RAWNSLEY, A. (2010) *The end of the party: the rise and fall of New Labour*. Viking: Penguin.

REVANS, R. (1982) *The origins and growth of action learning*. Bromley: Chartwell-Bratt.

ROWAN, J. (2001) The humanistic approach to action research. In: REASON, P. and BRADBURY, H. (eds). *The handbook of action research: participative inquiry and practice*. London: Sage. pp114–123.

SENGE, P. (1990) *The fifth discipline: the art and practice of the learning organisation*. New York: Doubleday.

SENGE, P. (2006) *The fifth discipline: the art and practice of the learning organization*. New York: Doubleday.

SENGE, P., ROSS, R., SMITH, B., ROBERTS, C. and KLEINER, A. (1994) *The fifth discipline fieldbook: strategies and tools for building a learning organisation.* London: Nicholas Brealey.

SHIPTON, H. (2006) Cohesion or confusion? Towards a typology for organizational learning research. *International Journal of Management Reviews.* Vol 8, No 4. pp233–252.

SHIPTON, H. and ZHOU, Q. (2008) Learning and development in organisations. In: ASTON CENTRE FOR HUMAN RESOURCES (ed.). *Strategic human resource management: building research-based practice.* London: CIPD. pp159–188.

SLIGO, J. (1996) Disseminating knowledge to build a learning organization. *The International Journal of Human Resource Management.* Vol 7, No 2. pp508–520

TSANG, E. (1997) Organizational learning and the learning organization: a dichotomy between prescriptive and descriptive research. *Human Relations.* Vol 50, No 1. pp73–89.

WALLOP, H. (2007) Northern Rock shares crash as customers queue. *Daily Telegraph.* 14 September. Available online at www.telegraph.co.uk/news/uknews/1563152/Northern-Rock-shares-crash-as-customers queue.

WALTON, J. (1999) *Strategic human resource development.* Harlow: Prentice Hall.

CHAPTER 15

ARMSTRONG, M. and MURLIS, H. (2007) *A handbook of remuneration strategy and practice.* 5th ed. London: Kogan Page.

ARROWSMITH, J. (2009) Regulating pay: the UK's national minimum wage. In: CORBY, S., PALMER, S. and LINDOP, E. (eds). *Rethinking reward.* Basingstoke: Palgrave Macmillan.

BACH, S., GIVAN, R.K. and FORTH, J. (2009) The public sector in transition. In: BROWN, W., BRYSON, A., FORTH, J. and WHITFIELD, K. (eds). *The evolution of the modern workplace.* Cambridge: Cambridge University Press.

BBC NEWS. (2010) What is a head teacher worth? 13 July. Available online www.bbc.co.uk/news/10612470

BEHREND, H. (1957) The effort bargain. *Industrial and Labour Relations Review.* Vol 10, No 4. pp503–515.

BLANCHFLOWER, D.G. and BRYSON, A. (2009) Trade union decline and the economics of the workplace. In: BROWN, W., BRYSON, A., FORTH, J. and WHITFIELD, K. (eds). *The evolution of the modern workplace.* Cambridge: Cambridge University Press.

BROWN, W., BRYSON, A. and FORTH, J. (2009) Competition and the retreat from collective bargaining. In: BROWN, W., BRYSON, A., FORTH, J. and WHITFIELD, K. (eds). *The evolution of the modern workplace.* Cambridge: Cambridge University Press.

BRYSON, A., WILLMAN, P., GOMEZ, R. and KRETSCHMER, T. (2007) *Employee voice and human resource management: an empirical analysis using British data*. London: Policy Studies Institute.

BUTCHER, T. (2005) The hourly earnings distribution before and after the national minimum wage. *Labour Market Trends*. October. pp427–435.

CADBURY, SIR A. (1992) *Report of the Committee on the Financial Aspects of Corporate Governance*. London: Gee Publishing.

CBI/WYATT. (1994) *Variable pay systems*. London: Confederation of British Industry.

CIPD. (2005) *Reward management*. London: CIPD.

CIPD. (2010) *Reward management*. Annual survey report. London: CIPD.

CORBY, S. (2009) Pay equity: gender and age. In: CORBY, S., PALMER, S. and LINDOP, E. (eds). *Rethinking reward*. Basingstoke: Palgrave Macmillan.

CORBY, S., STANWORTH, C. and GREEN, B. (2005) *Gender and the labour market in south east England. Volume 2. Employers' policies and practices*. London: SEEDA/ESF/University of Greenwich.

CROUCHER, R. and WHITE, G. (2007) Enforcing a national minimum wage: the British case. *Policy Studies*. Vol 28, No 2. pp145–161.

DICKENS, R. and MANNING, A. (2003) Minimum wage, minimum impact. In: DICKENS, R., GREGG, P. and WADSWORTH, J. (eds). *The labour market under New Labour: the state of working Britain*. Basingstoke: Palgrave Macmillan.

DOBBS, C. (2007) Patterns of pay: results of the annual survey of hours and earnings, 1997 to 2006. *Economic and Labour Market Review*. Vol 1, No 2. pp44–50.

FIGART, D.M. (2001) Wage setting under Fordism: the rise of job evaluation and ideology of equal pay. *Review of Political Economy*. Vol 13, No 4. pp405–425.

FORTH, J. and MILLWARD, N. (2000) *The determinants of pay levels and fringe benefit provision in Britain*. Discussion paper 171. London: National Institute of Economic and Social Research.

GOMEZ-MEJIA, L. (1993) *Compensation, organisation and firm performance*. San Francisco: Southwestern.

GOMEZ-MEJIA, L.R. and BALKIN, D.B (1992) Determinants of faculty pay: an agency theory perspective. *Academy of Management Journal*. Vol 35, No 5. pp921–955.

GOSPEL, H. (1992) *Markets, firms and the management of labour in modern Britain*. Cambridge: Cambridge University Press.

GRABHAM, A. (2003) Composition of pay. In: *Labour Market Trends*. London: Office for National Statistics. pp397–405.

GREENBURY, SIR R. (1995) *Report of the study group on directors' remuneration*. London: Gee Publishing.

GUEST, D. (1990) Human resource management and the American dream. *Journal of Management Studies*. Vol 27, No 4. pp387–397.

HAMPEL, SIR R. (1998) *Committee on Corporate Governance: final report*. London: Gee Publishing.

HEERY, E. (1996) Risk, representation and the new pay. *Personnel Review*. Vol 25, No 6. pp54–65.

HEERY, E. (2009) Worker voice and reward management. In: WHITE, G. and DRUKER, J. (eds). *Reward management: a critical text*. 2nd ed. Abingdon: Routledge.

HIGGS, D. (2003) *Review of the role and effectiveness of non-executive directors*. Available online at www.bis.gov.uk/files/file23012.pdf

HOUSE OF COMMONS. (2009) Top pay in the public sector – 6th report of session 2009–10 volume 1. *House of Commons Public Administration Select Committee*. London: The Stationery Office.

IDS. (2004) The pros and cons of market-related pay. *IDS Pay Report*. 907. June. pp8–9. London: Incomes Data Services.

IDS. (2006) *Directors' pay report 2006*. London: Incomes Data Services.

KERSLEY, B., ALPIN, C., FORTH, J., BRYSON, A., BEWLEY, H., DIX, G. and OXENBRIDGE, S. (2006) *Inside the workplace: findings from the 2004 Workplace Employment Relations Survey*. London: Routledge.

KESSLER, I. (2007) Reward choices: strategy and equity. In: STOREY, J. (ed.). *Human resource management: a critical text*. 3rd ed. London: Thomson.

LAWLER, E.E. (1990) *Strategic pay: aligning organisational strategies and pay systems*. San Francisco: Jossey-Bass.

LAWLER, E.E. (1995) The new pay: a strategic approach? *Compensation and Benefits Review*. Vol 27. July–August. pp14–22.

LEGGE, K. (1995) *Human resource management: rhetorics and realities*. Basingstoke: Macmillan Business.

LINDOP, E. (2009) Employee voice in pay determination. In: CORBY, S., PALMER, S. and LINDOP, E. (eds). *Rethinking reward*. Basingstoke: Palgrave Macmillan.

LOW PAY COMMISSION. (2007) *National minimum wage: Low Pay Commission report 2007*. London: The Stationery Office.

MACHIN, S. (2003) Wage inequality since 1975. In: DICKENS, R., GREGG, P. and WADSWORTH, J. (eds). *The labour market under New Labour: the state of working Britain*. Basingstoke: Palgrave Macmillan.

MAHONEY, T.A. (1992) Multiple pay contingencies: strategic design of compensation. In: SALAMON, G. (ed.). *Human resource strategies*. London: Sage.

MILLWARD, N., BRYSON, A. and FORTH, J. (2000) *All change at work: British employment relations 1980–1998 as portrayed by the Workplace Industrial Relations Survey series*. London: Routledge.

NATIONAL EQUALITY PANEL. (2010) *An anatomy of economic inequality in the UK*. London: Government Equalities Office.

ONS. (2004) Income: gaps in income and wealth remain large. Press release. 17 May. London: Office for National Statistics.

ONS. (2009) Gender pay gap. Available online at www.statistics.gov.uk/cci/nugget.asp?id=167

PENDLETON, A., WHITFIELD, K. and BRYSON, A. (2009) The changing use of contingent pay at the modern British workplace. In: BROWN, W., BRYSON, A., FORTH, J. and WHITFIELD, K. (eds). *The evolution of the modern workplace*. Cambridge: Cambridge University Press.

PERKINS, S. and WHITE, G. (2010) Modernising pay in the UK public services: trends and implications. *Human Resource Management Journal*. Vol 20, No 3. pp244–257.

PRITCHARD, D. and MURLIS, H. (1992) *Jobs, roles and people: the new world of job evaluation*. London: Nicholas Brealey.

SCHUSTER, J.R. and ZINGHEIM, P. (1992) *The new pay: linking employee and organisational performance*. New York: Lexington Books.

SISSON, K. (1994) Personnel management paradigms, practice and prospects. In: SISSON, K. (ed.). *Personnel management: a comprehensive guide to theory and practice in Britain*. Oxford: Blackwell.

STOREY, J. (1992) *Developments in the management of human resources*. Oxford: Blackwell.

THOMSON, M. (2009) Salary progression systems. In: WHITE, G. and DRUKER, J. (eds). *Reward management: a critical text*. 2nd ed. Abingdon: Routledge.

TREVOR, J. (2008) *Can compensation be strategic? A review of compensation management practice in leading multinational firms*. Working paper. Cambridge: Judge Business School.

TREVOR, J. (2009) Can pay be strategic? In: CORBY, S., PALMER, S. and LINDOP, E. (eds). *Rethinking reward*. Basingstoke: Palgrave Macmillan.

WALKER, D. (2009) *A review of corporate governance in UK banks and other financial industry entities*. 16 July. London: HM Treasury.

WHITE, G. (2009) Determining pay. In: WHITE, G. and DRUKER, J. (eds). *Reward management: a critical text*. 2nd ed. Abingdon: Routledge.

WILLMAN, P., GOMEZ, R. and BRYSON, A. (2009) Voice at the workplace: where do we find it, why is it there and where is it going? In: BROWN, W., BRYSON, A., FORTH, J. and WHITFIELD, K. (eds). *The evolution of the modern workplace*. Cambridge: Cambridge University Press.

CHAPTER 16

ACKER, J. (1990) Hierarchies, jobs, bodies: a theory of gendered organizations. *Gender and Society*. Vol 4, No 2. pp139–158.

BACK-WIKLUND, M. and PLANTIN, L. (2007) The workplace as an arena for negotiating the work–family boundary: a case study of two Swedish social services agencies. In: CROMPTON, R., LEWIS, S. and LYONETTE, C. (eds). *Women, men, work and family in Europe*. Basingstoke: Palgrave. pp171–189.

BAILYN, L. (2006) *Breaking the mold*. 2nd ed. Ithaca, NY: Cornell University Press.

BBC NEWS. (2005a) BA 'excludes mothers as pilots'. 10 January. Available online at http://news.bbc.co.uk/go/pr/fr/-/1/hi/uk/4160447.stm

BBC NEWS. (2005b) BA pilot wins discrimination case. 22 April. Available online at http://news.bbc.co.uk/go/pr/fr/-/1/hi/england/dorset/4471851.stm

BRANDT, B. and KVANDE, E. (2002) Reflexive fathers: negotiating parental leave and working life. *Gender, Work and Organizations*. Vol 9, No 2. pp186–203.

BRITTON, D.M. (2000) The epistemology of the gendered organization. *Gender and Society*. Vol 14, No 3. pp418–435.

CASPER, W.J., WELTMAN, D. and KWESIGA, E. (2007) Beyond family-friendly: the construct and measurement of singles-friendly work culture. *Journal of Vocational Behaviour*. Vol 70. pp478–501.

CHATRAKUL NA AYUDHYA, U. (2009) Too much of one and less of the other: graduates' conceptualizations and expectations of 'work–life balance'. Thesis for the Doctor of Philosophy in Psychology. Manchester Metropolitan University.

CHATRAKUL NA AYUDHYA, U. and LEWIS, S. (2010) From 'balancers' to 'integrators'? Young professionals talk about 'work' and 'life' in the UK. In: KAISER, S., RINGLSTETTER, M., PINA E CUNHA, M. and EIKHOF, D.R. (eds). *Creating balance? International perspectives on the work–life integration of professionals*. Berlin: Springer Science.

CROMPTON, R., LEWIS, S. and LYONETTE, C. (2007) Continuities, change and transformations. In: CROMPTON, R., LEWIS, S. and LYONETTE, C. (eds). *Women, men, work and family in Europe*. Basingstoke: Palgrave. pp230–244.

FLEETWOOD, S. (2007) Re-thinking work–life balance: editor's introduction. *International Journal of Human Resource Management*. Vol 18, No 3. pp351–359.

GAMBLES, R., LEWIS, S. and RAPOPORT, R. (2006) *The myth of work–life balance: the challenge of our time for men, women and societies.* Chichester: Wiley.

GOVERNMENT EQUALITIES OFFICE (GEO). (2010) Gender pay gap. Available online at www.equalities.gov.uk/what_we_do/women_and_work/gender_pay_gap.asp

HAAS, L. and HWANG, P. (2007) Gender and organizational culture. *Gender and Society.* Vol 21. pp52–79.

HAAS, L., ALLARD, K. and HWANG, P. (2002) The impact of organizational culture on men's use of parental leave in Sweden. *Community, Work and Family.* Vol 5, No 3. pp319–342.

HAMMER, L.B., KOSSEK, E.E., BODNER, T., ANGER, K. and ZIMMERMAN, K. (2010 forthcoming) Clarifying work–family intervention processes: the roles of work–family conflict and family supportive supervisor behaviors. *Journal of Applied Psychology.*

HAMMER, L., KOSSEK, E., YRAGUI, N., BODNER, T. and HANSEN, G. (2009) Development and validation of a multi-dimensional scale of family supportive supervisor behaviors. *Journal of Management.* Vol 35. pp837–856.

HOLT, H. and LEWIS, S. (2010 forthcoming) You can stand on your head and still end up with lower pay: gliding segregation and gendered work practices in Danish 'family-friendly' workplaces. *Gender, Work and Organization.*

HOLT, H., GEERDSEN, L.P., CHRISTENSEN, G., KLITGAARD, C. and LIND, M.L. (2006) *Det kønsopdelte arbejdsmarked-en kvantitativ og kvalitativ belysning (The gender segregated labour market – a quantitative and qualitative illustration).* Report No. 2. Copenhagen: Danish National Institute of Social Research.

KOSSEK, E. and HAMMER, L. (2008) Work/life training for supervisors gets big results. *Harvard Business Review.* November. p36.

LEWIS, S. (1997) Family friendly policies: organizational change or playing about at the margins? *Gender, Work and Organization.* Vol 4, No 1. pp13–23.

LEWIS, S. (2001) Restructuring workplace cultures: the ultimate work–family challenge? *Women in Management Review.* Vol 16, No 1. pp21–29.

LEWIS, S. and COOPER, C.L. (2005) *Work–life integration: case studies of organisational change,* Chichester: Wiley.

LEWIS, S. and HUMBERT, A. (2010) Discourse or reality? Work–life balance. flexible working policies and gendered organisations. *Equality, Diversity and Inclusion.* Vol 29, No 3. pp239–254.

LEWIS, S. and ROPER, I. (2008) Flexibility and work–life balance. In: MULLER-CAMEN, M., CROUCHER, R. and LEIGH, S. (eds). *Human resource management: a case study approach.* London: Chartered Institute of Personnel and Development. pp181–199.

LEWIS, S., GAMBLES, R. and RAPOPORT, R. (2007) The constraints of a 'work–

life balance' approach: an international perspective. *International Journal of Human Resource Management.* Vol 18, No 3. pp360–373.

MARTIN, P. and COLLINSON, D. (2002) Over the pond and across the water: developing the field of gendered organizations. *Gender, Work and Organization.* Vol 9, No 3. pp244–265.

OFFICE FOR NATIONAL STATISTICS (ONS). (2010a) *Focus on gender: work and family.* Available online at www.statistics.gov.uk/cci/nugget.asp?id=1655

OFFICE FOR NATIONAL STATISTICS (ONS). (2010b) *Focus on gender: working lives.* Available online at www.statistics.gov.uk/cci/nugget.asp?id=1654

OFFICE FOR NATIONAL STATISTICS (ONS). (2010c) *Labour market: gender pay gap.* Available online at www.statistics.gov.uk/cci/nugget.asp?id=167

RAPOPORT, R., BAILYN, L., FLETCHER, J. and PRUITT, B. (2002) *Beyond work–family balance: advancing gender equity and workplace performance.* London: Jossey-Bass Wiley.

REES, B. and GARNSEY, E. (2003) Analysing competence: gender and identity at work. *Gender, Work and Organization.* Vol 10, No 5. pp551–578.

ROSENSTOCK M., JENSEN, S., BOLL, J., HOLT, H. and WIESE, N. (2008) *Virksomheders sociale engagement – Årbog 2007 (Corporate social responsibility – yearbook 2007).* Report No. 3. Copenhagen: Danish National Institute of Social Research.

SWANBERG, E.J. (2004) Illuminating gendered organization assumptions: an important step in creating a family-friendly organization: a case study. *Community, Work and Family.* Vol 1, No 1. pp3–28.

YOUNG, M.B. (1999) Work–family backlash: begging the question, what's fair? *The Annals of the American Academy of Political and Social Science.* Vol 562, No 1. pp32–46.

CHAPTER 17

ACUNA, R.F. (2010) The illusive race question and class. In: HOWARD, Z. (ed.). Occasional paper No 59, *People history of the United States.* Available online at http://all4ed.org/htpp://institutionalracism.net/default.aspx

AIGNER, D.J. and CAIN, G.G. (1977) Statistical theories of discrimination in labour markets. *ILR Review.* Vol 30, No 2. pp175–187.

ANNUAL POPULATION SURVEY. (2004a) *Focus on ethnicity and identity.* Office for National Statistics. Available online at www.statistics.gov.uk

ANNUAL POPULATION SURVEY. (2004b) *Ethnicity and identity: labour market: non-white unemployment highest.* Office for National Statistics. Available online at www.statistics.gov.uk

BAINS, B. (2007) *Greater London: an overview of results; total change: projected population change by ethnic group.* Greater London Authority DMAG Briefing 2008-03, February 2008, GLA 2007 Round Ethnic Group Population Projections. Available online at www.london.gov.uk/gla/publications/factsandfigures/dmag-update-2008-03.pdf

BBC NEWS. (2007) To become plural city. BBC News. 11 September. Available online at http://news.bbc.co.uk/1/hi/england/leicestershire/6988815.stm

CASTLES, S. (2002) Migration and community formation under conditions of globalization. *The Center for Migration Studies of New York.* Vol 36, No 4. pp1143–1168.

COMMISSION FOR RACIAL EQUALITY. (2007) *What is racism and institutional racism?* Available online at www.cre.gov.uk/

EQUALITY ACT. (2010) Chapter 15: Part 6 Education, Chapter 2 Further and Higher Education, 92 Further and Higher Education Courses. Available online at www.opsi.gov.uk/acts/acts2010/ukpga_20100015_en_10

GILLIGAN, A. (2008) The problem with PC PCs. *Prospect Magazine.* Issue 152. 23 November. Available online at www.prospectmagazine.co.uk/2008/11/theproblemwithpcpcs/

GRAY, S. (2008) Tarique Ghaffur settles out of court with Met Commissioner. *Guardian.* Available online at www.guardian.co.uk/uk/2008/nov/25/ian-blair-tarique-ghaffur-police

GRIEVE, G.D. and FRENCH, J. (2000) Does institutional racism exist in the Metropolitan Police Service? In: GREEN, G.D., FRENCH, J., IGNATIEF, M., O'BRIEN, M. and SKIDELSKY, R. (eds). *Institutional racism and the police: fact or fiction?* London: Institute for the Study of Civil Society. pp7–20.

GROSFOGUEL, R. (1999) *Cultural racism and colonial Caribbean migrants in core zones of the capitalist world-economy.* Reprint from review: Fernand Braudel Center, XXII/4. pp409–434.

HENRY, B.R., HOUSTON, S. and MOONEY, G.H. (2004) Institutional racism in Australian healthcare: a plea for decency – fairness and compassion are the bases for improving Aboriginal health. *Indigenous Health Viewpoint MJA.* Vol 180. p517.

JUSSIM, L. (1991) Social perception and social reality: a reflective-construction model. *Psychological Review.* Vol 98, No 1. pp54–73.

JUSSIM, L., ECCLES, J. and MADON, S. (1996) Social perception, social stereotypes and teacher expectation: accuracy and the quest for the self-fulfilling prophecy. *Advances in Experimental Psychology.* Vol 28. pp281–388.

LAW, I., PHILIPS, D. and TURNEY, L. (eds) (2004) *Institutional racism in higher education.* Stoke on Trent: Trentham Books.

MAJORS, R. (2001) Cool pose: black masculinity and sports. In: WHITEHEAD, S.M. and BARRETT, F. (eds). *Masculinities reader.* Cambridge: Polity Press in association with Blackwell. pp209–218.

MCGRATH, J.E., BERDAHL, J.L. and ARROW, H. (1995) Traits, expectations, culture, and clout: the dynamics of diversity in work groups. In: JACKSON, S.E. and RUDERMAN, M.N. (eds). *Diversity in work teams.* Washington, DC: American Psychological Association. pp17–45.

MIYAZAKE, H. (1977) The rat race and internal labour markets. *Bell Journal of Economics.* Vol 8, No 2. pp394–418.

NATIONAL STATISTICS. (2002) *Minority ethnic groups in the UK.* Available online at www.statistics.gov.uk/statbase/Product.asp?vink=9763

NIEMEYER, G.O. (2004) The function of stereotypes in visual perception. *Documenta Opthalmalogica.* Vol 106, No 1. pp61–66.

OGBONNA, E. and HARRIS, L. (2006) The dynamics of employee relationships in an ethnically diverse workforce. *Human Relations.* Vol 59, No 3. pp379–407.

PRICE, A. (2007) *Human resource management in a business context.* 3rd ed. London: Thompson Learning.

SARGEANT, M. and LEWIS, D. (2008) *Employment law.* 4th ed. Harlow: Pearson Education.

SHULTZ, K.S., MORTON, K.R. and WECKERLE, J.R. (1998) The influence of push and pull factors on voluntary and involuntary early retirees' retirement decision and adjustment. *Journal of Vocational Behaviour.* Vol 53, No 1. pp45–57.

SIVANANDAN, A. (1976) Race, class and the state: the black experience in Britain. *Race and Class.* Vol 48, No 2. pp38–60.

SIVANANDAN, A. (2001) Poverty is the new black. *Race and Class*, 43, No 2. pp1–5.

SMITH, E.R. and MACKIE, D. (2010) *Social psychology.* 2nd ed. Hove: Psychology Press.

VAN DIJK, T.A. (2002) Discourse and racism. In: GOLDBERG, D. and SOLOMOS, J. (eds). *The Blackwell companion to racial and ethnic studies.* Oxford: Blackwell. pp145–159.

WILLEY, B. (2003) *Employment law in context – an introduction for HR professionals.* 2nd ed. Harlow: Pearson Education.

WILSON, D. (2010) What price respect: exploring the notion of respect in a 21st century global learning environment. *Contemporary Issues in Education Research.* Vol 3, No 1.

ZAVALA, M., DIAZ-DIOCARETZ, M. and VAN DIJK, T.A. (1987) *Critical theory – approaches to discourse poetics and psychiatry.* Philadelphia: John Benjamins.

CHAPTER 18

BAMBRA, C. and POPE, D. (2007) What are the effects of anti-discriminatory legislation on socioeconomic inequalities in the employment consequences of ill health and disability? *Journal of Epidemiology and Community Health.* Vol 61. pp421–426.

BARNES, C. and MERCER, G. (2005) Disability, work, and welfare: challenging the social exclusion of disabled people. *Work, Employment and Society.* Vol 19, No 3. pp527–545.

BBC NEWS. (2009a) Disabled woman sues clothes store. 24 June. Available online at http://news.bbc.co.uk/1/hi/england/london/8116231.stm

BBC NEWS. (2009b) Woman wins clothes store tribunal. 13 August. Available online at http://news.bbc.co.uk/1/hi/8200140.stm

BELL, D. and HEITMUELLER, A. (2009) The Disability Discrimination Act in the UK: helping or hindering employment among the disabled? *Journal of Health Economics.* Vol 28, No 2. pp465–480. Available online at www.sciencedirect. com/science?_ob=ArticleURL&_udi=B6V8K-4TVJNDX-1&_user=10&_ coverDate=03%2F31%2F2009&_rdoc=1&_fmt=high&_orig=search&_sort=d&_ docanchor=&view=c&_searchStrId=1247902002&_rerunOrigin=scholar. google&_acct=C000050221&_version=1&_urlVersion=0&_userid=10&md5=310 be5ab25b8ed89402a08e4ef826c7d – afn1

BERTHOUD, R. (2008) Disability employment penalties in Britain. *Work, Employment and Society.* Vol 22, No 1. pp129–148.

CHANDLER, P. (2003) *An A–Z of employment law: a complete reference source for managers.* London: Kogan.

DEAL, M. (2007) Aversive disablism: subtle prejudice toward disabled people. *Disability and Society.* Vol 22, No 1. pp93–100.

DIBBEN, P., JAMES, P., CUNNINGHAM, I. and SMYTHE, D. (2002) Employers and employees with disabilities in the UK: an economically beneficial relationship? *International Journal of Social Economics.* Vol 29, No 6. pp453–467.

DIRECTGOV. (2010) *Disabled people.* Available online at www.direct.gov.uk/en/ DisabledPeople/Employmentsupport/LookingForWork/DG_4000314

DISABILITY DISCRIMINATION ACT. (1995) Disability Discrimination Act 1995 – Chapter 50. Office of Public Sector Information. Available online at www. opsi.gov.uk/acts/acts1995/ukpga_19950050_en_1

DISABILITY DISCRIMINATION ACT. (2005) Disability Discrimination Act 2005 – Chapter 13. Office of Public Sector Information. Available online at www. opsi.gov.uk/acts/acts2005/ukpga_20050013_en_1

FOSTER, D. (2007) Legal obligation or personal lottery? Employee experiences of disability and the negotiation of adjustments in the public sector workplace. *Work, Employment and Society.* Vol 21, No 1. pp67–84.

GOODING, C. (2000) Disability Discrimination Act: from statute to practice. *Critical Social Policy.* Vol 20, No 4. pp533–549.

GOSS, D., GOSS, F. and ADAM-SMITH, D. (2000) Disability and employment: a comparative critique of UK legislation. *The International Journal of Human Resource Management.* Vol 11, No 4. pp807–821.

GREWAL, I., JOY, S., LEWIS, J., SWALES, K. and WOODFIELD, K. (2002) *Disabled for life? Attitudes towards and experiences of disability in Britain.* Research Report No. 173. Leeds: Department for Work and Pensions.

JACKSON, C.J., FURNHAM, A. and WILLEN, K. (2000) Employer willingness to comply with the Disability Discrimination Act regarding staff selection in the UK. *Journal of Occupational and Organizational Psychology.* Vol 73, No 1. pp119–129.

JACOBY, A., GORRY, J. and BAKER, G.A. (2005) Employers' attitudes to employment of people with epilepsy: still the same old story? *Epilepsia.* Vol 46, No 12. pp1978–1987.

JOBCENTRE PLUS. (2010) Part of the Department for Work and Pensions. Available online at www.jobcentreplus.gov.uk/JCP/index.html

JONES, M.K. and JONES, J. (2008) The labour market impact of the UK Disability Discrimination Act: evidence from the repeal of the small firm exemption. *Bulletin of Economic Research.* Vol 60, No 3. pp289–306.

KONUR, O. (2007) A judicial outcome analysis of the Disability Discrimination Act: a windfall for employers? *Disability and Society.* Vol 22, No 2. pp187–204.

MERCER, C. and MERCER, G. (2005) Disability, work, and welfare: challenging the social exclusion of disabled people. *Work, Employment and Society.* Vol 19, No 3. pp572–545.

ODI ANNUAL REPORT. (2009) *Delivering our vision – annual progress report on improving the life chances of disabled people.* Office for Disability Issues, HM Government. Available online at www.officefordisability.gov.uk/docs/res/annual-report/2009-annual-report-s.pdf

ODI. (2010) *Disability equality indicators.* Office for Disability Issues. Available online at www.officefordisability.gov.uk/research/indicators.php#employ

PETTS, J. (2008) Commentary: prognosis for disability discrimination following McDougall. *Industrial Law Journal.* Vol 37, No 3. pp268–278.

PIDD, H. (2009) Disabled student sues Abercrombie & Fitch for discrimination. *Guardian.* 24 June. Available online at www.guardian.co.uk/money/2009/jun/24/abercrombie-fitch-tribunal-riam-dean

ROULSTONE, A. and WARREN, J. (2006) Applying a barriers approach to monitoring disabled people's employment: implications for the Disability Discrimination Act 2005. *Disability and Society*. Vol 21, No 2. pp115–131.

SIMM, C., ASTON, J., WILLIAMS, C., HILL, D., BELLIS, A. and MEAGER, N. (2007) *Organisations' responses to the Disability Discrimination Act*. DWP Research Report No 410. Leeds: Corporate Document Services.

STALKER, K. and LERPINIERE, J. (2009) 'It's against our law, never mind anyone else's': the Disability Discrimination Act 1995 and adults with learning disabilities. *Disability and Society*. Vol 24, No 7. pp829–843.

STEVENS, G.R. (2002) Employers' perceptions and practice in the employability of disabled people: a survey of companies in south east UK. *Disability and Society*. Vol 17, No 7. pp779–796.

STUART, H. (2006) Mental illness and employment discrimination. *Current Opinion in Psychiatry*. Vol 19, No 5. pp522–526.

TRIBUNALS SERVICE: EMPLOYMENT. (2010) Available online at www. employmenttribunals.gov.uk/

WILLIAMS, A.N. (2008) Are tribunals given appropriate and sufficient evidence for disability claims? *Occupational Medicine*. Vol 58, No 1. pp35–40.

WOODHAMS, C. and CORBY, S. (2003) Defining disability in theory and practice: a critique of the British Disability Discrimination Act 1995. *Journal of Social Policy*. Vol 32, No 2. pp159–178.

WOODHAMS, C. and CORBY, S. (2007) Then and now: disability legislation and employers' practices in the UK. *British Journal of Industrial Relations*. Vol 45, No 3. pp556–580.

WOODHAMS, C. and DANIELI, A. (2000) Disability and diversity – a difference too far? *Personnel Review*. Vol 29, No 3. pp402–416.

CHAPTER 19

APPELBAUM, E., BAILEY, T., BERG, P. and KALLEBERG, A. (2000) *Manufacturing advantage*. Ithaca, NY: ILR Press.

BERR. (2008) *Manufacturing: new challenges, new opportunities*. London: Department for Business, Enterprise and Regulatory Reform.

BOTERO, J., DJANKOV, S., LA PORTA, R., LOPEZ-DE-SILANES, S. and SHLEIFER, A. (2004) The regulation of labour. *Quarterly Journal of Economics*. Vol 119. pp1339–1382.

BOYER, R. (2006) How do institutions cohere and change? In: WOOD, G. and JAMES, P. (eds). *Institutions, production and working life*. Oxford: Oxford University Press.

BREWSTER, C., WOOD, G., CROUCHER, R. and BROOKES, M. (2007)

Collective and individual voice: convergence in Europe? *International Journal of Human Resource Management*. Vol 18, No 7. pp1246–1262.

BUCHANAN, D. and PRESTON, D. (1992) Life in the cell: supervision and teamwork in a manufacturing systems engineering environment. *Human Resource Management Journal*. Vol 2, No 4. pp55–76.

CHILD, J. and PARTRIDGE, A. (1982) *Lost managers*. London: Cambridge University Press.

COHEN, R. (1994) Resistance and hidden forms of consciousness amongst African workers. In: WEBSTER, E. (ed.). *Work and industrialisation in South Africa: an introductory reader*. Johannesburg: Ravan.

COLLINGS, D. and WOOD, G. (eds) (2009) *Human resource management: a critical approach*. London: Routledge.

COOKE, E. (2009) Sweatshops defy the minimum wage. *Independent*. 28 March. Available online at www.independent.co.uk/news/sweatshops-defy-minimum-wage-1083562.html

CROUCH, C. (2005) Three meanings of complementarity. *Socio-Economic Review*. Vol 3. pp359–363.

DORE, R. (2000) *Stock market capitalism: welfare capitalism*. Cambridge: Cambridge University Press.

GOERGEN, M., BREWSTER, C. and WOOD, G. (2009) Corporate governance and training. *Journal of Industrial Relations*. Vol 51, No 4. pp459–487.

GOODERHAM, P., NORDHAUG, O. and RINGDAL, K. (2006) National embeddedness and calculative human resource management in US subsidiaries in Europe and Australia. *Human Relations*. Vol 59, No 11. pp1491–1513.

GOULD, M. and CAMPBELL, A. (1986) *Strategic decision making: the corporate role. Vol. 1: Strategic management styles*. London: London Business School, Centre for Business Strategy.

GRABE, S. and SILTBERER, P. (1956) *Selection and training of foremen in Europe*. Project No.234. Paris: OPEC (EPA).

GRUGULIS, I. (2009) Human resource development. In: COLLINGS, D. and WOOD, G. (eds). *Human resource management: a critical approach*. London: Routledge.

GUEST, D. (1987) Human resource management & industrial relations. *Journal of Management Studies*. Vol 24, No 5. pp503–521.

GWENT TEC. (1999) *Team leader research*. Final report. March.

HALE, C. (1986) What do managers do? A critical review of evidence. *Journal of Management Studies*. Vol 23, No 1. pp88–115.

HALES, C. (2005) Rooted in supervision, branching into management: continuity and change in the role of first-line managers. *Journal of Management Studies*. Vol 42, No 3. pp471–507.

HALL, P. and SOSKICE, D. (eds) (2001) *Varieties of capitalism: the institutional basis of competitive advantage*. Oxford: Oxford University Press.

HALL, R. (2010) Renewing and revising the engagement between labour process theory and technology. In: THOMPSON, P. and SMITH, C. (eds). *Working life: renewing labour process analysis*. London: Palgrave.

HARCOURT, M., ROPER, I. and WOOD, G. (2007) The importance of legislated employment protection for worker commitment in coordinated market economies. *Journal of Economic Issues*. Vol 41. pp961–980.

HC. (2009) *Manufacturing*. House of Commons Library Note SN/EP/1942.

IDS. (1987) *Supervising changes*. Study 386. May. London: Incomes Data Services Ltd.

INDEPENDENT. (2010) British manufacturing celebrates a 'blistering' export-led recovery. 2 June. Available online at www.independent.co.uk/news/business/news/british-manufacturing-celebrates-a-blistering-exportled-recovery-1988857. html

IRS EMPLOYMENT REVIEW. (2000) *Holding the line: industrial relations services*. In ACAS Advisory Booklet: *Supervision*. London: ACAS.

JAQUES, E. (1976) *A general theory of bureaucracy*. London: Heinemann Educational Books.

KOCHAN, T. and OSTERMAN, P. (2002) The mutual gains enterprise. In: MABEY, C., SALAMON, G. and MACNEIL, C. (eds). Line managers: facilitators of knowledge sharing in teams. *Employee Relations*. Vol 25, No 3. pp294–307.

KIRKPATRICK, I., DAVIS, A. and OLIVER, N. (1992) Decentralisation: friend or foe of human resource management? In: BLYTON, P. and TURNBULL, P. (eds). *Reassessing human resource management*. London: Sage.

LOWE, J. (1992) Locating the line: the front-line supervisor and human resource management. In: BLYTON, P. and TURNBULL, P. (eds). *Reassessing human resource management*. London: Sage. pp148–168.

MACEWAN, A. (1997) *Neo-liberalism or democracy*. London: Zed.

MACNEIL, C. (2003) Line managers: facilitators of knowledge sharing in teams. *Employee Relations*. Vol 25, No 3. pp294–307.

MARSDEN, D. (1999) *A theory of employment systems*. Oxford: Oxford University Press.

MARTINS, L. (2007) A strategic framework for managing first-tier managers. *Management Decision*. Vol 45, No 3. pp616–641.

MARTINS, L. (2008) The strategic management of first-tier-managers: a British aerospace engineering/manufacturing company case study. Unpublished PhD thesis, Middlesex University.

MARTINS, L. (2009) The nature of the changing role of first tier mangers: a long-cycle approach. *Journal of Organisational Change Management*. Vol 22, No 1. pp92–123.

MCGOVERN, P., GRATTON, L., HOPE-HAILEY, V., STILES, P. and TRUSS, C. (1997) Human resource management on the line. *Human Resource Management Journal*. Vol 7, No 4. pp12–29.

MOODY, K. (1997) *Workers in a lean world*. London: Verso.

NOWPUBLIC. (2009) *Sweatshops: capitalism's demons*. Available online at www.nowpublic.com/world/sweatshops-capitalisms-demons

POLLIN, R. (2007) *Contours of descent*. London: Verso.

RAYNER, C. and ADAM-SMITH, D. (2009) *Managing and leading people*. 2nd ed. London: CIPD.

STOREY, J. (1992) *Developments in the management of human resources*. Oxford: Blackwell.

STOREY, J. (2001) Human resource management today: an assessment. In: STOREY, J. (ed.). *Human resource management: a critical text*. London: Thomson Learning.

STOREY, J. (2007) *Strategic human resource management*. London: Sage.

THELEN, K. (2001) Varieties of labour politics in developed democracies. In: HALL, P. and SOSKICE, D. (eds). *Varieties of capitalism: the institutional foundations of competitive advantage*. Oxford: Oxford University Press.

THOMPSON, P. and SMITH, C. (2010) Introduction: labour process theory in retrospect and prospect 2010 – renewing and revising the engagement between labour process theory and technology. In THOMPSON, P. and SMITH, C. (eds). *Working life: renewing labour process analysis*. London: Palgrave.

THORNHILL, A. and SAUNDERS, M. (1998) The meanings, consequences and implications of the management of downsizing and redundancy: a review. *Personnel Review*. Vol 27, No 4. pp271–295.

THURLEY, K. and HAMBLIN, A. (1964) *The supervisor and his job, problems of progress in industry*. No 13. DSIR. London: HMSO.

THURLEY, K. and WIRDENIUS, H. (1973) *Supervision: a reappraisal*. London: Heinemann.

WOOD, G. and WRIGHT, M. (2009) Private equity: a review and synthesis. *International Journal of Management Reviews*. Vol 11, No 4. pp361–380.

WOODALL, J. and WINSTANLEY, D. (1998) *Management development*. Oxford: Blackwell.

WRIGHT, E.O. and DWYER, R. (2006) The pattern of job expansion in the USA. In: WOOD, G. and JAMES, P. (eds). *Institutions, production and working life*. Oxford: Oxford University Press.

CHAPTER 20

ANDERSON, S., KLEIN PEARO, L. and WIDENER, S.K. (2008) Drivers of service satisfaction: linking customer satisfaction to the service concept and customer characteristics. *Journal of Service Research*. Vol 10, No 4. pp365–381.

BARON, S., HARRIS, K. and HILTON, T. (2009) *Services marketing: text and cases*. 3rd ed. Basingstoke: Palgrave Macmillan.

BORUCKI, C.C. and BURKE, M.J. (1999) An examination of service-related antecedents to retail store performance. *Journal of Organizational Behaviour*. Vol 20. pp943–962.

BRASSINGTON, F. and PETTITT, S. (2003) *Principles of marketing*. 3rd ed. Harlow: Pearson Education Limited.

CLINTON, M. and WOOLLARD, S. (2010) *From recession to recovery? The state of human resources survey 2010*. London: King's College London HRM Learning Board in association with Speechly Bircham.

DEAN, A.M. and RAINNIE, A. (2009) Frontline employees' views on organizational factors that affect the delivery of service quality in call centers. *Journal of Services Marketing*. Vol 23, No 5. pp326–337.

DENHAM LINCOLN, N., TRAVERS, C., ACKERS, P. and WILKINSON, A. (2002) The meaning of empowerment: the interdisciplinary etymology of a new management concept. *International Journal of Management Reviews*. Vol 4, No 3. pp271–290.

EATON, S.C. (2000) Beyond unloving care: linking human resource management and patient care quality in nursing homes. *International Journal of Human Resource Management*. Vol 11, No 3. pp591–616.

EUROSTAT. (2009) *European business: facts and figures*. Luxembourg: Office for Official Publications of the European Communities.

GIARDINI, A. and FRESE, M. (2008) Linking service employees' emotional competence to customer satisfaction: a multilevel approach. *Journal of Organizational Behavior*. Vol 29. pp155–170.

GUEST, D.E., CLINTON, M. and WOOLLARD, S. (2009) *The state of human resources survey 2009: riding the recession? The state of HR in the current economic downturn*. London: King's College London/Speechly Bircham.

HAUSKNECHT, J.P., TREVOR, C.O. and HOWARD, M.J. (2009) Unit-level voluntary turnover rates and customer service quality: implications of group

cohesiveness, newcomer concentration and size. *Journal of Applied Psychology.*
Vol 94, No 4. pp1068–1075.

ILO. (2006) *Global employment trends brief.* Geneva: International Labour
Organization.

JOBBER, D. (2007) *Principles and practice of marketing.* 5th ed. Maidenhead:
McGraw-Hill Education.

KERSLEY, B., ALPIN, C., FORTH, J., BRYSON, A., BEWLEY, H., DIX, G. and
OXENBRIDGE, S. (2006) *Inside the workplace: findings from the 2004 Workplace
Employment Relations Survey.* Abingdon: Routledge.

KNUTSON, B., STEVENS, P., WULLAERT, C., PATTON, M. and YOKOYAMA,
F. (1990) LODGSERV: a service quality index for the lodging industry. *Hospitality
Research Journal.* Vol 14, No 2. pp277–284.

KORCZYNSKI, M. (2002) *Human resource management in service work.*
Basingstoke: Palgrave Macmillan.

KOTLER, P., ARMSTRONG, G., SAUNDERS, J. and WONG, V. (2002) *Principles
of marketing.* 3rd ed. Harlow: Pearson Education Limited.

LIAO, H. and CHUANG, A. (2004) A multilevel investigation of factors
influencing employee service performance and customer outcomes. *Academy of
Management Journal.* Vol 47, No 1. pp41–58.

LIAO, H., TOYA, K., LEPAK, D.P. and HONG, Y. (2009) Do they see eye to eye?
Management and employee perspectives of high-performance work systems and
influence processes on service quality. *Journal of Applied Psychology.* Vol 94, No 2.
pp371–391.

LOVEMAN, G.W. (1998) Employee satisfaction, customer loyalty, and financial
performance: an empirical examination of the service profit chain in retail
banking. *Journal of Service Research.* Vol 1, No 1. pp18–31.

LYTLE, R.S., HOM, P.W. and MOKWA, M.P. (1998) SERV*OR: a managerial
measure of organizational service-orientation. *Journal of Retailing.* Vol 74, No 4.
pp455–489.

MAYER, D.M., EHRHART, M.G. and SCHNEIDER, B. (2009) Service attribute
boundary conditions of the service climate–customer satisfaction link. *Academy
of Management Journal.* Vol 52, No 5. pp1034–1050.

NELIS, D., QUOIDBACH, J., MIKOLAJCZAK, M. and HANSENNE, M. (2009)
Increasing emotional intelligence: (how) is it possible? *Personality and Individual
Differences.* Vol 47. pp36–41.

PALMER, A. (2008) *Principles of services marketing.* 5th ed. Maidenhead:
McGraw-Hill Education.

PARASURAMAN, A. and ZEITHAML, V.A. (2002) Understanding and
improving service quality: a literature review and research agenda. In: WEITZ,

B. and WENSLEY, R. (eds). *Handbook of marketing.* London: Sage Publications. pp339–367.

PARASURAMAN, A., ZEITHAML, V.A. and BERRY, L.L. (1985) A conceptual model of service quality and its implications for future research. *Journal of Marketing.* Vol 49, No 4. pp41–50.

PECCEI, R. and ROSENTHAL, P. (1997) The antecedents of employee commitment to customer service: evidence from a UK service context. *The International Journal of Human Resource Management.* Vol 8, No 1. pp66–86.

PECCEI, R. and ROSENTHAL, P. (2001) Delivering customer-oriented behaviour through empowerment: an empirical test of HRM assumptions. *Journal of Management Studies.* Vol 38, No 6. pp831–857.

REIDENBACH, R.E. and SANDIFER-SMALLWOOD, B. (1990) Exploring perceptions of hospital operations by a modified SERVQUAL approach. *Journal of Health Care Marketing.* Vol 10, No 4. pp47–55.

SALVAGGIO, A.N., SCHNEIDER, B., NISHII, L.H., MAYER, D.M., RAMESH, A. and LYON, J.S. (2007) Manager personality, manager service quality orientation and service climate: test of a model. *Journal of Applied Psychology.* Vol 92, No 6. pp1741–1750.

SCHMIT, M.J. and ALLSCHEID, S.P. (1995) Employee attitudes and customer satisfaction: making theoretical and empirical connections. *Personnel Psychology.* Vol 48. pp521–536.

SCHNEIDER, B. (1990) The climate for service: an application of the climate construct. In: SCHNEIDER, B. (ed.). *Organizational climate and culture.* San Francisco, CA: Jossey-Bass Publishers. pp383–412.

SCHNEIDER, B. and BOWEN, D.E. (1985) Employee and customer perceptions of service in banks: replication and extension. *Journal of Applied Psychology.* Vol 70, No 3. pp423–433.

SCHNEIDER, B. and BOWEN, D.E. (1993) The service organization: human resources management is crucial. *Organizational Dynamics.* Vol 21, No 4. pp39–52.

SCHNEIDER, B. and WHITE, S.S. (2004) *Service quality: research perspectives* Thousand Oaks, CA: Sage Publications.

SCHNEIDER, B., PARKINGTON, J.J. and BUXTON, V.M. (1980) Employee and customer perceptions of service in banks. *Administrative Science Quarterly.* Vol 25. pp252–267.

SCHNEIDER, B., WHITE, S.S. and PAUL, M.C. (1998) Linking service climate and customer perceptions of service quality: test of a causal model. *Journal of Applied Psychology.* Vol 83, No 2. pp150–163.

SCHNEIDER, B., EHRHART, M.G., MAYER, D.M., SALTZ, J.L. and NILES-JOLLY, K. (2005) Understanding organization–customer links in service settings. *Academy of Management Journal.* Vol 48, No 6. pp1017–1032.

STEVENS, P., KNUTSON, B. and PATTON, M. (1995) DINESERV: a tool for measuring service quality in restaurants. *Cornell Hotel and Restaurant Administration Quarterly.* Vol 2. pp56–60.

SUSSKIND, A.M., KACMAR, K.M. and BORCHGREVINK, C.P. (2003) Customer service providers' attitudes relating to customer service and customer satisfaction in the customer–server exchange. *Journal of Applied Psychology.* Vol 88, No 1. pp179–187.

VROOM, V.H. (1964) *Work and motivation.* New York: John Wiley and Sons.

WOODSIDE, A.G., FREY, L.L. and DALY, R.T. (1989) Linking service quality, customer satisfaction and behavioural intention. *Journal of Health Care Marketing.* Vol 9, No 4. pp5–17.

ZEITHAML, V.A., BERRY, L.L. and PARASURAMAN, A. (1996) The behavioural consequences of service quality. *Journal of Marketing.* Vol 60, No 2. pp31–46.

CHAPTER 21

ACKROYD, S. (1995) From public administration to public sector management: understanding contemporary change in British public services. *International Journal of Public Sector Management.* Vol 8, No 2. pp19–32.

BACH, S. (1999) Europe: changing public service employment relations. In: BACH, S.L., BORDOGNA, G., DELLA ROCCA, G. and WINCHESTER, D. (eds). *Public service employment relations in Europe: transformation, modernisation or inertia?* London: Routledge.

BACH, S. (2004) *Employment relations and the health service.* London: Routledge.

BACH, S. and WINCHESTER, D. (2003) Industrial relations in the public sector. In: EDWARDS, P. (ed.). *Industrial relations: theory and practice.* 2nd ed. Oxford: Blackwell.

BACH, S., BORDOGNA, L., DELLA ROCCA, G. and WINCHESTER, D. (eds). (1999) *Public service employment relations in Europe: transformation, modernisation or inertia?* London: Routledge.

BATSTONE E., FERNER, A. and TERRY, M. (1984) *Consent and efficiency.* Oxford: Blackwell.

BBC. (2010) Hospital left patients 'sobbing and humiliated'. Nick Triggle. 24 February. Available online at http://news.bbc.co.uk/1/hi/health/8531441.stm

BEALE, D. (2005) The promotions and prospects of partnership at Inland Revenue: employer and union hand in hand? In: STUART, M. and MARTÍNEZ

LUCIO, M. (eds). *Partnership and modernisation in employment relations.* London: Routledge. pp137–153.

BERR. (2008) The market for public services in the UK. *Oxford Economics.* January.

BEWLEY, H. (2006) Raising the standard? The regulation of employment, and public sector employment policy. *British Journal of Industrial Relations.* Vol 44, No 2. pp351–372.

BORINS, A. (2002) Leadership and innovation in the public sector. *Leadership and Organisational Development Journal.* Vol 23, No 8. pp467–476.

BOYNE, G.A., JENKINS, G. and POOLE, M. (1999) Human resource management in the public and private sectors: an empirical comparison. *Public Administration.* Vol 77. pp407–420.

BRIGNALL, S. and MODELL, S. (2000) An institutional perspective on performance measurement and management in the new public sector. *Management Accounting Research.* Vol 11. pp281–306.

COLLING, T. (1995) Contracting public services: the management of compulsory competitive tendering in two county councils. *Human Resources Management Journal.* Vol 4, No 3. pp1–15.

CORBY, S. (2007) Equality and modernisation. In: DIBBEN, P., JAMES, P., ROPER, I. and WOOD, G. (eds). *Modernising work in public services.* London: Palgrave.

CUNNINGHAM, I. and JAMES, P. (2007) Trade unions and the public sector: a story of 'internal' institutional stability and declining regulatory reach. In: DIBBEN, P., JAMES, P., ROPER, I. and WOOD, G. (eds). *Modernising work in public services.* London: Palgrave.

DIBBEN, P., WOOD, G. and ROPER, I. (eds) (2004) *Contesting public sector reforms – critical perspectives, international debates.* Basingstoke: Palgrave Macmillan.

FARNHAM, D. and GILES, L. (1996) People management and employment relations. In: FARNHAM, D. and HORTON, S. (eds). *Managing the new public services.* London: Macmillan.

FINLAYSON, A. (2003) *Making sense of New Labour.* London: Lawrence & Wishart.

FORD, J. (2006) Discourse of leadership: gender, identity and contradiction in a UK public service organisation. *Leadership.* Vol 2, No 1. pp77–99

GOULD-WILLIAMS, J. (2004) The effects of 'high commitment' HRM practices on employee attitude. *Public Administration.* Vol 82, No 1. pp63–81.

GREY, A. (2009) Employee participation in a local college. Master's dissertation, Manchester University.

GRIMSHAW, D. and ROPER, I. (2007) *Partnership: transforming the employment relationship in public services delivery.* In: DIBBEN, P., JAMES, P., ROPER, I. and WOOD, G. (eds). *Modernising work in public services: redefining roles and relationships in Britain's changing workplace.* London: Palgrave.

GRIMSHAW, D., BEYNON, H., RUBERY, J. and WARD, K. (2000) The Blairing of the public and private sectors: towards the corporate economy. Paper presented at the International Annual Labour Process Conference, Strathclyde University.

HALL, S. (1988) *The hard road to renewal.* London: Verso.

HOEL, H. and BEALE, D. (2006) Workplace bullying, psychological perspectives and industrial relations: towards a contextualized and interdisciplinary approach. *British Journal of Industrial Relations.* Vol 44, No 2. pp239–262.

HOOD, C. (1991) A public management for all seasons? *Public Administration.* Vol 69, No 1. pp3–19.

KIRKPATRICK, I. (2006) Post Fordism and organisational change within the state administration. In: ALONSO, L.E. and MARTÍNEZ LUCIO, M. (eds). *Employment relations in a changing society.* London: Palgrave Macmillan.

KIRKPATRICK, I. and MARTÍNEZ LUCIO, M. (eds) (1995) *The politics of quality in the public sector.* London: Routledge.

LAWLER, J. (2009) Individualisation and public sector leadership. *Public Administration.* Vol 86, No 1. pp21–34.

LEWIS, D. and GUNN, R. (2007) Workplace bullying in the public sector: understanding the racial dimension. *Public Administration.* Vol 85, No 3. pp641–665.

LUPTON, B. and SHAW, S. (2001) Are public sector personnel managers the profession's poor relations? *Human Resource Management Journal.* Vol 11, No 3. pp23–38.

MACKENZIE, R. (2002) The migration of bureaucracy: contracting and the regulation of labour in the telecommunications industry. *Work, Employment and Society.* Vol 16, No 4. pp599–616.

MARTÍNEZ LUCIO, M. (2007) Trade unions and employment relations in the context of public sector change: the public sector, old welfare states and the politics of managerialism. *International Journal of Public Service Management.* Vol 20, No 1. pp5–15.

MARTÍNEZ LUCIO, M. and MACKENZIE, R. (1999) The impact of quality management on public sector industrial relations. In: CORBY, S. and WHITE, G. (eds). *Public sector employee relations.* London: Routledge.

MARTÍNEZ LUCIO, M. and NOON, M. (1994) Organisational change and the tensions of decentralisation: the case of Royal Mail. *Human Resource Management Journal.* Vol. 5. pp65–78.

MARTÍNEZ LUCIO, M. and STUART, M. (2007) Sustaining new industrial relations in the public sector: the politics of trust and co-operation in the context of organisational dementia and disarticulation. In: DIBBEN, P., JAMES, P., ROPER, I. and WOOD, G. (eds). *Modernising work in public services*. Basingstoke: Palgrave Macmillan.

MARTÍNEZ LUCIO, M., NOON, M. and JENKINS, S. (1997) Constructing the market: commercialisation and privatisation in the Royal Mail. *Public Administration*. Vol 75. pp271–86.

ONS. (2005) *Public sector employment trends*. London: HMSO.

ONS. (2009) *Public sector employment*. Statistical bulletin Q3. London: HMSO.

OSWICK, C. and GRANT, D. (1996) Personnel management in the public sector: power, roles and relationships. *Personnel Review*. Vol 25, No 2. pp4–18.

PERRETT, R., MARTÍNEZ LUCIO, M. and CRAIG, S. (2007) *A bitter pill to swallow: preliminary results from a survey of UNISON safety representatives*. London: UNISON.

POLLOCK, A.M. (2005) *NHS plc: the privatisation of our health care*. London: Verso Books.

PROWSE, P. and PROWSE, J. (2007) Is there still a public sector model of employment relations in the United Kingdom. *International Journal of Public Services Management*. Vol 20, No 1. pp48–62.

ROPER, I., HIGGINS, P. and JAMES, P. (2007) Shaping the bargaining agenda? The Audit Commission and local government industrial relations. *International Journal of Human Resource Management*. Vol 18, No 9. pp1589–1607.

SMITH, K. (2003) *A New Labour nightmare – the return of the awkward squad*. London: Verso.

SMITH, P. and MORTON, G. (2001) New Labour's reform of Britain's employment law: the devil is not only in the details but in the values and policy too. *British Journal of Industrial Relations*. Vol 39, No 1. pp119–138.

SMITH, P. and MORTON, G. (2006) Nine years of New Labour: neoliberalism and workers' rights. *British Journal of Industrial Relations*. Vol 44, No 3. pp401–420.

STUART, M. and MARTÍNEZ LUCIO, M. (eds) (2005) Introduction. In: *Partnership and the modernisation of employment relations*. London: Routledge.

STUART, M. and MARTÍNEZ LUCIO, M. (2008) The new benchmarking and advisory state: the role of the British Advisory, Conciliation and Arbitration Service in facilitating labour–management consultation in public sector transformation. *Journal of Industrial Relations*. Vol 50. pp736–751.

TERRY, L.D. (1998) Administrative leadership: neo-managerialism and the public management movement. *Public Administration Review*. Vol 58, No 3. pp194–200.

UPCHURCH, M., DANFORD, A., RICHARDSON, M. and TAILBY, S. (2008) *The realities of partnership at work*. London: Palgrave.

WINCHESTER, D. (1983) Industrial relations in the public sector. In: BAIN, G. (ed.). *Industrial relations in Britain*. Oxford: Blackwell.

CHAPTER 22

BAINES, D. (2004) Caring for nothing: work organisation and unwaged labour in social services. *Work, Employment and Society*. Vol 18, No 2. pp267–295.

BALL, C. (1992) Remuneration policies and employment practices: some dilemmas in the voluntary sector. In: BATSLEER, J., CORNFORTH, C. and PATON, R. (eds). *Issues in voluntary and non-profit management*. Wokingham: Addison-Wesley. pp69–81.

BARNARD, J., BROACH, S. and WAKEFIELD, V. (2004) *Social care: the growing crisis*. Report on recruitment and retention issues in the voluntary sector. London: Social Care Employers Consortium.

BRANDL, J. and GUTTEL, W.H. (2007) Organisational antecedents of pay-for-performance systems in nonprofit organisations. *Voluntas: International Journal of Voluntary and Nonprofit Organisations*. Vol 19, No 2. pp176–199.

BRESNAN. M. (1996) An organisational perspective on changing buyer–supplier relations: a critical review of the evidence. *Organisation*. Vol 3, No 1. pp121–146.

CARR, S. (2008) *Personalisation: a rough guide*. London: Social Care Institute for Excellence.

CHILD, J. (1972) Organisation structure, environment and performance: the role of strategic choice. *Sociology*. Vol 6, No 1. pp1–22.

CLARK, J., DOBBS, J., KANE, D. and WILDING, K. (2009) *The state and the voluntary sector: recent trends in government funding and public service delivery*. London: NCVO.

COMMUNITY CARE PROVIDERS SCOTLAND. (2007) Qualification rates and training costs for voluntary sector care providers. Edinburgh: CCPS.

CUNNINGHAM, I. (2000) Prospects for union growth in the UK voluntary sector: the impact of the Employment Relations Act 1999. *Industrial Relations Journal*. Vol 31, No 3. pp192–206.

CUNNINGHAM, I. (2001) Sweet charity! Managing employee commitment in the UK voluntary sector. *Employee Relations Journal*. Vol 23, No 3. pp226–240.

CUNNINGHAM, I. and JAMES, P. (2007) *False economy? The costs of contracting and workforce insecurity in the voluntary sector*. London: Unison.

CUNNINGHAM, I. (2008) *Employment relations in the voluntary sector*. London: Routledge.

CUNNINGHAM, I. and JAMES, P. (2010) Strategies for union renewal in the context of public sector outsourcing. *Economic and Industrial Democracy*. Vol 31. pp34–61.

CUNNINGHAM, I. and NICKSON, D. (2009) *A gathering storm? Procurement, re-tendering and the voluntary sector social care workforce*. Scottish Centre for Employment Research. Glasgow: University of Strathclyde.

DAVIES, S. (2007) *Third sector provision of local government and health services*. London: Unison.

DIMAGGIO, P.J. and POWELL, W.W. (1983) The iron cage revisited: institutional isomorphism and collective rationality in organisational fields. *American Sociological Review*. Vol 35. pp147–160.

FORD, J., QUIGLARS, D. and RUGG, J. (1998) *Creating jobs: the employment potential of domiciliary care*. Joseph Rowntree Foundation, Community care into practice series. Bristol: The Policy Press.

HARRIS, M., ROCHESTER, C. and HALFPENNY, P. (2001) Voluntary organisations and social policy: twenty years of change. In: HARRIS, M. and ROCHESTER, C. (eds). *Voluntary organisations and social policy in Britain: perspectives on change and choice*. Basingstoke: Palgrave. pp1–20.

HELP THE AGED. (2008) *Personalisation in social care: progress in the UK and abroad*. London: Help the Aged.

HEMS, L. and PASSEY, A. (1999) *The voluntary sector almanac*. London: National Council for Voluntary Organisations.

HUNTER, L., BEAUMONT, P. and SINCLAIR, D. (1996) A partnership route to HRM. *Journal of Management Studies*. Vol 33, No 2. pp235–257.

1 INCOMES DATA SERVICES. (2001) Pay in the voluntary sector. *IDS Report: Pay and Conditions and Labour Market Changes*. March. pp16–19.

2 INCOMES DATA SERVICES. (2002) Pay in charities. *IDS Report: Pay and Conditions and Labour Market Changes*. January. pp10–15.

3 INCOMES DATA SERVICES. (2005) Pay and conditions in social care. *IDS Pay Report 926*. April. pp15–18.

4 INCOMES DATA SERVICES. (2007) Pay and conditions in housing and social care 2007. *IDS Pay Report 976*. pp13–16.

JOHNSON, N., JENKINSON, S., KENDALL, I., BRADSHAW, Y. and BLACKMORE, M. (1998) Regulating for quality in the voluntary sector. *Journal of Social Policy*. Vol 27, No 3. pp307–328.

KENDALL, J. (2003) *The voluntary sector*. London: Routledge.

KENDALL, J. and ALMOND, S. (1998) The UK voluntary (third) sector in comparative perspective: exceptional growth and transformation. Unpublished paper, University of Kent, Canterbury.

KENDALL, J. and KNAPP, M. (1996) *The voluntary sector in the UK*. John Hopkins Nonprofit Sector Series. Manchester: Manchester University Press.

KNAPP, M., HARDY, B. and FORDER, J. (2001) Commissioning for quality: ten years of social care markets in England. *Journal of Social Policy*. Vol 30, No 2. pp283–306.

LEADBETTER, C. and LOWNSBROUGH, H. (2005) *Personalisation and participation: the future of social care in Scotland*. London: Demos.

LEGGE, K. (2007) Networked organisations and the negation of HRM? In: STOREY, J. (ed.). *Human resource management: a critical text*. 3rd ed. London: Thomson. pp39–56.

LEITER, J. (2005) Structural isomorphism in Australian nonprofit organisations. *Voluntas: International Journal of Voluntary and Nonprofit Organisations*. Vol 16, No 1. pp1–31.

MARCHINGTON, M., GRIMSHAW, D., RUBERY, J. and WILMOTT, H. (2005) *Fragmenting work: blurring organisational boundaries and disordering hierarchies*. Oxford: Oxford University Press.

MCMULLEN, K. and BRISBOIS, R. (2003) *Coping with change: human resource management in Canada's non-profit sector*. Canadian Policy Research Networks Series on Human Resources in the Non-Profit Sector. No 4. December.

MEYER, J.W. and ROWAN, B. (1977) Institutionalized organisations: formal structure as myth and ceremony. *American Journal of Sociology*. Vol 83, No 2. pp340–363.

MIRVIS, P. (1992) The quality of employment in the nonprofit sector: an update on employee attitudes in nonprofits versus business and government. *Nonprofit Management and Leadership*. Vol 3, No 1. pp23–41.

NATIONAL COUNCIL FOR VOLUNTARY ORGANISATIONS (NCVO). (2007) *Almanac 2007, Volunteering – Formal Volunteering is Slowly Increasing*. Available online at www.ncvo-vol.org.uk/node/295

NICKSON, D., WARHURST, C., DUTTON, E. and HURRELL, S. (2008) A job to believe in: recruitment in the Scottish voluntary sector. *Human Resource Management* Journal. Vol 18, No 1. pp20–35.

ONYX, J. and MACLEAN, M. (1996) Careers in the third sector. *Nonprofit Management and Leadership*. Vol 6, No 4. pp331–345.

ORLANS, V. (1992) Stress in voluntary and non-profit organisations. In: BATSLEER, J., CORNFORTH, C. and PATON, R. (eds). *Issues in voluntary and non-profit management*. Wokingham: Addison-Wesley. pp36–46.

OSBORNE, S.P. (1997) Managing the coordination of social services in the mixed economy of welfare: competition, cooperation or common cause? *British Journal of Management.* Vol 8. pp317–328.

OSBORNE, S.P. (1998) *Voluntary organisations and innovation in public services.* London: Routledge.

PARRY, E., KELLIHER, C., MILLS, T. and TYSON, S. (2005) Comparing HRM in the voluntary and public sectors. *Personnel Review.* Vol 34, No 5. pp588–602.

PASSEY, A., HEMS, L. and JAZ, P. (2000) *The voluntary sector almanac.* London: National Council for Voluntary Organizations.

PATON, R. and CORNFORTH, C. (1992) What's different about managing in voluntary and non-profit organisations. In: BATSLEER, J., CORNFORTH, C. and PATON, R. (eds). *Issues in voluntary and non-profit management.* Wokingham: Addison Wesley. pp36–46.

PATON, R. and FOOT, J. (2000) Nonprofits' use of awards to improve and demonstrate performance: valuable discipline or burdensome formalities? *Voluntas: International Journal of Voluntary and Nonprofit Organisations.* Vol 11, No 4. pp329–353.

PERRI, S. and KENDALL, J. (1997) Introduction. In: PERRI, S. and KENDALL, J. (eds). *The contract culture in public services.* Aldershot: Ashgate. pp1–15.

POLLIT, C. (1995) *Managerialism and public services.* Oxford: Blackwell.

REMUNERATION ECONOMICS. (2002) *15th annual voluntary sector salary survey.* Available online at www.celre.co.uk

REMUNERATION ECONOMICS. (2006) *19th annual voluntary sector salary survey.* Available online at www.celre.co.uk

RIDDER, H.G. and MCCANDLESS, A. (2008) Influences on the architecture of human resource management in nonprofit organisations: an analytical framework. *Nonprofit and Voluntary Sector Quarterly.* Vol 20, No 10. pp1–18.

RUBERY, J., EARNSHAW, J., MARCHINGTON, M., COOKE, F.L. and VINCENT, S. (2002) Changing organisational forms and the employment relationship. *Journal of Management Studies.* Vol 39, No 5. pp645–72.

SAKO, M. (1992) *Prices, quality and trust: inter-firm relations in Britain and Japan.* Cambridge: Cambridge University Press.

SAUNDERS, R. (2004) *Passion and commitment under stress: human resource issues in Canada's non-profit sector – a synthesis report.* Canadian Policy Research Networks Series on Human Resources in the Non-Profit Sector. No 5. January.

SCOTTISH COUNCIL FOR VOLUNTARY ORGANISATIONS. (2004) *Voluntary sector Scottish sector profile, 2004.* Edinburgh: SCVO.

SCOTTISH SOCIAL SERVICES COUNCIL. (2008) *Skills for care and development sector skills agreement stage 5 – Scotland*. Edinburgh SSSC. March.

SHAH, R. (2004) *Labour market information report*. Edinburgh: SCVO.

SIMMS, M. (2003) Union organizing in a not-for-profit organisation. In: GALL, G. (ed.). *Union organizing: campaigning for trade union recognition*. London: Routledge. pp97–113.

SIMMS, M. (2007) Managed activism: two union organising campaigns in the not-for-profit sector. *Industrial Relations Journal*. Vol 38, No 2. pp119–135.

SINGER, M.I. and YANKEY, J.A. (1991) Organisational metamorphosis: a study of eighteen nonprofit mergers, acquisitions and consolidations. *Nonprofit Management and Leadership*. Vol 1, No 4. pp357–369.

SOCIAL CARE INSTITUTE FOR EXCELLENCE. (2009) *At a glance 13: personalisation briefing: implications for voluntary sector service providers*. Available online at www.scie.org.uk/publications/ataglance/ataglance13.asp

TAYLOR, M. and BASSI, A. (1998) Unpacking the state: the implications for the third sector of changing relationships between national and local government. *Voluntas: International Journal of Voluntary and Nonprofit Organisations*. Vol 9, No 2. pp113–135.

TINNING, W. (2010) Quarriers staff in one-day strike over pay. *The Herald*. 26 April. Available online at www.heraldscotland.com/quarriers-staff-in-one-day-strike-over-pay-1.856870

TONKISS, F. and PASSEY, A. (1999) Trust, confidence and voluntary organisations: between values and institutions. *Sociology*. Vol 33, No 2. pp257–274.

TRUSS, C. (2004) Who's in the driving seat managing human resources in a franchise firm? *Human Resource Management Journal*. Vol 11, No 4. pp3–21.

UNISON. (2006) *Community and voluntary sector*. Available online at www.unison.org.uk/voluntary

VINCENT, J. and HARROW, J. (2005) Comparing thistles and roses: the application of governmental–voluntary sector relations theory to Scotland and England. *Voluntas: International Journal of Voluntary and Nonprofit Organisations*. Vol 16, No 4. pp375–395.

WAINWRIGHT, S., CLARK, J., GRIFFITH, M., JOCHUM, V. and WILDING, K. (2006) *The UK voluntary sector almanac 2006*. London: NCVO Publications.

WALSH, K. (1995) *Public services and market mechanisms*. Basingstoke: Macmillan.

WHELAN, R. (1999) *Involuntary action: how voluntary is the 'voluntary' sector?* London: Institute of Economic Affairs.

WILDING, K., COLLINS, G., JOCHUM, V. and WAINRIGHT, S. (2004) *The UK voluntary sector almanac 2004*. London: NCVO Publications.

YEANDLE, S. and STIELL, B. (2007) Issues in the development of the direct payments scheme for older people in England. In: UNGERSON, C. and YEANDLE, S. (eds). *Cash for care in developed welfare states*. Basingstoke: Palgrave.

ZIMMECK, M. (1998) *To boldly go: the voluntary sector and voluntary action in the new world of work*. London: Royal Society of Arts.

CHAPTER 23

ALLEN, J.M. and HART, M. (1998) Training older workers: implications for HRD/HPT professionals. *Performance Improvement Quarterly*. Vol 11, No 4. pp91–102.

BENACH, J. and MUNTANER, C. (2007) Precarious employment and health: developing a research agenda. *Journal of Epidemiology and Community Health*. Vol 61. pp276–277.

BEVAN, S. and THOMPSON, M. (1991) Performance management at the crossroads. *Personnel Management*. Vol 23, No 11. pp36–40.

BOHLE, P., QUINLAN, M., KENNEDY, D. and WILLIAMSON, A. (2004) Working hours, work–life conflict and health in precarious and 'permanent' employment. *Revista de Saúde Pública*. Vol 38. pp19–25.

BOYCE, A.S., RYAN, A.M., IMUS, A.L. and MORGESON, F.P. (2007) 'Non-permanent worker, permanent loser?' A model of the stigmatization of non-permanent workers. *Journal of Management*. Vol 33, No 1. pp5–29.

BROSCHAK, J.P., DAVIS-BLAKE, A. and BLOCK, E. (2008) Nonstandard, not substandard: the relationship among work arrangements, work attitudes, and job performance. *Work and Occupations*. Vol 35, No 1. pp3–43.

BRÜCKER, H. and DEFOORT, C. (2009) Inequality and the self-selection of international migrants: theory and new evidence. *International Journal of Manpower*. Vol 30, No 7. pp742–764.

BURGESS, J. and CONNELL, J. (2006) The influence of precarious employment on career development: the current situation in Australia. *Education and Training*. Vol 48, No 7. pp493–507.

BURGESS, J., CONNELL, J. and RASMUSSEN, E. (2005) Temporary agency work and precarious employment: a review of the current situation in Australia and New Zealand. *Management Revue*. Vol 16. pp351–369.

CAMPBELL, I. (2004) Casual work and casualisation: how does Australia compare? *Labour and Industry*. Vol 15, No 2. pp85–111.

CLARK, K. and DRINKWATER, S. (2008) The labour-market performance of recent migrants. *Oxford Review of Economic Policy*. Vol 24, No 3. pp496–517.

CONNELL, J. and BURGESS, J. (2006) The influence of precarious employment on career development: the current situation in Australia. *Education and Training*. Vol 48, No 7. pp493–507.

CRANFORD, C.J., VOSKO, L. and ZUKEWICH, N. (2003) Precarious employment in the Canadian labour market. *Just Labor*. Vol 3. pp6–22.

DÉMURGER, S., GURGAND, M., LI, S. and YUE, X. (2009) Migrants as second-class workers in urban China? A decomposition analysis. *Journal of Comparative Economics*. Vol 37, No 4. pp610–628.

GUEST, D.E. (2001) *Perspectives on work–life balance*. Discussion paper for the 2001 ENOP Symposium. Paris: ENOP.

HICKS, W.D. and KLIMOSKI, R.J. (1987) Entry into training programs and its effects on training outcomes: a field experiment. *Academy of Management Journal*. Vol 30. pp542–553.

HOUSEMAN, S.N. (1997) Flexible staffing arrangements in the US. *The Worklife Report*. Vol 10, No 4. p6.

HOUSEMAN, S.N. (2001) Why employers use flexible staffing arrangements: evidence from an establishment survey. *Industrial and Labor Relations Review*. Vol 55, No 1. pp149–179.

HUMAN RESOURCE MANAGEMENT INTERNATIONAL DIGEST. (2001) Boeing's long-distance approach to learning. *Human Resource Management International Digest*. Vol 9, No 1. pp10–11.

INTERNATIONAL LABOUR ORGANIZATION (ILO). (2004a) Half the world's workers living below US$2 a day poverty line ILO says new policies for promoting productivity growth and decent jobs could improve outlook for working poor. Available online at www.ilo.org/global/About_the_ILO/Media_and_public_information/Press_releases/lang--en/WCMS_005236/index.htm

INTERNATIONAL LABOUR ORGANIZATION (ILO). (2004b) *Towards a fair deal for migrant workers in the global economy*. Report VI, International Labour Conference, 92nd Session. Geneva: ILO.

INTERNATIONAL LABOUR ORGANIZATION (ILO). (2006) *Facts on decent work*. Available online at www.ilocarib.org.tt/portal/images/stories/contenido/pdf/Fact%20Sheets/FSDecentWork.pdf

INTERNATIONAL LABOUR ORGANIZATION (ILO). (2010a) *Labour migration*. Available online at www.ilo.org/global/Themes/Labour_migration/lang--en/index.htm

INTERNATIONAL LABOUR ORGANIZATION (ILO). (2010b) *Facing the global jobs crisis: migrant workers, a population at risk*. Available online at www.ilo.org/global/About_the_ILO/Media_and_public_information/Feature_stories/lang--en/WCMS_112537/index.htm

INTERNATIONAL METALWORKERS' FEDERATION. (2007) *Global action against precarious work.* Available online at www.imfmetal.org/files/07032015092779/WEB_spotlight_0107-2.pdf

JOHNSON, A. and SHARMAN, D. (1998) Innovation in all things. *Human Resource Management International Digest.* Vol 6, No 1. pp28–30.

LEWIS, S., SMITHSON, J. and KUGELBERG, C. (2002) Job insecurity and changing psychological contracts. In: BRANNEN, J., LEWIS, S., NILSEN, A. and SMITHSON, J. (eds). *Young Europeans: work and family: futures in transition.* London: Routledge. pp264–277.

LOCKE, E.A. and LATHAM, G.P. (2002) Building a practically useful theory of goal setting and task motivation. *The American Psychologist.* Vol 57, No 9. p705.

MACDONALD, F. and HOLM, S. (2002) Precarious work, uncertain futures. *Growth.* Vol 49, No 2. pp16–24.

MANCINELLI, S., MAZZANTI, M., PIVA, N. and PONTI, G. (2010) Education, reputation or network? Evidence on migrant workers employability. *Journal of Socio-Economics.* Vol 39, No 1. pp64–71.

MCDONALD, K.S. and HITE, L.M. (2008) A new era for career development and HRD. *Advances in Developing Human Resources.* Vol 10, No 1. pp86–103.

NOE, R.A. and WILK, S.L. (1993) Investigation of the factors that influence employees' participation in development activities. *Journal of Applied Psychology.* Vol 78, No 2. pp291–302.

OFFICE OF THE UNITED NATIONS HIGH COMMISSIONER FOR HUMAN RIGHTS (OHCHR). (2010) *Special rapporteur on the human rights of migrants.* Available online at www2.ohchr.org/english/issues/migration/rapporteur/

ORGANISATION FOR ECONOMIC CO-OPERATION AND DEVELOPMENT (OECD). (2009) *Employment outlook 2009.* Paris: OECD.

PATE, J., MARTIN, G., BEAUMONT, P. and MCGOLDRICK, J. (2000) Company-based lifelong learning: what's the pay-off for employers? *Journal of European Industrial Training.* Vol 24, No 2–4. pp149–157.

PETERS, L.H. and O'CONNOR, E.J. (1980) Situational constraints and work outcomes: the influence of a frequently overlooked constraint. *Academy of Management Review.* Vol 5. pp391–397.

PETERS, L.H., O'CONNOR, E.J. and RUDOLF, C.J. (1980) The behavior and affective consequences of performance-relevant situational variables. *Organizational Behavior and Human Performance.* Vol 25. pp79–96.

PETRIDOU, E. and CHATZIPANAGIOTOU, P. (2004) The planning process in managing organizations of continuing education: the case of Greek vocational training institutions. *The International Journal of Educational Management*. Vol 18, No 4–5. pp215–223.

PIOTRKOWSKI, C.S. (1979) *Work and the family system: a naturalistic study of working-class and lower-middle-class families.* New York: Free Press.

PORTWOOD, D. (1993) Work-based learning has arrived. *Management Development Review*. Vol 6, No 6. pp36–38.

POTTS, R. (1996) *Humanity's descent: the consequences of ecological instability.* New York: Morrow.

QUINLAN, M., MAYHEW, C. and BOHLE, P. (2001) The global expansion of precarious employment, work disorganization, and consequences for occupational health: a review of recent research. *International Journal of Health Services*. Vol 31, No 2. pp335–414.

READ, C.W. and KLEINER, B.H. (1996) Which training methods are effective? *Management Development Review*. Vol 9, No 2. pp24–29.

REITZ, J.G. (2007a) Immigrant employment success in Canada, part I: individual and contextual causes. *Journal of International Migration and Integration*. Vol 8, No 1. pp11–36.

REITZ, J.G. (2007b) Immigrant employment success in Canada, part II: understanding the decline. *Journal of International Migration and Integration*. Vol 8, No 1. pp37–62.

RODGERS, G. (1989) Precarious work in western Europe. In: RODGERS, G. and RODGERS, J. (eds). *Precarious jobs in labour market regulation: the growth of atypical employment in western Europe.* Belgium: International Institute for Labour Studies. pp1–16.

RUBINSTEIN, S.P. and RYAN, J. (1996) Survival for quality and unions. *Quality Progress.* Vol 29, No 7. p50.

SAMBROOK, S. and STEWART, J. (2000) Factors influencing learning in European learning oriented organisations: issues for management. *Journal of European Industrial Training*. Vol 24, No 2–4. pp209–219.

SCHERER, S. (2009) The social consequences of insecure jobs. *Social Indicators Research*. Vol 93, No 3. pp527–547.

SMITH, I.W. (2004) Continuing professional development and workplace learning 10: human resource development – the policy imperative. *Library Management*. Vol 25, No 8–9. pp401–403.

SMOLA, K.W. and SUTTON, C.D. (2002) Generational differences: revisiting generational work values for the new millennium. *Journal of Organizational Behavior*. Vol 23. pp263–382.

STURGES, J. and GUEST, D. (2004) Working to live or living to work? Work/life balance early in the career. *Human Resources Management Journal*. Vol 1, No 4. pp5–20.

THITE, M. (2001) Help us but help yourself: the paradox of contemporary career management. *Career Development International.* Vol 6, No 6. pp312–317.

TOWERS WATSON. (2010) *The shape of the emerging 'deal': insights from Towers Watson's 2010 Global Workforce Study.* Available online at www.towerswatson.com/assets/pdf/global-workforce-study/TWGWS_Exec_Summary.pdf

VASILEVA, K. (2009) *Citizens of European countries account for the majority of the foreign population in EU-27 in 2008.* Eurostat, Report no. 94/2009. Luxembourg: Eurostat.

VERMA, A., CHANG, Y.C., KIM, H.J. and RAINBOTH, S. (2009) Realizing the Korean dream for work–family balance: employer policies for sustainable societies. *National Human Resource Development Journal, Special Issue on Work–Life Balance.* July 2/3. pp29–52.

VERMA, A., SHANTZ, A., CHANG, Y.C. and KIM, H.J. (2005) *Lifelong learning in organizations: theory and evidence from leading corporations.* Report made to Kyung-Hee University and Yuhan-Kimberly, Seoul, South Korea.

WANG, Z. (2005) Convicted migrant worker killer waits for final verdict. *China Daily.* Available online at www.chinadaily.com.cn/english/doc/2005-09/21/content_479492.htm

ZEDECK, S. and MOSIER, K.L. (1990) Work in the family and employing organizations. *American Psychologist.* Vol 45. pp240–251.

Index